THE TIMES
FOOTBALL
YEARBOOK 2003-04

Times Books
an imprint of
Collins
77-85 Fulham Palace Road
London
W6 8JB

First published 2003
10 9 8 7 6 5 4 3 2 1 04 03

Printed and bound in the UK by
Butler & Tanner, Frome, Somerset
ISBN 0 00 717358 X

THE TIMES FOOTBALL
YEARBOOK 2003-04

EDITED BY RICHARD WHITEHEAD AND KEITH PIKE

 Collins

CONTENTS

351

233

Discover how Sir Bobby Robson pointed the way into the Champions League for Newcastle United and how Ivan Campo *(below left)* was one of the exotic talents that helped to keep Bolton Wanderers in the top flight

65

Epic cup action of came from Shrewsbury Town's victory over Everton *(right)* and Celtic's run to the Uefa Cup final *(above left)*

325

CREDITS

Editors

Richard Whitehead and Keith Pike

Design

Mike Krage and Kit Gregory

Picture research

Kate Cash

Photographs

All photographs Getty Images apart from pages 389, 390, 391, 392, 393 — Hulton Getty; pages 24, 292, 299 — Press Association; pages 343, 345, 364, 367 — Times Newspapers Ltd

Contributors

Tim Austin, Simon Barnes, Angus Batey, Malcolm Boyden, Rick Broadbent, Tony Cascarino, George Caulkin, Paul Connolly, Daniel Crewe, Tom Dart, John Dawkins, Matt Dickinson, Bill Edgar, Chris Gill, Walter Gammie, Phil Gordon, Richard Guy, Gavin Hadland, Richard Hakin, Geoff Harwood, Alan Kay, Oliver Kay, Steve Keenan, Russell Kempson, Shaun Keogh, Simon Kuper, Peter Lansley, Kevin McCarra, David McVay, Tim Miller, Phil Myers, Ashling O'Connor, Catherine Riley, Alyson Rudd, Owen Slot, Nick Szczepanik, Howard Wheatcroft, Nigel Williamson, Martin Woods

Photographers

Marc Aspland, Scott Barbour, Shaun Botterill, Clive Brunskill, Mark Bryn Lennon, Giuseppe Cacace, David Cannon, Phil Cole, Dave Etheridge Barnes, Stuart Franklin, Mike Finn-Kelcey, Stu Forster, Laurence Griffiths, Mike Hewitt, Harry Howe, Ross Kinnaird, Christopher Lee, Alex Livesey, Clive Mason, Jamie McDonald, Gary M Prior, Pete Norton, Ben Radford, Dave Rogers, Clive Rose, Tom Shaw, Michael Steele, Mark Thompson

Production

Steve Gibbs

Photographic imaging

Gary Hedgman

Tables and results

John Silva

Thanks to

Myles Archibald, Keith Blackmore, George Brock, Rory Campbell, Tomaso Capuano, Tim Hallissey, Robert Hands, Adam Hirschovits, Ian Passingham, Fritha Saunders, Mark Trowbridge, Richard Whiting

RICHARD WHITEHEAD

Richard Whitehead, 42, joined *The Times* in 1995 and has been in sports journalism for more than 20 years. He edits the paper's innovative and popular Handbook magazines and has been contributing football history features to the Saturday edition for the past six years. An Aston Villa supporter, he is the author of *Children of the Revolution: Aston Villa in the 1970s* and is working on a complete history of the club in the FA Cup.

KEITH PIKE

Keith Pike, 48, joined *The Times* in 1990. He spent his formative years thrilling to the goalscoring exploits of Jimmy Greaves at White Hart Lane and has a more than passing affection for Barnet. An enthusiastic and dedicated compiler of football statistics, he keeps a detailed record of each season and has written the Premiership match summaries that are one of the prime attractions of this book. He is also a keen amateur footballer (retired) and cricketer (unrequired) with Roving Reporters.

INTRODUCTION

KEITH BLACKMORE, Head of Sport, The Times

IT HAS ONLY TAKEN 130 years but here it is at last: a football annual you can actually read. There have been plenty of dusty old statistics books, of course, but the first *Times Football Yearbook* offers much more than just scorers, attendances and appearances. The editors of this book have been able to draw on a rich vein of material — the work of the award-winning football writers of *The Times*. Dip into one of the Premiership club reports and find a fresh appraisal of the season or take the plunge and follow Simon Barnes's odyssey from Ronaldinho to Rooney. Wherever you look you will find writing of the quality of a Beckham cross.

Beyond the Premiership there are reviews of all the divisions of the Nationwide League, non-league, women's football and full accounts of the European competitions and the performances of the international teams. As a nod to a slightly better established sporting yearbook, our editors have also chosen their own Five Footballers of the Year. Have a look. You may be surprised by their selection.

This is the 2002-03 season as it really happened. Enjoy it again.

FIVE FOOTBALLERS OF THE YEAR

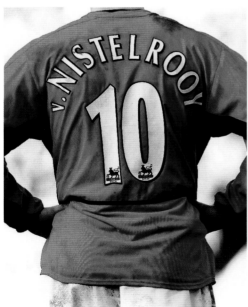

ONE SEASON, FIVE PLAYERS: Over the course of 2002-03, many footballers forced their way into the headlines for their performances, but only a few consistently displayed the special qualities required to become a *Times Football Yearbook* footballer of the year. Step forward Thierry Henry, Paul Merson, Chris Marsden, Ruud van Nistelrooy and Brad Friedel

BRAD FRIEDEL

OLIVER KAY

IN THEIR INFINITE WISDOM, the Department for Education and Skills decided in July 2000 that Brad Friedel no longer merited a work permit to play in England. His three-year spell at Liverpool had been so unproductive that the authorities would not let him return to the country from a holiday in his native United States. They finally relented on the condition that he did not set foot on his employer's premises. It was, he would later say in his Ohio drawl, "kind of strange".

Strange, too, that the only manager to come to his rescue was Graeme Souness, who was attempting to guide Blackburn Rovers back into the Premiership. Friedel and Souness went back a long way, to their time together at Galatasaray in the mid-1990s, but this was no old pals' act. Souness, incredulous at finding the United States goalkeeper on the scrapheap, was no less astonished at being able to sign him on a free transfer in November 2000, with a work permit finally granted at the fourth time of asking.

At times last season, when he was by some distance the outstanding goalkeeper in the Premiership, Friedel may have been tempted to contact his old friends in the Civil Service. Certainly, the notion that he did not fill the criteria to play in England appeared laughable. More than one manager, in addition to Souness, named him as

'Souness was astonished that he was able to sign him on a free transfer'

their player of the year. Plaudits also came from his fellow professionals, who voted him ahead of Carlo Cudicini in the Premiership representative team at the PFA awards.

Blackburn qualified for the Uefa Cup on the back of the fifth-best defensive record in the Premiership, but not even Souness would dare to claim they had the fifth-best defence. Friedel, at times, was a one-man barrier and never more so than at Highbury in October, when he produced an astonishing performance in a 2-1 win over Arsenal. Of all the points that Arsenal squandered over the course of the campaign, none frustrated Arsene

Wenger more than the three that Friedel denied them virtually on his own. As brave as he was athletic, he also threw in a couple of penalty saves during the campaign that helped to get his club into Europe.

Sir Alex Ferguson, the Manchester United manager, was certainly impressed, putting Friedel at the top of a list of contenders to replace the erratic Fabien Barthez at the end of the summer. Wenger, too, made the American his first choice to succeed David Seaman. Souness, though, was adamant that his most prized asset should not be sold. The Blackburn manager insisted that there was no price that would reflect Friedel's true value to the club.

Wherever his future lay, he would always feel a loyalty to Souness, the man who saved his career when other managers were not giving him a second glance. At that point, tangled up in red tape, Friedel was at rock bottom. Now, less than three years on, he has worked himself up to the very pinnacle of his profession.

THIERRY HENRY

ALYSON RUDD

THIERRY HENRY MUST BE a fabulous player. How else can he get away with wearing socks pulled up over his knees that make him look like a cancan girl? When football writers explained why they voted him Footballer of the Year, they all said in one form or another that he brought something special to the game. Yes, Ruud van Nistelrooy scored more goals, but Henry's were more aesthetically pleasing and, in any case, the France forward set up as many as he scored. We all like an unselfish talent.

The writers are also supposed to take into account how a player's personality enhances the game and Henry, despite his star status, always has time for the media and is without fail polite and modest while expressing his enthusiasm for his club and his team-mates. And he talks as he plays, without punctuation, without uncomfortable hesitation, almost in a stream of consciousness. He is the James Joyce of the Premiership.

Henry is also every defender's nightmare. How on earth do you keep track of him? He wanders all over the

'Against Chelsea he scored a goal that illustrated his ease with the ball and his elegance'

pitch for a start and then, just when you have figured out why he is heading for the right flank, he will accelerate towards goal, leaving his marker looking leaden-footed.

The goal that best summed him up was the one against Chelsea in the FA Cup quarter-final when, with his back to goal, he spun the ball around the goalkeeper and in one fluid movement scored. This is not the trickiest thing Henry has pulled off, but it illustrates his ease with the ball and his innate elegance.

He revels in playing alongside those with alert minds. There was not much beauty on show in the FA Cup Final against Southampton, but what little there was involved Henry releasing or accepting a lightning-quick pass. Dennis Bergkamp is no spring chicken, but when he has Henry to pass to we can all see how fast the Dutchman's brain remains. Henry won new fans in that match for

staying on his feet under the challenge of Claus Lundekvam. A penalty then, in the opening minute, would have killed the game off, but Henry always has his eye on the more pleasing option and a spot kick is not as lovely as a beautifully struck goal from open play.

Henry began his Highbury life looking out of place, neither a winger nor a true striker, but he has created a new position. He is not quite an off-striker, more of an on-off striker. Which makes him sound moody, but really means that he can switch effortlessly from the role of provider to goalscorer faster than any other player in Britain. His critics think he should score more goals and more tap-ins, but why plead for a more rounded striker when you can have one as delightfully individual and inspirational as Thierry Henry — with socks pulled over the knee.

CHRIS MARSDEN

NICK SZCZEPANIK

WHEN CHRIS MARSDEN JOINED Southampton from Birmingham City in February 1999, the club's supporters were distinctly underwhelmed at the signing of a veteran midfield player who had spent his entire professional career outside the top flight, bar a handful of games on loan to Coventry City. There seemed little promise in a curriculum vitae that included spells at Huddersfield Town, Notts County and Stockport County. Four years on, Marsden, those same supporters' player of the year for 2002, was one of the driving forces as the team finished eighth in the Premiership, reached the club's first FA Cup Final since 1976 and qualified for Europe.

To enjoy the best season of your career at 34 seems the stuff of dreams, especially when a "journeyman" tag has been hung constantly around your neck, but Marsden, an articulate and witty speaker, has no objection to labels. "If somebody had said when I left school, 'You'll be playing football for practically the next 18-20 years', I'd have snapped their hand off, at any level," he said before the Cup Final. "But to be where we are, eighth, in Europe and in the FA Cup Final, I won't say is a dream come true, because it's what you aim for — but it's going as well as can be expected."

That remark also shows a gift for understatement.

'He admits that Bridge has everything he lacks — youth, pace, hair'

Although James Beattie took many of the headlines as Southampton briefly gatecrashed the top six, the combative Marsden was as influential as anyone in the increasingly confident performances given by a team growing into its handsome St Mary's Stadium and took over as captain for most of the second half of the season after Jason Dodd was injured. He credits modern approaches to nutrition and fitness for extending his career, but also Gordon Strachan, the Southampton manager, and the players around him.

It was Strachan who moved him away from what had seemed his natural habitat in the centre of midfield to a wide position, where he has formed a formidable left wing partnership with Wayne Bridge. Bridge is often regarded as the more potent threat down the flank — Bridge, Marsden admits, has everything he lacks, "youth, pace, hair" — but in the FA Cup semi-final against Watford it was Marsden who flew down the left before crossing for Brett Ormerod to head the opening goal.

Marsden's fluke overhead effort had also set Saints on the way in their quarter-final against Wolverhampton Wanderers, so it was Sod's Law that a knee problem, his first injury of the season, should put his Cup Final place in doubt. However, he was never going to miss the chance to lead the team out, even if it meant risking long-term damage. Whether that decision was justified purely on football grounds is arguable, but nobody who has met this engaging character would have begrudged him his day on the big stage. And the disappointment of a generally low-key 1-0 defeat by Arsenal will surely be forgotten when the Uefa Cup comes around.

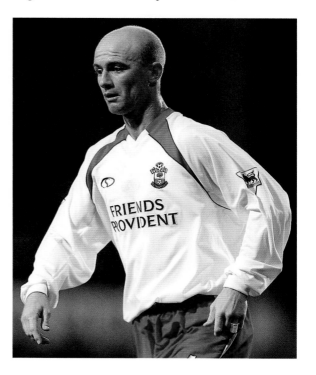

PAUL MERSON

RICK BROADBENT

MILLWALL SUPPORTERS ARE not the most accommodating bunch in the country. Combining the generosity of Uriah Heep with the natural balm of a box set of *The Sopranos*, they are generally best left alone. It is these traits that made it all the more remarkable when they rose as one and gave a standing ovation to Paul Merson as he was substituted at the New Den in March. Not bad considering the Portsmouth captain had just scored the final goal in a 5-0 victory.

Maybe it was the fact there was something irresistible to even the stoniest of hearts in Merson's renaissance. Here was a man who has battled his demons ever since his vices were laid bare in that tearful confessional in 1994. It was one for the hopeless romantics.

Back in August it had been easy to dismiss Portsmouth as a band of thirtysomething mercenaries after Harry Redknapp had trawled the top flight for fading stars in an attempt to revive the South Coast club. None of those myriad deals would prove as astute as the one that rescued Merson from a life of strife at Aston Villa. The pace may have slowed, the years of excess having taken their toll, but the mind was as sharp as ever.

Given the rise of young players such as Matthew Taylor, it would be an exaggeration to say that the 35-year-old carried Portsmouth, but few players have bestrode their side with such magnificence. The creative

> 'Villa supporters were left to wonder whether Mark Kinsella really was a better player'

streak was given licence by a more central position and, for all his own fears about surviving the first division treadmill, he played 49 games and scored 12 goals. If he had intended to prove a point to Graham Taylor, the manager who allowed him to leave Villa Park for free, he had done so with lashings of nostalgia.

Taylor's comment that he was a football manager and not a social worker suggested he had grown weary of Merson's foibles. Merson responded by saying: "Villa ain't a little car showroom on some street corner who have to wheel and deal."

When Taylor resigned at the end of Merson's glittering season, a rush of *Schadenfreude* could have been excused. But then Merson appeared on a television documentary and confirmed he was still addicted to gambling and had sent his wife a suicidal text message. It was clear the excess baggage remained. "I am powerless and my life has become unmanageable," he said. "I'm glad I'm not brave enough to kill myself."

And so what appeared a happy revival was in fact the saddest story, his moral courage failing to disguise the fact that his life had become a morality play.

On the pitch he was a joy to watch. By coming in from the wings, both literally and figuratively, he had rolled back the years and become what journalists used to call a schemer. Villa could only look from afar and wonder whether Mark Kinsella really was a better player. That Merson achieved it all while suffering so intensely only served to underline his achievement.

RUUD VAN NISTELROOY

BILL EDGAR

RUUD VAN NISTELROOY receives the ball on the left touchline at Highbury and proceeds to shrug off the challenges of Sol Campbell and Martin Keown. Fifty yards and a few seconds later, the ball hits the Arsenal net in what proves a pivotal moment in Manchester United's successful title charge. Brutally executed, the goal epitomised the Holland striker. Self-assurance enabled him to embark on an ambitious attempt to beat two England centre backs, a cute flick saw off Campbell, raw aggression kept Keown at bay and utter coolness allowed him to finish off his own move.

A month before, Van Nistelrooy had scored a similar, but even better, solo goal against Fulham after collecting the ball in the centre circle, providing further evidence of how he has learnt to fend for himself — a necessary attribute for him at Old Trafford. Not only has he lacked a regular strike partner in his two years at United, he has often played alone at the head of a 4-5-1 formation.

In many ways the Dutchman resembles a classic English centre forward. Aggressive and resilient, he has a remarkable ability to keep possession when surrounded by several opponents before laying off the ball to a

'His tally in the Champions League proves that he is no flat-track bully'

colleague. His extraordinary goalscoring hints at single-mindedness, but he has a gift for teamwork that Michael Owen can only dream about.

While Van Nistelrooy lacks the grace of Thierry Henry, his strength and clever link-up play give Ryan Giggs and Co the room to demonstrate their flair. His colleagues appreciate him as much as the adoring fans who mark each of his goals with the shout "Ruuuud".

And those goals have come with remarkable regularity. Having managed to score in ten successive games in his first season with United, a feat that most strikers do not even approach throughout their careers, he did so again in the final ten matches of last term.

In all he has scored 80 goals in 101 appearances for United, many of which have come decisively from the

penalty spot, but he is no flat-track bully. A goal tally of 24 in 25 Champions League matches, including strikes in both legs of the epic quarter-final against Real Madrid last season, testifies to his effectiveness at the highest level.

Yet Van Nistelrooy was hardly feared around Europe when he joined United from PSV Eindhoven at the age of 25. Sir Alex Ferguson, though, was convinced enough to remain determined to take him to Old Trafford even when a serious cruciate ligament injury, suffered shortly after he had failed a medical at United, kept him out of action for nine months.

Ferguson stayed in regular contact with his quarry, offering him the use of the club's training facilities, and he revived the £19 million move once the striker had regained fitness. The manager's doggedness has been repaid handsomely.

THE DOUBLE Double may have eluded his club, but Thierry Henry found himself in elite company when he picked up the PFA Player of the Year trophy, which he can now put on his shelf alongside the Footballer of the Year award. The Arsenal striker, scorer of 32 goals last season, including 24 in the Premiership, became the eleventh player to capture both awards since the PFA decided in 1974 to recognise the achievements of its members, the Football Writers' Association having given its original award to Stanley Matthews in 1948.

Henry follows in the bootsteps of Terry McDermott (1980), Kenny Dalglish (1983), Ian Rush (1984), Gary Lineker (1986), Clive Allen (1987), John Barnes (1988), Dennis Bergkamp (1998), David Ginola (1999), Roy Keane (2000) and Teddy Sheringham (2001). The four previous Footballers of the Year from Arsenal are Joe Mercer (1950), Frank McLintock (1971), Bergkamp and Robert Pires (2002).

PFA AWARDS
Player of the Year: Thierry Henry (Arsenal)
Young Player of the Year: Jermaine Jenas (Newcastle United)
Player of the Decade: Alan Shearer
Merit award: Sir Bobby Robson
Premiership team of the year: Brad Friedel (Blackburn Rovers) — **Stephen Carr** (Tottenham Hotspur), **Sol Campbell** (Arsenal), **William Gallas** (Chelsea), **Ashley Cole** (Arsenal) — **Kieron Dyer** (Newcastle United), **Patrick Vieira** (Arsenal), **Paul Scholes** (Manchester United), **Robert Pires** (Arsenal) — **Alan Shearer** (Newcastle United), **Thierry Henry** (Arsenal)

BARCLAYCARD PREMIERSHIP AWARD
Manager of the year: Sir Alex Ferguson (Manchester United)

LEAGUE MANAGERS ASSOCIATION AWARDS
Manager of the year: David Moyes (Everton)
First division: Harry Redknapp (Portsmouth)
Second division: Paul Jewell (Wigan Athletic)
Third division: Denis Smith (Wrexham)

FROM RONALDINHO TO ROONEY

SIMON BARNES, Chief Sports Writer

Hot radish
Pierced my tongue,
While the autumn wind
Pierced my heart.
— Matsuo Basho

SO THE SEASON BEGAN with memories of Japan and the World Cup still fresh. A new season seemed dreadfully anticlimactic: too soon and too much. I had been six weeks out there, watching football and learning Japan. In short, I had a hangover like the gardens of Babylon.

Jeeves used to serve Bertie with a morning-after reviver: "For a moment I felt as if somebody had touched off a bomb inside the old bean and was strolling down my throat with a lighted torch, and then everything seemed suddenly to get all right. The sun shone in through the window; birds twittered in the tree-tops; and, generally speaking, hope dawned once more." That was Arsenal. They made the new season — brief, damp autumn days and ever longer nights — seem worthwhile. It was what some observers were to call the too-sexy-for-my-shirt period and Sir Alex Ferguson was to call triumphalism, but it was great while it lasted.

Perhaps there was something hollow at the heart of it all. Perhaps there was a fragility beneath all the easy assumption of individual and corporate pre-eminence. But in football, as in Zen, it is best to live in the moment. "We're so great!" the Arsenal players said in speech bubbles on the cover of *When Saturday Comes*. "And so modest!" It takes a certain quality — and it is not modesty — for a goalkeeper to sign himself "Safe Hands", but that has long been the habit of David Seaman, then the Arsenal and England goalkeeper. Seaman made a brilliant save that turned the match in England's favour in the famous 5-1 defeat of Germany. I'd like to say that for the sake of fairness before I put the boot in.

In the World Cup, Seaman conceded the winning goal

The gloves are off: Seaman may have saved his best for Munich, but his mistakes in the World Cup finals against Brazil and then in the Euro 2004 qualifier against Macedonia cost him his cherished position as the England No 1

Teenage kicks: Rooney burst on to the scene at 16 with a goal of stunning impact and a talent that made anything seem possible

against Brazil from Ronaldinho's 35-yard free kick. Seaman has always been vulnerable to the unexpected; a first-class goalkeeper when it comes to the ordinary, but routinely undone by the extraordinary. And so it was déjà vu all over again when England played Macedonia at St Mary's Stadium in October.

These are the worst kind of fixtures, for England anyway: a must-win qualifier for Euro 2004 against a lesser footballing nation. Bring on the flat-track bullies. Let's crush them. Time after time, that is exactly what doesn't happen, and it was what didn't happen that night.

The most obvious reason for England's failure was Seaman, who let a corner from Artim Sakiri fly over his head into the goal. It was a freak goal scored against a man who is vulnerable to the freakish. England put up a poor performance all round, of that there is no question. But Seaman had to shoulder the blame and he was to lose his England place as a result: a keeper of high and lofty competence who consistently fell short of brilliance.

So much for a footballer passing through his personal autumn. Let us get on to spring. It was a spring that began in October with a moment of unbelievable hope. It is the sort of thing we love best in sport, perhaps even

more than the greatest achievement: that early quickening of talent, that sudden feeling of discovery, that miraculous feeling that anything is possible.

Wayne Rooney. This was his season. Hope is an ineluctable aspect of sport, and Rooney embodied hope. He was 17 in October. He scored what, in terms of impact, was unquestionably the goal of the season, when he blasted the winner for Everton against Arsenal — in retrospect, a goal that can be seen as the first real evidence of Arsenal's fallibility.

Perhaps it was the goal that settled the championship. It certainly made Rooney everybody's player of the season, for the way in which he filled us all with such good cheer as much as anything. There was a feeling that he might, just might, be something very special indeed.

Pele was a prodigy at 17, so was Diego Maradona. Rooney followed his winner against Arsenal with another spectacular strike against Leeds United, which kept them firmly on the downward slope. But it was Rooney that fascinated. A youthful flash in the pan? A real player of substance and permanence? Plenty of promising youngsters fail to train on, but the few rare geniuses of sport tend to show their ability alarmingly early.

Meanwhile, the other story of the season was the continuing failure of Manchester United. By the very highest terms, Ferguson was failing: this was clearly Arsenal's season. A shareholder made a speech of criticism at the club's annual meeting and Ferguson told him: "You are an idiot." The pressure of criticism was getting to him; in particular, criticism of his expensive flop, Juan Sebastian Veron.

It had become crucial to Ferguson's personal myth that Veron should become a howling success. Perhaps if Veron had stayed sound, he would have cost Ferguson his rewards of the season. As it was, Veron got injured — the best thing that could have happened for United. It is hard to remember now, I know, but Ferguson was feeling more pressure than he had done for years and it was not adding to his reputation for charm and courtesy.

But that's enough about football. Let's talk about money. We had the revelation that Michael Owen lost

£30,000 when gambling with team-mates at the World Cup — call that fifty quid if it had been you and me. This showed nothing but the fact that Owen is a human being rather than the cardboard cut-out "role model" figure that he presents to the world.

Farnborough Town did the underdog stuff in the FA Cup and their reward was a home tie against Arsenal, the holders. So, of course, they played the match at Highbury — and got routinely and tediously thumped — in order to make money. The crassest part of a crass business was the fact that the Football Association allowed them to do it. We pay our money — in admission, in satellite subscription, in licence fees — in order to watch football, and mostly we do so ungrudgingly. But when people take our money and our loyalty for granted and deny us such pleasures as unpredictability and romance, we are entitled to feel hard-done-by. Moral: the people most out of touch with what sport is all about are those who administer it.

I suppose you can't expect Sven to understand about Australians. You don't run into them much in Sweden and you don't get much chance to watch Test cricket in Italy. So when Sven-Goran Eriksson, the England head coach, decided to use the friendly against Australia as a practice kickabout, with a different side for each half, someone should have told him that the Australians would treat it as a real football match. Australia won 3-1, England were hopeless and a chap called Rooney made a debut that was overshadowed by the awfulness of the result.

This added a seemly measure of fear to England's next home qualifier, against Turkey at the Stadium of Light in Sunderland. It was the best of games, it was the worst of games. It was a night of bitter passion and deep commitment, and England played wonderfully well — and Rooney, winning his third cap, started the match and had a blinder. For once that cautious man, Eriksson, gambled — and gambled big. Perhaps he was incensed by Ferguson's comment that he was "a safe pair of hands". Whatever the reason, Eriksson played the gamble of his life and found himself on a winner.

At 16, Rooney swaggered into Premiership football and

Don't fade away: Arsenal may have played football that was too sexy for their shirts at the start of the season, but it was Manchester United who were dressed for the kill at the end of the campaign

looked the part at once. Now he was doing the same thing in England's biggest match since the World Cup. It was a stunning performance, one that means we no longer hope for good things from Rooney. We expect them.

All the same, it was a horrible night. To be there was to feel your skin crawl. There were nearly 100 arrests before the game, the night was filled with racist chanting, the Turkish anthem was inaudible under the booing, there were pitch invasions and the match took place in an atmosphere of poisonous hatred. There was a punch-up in the tunnel and damn near one on the pitch as England players went out of their way to provoke.

There is no doubt that the passion of the supporters drove England forward and inspired their best performance since they beat Denmark in the World Cup's second round. It was dark, hysterical, disturbing:

also powerful, thrilling, inspiring. Moral: sporting passion is not a simple thing.

The domestic season ended with Arsenal blowing their eight-point Premiership lead, mainly because Manchester United put pressure on them with a renewed taste for winning. Arsenal cracked under the strain and the FA Cup was scant consolation.

It was another season when United failed — but failed only at the very highest level, going out in the quarter-finals of the European Cup to Real Madrid. But they reasserted domestic hegemony: the natural and inevitable winners of the Premiership. And then, at last, a brief summer's pause.

> *Clouds now and then*
> *Giving men relief*
> *From moon-viewing.*

Friendly fire: while Eriksson used the fixture as a practice match, fielding a different XI in each half, Australia marched into Upton Park in February to deliver a painful lesson to England

IS THERE AN OLD FIRM IN ENGLAND?

TONY CASCARINO

WE ARE NEARING A pivotal moment in the game. If there is another season in which Manchester United and Arsenal dominate the Premiership, England will almost have its very own Old Firm. In the past few seasons, that pair have lost sight of the 18 teams below them, striding in concert to the climax of the campaign, as Celtic and Rangers have done on countless occasions since the professional game began in Scotland.

For years, people in England have scoffed at Scotland. Ha! Those Jocks! Only two teams can win the league there! The Premiership is not quite as predictable yet, but it is getting there. Imagine it: just as mundane, just as uncompetitive, just as boring, just as many one-sided matches — and the championship pretty much decided by two matches a season plus the odd slip-up.

Sounds ridiculous? Well, consider this. For five of the past six seasons, United and Arsenal have finished in the top two (United were third in the other and Arsenal were third in 1997). It has happened eight times in as many seasons in Scotland. United have won eight of the 11 Premiership trophies, the same number as Rangers in the same period, and Arsenal two. Like trinkets, Rangers have amassed 50 titles and Celtic 38, leaving just 18 for the rest, the last in 1985.

Who is to say that in 95 years' time, when the Premiership will also have been competed for 106 times, that United and Arsenal will not have replicated those figures? Newcastle United, Chelsea and Liverpool would be also-rans. The bookies think that is the case now. As the new season loomed, William Hill were offering 2-1 on any team apart from Arsenal and United finishing in the top two.

Maybe this was what Arsene Wenger was hinting at when he said in September that it was not impossible for his team to go through the domestic season unbeaten. At the time, Arsenal had not lost in 27 league matches and it seemed a reasonable answer to a question to their manager, even if many people who admired his team's exquisite rhythm thought that it was something he should have kept private.

A little over ten years ago, a competitiveness existed that made football intriguing for supporters. When was the last time a team came out of the pack to challenge? Arguably, Everton were that team in 2002-03, but they still finished 19 points behind Arsenal. Newcastle have had two good seasons, yet each time they were nine points behind the team in second.

The title race and relegation scrap this season were great for the neutral, but I am not alone in being bothered that the division could fragment further into at least five leagues. Alan Curbishley, the Charlton Athletic manager, said it would not be good for the league if United and Arsenal establish a championship duopoly. "While clubs have tried to break it, and some spent almost £100 million in the process, no one has managed to achieve it," Curbishley said. "I wouldn't like to think it is going to become like Scotland, when everything is

THE TWO TIMES TABLE

	P	W	D	L	F	A	GD	Pts
1997-98								
Arsenal	38	23	9	6	68	33	35	78
Manchester Utd	38	23	8	7	73	26	47	77
Liverpool	38	18	11	9	68	42	26	65
1998-99								
Manchester Utd	38	22	13	3	80	37	43	79
Arsenal	38	22	12	4	59	17	42	78
Chelsea	38	20	15	3	57	30	27	75
1999-2000								
Manchester Utd	38	28	7	3	97	45	52	91
Arsenal	38	22	7	9	73	43	30	73
Leeds Utd	38	21	6	11	58	43	15	69
2000-01								
Manchester Utd	38	24	8	6	79	31	48	80
Arsenal	38	20	10	8	63	38	25	70
Liverpool	38	20	9	9	71	39	32	69
2001-02								
Arsenal	38	26	9	3	79	36	43	87
Liverpool	38	24	8	6	67	30	37	80
Manchester Utd	38	24	5	9	87	45	42	77
2002-03								
Manchester Utd	38	25	8	5	74	34	40	83
Arsenal	38	23	9	6	85	42	43	78
Newcastle Utd	38	21	6	11	63	48	15	69

decided when Celtic and Rangers play each other." The inevitability of such dominance stultifies the rest. Teams are trapped by a familiar paradox: that, by investing in success, they risk crippling themselves financially.

Two years ago Leeds United were close to the European Cup final, but two managers, one chairman and more than £70 million of debt later, they found themselves close to administration. Chelsea, too, have incurred a large debt. "It is up to the rest of us to try and compete more, but that's difficult because no one wants to see clubs spending money they haven't got," Curbishley said.

It is not the fault of United and Arsenal that they are dominant. Liverpool, who could have challenged, wasted money on mediocre players and are burdened by Gerard Houllier's style of play. Success for Houllier and his counterparts at Newcastle and Chelsea is now qualifying for the Champions League, which has undermined the domestic league. The problem is partly self-perpetuating, because the best players only want to join the teams playing in the Champions League.

England once prided itself on having the most competitive league in Europe. David and Goliath stories are now reserved for cup competitions, and even here the names of the winners are increasingly familiar. Since the Premiership began 11 years ago, Arsenal have won the FA Cup four times and United three.

Of course, the romantic view of the Premiership is supported by Bolton Wanderers winning at Old Trafford and drawing with Arsenal, but we need to be careful if we are not going to arrive at a situation such as the one in Scotland, where this season the top two each dropped only 17 points in 38 matches. Only Motherwell beat both Rangers and Celtic. The Old Firm are mired in a mediocrity that is killing them.

The achievement by the top two in England is all the more extraordinary when you consider that United have had a wobbly back four and Arsenal have had to replace their legendary defence in the past three seasons. Even allowing for the mediocre calibre of players they have brought in, such as Pascal Cygan, they have still finished in the top two.

Three seasons ago when there was a chance that Arsenal would not make one of the Champions League spots, they simply moved up a gear and won enough matches to finish second. And maybe that's why Arsenal,

Money can't buy you happiness: as Manchester United and Arsenal continue to battle for the title, the days when the likes of Blackburn Rovers could use Jack Walker's chequebook to fund a tilt at glory by an outsider have probably vanished

and to a lesser extent United, have not imposed themselves in the Champions League, where they have been shown to be tactically naive. They have not been fully tested week in, week out and players can find it difficult just to step up another gear automatically. Likewise, Celtic and Rangers have failed to impose themselves in Europe's top competition.

Scotland and parts of Scandinavia clarify the perils of such domination. When I played for Celtic it was expected that we would beat every other team and the only match supporters relished was the derby against Rangers. A stale domestic league produces stale teams and stale football — and players who aren't up for every match.

Things were different when Liverpool dominated English football in the 1970s and 80s. While they were winning ten league championships, nine different teams finished second. History shows that their period of mastery came to an end, but it is not a guide to the future because football is different now. Liverpool were not suffused with money from their marketing activities, as United are with their shops around the world funnelling cash back to Old Trafford. I supported Liverpool as a kid, but rarely bought any paraphernalia. Nowadays, every United fan around the world wants something with the club's name on it.

So, what is going to change things? In the past, clubs wanting to challenge could buy success. Blackburn Rovers were the last team to do that, when Jack Walker, the late owner, spent about £25 million and broke the British transfer record twice to sign Alan Shearer and Chris Sutton. Nowadays, though, it would simply cost too much. Only Manchester United can spend £58 million on Juan Sebastian Veron and Rio Ferdinand to help them to win the championship.

The sale of David Beckham to Real Madrid will make little difference to United and even if they lost Ruud van Nistelrooy, Roy Keane and a few others, they would at worst come second. If Newcastle lost Shearer or Craig Bellamy, I would question if they would finish in the top four.

Where would it end if clubs could open their chequebook and win the league? Money alone cannot explain why United and Arsenal are dominant, or why the team that wins the league can waltz to a 6-2 win away to the third-placed team, Newcastle.

There are, though, a few things that may alter the balance. If Sir Alex Ferguson relinquishes his grip on United, they may stutter for a short while, but I believe that their infrastructure is too strong to topple the ship, whoever the next manager is. Another is Arsenal's planned new stadium at Ashburton Grove. There is a small difference between the clubs on the field at the moment, but Old Trafford holds 67,000 paying customers to Arsenal's 38,000.

Wenger probably wants two or three players, but Arsenal also need to be able to fund the interest payments on the loan to build their new stadium. Without the stadium, there would be a question mark over Wenger's future. If he left, it would be a catalyst for an exodus and their apparent privilege to a top-two place.

Ferguson, when the manager of Aberdeen, broke the Old Firm's dominance in Scotland, but which managers in England could do that? Or will it take Martin O'Neill to head south? Can the Premiership really claim to be the best league in Europe if it effectively has only two teams capable of winning it?

Firm favourites: but is England heading for the same dull scenario?

THE RETURN OF REALITY

ASHLING O'CONNOR

ON AUGUST 1, 2002, THE two most senior executives at the Football League trudged out of the High Court with news that would strike at the heart of the game, shaking its already precarious financial structure. From the steps of the court-house, Keith Harris, the League's chairman, and David Burns, the chief executive, announced that they had lost their ill-advised lawsuit against Carlton Communications and Granada, the owners of ITV Digital.

Failure to hold the country's two biggest television groups to account meant that the League's 72 clubs would forfeit £132 million of media revenues over the next two seasons. The League had failed to secure parent company guarantees for its £315 million, three-year rights deal, so when ITV Digital ceased to exist, so too did the promised money that clubs had budgeted for. In his brusque summation, Mr Justice Langley said that the League's case "looked just as unpromising at the finish as it looked at the start".

This was the moment when football's bubble burst. Reality would come home to roost during the 2002-03 season in the first big hangover since 1992, when the Premiership party began making millionaires out of footballers and turning clubs into brands.

The months after the ITV Digital bankruptcy witnessed the financial failure of some lower division clubs that had racked up unserviceable debts. Experts in corporate recovery would be kept busy trying to restructure clubs whose wage-bills had spiralled out of control as the transfer market crashed.

Neither were Premiership clubs immune from the consequences. Drunk on the sweet taste of a £1.6 billion media rights bonanza, the 20 member clubs went on a spending frenzy, frittering away the money inside two years. The most catastrophic example of a failed bid for glory was Leeds United, mired in £79 million of debt after banking on a season in the Champions League that failed to transpire. Happy to watch Peter Ridsdale throw money around on the promise of European success, the fans were as quick to turn on their chairman when the walls came tumbling down.

Football was greedy. This was the season it paid the price. In June, 586 players — about 20 per cent of the Premiership and Nationwide League workforce — were released by their clubs when their contracts expired. Around one-third of them are unlikely to find a way back into the professional game.

For Harris and Burns, the cost was their jobs. Backbiting from disgruntled football chairmen made their positions untenable and they resigned. Burns, a Sheffield Wednesday supporter with a background in the tourism industry, was relieved. "Keith, just think — you've given the asylum back to the lunatics," he said.

The legacy of ITV Digital was damaging. Clubs' income per season dropped dramatically. Central payments for a first division club fell from £1.9 million to £586,625; for a second division club from £795,000 to £285,041; and for a third division club from £557,000 to £199,333. They would struggle to fill the hole in their budgets while players were tied into fixed-term contracts as long as five years, some paid vast sums just to sit on the substitutes' bench. Notts County, the oldest League club, was already in administration before the start of the season, but many more would follow as winter approached. Eight clubs — among them Wimbledon —

Crozier's downfall revealed a sport "being torn apart"

Wise, left, ended up playing against his old club for Millwall. He claimed he was sacked by Leicester City because he was too expensive

would seek protection from their creditors while they tried to put their financial affairs in order.

On October 21, the most high-profile casualty came to light. Leicester City was put into the hands of administrators at Deloitte & Touche with debts that would eventually be shown to be more than £50 million. The club could barely pay its players and Dennis Wise, their midfield player, threatened to sue after he was sacked for breaking a team-mate's jaw, claiming that he was being offloaded only because he was too expensive.

The reaction to Leicester's plight was swift. Gary Lineker, their most famous alumnus, spearheaded a campaign to raise £5 million to buy the first division club out of administration. Emile Heskey, the Liverpool striker who started his career at Filbert Street, chipped in, as did Jon Holmes, managing director of SFX Europe, the sports agency. Financial disaster did not derail Leicester on the pitch, though. Against the odds, Micky Adams, the manager, strung together wins. Patience and temerity paid off. While the campaign to buy the club out of administration was progressing, so too did the team's bid for a quick return to the Premiership.

However, Leicester's eventual double success — promotion and an exit from administration — was not celebrated by all. Rivals with similar money troubles felt that the club had benefited unfairly from the process that allowed it to eliminate 90 per cent of its debt and start afresh in the top flight. The knee-jerk reaction from the League to this perceived competitive advantage showed the sport's rulers, in the eyes of the City at least, still to be out of touch with business realities.

The introduction of sporting sanctions for clubs that go into administration was the first significant proposal by Sir Brian Mawhinney, the League's new chairman. The no-nonsense former Secretary of State for Northern Ireland was clear: the bankruptcy courts would no longer be the easy way out for football's poor financial managers. He proposed that offending clubs should have points deducted — or even suffer relegation in extreme cases — against a backdrop of substantial criticism from insolvency experts, who claimed that the changes might encourage club directors to trade unlawfully to avoid punishment. The split in opinion, which led to a vote on the proposals being delayed to the end of the summer, underlined what most already knew: that despite the best intentions, it would remain impossible to align totally the interests of football with the strict logic of business.

It was a quandary all too familiar to Adam Crozier, whose downfall as chief executive of the Football Association revealed a sport being torn apart by divergent commercial interests. The club versus country debate raged throughout the season, failing to die even after Crozier's resignation on October 31. The issue that brought the Premier League's displeasure with Crozier to a head was his signing of key multimillion-pound deals with sponsors that demanded the time of England players, drawing them away from the clubs that paid their wages. But it was the former Saatchi & Saatchi executive's apparent disregard for the protocol of "decision by committee" that was the underlying tension.

Even the coup of Crozier's tenure, the financing of the new Wembley Stadium, was tainted. Crozier achieved what a posse of FA suits and politicians had failed to do over the preceding seven years. He negotiated for a German bank (WestLB) to underwrite a £426 million loan to the FA to enable the construction of the 90,000-seater stadium. The Government, which had committed £120 million of public money to the project, was relieved to be rid of its expensive albatross. The FA whooped at the prospect of a glorious new home for the England team. Yet there was already growing unease about football mortgaging its future and some in the FA, particularly at the grassroots level, thought it was too much of a stretch for the national game's finances.

Just how much of a stretch only became apparent after Crozier's departure, despite an assurance from Geoff Thompson, the chairman, that the FA was being left "in a very strong position financially". The FA was forced to take out a £130 million bridging loan to see it through a short-term cashflow crisis midway through the season. A round of redundancies was also implemented to cut huge operating costs of more than £120 million a year.

The extent of the mess the FA had got itself into was underlined by the appointment in May of a corporate recovery expert as Crozier's successor. Mark Palios, a former Tranmere Rovers player, had the credentials for

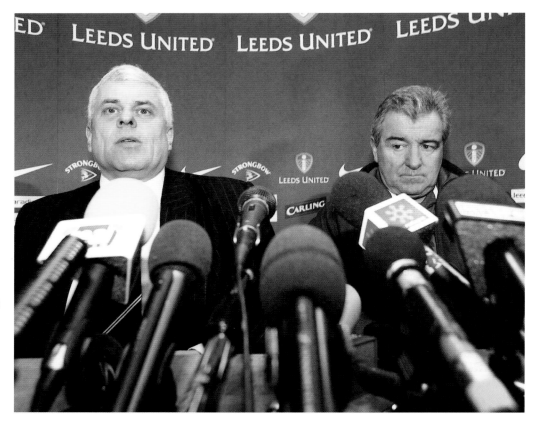

The chill financial wind blew through Elland Road as Leeds United found themselves saddled with huge debts after a failed attempt to buy success in Europe

turning round organisations in distress. Whether he would be given the teeth to keep the Premier League's ambitions in check remained unclear.

If not, some feared the chasm between the Premiership and the rest would only widen, to the sport's financial and cultural detriment. A club relegated from the Premiership goes over the edge of a steep cliff. They are barely able to survive the fall, which chops at least £15 million off the top line in lost TV revenues, even with parachute payments worth £10 million over two seasons — as Leicester discovered the hard way. It is an unhappy precedent for Sunderland, who went down with debts of £26 million. Or West Ham United, facing life in the first division with even larger debts and a roster of expensive players to pay should they not be sold.

The only club getting richer all the time is Manchester United, more so after the £23 million sale of one of their most valuable assets — David Beckham. The pure profit is expected to put them further out of reach. Even Arsenal, hamstrung by a 38,500-capacity stadium, are struggling to keep up. United's inexorable rise looks impossible to stop as they leave the rest of football farther and farther behind.

This would have happened even without the ITV Digital fiasco. It was an outcome determined by the creation of the Premier League, designed to provide a feast to a privileged few. The disappearance of the one source of income supposed to keep the smaller clubs within touching distance of football's top table merely accelerated the onset of the League's famine.

THE BARCLAYCARD PREMIERSHIP

MATT DICKINSON, Chief Football Correspondent

TAKEN MOMENTS AFTER Manchester United had secured a 2-2 draw at Highbury in the closing weeks of the season, the picture depicts a beaming Sir Alex Ferguson triumphantly striding to share his delight with the club's supporters. But it is not the foreground that is telling, so much as the expression of Gary Neville in softer focus. The full back is staring at his manager as if he has gone stark raving mad.

It would take a thousand photographs to tell the full tale of a league season, especially one with all the human drama that enveloped Peter Ridsdale, Glenn Roeder, Trevor Brooking and David Beckham, to name only the most obvious. But that image does better than any in picking up the main thread. United's championship was, more than anything, a victory for Ferguson. As the picture from Highbury shows, the Scot believed even when his own players doubted themselves. Ferguson led his team boldly, and daringly, from the front.

His eighth title in 11 campaigns glows even brighter in the context of the previous year, when, having reversed his decision to retire, he had seen Arsenal steal the crown. The perception of Ferguson as a fading force was gaining ground even among those whom he would count as allies. He needed to pull off something dramatic to reverse the tide and his team's run of 15 wins in 18 matches to overhaul Arsenal was an unarguable statement that he, and United, remain the tyrants of the English game.

Although the six goals away to Newcastle United in April provided the season's single outstanding display so soon after the chastening defeat in Madrid, the championship was a triumph of will as much as great football, which is why Ferguson regards it as his best yet. He likes the game to be played with adventure and, in Paul Scholes and Ruud van Nistelrooy, he had two players near their peak for most of the campaign.

The rest, though, were fitful, with Ryan Giggs, Roy Keane, Fabien Barthez, Beckham and the entire defence enduring months of crisis, despite the £30 million spent on Rio Ferdinand. The 3-1 defeat away to Manchester City in November can be regarded as the low point in a

FINAL TABLE

	Played	Won	Drawn	Lost	For	Against	Won	Drawn	Lost	For	Against	Points	Goal Diff
				HOME					AWAY				
Manchester United	38	16	2	1	42	12	9	6	4	32	22	83	40
Arsenal	38	15	2	2	47	20	8	7	4	38	22	78	43
Newcastle United	38	15	2	2	36	17	6	4	9	27	31	69	15
Chelsea	38	12	5	2	41	15	7	5	7	27	23	67	30
Liverpool	38	9	8	2	30	16	9	2	8	31	25	64	20
Blackburn Rovers	38	9	7	3	24	15	7	5	7	28	28	60	9
Everton	38	11	5	3	28	19	6	3	10	20	30	59	-1
Southampton	38	9	8	2	25	16	4	5	10	18	30	52	-3
Manchester City	38	9	2	8	28	26	6	4	9	19	28	51	-7
Tottenham Hotspur	38	9	4	6	30	29	5	4	10	21	33	50	-11
Middlesbrough	38	10	7	2	36	21	3	3	13	12	23	49	4
Charlton Athletic	38	8	3	8	26	30	6	4	9	19	26	49	-11
Birmingham City	38	8	5	6	25	23	5	4	10	16	26	48	-8
Fulham	38	11	3	5	26	18	2	6	11	15	32	48	-9
Leeds United	38	7	3	9	25	26	7	2	10	33	31	47	1
Aston Villa	38	11	2	6	25	14	1	7	11	17	33	45	-5
Bolton Wanderers	38	7	8	4	27	24	3	6	10	14	27	44	-10
West Ham United	38	5	7	7	21	24	5	5	9	21	35	42	-17
West Bromwich Albion	38	3	5	11	17	34	3	3	13	12	31	26	-36
Sunderland	38	3	2	14	11	31	1	5	13	10	34	19	-44

decade of domestic dominance, but Ferguson's ability continually to inspire his squad of millionaires and serial trophy-winners can never again be underestimated. "We never gave up, that's what got us the title," he said. "You can't deny a team when they put a run together like we did."

An eighth championship medal enabled Giggs to equal the record shared by Alan Hansen and Phil Neal, and this was one of the most memorable for the Welshman because Arsenal had proved themselves such worthy adversaries. Scorn for allowing a second successive championship to slip away should be tempered by generous praise for their enthralling football. As Ferguson was to acknowledge, it was the challenge from Highbury that had relit the fires within him and the jousting between the Scotsman and Arsene Wenger never failed to entertain.

Consecutive titles would have allowed Wenger to claim pre-eminence and the breathtaking adventure of early season suggested that his team was unstoppable. "We had it in our hands," Wenger said, but the lack of adequate defensive cover was increasingly exposed and finally laid bare when they squandered a 2-0 lead away to Bolton Wanderers. "If we won at Bolton, we would certainly win the championship," Wenger said. "It was very, very close. As close as that."

Wenger went on to add that "as long as it is a disaster to come second then it is not too bad", and Liverpool had more reason than most to envy Arsenal's position as runners-up. Gerard Houllier's team failed even to qualify for the Champions League after a season that was a significant step backwards, even though they did beat a distracted United to lift the Worthington Cup.

It was small beer for supporters who had expected to challenge for the Premiership and even the European Cup, but Liverpool's winter slump of 11 games without a win was one of the most startling features of the domestic campaign. Not one of the three summer signings — Bruno Cheyrou, Salif Diao or El-Hadji Diouf — made an impact and they never looked capable of beating Chelsea, thereby leaping into fourth place, on the final day.

Among the season's winners were David Moyes at

Managing nicely: Ferguson took huge delight in what he believes is his greatest triumph to date

LEADING SCORERS		Total
Ruud van Nistelrooy	Manchester United	25
Thierry Henry	Arsenal	24
James Beattie	Southampton	23
Mark Viduka	Leeds United	20
Michael Owen	Liverpool	19
Alan Shearer	Newcastle United	17
Nicolas Anelka	Manchester City	14
Robbie Keane	Tottenham, 1 for Leeds	14
Harry Kewell	Leeds United	14
Robert Pires	Arsenal	14
Paul Scholes	Manchester United	14
Gianfranco Zola	Chelsea	14
Teddy Sheringham	Tottenham	12
Jimmy Floyd Hasselbaink	Chelsea	11
Tomasz Radzinski	Everton	11
Kevin Campbell	Everton	10
Dion Dublin	Aston Villa	10
Jason Euell	Charlton Athletic	10
Eidur Gudjohnsen	Chelsea	10
Sylvain Wiltord	Arsenal	10

Everton and Alan Curbishley at Charlton Athletic, even if they did not finish with prizes, while the losers included the hapless Howard Wilkinson, who talked Sunderland into giving him the chance to escape his desk at the FA. How they paid for it in a season when none of their three managers could save them from the worst record in the Premiership's 11 seasons.

It was not until the final whistle of the final game that West Ham United knew that they would be accompanying Sunderland and West Bromwich Albion into the Nationwide League and penury. There was little hope that they might save themselves, but nothing could be discounted after Brooking's Clark Kent transformation from fence-sitting pundit to dugout-thumping coach.

Summoned to save his club when Roeder was found to have a brain tumour on Easter Monday, Brooking donned his Superman cape and led them to wins against Manchester City and Chelsea. It would have been one of the best tales of this or any season if he had steered them

to safety, but a paltry haul of six points from 42 over the winter had left him far too much to do.

Criticising Roeder's judgment became a sensitive subject in the light of his illness, but he must take his share of the blame. Trevor Sinclair, Frederic Kanoute and Paolo Di Canio were notable underachievers, even if the latter managed a typically melodramatic finale to his career at Upton Park by scoring in his last two matches after Brooking had summoned him from exile.

Di Canio's tantrums were a constant source of back-page stories, but, for a gripping soap opera, Elland Road was the only place to be. A little belatedly, Leeds United provided a cautionary tale of football's excesses as, a couple of seasons after reaching the European Cup semi-finals, they were forced to dismantle the team with such a lack of regard for performance that they only avoided relegation on the penultimate weekend.

Even the chirpy Terry Venables gave up trying to paint a rosy picture as the best players went and tales of extravagance emerged. From the £4 million pay-off to

Heading for trouble: Keown's late own goal in the draw away to Bolton Wanderers, when Arsenal contrived to surrender a 2-0 lead, proved to be one of the most important twists in their thrilling race with Manchester United for the title

David O'Leary to the £20 a month allowance for goldfish in the chairman's office, Ridsdale's overspending became a source of weekly bemusement. One of his last acts before he was ousted was to grant Peter Reid a £500,000 bonus for keeping Leeds in the top division. "Living the dream" was how Ridsdale described his time in charge, but he left behind more than £70 million of debts and a team in which everyone was for sale.

Departing the game along with Ridsdale — and surely not coming back, at least in positions of seniority — were Wilkinson and Graham Taylor, who made a mistake in believing that he could still cut it with the leading managers. On the playing side, Peter Schmeichel bade farewell after a brilliant career, and who could blame him after a season playing behind Manchester City's defence?

Winning battles for the older generation were Alan Shearer and the evergreen Gianfranco Zola, while Wayne Rooney was the new teenage sensation. From schoolboy to England's first-choice XI in under a year, the Everton prodigy has broken half a dozen records already. He was still 16 and earning £80 a week when he scored his spectacular goal to beat Arsenal.

Rooney's rise was one of the defining stories of the season and two other random tales spring to mind. Sam Allardyce admitted to signing three players he had never seen and yet still kept Bolton in the Premiership. It made more sense than Leeds laying off the tea ladies and then revealing that they were still paying Robbie Fowler £10,000 a week, even after he moved to Maine Road.

It is from Old Trafford that all the best back-page headlines come and this was a vintage season on and off the field. United's recovery from a faltering start made it one of the most memorable league campaigns and they set the agenda from first kick to last. The campaign began with Keane's controversial autobiography and it finished with Beckham appearing to say farewell to Old Trafford. He was still nursing the wounds inflicted by his manager after Ferguson had hit him with a stray boot and, in that crucial draw at Highbury, left him to stew on the bench.

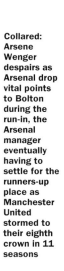

Collared: Arsene Wenger despairs as Arsenal drop vital points to Bolton during the run-in, the Arsenal manager eventually having to settle for the runners-up place as Manchester United stormed to their eighth crown in 11 seasons

AVERAGE ATTENDANCES	
Manchester United	67,601
Newcastle United	51,923
Liverpool	43,242
Chelsea	39,784
Sunderland	39,698
Leeds United	39,124
Everton	38,480
Arsenal	38,041
Tottenham Hotspur	35,897
Aston Villa	35,080
Manchester City	34,564
West Ham United	34,432
Middlesbrough	31,025
Southampton	30,680
Birmingham City	28,883
West Bromwich Albion	26,730
Charlton Athletic	26,255
Blackburn Rovers	26,225
Bolton Wanderers	25,016
Fulham	16,707

MANCHESTER UNITED

PREMIERSHIP

	P	W	D	L	F	A	Pts
Man Utd	**38**	**25**	**8**	**5**	**74**	**34**	**83**
Arsenal	38	23	9	6	85	42	78
Newcastle	38	21	6	11	63	48	69
Chelsea	38	19	10	9	68	38	67
Liverpool	38	18	10	10	61	41	64
Blackburn	38	16	12	10	52	43	60
Everton	38	17	8	13	48	49	59
Southampton	38	13	13	12	43	46	52
Man City	38	15	6	17	47	54	51
Tottenham	38	14	8	16	51	62	50
Middlesbrough	38	13	10	15	48	44	49
Charlton	38	14	7	17	45	56	49
Birmingham	38	13	9	16	41	49	48
Fulham	38	13	9	16	41	50	48
Leeds	38	14	5	19	58	57	47
Aston Villa	38	12	9	17	42	47	45
Bolton	38	10	14	14	41	51	44
West Ham	38	10	12	16	42	59	42
West Brom	38	6	8	24	29	65	26
Sunderland	38	4	7	27	21	65	19

FA CUP
Fifth round

WORTHINGTON CUP
Runners-up

CHAMPIONS LEAGUE
Quarter-finals

Written off by some, Roy Keane relished his fourth title as United captain

THE GAMES

Wednesday August 14
ZALAEGERSZEG (a)
Champions League, 3rd qualifying rnd, 1st leg
Lost 0-1   HT 0-0   Att 40,000
Carroll — Brown (P Neville 6), O'Shea, Blanc, Silvestre —
Beckham, Keane, Veron, Giggs — Van Nistelrooy,
Solskjaer (Forlan 80) *Subs not used* Scholes, Butt,
Stewart, Williams, Tierney *Booked* Beckham, Van
Nistelrooy
Referee **W Stark (Germany)**

An ankle injury rules Ferdinand, their £30 million recruit,
out of his debut, a number of chances go begging and
Koplarovics adds insult to injury by winning the match in
the last minute after a mistake by Phil Neville.

Saturday August 17
WEST BROMWICH ALBION (h)
Won 1-0   HT 0-0   Att 67,645   Position 4th
Carroll — P Neville (Scholes 71), O'Shea, Blanc, Silvestre
(Forlan 77) — Butt — Beckham, Keane, Veron (Solskjaer
59), Giggs — Van Nistelrooy *Subs not used* Williams,
Tierney *Booked* Keane
Scorer **Solskjaer 78**
Referee **S Bennett**

As the furore over Keane's autobiography reaches fever
pitch, United focus on beating the Premiership
newcomers and have to wait until the 78th minute for
Solskjaer to oblige with his hundredth goal for the club.

Friday August 23
CHELSEA (a)
Drew 2-2   HT 1-2   Att 41,541   Position 2nd
Carroll — P Neville, O'Shea, Blanc, Silvestre — Beckham,
Keane, Butt, Giggs (Veron 84) — Van Nistelrooy (Forlan
90), Scholes (Solskjaer 78) *Subs not used* Williams,
Tierney *Booked* Beckham, Neville
Scorers **Beckham 26, Giggs 66**
Report page 78

Tuesday August 27
ZALAEGERSZEG (h)
Champions League, 3rd qualifying rnd, 2nd leg
Won 5-0 (win 5-1 on agg)   HT 3-0   Att 66,814
Carroll — P Neville, Ferdinand (O'Shea 68), Blanc,
Silvestre — Beckham (Forlan 72), Keane, Veron, Giggs —
Van Nistelrooy, Scholes (Solskjaer 49) *Subs not used*
Williams, Chadwick, Stewart, Tierney
Scorers **Van Nistelrooy 6, 76 (pen), Beckham 15,
Scholes 21, Solskjaer 84**
Referee **L Batista (Portugal)**

Ferdinand is allowed an easy belated introduction as
Van Nistelrooy begins the rout, adding a penalty —
Keane prevents Forlan from taking the kick — when Ilic,
the former Charlton Athletic goalkeeper, brings him
down and is harshly sent off.

Saturday August 31
SUNDERLAND (a)
Drew 1-1   HT 1-0   Att 47,586   Position 8th
Carroll — P Neville (Forlan 90), Ferdinand, Blanc,
Silvestre (O'Shea 26) — Beckham, Keane, Veron, Giggs
— Van Nistelrooy, Solskjaer *Subs not used* Stewart,
Williams, Chadwick *Booked* Beckham, Neville *Sent off*
Keane 90
Scorer **Giggs 7**
Report page 270

Tuesday September 3
MIDDLESBROUGH (h)
Won 1-0   HT 1-0   Att 67,464   Position 4th

EVEN BY MANCHESTER UNITED'S STANDARDS it was an
extraordinary season. And that was only off the field. Indeed, it
would have been no great surprise to see a clutch of first-teamers
turn up at one of the TV soap awards ceremonies, with Ruud van
Nistelrooy stepping forward to pick up the gongs, if only to make up
for the individual football awards he so astonishingly missed out on.

The season started with the club splashing a British record
transfer fee of £30 million for Rio Ferdinand — right at the peak of
the market and at a price he has yet to justify. Mind you, he is not
alone — an even higher-profile team-mate consistently hits greater
heights for country rather than club. The headlines then gathered
momentum, staggering through a variety of barely believable stories
that stretched from takeover talk and the "Coolmore Mafia", the
alleged selection of Sven-Goran Eriksson as Sir Alex Ferguson's
replacement, David Beckham and Bootgate, fevered speculation
over the England captain and a possible move to Madrid,
culminating in Nelson Mandela getting the chance to meet
Beckham and a row over appearance money.

Mix in a by no means vintage Ferguson team producing one of
the most astonishing championship successes in the long history of
the competition (and that's not just the Premiership), plus the
staggering individual efforts of Van Nistelrooy, and it all adds up to
just another season in the history of the world's most dramatic
football club.

But do not let the off-field distractions detract from a title win of
immense character that was grudgingly admired everywhere apart
from Highbury, Anfield, Elland Road, Maine Road, etc, etc. From
the depths of a humiliating 3-1 defeat at the hands of Manchester
City in November, a result that had many fans calling for root-and-
branch surgery on and off the field, Ferguson somehow conjured a
series of results after Christmas and stalked Arsene Wenger's
increasingly twitchy team before eventually eclipsing them. Highlights of that run included a 6-2 demolition of title pretenders Newcastle United, a 4-0 stroll against Liverpool and then the decisive 2-2
draw away to Arsenal that finished with Ferguson's now famous
clenched-fist victory salute. And how right he was to celebrate.

A series of perfectly timed comments in the newspapers and
behind the dressing-room door fired up his own players and reeled
in an Arsenal side that found out how tough it is to win the title
from the front. Not that Wenger's side were on the radar when an
indifferent start to the season, including a draw away to Sunderland
and defeats by Bolton Wanderers and Leeds United, culminated in
that City shocker. Fergie told a few home truths, results began to

The destruction of Newcastle United was a key moment in the big title push

pick up and, apart from a blip that saw consecutive defeats by Blackburn Rovers and Middlesbrough over Christmas, the rest is legend. Not that it was down to any great tactical switch or sudden surge in form by an individual, rather the sheer bloody-mindedness of a manager and his players.

Indeed, when it came to tactics, Fergie again showed why he will not go down as one of the game's great coaches. Nobody seems certain of his best XI and his constant tinkering during games, particularly in defence, is sometimes difficult to fathom for players and fans alike. Indeed, the team's domestic cup disappointments were down to the inability to outwit an incredibly one-dimensional Liverpool team in the Worthington Cup final and then a desire to kick lumps out of an Arsenal side that had been comprehensively outplayed at the same ground just three months previously.

And then there was Europe. Consecutive European Cup finals in Glasgow and Manchester were tailor-made for Fergie to move out on his own as Britain's greatest manager. And the fact that he has failed to add to that single success in 1999 will always leave a question mark against his record when it is held up against the very best. Yes, his teams have done consistently better than anybody else in the competition's present format; yes, the 3-0 win against Juventus, the eventual finalists, in Turin was absolutely stunning; and yes, the second-leg defeat of Real Madrid was probably the game of the season. But then you remember that, under Ferguson, United have reached the final as often as Borussia Dortmund and Bayer Leverkusen.

He talks incessantly about his desire to improve that record, but for United to have real status among the elite of European football, not just as a money-making machine, they have got to start winning the big one on a regular basis instead of winning the league for fun.

Barthez — P Neville, Ferdinand, Blanc, Silvestre — Beckham (O'Shea 90), Veron, Butt, Giggs — Van Nistelrooy (Solskjaer 70), Scholes (Forlan 78) *Subs not used* Pugh, Ricardo *Booked* Veron
Scorer Van Nistelrooy 28 (pen)
Referee **M Riley**

Scholes, ruled unfit for England duty against Portugal in four days' time, controversially turns out for United, who edge past Middlesbrough with Van Nistelrooy's penalty, awarded when Ehiogu holds him back.

Wednesday September 11
BOLTON WANDERERS (h)
Lost 0-1 HT 0-0 Att 67,623 Position 7th
Barthez — P Neville, Ferdinand, Blanc, Silvestre — Beckham, Veron (Forlan 76), Butt, Giggs — Van Nistelrooy, Solskjaer *Subs not used* O'Shea, Stewart, Chadwick, Ricardo *Booked* Neville
Referee **G Barber**
Attendance **67,623**
Position **7th**

Lightning never strikes twice? Ask United, rudderless without the injured Keane, who lose at home to Bolton for the second season running, with Nolan again the executioner. His 77th-minute strike finds its way through a crowded area and under Barthez.

Saturday September 14
LEEDS UNITED (a)
Lost 0-1 HT 0-0 Att 39,622 Position 9th
Barthez — O'Shea, Ferdinand, Blanc, Silvestre — Beckham, P Neville, Butt (Chadwick 63), Giggs — Van Nistelrooy (Forlan 71), Solskjaer *Substitutes not used* Ricardo, Pugh, Roche *Booked* Solskjaer
Report page 211

Wednesday September 18
MACCABI HAIFA (h)
Champions League
Won 5-2 HT 2-1 Att 63,439
Barthez (Ricardo 68) — O'Shea, Ferdinand, Blanc, Silvestre — Beckham, P Neville, Veron, Giggs (Forlan 56) — Van Nistelrooy (Pugh 75), Solskjaer *Subs not used* G Neville, May, Stewart, Chadwick
Scorers Giggs 10, Solskjaer 35, Veron 46, Van Nistelrooy 54, Forlan 89 (pen)
Referee **P Allaerts (Belgium)**

Shock waves shake Old Trafford when Katan gives Maccabi the lead, but by the time Cohen adds a second, United have run in four and delight gives way to delirium when Forlan, on his 27th appearance, finally gets his first United goal with a late penalty.

Saturday September 21
TOTTENHAM HOTSPUR (h)
Won 1-0 HT 0-0 Att 67,611 Position 7th
Barthez — P Neville, Ferdinand, O'Shea, Silvestre — Beckham, Veron (G Neville 76), Butt, Giggs (Pugh 85) — Van Nistelrooy, Solskjaer (Forlan 76) *Subs not used* Ricardo, Stewart *Booked* Van Nistelrooy
Scorer Van Nistelrooy 63 (pen)
Referee **R Styles**

Barthez saves well from Richards early on as United try to stave off a third successive Premiership defeat and they secure a deserved victory when Doherty fouls Solskjaer and Van Nistelrooy converts the penalty.

Tuesday September 24
BAYER LEVERKUSEN (a)
Champions League
Won 2-1 HT 2-0 Att 22,500

Barthez — O'Shea (G Neville ht), Ferdinand, Blanc, Silvestre — Beckham, P Neville, Butt, Veron (Solskjaer 87) — Giggs — Van Nistelrooy (Forlan ht) *Subs not used* Ricardo, May, Stewart, Pugh *Booked* Butt, Ferdinand
Scorer **Van Nistelrooy 31, 44**
Referee **J Wegereef (the Netherlands)**

Revenge for last season's defeat in the European Cup semi-finals is delivered by Van Nistelrooy, who scores twice before a hamstring injury forces his withdrawal.

Saturday September 28
CHARLTON ATHLETIC (a)
Won 3-1   HT 0-1   Att 26,630   Position 4th
Barthez — O'Shea, Ferdinand, Blanc, P Neville — Forlan (Van Nistelrooy 56), Beckham, Butt (G Neville 70), Giggs — Solskjaer, Scholes *Subs not used* Ricardo, May, Stewart *Booked* Beckham, P Neville, Forlan
Scorers **Scholes 54, Giggs 83, Van Nistelrooy 90**
Report page 175

Tuesday October 1
OLYMPIAKOS (h)
Champions League
Won 4-0   HT 2-0   Att 66,902
Barthez — G Neville, Ferdinand, Blanc (O'Shea 69), Silvestre — Beckham, Butt, Veron, Giggs (Fortune 69) — Scholes (Forlan 78) — Solskjaer *Subs not used* Ricardo, P Neville, May, Stewart *Booked* Veron, Ferdinand, G Neville
Scorers **Giggs 19, Veron 26, Anatolakis 67 (og), Solskjaer 77**
Referee **G Vessiere (France)**

A brilliant chip from Veron is the highlight of United's thumping win over the Greeks, who have Ze Elias sent off for a bad foul on the Argentinian just before half-time. Uefa later deprives Giggs of a second goal.

Monday October 7
EVERTON (h)
Won 3-0   HT 0-0   Att 67,629   Position 4th
Barthez — G Neville, O'Shea, Blanc, Silvestre — Beckham, Butt (Forlan 85), Veron (Solskjaer 63), Giggs — Van Nistelrooy (P Neville 90), Scholes *Subs not used* Ricardo, Fortune
Scorers **Scholes 86, 90, Van Nistelrooy 90 (pen)**
Referee **M Riley**

Reports of a defensive job well done are already being written when Everton's world falls apart, conceding three goals in an extraordinary last four minutes. Scholes's double sandwiches a penalty from Van Nistelrooy.

Saturday October 19
FULHAM (a)
Drew 1-1   HT 0-1   Att 14,775   Position 3rd
Barthez — G Neville, O'Shea, Blanc, Silvestre (Forlan 80) — Beckham, P Neville (Fortune 59), Veron, Giggs — Scholes — Solskjaer *Subs not used* Ricardo, May, Richardson *Booked* Blanc, Beckham, Barthez
Scorer **Solskjaer 62**
Report page 201

Wednesday October 23
OLYMPIAKOS (a)
Champions League
Won 3-2   HT 1-0   Att 15,000
Barthez — G Neville, O'Shea, Blanc, Silvestre — Beckham (Chadwick 63), P Neville, Veron (Richardson 87), Giggs (Fortune 63) — Forlan, Scholes *Subs not used* Ricardo, May, Solskjaer, Roche *Booked* G Neville

MATCH OF THE SEASON

Arsenal 2   Manchester United 2
Highbury, Wednesday April 16, 2003
Matt Dickinson, Chief Football Correspondent

IT WAS A GAME THAT PROMISED everything and, on a night of raw intensity at Highbury, it delivered passion, controversy, an offside goal and a red card for an elbowing offence — everything, in fact, apart from a winner and an irrefutable pointer as to which of these extraordinarily well-matched sides will win the Barclaycard Premiership at the end of a campaign that now looks sure to go to the final week.

United will be most people's favourites after protecting their three-point advantage at the top, albeit having played a match more, but it would be a brave man who would bet against an Arsenal side that had the drive still to be attacking at the final whistle last night, even though, for the last seven minutes, they had been reduced to ten men.

Sol Campbell was the player dismissed, for swinging his right arm at the pursuing Ole Gunnar Solskjaer. It was not an offence that seemed in character for the England centre half, who will argue that he was only trying to use his outstretched hand, but even if there was no malicious intent, replays clearly showed some contact between elbow and nose.

Campbell looks certain to miss the last four matches of the season, including the FA Cup Final, after his second dismissal of the campaign. It is a massive blow to Arsene Wenger's hopes, possibly enough to make the difference between sides who could not be separated last night after 90 minutes of incessant and powerful football. No one can dispute Arsenal's fortitude, but there was good fortune in both their goals and it was United who celebrated as if the pendulum had just taken a significant swing their way.

United came into the match on a run of 11 wins and two draws in the Premiership and, if that form looked ominous for the home supporters, they were soon given plenty more reasons to fear the worst. Conceding the opening goal to Ruud van Nistelrooy was a huge blow to their fragile confidence; the loss of Patrick Vieira after barely a third of the match was enough to make some think of giving up and going home.

The Arsenal players had no choice but to soldier on without their captain, who started with so much strapping on his right knee that it could have been wrapped several times around Highbury. For all the 33 minutes that he could handle before being reduced to a hobble, Vieira was courageous in the tackle, but he must have sensed that this was not a match in which he could afford to be operating below his physical peak — not with Nicky Butt and Roy Keane planting a United flag in the centre of the pitch as they sought territorial domination.

Van Nistelrooy has Arsenal on the run in the big title showdown at Highbury

Led by their combative pair, Ferguson's men looked more powerful, more robust, from the kick-off. Keane clearly had been reading the papers telling of his passing as a midfield tyrant. When Thierry Henry wriggled around the back of the United defence, Keane was there to end the run with a full stop of a tackle. A rant at Rio Ferdinand was proof that Keane was on his game.

Of the Arsenal team, only the elusive Robert Pires seemed to have the upper hand against Wes Brown, his marker, in those early exchanges. The rest were being frustrated and, with a solid base behind them, the United attack must have been confident that chances would come soon enough, even in a match as tight and tense as this one. Paul Scholes might have scored when he misheaded a cross from Solskjaer and Van Nistelrooy lifted a good chance over the bar, but United were ahead by the 24th minute through a fine goal from the Dutchman.

The striker should have been stopped by Campbell, but the centre half, who has looked flawless in recent weeks, missed a chance to take man or ball. Van Nistelrooy nipped past him and used his speed to run clear of the Arsenal defence. Stuart Taylor, who found out he was playing only yesterday morning when David Seaman woke with a heavy cold, dived at the striker's feet, but the shot had already been clipped over him.

Arsenal needed something to cling to as they went in for their

Scorers **Blanc 21, Veron 59, Scholes 84**
Referee **P Collina (Italy)**

United make it four wins out of four and are through to the second stage for the seventh year in succession.

Saturday October 26
ASTON VILLA (h)
Drew 1-1   HT **0-1**   Att **67,619**   Position **4th**
Barthez — G Neville, Ferdinand, Blanc, Silvestre — Beckham, P Neville (Fortune 60), Veron, Forlan — Scholes — Solskjaer *Subs not used* Ricardo, O'Shea, Roche, Richardson *Booked* Beckham
Scorer **Forlan 77**
Referee **G Poll**

A much-changed Villa team produces a much-improved performance, but after Mellberg heads them in front, Forlan finally comes up trumps with his first league goal in 24 games.

Tuesday October 29
MACCABI HAIFA (a*)
Champions League
Lost 0-3   HT **0-1**   Att **22,000**   (* in Nicosia)
Ricardo — G Neville, Ferdinand, O'Shea, Silvestre — Richardson (Nardiello 61), P Neville, Scholes, Fortune — Forlan (Timm 78), Solskjaer *Subs not used* Carroll, May, Pugh, Roche, Lynch *Booked* Silvestre, O'Shea, Ricardo
Referee **A J Lopez Nieto (Spain)**

"No regrets" Sir Alex Ferguson insists, despite his barely recognisable selection suffering United's heaviest European defeat for eight years.

Saturday November 2
SOUTHAMPTON (h)
Won 2-1   HT **1-1**   Att **67,691**   Position **3rd**
Barthez — G Neville, Ferdinand, Blanc, Silvestre (Solskjaer 68) — Beckham, P Neville (Fortune 80), Veron, Giggs — Scholes — Van Nistelrooy (O'Shea 87) *Subs not used* Ricardo, Fortune
Scorers **P Neville 15, Forlan 85**
Referee **U Rennie**

Forlan celebrates his late winner against an unlucky Southampton by waving his shirt manically above his head . . . and is then unable to get it back on.

Tuesday November 5
LEICESTER CITY (h)
Worthington Cup, 3rd rnd
Won 2-0   HT **0-0**   Att **47,848**
Carroll — G Neville, Ferdinand, May, O'Shea — Forlan, Beckham, P Neville (Scholes 59), Fortune (Veron 65) — Solskjaer, Nardiello (Richardson 74) *Subs not used* Barthez, Pugh *Booked* Beckham, P Neville
Scorers **Beckham 80 (pen), Richardson 90**
Referee **C Foy**

Beckham's penalty and Richardson's first goal for the club, in the last minute, take United through.

Saturday November 9
MANCHESTER CITY (a)
Lost 1-3   HT **1-2**   Att **34,649**   Position **5th**
Barthez — G Neville (O'Shea 62), Ferdinand, Blanc, Silvestre — Solskjaer, P Neville, Veron (Forlan 62), Giggs — Scholes — Van Nistelrooy *Subs not used* Ricardo, May, Fortune *Booked* Solskjaer, P Neville
Scorer **Solskjaer 8**
Report page 141

Wednesday November 13
BAYER LEVERKUSEN (h)
Champions League
Won 2-0   HT **1-0**   Att **66,185**

Ricardo — O'Shea, Ferdinand, Blanc (G Neville 78), Silvestre — Beckham (Solskjaer 78), Veron, Fortune, Giggs (Chadwick 81) — Scholes — Van Nistelrooy *Subs not used* P Neville, Carroll, Forlan, Nardiello *Booked* Ricardo
Scorers **Veron 42, Van Nistelrooy 69**
Referee **V Hrinak (Slovakia)**

Old Trafford delights in the win that ensures United will be seeded for the second phase.

Sunday November 17
WEST HAM UNITED (a)
Drew 1-1 HT **1-0** Att **35,049** Position **5th**
Barthez — O'Shea, Brown, Blanc, Silvestre — Scholes, Veron, Fortune, Giggs — Van Nistelrooy, Solskjaer *Subs not used* Ricardo, P Neville, Forlan, Davis, Richardson
Scorer **Van Nistelrooy 38**
Report page 249

Saturday November 23
NEWCASTLE UNITED (h)
Won 5-3 HT **3-1** Att **67,619** Position **5th**
Barthez — O'Shea, Brown, Blanc (Roche 69), Silvestre — Solskjaer, Scholes, Fortune, Giggs — Forlan (Veron 80), Van Nistelrooy (Richardson 64) *Subs not used* Chadwick, Ricardo *Booked* Solskjaer, Van Nistelrooy
Scorers **Scholes 25, Van Nistelrooy 38, 45, 53, Solskjaer 55**
Referee **S Dunn**

A hat-trick inside 15 minutes by Van Nistelrooy settles a match of numerous thrills but untold defensive flaws. Lost somewhere amid the mayhem is Shearer's hundredth Premiership goal for Newcastle.

Tuesday November 26
FC BASLE (a)
Champions League
Won 3-1 HT **0-1** Att **29,501**
Barthez — P Neville, Brown (May 90), O'Shea, Silvestre — Solskjaer (Chadwick 90), Veron, Scholes, Fortune, Giggs — Van Nistelrooy (Forlan 73) *Subs not used* Ricardo, Stewart, Pugh, Richardson *Booked* Scholes, Fortune, Veron
Scorers **Van Nistelrooy 61, 63, Solskjaer 68**
Referee **V Ivanov (Russia)**

Trouble looms within 35 seconds of the second group stage starting, Gimenez giving Basle the lead, but the trusty Van Nistelrooy turns the tide.

Sunday December 1
LIVERPOOL (a)
Won 2-1 HT **0-0** Att **44,250** Position **4th**
Barthez — G Neville, Brown, Silvestre, O'Shea — Solskjaer, Scholes, Fortune (P Neville 82), Giggs — Van Nistelrooy (May 89), Forlan (Stewart 90) *Subs not used* Chadwick, Ricardo *Booked* Van Nistelrooy, Brown, Forlan, Silvestre
Scorer **Forlan 64, 67**
Report page 94

Tuesday December 3
BURNLEY (a)
Worthington Cup, 4th rnd
Won 2-0 HT **1-0** Att **22,034**
Carroll — P Neville, Brown, May, Silvestre — Chadwick, Stewart (Scholes 58), O'Shea, Pugh — Van Nistelrooy (Solskjaer ht), Forlan (Giggs 75) *Subs not used* Roche, Ricardo
Scorers **Forlan 35, Solskjaer 65**

The conquerors of Tottenham Hotspur are put in their place by a United side without its first-choice midfield.

An angry Campbell remonstrates with Solskjaer after his controversial red card

half-time talk and a better spell going into the interval must have raised their spirits. Whatever Wenger said, it helped to convince them that this match could yet be won and they forgot their self-pity not only to equalise but also to take the lead.

Their aggression and ambition was reflected by Ashley Cole's charge upfield six minutes after the restart, the full back taking the ball on the run from Pires. Dashing into the penalty area, Cole cut inside Brown and hit a right-foot shot that Barthez will have been confident of gathering.

That was until Henry appeared in his sights, the ball striking the back of the forward's legs and deflecting beyond the goalkeeper. Henry was credited with his twentieth Premiership strike of the season, but the goal belonged to Cole.

Fortunate then, Arsenal's luck knew no bounds when they took the lead 11 minutes later. Henry was at least a couple of yards offside when Gilberto picked him out with a low pass, but no flag was raised and the Frenchman turned and slipped the ball past the onrushing Barthez. From 1-0 down to 2-1 up; Highbury was delirious.

If only the players had not joined the celebrations, allowing United the softest of equalisers a minute later when Solskjaer's cross was headed in at the far post by Ryan Giggs as Lauren and Fredrik Ljungberg stood by. Wenger was apoplectic on the sidelines, but he could not complain about the result.

ARSENAL (4-4-2): S Taylor — Lauren, M Keown, S Campbell, A Cole — F Ljungberg, P Vieira (sub: Edu, 33min), Gilberto, R Pires (sub: Kanu, 80) — T Henry, D Bergkamp (sub: S Wiltord, 75). **Substitutes not used:** G Warmuz, O Luzhny. **Sent off:** Campbell.
MANCHESTER UNITED (4-4-1-1): F Barthez — W Brown, R Ferdinand, M Silvestre, J O'Shea (sub: G Neville, 46) — O G Solskjaer, R Keane, N Butt, P Scholes — R Giggs — R van Nistelrooy. **Substitutes not used:** P Neville, D Beckham, Ricardo, Q Fortune. **Booked:** Keane, Butt. **Referee:** M Halsey.

THE MANAGER

Sir Alex Ferguson

Vintage stuff, like the red wine he is known to be fond of. Not the best operator in the transfer market or on the training ground, Ferguson is without peer when it comes to getting into players' heads and under opponents' skin. The 2002-03 title win will rightly go down as one of his finest and convince even more people that there cannot be life after Sir Alex. But there has to be, and perhaps the only thing left for him to do at Old Trafford, apart from multiple triumphs in Europe, is to identify his successor and possibly even groom him.

Howard Wheatcroft

APPEARANCES

	Prem	FAC	WC	Euro	Total
F Barthez	30	2	4	10	46
D Beckham	27 (4)	3	5	10 (3)	45 (7)
L Blanc	15 (4)	1	-	9	25 (4)
W Brown	22	1 (1)	5	6	34 (1)
N Butt	14 (4)	0 (2)	0 (1)	8	22 (7)
R Carroll	8 (2)	1	2	3	14 (2)
L Chadwick	0 (1)	-	1	0 (3)	1 (4)
R Ferdinand	27 (1)	3	4	11	45 (1)
D Fletcher	-	-	-	2	2
D Forlan	7 (18)	0 (2)	3 (2)	5 (8)	15 (30)
Q Fortune	5 (4)	-	1	3 (3)	9 (7)
R Giggs	32 (4)	3	4 (1)	13 (2)	52 (7)
R Keane	19 (2)	3	2	6	30 (2)
M Lynch	-	-	-	1	1
D May	0 (1)	-	2	0 (1)	2 (2)
D Nardiello	-	-	1	0 (1)	1 (1)
G Neville	19 (7)	3	5	8 (2)	35 (9)
P Neville	19 (6)	2	4	10 (2)	35 (8)
J O'Shea	26 (6)	1	3	12 (4)	42 (10)
D Pugh	0 (1)	-	1	1 (2)	2 (3)
Ricardo	0 (1)	-	-	3 (1)	3 (2)
K Richardson	0 (2)	1	0 (1)	2 (3)	3 (6)
L Roche	0 (1)	-	-	1	1 (1)
P Scholes	31 (2)	2 (1)	4 (2)	9 (1)	46 (6)
M Silvestre	34	2	5	13	54
O G Solskjaer	29 (8)	1 (1)	1 (3)	9 (5)	40 (17)
M Stewart	0 (1)	0 (1)	1	0 (1)	1 (3)
M Timm	-	-	-	0 (1)	0 (1)
R van Nistelrooy	33 (1)	3	4	10 (1)	50 (2)
J S Veron	21 (4)	1	4 (1)	11	37 (5)
D Webber	-	-	-	0 (1)	0 (1)

Saturday December 7
ARSENAL (h)
Won 2-0   HT 1-0   Att **67,650**   Position **3rd**
Barthez — G Neville, Brown, Silvestre, O'Shea — Veron, P Neville — Solskjaer, Scholes, Giggs — Van Nistelrooy
Subs not used Ricardo, May, Chadwick, Stewart, Forlan
Booked P Neville
Scorers **Veron 22, Scholes 77**
Referee **D Gallagher**

The title race is on. Victory would have taken the champions nine points clear of United, but Henry's bad miss ends Arsenal's streak of games with a goal at 56 and the hungrier side wins.

Wednesday December 11
DEPORTIVO LA CORUNA (h)
Champions League
Won 2-0   HT 1-0   Att **67,014**
Barthez — G Neville, Brown, Silvestre, O'Shea (Beckham 81) — Veron, P Neville, O'Shea (Forlan 81) — Solskjaer, Scholes, Giggs — Van Nistelrooy (Richardson 89) *Subs not used* Stewart, Ricardo, Chadwick, Pugh *Booked* Solskjaer, Veron
Scorer **Van Nistelrooy 7, 55**
Referee **T Hauge (Norway)**

An early header and a second on the rebound elevates Van Nistelrooy to the position of United's leading European goalscorer as he takes his tally to 20.

Saturday December 14
WEST HAM UNITED (h)
Won 3-0   HT 2-0   Att **67,555**   Position **2nd**
Barthez — G Neville, Brown, Silvestre, O'Shea (Blanc 73) — Solskjaer (Beckham ht), P Neville, Veron, Giggs — Van Nistelrooy, Scholes (Forlan 73) *Subs not used* Richardson, Ricardo
Scorers **Solskjaer 15, Veron 17, Schemmel 61 (og)**

Van Nistelrooy misses four clear chances, but it matters little as Veron contributes a Beckham-esque free kick.

Tuesday December 17
CHELSEA (h)
Worthington Cup, 5th rnd
Won 1-0   HT 0-0   Att **57,985**
Barthez — G Neville, Brown, Silvestre, O'Shea — Beckham, P Neville, Veron, Giggs — Scholes — Forlan
Subs not used Blanc, Stewart, Nardiello, Richardson, Carroll *Booked* P Neville
Scorer **Forlan 80**
Referee **S Bennett**

The biggest crowd — finals apart — that the League Cup has witnessed for 28 years sees Forlan, profiting from Zola's mistake, put a late winner through Cudicini's legs.

Sunday December 22
BLACKBURN ROVERS (a)
Lost 0-1   HT 0-1   Att **30,475**   Position **3rd**
Barthez — G Neville, Brown, Silvestre, O'Shea — Solskjaer, P Neville (Blanc 84), Scholes, Giggs (Beckham 70) — Van Nistelrooy, Forlan (Keane 59) *Subs not used* Richardson, Ricardo *Booked* G Neville
Report page 107

Thursday December 26
MIDDLESBROUGH (a)
Lost 1-3   HT 0-1   Att **34,673**   Position **3rd**
Barthez — G Neville (Beckham 72), Brown, Blanc, O'Shea (Ferdinand 83) — Veron, Keane — Solskjaer, Scholes, Giggs — Van Nistelrooy *Subs not used* P Neville, Ricardo, Forlan *Booked* Brown, Scholes
Scorer **Giggs 60**
Report page 167

Saturday December 28
BIRMINGHAM CITY (h)
Won 2-0   HT 1-0   Att 67,640   Position 3rd
Barthez — O'Shea, Ferdinand, Brown, Silvestre —
Beckham, Keane (Giggs 85), Veron, Scholes (Richardson
74) — Forlan, Solskjaer (P Neville 76) *Subs not used*
Ricardo, G Neville *Booked* Brown
Scorers **Forlan 37, Beckham 73**
Referee **M Dean**

Steve Bruce returns to Old Trafford and has no
complaints about defeat, Beckham setting up the first
and chipping the second himself in glorious style.

Wednesday January 1
SUNDERLAND (h)
Won 2-1   HT 0-1   Att 67,609   Position 2nd
Barthez (Carroll 29) — O'Shea (Giggs 63), Ferdinand,
Brown, Silvestre — Beckham, Keane, Veron (G Neville
90), Scholes — Forlan, Solskjaer *Subs not used*
P Neville, Richardson *Booked* Solskjaer, Ferdinand
Scorers **Beckham 81, Scholes 90**
Referee **G Poll**

One of the shock results of the season is on the cards
after Veron's own goal, but Beckham levels and, with
stoppage time beginning, Scholes heads a winner.

Saturday January 4
PORTSMOUTH (h)
FA Cup, 3rd rnd
Won 4-1   HT 2-1   Att 67,222
Carroll — G Neville, Ferdinand, Blanc, Silvestre (Brown
82) — Beckham, Keane (Stewart ht), P Neville,
Richardson (Scholes 59) — Giggs — Van Nistelrooy
Subs not used Forlan, Ricardo
Scorers **Van Nistelrooy 5 (pen), 81 (pen),**
Beckham 17, Scholes 90
Referee **A Wiley**

Portsmouth may be on a march back to the top flight,
but they are given a lesson in what to expect when they
get there. How much different it might have been had
Quashie not missed a sitter with United just 2-1 ahead?

Tuesday January 7
BLACKBURN ROVERS (h)
Worthington Cup, semi-final, 1st leg
Drew 1-1   HT 0-0   Att 62,740
Details page 338

Saturday January 11
WEST BROMWICH ALBION (a)
Won 3-1   HT 2-1   Att 27,129   Position 2nd
Barthez — G Neville, Ferdinand, Brown, Silvestre —
Beckham, Keane (O'Shea 81), P Neville, Solskjaer
(Forlan 68) — Scholes — Van Nistelrooy *Subs not used*
Blanc, Ricardo, Richardson *Booked* Scholes
Scorers **Van Nistelrooy 7, Scholes 23, Solskjaer 55**
Report page 264

Saturday January 18
CHELSEA (h)
Won 2-1   HT 1-1   Att 67,606   Position 2nd
Barthez — G Neville, Ferdinand, Brown, Silvestre (Veron
86) — Beckham, Keane, P Neville (Giggs ht), Solskjaer
— Scholes, Van Nistelrooy (Forlan 71) *Subs not used*
O'Shea, Carroll
Scorers **Scholes 39, Forlan 90**
Referee **P Durkin**

Chelsea draw first blood, but a mistake by Cudicini —
who later makes one of the saves of the season —
precedes an equaliser by Scholes and Forlan's volley.

The obvious choice is Ruud van
Nistelrooy, but in reality it has to be
John O'Shea. An unassuming young
Irishman who is a born winner and
one of the finest footballers of his
generation. His development from
fringe squad player to one of the
most talked-about talents in years
was staggering, and although Sir Alex
Ferguson speaks of a desire for
experience at the back, there must
be a place for this young man. Either
full back position, centre of defence
and even midfield all come naturally.
Go Johnny, go.
Howard Wheatcroft

STATS AND FACTS

● United's 2-0 FA Cup defeat by Arsenal was only the second time they had lost at home by more than one goal since August 1992 in any competition.

● Arsenal were the Premiership's leading goalscorers — United had held the honour for each for the previous eight seasons.

● United lost 1-0 away to Leeds United on September 14: their previous eight failures to score in the Premiership had all been at Old Trafford.

● Bolton Wanderers have recorded more wins over United (41) than vice versa (39).

● The first match featuring two managerial knights was played on November 23 when United, managed by Sir Alex Ferguson, faced Newcastle United, led by Sir Bobby Robson.

● The past 21 games between United and Liverpool have been televised live.

● In 15 Premiership matches with Laurent Blanc in the starting line-up, United won six, drew five and lost four. In the 23 matches without him, the team won 19, drew three and lost one.

● During Ryan Giggs's home goal drought for United in the Premiership, between April 2001 and April 2003, Ruud van Nistelrooy scored 26 league goals at Old Trafford.

● United's 4-0 home win over Liverpool in April was only the second time in 79 meetings between the clubs that one side had scored four times.

● When the domestic season ended, Ruud van Nistelrooy had scored in each of his previous 12 games (ten for Manchester United, two for Holland).

● Only one of United's past 165 domestic matches has finished goalless — at home to Charlton Athletic on the final day of the 2001-02 season.

● United and Liverpool have each won eight league titles in 11 seasons.

Bill Edgar

GOALSCORERS

	Prem	FAC	WC	Euro	Total
D Beckham	6	1	1 (p)	3	11 (1p)
L Blanc	-	-	-	1	1
W Brown	-	-	-	1	1
D Forlan	6	-	2	1 (p)	9 (1p)
R Giggs	8	2	-	4	14
G Neville	-	-	-	1	1
P Neville	1	1	-	-	2
K Richardson	-	-	1	-	1
P Scholes	14	1	3	2	20
M Silvestre	1	-	-	-	1
O G Solskjaer	9	1	1	4	15
R van Nistelrooy	25 (8p)	4 (2p)	1 (p)	14 (1p)	44 (12p)
J S Veron	2	-	-	4	6
Own goals	2	-	-	2	4

Wednesday January 22
BLACKBURN ROVERS (a)
Worthington Cup, semi-final, 2nd leg
Won 3-1 (win 4-2 on agg)   HT **2-1**   Att **29,048**
Details page 338

Sunday January 26
WEST HAM UNITED (h)
FA Cup, 4th rnd
Won 6-0   HT **2-0**   Att **67,181**
Barthez — G Neville, Ferdinand, O'Shea, P Neville — Beckham (Solskjaer 63), Keane, Veron (Butt 51) — Scholes (Forlan ht) — Van Nistelrooy, Giggs *Subs not used* Brown, Carroll *Booked* Veron
Scorers **Giggs 8, 29, Van Nistelrooy 49, 58, P Neville 50, Solskjaer 69**
Referee **S Bennett**

Glenn Roeder vows to fight on, but the West Ham manager admits their Cup demolition is "excruciating".

Saturday February 1
SOUTHAMPTON (a)
Won 2-0   HT **2-0**   Att **32,085**   Position **2nd**
Barthez (Carroll 39) — G Neville, Ferdinand, O'Shea, Silvestre — Beckham (Scholes 69), Keane, Veron — Giggs — Van Nistelrooy (Forlan 88), Solskjaer *Subs not used* P Neville, Brown
Scorers **Van Nistelrooy 15, Giggs 22**
Report page 132

Tuesday February 4
BIRMINGHAM CITY (a)
Won 1-0   HT **0-0**   Att **29,475**   Position **2nd**
Carroll — G Neville, Ferdinand, Brown, Silvestre — Beckham, Keane, Veron — Scholes — Van Nistelrooy (Solskjaer 82), Giggs *Subs not used* P Neville, Butt, Forlan, Ricardo *Booked* Keane
Scorer **Van Nistelrooy 56**
Referee **S Dunn**
Report page 193

Sunday February 9
MANCHESTER CITY (h)
Drew 1-1   HT **1-0**   Att **67,646**   Position **2nd**
Carroll — G Neville, Ferdinand, Brown, Silvestre — Beckham, Keane, Veron (Butt 77) — Scholes — Van Nistelrooy, Giggs (Solskjaer 89) *Subs not used* O'Shea, P Neville, Ricardo *Booked* G Neville
Scorer **Van Nistelrooy 18**
Referee **A Wiley**

With United hanging on to Van Nistelrooy's far-post finish, Kevin Keegan pulls off a masterstroke with a double substitution four minutes from time, Benarbia setting up Goater's equaliser with their first touches.

Saturday February 15
ARSENAL (h)
FA Cup, 5th rnd
Lost 0-2   HT **0-1**   Att **67,209**
Barthez — G Neville, Ferdinand, Brown, Silvestre — Beckham (Butt 83), Keane, Scholes, Solskjaer — Van Nistelrooy, Giggs (Forlan 71) *Subs not used* Ricardo, P Neville, O'Shea *Booked* Keane, Van Nistelrooy, Scholes
Referee **J Winter**

A flurry of yellow cards to start, a brace of goals to finish and a candidate for the worst miss ever in between from Giggs, who shoots over an open goal at 0-0. Arsenal have the last laugh, even if it is Beckham who ends the day in stitches.

Wednesday February 19
JUVENTUS (h)
Champions League

Won 2-1   HT 1-0   Att 66,703
Barthez — G Neville, Ferdinand, Brown, Silvestre (O'Shea
52) — Beckham, Keane, Butt, Giggs (Forlan 90) —
Scholes (Solskjaer 79) — Van Nistelrooy *Subs not used*
Ricardo, P Neville, Pugh, Fletcher *Booked* Keane,
Scholes
Scorers **Brown 3, Van Nistelrooy 85**
Referee **K M Nielsen (Denmark)**

All eyes are on Beckham after three days when his
wound captures more headlines than impending war
and he responds by setting up both goals.

Saturday February 22
BOLTON WANDERERS (a)
Drew 1-1   HT 0-0   Att 27,409   Position 2nd
Barthez — G Neville, Ferdinand, Brown (P Neville 64),
O'Shea — Beckham, Keane, Veron (Butt 80), Giggs
(Forlan 57) — Van Nistelrooy, Solskjaer *Subs not used*
Ricardo, Fletcher *Booked* Keane
Scorer **Solskjaer 90**
Report page 242

Tuesday February 25
JUVENTUS (a)
Champions League
Won 3-0   HT 2-0   Att 59,111
Barthez — G Neville, Ferdinand, Keane, O'Shea (Pugh
60) — Beckham, Butt, P Neville — Veron — Forlan (Giggs
8; Van Nistelrooy 48), Solskjaer *Subs not used* Roche,
Fletcher, Richardson, Carroll *Booked* P Neville
Scorers **Giggs 15, 41, Van Nistelrooy 63**
Referee **M Merk (Germany)**

Needing a point to guarantee a quarter-final place for a
record seventh season in succession, United get three
when Giggs scores twice.

Sunday March 2
LIVERPOOL
Worthington Cup, final (Cardiff)
Lost 0-2   HT 0-1   Att 74,500
Details page 338

Wednesday March 5
LEEDS UNITED (h)
Won 2-1   HT 1-0   Att 67,135   Position 2nd
Barthez — O'Shea, Ferdinand, Keane, Silvestre —
Beckham, Butt, Veron (P Neville 56), Fortune (Giggs 64)
— Scholes — Van Nistelrooy (G Neville 90) *Subs not
used* Fletcher, Carroll *Booked* Scholes
Scorers **Radebe 20 (og), Silvestre 79**
Referee **G Poll**

Unconvincing they may be, but United win their game in
hand on Arsenal thanks to two moments of quick
thinking by Beckham, whose cross forces Radebe's own
goal and whose quick thinking leads to Silvestre
heading the winner.

Wednesday March 12
FC BASLE (h)
Champions League
Drew 1-1   HT 0-1   Att 66,870
Carroll — G Neville, Ferdinand, Blanc (Scholes 73),
O'Shea — Solskjaer, Fletcher (Beckham 73), Butt,
P Neville, Richardson (Giggs ht) — Forlan *Subs not used*
Ricardo, Van Nistelrooy, Pugh, Webber *Booked* P Neville
Scorer **G Neville 53**
Referee **C Larsen (Denmark)**

Already qualified and fielding a weakened team that still
meets Uefa requirements, United are rescued by Gary
Neville's first goal in 82 European matches.

Saturday March 15
ASTON VILLA (a)
Won 1-0   HT 1-0   Att 42,602   Position 2nd

THE PLAYERS

FABIEN BARTHEZ
Goalkeeper
Born June 28, 1971,
Lavelanet, France
Ht 5ft 11in **Wt** 12st 8lb
Signed from AS Monaco, July
2000, £7.8m

DAVID BECKHAM
Midfield
Born May 2, 1975, Leytonstone
Ht 6ft 0in **Wt** 11st 12lb
Signed from trainee, January
1993

LAURENT BLANC
Defender
Born November 19, 1965,
Ales, France
Ht 6ft 4in **Wt** 13 9lb
Signed from Inter Milan, August
2001, free

WES BROWN
Defender
Born October 13, 1979,
Manchester
Ht 6ft 1in **Wt** 12st 4lb
Signed from trainee, November
1996

NICKY BUTT
Midfield
Born January 21, 1975,
Manchester
Ht 5ft 10in **Wt** 11st 3lb
Signed from trainee, January 1993

ROY CARROLL
Goalkeeper
Born September 30, 1977,
Enniskillen
Ht 6ft 2in **Wt** 12st 9lb
Signed from Wigan Athletic, July
2001, £2.5m

LUKE CHADWICK
Midfield
Born November 18, 1980,
Cambridge
Ht 5ft 11in **Wt** 11st 0lb
Signed from trainee, February
1999

RIO FERDINAND
Defender
Born November 8, 1978, Peckham
Ht 6ft 2in **Wt** 12st 1lb
Signed from Leeds United, July
2002, £30m

DARREN FLETCHER
Midfield
Born February 1, 1984, Edinburgh
Ht 6ft 0in **Wt** 13st 1lb
Signed from trainee, August 2000

DIEGO FORLAN
Forward
Born May 19, 1979, Montevideo
Ht 5ft 8in **Wt** 11st 11lb
Signed from Independiente,
January 2002, £7.5m

Fabien Barthez

QUINTON FORTUNE
Midfield
Born May 21, 1977, Cape Town
Ht 5ft 11in **Wt** 11st 11lb
Signed from Atletico Madrid,
August 1999, £1.5m

RYAN GIGGS
Forward
Born November 29, 1973, Cardiff
Ht 5ft 11in **Wt** 10st 9lb
Signed from trainee, December
1990

ROY KEANE
Midfield
Born August 10, 1971, Cork
Ht 5ft 10in **Wt** 12st 10lb
Signed from Nottingham Forest,
July 1993, £3.75m

MARK LYNCH
Defender
Born September 2, 1981,
Manchester
Ht 5ft 11in **Wt** 11st 3lb
Signed from trainee, August 2001

DAVID MAY
Defender
Born June 24, 1970, Oldham
Ht 6ft 0in **Wt** 13st 5lb
Signed from Blackburn Rovers,
July 1994, £1.4m

DANNY NARDIELLO
Forward
Born October 22, 1982, Coventry
Ht 5ft 11in **Wt** 11st 4lb
Signed from trainee, November
1999

GARY NEVILLE
Defender
Born February 18, 1975, Bury
Ht 5ft 11in **Wt** 12st 8lb
Signed from trainee, January
1993

PHIL NEVILLE
Defender
Born January 21, 1977, Bury
Ht 5ft 11in **Wt** 12st 0lb
Signed from trainee, June 1994

JOHN O'SHEA
Defender
Born April 30, 1981, Waterford
Ht 6ft 3in **Wt** 11st 12lb
Signed from Waterford United,
September 1998

DANNY PUGH
Midfield
Born October 19, 1982,
Manchester
Ht 6ft 0in **Wt** 12st 7lb
Signed from trainee, August 2002

RICARDO
Goalkeeper
Born December 31, 1971, Madrid
Ht 6ft 1in **Wt** 13st 8lb
Signed from Real Valladolid,
August 2002, £1.5m

Phil Neville

Barthez — G Neville, Ferdinand, Silvestre, O'Shea —
Beckham, Butt, Scholes, Giggs — Van Nistelrooy,
Solskjaer *Subs not used* Ricardo, P Neville, Blanc,
Forlan, Fletcher *Booked* Scholes
Scorer **Beckham 12**
Report page 231

Tuesday March 18
DEPORTIVO LA CORUNA (a)
Champions League
Lost 0-2 HT 0-1 Att 25,000
Ricardo — Roche (Stewart ht), Blanc, O'Shea — Lynch,
Fletcher, P Neville, Butt, Pugh — Forlan (Webber 72),
Giggs (Richardson 72) *Subs not used* May, Davis,
Carroll, Nardiello *Booked* P Neville
Referee **V Hrinak (Slovakia)**

With United already qualified, Sir Alex fields an almost
unrecognisable line-up that is, predictably, beaten.

Saturday March 22
FULHAM (h)
Won 3-0 HT 1-0 Att 67,706 Position 1st
Barthez — G Neville, Ferdinand, Brown, O'Shea —
Beckham, Butt, Scholes, Giggs — Van Nistelrooy,
Solskjaer *Subs not used* Blanc, Ricardo, Forlan, Fortune,
Fletcher *Booked* G Neville, Ferdinand
Scorer **Van Nistelrooy 45 (pen), 68, 90**
Referee **S Bennett**

United are back to full strength and back on top of the
Premiership. A record postwar Old Trafford attendance
sees Van Nistelrooy score a superb solo second goal.

Saturday April 5
LIVERPOOL (h)
Won 4-0 HT 1-0 Att 67,639 Position 2nd
Barthez — G Neville, Ferdinand, Brown, Silvestre (O'Shea
66) — Solskjaer, Keane, P Neville (Beckham 66), Giggs
— Scholes (Butt 79) — Van Nistelrooy *Subs not used*
Ricardo, Forlan *Booked* Silvestre
Scorers **Van Nistelrooy 5 (pen), 65 (pen), Giggs 78,
Solskjaer 90**
Referee **M Riley**

A difficult fixture for United is settled inside five minutes
as Hyypia hauls down Van Nistelrooy and sees red. The
Dutchman adds a second penalty and Liverpool's ten
men concede two more in the closing stages.

Tuesday April 8
REAL MADRID (a)
European Cup, quarter-final, 1st leg
Lost 1-3 HT 0-2 Att 75,000
Barthez — G Neville (Solskjaer 86), Ferdinand, Brown,
Silvestre (O'Shea 59) — Beckham, Keane, Butt, Giggs —
Scholes — Van Nistelrooy *Subs not used* Ricardo, Blanc,
Forlan, Fortune, Fletcher *Booked* Neville, Van Nistelrooy,
Scholes
Scorer **Van Nistelrooy 52**
Referee **A Frisk (Sweden)**

United are left in a real fix after the holders produce an
inspired display. Van Nistelrooy's header keeps United in
with a chance, but the look on the face of Ferguson —
charged by Uefa over his claim that the draw was rigged
— says it all.

Saturday April 12
NEWCASTLE UNITED (a)
Won 6-2 HT 4-1 Att 52,164 Position 1st
Barthez — Brown (Blanc 66), Ferdinand, Silvestre,
O'Shea (G Neville 49) — Solskjaer, Keane, Butt, Scholes
— Giggs (Forlan ht) — Van Nistelrooy *Subs not used*
Ricardo, P Neville
Scorers **Solskjaer 32, Scholes 34, 38, 52, Giggs 44,
Van Nistelrooy 58 (pen)**
Report page 75

Wednesday April 16
ARSENAL (a)
Drew 2-2   HT 1-0   Att 38,164   Position 1st
Barthez — Brown, Ferdinand, Silvestre, O'Shea
(G Neville ht) — Solskjaer, Keane, Butt, Scholes — Giggs
— Van Nistelrooy *Subs not used* P Neville, Beckham,
Ricardo, Fortune *Booked* Keane, Butt
Scorers **Van Nistelrooy 24, Giggs 63**
Report page 63

Saturday April 19
BLACKBURN ROVERS (h)
Won 3-1   HT 2-1   Att 67,626   Position 1st
Barthez (Ricardo ht) — Brown, Ferdinand, Silvestre,
P Neville — Butt (Keane 54), Fortune — Scholes —
Beckham, Van Nistelrooy, Giggs (Solskjaer 82) *Subs not
used* G Neville, Forlan
Scorers **Van Nistelrooy 20, Scholes 42, 61**
Referee **A D'Urso**

United overcome an awkward hurdle thanks to the
agility of Ricardo — a substitute for Barthez, he
concedes but then saves Dunn's penalty at 2-1 up —
and the poaching instincts of Scholes.

Wednesday April 23
REAL MADRID (h)
European Cup, quarter-final, 2nd leg
Won 4-3 (lose 5-6 on agg)   Att 66,708
Barthez — Brown, Ferdinand, Silvestre (P Neville 78),
O'Shea — Butt, Keane (Fortune 82) — Solskjaer, Veron
(Beckham 63), Giggs — Van Nistelrooy *Subs not used*
Ricardo, Blanc, Forlan, Fletcher *Booked* Veron, Fortune
Scorers **Van Nistelrooy 43, Helguera 52 (og),
Beckham 71, 84**
Referee **P Collina (Italy)**

United go out in a blaze of goals and near glory. With
Beckham, on the bench as Veron starts, scoring twice,
they get the four they need, but they have no answer to
the finishing of Ronaldo, whose hat-trick sees the
holders through to face Juventus in thrilling style.

Sunday April 27
TOTTENHAM HOTSPUR (a)
Won 2-0   HT 0-0   Att 36,073   Position 1st
Carroll — Brown (G Neville 55), Ferdinand, Silvestre,
O'Shea — Beckham, Keane, Scholes, Solskjaer (Fortune
72) — Van Nistelrooy, Giggs *Subs not used* Ricardo,
Blanc, Forlan
Scorers **Scholes 69, Van Nistelrooy 90**
Referee **J Winter**
Report page 160

Saturday May 3
CHARLTON ATHLETIC (h)
Won 4-1   HT 3-1   Att 67,721   Position 1st
Carroll — Brown, Ferdinand, Silvestre, O'Shea — Keane,
Scholes (Veron 69) — Beckham, Giggs (Butt 78),
Solskjaer (Forlan 78) — Van Nistelrooy *Subs not used*
P Neville, Barthez
Scorers **Beckham 11, Van Nistelrooy 32, 37, 53**

After Jensen, punishing Carroll's weak clearance,
cancels out Beckham's opener, Van Nistelrooy marks
his hundredth game with a brisk hat-trick to take his
side eight points clear.

Sunday May 11
EVERTON (a)
Won 2-1   HT 1-1   Att 40,168   Position 1st
Carroll — Brown (P Neville 40), Ferdinand, Silvestre,
O'Shea (Blanc ht) — Beckham, Keane, Scholes, Giggs —
Van Nistelrooy, Solskjaer (Fortune 76) *Subs not used*
Veron, Butt *Booked* Ferdinand, P Neville, Blanc
Scorers **Beckham 43, Van Nistelrooy 79 (pen)**
Report page 124

KIERAN RICHARDSON
Midfield
Born October 21, 1984, London
Signed from West Ham United,
July 2002, undisclosed

LEE ROCHE
Defender
Born October 28, 1980, Bolton
Ht 5ft 10in **Wt** 10st 12lb
Signed from trainee, February
1999

PAUL SCHOLES
Midfield
Born November 16, 1974,
Salford
Ht 5ft 7in **Wt** 11st 10lb
Signed from trainee, January
1993

MIKAEL SILVESTRE
Defender
Born August 9, 1977,
Tours, France
Ht 6ft 0in **Wt** 13st 1lb
Signed from Inter Milan,
September 1999, £4m

OLE GUNNAR SOLSKJAER
Forward
Born February 26, 1973,
Kristiansund, Norway
Ht 5ft 10in **Wt** 11st 10lb
Signed from Molde, July 1996,
£1.5m

MICHAEL STEWART
Midfield
Born February 26, 1981
Edinburgh
Ht 5ft 11in **Wt** 11st 11lb
Signed from trainee, March 1998

MADS TIMM
Forward
Born October 31, 1984, Odense
Signed from OB Odense, August
2002, free

RUUD VAN NISTELROOY
Forward
Born July 1, 1976, Oss,
the Netherlands
Ht 6ft 2in **Wt** 12st 13lb
Signed from PSV Eindhoven, July
2001, £19m

JUAN SEBASTIAN VERON
Midfield
Born March 9, 1975, Buenos Aires
Ht 6ft 1in **Wt** 12st 7lb
Signed from Lazio, July 2001,
£28.1m

DANNY WEBBER
Forward
Born December 28, 1981,
Manchester
Ht 5ft 9in **Wt** 10st 8lb
Signed from trainee, January
1999

Juan Sebastian Veron

ARSENAL

PREMIERSHIP

	P	W	D	L	F	A	Pts
Man Utd	38	25	8	5	74	34	83
Arsenal	**38**	**23**	**9**	**6**	**85**	**42**	**78**
Newcastle	38	21	6	11	63	48	69
Chelsea	38	19	10	9	68	38	67
Liverpool	38	18	10	10	61	41	64
Blackburn	38	16	12	10	52	43	60
Everton	38	17	8	13	48	49	59
Southampton	38	13	13	12	43	46	52
Man City	38	15	6	17	47	54	51
Tottenham	38	14	8	16	51	62	50
Middlesbro	38	13	10	15	48	44	49
Charlton	38	14	7	17	45	56	49
Birmingham	38	13	9	16	41	49	48
Fulham	38	13	9	16	41	50	48
Leeds	38	14	5	19	58	57	47
Aston Villa	38	12	9	17	42	47	45
Bolton	38	10	14	14	41	51	44
West Ham	38	10	12	16	42	59	42
West Brom	38	6	8	24	29	65	26
Sunderland	38	4	7	27	21	65	19

FA CUP
Winners

WORTHINGTON CUP
Third round

CHAMPIONS LEAGUE
Second group stage

Patrick Vieira, still the heart and lungs of Arsenal in 2002-03

THE GAMES

Sunday August 1
LIVERPOOL
Community Shield (Cardiff)
Won 1-0   HT 0-0   Att 67,337
Seaman — Lauren, Keown, Campbell, Cole — Parlour,
Vieira, Edu (Gilberto ht), Wiltord — Henry, Bergkamp
(Toure 86) *Subs not used* Cygan, Upson, Luzhny,
Aliadiere, Taylor *Booked* Vieira, Wiltord, Henry, Gilberto
Scorer **Gilberto 69**
Referee **A Wiley**

On the weekend that Tony Adams announces his
retirement, Gilberto, the £4.5 million signing from
Atletico Mineiro, comes on at half-time and launches a
new era with a deserved winner from Bergkamp's pass.
Gerrard's late tackle on Vieira angers Arsene Wenger.

Sunday August 18
BIRMINGHAM CITY (h)
Won 2-0   HT 2-0   Att 38,018   Position 3rd
Seaman — Lauren, Keown, Campbell, Cole — Parlour,
Vieira, Edu (Toure 86), Wiltord (Aliadiere 76) — Henry,
Bergkamp (Gilberto 31) *Subs not used* Luzhny, Taylor
Scorers **Henry 9, Wiltord 24**
Referee **M Riley**

Wiltord caps a brilliant first-half team display by finishing
a move the length of the Highbury pitch to put the
newcomers out of their misery. Henry sets up a
Premiership record fourteenth straight win with his free
kick opener, punishing Vaesen's error. Cole is criticised
for his role in Cisse's sending-off.

Saturday August 24
WEST HAM UNITED (a)
Drew 2-2   HT 0-1   Att 35,048   Position 4th
Seaman — Lauren (Toure 83), Keown, Campbell, Cole —
Parlour (Pennant 62), Vieira, Edu, Wiltord — Henry,
Bergkamp (Kanu ht) *Subs not used* Taylor, Luzhny
Booked Keown, Cole, Vieira, Edu, Bergkamp
Scorers **Henry 65, Wiltord 88**
Referee **N Barry**
Report page 246

Tuesday August 27
WEST BROMWICH ALBION (h)
Won 5-2   HT 3-0   Att 37,920   Position 1st
Seaman — Lauren, Keown, Campbell, Cole — Wiltord
(Aliadiere 82), Vieira, Edu (Toure 77), Gilberto, Edu — Henry,
Kanu (Parlour 66) *Subs not used* Taylor, Luzhny *Booked*
Keown, Campbell, Edu
Scorers **Cole 3, Lauren 21, Wiltord 24, 77,**
Aliadiere 90
Referee **P Durkin**

Cole blasts a ferociously struck opener and the match is
over after 24 minutes with Arsenal 3-0 up and cruising.
A splendid night is capped at the final whistle with the
news that Spurs have been displaced at the top of the
table on goal difference, while West Brom are sent to
the bottom.

Sunday September 1
CHELSEA (a)
Drew 1-1   HT 0-1   Att 40,037   Position 2nd
Seaman — Lauren, Keown, Campbell, Cole — Parlour,
Vieira, Gilberto, Edu (Toure 31) — Kanu (Cygan 83),
Wiltord (Aliadiere 90) *Subs not used* Taylor, Jeffers
Booked Vieira, Wiltord *Sent off* Vieira 50
Scorer **Toure 60**
Referee **A D'Urso**
Report page 78

FOR MANY CLUBS, TO FINISH second in the Premiership and
win the FA Cup would be a cause for celebration, but for Arsenal the
2002-2003 season will go down as one of underachievement. In a
classic case of the biter bit, Arsenal threw away an eight-point lead
to trail Manchester United home by five points, conceding the title
with barely a whimper.

At the start of the season, it seemed to be accepted that progress
for the champions would be measured only by success in Europe. In
the first stage of the Champions League, they were drawn in a
relatively easy group along with PSV Eindhoven, Borussia Dortmund and Auxerre. The first three matches yielded seven goals and
nine points, but a home defeat against Auxerre, followed by another
in Dortmund, made for a nervous final match against PSV.

The second stage brought a much stronger line-up of Roma,
Valencia and Ajax. A 3-1 defeat of Roma in the Olympic Stadium
added weight to the belief that this was going to be Arsenal's year,
but defeat by United in the league had had a more damaging effect
on the team than may have been imagined. Three days later, a tame
0-0 draw with Valencia at Highbury set the tone for the rest of the
group stage. In the final match, Arsene Wenger's side needed a
point at the Mestalla — or a Roma victory against Ajax — to qualify
for the last eight for only the third time. For the second season in
succession, however, Arsenal slipped out of the competition before
the knockout stage.

By now, things were also looking a little less certain in the league.
The weekend before the Valencia game, Arsenal had been beaten
2-0 by Blackburn Rovers at Ewood Park while Manchester United
won away to Aston Villa. Arsenal's lead had narrowed to two points,
injuries were starting to take their toll and the lack of defensive
cover was once again being exposed. The defence, so long the rock
on which Arsenal's success has been based, was now the rock on
which the team foundered and the sale of Matthew Upson to
Birmingham City was baffling. Oleg Luzhny proved an able deputy,
never more so than in the Cup Final, but now "The Horse" has been
let out of the Highbury stable, the defensive cupboard is bare. Igors
Stepanovs does not count, I'm afraid.

Arsenal's inability to hang on to a lead became more and more
apparent as the title run-in progressed and the visit of Everton
loomed. Wayne Rooney had dramatically announced his arrival in
October, when his scorching shot past David Seaman at Goodison
Park had inflicted Arsenal's first league defeat of the season and also
ended two records — the unbeaten run of 30 games in the Premiership and the undefeated away run of 23 matches — and his equaliser

Bergkamp leads awesome Arsenal's demolition of Charlton

at Highbury looked like condemning them to a fifth game without a win until Patrick Vieira's goal made sure of the points.

A 1-1 draw with Aston Villa left Arsenal level on points with United with six games to play. One of the most hyped matches in Premiership history came when United visited Highbury on April 16. Honours were even at 2-2, but the main talking point was Sol Campbell's dismissal for elbowing Ole Gunnar Solskjaer. The defensive linchpin received a four-match ban, which ruled him out of the last three Premiership matches as well as the Cup Final. His final appearance came in the 2-2 draw away to Bolton Wanderers, when Arsenal squandered a two-goal lead and the impetus in the title battle. The game was up after a home defeat by Leeds United with two matches to play and the title celebrations could begin at Old Trafford.

A 1-0 win over Southampton in the FA Cup Final proved scant consolation. Despite back-to-back victories over Manchester United and Chelsea in the fifth and sixth rounds, the air of "if only" is hanging heavy over Highbury.

The proposed move to Ashburton Grove is costing the club dear. Arsenal need a larger stadium to compete financially with United as a capacity of just under 39,000 does not bring in the revenue needed. United, with crowds of around 67,000, earn more than £1 million a match in gate receipts. Yet with costs of the new stadium escalating to about £400 million, Arsenal, who have long prided themselves on fiscal responsibility, announced a pre-tax loss of £22.3 million.

The new season — and the season beyond — should see the emphasis firmly back on the Premiership. In these unusually straitened times for Arsenal, success in Europe is undoubtedly important for the revenue it brings in. Real progress, though, is not measured simply by winning the domestic title, but by retaining it.

Tuesday September 10
MANCHESTER CITY (h)
Won 2-1   HT **2-1**   Att **37,878**   Position **1st**
Seaman — Luzhny, Keown, Campbell, Cole — Wiltord, Vieira, Gilberto, Edu (Toure 73) — Henry, Bergkamp *Subs not used* Taylor, Cygan, Kanu, Jeffers *Booked* Vieira
Scorers **Wiltord 26, Henry 42**
Referee **C Wilkes**

Anelka gets on the scoresheet on his much-hyped Highbury return, but his header is sandwiched by goals from Wiltord and Henry which take Arsenal back to the top. Benarbia is sent off towards the end of an exciting contest for his second bookable offence.

Saturday September 14
CHARLTON ATHLETIC (a)
Won 3-0   HT **1-0**   Att **26,080**   Position **1st**
Seaman — Luzhny, Keown, Campbell, Cole — Toure (Edu 66), Vieira, Gilberto, Wiltord (Cygan 86) — Henry, Bergkamp (Kanu 72) *Subs not used* Jeffers, Shaaban *Booked* Keown, Cole, Luzhny
Scorers **Henry 44, Wiltord 67, Edu 88**
Booked **Keown, Cole, Luzhny**
Referee **S Dunn**
Report page 175

Tuesday September 17
BORUSSIA DORTMUND (h)
Champions League
Won 2-0   HT **0-0**   Att **34,907**
Seaman — Luzhny (Lauren 73), Keown, Campbell, Cole — Ljungberg (Cygan 84), Vieira, Gilberto, Wiltord (Toure 89) — Henry, Bergkamp *Subs not used* Taylor, Jeffers, Pennant, Kanu
Scorers **Bergkamp 62, Ljungberg 77**
Referee **A Frisk (Sweden)**

The perfect start to a Champions League campaign, with Bergkamp setting Arsenal on their way with a deflected shot and Ljungberg celebrating his return from injury with the second goal after a dazzling move.

Saturday September 21
BOLTON WANDERERS (h)
Won 2-1   HT **1-0**   Att **37,974**   Position **1st**
Seaman — Lauren (Toure 85), Keown, Campbell, Cole — Wiltord (Jeffers 67), Gilberto, Parlour, Ljungberg (Bergkamp 67) — Henry, Kanu *Subs not used* Luzhny, Shaaban *Booked* Keown
Scorers **Henry 26, Kanu 90**
Referee **D Pugh**

Henry misses a penalty before opening the scoring, but Seaman's embarrassment at letting Farrelly's cross drift over his head for the equaliser is eased when Kanu grabs a last-minute winner against ten men, Campo having been unluckily sent off for two yellow cards.

Wednesday September 25
PSV EINDHOVEN (a)
Champions League
Won 4-0   HT **1-0**   Att **24,000**
Seaman — Lauren, Keown (Cygan 10), Campbell, Cole — Wiltord, Vieira, Gilberto, Ljungberg (Toure 85) — Henry, Bergkamp (Kanu 79) *Subs not used* Shaaban, Jeffers, Pennant, Luzhny *Booked* Lauren
Scorers **Gilberto 1, Ljungberg 66, Henry 81, 90**
Referee **L Michel (Slovakia)**

Gilberto makes an indelible mark with the fastest goal in Champions League history, timed at 20.07 seconds, with Henry exacting revenge on the Dutch fans who racially abuse him by scoring twice late on.

Saturday September 28
LEEDS UNITED (a)
Won 4-1 HT 2-0 Att **40,199** Position **1st**
Seaman — Lauren, Cygan, Campbell, Cole — Wiltord
(Pennant 79), Vieira, Gilberto, Toure (Luzhny 72) —
Henry, Kanu (Jeffers 90) *Subs not used* Ljungberg,
Shaaban *Booked* Campbell, Vieira
Scorers Kanu 9, 86, Toure 20, Henry 47
Referee **A Wiley**
Report page 211

Wednesday October 2
AUXERRE (a)
Champions League
Won 1-0 HT 0-0 Att **21,000**
Seaman — Lauren, Cygan, Campbell, Cole — Wiltord
(Luzhny 83), Vieira, Gilberto, Toure (Edu 60) — Henry
(Pennant 58), Kanu *Subs not used* Taylor, Ljungberg,
Jeffers, Stepanovs
Scorer **Gilberto 48**
Referee **F de Bleeckere (Belgium)**

Gilberto's goal adds the scalp of the French league
leaders to those of the German champions and Dutch
league leaders already claimed in the Champions
League. Benjami hits the bar with a late shot.

Sunday October 6
SUNDERLAND (h)
Won 3-1 HT 3-0 Att **37,902** Position **1st**
Seaman — Lauren, Cygan, Campbell, Cole — Wiltord
(Edu 78), Vieira, Gilberto, Ljungberg (Toure 78) — Henry
(Jeffers 78), Kanu *Subs not used* Taylor, Luzhny
Scorers Kanu 3, 9, Vieira 45
Referee **D Elleray**

Kanu's early strikes puts Arsenal in control well before
Sorensen, the Sunderland goalkeeper, suffers a
dislocated elbow, Vieira beating Myhre before half-time.
Craddock's consolation is the last goal scored under
Peter Reid, who is sacked the next day.

Saturday October 19
EVERTON (a)
Lost 1-2 HT 1-1 Att **39,038** Position **2nd**
Seaman — Lauren, Cygan, Campbell, Cole — Toure
(Wiltord 64), Vieira, Gilberto, Ljungberg (Edu 85) —
Henry, Kanu (Jeffers 71) *Subs not used* Luzhny,
Shaaban *Booked* Edu
Scorer **Ljungberg 8**
Report page 116

Tuesday October 22
AUXERRE (h)
Champions League
Lost 2-1 HT 0-2 Att **35,206**
Seaman — Lauren (Toure 76), Cygan, Campbell, Cole —
Wiltord, Vieira, Gilberto (Pires 71), Ljungberg — Henry,
Kanu *Subs not used* Shaaban, Edu, Pennant, Luzhny,
Stepanovs *Booked* Campbell, Vieira
Scorer **Kanu 53**
Referee **D Messina (Italy)**

Arsenal are caught cold at the start, with Kapo and
Fadiga putting Auxerre in control before Kanu halves the
deficit, and are deservedly beaten as defeat takes the
edge off the long-awaited return of Pires after surgery.

THE ☙ TIMES   Thursday November 28 2002

MATCH OF THE SEASON

AS Roma 1   Arsenal 3
Olympic Stadium, Wednesday November 27 2002
Russell Kempson in Rome

IT WILL GO DOWN AS ONE OF the most memorable evenings in Arsenal's star-spangled history. They travelled to the Eternal City in cautious mode but left on a high that they barely thought possible. AS Roma, the Serie A runners-up of last season, were defeated with an ease that bordered on contempt in the Stadio Olimpico.

Teamwork and honest graft laid the foundations for this startling victory in the opening fixture of the second group stage of the Champions League and Thierry Henry applied the gloss finish with as good a hat-trick as can have been seen for a long time. He scored in the sixth, seventeenth and 75th minutes, after Roma had poached an early lead, to take his tally for the season to 13 goals.

Henry will take all the plaudits from this fascinating group B tie and deservedly so. He broke the hearts of Roma and set the scene nicely for the visit of Valencia, the Spanish champions, who had to share the points with Ajax last night, to Highbury a week on Tuesday. But his team-mates were exceptional, too.

"We had a difficult start but quickly came back into it in a great way," Arsene Wenger, the Arsenal manager, said. "At 1-1, I felt that Roma were too cautious. They did not want to be caught on the break. They were scared of our counter-attacking. In the second half, we were always in control. It was all about trying to find the right moment to score and we did."

Fabio Capello, the Roma coach, accepted defeat generously. "Arsenal are the strongest team in Europe at the moment," he said. "They punish you at the first mistake and are always united. They run for each other the whole time. They never stop."

Wenger's grasp of percentages had appeared flawed the previous day. He reckoned that Oleg Luzhny, the full back, had only a "20 per cent" chance of playing because of a hamstring injury and that the chances of David Seaman, the goalkeeper, who has a recurring groin problem, were "90 per cent". When reality beckoned, Luzhny passed a fitness test and Seaman did not. Rami Shaaban replaced him.

When the Arsenal players walked out for an inspection of the pitch, they were greeted with hoots of derision by the Roma Ultras. In the same stadium two years ago, when Arsenal played Lazio, Patrick Vieira was subjected to racist taunts by Sinisa Mihajlovic, the Yugoslavia and Lazio defender, during the game; the Stadio Olimpico is a magnificent but hostile, daunting venue.

With four minutes gone, the volume of hostility went up a notch as Roma went ahead. Sol Campbell tried to make up lost ground but Antonio Cassano's shot took a slight deflection off him, trickled past Shaaban and on to his near post. It looked as if the ball might roll

The brilliant Henry leaves Roma in ruins with a devastating hat-trick

along the goalline to safety, but the spin from striking the upright took it back into the net.

Two minutes later, Arsenal responded in incontrovertible fashion. Gilberto threaded a long pass away from the outstretched leg of Christian Panucci for Henry to run on to. That he did, with panache, and as he closed in on Francesco Antonioli, the goalkeeper, he curled the most accurate of shots past him. Touché.

Neither side was prepared to risk conceding another goal. Arsenal played it tight, with Vieira, as always, the guiding influence in midfield. Francesco Totti, the darling of the home fans, flitted menacingly but a touch too theatrically for Lubos Michel, the Slovakian referee, when he clearly dived under the challenge of Fredrik Ljungberg.

The Ultras could not believe it and were incandescent soon after, when Michel was not taken in by Cassano, who also performed his impression of a dying swan. Half-empty bottles of water rained down on to the athletics track when, a minute later, an offside decision went against Roma.

Through Totti, Roma always carried a threat, but, at times, the thrust and counter-thrust grew almost tedious. Yet it was intriguing, as the watching Sven-Goran Eriksson, the England head coach, probably would have agreed.

Saturday October 26
BLACKBURN ROVERS (h)
Lost 1-2   HT 1-1   Att **38,064**   Position **2nd**
Seaman — Lauren, Cygan, Campbell, Cole (Toure 86) — Wiltord, Gilberto, Edu (Pires 64), Ljungberg — Henry, Kanu (Bergkamp 64) *Subs not used* Taylor, Luzhny
Booked Henry
Scorer **Edu 45**
Referee **G Barber**

The slump goes on. Edu cancels out his early volleyed own goal, but despite relentless pressure and the harsh dismissal of Flitcroft for his second bookable offence, Arsenal can find no way past an inspired Friedel in the Blackburn goal after Yorke hits the 51st-minute winner.

Wednesday October 30
BORUSSIA DORTMUND (a)
Champions League
Lost 1-2   HT 1-1   Att **52,000**
Seaman — Lauren, Cygan, Campbell, Cole — Wiltord (Kanu 79), Vieira, Gilberto (Edu 80), Pires (Toure 67) — Henry, Ljungberg *Subs not used* Taylor, Jeffers, Luzhny, Stepanovs
Scorer **Henry 18**
Referee **M E Mejuto Gonzalez (Spain)**

A fourth successive 2-1 defeat makes it the worst sequence of results for Arsenal for 19 years, although even this reverse is not enough to stop them qualifying for the second phase. Henry's free kick puts them ahead, but Dortmund prevail through Gilberto's headed own goal and Rosicky's 63rd-minute penalty.

Sunday November 3
FULHAM (a)
Won 1-0   HT 1-0   Att **18,800**   Position **2nd**
Seaman — Lauren (Luzhny 65), Cygan, Campbell, Cole — Wiltord (Toure 83), Gilberto, Edu, Ljungberg — Henry, Bergkamp (Kanu 71) *Subs not used* Shaaban, Pires
Booked Edu, Cygan
Scorer **Marlet 31 (og)**
Referee **J Winter**
Report page 202

Wednesday November 6
SUNDERLAND (h)
Worthington Cup, 3rd rnd
Lost 2-3   HT 2-0   Att **19,059**
Taylor — Luzhny, Stepanovs, Tavlaridis, Toure — Pennant (Volz 81), Van Bronckhorst, Svard (Garry 81), Pires — Jeffers, Kanu *Subs not used* Shaaban, Sidwell, Thomas
Scorers **Pires 12, Jeffers 32**
Referee **A Wiley**

Arsenal's Worthington Cup reserves squander a 2-0 lead, a trio of headers from Kyle and Stewart — the latter pouncing twice — in 16 second-half minutes giving an equally denuded Sunderland side their first win under Howard Wilkinson's management.

Saturday November 9
NEWCASTLE UNITED (h)
Won 1-0   HT 1-0   Att **38,121**   Position **2nd**
Seaman — Luzhny, Cygan, Campbell, Cole — Wiltord (Edu 90), Vieira, Gilberto, Ljungberg — Henry, Bergkamp (Pires 70) *Subs not used* Taylor, Stepanovs, Toure
Scorer **Wiltord 24**
Referee **M Dean**

With Vieira and Bergkamp outstanding, Arsenal are back somewhere near their imperious best, Wiltord settling a hugely entertaining match, although Viana almost rescues a point when his shot hits the crossbar.

Tuesday November 12
PSV EINDHOVEN (h)
Champions League
Drew 0-0 HT 0-0 Att **35,274**
Shaaban — Luzhny, Cygan, Stepanovs, Toure — Pires,
Vieira (Gilberto 77), Edu, Van Bronckhorst — Henry
(Bergkamp 64), Jeffers (Wiltord 69) *Subs not used*
Taylor, Cole, Ljungberg, Tavlaridis *Booked* Toure
Sent off Toure 35
Referee **T H Ovrebo (Norway)**

Forced to play for most of the match with ten men after
Toure's dismissal for two fouls on Rommedahl, Arsenal
fail to score for the first time in 32 matches but still
qualify as group winners as Dortmund lose to Auxerre.

Saturday November 16
TOTTENHAM HOTSPUR (h)
Won 3-0 HT 1-0 Att **38,152** Position **1st**
Shaaban — Luzhny, Cygan, Campbell, Cole — Wiltord,
Vieira (Van Bronckhorst 78), Gilberto, Ljungberg —
Henry (Jeffers 75), Bergkamp (Pires 27) *Subs not used*
Taylor, Toure
Scorers **Henry 13, Ljungberg 55, Wiltord 71**
Referee **M Riley**

Ahead through Henry's breathtaking solo goal and well
on top even before the dreadfully harsh dismissal of
Davies (for a non-existent foul on Cole and a fractionally
mistimed challenge on Vieira), Arsenal go back to the
top with the sweetest and most convincing of victories.

Saturday November 23
SOUTHAMPTON (a)
Lost 2-3 HT 1-1 Att **31,797** Position **1st**
Seaman — Luzhny, Campbell, Cygan, Cole — Wiltord,
Vieira, Edu (Toure 61), Ljungberg (Pires 73) — Bergkamp
(Jeffers 73), Henry *Subs not used* Taylor, Gilberto
Booked Cole, Vieira *Sent off* Campbell 59
Scorers **Bergkamp 36, Pires 80**
Referee **P Durkin**
Report page 129

Wednesday November 27
AS ROMA (a)
Champions League
Won 3-1 HT 1-1 Att **70,000**
Shaaban — Luzhny, Campbell, Cygan, Cole — Ljungberg
(Edu 90), Vieira, Gilberto, Pires (Van Bronckhorst 78) —
Henry, Wiltord (Keown 84) *Subs not used* Taylor, Jeffers,
Stepanovs, Volz
Scorers **Henry 6, 70, 75**
Referee **L Michel (Slovakia)**

A tough group in the second phase looks even tougher
when Cassano gives Roma a fourth-minute lead, but the
Italians are then stunned by the Thierry Henry Show. He
immediately finishes a fine move and adds two more in
the second half, the last a free kick into the top corner.

Saturday November 30
ASTON VILLA (h)
Won 3-1 HT 1-0 Att **38,090** Position **1st**
Shaaban — Luzhny, Cygan, Campbell, Van Bronckhorst —
Toure (Keown 68), Vieira, Gilberto, Pires (Ljungberg 78)
— Henry, Bergkamp (Wiltord 72) *Subs not used* Taylor,
Jeffers *Booked* Henry, Luzhny
Scorers **Pires 17, Henry 49, 82 (pen)**
Referee **G Barber**

Henry's dead-ball expertise is to the fore again, another
unstoppable free kick doubling Arsenal's lead and a
cute penalty, chipped softly into the central space
Enckelman has vacated, easing Arsenal's nerves after
Hitzlsperger had given Villa some hope with a stunning
left-foot shot into the top far corner.

Arsenal have every right to look delighted with a magnificent display in Rome

With 15 minutes remaining, Arsenal stepped up a gear to apply the coup de grace. First, Henry crashed the ball in from close range after his initial header had bounced off Panucci. Then he curled in one of his trademark free kicks after Sylvain Wiltord had been fouled off the ball. Antonioli never saw it.

"It's wonderful to score a hat-trick," Henry said. "But the main thing is that we won. We have to keep our feet on the ground as this will mean nothing if we don't beat Valencia." Wenger said: "Thierry had an exceptional night. They were three different goals, but great goals. But it's not just about him. We kept the ball, defended very well and we got stronger and stronger in the middle. We won in Eindhoven, Auxerre and now here. Thierry could not do it all on his own. It's about the team."

That team now stands at the top of group B. Roma and their Ultras had been silenced. The job had been done superbly. Bring on Valencia.

AS ROMA (3-4-1-2): F Antonioli — C Panucci, J Zebina, W Samuel — Cafu, Emerson, Lima (sub: G Batistuta, 72min), V Candela — F Totti — A Cassano (sub: V Montella, 64), M Delvecchio (sub: G Guigou, 56). **Substitutes not used:** I Pelizzoli, Cufre, D Bombardini, J Guardiola. **Booked:** Samuel, Emerson, Batistuta.
ARSENAL (4-4-2): R Shaaban — O Luzhny, S Campbell, P Cygan, A Cole — F Ljungberg (sub: Edu, 90), P Vieira, Gilberto, R Pires (sub: G van Bronckhorst, 78) — T Henry, S Wiltord (sub: M Keown, 84). **Substitutes not used:** S Taylor, F Jeffers, I Stepanovs, M Volz.
Referee: L Michel (Slovakia).

THE MANAGER

Arsene Wenger

Will the fact that Arsenal were outfought by United rankle most, or the fact that he was for once out-thought by Sir Alex Ferguson? Arsene Wenger's statement that Arsenal were still the best team sounded like the words of a blinkered man. Still, he has been hamstrung by the board, which is treading a fine line between finding money to strengthen the squad and funding the new stadium. Wenger says he will honour his Highbury contract, but he cannot be relishing the weight of expectation on his shoulders this season.

Catherine Riley

APPEARANCES

	Prem	FAC	WC	Euro	Total
J Aliadiere	0 (3)	-	-	-	0 (3)
D Bentley	-	0 (1)	-	-	0 (1)
D Bergkamp	23 (6)	2 (2)	-	6 (1)	32* (9)
S Campbell	33	5	-	10	49*
A Cole	30 (1)	3	-	9	43* (1)
P Cygan	16 (2)	2	-	9 (2)	27 (4)
Edu	12 (6)	5 (1)	-	1 (3)	19* (10)
R Garry	1	-	0 (1)	-	1 (1)
Gilberto Silva	32 (3)	1 (2)	-	11 (1)	44 (7†)
T Henry	37	2 (3)	-	12	52*(3)
J Hoyte	0 (1)	-	-	-	0 (1)
F Jeffers	2 (14)	6	1	1 (4)	10 (18)
Kanu	9 (7)	1	1	2 (6)	13 (13)
M Keown	22 (2)	5	-	4 (1)	32* (3)
Lauren	26 (1)	6	-	9 (1)	42* (2)
F Ljungberg	19 (1)	3 (1)	-	7 (1)	29 (3)
O Luzhny	11 (6)	2	1	3 (1)	17 (7)
R Parlour	14 (5)	6	-	0 (2)	21* (7)
J Pennant	1 (4)	-	1	0 (1)	2 (5)
R Pires	21 (5)	5 (1)	1	8 (1)	35 (7)
D Seaman	28	5	-	9	43*
R Shaaban	3	-	-	2	5
I Stepanovs	2	-	1	1	4
S Svard	-	1	1	-	2
E Tavlaridis	0 (1)	-	1	-	1 (1)
S Taylor	7 (1)	2	1	1 (1)	11 (2)
K Toure	9 (17)	3 (2)	1	3 (4)	16 (24†)
M Upson	-	1	-	-	1
G van Bronckhorst	9 (11)	3 (2)	1	2 (2)	15 (15)
P Vieira	24	5	-	12	42*
M Volz	-	-	0 (1)	-	0 (1)
S Wiltord	27 (7)	3 (4)	-	10 (2)	41* (13)

(* denotes appearance and † substitute appearance in Community Shield)

Saturday December 7
MANCHESTER UNITED (a)
Lost 0-2 HT 0-1 Att **67,650** Position **1st**
Shaaban (Taylor 42) — Luzhny, Keown, Cygan, Cole — Ljungberg, Vieira, Gilberto, Pires (Toure 77) — Henry, Wiltord (Bergkamp 68) Subs not used Lauren, Van Bronckhorst
Report page 47

Tuesday December 10
VALENCIA (h)
Champions League
Drew 0-0 HT 0-0 Att **34,793**
Seaman — Lauren, Campbell, Cygan, Cole — Ljungberg (Wiltord 78), Vieira (Parlour 38), Gilberto, Pires (Kanu 83) — Henry, Bergkamp Subs not used Taylor, Keown, Edu, Luzhny
Referee **K M Nielsen (Denmark)**

The champions of England and Spain produce a low-key draw that fails to warm a bitterly cold crowd. Arsenal have a man advantage for the last 18 minutes after Angulo is sent off for flattening Cygan off the ball.

Sunday December 15
TOTTENHAM HOTSPUR (a)
Drew 1-1 HT 1-1 Att **36,076** Position **1st**
Seaman — Lauren, Keown, Campbell, Cole — Ljungberg (Toure 87), Gilberto, Parlour, Pires (Van Bronckhorst 79) — Henry, Bergkamp (Wiltord 70) Subs not used Taylor, Upson Booked Lauren, Parlour
Scorer **Pires 45 (pen)**
Report page 155

Saturday December 21
MIDDLESBROUGH (h)
Won 2-0 HT 1-0 Att **38,003** Position **1st**
Seaman — Lauren, Keown, Campbell, Cole — Wiltord, Gilberto, Van Bronckhorst, Ljungberg — Henry, Pires Subs not used Jeffers, Luzhny, Shaaban, Kanu, Toure Booked Cole
Scorers **Campbell 45, Pires 90**
Referee **S Dunn**

Arsene Wenger celebrates his 350th match in charge with his 200th victory, secured thanks to Campbell's header and a second from Pires. Middlesbrough's sorry afternoon is capped by a knee injury to Boateng and Wilkshire's 73rd-minute dismissal for two fouls.

Thursday December 26
WEST BROMWICH ALBION (a)
Won 2-1 HT 0-1 Att **27,025** Position **1st**
Seaman — Lauren, Keown, Campbell, Cole — Wiltord (Toure 78), Vieira, Gilberto, Van Bronckhorst (Pires 68) — Henry, Jeffers (Kanu 68) Subs not used Holloway, Upson
Scorers **Jeffers 48, Henry 85**
Report page 263

Sunday December 29
LIVERPOOL (h)
Drew 1-1 HT 0-0 Att **38,074** Position **1st**
Seaman — Lauren, Keown, Campbell, Cole — Wiltord (Jeffers 76), Vieira, Gilberto, Pires (Van Bronckhorst 84) — Henry, Kanu (Bergkamp 65) Subs not used Taylor, Luzhny Booked Campbell
Scorer **Henry 79 (pen)**

Arsenal go into 2003 five points clear after a disappointingly sterile draw with Liverpool, the result hingeing on two penalties. Murphy puts Liverpool ahead after Campbell's foul on Baros, but Arsenal's reply is much more contentious, Jeffers collapsing after minor contact from Riise.

Wednesday January 1
CHELSEA (h)
Won 3-2   HT 1-0   Att 38,096   Position 1st
Seaman — Luzhny, Keown, Campbell, Cole — Wiltord (Lauren 68), Vieira, Gilberto, Pires (Van Bronckhorst 57) — Henry, Bergkamp (Toure 80) *Subs not used* Taylor, Jeffers
Scorers **Desailly 9 (og), Van Bronckhorst 81, Henry 82**
Referee **U Rennie**

Four goals in the last nine minutes give an explosive end to a previously routine — and bookings-free — derby as Arsenal, 3-0 up, are given palpitations by Chelsea's unexpected riposte, Stanic and Petit, the Highbury old boy, bringing them within sight of a famous point.

Saturday January 4
OXFORD UNITED (h)
FA Cup, 3rd rnd
Won 2-0   HT 1-0   Att 34,432
Seaman — Luzhny, Keown, Upson, Van Bronckhorst — Toure (Bentley 77), Edu, Svard (Gilberto 77), Pires — Jeffers, Bergkamp (Wiltord 80) *Subs not used* Taylor, Stepanovs
Scorers **Bergkamp 15, McNiven 67 (og)**
Referee **C Wilkes**

Even a weakened Arsenal side is too good for third division opposition boasting seven wins in their previous eight games. Bergkamp chips his hundredth Arsenal goal and McNiven's own goal ends any doubts.

Sunday January 12
BIRMINGHAM CITY (a)
Won 4-0   HT 2-0   Att 29,505   Position 1st
Seaman — Lauren, Keown, Campbell, Cole — Wiltord, Gilberto, Edu (Van Bronckhorst 76), Pires (Toure 80) — Henry, Bergkamp (Jeffers 78) *Subs not used* Luzhny, Taylor *Booked* Lauren, Keown
Scorers **Henry 6, 70, Pires 29, Lauren 67**
Report page 192

Sunday January 19
WEST HAM UNITED (h)
Won 3-1   HT 1-1   Att 38,053   Position 1st
Seaman — Lauren, Keown, Campbell, Van Bronckhorst — Wiltord (Jeffers 86), Gilberto, Edu (Parlour 67), Pires — Henry, Bergkamp (Luzhny 86) *Subs not used* Taylor, Toure *Booked* Lauren, Parlour, Bergkamp
Scorer **Henry 13 (pen), 71, 86**
Referee **M Dean**

Arsenal are again five points clear; West Ham are just furious. Angered by the dismissal of Lomas for the foul that allows Henry to launch his hat-trick from the penalty spot, they are incandescent when Bergkamp gets away with an arm in Bowyer's face before crossing for Henry's second. his first headed Premiership goal.

Saturday January 25
FARNBOROUGH TOWN (a*)
FA Cup, 4th rnd
Won 5-1   HT 2-0   Att 35,108   (*at Highbury)
Taylor — Lauren, Campbell, Cygan, Van Bronckhorst — Toure (Wiltord 66), Vieira, Parlour, Pires (Bergkamp 66) — Jeffers, Kanu (Edu 76) *Subs not used* Seaman, Luzhny
Scorers **Campbell 19, Jeffers 23, 68, Bergkamp 74, Lauren 79**
Referee **A Wiley**

Arsenal are happy to let Farnborough take the money and run, the Nationwide Conference club's decision to switch the tie earning them around £300,000, but essentially ensuring the holders' progress.

PLAYER OF THE SEASON   Thierry Henry

Who to choose? Most had their moments, but Thierry Henry stood head and shoulders above the rest. He proved that his goalscoring ability is not a flash in the pan — his pace and sheer physical presence continues to unnerve even the hardiest of defences, while he became a much less selfish player last season, providing plenty of assistance to his team-mates up front. For standing up to be counted at the end of the season, for putting pen to paper and pledging his long-term future to the club, he deserves the accolade.
Catherine Riley

STATS AND FACTS

- Since April 1998 there have been only two instances of the away team scoring four times in the first 40 minutes of a Premiership game — both times achieved by Arsenal against Manchester City.

- Arsenal were the league's leading goalscorers — Manchester United had held the honour for each of the previous eight seasons.

- Only three own goals have been scored by Arsenal outfield players at Highbury since the Premier League's formation in 1992 and all have come from Brazilians — Edu and Silvinho against Middlesbrough in April 2001 and Edu against Blackburn Rovers on October 26, 2002.

- Arsenal's goal difference in the first halves of Premiership matches was plus 31. In the second halves it was plus 12.

- They are unbeaten in ten away London derbies in the Premiership.

- Arsene Wenger's team suffered four successive 2-1 defeats in October, to Everton, Auxerre, Blackburn Rovers and Borussia Dortmund.

- They won fewer points than Everton between mid-October and early February — 31 to 34.

- Arsenal have lost only one of their past 16 meetings with Tottenham Hotspur.

- Arsenal and Manchester United kicked off at the same time only six times last season in all competitions (Arsenal played 59 matches, United 63).

- None of Arsenal's past 96 domestic matches has finished goalless.

Bill Edgar

GOALSCORERS

	Prem	FAC	WC	Euro	Total
J Aliadiere	1	-	-	-	1
D Bergkamp	4	2	-	1	7
S Campbell	2	1	-	-	3
A Cole	1	-	-	-	1
P Cygan	1	-	-	-	1
Edu	2	1	-	-	3
Gilberto Silva	-	-	-	2	3*
T Henry	24 (3p)	1	-	7	32 (3p)
F Jeffers	2	3	1	-	6
Kanu	5	-	-	1	6
Lauren	2	2	-	-	4
F Ljungberg	6	1	-	2	9
J Pennant	3	-	-	-	3
R Pires	14 (1p)	1	1	-	16 (1p)
K Toure	2	-	-	-	2
G van Bronckhorst	1	-	-	-	1
P Vieira	3	-	-	1	4
S Wiltord	10	2	-	1	13
Own goals	2	2	-	-	4

(*Total includes goal in Community Shield)

Wednesday January 29
LIVERPOOL (a)
Drew 2-2 HT 1-0 Att 43,668 Position 1st
Seaman — Lauren, Campbell, Cygan, Cole — Parlour, Vieira, Gilberto, Pires — Henry, Bergkamp (Luzhny 85) *Subs not used* Jeffers, Wiltord, Taylor, Van Bronckhorst
Booked Cygan
Scorers **Pires 9, Bergkamp 63**
Report page 97

Saturday February 1
FULHAM (h)
Won 2-1 HT 1-1 Att 38,050 Position 1st
Seaman — Lauren (Toure 84), Keown, Campbell, Cole — Wiltord (Jeffers 69), Vieira, Gilberto (Van Bronckhorst 79), Pires — Henry, Bergkamp *Subs not used* Taylor, Cygan *Booked* Lauren, Henry, Toure
Scorer **Pires 17, 90**
Referee **E Wolstenholme**

Arsenal show the mettle of champions by winning despite playing only moderately well. Pires, with a header and a close-range effort with three seconds of the 90 minutes remaining, deflates Fulham, for whom Malbranque continues his scoring run with a volley.

Sunday February 9
NEWCASTLE UNITED (a)
Drew 1-1 HT 1-0 Att 52,157 Position 1st
Seaman — Lauren, Keown, Campbell, Cole — Wiltord (Van Bronckhorst 84), Vieira, Gilberto (Parlour 84), Pires — Henry, Bergkamp (Jeffers 78) *Subs not used* Taylor, Cygan *Booked* Lauren, Cole
Scorer **Henry 35**
Report page 73

Saturday February 15
MANCHESTER UNITED (a)
FA Cup, 5th rnd
Won 2-0 HT 1-0 Att 67,209
Seaman — Lauren, Keown, Campbell, Cole — Parlour, Vieira, Edu, Pires (Van Bronckhorst 84) — Jeffers (Henry 73), Wiltord (Toure 90) *Subs not used* Warmuz, Cygan *Booked* Vieira
Scorers **Edu 36, Wiltord 52**
Referee **J Winter**
Report page 49

Tuesday February 18
AJAX (h)
Champions League
Drew 1-1 HT 1-1 Att 35,427
Seaman (Taylor ht) — Lauren, Campbell, Cygan, Cole — Wiltord, Vieira, Gilberto (Jeffers 72), Pires — Henry, Bergkamp (Kanu 84) *Subs not used* Parlour, Van Bronckhorst, Edu, Stepanovs
Scorer **Wiltord 5**
Referee **L C Cortez Batista (Portugal)**

Despite another flying start through Wiltord, Arsenal fail to win at home for the fourth time in five Champions League matches this season, De Jong equalising and Ajax showing enough class to merit their point.

Saturday February 22
MANCHESTER CITY (a)
Won 5-1 HT 4-0 Att 34,960 Position 1st
Taylor — Lauren, Keown, Campbell, Van Bronckhorst — Wiltord (Jeffers 74), Vieira, Gilberto, Pires (Edu 74) — Henry, Bergkamp (Parlour 64) *Subs not used* Warmuz, Cygan
Scorers **Bergkamp 4, Pires 12, Henry 15, Campbell 19, Vieira 53**
Report page 146

Wednesday February 26
AJAX (a)
Champions League
Drew 0-0 HT 0-0 Att 51,500
Seaman — Lauren, Keown, Campbell, Cole — Wiltord
(Parlour 78), Vieira, Gilberto, Pires (Van Bronckhorst 86)
— Henry, Bergkamp (Jeffers 78) *Subs not used* Taylor,
Edu, Cygan, Toure *Booked* Vieira, Cole
Referee **V Ivanov (Russia)**

Arsene Wenger asks for a victory with style but gets
neither in a drab contest in which Cole's headed
clearance on the line from Chivu's free kick is the
nearest thing to a goal for either side.

Sunday March 2
CHARLTON ATHLETIC (h)
Won 2-0 HT 2-0 Att 38,015 Position 1st
Seaman — Toure, Keown, Campbell, Van Bronckhorst —
Ljungberg (Wiltord 64), Parlour, Edu, Pires (Gilberto 68)
— Henry, Jeffers *Subs not used* Cygan, Warmuz, Pennant
Booked Henry
Scorers **Jeffers 26, Pires 45**
Referee **R Styles**

As their closest challengers are losing one piece of
silverware in Cardiff, Arsenal stride on towards the main
prize as Henry's pace sets up the first-half goals that
end Charlton's winning streak and open up an
eight-point gap at the top of the Premiership.

Saturday March 8
CHELSEA (h)
FA Cup, 6th rnd
Drew 2-2 HT 2-1 Att 38,104
Seaman — Lauren, Keown, Campbell, Van Bronckhorst
— Parlour, Vieira, Edu, Ljungberg (Pires 64) — Henry
(Toure 84), Jeffers (Wiltord 64) *Subs not used* Cygan,
Wormuz *Booked* Edu
Scorers **Jeffers 37, Henry 45**
Referee **P Durkin**

An excellent contest is overshadowed by the coins
thrown at Henry, who is in inspired form, and the
allegations of diving levelled at Jeffers after his tumble
under Cudicini's challenge, the goalkeeper saving the
subsequent penalty. Terry's opener and Lampard's
scrambled equaliser secure a deserved replay.

Tuesday March 11
AS ROMA (h)
Champions League
Drew 1-1 HT 1-1 Att 35,472
Seaman — Lauren (Kanu 87), Keown, Cygan, Van
Bronckhorst — Wiltord (Ljungberg 73), Vieira, Gilberto,
Pires — Henry, Bergkamp (Jeffers 73) *Subs not used*
Taylor, Parlour, Stepanovs, Toure *Booked* Van
Bronckhorst
Scorer **Vieira 12**
Referee **U Meier (Switzerland)**

Another patchy home performance in Europe leaves
Arsenal's qualification in doubt. Ahead through Vieira's
header and against ten men from the 22nd minute,
Arsenal concede a goal to Cassano before half-time and
are grateful when Montela heads over an open goal.

Saturday March 15
BLACKBURN ROVERS (a)
Lost 0-2 HT 0-1 Att 29,840 Position 1st
Taylor — Lauren, Keown (Gilberto 20), Cygan, Van
Bronckhorst — Ljungberg, Parlour, Edu (Jeffers 69),
Pires (Wiltord 69) — Henry, Bergkamp *Subs not used*
Warmuz, Toure *Booked* Parlour, Van Bronckhorst
Report page 110

THE PLAYERS

JEREMIE ALIADIERE
Forward
Born March 30, 1983,
Rambouillet, France
Ht 6ft 0in **Wt** 11st 0lb
Signed from trainee, March 2000

DAVID BENTLEY
Forward
Born August 27, 1984,
Peterborough
Ht 5ft 11in **Wt** 11st 0lb
Signed from trainee, summer
2000

DENNIS BERGKAMP
Forward
Born May 18, 1969, Amsterdam
Ht 6ft 0in **Wt** 12st 5lb
Signed from Inter Milan, July
1995, £7.5m

SOL CAMPBELL
Defender
Born September 18, 1974,
Newham
Ht 6ft 2in **Wt** 14st 1lb
Signed from Tottenham Hotspur,
July 2001, free

ASHLEY COLE
Defender
Born December 20, 1980,
Stepney
Ht 5ft 8in **Wt** 10st 10lb
Signed from trainee, November
1998

PASCAL CYGAN
Defender
Born April 29, 1974, Lens
Ht 6ft 3in **Wt** 13st 10lb
Signed from Lille, July 2002,
£2.1m

EDU
Midfield
Born May 15, 1978, Sao Paulo
Ht 6ft 1in **Wt** 11st 4lb
Signed from Corinthians, Brazil,
January 2001, £6m

RYAN GARRY
Defender
Born September 29, 1983,
Hornchurch
Ht 6ft 2in **Wt** 13st 0lb
Signed from trainee, June 2000

GILBERTO SILVA
Midfield
Born October 7, 1976,
Lagoa da Prata, Brazil
Ht 6ft 3in **Wt** 12st 7lb
Signed from Atletico Mineiro, July
2002, £4.5m

THIERRY HENRY
Forward
Born August 17, 1977, Paris
Ht 6ft 2in **Wt** 12st 6lb
Signed from Juventus, August
1999, £10.5m

Ashley Cole

JUSTIN HOYTE
Defender
Born November 20, 1984,
Waltham Forest
Ht 5ft 11in **Wt** 10st 7lb
Signed from trainee, June 2001

FRANCIS JEFFERS
Forward
Born January 25, 1981, Liverpool
Ht 5ft 9in **Wt** 10st 8lb
Signed from Everton, June 2001,
£8m

KANU
Forward
Born August 1, 1976,
Owerri, Nigeria
Ht 6ft 6in **Wt** 12st 8lb
Signed from Inter Milan, February
1999, £4.5m

MARTIN KEOWN
Defender
Born July 24, 1966, Oxford
Ht 6ft 1in **Wt** 12st 4lb
Signed from Everton, February
1993, £2m

LAUREN
Defender
Born January 19, 1977,
Lodhji Krib, Cameroon
Ht 5ft 11in **Wt** 11st 3lb
Signed from Real Mallorca, June
2000, £7.2m

FREDRIK LJUNGBERG
Midfield
Born April 16, 1977,
Vittsjo, Sweden
Ht 5ft 9in **Wt** 11st 11lb
Signed from BK Halmstad,
September 1998, £3m

OLEG LUZHNY
Defender
Born August 5, 1968, Kiev

Ht 6ft 0in **Wt** 12st 2lb
Signed from Dinamo Kiev, July
1999, £1.8m

RAY PARLOUR
Midfield
Born March 7, 1973, Romford
Ht 5ft 10in **Wt** 11st 13lb
Signed from trainee, July 1989

JERMAINE PENNANT
Midfield
Born January 15, 1983,
Nottingham
Ht 5ft 8in **Wt** 10st 1lb
Signed from Notts County,
January 1999, £1.5m

ROBERT PIRES
Midfield
Born October 29, 1973, Reims
Ht 6ft 1in **Wt** 11st 9lb
Signed from Marseilles, July 2000,
£6m

DAVID SEAMAN
Goalkeeper
Born September 19, 1963,
Rotherham
Ht 6ft 3in **Wt** 13st 0lb
Signed from QPR, May 1990,
£1.3m

Martin Keown

Wednesday March 19
VALENCIA (a)
Champions League
Lost 1-2 **HT** 0-1   Att **50,000**
Taylor — Lauren, Campbell, Cygan, Toure (Kanu 86) —
Wiltord (Jeffers 76), Vieira, Gilberto, Ljungberg
— Pires — Henry *Subs not used* Holloway, Parlour, Van
Bronckhorst, Edu, Stepanovs *Booked* Vieira, Pires
Scorer **Henry 49**
Referee **K Vassaras (Greece)**

Needing a draw to qualify — or for Roma to beat Ajax in
Italy — Arsenal get neither and the side widely regarded
as potential European champions, not least by
themselves, do not even reach the quarter-finals.

Sunday March 23
EVERTON (h)
Won 2-1 **HT** 1-0   Att **38,042**   Position **1st**
Taylor — Lauren, Campbell, Cygan, Van Bronckhorst —
Ljungberg, Vieira, Gilberto, Pires (Parlour 68) — Henry,
Bergkamp (Toure 86) *Subs not used* Jeffers, Wiltord,
Warmuz *Booked* Lauren, Henry
Scorers **Cygan 8, Vieira 64**
Referee **A Wiley**

Deprived of the leadership for just over 24 hours by
Manchester United, Arsenal battle back into pole
position when Cygan's header and Vieira's no-nonsense
finish sandwich another fine goal from Rooney.

Tuesday March 25
CHELSEA (a)
FA Cup, 6th rnd, replay
Won 3-1 **HT** 2-0   Att **41,456**
Taylor — Lauren, Campbell, Cygan, Toure — Parlour,
Vieira, Edu, Pires (Ljungberg 74) — Jeffers (Van
Bronckhorst 68), Wiltord (Henry 74) *Subs not used*
Warmuz, Bergkamp *Booked* Lauren, Cygan *Sent off*
Cygan 66
Scorers **Terry 25 (og), Wiltord 34, Lauren 82**
Report page 87

Saturday April 5
ASTON VILLA (a)
Drew 1-1 **HT** 0-0   Att **42,602**   Position **1st**
Taylor — Lauren, Campbell, Cygan, Toure (Cole 78) —
Parlour (Wiltord 78), Vieira, Gilberto, Ljungberg — Henry,
Bergkamp (Jeffers 85) *Subs not used* Edu, Warmuz
Booked Vieira, Jeffers
Scorer **Ljungberg 56**
Report page 231

Sunday April 13
SHEFFIELD UNITED
FA Cup, semi-final (Old Trafford)
Won 1-0 **HT** 1-0   Att **59,170**
Details page 332

Wednesday April 16
MANCHESTER UNITED (h)
Drew 2-2 **HT** 0-1   Att **38,164**   Position **2nd**
Taylor — Lauren, Keown, Campbell, Cole — Ljungberg,
Vieira (Edu 33), Gilberto, Pires (Kanu 80) — Henry,
Bergkamp (Wiltord 75) *Subs not used* Warmuz, Luzhny
Sent off Campbell 83
Scorer **Henry 51, 62**
Referee **M Halsey**

The most hyped match of the season lives up to its
billing but leaves both sides claiming injustice. Van
Nistelrooy brilliantly puts the leaders ahead, Henry
replies twice for the champions and Giggs's header
ensures that the title race stays alive. However,
Campbell is sent off for an alleged elbowing offence on
Solskjaer and may now be suspended for the Cup Final.

Saturday April 19
MIDDLESBROUGH (a)
Won 2-0   HT 0-0   Att 34,724   Position 2nd
Taylor — Lauren, Campbell, Cygan, Cole (Luzhny 83) — Ljungberg, Parlour, Gilberto, Pires (Van Bronckhorst 90) — Henry (Bergkamp 90), Wiltord *Subs not used* Keown, Warmuz *Booked* Henry
Scorers **Wiltord 48, Henry 82**
Report page 171

Saturday April 26
BOLTON WANDERERS (a)
Drew 2-2   HT 0-0   Att 27,253   Position 2nd
Seaman — Lauren (Van Bronckhorst 72), Campbell, Cygan (Keown 72), Cole — Ljungberg (Luzhny 59), Parlour, Gilberto, Pires — Henry, Wiltord *Subs not used* Bergkamp, Taylor *Booked* Henry, Parlour
Scorers **Wiltord 47, Pires 56**
Report page 244

Sunday May 4
LEEDS UNITED (h)
Lost 2-3   HT 1-1   Att 38,127   Position 2nd
Seaman — Toure (Kanu 70), Luzhny, Keown, Cole — Wiltord (Pennant 76), Parlour, Gilberto, Pires (Van Bronckhorst 80) — Henry, Bergkamp *Subs not used* Taylor, Stepanovs *Booked* Keown, Bergkamp
Scorers **Henry 31, Bergkamp 63**
Referee **A Wiley**

The title goes back to Old Trafford, even though Arsene Wenger insists that Arsenal are the better team. But they are not good enough to beat Leeds and prolong the championship race, twice coming from a goal down but losing to a late strike — scored by Viduka after he is allowed to run on from an offside position — that effectively secures Leeds's Premiership status.

Wednesday May 7
SOUTHAMPTON (h)
Won 6-1   HT 5-1   Att 38,052   Position 2nd
Taylor — Toure, Luzhny (Tavlaridis 77), Stepanovs, Garry — Pennant (Hoyte 90), Parlour, Van Bronckhorst, Pires (Bergkamp 62) — Henry, Kanu *Subs not used* Wiltord, Warmuz *Booked* Henry
Scorers **Pires 9, 23, 47, Pennant 16, 19, 26**
Referee **U Rennie**

The title has gone and now the curtain is brought down on Southampton after just 26 minutes of this Cup Final rehearsal, by which time Arsenal have romped into a 5-0 lead. Pennant, like many on the pitch unlikely to figure in Cardiff, marks his first Premiership start with a ten-minute hat-trick and Pires also gets three, the last a superlative lob from long range.

Sunday May 11
SUNDERLAND (a)
Won 4-0   HT 2-0   Att 40,188   Position 2nd
Seaman — Toure, Luzhny, Stepanovs, Cole — Ljungberg, Parlour (Van Bronckhorst ht), Gilberto, Pires (Pennant 64) — Henry, Bergkamp (Kanu 75) *Subs not used* Warmuz, Garry
Scorers **Henry 7, Ljungberg 39, 78, 88**
Report page 280

Saturday May 17
SOUTHAMPTON
FA Cup, Final (Cardiff)
Won 1-0   HT 1-0   Att 73,726
Details page 332

RAMI SHAABAN
Goalkeeper
Born June 30, 1975, Stockholm
Ht 6ft 4in **Wt** 14st 9lb
Signed from Djurgardens IF, August 2002, free

IGORS STEPANOVS
Defender
Born January 26, 1976, Ogre, Latvia
Ht 6ft 4in **Wt** 13st 5lb
Signed from Skonto Riga, Latvia, September 2000, £1m

SEBASTIAN SVARD
Defender
Born January 15, 1983, Hvidovre, Denmark
Ht 6ft 1in **Wt** 12st 11lb
Signed from FC Copenhagen, November 2000, nominal

EFSTATHIOS TAVLARIDIS
Defender
Born January 25, 1980, Serres, Greece
Ht 6ft 0in **Wt** 12st 11lb
Signed from Iraklis, Greece, September 2001, £600,000

STUART TAYLOR
Goalkeeper
Born November 28, 1980, Romford
Ht 6ft 5in **Wt** 13st 6lb
Signed from trainee, July 1998

KOLO TOURE
Midfield
Born March 19, 1981, Abidjan, Ivory Coast
Ht 6ft 0in **Wt** 12st 0lb
Signed from Asec Mimosas, February 2002, free

MATTHEW UPSON
(see Birmingham City)

GIOVANNI VAN BRONCKHORST
Midfield
Born February 5, 1975, Rotterdam
Ht 5ft 10in **Wt** 11st 9lb
Signed from Rangers, June 2001, £8.5m

PATRICK VIEIRA
Midfield
Born June 23, 1976, Dakar, Senegal
Ht 6ft 4in **Wt** 13st 0lb
Signed from AC Milan, August 1996, £3.5m

MORITZ VOLZ
Defender
Born January 21, 1983, Siegen, Germany
Ht 6ft 0in **Wt** 12st 7lb
Signed from Schalke 04, June 1999, free

SYLVAIN WILTORD
Forward
Born May 10, 1974, Paris
Ht 5ft 9in **Wt** 12st 4lb
Signed from Bordeaux, August 2000, £13m

Sylvain Wiltord

NEWCASTLE UNITED

PREMIERSHIP

	P	W	D	L	F	A	Pts
Man Utd	38	25	8	5	74	34	83
Arsenal	38	23	9	6	85	42	78
Newcastle	**38**	**21**	**6**	**11**	**63**	**48**	**69**
Chelsea	38	19	10	9	68	38	67
Liverpool	38	18	10	10	61	41	64
Blackburn	38	16	12	10	52	43	60
Everton	38	17	8	13	48	49	59
Southampton	38	13	13	12	43	46	52
Man City	38	15	6	17	47	54	51
Tottenham	38	14	8	16	51	62	50
Middlesbro	38	13	10	15	48	44	49
Charlton	38	14	7	17	45	56	49
Birmingham	38	13	9	16	41	49	48
Fulham	38	13	9	16	41	50	48
Leeds	38	14	5	19	58	57	47
Aston Villa	38	12	9	17	42	47	45
Bolton	38	10	14	14	41	51	44
West Ham	38	10	12	16	42	59	42
West Brom	38	6	8	24	29	65	26
Sunderland	38	4	7	27	21	65	19

FA CUP
Third round

WORTHINGTON CUP
Third round

CHAMPIONS LEAGUE
Second group stage

Jermaine Jenas, like Sir Bobby Robson's team, bristling with youthful promise

THE GAMES

Wednesday August 14
ZELJEZNICAR SARAJEVO (a)
Champions League, 3rd qualifying rnd, 1st leg
Won 1-0   HT 0-0   Att 35,000
Given — Hughes, Dabizas, Bramble, Bernard (Quinn 89)
— Solano, Dyer, Jenas, Viana (Elliott 89) — Shearer,
LuaLua (Ameobi 82) *Subs not used* Harper, O'Brien,
Griffin, Bassedas *Booked* Dabizas, LuaLua
Scorer **Dyer 56**
Referee **M Lubos (Slovakia)**

Newcastle begin their campaign with a daunting trip to
Bosnia-Herzegovina, where the scars of war are still
clearly visible in the city, and cap an encouragingly
gutsy performance with a goal of real class, as Dyer
finishes a splendid team move.

Monday August 19
WEST HAM UNITED (h)
Won 4-0   HT 0-0   Att 51,072   Position 1st
Given — Hughes, Dabizas, Bramble, Bernard — Solano
(McClen 87), Dyer, Jenas, Viana (Elliott 90) — Shearer,
LuaLua (Ameobi 81) *Subs not used* Harper, Griffin
Booked Shearer
Scorers **LuaLua 61, 72, Shearer 76, Solano 86**
Referee **P Durkin**

The first full weekend of the Premiership ends with
Newcastle on top of the table, West Ham at the bottom.
Sir Bobby Robson is doing cartwheels as LuaLua sparks
a burst of four goals in 25 minutes; Glenn Roeder's
team, with no Di Canio, no Kanoute and no threat,
crumbles ominously.

Saturday August 24
MANCHESTER CITY (a)
Lost 0-1   HT 0-1   Att 34,776   Position 10th
Given — Hughes, Dabizas, Bramble — Solano, Dyer,
Speed (Viana 73), Jenas, Bernard (Griffin 57) —
Shearer, LuaLua (Ameobi 73) *Subs not used* Harper,
O'Brien *Booked* Bernard
Report, page 138

Wednesday August 28
ZELJEZNICAR SARAJEVO (h)
Champions League, 3rd qualifying rnd, 2nd leg
Won 4-0 (win 5-0 on agg)   HT 2-0   Att 34,067
Given — Hughes, Dabizas (O'Brien 71), Bramble,
Bernard — Solano (Kerr 75), Dyer, Speed, Viana —
Shearer, LuaLua (Ameobi 51) *Subs not used* Harper,
Elliott, Jenas, Griffin *Booked* Dabizas
Scorers **Dyer 23, LuaLua 37, Viana 74, Shearer 80**
Referee **F De Bleeckere (Belgium)**

Dyer, the first-leg scorer, does it again with a neat lob
and this time the floodgates open, Viana and Shearer
scoring against ten men after Jahic is sent off for a
professional foul on Ameobi. The Champions League
proper beckons.

Monday September 2
LIVERPOOL (a)
Drew 2-2   HT 0-0   Att 43,241   Position 13th
Given — Hughes, Dabizas, Bramble, Bernard — Solano
(Jenas 64), Dyer, Speed, Viana (Robert 64) — Shearer,
LuaLua (Bellamy 64) *Subs not used* O'Brien, Harper
Booked Bernard, Speed
Scorers **Speed 80, Shearer 88**
Report page 90

NEWCASTLE UNITED'S SUPPORTERS should be looking
forward with unquenchable optimism after a season that stirred the
hearts even of non-believers. Yet to some fans — admittedly,
perhaps, a small minority — this sort of talk misses the point.

April 9, 2000: Wembley Stadium. And in an FA Cup semi-final
against Chelsea, for a brief moment — after Robert Lee's equaliser
— thoughts of victory and visions of a winnable final glimmered in
Geordie hearts. But Chelsea's second goal ended those dreams and,
for some Newcastle fans, ushered in an era of fatalistic realism that
has, perversely, heightened their enjoyment.

This was the day that some of the Toon Army finally realised
that it was not their club's destiny to win things. Since then,
watching Newcastle has been a joy: freed from the temptation to
dream, these Zen-like individuals have been able to gorge
themselves on a footballing feast.

Which is partly why the news that Newcastle have signed Lee
Bowyer has been greeted with such dismay by many. Aside from the
personal, political and social objections they have to the player, his
signing represents a decisive step away from the recent past.
Newcastle United, this signing says, is now a club where winning
has become everything.

Which, perhaps, is as it should be. After all, Newcastle have failed
to land a trophy in the past 34 years, an amazing (lack of)
achievement considering the riches that have been lavished on the
team in recent times. Yet such a controversial, possibly disruptive,
new signing has the whiff of unnecessary tinkering about it: last season, the present squad came so close to winning something that it
seems only increased application is required, not wholesale change.

On the negative side, Newcastle were occasionally found
wanting when the pressure was on and faded towards the end of the
season. The same could be said of Arsenal, a team they must
consistently match if they are to lift that elusive pot. A 1-0 defeat at
Highbury flattered Newcastle, who were unable to create a single
chance, though the 1-1 draw at St James' Park showed that they
were starting, at last, to get the measure of them.

Against Manchester United, though, Newcastle went backwards.
A calamitous defeat at Old Trafford was compounded in the return
fixture. Six goals in 26 minutes was harsh, but if the team has learnt
from the humbling experience, it was an invaluable lesson indeed.
But this was also a season of numerous highs, particularly in Europe.
Qualifying for the second group stage of the Champions League,
after losing their opening three matches, was unprecedented, as
were the scenes of jubilation in the De Kuip stadium in

Six points taken off Sunderland have rarely tasted sweeter

Rotterdam as travelling Geordies barmily celebrated Craig Bellamy's astonishing last-gasp winner that sealed second place in the group. Perhaps even more indicative of the squad's progress were the meetings with Juventus, the eventual runners-up. While the away game ended in defeat, there was little between the sides, while at home, a depleted Newcastle took the battle to the Italians and secured a notable victory.

The same passion carried them to within an inch of the knockout stages, but a superlative team effort away to Inter Milan effectively ended the campaign in a match besmirched by cynicism, bare-faced cheating and cowardly, if not dishonest, refereeing. And, while acknowledging Bayer Leverkusen were hardly the same team that had reached the final in 2002, for Newcastle to beat them twice, doing so away while deprived of the services of Bellamy and Alan Shearer, was a superb achievement.

What is most exciting for Newcastle supporters is that Sir Bobby Robson's squad continues to blend pace, passing, movement and creativity with experience and youth. Aaron Hughes, still only 23, has captained his country; Jermaine Jenas has made the step from under-21 to full international look easy; Shola Ameobi has shown that he can fill Shearer's boots in the most exacting of environments.

The one nagging worry is that the manager seems reluctant to utilise like-for-like replacements. Ameobi has been paired with Shearer when it is the tricky Lomana LuaLua who can best replace Bellamy. Youngsters who have played well when given the chance — Steve Caldwell, Jamie McClen, Michael Chopra — have watched non-specialists take their positions. Which makes the Bowyer signing seem all the more curious, especially given his form at West Ham United. Yet Robson was proved correct when he signed Bellamy, a player few rated. Another vindication for the grey knight would really not be a surprise.

Wednesday September 11
LEEDS UNITED (h)
Lost 0-2 HT **0-1** Att **51,730** Position **19th**
Given — Hughes, O'Brien (Griffin 83), Bramble, Bernard — Solano, Dyer, Speed (Viana 67), Robert — Shearer, Ameobi (Bellamy 67) *Subs not used* Jenas, Harper
Booked Bramble, Griffin, Speed
Referee **D Gallagher**

The only player on either side not to have got on the pitch when England played Portugal four days earlier, Robinson, the Leeds goalkeeper, makes up for lost time with a superb display to frustrate Newcastle. Expert strikes from Viduka and Smith at either end of the match win the points for his side.

Saturday September 14
CHELSEA (a)
Lost 0-3 HT **0-2** Att **39,746** Position **19th**
Given — Hughes, O'Brien, Dabizas, Bernard — Solano (Jenas 78), Dyer, Speed, Viana (Viana 78) — Shearer, Bellamy (Ameobi 78) *Subs not used* Harper, Bramble
Booked Bernard, Solano, Shearer, Speed
Report page 79

Wednesday September 18
DYNAMO KIEV (a)
Champions League
Lost 0-2 HT **0-1** Att **42,500**
Given — Griffin, O'Brien, Dabizas, Bernard (Robert 69) — Hughes (Solano 69) — Dyer, Speed, Viana (Ameobi 79), Bellamy *Subs not used* Harper, Jenas, Bramble, LuaLua *Booked* Hughes
Referee **E Iturralde (Spain)**

The margin may be 2-0, but Newcastle suffer an old-fashioned stuffing in Kiev, where goals from Shatskikh and Khatskevich scarcely reflect Dynamo's dominance. Worse is to follow as Bellamy is handed a three-match ban by Uefa for butting Ghioane, the Kiev defender, off the ball.

Saturday September 21
SUNDERLAND (h)
Won 2-0 HT **2-0** Att **52,181** Position **13th**
Given — Griffin, O'Brien, Dabizas, Hughes — Solano (Jenas 64), Dyer, Speed, Robert (Viana 77) — Shearer, Bellamy (Ameobi 86) *Subs not used* Harper, Bramble
Booked Robert, Bellamy
Scorers **Bellamy 2, Shearer 39**
Referee **M Riley**

The pressure on Peter Reid, the Sunderland manager, rises to almost intolerable levels after a poor, passionless display in a derby effectively settled in the 83 seconds it takes Bellamy to give Newcastle the lead. Shearer adds an unnecessary second; Reid's tenure has only three more matches to run.

Tuesday September 24
FEYENOORD (h)
Champions League
Lost 0-1 HT **0-1** Att **40,540**
Given — Griffin, O'Brien, Dabizas, Hughes — Solano, Dyer, Speed, Robert — Shearer, Bellamy (LuaLua 76) *Subs not used* Harper, Jenas, Bramble, Ameobi, Bernard, Viana
Referee **C Colombo (France)**

Early mistakes by Griffin and O'Brien, which present Pardo with the chance to score with a splendid volley, prove impossible for Newcastle to rectify, despite boundless enthusiasm that sees Bellamy hit the bar and Shearer have an effort cleared off the line.

Saturday September 28
BIRMINGHAM CITY (a)
Won 2-0 HT 1-0 Att 29,072 Position 10th
Given — Griffin, O'Brien, Dabizas, Hughes — Solano
(Jenas 79), Dyer, Speed, Robert (Viana 88) — Shearer,
LuaLua (Ameobi 79) *Subs not used* Harper, Bramble
Scorers **Solano 34, Ameobi 90**
Report page 187

Tuesday October 1
JUVENTUS (a)
Champions League
Lost 0-2 HT 0-0 Att 41,424
Given — O'Brien, Dabizas, Hughes — Griffin (Ameobi 79)
— Solano (Viana 70), Jenas (LuaLua 79), Speed, Robert
— Dyer — Shearer *Subs not used* Harper, Elliott,
Bramble, Bernard *Booked* Dabizas
Referee **R Temmink (the Netherlands)**

Played three, lost three. Newcastle's Champions League
hopes are now hanging by a thread despite a brave
performance in Turin. Robert misses a great first-half
chance and Shearer has a header wrongly disallowed
for offside at 1-0, but Del Piero's double proves
decisive.

Saturday October 5
WEST BROMWICH ALBION (h)
Won 2-1 HT 1-1 Att 52,142 Position 6th
Given — Griffin, Dabizas, O'Brien, Hughes — Solano
(Jenas 82), Dyer, Speed, Robert (Bernard 89) —
Shearer, Bellamy (LuaLua 82) *Subs not used* Ameobi,
Harper *Booked* O'Brien
Scorer **Shearer 45, 69**
Referee **C Foy**

Gary Megson, the West Bromwich Albion manager, is
furious — and television evidence backs his claims —
when O'Brien escapes after a "professional foul" on
Roberts and then Balis, scorer of the opening goal, is
penalised for the free kick that allows Shearer to
equalise. Shearer later rubs salt in the wounds with the
close-range winner.

Saturday October 19
BLACKBURN ROVERS (a)
Lost 2-5 HT 1-2 Att 27,307 Position 11th
Given — Hughes (Bernard 80), Dabizas, O'Brien, Griffin
(Bramble 75) — Solano, Jenas, Speed, Robert (Viana 75)
— Shearer, Bellamy *Subs not used* Ameobi, Harper
Booked Speed, Robert *Sent off* Dabizas 4
Scorer **Shearer 36 (pen), 48**
Report page 104

Wednesday October 23
JUVENTUS (h)
Champions League
Won 1-0 HT 0-0 Att 48,370
Harper — Griffin, Bramble, O'Brien, Hughes — Solano,
Jenas, Speed, Robert (Viana 85) — Shearer, LuaLua
(Ameobi 85) *Subs not used* Given, Elliott, Acuna, Kerr,
Bernard
Scorer **Griffin 62**
Referee **R Pedersen (Norway)**

Off the mark at last, though still bottom of group E,
Newcastle benefit from an overdue slice of luck when
Buffon, the previously faultless Juventus goalkeeper,
turns Griffin's low cross into his own net. Uefa
subsequently — and bizarrely — allows Griffin to keep
Newcastle's first goal in the Champions League,
although it is clearly an own goal.

MATCH OF THE SEASON

Feyenoord 2   Newcastle United 3
De Kuip Stadium, Wednesday November 13 2002
George Caulkin in Rotterdam

A RISK. SIR BOBBY ROBSON had described his decision to play
Craig Bellamy against Feyenoord as "a risk". Imagine that. To the
tune of £10 million, it paid off for Newcastle United last night as, con-
trary to all logic and expectation, they qualified for the second group
stage of the Champions League.

Two weeks ago, Bellamy was consulting a specialist, fearing
more surgery on his knee. Last night he scored twice as Newcastle
created history, becoming the first side to reach the second phase
after losing their opening three matches. On an evening of
unbearable tension and, finally, ecstasy, the drama that accompanied their achievement was extraordinary. They were helped on
their way by the gods of fortune, but they were heroic and defiant.

Bellamy scored in the final moments of each half, but his
renaissance was not the only surprise. A severely depleted Juventus
side did the unthinkable and beat Dynamo Kiev 2-1 away from
home, ensuring that a Newcastle victory would be good enough.
First it was in their grasp and then it was forfeited, a two-goal lead
amassed and tossed away. The winner came at the death.

The Dutch club, winners of the Uefa Cup last season, were
playing for everything that Newcastle were. They fought and clawed
their way back into the contest and, until Bellamy capitalised on a
rebound from Kieron Dyer's shot, they looked more likely to
progress. Instead, they finished bottom of group E. "Juve, Juve," a
jubilant batch of travelling supporters sang.

If starting with Bellamy, he of the dodgy leg and dodgier temperament, was a gamble by Robson, it was one brought about by the
weight of adverse statistics pressing down on his side. It was enough
for the gloomy to feast on: Newcastle had never previously won in
the Netherlands and never away in the Champions League. It was to
become the manager's finest night with his home-town club.

Events in the Olympiyskyi Stadium — where a Juventus team
shorn of Nedved, Thuram and Del Piero and staffed by a clutch of
youngsters were brilliantly playing for Tyneside — were far outside
their control, yet were still a niggling itch at the back of the head. In
spite of a vibrant, caustic atmosphere, it was a distraction to all, even
if Newcastle only discovered the result once back in their
dressing-room.

Bellamy's absence for six matches had, conveniently,
encapsulated a three-game suspension for a butting offence on
Tiberiu Ghioane in Ukraine. Within five minutes he was claiming a
penalty; as Robson has said, when the Wales striker is making noise,
you know he is back. His return had been trailed so heavily that it
was hardly a surprise, unlike Nolberto Solano's relegation to the

Ecstasy for Craig Bellamy after his last-minute goal in Rotterdam secured Newcastle's place in the second phase of the Champions League

Saturday October 26
CHARLTON ATHLETIC (h)
Won 2-1   HT 1-1   Att **51,670**   Position **8th**
Given — Griffin, Bramble, O'Brien, Hughes — Solano
(Viana 87), Jenas, Speed, Robert (Bernard 87) —
Shearer, Ameobi *Subs not used* Harper, Chopra,
Dabizas *Booked* Ameobi, Griffin
Scorers **Griffin 37, Robert 59**
Referee **A D'Urso**

Charlton must know that it is not going to be their day
when they discover that their shorts have been stolen
from the team hotel. Despite taking the lead in
borrowed kit, through Bartlett, they are beaten by goals
from the suddenly prolific Griffin and, in the second
half, Robert.

Tuesday October 29
DYNAMO KIEV (h)
Champions League
Won 2-1   HT 0-0   Att **40,185**
Harper — Griffin, Bramble (Dabizas 27), O'Brien (Bernard
ht), Hughes — Solano (Dyer 82), Jenas, Speed, Robert —
Shearer, Ameobi *Subs not used* Given, Acuna, LuaLua,
Viana *Booked* Ameobi
Scorers **Speed 58, Shearer 69 (pen)**
Referee **J A F Marin (Spain; rep J L Omar, Spain, ht)**

The Great Escape is still on after Newcastle come from
behind to beat Kiev, Speed equalising with a diving
header from Solano's corner before Shearer wins and
converts a penalty. "I knew he would not fail us," Sir
Bobby Robson says.

Monday November 4
MIDDLESBROUGH (h)
Won 2-0   HT 1-0   Att **51,558**   Position **8th**
Given — Griffin, Hughes, Caldwell, Bernard — Solano
(Dyer 71), Jenas, Speed, Robert (Viana 71) — Shearer,
Ameobi *Subs not used* Elliott, Harper, LuaLua *Booked*
Shearer, Griffin
Scorers **Ameobi 20, Caldwell 87**
Referee **G Barber**

For the second match running, Queudrue sees red in
the last minute for a second bookable offence as
Middlesbrough's night turns from bad to worse. The
better side in spells — Maccarone hits Given's post —
they lose to goals from Ameobi and Caldwell, who is
making his first start for 20 months.

Wednesday November 6
EVERTON (h)
Worthington Cup, 3rd rnd
Drew 3-3 (aet; lose 3-2 on pens) HT 0-1 Att **34,584**
Harper — Griffin, Dabizas, Caldwell, Elliott — Dyer, Viana,
Acuna (Solano 66), Bernard (Robert 66) — Cort, LuaLua
(Chopra 66) *Subs not used* Given, Hughes *Booked* Viana
Sent off Caldwell 112
Scorers **Dyer 77, 78, Pistone 100 (og)**
Referee **M Riley**

A cup-tie with just about everything sees Newcastle trail,
take the lead twice (the second time with an own goal),
taken into extra time after Caldwell's dismissal for
handling on the line and finally beaten in a shoot-out by
an Everton side for whom Rooney's introduction is
again decisive.

Saturday November 9
ARSENAL (a)
Lost 0-1 HT **0-1** Att **38,121** Position **9th**
Given — Griffin, Dabizas, O'Brien, Hughes — Solano (Ameobi 70), Jenas, Speed, Viana (Bernard 70) — Shearer, Dyer *Subs not used* Harper, LuaLua, Caldwell
Booked Viana, Griffin
Report page 57

Wednesday November 13
FEYENOORD (a)
Champions League
Won 3-2 HT **1-0** Att **45,000**
Given — Griffin, Dabizas, O'Brien, Hughes — Jenas, Dyer, Speed, Viana (Bernard 82) — Shearer, Bellamy *Subs not used* Harper, Solano, Acuna, LuaLua, Ameobi, Caldwell
Booked Griffin, Bellamy
Scorers **Bellamy 45, 90, Viana 49**
Referee **F-X Wack (Germany)**

Rarely has a place in football history been achieved in such dramatic style. Needing to win in the Netherlands and for Juventus to avoid defeat in Kiev to become the first side to qualify for the second stage after losing their first three matches, Newcastle surrender a 2-0 lead before Bellamy squeezes in a last-minute winner — a goal worth around £10 million to the club.

Saturday November 16
SOUTHAMPTON (h)
Won 2-1 HT **1-1** Att **51,812** Position **6th**
Given — Griffin, Caldwell, O'Brien (Dabizas 78), Hughes — Jenas, Dyer, Speed, Viana (Bernard 82) — Shearer, Ameobi *Subs not used* Solano, Harper, LuaLua *Booked* Shearer
Scorers **Ameobi 41, Hughes 54**
Referee **C Wilkes**

He does not score, but Shearer's brilliance is the difference between the sides, according to Gordon Strachan. The Southampton manager sees Beattie give his side the lead with a stunning volley, but Ameobi — set up by Dyer — and Hughes take Newcastle up to sixth place in the table.

Saturday November 23
MANCHESTER UNITED (a)
Lost 3-5 HT **1-3** Att **67,619** Position **8th**
Given — Griffin, O'Brien, Dabizas, Hughes — Jenas, Dyer, Speed, Bernard (Solano 72) — Bellamy, Shearer *Subs not used* Harper, Elliott, Acuna, Ameobi *Booked* Speed, Dabizas
Scorers **Bernard 35, Shearer 52, Bellamy 75**
Report page 46

Wednesday November 27
INTER MILAN (h)
Champions League
Lost 1-4 HT **0-3** Att **50,108**
Given — Griffin, Dabizas, O'Brien, Hughes (Caldwell 86) — Solano, Dyer, Speed, Viana (Robert ht) — Shearer, Bellamy *Subs not used* Acuna, Jenas, LuaLua, Ameobi, Harper *Sent off* Bellamy 6
Scorer **Solano 72**
Referee **S Bre (France)**

Here we go again; six minutes into the second phase, Newcastle's hopes are already fading. Behind after 67 seconds, they then lose Bellamy, not long back from a three-match European ban, who is sent off after tangling with Materazzi off the ball, while TV later catches Shearer elbowing Cannavaro, though he escapes immediate punishment. Inter go on to complete a resounding triumph.

substitutes' bench. Without any wingers in their team, Newcastle aimed to play through Feyenoord's defence rather than around it, to harry them with four natural midfield players. Given that the Dutch team had not scored in Europe since leaving St James' Park with a 1-0 victory in September, it was a viable tactic, designed to prey on attacking frailties.

Without approaching anything resembling peak fluency, Newcastle quietly manufactured the more prominent chances. Gary Speed twice darted forward from midfield to unsettle Patrick Lodewijks, while Bellamy was only thwarted by the Feyenoord goalkeeper when a heavy touch took the ball away from his toes. Bellamy's pace was the one constant source of menace. The risk of playing him had not been an idle fancy.

With virtually the final move of the opening period, he proved it decisively after a simple, effective move, tailor-made to exploit his qualities. A free kick from Shay Given, deep in his own territory, was nodded on by Alan Shearer and Bellamy shrugged off his marker and rolled his shot home from six yards. Meanwhile, the news from Ukraine was positive: Juventus were drawing 0-0.

By the 49th minute, Newcastle's lead had been doubled, with Dyer — another stellar performer — pinching the ball from Tomasz Rzasa, the left back, and lobbing it to the far post, where Viana caressed home a shot from 22 yards.

Suddenly, a tremor of electricity passed through the game. In the 65th minute, Feyenoord spied a route back into the contest, with Mariano Bombarda, a substitute, accepting a pass from Bonaventure Kalou and shooting as he fell. Soon, they were level. A header from Bombarda caught Newcastle leaden-footed and brought a searing volley from Anthony Lurling.

It was desperate stuff, addled by nerves, and there was only going to be one winner. "At 2-2, I thought we were heading for the second round of the Champions League," Bert van Marwijk, the Feyenoord coach, said. So did most rational observers. The linesman held up a board indicating three minutes of injury time. Then Dyer broke from midfield, Lodewijks could only parry his shot and Bellamy struck to spark pandemonium.

FEYENOORD (4-4-2): P Lodewijks — C Gyan, K van Wonderen, P Paauwe, T Rzasa — C-G Song (sub: M Bombarda, 51min), P Bosvelt, B Emerton, A Lurling — B Kalou, T Buffel.
Substitutes not used: C I'Ami, P Collen, F de Haan, R van Persie, S Pardo, G Loovens.
Booked: Paauwe, Bombarda.
NEWCASTLE UNITED (4-4-2): S Given — A Griffin, N Dabizas, A O'Brien, A Hughes — J Jenas, K Dyer, G Speed, H Viana (sub: O Bernard, 82) — A Shearer, C Bellamy.
Substitutes not used: S Harper, N Solano, C Acuna, L LuaLua, S Ameobi, S Caldwell.
Booked: Griffin, Bellamy.
Referee: F-X Wack (Germany).

THE MANAGER

Sir Bobby Robson

Even if judged purely on what he achieved in 2002-03, Sir Bobby remains a managerial giant. As well as an improved finish in the Premiership and a Champions League run only ended by an intransigent Portuguese referee and some abominable cheating by Inter Milan, the Grand Old Man of English football has built a fine, young, flair-packed squad that will surely improve with age. However, the arrival of Lee Bowyer will test even this living legend, with off-field problems already worrying the club. Robson will need all his considerable powers if he is to prevail.

Angus Batey

APPEARANCES

	Prem	FAC	WC	Euro	Total
C Acuna	2 (2)	1	1	-	4 (2)
D Ambrose	0 (1)	-	-	-	0 (1)
S Ameobi	8 (20)	0 (1)	-	4 (6)	12 (27)
C Bellamy	27 (2)	1	-	6	34 (2)
O Bernard	24 (6)	1	1	8 (2)	34 (8)
T Bramble	13 (3)	-	-	8	21 (3)
S Caldwell	12 (2)	-	1	1 (1)	14 (3)
M Chopra	0 (1)	-	0 (1)	0 (2)	0 (4)
C Cort	0 (1)	-	1	0 (1)	1 (2)
N Dabizas	13 (3)	0 (1)	1	7 (1)	21 (5)
K Dyer	33 (2)	-	1	11 (1)	45 (3)
R Elliott	0 (2)	-	1	0 (1)	1 (3)
S Given	38	1	-	12	51
A Griffin	22 (5)	1	1	11	35 (5)
S Harper	-	-	1	2	3
A Hughes	35	1	-	11 (1)	47 (1)
J Jenas	23 (9)	1	-	8	32 (9)
B Kerr	4 (4)	-	-	1 (1)	5 (5)
L LuaLua	5 (6)	0 (1)	1	5 (4)	11 (11)
J McClen	0 (1)	-	-	-	0 (1)
A O'Brien	26	1	-	11 (1)	38 (1)
W Quinn	-	-	-	0 (1)	0 (1)
L Robert	25 (2)	1	0 (1)	9 (2)	35 (5)
A Shearer	35	1	-	12	48
N Solano	29 (2)	1	0 (1)	10 (2)	40 (5)
G Speed	23 (1)	-	-	12	35 (1)
H Viana	11 (12)	-	1	5 (5)	17 (17)
J Woodgate	10	-	-	-	10

Sunday December 1
EVERTON (h)
Won 2-1 HT 0-1 Att **51,607** Position **6th**
Given — Griffin, Caldwell (Ameobi 81), O'Brien, Bernard — Solano, Dyer, Speed (Viana 81), Robert — Shearer, Bellamy *Subs not used* Harper, Jenas, Dabizas
Scorers **Shearer 86, Li Tie 89 (og)**
Referee **M Halsey**

Everton's seven-match winning streak comes to an end in sensational fashion. Ahead through Campbell but down to ten men from the 22nd minute after Yobo's dismissal, they concede a stunning late equaliser to Shearer, who rates his dipping, swerving volley his "best-ever" goal, and an even later winner, when Bellamy's shot is deflected in off Li Tie, who is later credited with an own goal.

Saturday December 7
ASTON VILLA (a)
Won 1-0 HT 0-0 Att **33,446** Position **6th**
Given — Griffin, Hughes, O'Brien, Bernard — Solano, Dyer, Jenas, Robert — Shearer, Bellamy *Subs not used* Harper, Acuna, LuaLua, Ameobi, Caldwell
Scorer **Shearer 82**
Report page 227

Wednesday December 11
BARCELONA (a)
Champions League
Lost 1-3 HT 1-2 Att **45,100**
Given — Griffin, Hughes, O'Brien, Bernard — Solano, Dyer, Speed, Robert — Ameobi, LuaLua (Chopra 83) *Subs not used* Harper, Acuna, Jenas, Cort, Caldwell, Dabizas *Booked* Ameobi
Scorer **Ameobi 24**
Referee **F De Bleeckere (Belgium)**

Forced by torrential rain to delay his return to the Nou Camp for 24 hours, Sir Bobby Robson sees his side, deprived of the suspended Shearer and Bellamy, compete well and draw level through the excellent Ameobi, but they eventually bow to Barcelona's superior marksmanship.

Saturday December 14
SOUTHAMPTON (a)
Drew 1-1 HT 0-0 Att **32,061** Position **6th**
Given — Griffin, Caldwell, O'Brien, Hughes — Jenas, Dyer, Speed, Robert — Shearer, Bellamy *Subs not used* Harper, Dabizas, Acuna, LuaLua, Ameobi
Scorer **Bellamy 50**
Report page 130

Saturday December 21
FULHAM (h)
Won 2-0 HT 1-0 Att **51,576** Position **4th**
Given — Griffin, Caldwell, O'Brien, Hughes — Solano (Ameobi 83), Dyer (Jenas 81), Speed (Acuna 87), Robert — Shearer, Bellamy *Subs not used* Harper, Dabizas
Scorers **Solano 8, Bellamy 70**
Referee **A Wiley**

A routine win for Newcastle is marred only by Shearer's miss from the penalty spot (playing the only Premiership side he is yet to score against). For Van der Sar, though, it is a nightmare: the Fulham goalkeeper is booked, injured and responsible for Solano's opener. They also have Wome sent off for a high, late challenge on Griffin.

Thursday December 26
BOLTON WANDERERS (a)
Lost 3-4 **HT 1-3** Att **27,314** Position **6th**
Given — Griffin, Caldwell, O'Brien, Hughes — Solano (Jenas 72), Dyer, Speed, Robert — Shearer, Ameobi (LuaLua 72) *Subs not used* Harper, Bellamy, Dabizas
Booked Shearer, LuaLua
Scorers **Shearer 8, 79, Ameobi 71**
Report page 239

Sunday December 29
TOTTENHAM HOTSPUR (h)
Won 2-1 **HT 1-0** Att **52,145** Position **4th**
Given — Hughes, Caldwell, O'Brien, Bernard — Solano (LuaLua ht), Dyer (Dabizas ht), Speed (Jenas 23), Robert — Shearer, Bellamy *Subs not used* Harper, Ameobi
Booked Dabizas
Scorers **Speed 17, Shearer 58**
Referee **S Bennett**

Newcastle win a thrilling match despite three early injuries and with Dabizas heading Spurs back into contention with a spectacular own goal. Glenn Hoddle is more concerned with the health of Ziege, having revealed that the defender spent Boxing Day "fighting for his life" after an emergency operation to remove a blood clot from his thigh.

Wednesday January 1
LIVERPOOL (h)
Won 1-0 **HT 1-0** Att **52,147** Position **4th**
Given — Griffin, Hughes, O'Brien, Bernard — Kerr (Ameobi 73), Jenas, Acuna (Elliott 73), Robert — Shearer, Bellamy *Subs not used* Harper, LuaLua, Dabizas *Booked* Jenas
Scorer **Robert 13**
Referee **D Gallagher**

Liverpool's run of league matches without a win is extended to ten — their worst since 1923 — as they fall to Robert's free kick, deflected by Baros, for a weakened Newcastle team on a sodden pitch that survives two inspections. Diao's sending-off compounds Liverpool's misery.

Sunday January 5
WOLVERHAMPTON WANDERERS (a)
FA Cup, 3rd rnd
Lost 2-3 **HT 2-2** Att **27,316**
Given — Griffin, Hughes, O'Brien (Dabizas ht), Bernard — Solano (LuaLua 76), Jenas, Acuna (Ameobi 84), Robert — Shearer, Bellamy *Subs not used* Harper, Kerr *Booked* Bernard
Scorers **Jenas 40, Shearer 43 (pen)**
Referee **R Styles**

The last tie of the round is also the best tie of the round, a meeting of two of the Cup's greatest names producing a magnificent spectacle of end-to-end attacking for a Sunday television audience. Newcastle trail 2-0 inside half an hour, are level by the break, but concede the winner to Ndah as Wolves hang on.

Saturday January 11
WEST HAM UNITED (a)
Drew 2-2 **HT 1-2** Att **35,048** Position **4th**
Given — Griffin, Caldwell, Hughes, Bernard — Jenas, Acuna (LuaLua 66), Dyer, Robert — Bellamy, Ameobi (Cort 86) *Subs not used* Harper, Solano, Dabizas
Booked Griffin
Scorers **Bellamy 9, Jenas 81**
Report page 252

PLAYER OF THE SEASON — Alan Shearer

While it may sound like the most tedious of choices, particularly in a season that saw the PFA young player award going to Tyneside for the second season running, Newcastle's player of the season was quite clearly Shearer. A continuing inspiration, he led the line superbly and played with passion that only a fan can bring, defying age, injury and his numerous critics to fire in 25 goals and briefly reignite talk of an England recall. It would have been sacrilege not long ago, yet now many Toon fans who saw both play are touting Shearer over Jackie Milburn as Newcastle's greatest No 9.
Angus Batey

STATS AND FACTS

● This season Sir Bobby Robson led Newcastle United against Fulham; 35 years earlier, in 1968, he managed the Fulham team that faced Newcastle in the top flight.

● Newcastle have not won any of their past 22 games away to Manchester United.

● Alan Shearer has finished either top scorer or joint top scorer for his club in each of the past 12 seasons, covering spells at Southampton, Blackburn Rovers and Newcastle.

● Newcastle are unbeaten in the 22 Premiership games that have immediately followed their 22 European matches under Robson.

● Perhaps the travelling is draining when the two clubs who are farthest apart geographically in the Premiership play each other. Of the 78 meetings between Newcastle United and Southampton, only seven have ended in away wins.

● Newcastle scored fewer league goals than Sunderland in the 2000-01 season, but in the subsequent two seasons they have outscored their great rivals by 137 goals to 50.

● Only one of Newcastle's past 102 games in all competitions has ended 0-0.

● The past two scorelines of 6-2 in the Premiership have both occurred at St James' Park: Newcastle United 2, Manchester United 6 in April 2003, and Newcastle United 6, Everton 2 in March the previous year.

● Jermaine Jenas and Sir Bobby Robson turned 20 and 70 respectively on the same day last season: February 18.

● Newcastle have managed only two wins in their past 14 matches against Manchester United. Both came at St James' Park, and each time Roy Keane was sent off.

Bill Edgar

GOALSCORERS

	Prem	FAC	WC	Euro	Total
S Ameobi	5	-	-	3	8
C Bellamy	7	-	-	2	9
O Bernard	2	-	-	-	2
S Caldwell	1	-	-	-	1
K Dyer	2	-	2	2	6
A Griffin	1	-	-	1	2
A Hughes	1	-	-	-	1
J Jenas	6	1	-	-	7
L LuaLua	2	-	-	2	4
L Robert	5	-	-	-	5
A Shearer	17 (2p)	1 (p)	-	7 (2p)	25 (5p)
N Solano	7 (1p)	-	-	1	8 (1p)
G Speed	2	-	-	1	3
H Viana	2	-	-	-	2
Own goals	3	-	1	-	4

Saturday January 18
MANCHESTER CITY (h)
Won 2-0 HT 1-0 Att 52,152 Position 3rd
Given — Hughes, Dabizas, Caldwell, Bernard — Solano (Kerr 90), Jenas, Dyer, Robert — Shearer, Bellamy *Subs not used* Elliott, Harper, LuaLua, Ameobi
Scorers **Shearer 1, Bellamy 64**
Referee **G Poll (rep C Webster 83)**

Newcastle's tenth successive home league win is on course after precisely 10.4 seconds, the time it takes for Shearer to charge down a clearance from Nash — in City's goal in place of the injured Schmeichel — and record the second-fastest Premiership goal in history.

Wednesday January 22
BOLTON WANDERERS (h)
Won 1-0 HT 1-0 Att 52,005 Position 3rd
Given — Hughes, Dabizas, Caldwell, Bernard — Solano (Kerr 84), Jenas, Dyer, Robert — Shearer, Bellamy *Subs not used* Elliott, Harper, LuaLua, Ameobi *Booked* Dabizas
Scorer **Jenas 18**
Referee **P Dowd**

Watched by an admiring Sven-Goran Eriksson, Jenas adds to his burgeoning reputation with a simple goal that is just enough to see off Bolton — who have two strong claims for penalties turned down and miss a routine chance through Gardner — and leaves them only two points behind Manchester United.

Wednesday January 29
TOTTENHAM HOTSPUR (a)
Won 1-0 HT 0-0 Att 36,084 Position 2nd
Given — O'Brien, Bramble, Dabizas, Bernard — Kerr (Solano 60), Jenas, Dyer, Robert — Shearer, Bellamy *Subs not used* Harper, Elliott, LuaLua, Ameobi *Booked* Bernard
Scorer **Jenas 90**
Report page 157

Sunday February 9
ARSENAL (h)
Drew 1-1 HT 0-1 Att 52,157 Position 3rd
Given — Hughes, O'Brien, Bramble, Bernard — Solano (Speed ht), Jenas, Dyer, Robert — Shearer (Ameobi 90), Bellamy *Subs not used* LuaLua, Caig, Dabizas *Booked* Shearer, Robert *Sent off* Robert 58
Scorer **Robert 53**
Referee **N Barry**

After 11 straight home league victories, Newcastle are finally held by the champions. But their streak ends in controversial circumstances, Robert — five minutes after cancelling out Henry's opener — being sent off for a second bookable offence. Sir Bobby Robson is none too impressed by Bergkamp's role in the fateful caution.

Tuesday February 18
BAYER LEVERKUSEN (a)
Champions League
Won 3-1 HT 3-1 Att 22,500
Given — Hughes, O'Brien, Bramble, Bernard — Jenas, Speed, Dyer, Robert — Ameobi (Cort 88), LuaLua (Chopra 83) *Subs not used* Harper, Acuna, Griffin, Kerr, Caldwell
Scorers **Ameobi 5, 15, LuaLua 32**
Referee **T Hauge (Norway)**

Sir Bobby Robson gets the 70th birthday present of his dreams: a German club in crisis on and off the field and a vital victory despite the absence of Shearer and Bellamy, both banned. Ameobi and LuaLua, their stand-ins, do the damage with all three goals.

Saturday February 22
LEEDS UNITED (a)
Won 3-0 HT 1-0 Att 40,025 Position 3rd
Given — Griffin (Dabizas 84), O'Brien, Bramble, Hughes
— Kerr (Ameobi 80), Dyer (Acuna 80), Speed, Robert —
Shearer, Bellamy Subs not used Caig, Chopra
Scorers **Dyer 17, 48, Shearer 54**
Report page 218

Wednesday February 26
BAYER LEVERKUSEN (h)
Champions League
Won 3-1 HT 3-0 Att 40,508
Given — Griffin, Caldwell, Bramble, Bernard — Kerr
(Viana 83), Dyer (Solano 70), Speed, Robert — Shearer
(LuaLua 81), Ameobi Subs not used Harper, O'Brien,
Cort, Hughes
Scorer **Shearer 5, 11, 36 (pen)**
Referee **C Bo-Larsen (Denmark)**

At last, Shearer breaks his duck with the first
Champions League goal of his career from open play, a
thunderous diving header. Within half an hour he has
completed a hat-trick from the spot after Given
concedes and saves a penalty at the other end. Babic's
goal for an outclassed Leverkusen cannot erase the
smiles on Tyneside.

Saturday March 1
CHELSEA (h)
Won 2-1 HT 1-1 Att 52,157 Position 3rd
Given — Hughes, O'Brien, Woodgate, Bernard —
Solano (Griffin 79), Dyer (Ameobi 88), Speed, Viana
(Bramble 72) — Shearer, Bellamy Subs not used
LuaLua, Caig
Scorers **Hasselbaink 31 (og), Bernard 53**
Referee **J Winter**

Third entertains fourth at lunchtime and, after
Hasselbaink's spectacular headed own goal and a
neat finish by Bernard sandwich Lampard's volley for
Chelsea, Newcastle sit down for tea with a
six-point cushion over their nearest pursuers.
Woodgate makes an assured debut at the heart of
their defence.

Wednesday March 5
MIDDLESBROUGH (a)
Lost 0-1 HT 0-0 Att 34,814 Position 3rd
Given — Hughes, Bramble, Woodgate, Bernard — Jenas,
Dyer, Speed (Viana 77), Robert (Ameobi 79) — Shearer,
Bellamy Subs not used Solano, O'Brien, Harper Booked
Bernard, Viana, Bramble
Report page 170

Tuesday March 11
INTER MILAN (a)
Champions League
Drew 2-2 HT 1-0 Att 53,459
Given — Griffin, O'Brien (Hughes 59), Bramble, Bernard
— Solano (LuaLua 83), Jenas, Speed, Robert (Viana 83)
— Shearer, Bellamy Subs not used Harper, Ameobi,
Kerr, Caldwell Booked Shearer, Bellamy, Bramble,
LuaLua
Scorer **Shearer 42, 49**
Referee **L Batista (Portugal)**

Qualification remains within Newcastle's reach after
Shearer's double — his first goals against Italian
opposition for club or country — caps a splendid team
performance in an absorbing contest, Inter twice
coming from behind through headers from Vieri and
Cordoba to maintain the advantage over United with
one game to go.

THE PLAYERS

CLARENCE ACUNA
Midfield
Born February 2, 1975, Rancagua,
Chile
Ht 5ft 10in **Wt** 11st 5lb
Signed from Universidad de Chile,
October 2000, £900,000

DARREN AMBROSE
Forward
Born February 29, 1984, Harlow
Ht 5ft 11in **Wt** 10st 5lb
Signed from Ipswich Town, March
2003, £1m

SHOLA AMEOBI
Forward
Born October 12, 1981, Zaria,
Nigeria
Ht 6ft 3in **Wt** 11st 9lb
Signed from trainee, October
1998

CRAIG BELLAMY
Forward
Born July 13, 1979, Cardiff
Ht 5ft 8in **Wt** 10st 10lb
Signed from Coventry City, July
2001, £6m

OLIVIER BERNARD
Defender
Born October 14, 1979, Paris
Ht 5ft 9in **Wt** 10st 7lb
Signed from Lyons, October
2000, free

TITUS BRAMBLE
Defender
Born July 31, 1981, Ipswich
Ht 6ft 2in **Wt** 13st 7lb
Signed from Ipswich Town, July
2002, £5m

STEVE CALDWELL
Defender
Born September 12, 1980, Stirling
Ht 6ft 3in **Wt** 11st 8lb
Signed from trainee, June 1997

MICHAEL CHOPRA
Forward
Born December 23, 1983,
Newcastle
Ht 5ft 9in **Wt** 11st 5lb
Signed from trainee, January
2002

CARL CORT
Forward
Born November 1, 1977,
Southwark
Ht 6ft 4in **Wt** 12st 7lb
Signed from Wimbledon, July
2000, £700,000

Shola Ameobi

NICOS DABIZAS
Defender
Born August 3, 1973, Ptolemaida, Greece
Ht 6ft 1in **Wt** 11st 8lb
Signed from Olympiakos, March 1998, £1.3m

KIERON DYER
Midfield
Born December 29, 1978, Ipswich
Ht 5ft 8in **Wt** 10st 4lb
Signed from Ipswich Town, July 1997, £6m

ROBBIE ELLIOTT
Defender
Born December 25, 1973, Gosforth
Ht 5ft 10in **Wt** 11st 6lb
Signed from Bolton Wanderers, July 2001, free

SHAY GIVEN
Goalkeeper
Born April 20, 1976, Lifford, Co Donegal
Ht 6ft 0in **Wt** 13st 4lb
Signed from Blackburn Rovers, July 1997, £1.5m

ANDY GRIFFIN
Defender
Born March 7, 1979, Billinge
Ht 5ft 10in **Wt** 10st 10lb
Signed from Stoke City, January 1998, £1.5m

STEVE HARPER
Goalkeeper
Born March 14, 1975, Easington
Ht 6ft 2in **Wt** 13st 0lb
Signed from Seaham Red Star, July 1993, free

AARON HUGHES
Defender
Born November 8, 1979, Cookstown

Ht 6ft 1in **Wt** 11st 2lb
Signed from trainee, March 1997

JERMAINE JENAS
Midfield
Born February 18, 1983, Nottingham
Ht 5ft 10in **Wt** 11st 2lb
Signed from Nottingham Forest, February 2002, £5m

BRIAN KERR
Midfield
Born October 12, 1981, Motherwell
Ht 5ft 10in **Wt** 11st 12lb
Signed from trainee, December 1998

Shay Given

Saturday March 15
CHARLTON ATHLETIC (a)
Won 2-0 HT 1-0 Att 26,728 Position 3rd
Given — Hughes, Bramble, Woodgate, Bernard — Solano (Ameobi 85), Jenas, Speed (Dyer 66), Viana (Griffin 75) — Shearer, Bellamy *Subs not used* Harper, LuaLua
Booked Hughes, Viana
Scorers **Shearer 33 (pen), Solano 49**
Report page 182

Wednesday March 19
BARCELONA (h)
Champions League
Lost 0-2 HT 0-0 Att 51,883
Given — Griffin, O'Brien, Bramble, Bernard — Solano (Ameobi 67), Dyer, Jenas, Robert (Viana 67) — Shearer, Bellamy *Subs not used* Harper, Hughes, LuaLua, Kerr, Caldwell *Booked* Bernard
Referee **J Wegereef (the Netherlands)**

Newcastle need to win to stand any chance of going through — although Inter Milan's defeat of Bayer Leverkusen would have rendered victory redundant — and they have enough opportunities, but each one falls to Bellamy and for once he cannot deliver. Kluivert, after Bramble's dawdling, and Motta get the goals that finally end their dream.

Saturday March 22
BLACKBURN ROVERS (h)
Won 5-1 HT 1-0 Att 52,106 Position 3rd
Given — Griffin, Woodgate, Bramble, Hughes — Solano (Jenas 65), Dyer, Speed, Robert (Viana 77) — Shearer (Ameobi 86), Bellamy *Subs not used* Harper, O'Brien
Booked Bramble
Scorers **Solano 24, Robert 61, Jenas 85, Gresko 89 (og), Bellamy 90**
Referee **N Barry**

Newcastle respond to their European exit in typically upbeat fashion, a burst of three goals in the last five minutes — including an own goal by Gresko — bringing Blackburn's run of four successive victories to a shuddering halt after Duff's well-struck equaliser for the visiting team.

Sunday April 6
EVERTON (a)
Lost 1-2 HT 1-1 Att 40,031 Position 3rd
Given — O'Brien (Griffin 78), Woodgate, Bramble, Bernard — Kerr (Ameobi 78), Dyer, Jenas, Robert — Shearer, Bellamy *Subs not used* Harper, Hughes, LuaLua *Booked* Woodgate, Ameobi
Scorer **Robert 40**
Report page 123

Saturday April 12
MANCHESTER UNITED (h)
Lost 2-6 HT 1-4 Att 52,164 Position 3rd
Given — Hughes, Woodgate, Bramble, Bernard — Solano (Ameobi 66), Dyer, Jenas, Robert (Viana 15; LuaLua 66) — Shearer, Bellamy *Subs not used* Harper, Griffin *Booked* Shearer
Scorers **Jenas 21, Ameobi 89**
Referee **S Dunn**

And then there were two. They open the scoring through Jenas's superb strike and close it via Ameobi, but in between times Newcastle are taken apart by an inspired performance from Manchester United, who inflict their heaviest home defeat for more than 40 years to remove them from the championship equation and throw down the Premiership title gauntlet to Arsenal.

Saturday April 19
FULHAM (a)
Lost 1-2 HT **1-0** Att **17,900** Position **3rd**
Given — Griffin, Woodgate, O'Brien, Bernard — Solano
(Caldwell 65), Dyer, Hughes, Viana (Ameobi 84) —
Shearer, Bellamy *Subs not used* Harper, Acuna, LuaLua
Booked Griffin *Sent off* Griffin 63
Scorer **Shearer 39**
Report page 208

Monday April 21
ASTON VILLA (h)
Drew 1-1 HT **1-0** Att **52,015** Position **4th**
Given — Griffin, Woodgate (Bramble 52), O'Brien,
Hughes — Solano, Dyer, Viana, Bernard (LuaLua 73) —
Shearer (Ameobi 74), Bellamy *Subs not used* Harper,
Acuna
Scorer **Solano 37**
Referee **J Winter**

Newcastle end their three-match losing run, but by
dropping two points to Aston Villa — Dublin heading the
equaliser after Solano's expert free kick opener — they
also surrender third place in the Premiership to Chelsea
and now have a real fight on their hands to return to
the Champions League.

Saturday April 26
SUNDERLAND (a)
Won 1-0 HT **1-0** Att **45,067** Position **3rd**
Given — Griffin, O'Brien (Caldwell 19), Woodgate,
Hughes — Solano, Dyer, Jenas, Viana (Bernard 72) —
Shearer (Ameobi 26), Bellamy *Subs not used* Harper,
LuaLua *Booked* Dyer, Viana, Griffin, Caldwell
Scorer **Solano 43 (pen)**
Report page 280

Saturday May 3
BIRMINGHAM CITY (h)
Won 1-0 HT **1-0** Att **52,146** Position **3rd**
Given — Hughes, Woodgate, Caldwell, Bernard —
Solano (Kerr 79), Dyer, Jenas, Viana (Robert 84) —
Bellamy, Ameobi *Subs not used* Harper, Bramble,
LuaLua
Scorer **Viana 42**
Referee **D Elleray**

David Elleray plays a final card trick in his last
appearance before retirement as England's most
famous referee sends off Upson, the Birmingham
defender, for a professional foul on Bellamy. Viana
scores the only goal from the resulting free kick and
with Chelsea and Liverpool losing, that is enough to
guarantee third place.

Sunday May 11
WEST BROMWICH ALBION (a)
Drew 2-2 HT **1-0** Att **27,036** Position **3rd**
Given — Griffin, O'Brien, Caldwell, Hughes — Solano
(Ambrose 76), Dyer (Kerr 90), Jenas, Viana — Ameobi,
LuaLua (Chopra 83) *Subs not used* Harper, Bramble
Scorers **Jenas 44, Viana 80**
Report page 268

LOMANA LUALUA
Forward
Born December 28, 1980,
Kinshasa, Zaire
Ht 5ft 8in **Wt** 12st 2lb
Signed from Colchester United,
September 2000, £2.25m

JAMIE McCLEN
Midfield
Born May 13, 1979, Newcastle
Ht 5ft 8in **Wt** 10st 7lb
Signed from trainee, August 1997

ANDY O'BRIEN
Defender
Born June 29, 1979, Harrogate
Ht 6ft 2in **Wt** 12st 4lb
Signed from Bradford City, March
2001, £2m

WAYNE QUINN
Defender
Born November 19, 1976, Truro
Ht 5ft 10in **Wt** 11st 12lb
Signed from Sheffield United,
January 2001, £750,000

LAURENT ROBERT
Midfield
Born May 21, 1975, Saint-Benoit,
France
Ht 5ft 8in **Wt** 11st 2lb
Signed from Paris Saint-Germain,
August 2001, £10.5m

ALAN SHEARER
Forward
Born August 13, 1970, Newcastle
Ht 5ft 11in **Wt** 12st 6lb
Signed from Blackburn Rovers,
July 1996, £15m

NOLBERTO SOLANO
Midfield
Born December 12, 1974,
Callao, Peru
Ht 5ft 8in **Wt** 10st 8lb
Signed from Boca Juniors, August
1998, £2.76m

GARY SPEED
Midfield
Born September 8, 1969, Deeside
Ht 5ft 10in **Wt** 12st 10lb
Signed from Everton, February
1998, £5.5m

HUGO VIANA
Midfield
Born January 15, 1983, Barcelos,
Portugal
Ht 5ft 9in **Wt** 11st 6lb
Signed from Sporting Lisbon, June
2002, £850,000

JONATHAN WOODGATE
Defender
Born January 22, 1980,
Middlesbrough
Ht 6ft 2in **Wt** 11st 2lb
Signed from Leeds United,
January 2003, £9m

Gary Speed

CHELSEA

PREMIERSHIP

	P	W	D	L	F	A	Pts
Man Utd	38	25	8	5	74	34	83
Arsenal	38	23	9	6	85	42	78
Newcastle	38	21	6	11	63	48	69
Chelsea	**38**	**19**	**10**	**9**	**68**	**38**	**67**
Liverpool	38	18	10	10	61	41	64
Blackburn	38	16	12	10	52	43	60
Everton	38	17	8	13	48	49	59
Southampton	38	13	13	12	43	46	52
Man City	38	15	6	17	47	54	51
Tottenham	38	14	8	16	51	62	50
Middlesbro	38	13	10	15	48	44	49
Charlton	38	14	7	17	45	56	49
Birmingham	38	13	9	16	41	49	48
Fulham	38	13	9	16	41	50	48
Leeds	38	14	5	19	58	57	47
Aston Villa	38	12	9	17	42	47	45
Bolton	38	10	14	14	41	51	44
West Ham	38	10	12	16	42	59	42
West Brom	38	6	8	24	29	65	26
Sunderland	38	4	7	27	21	65	19

FA CUP
Sixth round

WORTHINGTON CUP
Quarter-finals

UEFA CUP
First round

**Zola and Gudjohnsen celebrate
Champions League qualification**

THE GAMES

Saturday August 17
CHARLTON ATHLETIC (a)
Won 3-2 HT 1-2 Att 25,640 Position 3rd
Cudicini — Ferrer, Gallas, Desailly, Babayaro —
De Lucas, Lampard, Petit (Gudjohnsen 60), Zenden —
Hasselbaink (Gronkjaer 74), Zola (Cole 74) *Subs not
used* De Goey, Melchiot *Booked* Desailly, Babayaro,
Zenden
Scorers **Zola 43, Cole 74, Lampard 89**
Report page 174

Friday August 23
MANCHESTER UNITED (h)
Drew 2-2 HT 2-1 Att 41,541 Position 1st
Cudicini — Ferrer, Gallas, Desailly, Babayaro —
De Lucas, Lampard, Petit (Gronkjaer 73), Zenden —
Hasselbaink (Cole 80), Zola (Gudjohnsen 80) *Subs not
used* De Goey, Ferrer *Booked* Desailly, De Lucas,
Hasselbaink
Scorers **Gallas 3, Zenden 45**
Referee **G Poll**

Friday night football comes to the capital and two of
the title favourites serve up a tasty *hors-d'oeuvre* for
the weekend, with Chelsea twice taking the lead only
for United to show their fighting qualities through
Beckham and — with his hundredth goal for the
club — Giggs.

Wednesday August 28
SOUTHAMPTON (a)
Drew 1-1 HT 0-0 Att 31,208 Position 5th
Cudicini — Melchiot, Gallas, Desailly, Babayaro —
Gronkjaer, Lampard, De Lucas, Zenden (Stanic 85) —
Hasselbaink (Gudjohnsen ht), Zola *Subs not used*
De Goey, Ferrer, Keenan *Booked* Babayaro,
Gronkjaer
Scorer **Lampard 80**
Report page 126

Sunday September 1
ARSENAL (h)
Drew 1-1 HT 1-0 Att 40,037 Position 5th
Cudicini — Ferrer, Gallas, Desailly, Le Saux (Melchiot 65)
— Gronkjaer, Lampard, De Lucas, Zenden (Stanic 7) —
Gudjohnsen, Zola (Hasselbaink 67) *Subs not used*
De Goey, Morris *Booked* De Lucas, Lampard, Gronkjaer,
Melchiot, Le Saux
Scorer **Zola 34**
Referee **A D'Urso**

A typically feisty derby of eight yellow cards, including
two for Vieira, who sees red in Arsenal's colours for
the eighth time. The ten men hit back well, however,
Toure pouncing on the hour to cancel out the lead
given to Chelsea when Zola's long-range free kick
deceives Seaman.

Wednesday September 11
BLACKBURN ROVERS (a)
Won 3-2 HT 1-2 Att 22,999 Position 5th
Cudicini — Melchiot, Gallas, Desailly, Babayaro —
Gronkjaer (Gudjohnsen 77), Lampard, Morris
(De Lucas 87), Stanic (Zenden 72) — Hasselbaink, Zola
Subs not used Huth, De Goey *Booked* Babayaro,
Stanic, Morris
Scorers **Gronkjaer 38, Zola 52, 80**
Report page 102

WITH POUND SIGNS LIGHTING up the eyes of the club accountants and the players celebrating as if they had won the European Cup already, a sense of wellbeing settled on new Chelsea as they realised that they were back where they feel they belong ... rubbing shoulders with Europe's elite.

Yet when the Premiership fixture list spewed from the computer at Soho Square last summer and sent Liverpool to Stamford Bridge on the last day, somehow true Blues knew they would suffer to the final whistle if they were to secure the most precious prize of all, a money-spinning passport to the Champions League.

Chelsea being Chelsea, it was inevitable they would do it the hard way.

Sitting proudly in second place at the turn of the year, with talk of an improbable title challenge from a club straining under debts of more than £90 million, a finish in the top four appeared easy meat for a collection of players who have dined at football's top table. When it came down to it, though, they skidded and slid towards the finish line before finally raising their arms in exhausted triumph at Stamford Bridge in the match they called the "£15 million play-off".

It had all seemed so far off to forlorn supporters when Chelsea set out on a new campaign without two beans to rub together or a new signing worth the name, but the opening two fixtures set the pattern for a season in which recent form was to be turned on its head. The traditional banana skin that is Charlton Athletic was skipped over in a harum-scarum victory at The Valley, the ageless Gianfranco Zola's extra hours in the gym reaping dividends as the heavy goalscoring burden that was to be his all season descended on his slight shoulders.

Six days later, with the deity of television decreeing the opening home fixture should be on a Friday night, of all times, Manchester United swaggered into town for a 2-2 draw to begin a sequence that left Chelsea — previously so assured on the big occasion — with a mere five points from 18 against the three sides to finish above them.

If the newfound steel against the Premiership's whipping boys had reversed a trend, one thing was guaranteed — a humiliating exit from the Uefa Cup. It was Viking FK who inevitably did the raping and pillaging in the clubs' first-round tie, but Marcel Desailly's warriors proved they were made of sterner stuff than many of their predecessors with a rousing riposte. Losing only to a last-minute goal away to Liverpool, they embarked on a run of 11 unbeaten matches in the Premiership that left them breathing down the necks of Arsenal, the leaders, by Boxing Day.

As always with Chelsea, the words "all going" and "pear-shaped"

Chelsea's Friday night match against United was a cracker

are never far away and the loss of two points in a sterile home draw with Southampton prevented them from going top, before successive defeats by Leeds United and Arsenal brought them crashing back to earth. With Jimmy Floyd Hasselbaink a shadow of his former self after a serious leg injury and Eidur Gudjohnsen out of touch all season, it was Zola's renaissance in front of goal that kept the team from stumbling irretrievably.

Form dipped and peaked as only Chelsea's can and what should have been a foregone conclusion became a nervous struggle to keep afloat in a morass of wasted points — especially at home — as first Everton then Newcastle United and Liverpool clawed their way back into contention for a share of the Champions League gold.

West Ham United took six points off Chelsea in their relegation season and Blackburn Rovers tightened their Premiership hold over Stamford Bridge, indicating that the old chestnut of fragility was still to be totally cracked, but when they needed to be, Claudio Ranieri's men were strong.

The arrival of Carlton Cole, the head coach's young lion, with some exquisite goals and respectable showings in the FA and Worthington Cups — ended, respectively, by Arsenal, in a quarter-final replay, and Manchester United — promised much, but one thing mattered above all else to a club fighting for its very survival.

Cometh the hour, cometh the man and an unlikely hero emerged. Step forward Jesper Gronkjaer into Chelsea folklore. Hailed as a potential world-beater if only he could cross, pass or shoot, the lightning-quick winger confounded his critics by gliding into the penalty area to fire the goal that finally cut Liverpool adrift.

Of course, the Champions League qualifiers held the potential for further embarrassment to a team so capable of shooting itself in the foot but when it came to it on that all-or-nothing May afternoon, Chelsea had a Dane who could bring home the bacon.

Saturday September 14
NEWCASTLE UNITED (h)
Won 3-0 HT **2-0** Att **39,746** Position **3rd**
Cudicini — Melchiot, Gallas, Desailly, Stanic — De Lucas, Lampard, Morris, Zenden (Keenan 89) — Gudjohnsen (Hasselbaink 81), Zola (Gronkjaer 81) *Subs not used* De Goey, Huth *Booked* Gallas
Scorers **Gudjohnsen 14, 58, Zola 26**
Referee **B Knight**

Sir Bobby Robson is left to despair over the poverty of Newcastle's performance as they slip to their third defeat in four matches, leaving only West Ham below them in the table. Gudjohnsen's header sparks Chelsea's routine win, the suddenly prolific Zola adding a deflected free kick.

Thursday September 19
VIKING FK (h)
Uefa Cup, 1st rnd, 1st leg
Won 2-1 HT **1-0** Att **15,772**
Cudicini — Gallas, Huth, Desailly, Stanic — Gronkjaer, Morris, De Lucas, Zola (Oliveira 86) — Hasselbaink, Gudjohnsen (Lampard ht) *Subs not used* De Goey, Zenden, Ambrosetti, Kitamirike, Keenan *Booked* Huth
Scorers **Hasselbaink 43, De Lucas 69**
Referee **M Tokat (Turkey)**

Another European embarrassment looms for Chelsea after Ben Wright, a striker who has plied his trade with the likes of Kettering Town, Woking and Bristol City, heads a last-minute goal for the Norwegians after Hasselbaink's first of the season and De Lucas's first for the club.

Monday September 23
FULHAM (a)
Drew 0-0 HT **0-0** Att **16,503** Position **3rd**
Cudicini — Melchiot, Gallas, Huth, Stanic — De Lucas, Lampard, Morris, Zenden (Gronkjaer 66) — Hasselbaink, Zola (Gudjohnsen 74) *Subs not used* De Goey, Bogarde, Keenan
Report page 200

Saturday September 28
WEST HAM UNITED (h)
Lost 2-3 HT **1-1** Att **38,929** Position **5th**
Cudicini — Melchiot, Gallas, Huth, Stanic — Gronkjaer, Lampard, Morris, Zenden (Zola 63) — Hasselbaink, Gudjohnsen *Subs not used* De Goey, De Lucas, Terry, Nicolas *Booked* Huth
Scorers **Hasselbaink 21 (pen), Zola 74**
Referee **M Dean**

One of the games of the season features one of the goals of the season, Di Canio teeing up and dispatching a sensational volley to put West Ham 2-1 ahead, then punishing hesitancy in the Chelsea defence six minutes from time to secure a first win of the season for Glenn Roeder's side.

Thursday October 3
VIKING FK (a)
Uefa Cup, 1st rnd, 2nd leg
Lost 2-4 (lose 4-5 on agg) HT 1-2 Att 5,500
Cudicini — Gallas, Terry, Huth, Le Saux — Gronkjaer, Lampard, Petit (Morris 62), Stanic (Zenden 89) — Hasselbaink (Gudjohnsen 80), Zola *Subs not used* De Goey, Bogarde, Ambrosetti, Kitamirike
Scorers **Lampard 45, Terry 62**
Referee **J van Hulten (the Netherlands)**

To the list of minnows including St Gallen and Hapoel Tel-Aviv can now be added the name of Viking FK after the part-timers from the Norwegian port of Stavanger embarrass Chelsea in the Uefa Cup, Erik Nevland, once of Manchester United, clinching a famous victory in the 87th minute.

Sunday October 6
LIVERPOOL (a)
Lost 0-1 HT 0-0 Att 43,856 Position 7th
Cudicini — Melchiot, Gallas, Desailly, Le Saux — Gronkjaer, Lampard, Petit, Stanic (Morris ht) — Hasselbaink (Gudjohnsen ht), Zola *Subs not used* De Goey, Zenden, Terry *Booked* Gronkjaer, Stanic
Report page 92

Saturday October 19
MANCHESTER CITY (a)
Won 3-0 HT 0-0 Att 34,953 Position 5th
Cudicini — Melchiot, Gallas, Desailly, Le Saux — De Lucas, Lampard, Petit, Morris — Hasselbaink, Zola (Oliveira 88) *Subs not used* Pidgeley, Ferrer, Terry, Gudjohnsen *Booked* De Lucas, Lampard
Scorers **Zola 69, 84, Hasselbaink 85**
Report page 140

Saturday October 26
WEST BROMWICH ALBION (h)
Won 2-0 HT 1-0 Att 40,893 Position 3rd
Cudicini — Melchiot, Gallas, Desailly, Le Saux — Gronkjaer (Terry 80), Lampard, Petit (Morris 73), De Lucas — Hasselbaink, Zola *Subs not used* Pidgeley, Gudjohnsen, Oliveira
Scorers **Hasselbaink 30, Le Saux 55**
Referee **S Dunn**

Chelsea are in control from the moment Hasselbaink profits from Petit's pass. Le Saux pops up for the second, but Albion refuse to go quietly and both Johnson and Clement, the former Chelsea defender, hit the woodwork before defeat pushes Gary Megson's side back into the bottom three.

Sunday November 3
TOTTENHAM HOTSPUR (a)
Drew 0-0 HT 0-0 Att 36,049 Position 4th
Cudicini — Melchiot, Gallas, Desailly, Babayaro — Morris, Lampard, Petit, De Lucas (Oliveira 82) — Hasselbaink (Gudjohnsen 43), Zola *Subs not used* Pidgeley, Ferrer, Terry *Booked* De Lucas, Morris
Report page 153

Chelsea 2   Liverpool 1
Stamford Bridge, Sunday May 11 2003
Owen Slot

PARTY TIME AT STAMFORD BRIDGE, A £20 million party, you may have heard. The gateway to the Champions League. The most valuable victory in the history of the Premiership. Or ever, depending on which hyperbole you prefer. The view of Ken Bates, the Chelsea chairman, was that this was "the real Cup Final, not next week at the Millennium Stadium".

In which case, you wonder if someone forgot to tell Liverpool. Granted the opportunity of pulling off a rescue mission on a season of woe, they have now contrived to lose their last two games, dying out quietly, barely raising their voices, never raging like giants.

The impression in the build-up to this fixture was that it was less a football match and more an extended financial transaction. But put the cash on the table and dangle a ticket to Europe's high table, and still you don't seem to inspire Liverpool.

The best man in a Liverpool shirt was the man who got sent off. Steven Gerrard played with a determination that matched the occasion, passion and urgency to the fore, but his frustration was reflected in the increasing aggression in his challenges and two yellow cards in the last ten minutes were his undoing. After the second, a high foot left trailing into a late tackle on Graeme Le Saux, he didn't even bother to turn to see the colour of the referee's card.

And he didn't receive a word of criticism from Gerard Houllier. Quite the opposite. In reference to the attitude with which he plays the game, Houllier said: "I sometimes wish I had a couple more like that."

A couple more would maybe have brought Liverpool close. As it was, they didn't even get there. A draw would have taken the rewards to Chelsea, so you might have expected to see Liverpool hammering away at the opposition goal, but Michael Owen was silenced effectively by Marcel Desailly. He produced just one save from Carlo Cudicini in the first minute and thereafter the Chelsea goalkeeper was only required once again and that was from a 30-yard shot from Gerrard.

When it was done, Owen made straight for the tunnel but was pushed back on to the field by Phil Thompson. The travelling fans have been given little else this season, so a vote of thanks was the least they deserved.

Then the stage was left for Chelsea to do their own cup final day cameo. A lap of honour was applauded by an almost-full stadium, the camera lingering repeatedly on their foreign favourite, Gianfranco Zola, a reference perhaps to Bates's programme declaration that "today is tinged with sadness" because "we have seen some familiar faces for the last time".

His objective achieved, Ranieri takes the plaudits from the fans

The brilliant Italian has featured regularly and highly in the line-up for Chelsea's supposed great summer sale, but now that their bank accounts look suddenly so considerably less red, gleeful shoppers may instead be disappointed.

After weathering a difficult first quarter of an hour, Chelsea maintained control for the majority of the game. The opening was certainly frantic. Liverpool went ahead from a curling free kick from Danny Murphy that Sami Hyypia nodded in at the far post but, two minutes later, Chelsea emptied any reserves of confidence that the visiting team may have been building by scoring a copycat goal, Desailly heading in a curling cross from Jesper Gronkjaer.

The winner, a splendid individual effort from Gronkjaer, came soon after. The Dane received a pass from Mario Melchiot and drove forward to the edge of the penalty box, brushing off a challenge from John Arne Riise and striking his shot before Djimi Traore could mount a second challenge. The strike was left-footed, low and curling fast round a melee in the box so that Jerzy Dudek

Wednesday November 6
GILLINGHAM (h)
Worthington Cup, 3rd rnd
Won 2-1   HT 1-0   Att 28,033
Cudicini — Ferrer, Gallas, Terry, Babayaro — De Lucas (Bogarde 69), Lampard, Morris, Le Saux (Oliveira 61) — Cole (Gronkjaer 64), Zola *Subs not used* Pidgeley, Petit
Scorer **Cole 20, 52**
Referee **A D'Urso**

Cole, a scorer on the opening day of the season but forced to put his injured feet up since then, returns with two goals to put paid to Gillingham's Worthington Cup hopes. Cole finishes from Gallas's pass and then heads in Morris's cross before King's late consolation effort.

Saturday November 9
BIRMINGHAM CITY (h)
Won 3-0   HT 3-0   Att 35,237   Position 3rd
Cudicini — Melchiot, Gallas, Desailly (Terry 77), Babayaro — Morris, Lampard, Petit, Le Saux (Gronkjaer 74) — Gudjohnsen (Cole 71), Zola *Subs not used* Pidgeley, De Lucas *Booked* Desailly
Scorers **Gudjohnsen 3, 31, Zola 42**
Referee **D Pugh**

The irrepressible Zola is now the Premiership's leading scorer. Not content with setting up both of Gudjohnsen's goals, the Italian adds a beautiful third as Birmingham are crushed. But the headlines the next day are taken by Mark Bosnich and stories of a failed drugs test.

Saturday November 16
MIDDLESBROUGH (h)
Won 1-0   HT 0-0   Att 39,064   Position 3rd
Cudicini — Melchiot, Gallas, Desailly, Babayaro — Le Saux (Terry 85), Lampard, Petit, Morris (Gronkjaer ht) — Gudjohnsen (Hasselbaink 76), Zola *Subs not used* Pidgeley, De Lucas *Booked* Petit, Melchiot
Scorer **Babayaro 47**
Referee **P Dowd**

Babayaro's first Premiership goal for more than three years and another resolute display by the Chelsea defence — they have now kept five successive clean sheets in the league for the first time since 1911 — see off Middlesbrough, for whom Boateng is criticised, though unpunished, for a robust challenge on Zola.

Saturday November 23
BOLTON WANDERERS (a)
Drew 1-1   HT 0-0   Att 25,476   Position 4th
Cudicini — Melchiot, Gallas, Desailly, Babayaro — Gronkjaer (Hasselbaink ht), Lampard, Petit, Le Saux (Morris 72) — Gudjohnsen, Zola *Subs not used* De Goey, Terry, Stanic *Booked* Gallas, Desailly, Hasselbaink, Melchiot *Sent off* Babayaro 77
Scorer **Hasselbaink 90**
Report page 237

Saturday November 30
SUNDERLAND (h)
Won 3-0 HT 0-0   Att **38,946**   Position **3rd**
Cudicini — Melchiot, Gallas, Desailly, Le Saux —
De Lucas (Gudjohnsen ht), Lampard, Morris (Petit ht),
Gronkjaer (Stanic 81) — Hasselbaink, Zola *Subs not
used* De Goey, Terry
Scorers **Gallas 58, Desailly 84, Hasselbaink 89**
Referee **S Bennett**

Sunderland's desperate resistance is finally broken by
Chelsea's centre halves, Gallas and Desailly — "my
extra-terrestrials", Claudio Ranieri calls them — before
Hasselbaink gives the scoreline a more realistic look.
But for Macho's athleticism, Sunderland would have
suffered far heavier punishment.

Wednesday December 4
EVERTON (h)
Worthington Cup, 4th rnd
Won 4-1 HT 2-0   Att **32,322**
Cudicini — Melchiot, Gallas, Terry, Babayaro — Gronkjaer
(De Lucas 64), Lampard, Petit, Stanic (Morris 71) —
Hasselbaink, Zola (Gudjohnsen 58) *Subs not used* De
Goey, Desailly
Scorers **Hasselbaink 26, 71, Petit 44, Stanic 69**
Referee **P Durkin**

The tie of the round goes emphatically Chelsea's way,
with Zola's brilliant passes setting up the first two
goals as Everton are nearly swamped. Hasselbaink
has already scored his second — Chelsea's fourth —
before Rooney has a horribly weak penalty saved by
Cudicini.

Saturday December 7
EVERTON (a)
Won 3-1 HT 2-1   Att **39,396**   Position **2nd**
Cudicini — Melchiot, Gallas, Desailly, Le Saux — De
Lucas (Terry 76), Lampard, Petit, Stanic (Gronkjaer 60)
— Hasselbaink (Gudjohnsen 89), Zola *Subs not used*
De Goey, Morris *Booked* Gallas, De Lucas, Lampard,
Hasselbaink, Gronkjaer, Stanic
Scorers **Stanic 5, Hasselbaink 28, Gronkjaer 90**
Report page 118

Saturday December 14
MIDDLESBROUGH (a)
Drew 1-1 HT 1-1   Att **29,160**   Position **3rd**
Cudicini — Melchiot, Gallas, Terry, Le Saux — Gronkjaer
(De Lucas 73), Lampard, Petit, Stanic (Zenden 68) —
Hasselbaink (Gudjohnsen 89), Zola *Subs not used*
De Goey, Morris *Booked* Petit
Scorer **Terry 42**
Report page 167

Tuesday December 17
MANCHESTER UNITED (a)
Worthington Cup, 5th rnd
Lost 0-1 HT 0-0   Att **57,985**
Cudicini — Melchiot, Gallas, Terry, Le Saux — De
Lucas (Zenden 66), Lampard, Morris, Stanic —
Hasselbaink (Gudjohnsen 78), Zola *Subs not used*
Ferrer, Desailly, De Goey *Booked* Stanic, Terry
Report page 47

Gronkjaer celebrates the most valuable goal of the season

was barely sighted until the ball was inside the right side-netting of
his goal.

The chances thereafter fell more to Chelsea. Liverpool will not
enjoy recalling Owen's miss from eight yards or the time that they
did succeed in bundling the ball into the net, but only with the
assistance of Milan Baros's right hand. Chelsea, for whom Melchiot
hit the post, were more deserving of the huge rewards on offer.

"I wouldn't say it's a disappointing season," Houllier said. The
fans would disagree. Houllier cited the Worthington Cup victory as
evidence — which is scraping the barrel. He also said that refereeing
decisions had let down their campaign — which left the barrel
completely dry.

CHELSEA (4-4-2): C Cudicini — M Melchiot, W Gallas, M Desailly, C Babayaro J Gronkjaer (sub: M Stanic, 68min), E Petit, F Lampard, G Le Saux, E Gudjohnsen (sub: G Zola, 73), J F Hasselbaink (sub: C Cole, 80). **Substitutes not used:** E De Goey, J Morris. **Booked:** Gallas, Le Saux, Hasselbaink.
LIVERPOOL (4-4-2): J Dudek — J Carragher, S Hyypia, D Traore, J A Riise (sub: B Cheyrou, 75) — E-H Diouf (sub: P Berger, 63), S Diao (sub: E Heskey, 46), S Gerrard, D Murphy — M Baros, M Owen. **Substitutes not used:** P Arphexad, I Biscan. **Booked:** Gerrard. **Sent off:** Gerrard.
Referee: A Wiley.

THE MANAGER

Claudio Ranieri

"Everybody know the club needa little money," Claudio Ranieri said in his charmingly eccentric English from behind a grin as wide as Stamford Bridge. While the defeat of Liverpool had turned a fast buck for Chelsea, the jury remains out. For all that the Italian has transformed a group of talented individuals into a tight unit, his tactical decisions still have supporters scratching their heads and he has no silverware to show for nigh on three years at the club. "The money is very [turns to interpreter] . . . welcome," the head coach added. Even Ken Bates, a hard-nosed chairman, cannot disagree with that.

Geoff Harwood

APPEARANCES

	Prem	FAC	WC	Euro	Total
C Babayaro	16 (3)	3	2	-	21 (3)
W Bogarde	-	-	0 (1)	-	0 (1)
C Cole	2 (11)	0 (2)	1	-	3 (13)
C Cudicini	36	5	3	2	46
E De Goey	2	0 (1)	-	-	2 (1)
E De Lucas	17 (8)	1 (1)	2 (1)	1	21 (10)
M Desailly	30 (1)	1	-	1	32 (1)
A Ferrer	3	-	1	-	4
W Gallas	36 (2)	5	3	2	46 (2)
J Gronkjaer	20 (10)	2 (3)	1 (1)	2	25 (14)
E Gudjohnsen	20 (15)	3 (2)	0 (2)	1 (1)	24 (20)
J F Hasselbaink	27 (9)	4	2	2	35 (9)
R Huth	2	0 (1)	-	2	4 (1)
J Keenan	0 (1)	-	-	-	0 (1)
F Lampard	37 (1)	5	3	1 (1)	46 (2)
G Le Saux	27 (1)	3	2	1	33 (1)
M Melchiot	31 (3)	4 (1)	2	-	37 (4)
J Morris	19 (6)	2 (1)	2 (1)	1 (1)	24 (9)
F Oliveira	0 (3)	-	0 (1)	0 (1)	0 (5)
E Petit	23 (1)	5	1	1	30 (1)
M Stanic	13 (5)	3	2	2	20 (5)
J Terry	16 (4)	5	3	1	25 (4)
B Zenden	11 (10)	1 (3)	0 (1)	0 (1)	12 (15)
G Zola	30 (8)	3	3	2	38 (8)

Saturday December 21
ASTON VILLA (h)
Won 2-0 HT 1-0 Att **38,284** Position **2nd**
Cudicini — Melchiot, Gallas, Terry, Le Saux — Stanic (Gronkjaer 55), Lampard, Morris, Zenden (Babayaro 67) — Hasselbaink (Zola 77), Gudjohnsen *Subs not used* De Goey, Ferrer
Scorers **Gudjohnsen 42, Lampard 57**
Referee **M Riley**

Hendrie and Mellberg go close for Aston Villa early on, the latter hitting the bar, and Cudicini makes two fine late saves, but in between Chelsea deservedly win the game through Gudjohnsen and Lampard, who scores a freak second when his intended cross sails over Enckelman.

Thursday December 26
SOUTHAMPTON (h)
Drew 0-0 HT 0-0 Att **39,428** Position **2nd**
De Goey — Melchiot (Gallas 86), Desailly, Terry, Babayaro — De Lucas (Gudjohnsen 81), Morris, Petit, Zenden (Lampard 85) — Hasselbaink, Zola *Subs not used* Pidgeley, Gronkjaer *Booked* Melchiot
Referee **P Durkin**

Chelsea are the latest side to discover that Southampton, for whom Bridge, their England defender, breaks Shearer's Premiership record by making his 109th successive appearance, are not to be easily beaten, although Zola does put an early sitter against the post and Niemi is forced to make a brilliant late save from Gallas.

Saturday December 28
LEEDS UNITED (a)
Lost 0-2 HT 0-2 Att **40,122** Position **2nd**
De Goey — Ferrer (Hasselbaink ht), Gallas, Desailly, Le Saux — Gronkjaer (De Lucas ht), Lampard, Morris, Stanic — Gudjohnsen, Zola *Subs not used* Pidgeley, Babayaro, Terry
Report page 216

Wednesday January 1
ARSENAL (a)
Lost 2-3 HT 0-1 Att **38,096** Position **3rd**
Cudicini — Melchiot, Gallas, Desailly, Babayaro — De Lucas (Gronkjaer 57), Lampard, Petit, Le Saux (Gudjohnsen 71) — Hasselbaink, Zola (Stanic 80) *Subs not used* De Goey, Terry
Scorers **Stanic 85, Petit 86**
Report page 60

Saturday January 4
MIDDLESBROUGH (h)
FA Cup, 3rd rnd
Won 1-0 HT 1-0 Att 29,796
Cudicini — Gallas, Terry, Desailly, Babayaro — Gronkjaer (Melchiot 90), Lampard, Petit, Stanic (Zenden 60) — Hasselbaink, Gudjohnsen (De Goey 64) *Subs not used* Morris, Zola *Booked* Gudjohnsen, Terry *Sent off* Cudicini 64
Scorer **Stanic 39**
Referee **M Halsey**

A poor tie on another poor pitch ignites when Cudicini is caught by a late challenge from Windass and a melee ensues after which the Chelsea goalkeeper is sent off for allegedly putting his knee into the Middlesbrough forward's face by way of retaliation. Stanic deservedly wins the tie for Chelsea nonetheless in the first half.

Saturday January 11
CHARLTON ATHLETIC (h)
Won 4-1 HT 3-1 Att 37,284 Position 3rd
Cudicini — Gallas, Desailly, Terry (Morris 23), Babayaro — Gronkjaer (Zenden 81), Lampard, Petit, Le Saux (Zola 79) — Hasselbaink, Gudjohnsen *Subs not used* De Goey, Cole *Booked* Desailly, Petit, Gudjohnsen, Le Saux
Scorers **Hasselbaink 3 (pen), Gallas 11, Gudjohnsen 34, Le Saux 54**
Referee **M Dean**

On the weekend that he reveals that he has lost £400,000 in five months at a casino, it is a fair bet that Gudjohnsen will get on the scoresheet and he duly obliges with the third goal in a comprehensive victory over Charlton, who four days later demand a rematch because the Stamford Bridge pitch resembles a beach.

Saturday January 18
MANCHESTER UNITED (a)
Lost 1-2 HT 1-1 Att 67,606 Position 4th
Cudicini — Melchiot, Gallas, Desailly, Babayaro — Gronkjaer (De Lucas 56), Lampard, Petit, Le Saux — Hasselbaink (Zola 16), Gudjohnsen (Zenden 84) *Subs not used* Morris, De Goey
Scorer **Gudjohnsen 30**
Report page 48

Sunday January 26
SHREWSBURY TOWN (a)
FA Cup, 4th rnd
Won 4-0 HT 1-0 Att 7,950
Cudicini — Melchiot, Gallas, Terry, Babayaro (Cole ht) — Zenden, Lampard (Morris 56), Petit, Le Saux — Gudjohnsen (Gronkjaer 63), Zola *Subs not used* De Goey, Huth
Scorers **Zola 40, 73, Cole 53, Morris 80**
Referee **M Riley**

Gay Meadow may have been Everton's Cup graveyard, but Chelsea are alive and kicking thanks to Zola, who returns to his early-season goalscoring form with a double, the second a beautifully judged chip, and crosses for Cole's header. Morris weighs in with a fine curling effort.

PLAYER OF THE SEASON Gianfranco Zola

The Barclaycard Golden Gloves award — the result of a national TV poll — was placed in the safe hands of Carlo Cudicini, but there was no doubt who the fans turned to in their moment of triumph. At 37, Gianfranco Zola had bounced off the bench full of boyish enthusiasm to give a cameo display of keeping the ball as the clock ticked away against Liverpool on the last day of the season. It was his goalscoring contribution, though, that made him the crucial cog in Chelsea's wheel throughout a season when the usual front pair of Hasselbaink and Gudjohnsen misfired.
Geoff Harwood

STATS AND FACTS

- Chelsea's past 11 home matches against Blackburn Rovers have produced either a draw or a one-goal win for Blackburn.

- On November 16, Chelsea kept their fifth successive clean sheet in the league, their first such sequence since 1911.

- In their League Cup semi-final second leg at Stamford Bridge in February 1998, Chelsea took the lead against Arsenal via a Gianfranco Zola free kick in the first half before Patrick Vieira was sent off for a booking in each half. In September 2002, at the same ground, the same happened.

- Chelsea's past nine defeats against Middlesbrough have all come at home.

- When Chelsea met Arsenal in an FA Cup quarter-final it was the second successive season that Highbury had staged an FA Cup tie between the previous year's finalists, Arsenal having beaten Liverpool a year before.

- The only teams to have beaten Chelsea in the FA Cup over the past eight seasons are Manchester United (three times) and Arsenal (three times). Chelsea won in 1997 and 2000.

- Aside from a League Cup match in which their opponents fielded a reserve side, Chelsea have not won in 16 games away to Arsenal.

- Chelsea have not lost any of their past 12 games against Fulham.

- There have been no away wins in the past 24 meetings between Chelsea and Liverpool.

- Chelsea have won their past nine home games against Bolton Wanderers.

Bill Edgar

GOALSCORERS

	Prem	FAC	WC	Euro	Total
C Babayaro	1	-	-	-	1
C Cole	3	1	2	-	6
E De Lucas	-	-	-	1	1
M Desailly	2	-	-	-	2
W Gallas	4	-	-	-	4
J Gronkjaer	4	1	-	-	5
E Gudjohnsen	10	-	-	-	10
J F Hasselbaink	11 (3p)	1	2	1	15 (3p)
F Lampard	6	1	-	1	8
G Le Saux	2	-	-	-	2
J Morris	-	1	-	-	1
E Petit	1	-	1	-	2
M Stanic	4	1	1	-	6
J Terry	3	2	-	1	6
B Zenden	1	-	-	-	1
G Zola	14	2	-	-	16
Own goals	2	-	-	-	2

Tuesday January 28
LEEDS UNITED (h)
Won 3-2 HT 0-1 Att 39,738 Position 4th
Cudicini — Gallas, Desailly, Terry, Babayaro (Cole 36) — Gronkjaer, Lampard, Morris, Le Saux — Gudjohnsen, Zola (Zenden 65) *Subs not used* De Goey, Melchiot, Petit *Booked* Cole, Le Saux
Scorers **Gudjohnsen 57, Lampard 80, Matteo 83 (og)**
Referee **J Winter**

As Fowler resumes transfer negotiations with Manchester City, Leeds are dealt another blow when they twice lead Chelsea only for Lampard — with the cross that invites Gudjohnsen's majestic bicycle kick, a shot deflected off Matteo and finally the effort turned into his own net by the same Leeds defender — to settle the match.

Saturday February 1
TOTTENHAM HOTSPUR (h)
Drew 1-1 HT 1-1 Att 41,384 Position 4th
Cudicini — Gallas, Desailly, Terry, Le Saux (Hasselbaink 72) — Gronkjaer (Cole 87), Lampard, Petit, Zenden (Melchiot ht) — Gudjohnsen, Zola *Subs not used* De Goey, Morris *Booked* Petit
Scorer **Zola 40**
Referee **P Durkin**

Rarely can a match have produced two such contrasting goals, Sheringham poking in Tottenham's opener from inches and Zola replying with a long-range free kick of breathtaking swerve and dip. Spurs may not have ended their depressingly long sequence of league matches without a win against Chelsea, but they deserve this point.

Saturday February 8
BIRMINGHAM CITY (a)
Won 3-1 HT 1-0 Att 29,475 Position 3rd
Cudicini — Melchiot, Desailly, Terry, Gallas — Gronkjaer (De Lucas 74), Lampard (Morris 62), Petit, Le Saux — Gudjohnsen, Zola (Hasselbaink ht) *Subs not used* De Goey, Cole *Booked* Desailly, De Lucas, Petit, Terry
Scorers **Zola 44, Gudjohnsen 49, Hasselbaink 69 (pen)**
Report page 193

Sunday February 16
STOKE CITY (a)
FA Cup, 5th rnd
Won 2-0 HT 0-0 Att 26,615
Cudicini — Melchiot, Gallas, Terry, Le Saux — De Lucas (Gronkjaer 61), Lampard, Petit (Huth 81), Stanic (Cole 87) — Hasselbaink, Gudjohnsen *Subs not used* Evans, Zenden
Scorers **Hasselbaink 52, Gronkjaer 76**
Referee **R Styles**

Without Zola, Chelsea still have too much guile and gumption for hard-working, relegation-threatened first-division opponents. Hasselbaink and Gronkjaer, the latter after a determined run at the Stoke defence, put them through to the last eight.

Saturday February 22
BLACKBURN ROVERS (h)
Lost 1-2 HT 0-0 Att 40,850 Position 4th
Cudicini — Melchiot, Gallas, Terry, Le Saux (Babayaro 18) — Gronkjaer (Zola ht), Lampard, Morris, Stanic (Zenden 65) — Hasselbaink, Gudjohnsen *Subs not used* Evans, De Lucas *Booked* Gallas, Stanic
Scorer **Hasselbaink 90**
Referee **G Poll**

What Claudio Ranieri calls Chelsea's worst display of the season still looks likely to earn a point until Yorke, with a header, and Dunn — recalled by Graeme Souness after having his attitude questioned by the Blackburn manager — score in the last four minutes. Hasselbaink replies with a free kick as Zola marks his 300th Chelsea appearance with a defeat.

Saturday March 1
NEWCASTLE UNITED (a)
Lost 1-2 HT 1-1 Att 52,157 Position 5th
Cudicini — Melchiot, Gallas, Terry, Babayaro (Cole 77) — Gronkjaer (Zola 67), Morris, Lampard, Stanic (Zenden 67) — Hasselbaink, Gudjohnsen *Subs not used* Evans, Huth *Booked* Cole
Scorer **Lampard 37**
Report page 74

Saturday March 8
ARSENAL (a)
FA Cup, 6th rnd
Drew 2-2 HT 1-2 Att 38,104
Cudicini — Melchiot, Gallas, Terry, Babayaro — Gronkjaer (Gudjohnsen 72), Lampard, Petit (De Lucas 72), Morris — Hasselbaink, Zola (Zenden ht) *Subs not used* Huth, Evans *Booked* Cudicini, Morris
Scorers **Terry 3, Lampard 84**
Report page 62

Sunday March 16
WEST BROMWICH ALBION (a)
Won 2-0 HT 1-0 Att 27,024 Position 4th
Cudicini — Melchiot, Terry, Gallas — Stanic (De Lucas 73), Morris, Lampard, Le Saux (Desailly 82) — Zola — Hasselbaink, Gudjohnsen (Gronkjaer 55) *Subs not used* De Goey, Cole
Scorers **Stanic 38, Zola 56**
Report page 266

Saturday March 22
MANCHESTER CITY (h)
Won 5-0 HT 2-0 Att 41,105 Position 4th
Cudicini — Melchiot, Terry, Gallas — Stanic, Lampard, Morris, Le Saux (Zenden 55) — Zola (De Lucas 65) — Hasselbaink (Cole 61), Gudjohnsen *Subs not used* De Goey, Desailly *Booked* Terry
Scorers **Hasselbaink 37, Terry 43, Stanic 58, Lampard 69, Gallas 79**
Referee **P Dowd**

With a goal, an assist and an England call-up to follow the next day, Terry is among the delighted Chelsea corps after their rout of Manchester City, who have Schmeichel to thank for preventing a heavier defeat and Sun sent off for two bookable offences after his arrival as a substitute, all to Kevin Keegan's ill-disguised embarrassment.

THE PLAYERS

CELESTINE BABAYARO
Defender
Born August 29, 1978, Kaduna, Nigeria
Ht 5ft 8in **Wt** 11st 0lb
Signed from Anderlecht, June 1997, £2.25m

WINSTON BOGARDE
Defender
Born October 22, 1970, Rotterdam
Ht 6ft 3in **Wt** 14st 4lb
Signed from Barcelona, August 2000, free

CARLTON COLE
Forward
Born November 12, 1983, Croydon
Ht 6ft 3in **Wt** 13st 4lb
Signed from trainee, October 2000

CARLO CUDICINI
Goalkeeper
Born September 6, 1973, Milan
Ht 6ft 1in **Wt** 12st 3lb
Signed from Castel Di Sangro, Italy, July 1999, £160,000

ED DE GOEY
Goalkeeper
Born December 20, 1966, Gouda, Holland
Ht 6ft 6in **Wt** 15st 0lb
Signed from Feyenoord, July 1997, £2.25m

ENRIQUE DE LUCAS
Midfield
Born August 17, 1978, Llobregat, Spain
Ht 5ft 10in **Wt** 10st 7lb
Signed from Espanyol, July 2002, free

MARCEL DESAILLY
Defender
Born September 7, 1968, Accra, Ghana
Ht 6ft 1in **Wt** 13st 5lb
Signed from AC Milan, July 1998, £4.6m

ALBERT FERRER
Defender
Born June 6, 1970, Barcelona
Ht 5ft 7in **Wt** 10st 6lb
Signed from Barcelona, August 1998, £2.2m

Carlo Cudicini

WILLIAM GALLAS
Defender
Born August 17, 1977, Paris
Ht 6ft 1in **Wt** 12st 7lb
Signed from Marseilles, May
2001, £6.2m

JESPER GRONKJAER
Midfield
Born August 12, 1977,
Nuuk, Denmark
Ht 6ft 1in **Wt** 12st 8lb
Signed from Ajax, December
2000, £7.8m

EIDUR GUDJOHNSEN
Forward
Born September 15, 1978,
Reykjavik
Ht 6ft 1in **Wt** 13st 0lb
Signed from Bolton Wanderers,
June 2000, £4m

JIMMY FLOYD HASSELBAINK
Forward
Born March 27, 1972,
Paramaribo, Surinam
Ht 5ft 10in **Wt** 13st 4lb
Signed from Atletico Madrid, June
2000, £15m

ROBERT HUTH
Defender
Born August 18, 1984, Berlin
Ht 6ft 2in **Wt** 12st 12lb
Signed from trainee, August 2001

JOE KEENAN
Midfield
Born October 14, 1982,
Southampton
Ht 5ft 7in **Wt** 10st 8lb
Signed from trainee, October
1999

FRANK LAMPARD
Midfield
Born June 20, 1978, Romford
Ht 6ft 0in **Wt** 12st 6lb
Signed from West Ham United,
June 2001, £11m

GRAEME LE SAUX
Defender
Born October 17, 1968, Jersey
Ht 5ft 10in **Wt** 12st 2lb
Signed from Blackburn Rovers,
August 1997, £5m

Frank Lampard

Tuesday March 25
ARSENAL (h)
FA Cup, 6th rnd, replay
Lost 1-3 HT 0-2 Att 41,456
Cudicini — Melchiot, Terry, Gallas — Stanic (Gronkjaer
35), Morris, Lampard, Petit (Gudjohnsen 59), Le Saux
— Hasselbaink, Zola *Subs not used* De Goey, Desailly
Booked Stanic
Scorer **Terry 79**
Referee **D Elleray**

Inspired by Vieira, who creates the first two goals — the
first put through his own net by Terry — Arsenal keep
their double Double hopes alive with a masterful
display of the counter-attacking art, their joy tempered
only by the dismissal of Cygan for his second (and
seemingly innocuous) foul on Hasselbaink, plus the cut
head sustained by Henry, who is hit by a missile thrown
from the crowd.

Saturday April 5
SUNDERLAND (a)
Won 2-1 HT 0-1 Att 40,011 Position 4th
Cudicini — Melchiot, Desailly, Terry, Gallas — De Lucas
(Cole ht), Lampard, Morris, Le Saux — Hasselbaink
(Oliveira 90), Zola (Zenden 88) *Subs not used* De Goey,
Huth *Booked* Cole
Scorers **Zola 52, Cole 85**
Report page 279

Saturday April 12
BOLTON WANDERERS (h)
Won 1-0 HT 0-0 Att 39,852 Position 4th
Cudicini — Melchiot, Desailly, Terry, Le Saux — Zenden
(De Lucas 58), Lampard, Petit — Zola (Gudjohnsen 86)
— Hasselbaink, Cole (Gallas 75) *Subs not used* De Goey,
Babayaro *Booked* Zenden
Scorer **Cole 58**
Referee **G Barber**

Both sides are confident after three successive league
wins, but it is Chelsea who keep their run going thanks
to another goal from the rapidly emerging Cole, who
converts Petit's pass to keep them on course for the
Champions League and Bolton firmly in relegation
trouble.

Saturday April 19
ASTON VILLA (a)
Lost 1-2 HT 0-1 Att 39,358 Position 4th
Cudicini — Melchiot (Hasselbaink ht), Desailly, Terry,
Gallas — De Lucas, Lampard, Petit, Le Saux (Babayaro
66) — Cole, Zola (Gudjohnsen 66) *Subs not used*
De Goey, Zenden
Scorer **Terry 89**
Report page 232

Monday April 21
EVERTON (h)
Won 4-1 **HT 1-0** Att **40,875** Position **3rd**
Cudicini — Melchiot, Desailly, Terry, Gallas — De Lucas,
Lampard, Petit, Gronkjaer (Le Saux 87) — Hasselbaink
(Zola 82), Gudjohnsen (Cole 85) *Subs not used* De
Goey, Stanic *Booked* De Lucas
Scorers **Gudjohnsen 25, Hasselbaink 48,
Gronkjaer 62, Zola 90**
Referee **M Riley**

Perhaps a decisive moment in the race for a
Champions League place, with Chelsea overtaking
Newcastle United on the back of a comprehensive win
— Zola steals the show with a marvellous fourth goal,
lobbed over Wright on the run from an angle — and
Everton almost removed from the equation after a
second successive defeat.

Saturday April 26
FULHAM (h)
Drew 1-1 **HT 1-0** Att **40,792** Position **4th**
Cudicini — Gallas (Melchiot 72), Desailly, Terry,
Le Saux — De Lucas (Morris 72), Lampard, Petit,
Gronkjaer (Gudjohnsen 60) — Hasselbaink, Zola
Subs not used De Goey, Cole *Booked* Terry, Petit,
Gronkjaer
Scorer **Goma 39 (og)**
Referee **D Elleray**

They are unable to reach an agreement to share a
ground, but the West London neighbours share the
spoils at Stamford Bridge when Goma's own goal,
forced by Terry, is cancelled out by Boa Morte. Taylor,
in the Fulham goal, is in brilliant form, with one brave,
close-range save from Lampard drawing comparisons
with some of the best ever seen.

Saturday May 3
WEST HAM UNITED (a)
Lost 0-1 **HT 0-0** Att **35,042** Position **4th**
Cudicini — Melchiot, Gallas, Desailly, Babayaro — Morris
(Zenden 77), Lampard, Petit, Le Saux — Gudjohnsen
(Hasselbaink 71), Zola (Cole 71) *Subs not used* De
Goey, Stanic *Booked* Morris
Report page 256

Sunday May 11
LIVERPOOL (h)
Won 2-1 **HT 2-1** Att **41,911** Position **4th**
Cudicini — Melchiot, Gallas, Desailly, Babayaro —
Gronkjaer (Stanic 68), Lampard, Petit, Le Saux —
Hasselbaink (Cole 80), Gudjohnsen (Zola 73) *Subs not
used* De Goey, Morris *Booked* Gallas, Le Saux,
Hasselbaink
Scorers **Desailly 14, Gronkjaer 27**
Referee **A Wiley**

The £20 million match. Liverpool need to win to
deprive Chelsea of the fourth Champions League place
and duly take the lead through Hyypia's header, but
Desailly replies in kind and Gronkjaer leaves the
Merseysiders, who have Gerrard sent off for late fouls
on Zola and Le Saux, out of pocket.

MARIO MELCHIOT
Defender
Born November 4, 1976,
Amsterdam
Ht 6ft 1in **Wt** 11st 8lb
Signed from Ajax, July 1999, free

JODY MORRIS
Midfield
Born December 22, 1978,
Hammersmith
Ht 5ft 5in **Wt** 10st 12lb
Signed from trainee, January
1996

FILIPE OLIVEIRA
Midfield
Born May 27, 1984, Braga,
Portugal
Ht 5ft 10in **Wt** 10st 12lb
Signed from FC Porto, August
2001, £500,000

EMMANUEL PETIT
Midfield
Born September 22, 1970,
Dieppe
Ht 6ft 1in **Wt** 12st 8lb
Signed from Barcelona, July 2001,
£7.5m

MARIO STANIC
Defender
Born April 10, 1972, Sarajevo
Ht 6ft 2in **Wt** 12st 12lb
Signed from Parma, July 2000,
£5.6m

JOHN TERRY
Defender
Born December 7, 1980, Barking
Ht 6ft 0in **Wt** 12st 4lb
Signed from trainee, March
1998

BOUDEWIJN ZENDEN
Midfield
Born August 15, 1976, Maastricht
Ht 5ft 9in **Wt** 11st 5lb
Signed from Barcelona, August
2001, £7.5m

GIANFRANCO ZOLA
Forward
Born July 5, 1966, Oliena, Italy
Ht 5ft 6in **Wt** 10st 10lb
Signed from Parma, November
1996, £4.5m

Boudewijn Zenden

LIVERPOOL

PREMIERSHIP

	P	W	D	L	F	A	Pts
Man Utd	38	25	8	5	74	34	83
Arsenal	38	23	9	6	85	42	78
Newcastle	38	21	6	11	63	48	69
Chelsea	38	19	10	9	68	38	67
Liverpool	**38**	**18**	**10**	**10**	**61**	**41**	**64**
Blackburn	38	16	12	10	52	43	60
Everton	38	17	8	13	48	49	59
Southampton	38	13	13	12	43	46	52
Man City	38	15	6	17	47	54	51
Tottenham	38	14	8	16	51	62	50
Middlesbro	38	13	10	15	48	44	49
Charlton	38	14	7	17	45	56	49
Birmingham	38	13	9	16	41	49	48
Fulham	38	13	9	16	41	50	48
Leeds	38	14	5	19	58	57	47
Aston Villa	38	12	9	17	42	47	45
Bolton	38	10	14	14	41	51	44
West Ham	38	10	12	16	42	59	42
West Brom	38	6	8	24	29	65	26
Sunderland	38	4	7	27	21	65	19

FA CUP
Fourth round

WORTHINGTON CUP
Winners

CHAMPIONS LEAGUE
First group stage

UEFA CUP
Quarter-finals

**Gerard Houllier won a trophy but found
his managerial credentials questioned**

THE GAMES

Sunday August 11
ARSENAL
Community Shield (Cardiff)
Lost 0-1   HT 0-0   Att 67,337
Dudek — Xavier (Babbel 78), Henchoz, Hyypia, Traore (Cheyrou 88) — Gerrard, Hamann (Murphy 67), Riise, Diouf — Owen (Smicer 85), Heskey (Baros 74) *Subs not used* Kirkland, Carragher *Booked* Gerrard, Murphy
Report page 54

Sunday August 18
ASTON VILLA (a)
Won 1-0   HT 0-0   Att 41,183   Position 6th
Dudek — Xavier, Henchoz, Hyypia, Traore — Murphy, Hamann, Gerrard, Riise — Owen (Heskey 81), Diouf (Carragher 90) *Subs not used* Smicer, Kirkland, Cheyrou *Booked* Hamann, Diouf, Murphy
Scorer **Riise 47**
Report page 223

Saturday August 24
SOUTHAMPTON (h)
Won 3-0   HT 1-0   Att 43,058   Position 2nd
Dudek — Xavier, Henchoz, Hyypia, Traore — Murphy, Hamann, Gerrard (Cheyrou 85), Heskey — Owen (Riise 72), Diouf (Smicer 81) *Subs not used* Kirkland, Carragher
Scorers **Diouf 3, 51, Murphy 90 (pen)**
Referee **J Winter**

Southampton are accused of "propaganda football" by Gordon Strachan. Whether that is good or bad is not clear, but the manager is furious at Liverpool's easy win to suggest they had better not repeat it.

Wednesday August 28
BLACKBURN ROVERS (a)
Drew 2-2   HT 1-1   Att 29,207   Position 2nd
Dudek — Xavier, Henchoz, Hyypia, Traore — Murphy, Hamann, Gerrard, Riise (Diao 87) — Owen (Heskey 64), Diouf (Smicer 64) *Subs not used* Kirkland, Carragher *Booked* Murphy
Scorers **Murphy 31, Riise 77**
Referee **S Bennett**
Report page 102

Monday September 2
NEWCASTLE UNITED (h)
Drew 2-2   HT 0-0   Att 43,241   Position 3rd
Dudek — Xavier, Henchoz, Hyypia, Traore — Gerrard (Cheyrou 84), Hamann — Smicer (Diouf 68), Murphy, Heskey — Owen *Subs not used* Riise, Kirkland, Carragher *Booked* Hamann
Scorers **Hamann 53, Owen 73 (pen)**
Referee **G Poll**

Outplayed, trailing 2-0 and with just ten minutes to go, Newcastle somehow salvage a point. Sir Bobby Robson's triple substitution pays dividends with a goal from Speed and then a powerful header from Shearer.

Wednesday September 11
BIRMINGHAM CITY (h)
Drew 2-2   HT 1-0   Att 43,113   Position 4th
Dudek — Carragher, Henchoz (Heskey ht), Hyypia, Traore — Murphy, Hamann, Gerrard, Riise (Diao 71) — Owen, Diouf (Berger 79) *Subs not used* Baros, Kirkland
Scorers **Murphy 25, Gerrard 49**
Referee **N Barry**

Again Liverpool lead 2-0 with time almost up and again they take only one point as Birmingham, with Morrison punishing Traore's mistake and then equalising with a brilliant last-minute header, snatch an unlikely draw.

A DAMP SQUIB — OR WAS IT A plateau? A worrying dip in form — or was it a PLATEAU? A troubling downturn in fortunes — or was it a *plateau*?

Gerard Houllier chose to call the 2002-03 season a plateau. And not just any old plateau. It was, he said, something he had been anticipating after the triumphs and progress of the previous two years. This would be plausible if only Houllier had not foreseen something quite different at the end of the previous campaign.

Liverpool, he said, would take small steps forward, and that was why no one should be critical of the second-place finish in 2002. It was one step on from the third-place finish the season before. There was only one logical conclusion. Be patient and the title, first place, would be the next step. Instead, the team reached a plateau, finishing below Chelsea and outside of the Champions League placings. The fans felt perplexed as well as disappointed. Suddenly the holy grail of a Premiership title seemed farther away than ever.

Most clubs at this juncture can point to lack of financial muscle as a significant factor in stalling ambition. Leeds United fell farther from grace than did Liverpool, but in some respects it is a wonder they still exist, let alone remain in the Premiership. No, Liverpool had more traditional excuses to hand. Players lost form, confidence wobbled and the team were flung around in a curious cycle of wonderment and hopelessness. It was a puzzling season.

There was a trophy, but simply to look at the stark fact that Liverpool won the Worthington Cup is insufficient. The statistic looks paltry, but the winning was wonderful. Liverpool outsmarted Manchester United in every way; on the streets of Cardiff, in the stands and on the pitch.

Was there something of the sick man about Liverpool? The man who, although ill, manages to spruce himself up for a big party and fool all his friends that he is in fine fettle? Cardiff felt like that. Liverpool were magnificent. There were hints for sure that maybe something was amiss, for they began hesitantly, but by the end it all seemed so rosy. The story was near perfect.

Liverpool's heroes were three players for whom the season had been soured. Jerzy Dudek, back only because of injury to Chris Kirkland, performed majestically in goal. Steven Gerrard was masterful and composed and determined, all the qualities his manager had publicly hinted he lacked. And Michael Owen, for whom the posts in most matches had shifted by two inches, rediscovered that impressive, clinical eye. He had what must have felt like hours to beat Fabien Barthez as he homed in on Dietmar Hamann's pass, and therefore had time to dwell on the criticisms

LIVERPOOL

PREMIERSHIP

	P	W	D	L	F	A	Pts
Man Utd	38	25	8	5	74	34	83
Arsenal	38	23	9	6	85	42	78
Newcastle	38	21	6	11	63	48	69
Chelsea	38	19	10	9	68	38	67
Liverpool	**38**	**18**	**10**	**10**	**61**	**41**	**64**
Blackburn	38	16	12	10	52	43	60
Everton	38	17	8	13	48	49	59
Southampton	38	13	13	12	43	46	52
Man City	38	15	6	17	47	54	51
Tottenham	38	14	8	16	51	62	50
Middlesbro	38	13	10	15	48	44	49
Charlton	38	14	7	17	45	56	49
Birmingham	38	13	9	16	41	49	48
Fulham	38	13	9	16	41	50	48
Leeds	38	14	5	19	58	57	47
Aston Villa	38	12	9	17	42	47	45
Bolton	38	10	14	14	41	51	44
West Ham	38	10	12	16	42	59	42
West Brom	38	6	8	24	29	65	26
Sunderland	38	4	7	27	21	65	19

FA CUP
Fourth round

WORTHINGTON CUP
Winners

CHAMPIONS LEAGUE
First group stage

UEFA CUP
Quarter-finals

Gerard Houllier won a trophy but found his managerial credentials questioned

THE GAMES

Alyson Rudd

Sunday August 11
ARSENAL
Community Shield (Cardiff)
Lost 0-1   HT 0-0   Att 67,337
Dudek — Xavier (Babbel 78), Henchoz, Hyypia, Traore
(Cheyrou 88) — Gerrard, Hamann (Murphy 67), Riise,
Diouf — Owen (Smicer 85), Heskey (Baros 74) *Subs not
used* Kirkland, Carragher *Booked* Gerrard, Murphy
Report page 54

Sunday August 18
ASTON VILLA (a)
Won 1-0   HT 0-0   Att 41,183   Position 6th
Dudek — Xavier, Henchoz, Hyypia, Traore — Murphy,
Hamann, Gerrard, Riise — Owen (Heskey 81), Diouf
(Carragher 90) *Subs not used* Smicer, Kirkland, Cheyrou
Booked Hamann, Diouf, Murphy
Scorer **Riise 47**
Report page 223

Saturday August 24
SOUTHAMPTON (h)
Won 3-0   HT 1-0   Att 43,058   Position 2nd
Dudek — Xavier, Henchoz, Hyypia, Traore — Murphy,
Hamann, Gerrard (Cheyrou 85), Heskey — Owen (Riise
72), Diouf (Smicer 81) *Subs not used* Kirkland,
Carragher
Scorers **Diouf 3, 51, Murphy 90 (pen)**
Referee **J Winter**

Southampton are accused of "propaganda football" by
Gordon Strachan. Whether that is good or bad is not
clear, but the manager is furious at Liverpool's easy win
to suggest they had better not repeat it.

Wednesday August 28
BLACKBURN ROVERS (a)
Drew 2-2   HT 1-1   Att 29,207   Position 2nd
Dudek — Xavier, Henchoz, Hyypia, Traore — Murphy,
Hamann, Gerrard, Riise (Diao 87) — Owen (Heskey 64),
Diouf (Smicer 64) *Subs not used* Kirkland, Carragher
Booked Murphy
Scorers **Murphy 31, Riise 77**
Referee **S Bennett**
Report page 102

Monday September 2
NEWCASTLE UNITED (h)
Drew 2-2   HT 0-0   Att 43,241   Position 3rd
Dudek — Xavier, Henchoz, Hyypia, Traore — Gerrard
(Cheyrou 84), Hamann — Smicer (Diouf 68), Murphy,
Heskey — Owen *Subs not used* Riise, Kirkland,
Carragher *Booked* Hamann
Scorers **Hamann 53, Owen 73 (pen)**
Referee **G Poll**

Outplayed, trailing 2-0 and with just ten minutes to go,
Newcastle somehow salvage a point. Sir Bobby
Robson's triple substitution pays dividends with a goal
from Speed and then a powerful header from Shearer.

Wednesday September 11
BIRMINGHAM CITY (h)
Drew 2-2   HT 1-0   Att 43,113   Position 4th
Dudek — Carragher, Henchoz (Heskey ht), Hyypia, Traore
— Murphy, Hamann, Gerrard, Riise (Diao 71) — Owen,
Diouf (Berger 79) *Subs not used* Baros, Kirkland
Scorers **Murphy 25, Gerrard 49**
Referee **N Barry**

Again Liverpool lead 2-0 with time almost up and again
they take only one point as Birmingham, with Morrison
punishing Traore's mistake and then equalising with a
brilliant last-minute header, snatch an unlikely draw.

A DAMP SQUIB — OR WAS IT A plateau? A worrying dip in form
— or was it a PLATEAU? A troubling downturn in fortunes — or
was it a *plateau*?

Gerard Houllier chose to call the 2002-03 season a plateau. And
not just any old plateau. It was, he said, something he had been
anticipating after the triumphs and progress of the previous two
years. This would be plausible if only Houllier had not foreseen
something quite different at the end of the previous campaign.

Liverpool, he said, would take small steps forward, and that was
why no one should be critical of the second-place finish in 2002. It
was one step on from the third-place finish the season before. There
was only one logical conclusion. Be patient and the title, first place,
would be the next step. Instead, the team reached a plateau,
finishing below Chelsea and outside of the Champions League
placings. The fans felt perplexed as well as disappointed. Suddenly
the holy grail of a Premiership title seemed farther away than ever.

Most clubs at this juncture can point to lack of financial muscle
as a significant factor in stalling ambition. Leeds United fell farther
from grace than did Liverpool, but in some respects it is a wonder
they still exist, let alone remain in the Premiership. No, Liverpool
had more traditional excuses to hand. Players lost form, confidence
wobbled and the team were flung around in a curious cycle of
wonderment and hopelessness. It was a puzzling season.

There was a trophy, but simply to look at the stark fact that
Liverpool won the Worthington Cup is insufficient. The statistic
looks paltry, but the winning was wonderful. Liverpool outsmarted
Manchester United in every way; on the streets of Cardiff, in the
stands and on the pitch.

Was there something of the sick man about Liverpool? The man
who, although ill, manages to spruce himself up for a big party and
fool all his friends that he is in fine fettle? Cardiff felt like that.
Liverpool were magnificent. There were hints for sure that maybe
something was amiss, for they began hesitantly, but by the end it all
seemed so rosy. The story was near perfect.

Liverpool's heroes were three players for whom the season had
been soured. Jerzy Dudek, back only because of injury to Chris
Kirkland, performed majestically in goal. Steven Gerrard was
masterful and composed and determined, all the qualities his
manager had publicly hinted he lacked. And Michael Owen, for
whom the posts in most matches had shifted by two inches,
rediscovered that impressive, clinical eye. He had what must have
felt like hours to beat Fabien Barthez as he homed in on Dietmar
Hamann's pass, and therefore had time to dwell on the criticisms

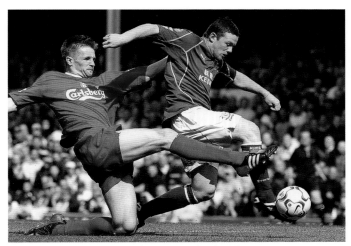

Liverpool only just caught up with a Rooney-inspired Everton

and all the chances he might have put away. A lesser man, most men in fact, would have felt their heart skip and fluffed the chance. Owen, though, back on the big stage, was lethal and United were felled.

All those who scoff at the victory should think back to Owen's delight and the fans' delirium that day. No matter what else is happening in a season, to beat the old enemy on a grand stage is enormously fulfilling. It was fun, it was the end of the pain, it was the start of the push to greater glory. Only it wasn't.

The signs had been there from the off that Liverpool lacked calm efficiency. Gary McAllister had provided a level-headedness that a young, multinational side now sorely missed and three successive 2-2 draws, all games that seemed to have been won, early in the season rammed it home that this side were low on maturity.

They also lacked class when up against the classiest and Valencia's performances in the Champions League made fans wonder why the truly European and decidedly classy playmaker, Jari Litmanen, had been allowed to leave. Valencia's elegance apart, Liverpool could still have progressed to the second group stage but for the spooky games against FC Basle, which produced nothing that was expected and everything that makes football almost comical.

As Liverpool faltered in the league, the party line was that these two drawn and draining matches knocked the stuffing out of the team. But Liverpool were already unpredictable and lacking cohesion.

Take the last game. That great cup side, Liverpool, treat the match at Stamford Bridge as a cup final and end up playing as if it was a pre-season testimonial. It was a passionless way to forego another bite at the Champions League cherry. But maybe a plateau is necessarily passionless.

Saturday September 14
BOLTON WANDERERS (a)
Won 3-2 HT **1-0** Att **27,328** Position **4th**
Dudek — Carragher, Diao, Hyypia, Traore — Murphy, Hamann, Gerrard, Heskey — Cheyrou (Riise 85) — Baros *Subs not used* Berger, Diouf, Owen, Kirkland *Booked* Hamann, Baros
Scorers **Baros 45, 72, Heskey 88**
Report page 235

Tuesday September 17
VALENCIA (a)
Champions League
Lost 0-2 HT **0-2** Att **43,000**
Dudek — Carragher, Diao (Cheyrou ht), Hyypia, Traore — Murphy (Baros 76), Hamann, Gerrard, Riise — Diouf (Owen ht) — Heskey *Subs not used* Babbel, Biscan, Berger, Kirkland *Booked* Traore, Hamann *Sent off* Hamann 77
Referee **H Frandel (Germany)**

On the back foot throughout, Liverpool can only be grateful that Valencia ease up after taking charge through Aimar, who is in majestic form, and Baraja in the first half. Hamann's dismissal for a second bookable offence completes a sorry first Champions League outing.

Saturday September 21
WEST BROMWICH ALBION (h)
Won 2-0 HT **0-0** Att **43,830** Position **2nd**
Dudek — Carragher, Henchoz, Hyypia, Riise — Gerrard, Hamann, Murphy — Cheyrou (Diao 88) — Owen, Baros (Heskey 75) *Subs not used* Traore, Diouf, Kirkland *Booked* Heskey, Murphy
Scorers **Baros 56, Riise 90**
Referee **D Elleray**

Joe Murphy's first touch as an Albion player is to save Owen's penalty after replacing Hoult — sent off for hauling down the out-of-form England striker — between the posts. His dramatic entry cannot prevent a Liverpool win, but Albion are denied a clear penalty of their own when Hyypia fells Roberts.

Wednesday September 25
FC BASLE (h)
Champions League
Drew 1-1 HT **1-1** Att **37,634**
Dudek — Carragher, Henchoz, Hyypia, Riise — Murphy, Gerrard, Cheyrou, Heskey (Diouf 70) — Owen (Berger 78), Baros *Subs not used* Babbel, Traore, Biscan, Diao, Kirkland *Booked* Diouf
Scorer **Baros 34**
Referee **D van Egmond (Netherlands)**

Forget the scoreline, this is a 1-1 massacre. Liverpool attack relentlessly, hitting the woodwork three times, but Baros's goal is cancelled out when Rossi finishes a rare Basle attack just before half-time and the Swiss hang on for an undeserved point.

Saturday September 28
MANCHESTER CITY (a)
Won 3-0 HT **1-0** Att **35,131** Position **2nd**
Dudek — Carragher, Traore, Hyypia, Riise — Gerrard (Diao 89), Hamann, Murphy, Heskey — Owen, Baros (Diouf 59) *Subs not used* Berger, Cheyrou, Kirkland
Scorer **Owen 6, 64, 89**
Report page 139

Wednesday October 2
SPARTAK MOSCOW (h)
Champions League
Won 5-0 HT 3-0 Att **40,812**
Dudek — Carragher, Henchoz (Traore 67), Hyypia, Riise
— Gerrard (Diao 76), Hamann, Cheyrou (Diouf 82),
Murphy — Owen, Heskey *Subs not used* Kirkland,
Berger, Biscan, Baros *Booked* Henchoz
Scorers **Heskey 7, 89, Cheyrou 14,**
Hyypia 28, Diao 81
Referee **A Hamer (Luxembourg)**

Heskey begins and ends the rout of dismal opponents
and it is one-way traffic in between times, Diao and
Cheyrou registering their first Liverpool goals.

Sunday October 6
CHELSEA (h)
Won 1-0 HT 0-0 Att **43,856** Position **2nd**
Dudek — Carragher, Henchoz (Traore 40), Hyypia, Riise
— Gerrard, Hamann, Murphy (Diao 75), Cheyrou (Baros
71) — Owen, Heskey *Subs not used* Kirkland, Diouf
Scorer **Owen 89**
Referee **M Riley**

The Anfield curse strikes again for Chelsea, beaten at
the death for the second season running. This time it is
Owen who snatches a fortuitous three points, pouncing
after Heskey's shot is pushed on to a post. After their
Uefa Cup elimination by Viking, it is particularly galling
for Claudio Ranieri's team.

Saturday October 19
LEEDS UNITED (a)
Won 1-0 HT 0-0 Att **40,187** Position **1st**
Dudek — Carragher, Traore, Hyypia, Riise — Murphy,
Hamann, Diao, Cheyrou — Baros (Owen 70), Diouf *Subs
not used* Babbel, Biscan, Smicer, Arphexad *Booked*
Carragher, Diouf
Scorer **Diao 66**
Report page 212

Tuesday October 22
SPARTAK MOSCOW (a)
Champions League
Won 3-1 HT 1-1 Att **10,000**
Dudek — Carragher, Traore, Hyypia, Riise — Murphy,
Hamann, Diao, Heskey (Vignal 66; Biscan 76) — Owen,
Baros (Diouf 70) *Subs not used* Arphexad, Babbel,
Mellor, Smicer
Scorer **Owen 29, 70, 80**
Referee **K Plautz (Austria)**

Trailing to a 23rd-minute goal from Danishevskiy,
Liverpool, via the rejuvenated Owen, complete a
double over the Russians. Owen's hat-trick, his ninth
for the club, is a classic of the genre: header, left foot,
right foot.

Saturday October 26
TOTTENHAM HOTSPUR (h)
Won 2-1 HT 0-0 Att **44,084** Position **1st**
Dudek — Carragher, Traore, Hyypia, Riise — Gerrard
(Smicer 68), Hamann, Diao, Murphy — Owen, Diouf
(Baros 58) *Subs not used* Kirkland, Babbel, Cheyrou
Booked Smicer, Diao
Scorers **Murphy 72, Owen 86 (pen)**
Referee **M Riley**

Liverpool's sixth straight win is tinged with fortune.
Murphy gives them the lead with a superb free kick, but
after Richards heads Tottenham's equaliser they need a
late penalty — won and converted by Owen, who tempts
Carr into a rash tackle — to keep their run going.

MATCH OF THE SEASON

Liverpool 2   Manchester United 0
Millennium Stadium, Sunday March 2, 2003
Matt Dickinson, Chief Football Correspondent

MANCHESTER UNITED WANTED victory, Liverpool needed it
and there is a mighty difference between the two. If the
Worthington Cup is to have meaning, it needs the victors to cherish
the trophy and the cup found a loving owner in Gerard Houllier and
his conquering team.

Houllier was the manager under pressure, Liverpool the side
under scrutiny in Cardiff as, perversely, they became the first
underdogs to come into a leading final bearing the greater
expectations. They responded with a triumph that has made the
Frenchman's seat just a little more comfortable as he tries to steer
his club through choppy waters. "This went beyond the trophy," he
said after match-winning performances from Jerzy Dudek, Steven
Gerrard and Michael Owen.

Victory could never mean the same for United as they chase
greater prizes and they will be more angry at losing to Liverpool
than missing the silverware. Sir Alex Ferguson can live without the
Worthington Cup, a competition he would have won more than
once in his 17 years at Old Trafford if it was that important to him,
but the damage to his pride will have hurt.

The United manager congratulated the Liverpool players at the
final whistle and it is a shame that he could not bring himself to
show similar courtesy to the press and, more importantly, to the
sponsor, who should be able to expect some co-operation for the
millions of pounds invested. Ferguson was happy to take the same
company's award of a lifetime's supply of Carling for his managerial
achievements and his no-show, apart from a few television
soundbites, was insulting.

Perhaps it was the realisation that he may have lost two trophies
in one afternoon, because Arsenal's victory over Charlton Athletic
extended their lead at the top of the Barclaycard Premiership to
eight points. United still have to travel to Highbury and Newcastle
so Ferguson may need to win the European Cup to avoid a second
successive barren season — the first time that would have happened
since Remi Moses and Peter Davenport were at Old Trafford in
1989.

United must also still welcome Liverpool to Old Trafford on
April 5 and defeat yesterday confirmed the Merseyside club as
Ferguson's bogey team. Liverpool have now won six out of seven
games against their Manchester rivals, and that one blip may have
been avoided but for Dudek's calamitous afternoon.

Perhaps sensing that his goalkeeper might quiver at the first
sight of United's attack since his dreadful error at Anfield in
December, Houllier pulled Dudek aside last week for a chat. "I

Liverpool stood firm against United in the final reckoning

said to him, 'I can feel you will be the hero,' and he deserved to be man of the match," the manager said. "In football, you can go from rock bottom to being a hero."

As Ferguson admitted, Dudek's reliability allowed Liverpool to defend deep inside their own penalty area, but the goalkeeper could not have complained if the individual prize had gone to Gerrard. The England midfield player has been improving with every game over the past couple of months and this was him back to the peak of form. He was ably assisted in midfield by Danny Murphy and El-Hadji Diouf, who was clattering into tackles from the kick-off. Dietmar Hamann was the least notable of Liverpool's midfield players but he still had a decisive influence in setting up their second goal for Owen.

The first strike came from the swinging right foot of Gerrard and, in games as tight as this one, the early breakthrough often proves decisive, although it would be unfair to say that it came out of the blue. United had enjoyed the better of a dreadful opening spell and Ruud van Nistelrooy almost poked in a cross from Ryan Giggs, but Liverpool had cast off their inhibitions even before they took the lead in the 39th minute.

Owen had dashed past Rio Ferdinand, Murphy chipped over the crossbar and Diouf failed to spot the run of Emile Heskey in a period of sustained pressure that was rewarded with the goal. David Beckham paid for his failure to close down Gerrard when his England team-mate's shot cannoned off his shin and over Fabien Barthez from 25 yards.

United might have equalised just before the interval, when Stephane Henchoz cleared off the line from Paul Scholes, but, while they had plenty of chances after the interval, they never reduced Liverpool's defence to panic. Roy Keane vented his frustration on

Wednesday October 30
VALENCIA (h)
Champions League
Lost 0-1   HT 0-1   Att 41,831
Dudek — Carragher (Cheyrou 82), Traore, Hyypia, Riise — Hamann — Gerrard, Diao, Murphy (Smicer 61) — Owen, Heskey (Baros 61) *Subs not used* Kirkland, Babbel, Biscan, Diouf
Referee **T Hauge (Norway)**

Gerrard and Owen waste openings for Liverpool, but they are deservedly beaten by a classy Valencia side who qualify comfortably for the second phase with Rufete's first-half goal, which takes a deflection off Hyypia.

Saturday November 2
WEST HAM UNITED (h)
Won 2-0   HT 1-0   Att 44,048   Position 1st
Dudek — Carragher, Traore, Hyypia, Riise — Diao, Hamann — Murphy, Smicer (Gerrard 70), Heskey — Owen *Subs not used* Cheyrou, Diouf, Baros, Kirkland
Scorer **Owen 28, 55**
Referee **E Wolstenholme**

Is it too early to send the championship trophy to Anfield? Liverpool are seven points clear of Arsenal, for 24 hours at least, after Owen's superbly executed double polishes off a West Ham side whose own revival seems to have been ended.

Wednesday November 6
SOUTHAMPTON (h)
Worthington Cup, 3rd rnd
Won 3-1   HT 1-0   Att 35,870
Kirkland — Ostemobor (Traore 70), Babbel, Biscan, Vignal — Smicer (Diao 76), Gerrard, Berger, Cheyrou — Diouf, Baros (Heskey 65) *Subs not used* Diomede, Arphexad *Booked* Smicer
Scorers **Berger 45, Diouf 57, Baros 60**
Referee **P Dowd**

Given his first start of the season as Gerard Houllier makes ten changes, Kirkland responds with a brilliant display that sees Liverpool scrape past a more recognisable Southampton line-up. Delgado gets his first goal for Gordon Strachan's side.

Saturday November 9
MIDDLESBROUGH (a)
Lost 0-1   HT 0-0   Att 34,747   Position 1st
Dudek — Carragher, Traore, Hyypia, Riise — Gerrard (Smicer 68), Hamann, Diao, Heskey — Murphy (Baros 86) — Owen *Subs not used* Babbel, Kirkland, Biscan
Report page 165

Tuesday November 12
FC BASLE (a)
Champions League
Drew 3-3   HT 0-3   Att 35,000
Dudek — Carragher (Diouf 79), Traore, Hyypia, Riise — Murphy, Hamann, Gerrard (Diao ht) — Smicer — Owen *Subs not used* Kirkland, Babbel, Biscan, Cheyrou *Booked* Murphy, Smicer
Scorers **Murphy 61, Smicer 64, Owen 85**
Referee **C Colombo (France)**

Three days after losing the last unbeaten league record in England, Liverpool go out of the Champions League in a blaze of goals and near-glory. Needing to win to qualify for the second phase, they are 3-0 down inside half an hour but fall just short after an astonishing second-half recovery.

Sunday November 17
SUNDERLAND (h)
Drew 0-0   HT 0-0   Att **43,074**   Position **2nd**
Dudek — Babbel, Traore, Hyypia, Carragher (Riise 67)
— Diao, Hamann, Murphy — Smicer (Diouf 67) — Owen,
Heskey *Subs not used* Gerrard, Baros, Kirkland
Referee **A D'Urso**

No shots (to Liverpool's 24), no corners (to Liverpool's
12), Sunderland put up the shutters to give Gerard
Houllier's team an afternoon of utter frustration. Gerrard
kicks his heels on the Liverpool bench after his attitude
is criticised by his manager.

Saturday November 23
FULHAM (a)
Lost 2-3   HT 0-2   Att **18,144**   Position **2nd**
Dudek — Babbel (Baros ht), Traore, Hyypia, Carragher —
Murphy, Hamann, Diao (Gerrard ht), Riise — Heskey
(Smicer 77), Owen *Subs not used* Kirkland, Cheyrou
Booked Traore
Scorers **Hamann 62, Baros 86**
Report page 203

Thursday November 28
VITESSE ARNHEM (a)
Uefa Cup, 3rd rnd, 1st leg
Won 1-0   HT 1-0   Att **28,000**
Dudek — Babbel, Henchoz, Hyypia, Traore — Gerrard,
Diao, Murphy — Cheyrou (Smicer 9) — Owen, Baros
(Heskey 74) *Subs not used* Diouf, Kirkland, Carragher,
Biscan, Welsh *Booked* Diao
Scorer **Owen 26**
Referee **M Mejuto-Gonzalez (Spain)**

Relegated to the minor European competition, Liverpool
make a winning start thanks to a goal by Owen.

Sunday December 1
MANCHESTER UNITED (h)
Lost 1-1   HT 0-0   Att **44,250**   Position **2nd**
Dudek — Carragher, Henchoz, Hyypia, Traore (Riise 79)
— Gerrard, Hamann, Murphy — Smicer (Diouf 70) —
Owen, Baros (Heskey 58) *Subs not used* Diao, Kirkland
Booked Smicer
Scorer **Hyypia 82**
Referee **A Wiley**

The Dudek horror show. Liverpool's goalkeeper lets
Carragher's back-header through his arms and is then
beaten at the near post, Forlan profiting twice for
United. Hyypia halves the deficit, but Barthez ensures an
away win with a brilliant save from Hamann.

Wednesday December 4
IPSWICH TOWN (h)
Worthington Cup, 4th rnd
Drew 1-1 (aet; win 5-4 on pens) HT 0-1 Att **26,305**
Dudek — Xavier, Babbel (Carragher ht), Biscan, Vignal —
Gerrard, Diao, Riise — Smicer (Welsh 83) — Diouf, Mellor
(Baros 76) *Subs not used* Ostemobor, Arphexad
Scorer **Diouf 54 (pen)**
Referee **D Gallagher**

Told that he would be dropped but unexpectedly
reprieved, Dudek is beaten by Miller, but a penalty
takes the game into extra time and a shoot-out.

Saturday December 7
CHARLTON ATHLETIC (a)
Lost 0-2   HT 0-1   Att **26,694**   Position **4th**
Kirkland — Carragher, Henchoz, Hyypia, Traore (Baros
60) — Murphy, Hamann, Gerrard, Heskey (Riise 36) —
Owen, Diouf *Subs not used* Dudek, Smicer, Diao
Booked Henchoz, Traore, Hamann
Report page 178

Owen applies a gloss finish to Liverpool's Cardiff triumph

Mikael Silvestre and Juan Sebastian Veron for two moments of
carelessness, but they were no more culpable than any of their
team-mates.

For all the United possession in the second half, it was Liverpool
who created the best opportunity, in the 64th minute, when Milan
Baros, on for the hamstrung Heskey, broke on the counter-attack
and fed Gerrard, who was thwarted by Barthez at the near post.
Dudek was kept busy at the other end, but, with the exception of
one block from Van Nistelrooy, most of the saves would be regarded
as routine in circumstances other than a cup final.

Owen's goal, in the 87th minute, was also the type he has scored
a hundred times, but it required steely nerve. After mistakes by
Silvestre and Ferdinand, Hamann stole possession and invited the
England striker to sprint clear. Running towards the end where he
scored twice against Arsenal to steal the FA Cup two years ago, the
old confidence came surging back through the England forward,
who buried his shot into the bottom corner.

Some of the questions about Owen and Gerrard's form were
always going to be answered soon enough, but Houllier may face a
renewed inquisition if he misses out on the Champions League. At
least victory yesterday gave him room to breathe. "In the 11 months
since I came back from the heart problem, we have reached the
quarter-finals of the European Cup, finished second in the league,
won the Worthington Cup and we are still in the Uefa Cup," he said.
"That is not a bad record."

LIVERPOOL (4-4-2): J Dudek — J Carragher, S Henchoz, S Hyypia, J A Riise — E-H Diouf (sub: I Biscan,
90min), D Hamann, S Gerrard, D Murphy — E Heskey (sub: M Baros, 61; sub: V Smicer 89), M Owen.
Substitutes not used: P Arphexad, D Traore. **Booked:** Henchoz.
MANCHESTER UNITED (4-4-1-1): F Barthez — G Neville, R Ferdinand, W Brown (sub: O G Solskjaer,
74), M Silvestre — D Beckham, R Keane, J S Veron, R Giggs — P Scholes — R van Nistelrooy.
Substitutes not used: J O'Shea, P Neville, N Butt, R Carroll.
Referee: P Durkin.

THE MANAGER

Gerard Houllier

Funny how things turn out. Gerard Houllier was the most adored and respected of managers. His recovery from heart surgery and commitment to the cause immediately installed him in Scouse folklore, but as last season unfolded, doubts set in over whether the man influential enough to be awarded an honorary OBE knew a good signing when he saw one and whether he could inspire a team to more than pragmatic victories. There were concerns, too, that he did not take quite the full share of responsibility for poor performances.

Alyson Rudd

APPEARANCES

	Prem	FAC	WC	Euro	Total
M Babbel	2	-	3	1	6 (†1)
M Baros	17 (10)	0 (1)	2 (2)	3 (6)	22 (†20)
P Berger	0 (2)	-	1	0 (1)	1 (3)
I Biscan	3 (3)	0 (1)	2 (1)	0 (3)	5 (8)
J Carragher	34 (1)	3	3 (2)	11	51 (3)
B Cheyrou	8 (11)	2	1 (1)	3 (2)	14 (†15)
S Diao	13 (13)	1 (1)	3 (1)	5 (3)	22 (18)
E-H Diouf	21 (8)	3	5	5 (4)	35* (12)
J Dudek	30	1 (1)	2	11	45* (1)
S Gerrard	32 (2)	2	6	11	52* (2)
D Hamann	29 (1)	1	1	7 (2)	39* (3)
S Henchoz	19	2	4	6	32*
E Heskey	22 (10)	2 (1)	2 (3)	10 (1)	37* (15)
S Hyypia	36	3	4	12	56*
C Kirkland	8	2	4	1	15
N Mellor	1 (2)	1	2	-	4 (2)
D Murphy	36	3	4	12	55 (†1)
J Ostemobor	-	-	1	-	1
M Owen	32 (3)	2	3 (1)	11 (1)	49* (5)
J A Riise	31 (6)	2 (1)	4	10 (1)	48* (8)
V Smicer	10 (11)	1	4 (1)	3 (3)	18 (†16)
D Traore	30 (2)	2	2 (1)	10 (1)	45* (4)
G Vignal	0 (1)	-	2	0 (1)	2 (2)
J Welsh	-	-	0 (1)	-	0 (1)
A Xavier	4	-	1	-	6*

(Total includes *appearance in Community Shield and † substitute appearance in Community Shield)

Thursday December 12
VITESSE ARNHEM (h)
Uefa Cup, 3rd rnd, 2nd leg
Won 1-0 (win 2-0 on agg) **HT 1-0** Att **23,576**
Kirkland — Carragher, Henchoz, Hyypia, Traore — Murphy, Gerrard, Diao (Hamann 68), Smicer (Baros 88) — Owen, Diouf (Riise 78) *Subs not used* Dudek, Babbel, Biscan, Mellor *Booked* Henchoz
Scorer **Owen 21**
Referee **W Stark (Germany)**

A half-empty Anfield includes Ian Rush among its number and he sees Owen move to within one strike of his club record with his nineteenth European goal.

Sunday December 15
SUNDERLAND (a)
Lost 1-2 **HT 0-1** Att **37,118** Position **5th**
Kirkland — Carragher, Henchoz, Biscan (Diouf 64), Traore — Murphy, Hamann (Riise ht), Gerrard, Smicer — Owen, Baros (Diao 72) *Subs not used* Dudek, Babbel *Booked* Murphy, Carragher
Scorer **Baros 68**
Report page 274

Wednesday December 18
ASTON VILLA (a)
Worthington Cup, 5th rnd
Won 4-3 **HT 1-1** Att **38,530**
Kirkland — Babbel (Carragher 39), Henchoz, Hyypia, Traore — Murphy, Diao, Gerrard, Riise — Owen (Heskey 76), Baros *Subs not used* Dudek, Smicer, Diouf *Booked* Henchoz, Hyypia, Murphy
Scorers **Murphy 27, 90, Baros 54, Gerrard 67**
Report page 228

Sunday December 22
EVERTON (h)
Drew 0-0 **HT 0-0** Att **44,025** Position **5th**
Kirkland — Carragher, Henchoz, Hyypia, Traore (Heskey 52) — Murphy, Gerrard, Diao (Smicer 52), Riise — Owen, Baros *Subs not used* Biscan, Diouf, Dudek *Booked* Henchoz, Traore, Carragher
Referee **G Poll**

Everton will spend Christmas above their neighbours for the first time since 1985 after a tight, bruising derby in which Rooney's shot, deflected on to the bar by Henchoz, is overtaken as a talking point by Gerrard's two-footed jump tackle on Naysmith.

Thursday December 26
BLACKBURN ROVERS (h)
Drew 1-1 **HT 1-0** Att **43,075** Position **5th**
Kirkland — Carragher, Henchoz, Hyypia, Traore (Diouf 83) — Smicer (Biscan 65), Gerrard, Murphy, Riise — Owen, Heskey (Baros 58) *Subs not used* Arphexad, Diao *Booked* Traore
Scorer **Riise 17**
Referee **N Barry**

Liverpool's worst league run for almost 50 years is extended by a goal of spectacular brilliance from Cole, who sends a dipping, 32-yard volley over Kirkland in the 77th minute to cancel out Riise's deflected opener.

Sunday December 29
ARSENAL (a)
Drew 1-1 **HT 0-0** Att **38,074** Position **6th**
Kirkland — Carragher, Henchoz, Hyypia, Riise — Murphy, Gerrard, Diao, Cheyrou (Traore 79) — Owen (Diouf 33), Baros (Biscan 86) *Subs not used* Arphexad, Mellor *Booked* Riise, Murphy, Diao
Scorer **Murphy 70 (pen)**
Report page 59

Wednesday January 1
NEWCASTLE UNITED (a)
Lost 0-1   HT 0-1   Att 52,147   Position **7th**
Kirkland — Carragher, Henchoz, Hyypia, Riise — Biscan,
Gerrard, Diao, Cheyrou (Smicer 59) — Diouf (Vignal 79),
Baros (Mellor 55) *Subs not used* Arphexad, Traore
Booked Cheyrou, Diao, Diouf, Gerrard *Sent off* Diao 66
Report page 72

Sunday January 5
MANCHESTER CITY (a)
FA Cup, 3rd rnd
Won 1-0   HT 0-0   Att 28,586
Kirkland — Carragher, Henchoz, Hyypia, Traore —
Gerrard, Diao — Diouf, Murphy, Smicer (Riise 86) —
Mellor (Heskey 74) *Subs not used* Cheyrou, Baros,
Dudek *Booked* Hyypia, Murphy, Smicer
Scorer **Murphy 47 (pen)**
Report page 144

Wednesday January 8
SHEFFIELD UNITED (a)
Worthington Cup, semi-final, 1st leg
Lost 1-2   HT 1-0   Att 30,095
Details page 338

Saturday January 11
ASTON VILLA (h)
Drew 1-1   HT 1-0   Att 43,210   Position **7th**
Kirkland — Carragher, Henchoz, Hyypia, Riise — Murphy,
Gerrard, Diao (Cheyrou 73), Diouf (Smicer 61) — Owen,
Mellor (Heskey 61) *Subs not used* Traore, Dudek
Booked Henchoz
Scorer **Owen 38**
Referee **P Durkin**

Odds-on to end their dismal run against Villa's poor
travellers, Liverpool get on top and take the lead
through Owen, but end up grateful that Dublin, having
equalised from the penalty spot after Hyypia's foul on
Barry, misses three clear chances to secure Villa's first
league win on the road.

Saturday January 18
SOUTHAMPTON (a)
Won 1-0   HT 1-0   Att 32,104   Position **6th**
Kirkland — Carragher, Henchoz, Hyypia, Traore — Diouf,
Gerrard, Murphy, Riise — Heskey, Owen *Subs not used*
Dudek, Smicer, Biscan, Cheyrou, Baros
Scorer **Heskey 14**
Report page 131

Tuesday January 21
SHEFFIELD UNITED (h)
Worthington Cup, semi-final, 2nd leg
Won 2-0 (aet; win 3-2 on agg)   HT 1-0   Att 43,837
Details page 338

Sunday January 26
CRYSTAL PALACE (a)
FA Cup, 4th rnd
Drew 0-0   HT 0-0   Att 26,054
Kirkland (Dudek 25) — Carragher, Hyypia, Traore, Riise
— Diouf (Biscan 86), Gerrard, Murphy, Cheyrou (Diao 90)
— Heskey, Owen *Subs not used* Baros, Mellor *Booked*
Cheyrou, Carragher
Referee **R Styles**

Liverpool pay a high price for their place in the
fifth-round draw, Kirkland suffering medial knee
ligament damage in an accidental collision with Adebola
that will rule him out for the season. Heskey, with a
timely flick of the boot, ensures that Dudek, Kirkland's
replacement, is not beaten by Popovic's header.

PLAYER OF THE SEASON
Jerzy Dudek

So many fine players were at some
point or another hugely disappointing
— but as we all know, the mistakes
made by a goalkeeper are more
obvious and more humiliating. Dudek
was far from alone in finding himself
flapping about, but he was isolated
by his manager in the degree to
which he was punished for his errors.
His dignity in despair and the manner
in which he rallied to the cause when
Chris Kirkland, his replacement, was
hurt were impressive. Man of the
match in Cardiff, he was man of the
season for Liverpool.
Alyson Rudd

STATS AND FACTS

● Michael Owen scored four for Liverpool away to West Bromwich Albion in April, which was only one fewer than Albion's joint top scorers, Danny Dichio and Scott Dobie, managed all season in the Premiership.

● In the autumn, they lost four league games in a row for the first time since 1993.

● Since 1980, Liverpool have won 14 of the 18 domestic and European finals in which they have played.

● Liverpool are unbeaten in 35 home games against West Ham United.

● Having not lost a two-goal lead at Anfield since their 2-2 FA Cup draw against Brighton & Hove Albion on January 26, 1991 (a period of 304 home matches), Liverpool did so twice in successive home games in September, against Newcastle United and Birmingham City.

● Never before in a fixture first played in 1894 has the first Merseyside derby of the campaign come so late in the season as the meeting on December 22 at Anfield.

● Liverpool have finished above Everton in the table every year since 1965 except for the latter's title triumphs of 1970, 1985 and 1987.

● Michael Owen and Emile Heskey scored in the same home match for the first time when Fulham were beaten 2-0 in April 2003.

● For the second successive season Liverpool won 6-0 away to a side relegated at the end of the campaign — they beat West Bromwich Albion in April and beat Ipswich Town just over a year earlier.

● Liverpool and Manchester United have each managed eight league titles in 11 seasons, missing out in the third, sixth and tenth years of that period (Liverpool from 1975-76 to 1985-86; United from 1992-93 to 2002-03).

Bill Edgar

GOALSCORERS

	Prem	FAC	WC	Euro	Total
M Baros	9	-	2	1	12
P Berger	-	-	1	-	1
B Cheyrou	-	-	-	1	1
S Diao	1	-	-	1	2
E-H Diouf	3	-	3 (1p)	-	6 (1p)
S Gerrard	5	-	2	-	7
D Hamann	2	-	-	-	2
E Heskey	6	-	-	3	9
S Hyypia	3	-	-	2	5
N Mellor	-	-	1	-	1
D Murphy	7 (2p)	1 (p)	2	2	12 (3p)
M Owen	19 (2p)	-	2	7	28 (2p)
J A Riise	6	-	-	-	6
V Smicer	-	-	-	1	1

Wednesday January 29
ARSENAL (h)
Drew 2-2   HT 0-1   Att 43,668   Position 6th
Dudek — Carragher, Henchoz, Hyypia, Riise — Diouf (Baros 82), Gerrard, Murphy (Diao 79), Cheyrou (Smicer 69) — Heskey, Owen *Subs not used* Arphexad, Traore *Booked* Diouf
Scorers **Riise 52, Heskey 90**
Referee **M Halsey**

With Sir Alex Ferguson sitting uncomfortably at Anfield, a Henry-inspired Arsenal are twice ahead through Pires and Bergkamp and about to open up a seven-point lead at the top. Heskey, though, profits from the award of a disputed corner to head a stoppage-time equaliser.

Sunday February 2
WEST HAM UNITED (a)
Won 3-0   HT 2-0   Att 35,033   Position 6th
Dudek — Carragher, Henchoz, Hyypia, Riise — Diouf, Gerrard, Murphy (Hamman 82), Smicer (Cheyrou 78) — Heskey, Baros (Owen 72) *Subs not used* Arphexad, Traroe
Scorers **Baros 7, Gerrard 9, Heskey 67**
Report page 253

Wednesday February 5
CRYSTAL PALACE (h)
FA Cup, 4th rnd replay
Lost 0-2   HT 0-0   Att 35,109
Dudek — Carragher, Henchoz, Hyypia, Riise — Diouf, Hamann, Murphy (Baros 67), Cheyrou — Heskey, Owen *Subs not used* Traore, Biscan, Diao, Arphexad
Referee **P Dowd**

All the pressure and all the chances count for nothing as Palace stun Anfield through Gray, who thumps a fine 55th-minute goal past Dudek and, with his side now down to ten men after Freedman's elbow into Hyypia's face, forces Henchoz into conceding the own goal that seals Liverpool's fate.

Saturday February 8
MIDDLESBROUGH (h)
Drew 1-1   HT 0-1   Att 42,247   Position 6th
Dudek — Carragher, Henchoz, Hyypia, Riise — Diouf, Hamann, Murphy, Smicer (Diao 60) — Heskey (Baros ht), Owen *Subs not used* Traore, Cheyrou, Arphexad
Scorer **Riise 74**
Referee **S Bennett**

After more than 13 hours spread over ten matches since September, Middlesbrough's long wait for an away goal is over — and a fine goal it is, Geremi beating Dudek with a stunning free kick. Liverpool, though, gain a deserved point when Owen slaloms through the area to set up Riise's equaliser.

Thursday February 20
AUXERRE (a)
Uefa Cup, 4th rnd, 1st leg
Won 1-0   HT 0-0   Att 20,452
Dudek — Carragher, Henchoz (Diao 69), Hyypia, Traore — Diouf, Gerrard, Murphy, Riise — Heskey, Owen (Baros 90) *Subs not used* Babbel, Biscan, Hamann, Cheyrou, Arphexad *Booked* Diouf
Scorer **Hyypia 73**
Referee **M De Santis (Italy)**

After misses by Owen and Heskey, Hyypia shows Liverpool's forwards how to do it when he poaches the goal that gives Houllier a satisfying victory on his return to his native France and strengthens the prospect of a quarter-final showdown with Celtic.

Sunday February 23
BIRMINGHAM CITY (a)
Lost 1-2   HT 0-1   Att 29,449   Position 7th
Dudek — Carragher (Owen 63), Hyypia, Traore, Riise
— Murphy, Hamann, Diao, Cheyrou (Mellor 84) —
Heskey, Baros *Subs not used* Babbel, Arphexad, Biscan
Booked Diao
Scorer **Owen 77**
Report page 194

Thursday February 27
AUXERRE (h)
Uefa Cup, 4th rnd, 2nd leg
Won 2-0 (win 3-0 on agg)   HT 0-0   Att 34,252
Dudek — Carragher, Henchoz (Biscan 77), Hyypia,
Traore (Smicer ht) — Diouf (Hamann 62), Gerrard,
Murphy, Riise — Heskey, Owen *Subs not used* Diao,
Cheyrou, Baros, Arphexad *Booked* Traore
Scorers **Owen 67, Murphy 73**
Referee **A J Lopez Nieto (Spain)**

Liverpool pose little threat — although neither do
Auxerre — until Murphy releases Owen for the opener,
and when Murphy's long-range effort is fumbled into his
own net by Cool they are through to a quarter-final
meeting with Celtic, who edge past VfB Stuttgart earlier
in the day.

Sunday March 2
MANCHESTER UNITED
Worthington Cup, final (Cardiff)
Won 2-0   HT 1-0   Att 74,500
Details page 338

Saturday March 8
BOLTON WANDERERS (h)
Won 2-0   HT 1-0   Att 41,462   Position 6th
Dudek — Carragher, Traore, Hyypia, Riise — Gerrard
(Diao 72), Hamann — Diouf, Murphy, Smicer (Cheyrou
58) — Owen *Subs not used* Biscan, Baros, Arphexad
Scorers **Diouf 44, Owen 67**
Referee **G Barber**

With most attention focused on the FA Cup
quarter-finals, Liverpool quietly — if unconvincingly — win
the match in hand that they and Bolton have on the
rest. Owen sets up Diouf for the opener, Diouf returning
the compliment for their first home league win since
November 2.

Thursday March 13
CELTIC (a)
Uefa Cup, quarter-final, 1st leg
Drew 1-1   HT 1-1   Att 59,759
Dudek — Carragher, Traore, Hyypia, Riise — Diouf
(Biscan 90), Gerrard, Hamann, Murphy — Heskey, Owen
Subs not used Diao, Cheyrou, Smicer, Baros, Mellor,
Arphexad
Scorer **Heskey 17**
Referee **T Hauge (Norway)**

Behind within three minutes to the returning Larsson,
Liverpool edge the first leg once Heskey has dragged
them level, but the match will be remembered only for
Diouf's spat with Celtic fans at the death, the night
ending with the striker being withdrawn for his own
safety and interviewed by police.

MARKUS BABBEL
Defender
Born September 8, 1972, Munich
Ht 6ft 3in **Wt** 12st 10lb
Signed from Bayern Munich, July
2000, free

MILAN BAROS
Forward
Born October 28, 1981,
Ostrava, Czech Republic
Ht 6ft 0in **Wt** 11st 12lb
Signed from Banik Ostrava,
December 2001, £3.4m

PATRIK BERGER
Midfield
Born November 10, 1973,
Prague
Ht 6ft 1in **Wt** 12st 6lb
Signed from Borussia Dortmund,
August 1996, £3.25m

IGOR BISCAN
Defender
Born May 4, 1978, Zagreb
Ht 6ft 3in **Wt** 12st 8lb
Signed from Dynamo Zagreb,
December 2000, £3.5m

JAMIE CARRAGHER
Defender
Born January 28, 1978, Bootle
Ht 6ft 1in **Wt** 13st 0lb
Signed from trainee, October
1996

BRUNO CHEYROU
Midfield
Born May 10, 1978,
Suresnes, France
Ht 6ft 1in **Wt** 12st 6lb
Signed from Lille, July 2002,
£3.7m

SALIF DIAO
Midfield
Born February 10, 1977,
Kadougou, Senegal
Ht 6ft 0in **Wt** 11st 5lb
Signed from Sedan, August 2002,
£5m

EL-HADJI DIOUF
Midfield
Born January 15, 1981,
Dakar, Senegal
Ht 5ft 9in **Wt** 11st 8lb
Signed from Lens, June 2002,
£10m

JERZY DUDEK
Goalkeeper
Born March 23, 1973,
Rybnik, Poland
Ht 6ft 2in **Wt** 12st 10lb
Signed from Feyenoord, August
2001, £4.85m

Jamie Carragher

STEVEN GERRARD
Midfield
Born May 30, 1980, Huyton
Ht 6ft 2in **Wt** 12st 4lb
Signed from trainee, February 1998

DIETMAR HAMANN
Midfield
Born August 27, 1973, Waldsasson, Germany
Ht 6ft 3in **Wt** 12st 2lb
Signed from Newcastle United, July 1999, £8m

STEPHANE HENCHOZ
Defender
Born September 7, 1974, Billens, Switzerland
Ht 6ft 1in **Wt** 12st 10lb
Signed from Blackburn Rovers, July 1999, £3.75m

EMILE HESKEY
Forward
Born January 11, 1978, Leicester
Ht 6ft 2in **Wt** 13st 12lb
Signed from Leicester City, March 2000, £11m

SAMI HYYPIA
Defender
Born October 7, 1973, Porvoo, Finland
Ht 6ft 4in **Wt** 13st 5lb
Signed from Willem II, Holland, £2.6m

CHRIS KIRKLAND
Goalkeeper
Born May 2, 1981, Leicester
Ht 6ft 3in **Wt** 11st 7lb
Signed from Coventry City, August 2001, £6m

NEIL MELLOR
Forward
Born November 4, 1982, Sheffield
Ht 5ft 11in **Wt** 11st 11lb
Signed from trainee, July 2002

DANNY MURPHY
Midfield
Born March 18, 1977, Chester
Ht 5ft 9in **Wt** 10st 8lb
Signed from Crewe Alexandra, July 1997, £1.5m

Sami Hyypia

Sunday March 16
TOTTENHAM HOTSPUR (a)
Won 3-2 **HT 0-0** Att **36,077** Position **6th**
Dudek — Carragher, Traore, Hyypia, Riise — Diouf, Gerrard, Hamann (Diao 87), Murphy — Heskey, Owen
Subs not used Arphexad, Baros, Smicer, Biscan
Booked Hamann
Scorers **Owen 51, Heskey 72, Gerrard 82**
Report page 158

Thursday March 20
CELTIC (h)
Uefa Cup, quarter-final, 2nd leg
Lost 0-2 (lose 1-3 on agg) **HT 0-1** Att **44,238**
Dudek — Carragher, Traore, Hyypia, Riise — Murphy, Gerrard, Hamann (Baros 56) — Heskey, Owen
Subs not used Biscan, Diao, Berger, Cheyrou, Mellor, Arphexad
Referee **M Merk (Germany)**

With the disgraced Diouf sensibly withdrawn from the firing line, Liverpool lack the firepower to trouble an improved Celtic, Heskey wasting their one real chance, and Martin O'Neill's side secure a deserved triumph through Thompson's free kick just before half-time and Hartson's fine clincher.

Sunday March 23
LEEDS UNITED (h)
Won 3-1 **HT 2-1** Att **43,021** Position **5th**
Dudek — Carragher, Traore, Hyypia, Riise — Diouf, Gerrard, Hamann (Diao 79), Murphy — Heskey (Baros 79), Owen *Subs not used* Biscan, Smicer, Arphexad
Scorers **Owen 12, Murphy 20, Gerrard 73**
Referee **A D'Urso**

Three days after Terry Venables's brief and troubled reign at Elland Road ends in the sack, Peter Reid — given eight games in which to stake a claim for the job — sees his new side well beaten as Liverpool put their European exit behind them. Murphy's goal, a superb shot into the top far corner, is the pick of their three.

Saturday April 5
MANCHESTER UNITED (a)
Lost 0-4 **HT 0-1** Att **67,639** Position **5th**
Dudek — Carragher, Traore, Hyypia, Riise — Murphy (Cheyrou 80), Gerrard, Hamann, Diouf (Smicer 71) — Heskey, Baros (Biscan 6) *Subs not used* Arphexad, Mellor *Booked* Diouf, Gerrard, Murphy *Sent off* Hyypia 4
Report page 51

Saturday April 12
FULHAM (h)
Won 2-0 **HT 1-0** Att **42,120** Position **6th**
Dudek — Carragher, Hyypia, Traore, Riise — Heskey, Gerrard, Hamann, Smicer (Cheyrou 90) — Owen, Baros
Subs not used Arphexad, Biscan, Diao, Mellor *Booked* Heskey
Scorers **Heskey 36, Owen 59**
Referee **A Wiley**

"We're right in it," Taylor, the Fulham goalkeeper, admits after another toothless display sees his side dragged ever nearer the relegation zone. Heskey and Owen, the latter after missing a far easier chance, complete a routine victory for Liverpool, for whom the Merseyside derby is now looming large.

Saturday April 19
EVERTON (a)
Won 2-1 HT 1-0 Att **40,162** Position **5th**
Dudek — Carragher, Biscan (Diao 9), Traore, Riise —
Heskey, Gerrard, Hamann, Murphy — Owen, Baros
(Diouf 66) *Subs not used* Cheyrou, Smicer, Arphexad
Booked Gerrard, Baros, Hamann
Scorers **Owen 31, Murphy 64**
Report page 123

Monday April 21
CHARLTON ATHLETIC (h)
Won 2-1 HT 0-0 Att **42,010** Position **5th**
Dudek — Carragher, Hyypia, Traore, Riise — Diouf
(Cheyrou 74), Gerrard, Hamann, Murphy (Smicer 74)
— Owen, Heskey (Baros ht) *Subs not used* Arphexad,
Diao
Scorers **Hyypia 86, Gerrard 90**
Referee **S Dunn**

The late, late show. Behind after Bartlett punishes
Traore's bad slip, Liverpool level through Hyypia four
minutes from time, seem to preserve a point when
Dudek saves brilliantly from Euell's header, and then
take all three in stoppage time when Gerrard sends a
low shot under Kiely as Charlton lament their poor
fortune.

Saturday April 26
WEST BROMWICH ALBION (a)
Won 6-0 HT 1-0 Att **27,128** Position **5th**
Dudek — Carragher, Hyypia, Traore, Riise (Diao 79) —
Diouf (Heskey 68), Gerrard, Hamann, Murphy (Cheyrou
83) — Baros, Owen *Subs not used* Smicer, Arphexad
Booked Traore
Scorers **Owen 15, 49, 61, 67, Baros 47, 84**
Report page 268

Saturday May 3
MANCHESTER CITY (h)
Lost 1-2 HT 0-0 Att **44,220** Position **5th**
Dudek — Carragher, Hyypia, Traore, Riise — Murphy,
Gerrard, Hamann (Cheyrou 78), Diouf (Heskey 78) —
Baros, Owen *Subs not used* Arphexad, Diao, Biscan
Booked Heskey, Hamann
Scorer **Baros 59**
Referee **N Barry**

Denied two possible penalties and thwarted by the
brilliance of Schmeichel, whose save from Diouf almost
defies comprehension, Liverpool are sunk by the striker
they rejected, Anelka equalising from the spot and then
belting home the stoppage-time volley that leaves his
old club needing to win away to Chelsea on the last day
to qualify for the Champions League.

Sunday May 11
CHELSEA (a)
Lost 1-2 HT 1-2 Att **41,911** Position **5th**
Dudek — Carragher, Hyypia, Traore, Riise (Cheyrou 75)
— Diouf (Berger 63), Diao (Heskey ht), Gerrard, Murphy
— Baros, Owen *Subs not used* Arphexad, Biscan *Booked*
Gerrard *Sent off* Gerrard 90
Scorer **Hyypia 11**
Report page 88

JON OSTEMOBOR
Defender
Born March 23, 1983, Liverpool
Signed from trainee, July 2002

MICHAEL OWEN
Forward
Born December 14, 1979,
Chester
Ht 5ft 9in **Wt** 11st 2lb
Signed from trainee, December
1996

JOHN ARNE RIISE
Defender
Born September 24, 1980,
Molde, Norway
Ht 6ft 1in **Wt** 12st 6lb
Signed from AS Monaco, July
2001, £4m

VLADIMIR SMICER
Midfield
Born May 24, 1973, Decin,
Czech Republic
Ht 5ft 11in **Wt** 11st 3lb
Signed from Lens, July 1999,
£3.75m

DJIMI TRAORE
Defender
Born March 1, 1980, Paris
Ht 6ft 3in **Wt** 13st 10lb
Signed from Laval, France,
February 1999, £550,000

GREGORY VIGNAL
Defender
Born July 19, 1981, Montpellier
Ht 6ft 0in **Wt** 12st 4lb
Signed from Montpellier,
September 2000, £500,000

JOHN WELSH
Defender
Born January 1, 1984, Liverpool
Signed from trainee, July 2002

ABEL XAVIER
Defender
Born November 30, 1972,
Nampula, Mozambique
Ht 6ft 2in **Wt** 13st 6lb
Signed from Everton, January
2002, £800,000

John Arne Riise

BLACKBURN ROVERS

ARTE ET LABORE

PREMIERSHIP

	P	W	D	L	F	A	Pts
Man Utd	38	25	8	5	74	34	83
Arsenal	38	23	9	6	85	42	78
Newcastle	38	21	6	11	63	48	69
Chelsea	38	19	10	9	68	38	67
Liverpool	38	18	10	10	61	41	64
Blackburn	**38**	**16**	**12**	**10**	**52**	**43**	**60**
Everton	38	17	8	13	48	49	59
Southampton	38	13	13	12	43	46	52
Man City	38	15	6	17	47	54	51
Tottenham	38	14	8	16	51	62	50
Middlesbro	38	13	10	15	48	44	49
Charlton	38	14	7	17	45	56	49
Birmingham	38	13	9	16	41	49	48
Fulham	38	13	9	16	41	50	48
Leeds	38	14	5	19	58	57	47
Aston Villa	38	12	9	17	42	47	45
Bolton	38	10	14	14	41	51	44
West Ham	38	10	12	16	42	59	42
West Brom	38	6	8	24	29	65	26
Sunderland	38	4	7	27	21	65	19

FA CUP
Fourth round

WORTHINGTON CUP
Semi-finals

UEFA CUP
Second round

Damien Duff celebrates his goal at The Hawthorns in September

THE GAMES

John Dawkins

Saturday August 17
SUNDERLAND (h)
Drew 0-0 HT 0-0 Att **27,122** Position **7th**
Friedel — Neill, Taylor, Short, Johansson — Gillespie (Hignett 80), Dunn, Tugay, Duff — Cole, Yorke Subs *not used* Grabbi, Hakan Unsal, Berg, Kelly Booked Cole
Referee **D Elleray**

The much-vaunted former Manchester United partnership of Cole and Yorke is reformed, but to little effect on opening day, when the nearest thing to a goal comes as Friedel keeps out Reyna's long-range effort for Sunderland. The visiting team play with just one up front and are happy with a point.

Saturday August 24
BIRMINGHAM CITY (a)
Won 1-0 HT 1-0 Att **28,563** Position **9th**
Friedel — Neill, Taylor, Short, Johansson — Dunn, Flitcroft, Tugay (Berg 58), Duff — Cole, Yorke Subs *not used* Kelly, Grabbi, Hignett, Hakan Unsal Booked Johansson, Berg
Scorer **Yorke 13**
Report page 186

Wednesday August 28
LIVERPOOL (h)
Drew 2-2 HT 1-1 Att **29,207** Position **7th**
Friedel — Neill, Taylor, Short (Grabbi 82), Johansson — Dunn, Flitcroft, Tugay, Duff — Cole, Yorke Subs *not used* Kelly, Hignett, Mahon, Berg Booked Cole, Yorke, Grabbi
Scorers **Dunn 16, Grabbi 83**
Referee **S Bennett**

Graeme Souness, banished to the stands for his protests over an alleged elbowing offence by Heskey, sees Grabbi head an equaliser within a minute of coming on, Liverpool having recovered from Dunn's opener to lead through Murphy's fine shot and Riise's header in a thriller.

Saturday August 31
MIDDLESBROUGH (a)
Lost 0-1 HT 0-0 Att **28,270** Position **10th**
Friedel — Neill, Taylor, Short, Johansson — Thompson (Tugay 82), Flitcroft, Dunn, Duff — Yorke, Cole Subs *not used* Kelly, Hignett, Grabbi, Berg Booked Johansson, Tugay, Thompson
Report page 162

Wednesday September 11
CHELSEA (h)
Lost 2-3 HT 2-1 Att **22,999** Position **14th**
Friedel — Neill, Taylor, Short, Johansson (Grabbi 81) — Thompson, Flitcroft, Tugay (Gillespie 65), Dunn — Cole, Yorke Subs *not used* Hignett, Berg, Kelly Booked Johansson, Thompson
Scorers **Dunn 18 (pen), Thompson 45**
Referee **M Riley**

Twice behind in the first half, through Dunn's penalty and Thompson's 20-yard shot, Chelsea maintain their unbeaten start thanks to the genius of Zola. A mis-hit shot by Gronkjaer, who had scored earlier, allows the little Italian to level with a header and he cuts in from the left to curl in a delicious eightieth-minute winner.

THE END-OF-TERM REPORT makes for satisfying reading for Blackburn Rovers supporters: sixth place in the Premiership, another season in Europe to savour, a stout defence of the Worthington Cup won at Cardiff in February 2002 and evidence that the acclaimed academy at Brockhall is bearing more fruit with the under-19 team winning the national cup competition. Ewood Park has rarely been happier since the halcyon days of 1995 but, looking back over the past nine months, Graeme Souness might reflect on an opportunity missed.

The intervening years since that glorious championship-winning season have certainly been a rollercoaster ride. Rewind four seasons, when they were relegated amid acrimony in the boardroom and indifference on the pitch, and the club that the late Jack Walker rebuilt seemed to be heading for oblivion. Or worse still, Burnley.

Fast-forward to the summer of 2003 and the transformation has been remarkable. Promotion was achieved at the second attempt, the following year the Worthington Cup was secured in a wonderful day at the Millennium Stadium, the club's first cup success in 74 years, and on the final day of this season Rovers snatched the last Uefa Cup place from a faltering and overachieving Everton thanks to a 4-0 victory away to Tottenham Hotspur. Not bad, as Souness said, for "a small club from East Lancashire".

Souness's tongue may have been in his cheek when he made that remark, but the Scot deserves much of the credit for turning the club around.

Appointed in early 2000 — albeit not as first choice by the board, who had initially targeted Sunderland's Peter Reid, and not universally welcomed by sections of the Ewood faithful — to sort out the mess left by Brian Kidd's disastrous tenure, Souness has won over the doubters by returning Rovers to the pinnacle of the English game that they dominated briefly under Kenny Dalglish nearly a decade ago. Even the metropolitan-based media, so disparaging of Walker's "big-spending Blackburn" when they "bought" the title, have gone soft on Rovers and praised them for the quality of their football this season.

Convention has it that managers mould teams in their own image, but unlikely as it may seem, for those who remember him 20 years ago as the hard-man assassin in Liverpool's midfield, Souness has assembled one of the most skilful and talented squads in Blackburn's history. Dalglish's championship-winning team were resilient, physical, and when they had to be, downright bloody-minded, but, man for man, they would struggle to match Souness's present side for sheer ability. From Brad Friedel, the Premiership's

Hugs all round after another goal in the last-day rout of Tottenham Hotspur

goalkeeper of the year — to Martin Taylor in defence, to Tugay in midfield and to Andrew Cole and Damien Duff in attack — Blackburn have players coveted by Premiership managers. The apogee this season came away to Celtic in October when Rovers, with a scintillating display of passing and movement, silenced 60,000 Glaswegian voices when they gave the Scottish champions the run-around in the Uefa Cup.

That Blackburn lost the match to a Henrik Larsson goal in the final minutes — and the tie overall after an ineffectual performance in the second leg at Ewood — perhaps sums up 2002-03. After an encouraging start, inconsistency, and poor results against the lower teams, particularly when the team's form dipped in mid-season, were extremely costly. Victories over Manchester United and Newcastle United at home, Chelsea away and, best of all, a famous double triumph over Arsenal, have been tempered by the surrender of four points to West Ham United and Sunderland while home points were dropped against the likes of West Bromwich Albion and Bolton Wanderers.

Although earning another crack at the Uefa Cup was a reason for celebration, supporters, players and manager alike expressed their disappointment that Rovers were just out of reach of a Champions League place. After maintaining all season that survival was his sole aim, Souness dropped his guard after the triumph at White Hart Lane and admitted that with better results against the weaker teams and better luck with injuries — Matt Jansen missed virtually the whole season, while Duff, David Dunn and Henning Berg were out for large parts of the campaign — his team would be competing with the big boys in a "different European competition" in August. The fact that a workmanlike side such as Chelsea did qualify for the Champions League proved that this was not a case of Souness indulging in delusions of grandeur.

Sunday September 15
MANCHESTER CITY (a)
Drew 2-2   HT 1-0   Att **34,130**   Position **13th**
Friedel — Taylor, Berg, Short, Neill — Gillespie (Mahon 78), Flitcroft, Dunn, Thompson (Tugay 85) — Cole (Grabbi 56), Yorke *Subs not used* Kelly, Johansson
Booked Neill, Gillespie, Grabbi
Scorers **Thompson 25, Cole 54**
Report page 139

Thursday September 19
CSKA SOFIA (h)
Uefa Cup, 1st rnd, 1st leg
Drew 1-1   HT 1-1   Att **18,300**
Friedel — Neill, Taylor, Todd, Johansson — Hignett, Danns (Berg 70), Tugay, Dunn — Grabbi (Ostenstad 62), Yorke (Gillespie 12) *Subs not used* Mahon, Curtis, Douglas, Kelly *Booked* Danns
Scorer **Grabbi 29**
Referee **B Coue (France)**

Deprived of Yorke, who pulls a hamstring early on, and then a goal behind to Dimitrov after 23 minutes, a weakened Blackburn side recover to earn a draw against the Bulgarians, who finish with ten men after the 75th-minute dismissal of Tomovski for a second bookable offence.

Sunday September 22
LEEDS UNITED (h)
Won 1-0   HT 1-0   Att **25,415**   Position **9th**
Friedel — Taylor, Berg, Short, Neill — Tugay — Gillespie, Flitcroft, Dunn (Danns 90), Thompson — Ostenstad (Grabbi 67) *Subs not used* Hignett, Johansson, Kelly *Booked* Neill
Scorer **Flitcroft 24**
Referee **G Poll**

The breaks that Blackburn feel are overdue arrive in force against Leeds, with Gillespie getting away with a clear pull on Harte's shirt before setting up the winner for Flitcroft and Friedel saving Smith's weak second-half penalty, awarded for handball by Berg.

Monday September 30
WEST BROMWICH ALBION (a)
Won 2-0   HT 0-0   Att **25,170**   Position **8th**
Friedel — Taylor, Berg, Johansson, Neill — Tugay — Thompson, Flitcroft (Cole 19), Dunn (Gillespie 60), Duff — Ostenstad (Yorke ht) *Subs not used* Kelly, Todd *Booked* Johansson
Scorers **Yorke 72 (pen), Duff 76**
Report page 259

Thursday October 3
CSKA SOFIA (a)
Uefa Cup, 1st rnd, 2nd leg
Drew 3-3   (aet; 4-4 on agg; win on away goals)
HT 1-0   Att **21,000**
Friedel — Taylor, Berg, Johansson, Neill — Thompson, Tugay (Gillespie 62), Dunn, Duff — Cole (Mahon 85), Ostenstad (Grabbi 60) *Subs not used* Kelly, Todd, Hignett, Danns *Booked* Neill, Ostenstad
Scorers **Thompson 30, Ostenstad 56, Duff 58**
Referee **A Yelet (Israel)**

Three-nil up and cruising with more than an hour gone, Blackburn are forced to hang on to progress on the away-goals rule after CSKA stage an unlikely fightback, forcing extra time with an 88th-minute penalty conceded by Neill. The Israeli referee needs to be escorted from the pitch by riot police after dismissing Dimitriov for pushing Thompson.

Sunday October 6
TOTTENHAM HOTSPUR (h)
Lost 1-2   HT 0-1   Att 26,203   Position 10th
Friedel — Taylor, Berg (Gillespie ht), Johansson, Neill
— Thompson, Tugay, Flitcroft, Dunn (Grabbi 69) —
Cole (Ostenstad ht), Duff *Subs not used* Kelly, Todd
Booked Berg
Scorer **Ostenstad 59**
Referee **A D'Urso**

Keane, after four games without a goal, is off and
running with a ferocious shot to give Spurs an early
lead, and though Ostenstad levels just before the hour,
a Blackburn team exhausted from their midweek Uefa
Cup exertions, according to Graeme Souness, are
beaten in the 89th minute when Redknapp's mis-hit
shot loops in for the winner.

Saturday October 19
NEWCASTLE UNITED (h)
Won 5-2   HT 2-1   Att 27,307   Position 8th
Friedel — Neill, Taylor, Berg, Johansson — Gillespie
(Tugay 64), Flitcroft, Dunn, Thompson — Yorke
(Jansen 64), Ostenstad (Grabbi 78) *Subs not used*
Curtis, Kelly
Scorers **Dunn 5 (pen), 8, Taylor 55, 74,
Griffin 65 (og)**
Referee **A Wiley**

Shearer's 200th and 201st goals of his club career are
of little consolation to him or Newcastle. Playing with
ten men from the fourth minute after Dabizas
concedes a penalty for handling on the line, they are
swamped by a rampant Blackburn, for whom Taylor
grabs his first goals for the club.

Saturday October 26
ARSENAL (a)
Won 2-1   HT 1-1   Att 38,064   Position 7th
Friedel — Neill, Taylor, Berg, Johansson — Thompson,
Tugay (Gillespie 66), Flitcroft, Dunn (Jansen 86)
— Yorke, Ostenstad (Short 86) *Subs not used* Kelly,
Grabbi *Booked* Johansson, Flitcroft, Ostenstad *Sent off*
Flitcroft 79
Scorers **Edu 6 (og), Yorke 51**
Report page 57

Thursday October 31
CELTIC (a)
Uefa Cup, 2nd rnd, 1st leg
Lost 0-1   HT 0-0   Att 59,553
Friedel — Neill, Taylor, Short, Johansson — Thompson,
Tugay, Flitcroft, Duff (Dunn 66) — Yorke, Ostenstad
(Cole ht) *Subs not used* Kelly, Jansen, Grabbi, Gillespie,
Douglas *Booked* Neill
Referee **H Albrecht (Germany)**

Blackburn win the first engagement in the so-called
Battle of Britain in all departments — except where it
matters. Celtic are outplayed for long periods but earn
a precious advantage when Larsson strikes with five
minutes to go. It is his 22nd goal in European
competition, a record north of the border.

MATCH OF THE SEASON

Blackburn Rovers 5   Newcastle United 2
Ewood Park, Saturday October 19 2002
Rick Broadbent

THE STORY SO FAR: England's plan for world domination has
been jeopardised by a maverick band of Eastern Europeans. The
mysterious Svengali at HQ has five months to recover the magic
formula, but his position has been undermined by his defence minister who has been responsible for several leaks. Who can save him
now? "Not me," Alan Shearer says. England's premier striker of
modern times stated the case for international retirement as he
notched his 300th and 301st club goals.

"I miss the thrill of going out and hearing the anthems, but I
don't miss being away from home for ten days at a time," he said
after a ripsnorter on his old stomping ground. "I definitely made the
right decision and it's probably given me another year on my
career."

The Toon Army chanted "England's number one," as Shearer's
goals, a typically assured penalty and an exquisite, if unmarked,
header, dragged ten-men Newcastle United back to 2-2 shortly after
the break. "Couldn't do any worse than Seaman," one wag opined.
Shearer, himself, gave his support to the England goalkeeper. "I've
had criticism myself and it certainly gave me something to prove to
people," he said. "David's big enough to deal with it and, until someone comes and takes the jersey off him, he's still England's No 1.
People have had their chance but nobody's taken it."

Shearer's landmark led to glowing appraisals. "Historical,
marvellous, colossal," Sir Bobby Robson said as he thumbed his
thesaurus. Graeme Souness's eulogy was just as heartfelt. "He's a
very special player, the best British striker I've seen in my time."

It was a tale of two strikers, of old England and new, an anodyne
hero and a part-time singer who spent four days in a coma after a
road accident in Rome. If Shearer was glum-faced after a drubbing,
the presence of Matt Jansen provided perspective. He made his
return to a standing ovation after overcoming the head injuries he
sustained on his summer holiday. "I've only played one reserve
game so didn't expect to come back this soon," Jansen said. "The
reaction of the fans was brilliant but it's still rehabilitation for me."

Jansen, who was knocking on the England door last season, has
made a remarkable recovery. "There was genuine fear that he would
not play again," Souness said. "For someone who loves playing so
much that would have been like cutting off his leg."

His comeback added another chapter to an enduring romance.
Blackburn's games these days are true bodice rippers — all passion,
twists and lusty midfield players with their hearts set on England.
They are a neutral's dream. Full of flair and foibles, they have
squandered leads against Liverpool, Chelsea, Manchester City and

Matt Jansen made a surprise comeback in the thrashing of Newcastle United

Sunday November 3
ASTON VILLA (h)
Drew 0-0 HT 0-0 Att 23,004 Position 7th
Friedel — Neill, Taylor, Short, Johansson — Thompson
(Tugay 76), Flitcroft, Dunn (Gillespie 65), Duff — Yorke
(Ostenstad 65), Cole *Subs not used* Grabbi, Kelly
Booked Duff
Referee **M Dean**

Graeme Souness blames tiredness — again — for
Blackburn's lacklustre display, although had Cole's
header not been pushed on to a post by Enckelman
early on, the match might have improved. Aston Villa,
though, would have won but for Dublin's shocking miss
in the 75th minute, when he inexplicably shoots wide of
an open goal.

Wednesday November 6
WALSALL (h)
Worthington Cup, 3rd rnd
Drew 2-2 (aet; win 5-4 on pens) HT 1-0 Att 9,486
Kelly — Pelzer (McEveley 30), Todd, Curtis, Johansson
— Gillespie, Dunn, Danns (Douglas 63), Mahon —
Jansen (Richards 80), Grabbi *Subs not used*
Ostenstad, Robinson
Scorers **Grabbi 45 (pen)**, Roper 105 (og)
Referee **N Barry**

After the sides swap penalties in normal time,
Blackburn's "reserves" go behind in extra time and
need Roper's own goal to prevent defeat to the
Nationwide League first division side. Having forced a
shoot-out, though, Kelly makes the decisive save from
Wrack to put Blackburn through.

Saturday November 9
SOUTHAMPTON (a)
Drew 1-1 HT 0-1 Att 30,059 Position 7th
Friedel — Neill, Taylor (Todd 63), Short, Curtis
(Ostenstad 68) — Gillespie, Tugay, Dunn, Thompson —
Cole, Yorke *Subs not used* Kelly, Jansen, Grabbi
Booked Tugay *Sent off* Tugay 76
Scorer **Cole 90**
Report page 129

Thursday November 14
CELTIC (h)
Uefa Cup, 2nd rnd, 2nd leg
Lost 0-2 (lose 3-0 on agg) HT 0-1 Att 29,698
Friedel — Neill, Short, Johansson, Curtis (Gillespie ht)
— Thompson, Tugay, Dunn, Duff — Cole, Yorke (Jansen
64) *Subs not used* Todd, Grabbi, Ostenstad, Douglas,
Kelly *Booked* Neill
Referee **C Bolognini (Italy)**

The roles are reversed in the second Uefa Cup meeting
— Celtic are much the better side this time — but not
the scoreline. Martin O'Neill's side complete a
comfortable passage, with Larsson on target again in
the fifteenth minute and — who else? — Sutton rubbing
it in with a 68th-minute header on his Ewood Park
return.

Sunday November 17
EVERTON (h)
Lost 0-1   HT 0-1   Att 26,496   Position 8th
Friedel — Neill, Short, Johansson, Curtis (Yorke 69) —
Thompson, Tugay, Dunn, Duff — Cole, Ostenstad *Subs
not used* Jansen, Grabbi, Todd, Robinson *Booked* Short,
Johansson, Ostenstad
Referee **G Poll**

Carsley's pass, Campbell's nineteenth-minute goal,
and Everton are on their way to a fourth successive
1-0 league win, their best run since the heady days of
1986-87. A bad week for Blackburn is completed when
Cole's lob in the last few seconds is saved by Wright.

Sunday November 24
CHARLTON ATHLETIC (a)
Lost 1-3   HT 0-0   Att 26,152   Position 9th
Kelly — Curtis (Grabbi 78), Taylor, Short, Neill —
Thompson (Gillespie 87), Todd, Dunn, Duff — Cole,
Ostenstad (Yorke 53) *Subs not used* Robinson,
Jansen *Booked* Todd
Scorer **Thompson 60**
Report page 178

Saturday November 30
FULHAM (h)
Won 2-1   HT 1-0   Att 21,096   Position 8th
Friedel — Neill, Short, Todd, Johansson — Thompson,
Tugay, Dunn (Douglas 90), Duff — Cole, Yorke *Subs
not used* Kelly, Jansen, Grabbi, Ostenstad *Booked*
Dunn
Scorers **Yorke 35, Brevett 77 (og)**
Referee **P Dowd**

Blackburn's luckiest win of the season, Graeme
Souness admits. Ahead through Yorke, they are pegged
back by Marlet and need Friedel's 68th-minute penalty
save from the same player to stay on terms before
Fulham gift them the winner, Van der Sar hitting
Brevett with his clearance for a decisive own goal.

Wednesday December 4
ROTHERHAM UNITED (h)
Worthington Cup, 4th rnd
Won 4-0   HT 4-0   Att 11,220
Kelly — Neill, Johansson, Todd, McEveley — Thompson,
Tugay (Flitcroft 62), Danns, Duff — Cole (Grabbi 73),
Yorke (Ostenstad 73) *Subs not used* Gillespie, Robinson
Booked Thompson
Goals **Yorke 12, 39, Cole 16, Duff 43**
Referee **M Messias**

Hakan Sukur is paraded on the pitch before kick-off and
his arrival seems to act as a spur to Rovers in a
rampant first half. Yorke begins the fun and Cole's goal
means that the former Old Trafford team-mates have
got on the scoresheet together for the first time since
being reunited.

Saturday December 7
BOLTON WANDERERS (a)
Drew 1-1   HT 0-1   Att 24,556   Position 9th
Friedel — Neill, Taylor, Short, McEveley (Johansson 52)
— Thompson, Flitcroft, Dunn (Tugay 11), Duff — Cole,
Yorke *Subs not used* Kelly, Ostenstad, Todd *Booked*
Tugay, Thompson
Scorer **Short 90**
Report page 238

Egil Ostenstad adds to the discomfort of the Newcastle defence

CSKA Sofia. Even against a side reduced to ten men for 87 minutes
after Nikos Dabizas was sent off for handball, they dithered their
way to a happy ending. After David Dunn's brace was cancelled out
by Shearer, Martin Taylor restored the advantage with a neat half-
volley. Shay Given then spilt Keith Gillespie's header against Andy
Griffin's legs and Taylor headed a fifth, but neither Celtic nor
Juventus will be unduly worried.

On the plus side, David Thompson's form continues to dazzle
while Shearer still looks good enough for a bigger stage.

Given his superb record at Blackburn — 112 goals in 136 games
— the reception he received from the home contingent was
shameful. "They don't boo bad players do they?" he suggested.
"They do at Sunderland," came the reply and, with that, even
Shearer departed Ewood Park with a smile on his face.

BLACKBURN ROVERS (4-4-2): B Friedel — N-E Johansson, H Berg, M Taylor, L Neill — K Gillespie (sub:
Tugay, 65min), G Flitcroft, D Dunn, D Thompson — D Yorke (sub: M Jansen, 65), E Ostenstad (sub: C
Grabbi, 78). **Substitutes not used:** J Curtis, A Kelly.
NEWCASTLE UNITED (4-4-2): S Given — A Hughes (sub: O Bernard, 80), A O'Brien, N Dabizas, A Grif-
fin (sub: T Bramble, 75) — N Solano, J Jenas, G Speed, L Robert (sub: H Viana, 75) — C Bellamy, A
Shearer. **Substitutes not used:** S Ameobi, S Harper. **Booked:** Robert, Speed. **Sent off:** Dabizas.
Referee: A Wiley.

THE MANAGER

Graeme Souness

After a patchy record with Liverpool, Southampton and Galatasaray, Souness has found the perfect niche at Ewood. He had a reputation for being a tea-cup thrower, but the new, mellow Souness has quietly steered the club from the lower reaches of the first division into the country's top six. He still enjoys the occasional confrontation — Cole, Yorke, Sukur and Dunn all had disputes during the season — but after the weak leadership of the Hodgson-Kidd era, Rovers needed strong management.
John Dawkins

APPEARANCES

	Prem	FAC	WC	Euro	Total
H Berg	15 (1)	1	-	1 (1)	17 (2)
S I Bjornebye	-	-	1	-	1
A Cole	32 (2)	2	4	2 (1)	40 (3)
J Curtis	5	-	1	1	7
N Danns	1 (1)	1	2	1	5 (1)
J Douglas	0 (1)	1 (2)	0 (1)	-	1 (4)
D Duff	26	-	2	3	31
D Dunn	26 (2)	2	2	3 (1)	33 (3)
G Flitcroft	33	2	3 (1)	1	39 (1)
B Friedel	37	3	3	4	47
P Gallagher	0 (1)	-	-	-	0 (1)
K Gillespie	10 (15)	0 (2)	2 (2)	0 (3)	12 (22)
C Grabbi	1 (10)	0 (1)	1 (1)	1 (1)	3 (13)
V Gresko	10	-	-	-	10
Hakan Sukur	7 (2)	-	-	-	7 (2)
C Hignett	1 (2)	-	-	1	2 (2)
M Jansen	0 (7)	2	1 (2)	0 (1)	3 (10)
N-E Johansson	20 (10)	1 (1)	2 (1)	4	27 (12)
A Kelly	1	-	2	-	3
A Mahon	0 (2)	-	1	0 (1)	1 (3)
J McEveley	9	2	3 (1)	-	14 (1)
L Neill	34	3	4	4	45
E Ostenstad	8 (9)	1 (2)	0 (2)	2 (1)	11 (14)
M S Pelzer	-	-	1	-	1
M Richards	-	-	1	-	1
C Short	26 (1)	-	1	2	29 (1)
M Taylor	29 (4)	3	3	3	38 (4)
D Thompson	23	2	4	3	32
A Todd	7 (5)	2	4	1	14 (5)
Tugay Kerimoglu	32 (5)	2 (1)	4	4	42 (6)
D Yorke	25 (8)	3	4	3	35 (8)

Saturday December 14
EVERTON (a)
Lost 1-2   HT 1-2   Att 36,578   Position 10th
Friedel — Neill, Taylor, Short, McEveley (Gillespie 45) — Thompson, Tugay, Flitcroft (Johansson 76), Duff — Cole, Yorke *Subs not used* Kelly, Ostenstad, Danns
Booked Neill, Thompson *Sent off* Neill 74
Scorer **Cole 6**
Report page 119

Tuesday December 17
WIGAN ATHLETIC (a)
Worthington Cup, 5th rnd
Won 2-0   HT 1-0   Att 16,922
Friedel — Neill, Taylor, Short, Bjornebye (Johansson 83) — Thompson, Tugay, Flitcroft, Gillespie — Cole (Jansen 84), Yorke (Ostenstad 84) *Subs not used* Kelly, Danns
Booked Flitcroft
Scorer **Cole 16, 80**
Referee **A D'Urso**

In front of a record crowd for the thriving second division club, Cole's finishing proves the decisive factor in a tight tie. He latches on to defence-splitting passes from Tugay and Thompson in turn, while Graeme Souness watches the second half from the stand after being dismissed from the dug-out (again).

Sunday December 22
MANCHESTER UNITED (h)
Won 1-0   HT 1-0   Att 30,475   Position 9th
Friedel — Neill, Taylor, Short, Johansson — Dunn (Gillespie 55), Tugay, Thompson, Duff — Cole, Yorke *Subs not used* Todd, Jansen, Ostenstad, Kelly
Scorer **Flitcroft 40**
Referee **D Elleray**

Keane returns for United after five tumultuous months, but he is subdued and with Van Nistelrooy missing two great chances, their run of eight successive victories in all competitions is ended by Flitcroft's strike for Blackburn. It is, according to Graeme Souness, a "monster win" for his Rovers side.

Thursday December 26
LIVERPOOL (a)
Drew 1-1   HT 0-1   Att 43,075   Position 10th
Friedel — Neill, Taylor, Short, Johansson (Ostenstad 52) — Thompson, Tugay, Flitcroft, Duff — Cole, Yorke *Subs not used* Todd, Kelly, Curtis, Danns *Booked* Neill
Scorer **Cole 77**
Report page 95

Saturday December 28
WEST HAM UNITED (h)
Drew 2-2   HT 1-1   Att 24,998   Position 11th
Friedel — Curtis (Yorke ht), Taylor, Short (Todd 62), Johansson — Thompson, Tugay, Flitcroft, Duff (Gillespie 62) — Cole, Ostenstad *Subs not used* Danns, Kelly
Booked Cole, Thompson, Todd
Scorers **Duff 4, Cole 78**
Referee **A Wiley**

On the ground where they were humiliated 7-1 the previous season, West Ham start dreadfully again when James fumbles Duff's fourth-minute shot into his own net, but they twice come from behind to take a point, Defoe pouncing after Pearce, a former Rover, heads down four minutes from time.

Wednesday January 1
MIDDLESBROUGH (h)
Won 1-0   HT 0-0   Att 23,413   Position 8th
Friedel — Neill, Taylor, Johansson, McEveley (Todd
74) — Danns (Gillespie ht), Tugay, Flitcroft, Thompson
— Cole, Yorke (Ostenstad 84) *Subs not used*
Kelly, Dunn
Scorer **Yorke 57**
Referee **D Pugh**

The early loss of Ehiogu with two broken ribs and a
punctured lung, injuries sustained in a collision with
Friedel, does not augur well for Middlesbrough and they
duly go on to lose their eighth successive away match
when Yorke combines with Cole before volleying a
close-range winner.

Saturday January 4
ASTON VILLA (a)
FA Cup, 3rd rnd
Won 4-1   HT 1-1   Att 23,884
Friedel — Neill, Taylor, Todd, McEveley — Danns
(Tugay ht), Flitcroft, Yorke (Douglas 75), Dunn —
Ostenstad (Gillespie ht), Jansen *Subs not used* Kelly,
Johansson
Scorers **Jansen 17, 60, Yorke 52, 71**
Report page 229

Tuesday January 7
MANCHESTER UNITED (a)
Worthington Cup, semi-final, 1st leg
Drew 1-1   HT 0-0   Att 62,740
Details page 338

Saturday January 11
SUNDERLAND (a)
Drew 0-0   HT 0-0   Att 36,529   Position 9th
Friedel — Neill (Mahon 74), Taylor, Todd, Johansson —
Thompson (Gillespie 57), Tugay, Flitcroft, Duff
(Jansen 79) — Cole, Yorke *Subs not used* Kelly,
Ostenstad *Booked* Tugay, Thompson, Todd
Report page 276

Saturday January 18
BIRMINGHAM CITY (h)
Drew 1-1   HT 1-0   Att 23,331   Position 9th
Friedel — Neill, Todd, Taylor, McEveley — Thompson,
Tugay, Flitcroft, Duff — Cole (Jansen 73), Yorke
(Johansson 35) *Subs not used* Gillespie, Ostenstad,
Kelly *Booked* Neill, Tugay *Sent off* Todd 28
Scorer **Duff 19**
Referee **C Wilkes**

After what Birmingham — and television viewers later in
the evening — might believe is the deliberate targeting
of the outstanding Dugarry, Todd is dismissed for a
crude kick at the prostrate Frenchman. By then,
Blackburn are ahead, but their remaining ten men
crack seven minutes from time when John, the City
substitute, rises unchallenged to meet a cross from
Lazaridis.

Brad Friedel has been consistently brilliant in goal, Damien Duff has dazzled occasionally on the wing, but Rovers as a team just do not function properly when one player is missing. Stand up Garry Flitcroft. Every club has one. Unsung and sometimes unloved by the fans, he is the grafting, hard-working player who supplies the platform in midfield that allows more exotic talents to flourish. Tugay, for example, is certainly never the same performer for Rovers when Flitcroft is absent. Signed from Manchester City way back in March 1996, the 30-year-old club captain stuck by Rovers in the darkest days under Brian Kidd and has been rewarded by having his contract extended to 2006.

John Dawkins

STATS AND FACTS

● The past 11 meetings between Chelsea and Blackburn at Stamford Bridge have ended either in a draw or a one-goal win for Rovers.

● Rovers' 5-2 home win over Newcastle United was the only time they scored more than four in the Premiership, while their 5-1 defeat away to Newcastle was the one occasion when they conceded more than four.

● Blackburn could have fielded the following alliterative midfield: David Dunn, Darren Dunning, Neil Danns, Damien Duff.

● In December, Andrew Cole and Dwight Yorke scored in the same game for the first time in two years, nine months. The pair had only been at different clubs for half a season in that period.

Bill Edgar

GOALSCORERS

	Prem	FAC	WC	Euro	Total
H Berg	1	-	-	-	1
A Cole	7	2	4	-	13
D Duff	9	-	1	1	11
D Dunn	8 (4p)	-	-	-	8 (4p)
G Flitcroft	2	2	-	-	4
C Grabbi	1	-	1 (p)	1	3 (1p)
Hakan Sukur	2	-	-	-	2
C Hignett	1	-	-	-	1
M Jansen	-	2	-	-	2
E Ostenstad	1	-	-	-	1
C Short	1	-	-	-	1
M Taylor	2	-	-	-	2
D Thompson	4	-	1	1	6
A Todd	1	-	-	-	1
Tugay Kerimoglu	1	-	-	-	1
D Yorke	8 (1p)	3	2	-	13 (1p)
Own goals	3	-	1	-	4

Wednesday January 22
MANCHESTER UNITED (h)
Worthington Cup, semi-final, 2nd leg
Lost 1-3   (lose 2-4 on agg)   HT 1-2   Att 29,048
Details page 338

Saturday January 25
SUNDERLAND (h)
FA Cup, 4th rnd
Drew 3-3   HT 1-1   Att 14,315
Friedel — Douglas (Ostenstad 60), Todd, Taylor, Neill — Thompson, Tugay, Yorke, Dunn (Johansson 83) — Cole, Jansen (Gillespie ht) *Subs not used* Robinson, Short *Booked* Dunn
Scorers **Cole 14, 73, Yorke 90**
Referee **D Elleray**

Both sides are desperate to avoid a replay and go all-out for victory in a thriller. The inevitable result? A replay, ensured when Yorke equalises in stoppage time from Neill's long ball after Sunderland had led 1-0 and 3-1, their third goal converted by the deserving Phillips after Craddock's clever back-heel.

Wednesday January 29
WEST HAM UNITED (a)
Lost 1-2   HT 1-0   Att 34,743   Position 11th
Friedel — Neill, Todd, Taylor, McEveley (Jansen 90) — Gillespie (Johansson 70), Tugay, Flitcroft, Thompson — Cole, Yorke (Ostenstad 84) *Subs not used* Robinson, Douglas *Booked* McEveley
Scorer **Yorke 38**
Report page 253

Sunday February 2
ASTON VILLA (a)
Lost 0-3   HT 0-2   Att 29,171   Position 12th
Friedel — Curtis (Ostenstad ht), Taylor, Johansson, McEveley — Thompson (Gillespie 69), Tugay, Flitcroft, Gresko (Jansen 77) — Cole, Yorke *Subs not used* Kelly, Douglas *Booked* Taylor, Johansson, Flitcroft, Thompson, McEveley
Report page 230

Wednesday February 5
SUNDERLAND (a)
FA Cup, 4th rnd replay
Drew 2-2   (aet; lose 3-0 on pens)   HT 0-1   Att 15,745
Friedel — Neill, Berg, Taylor, McEveley (Douglas ht) — Thompson, Tugay, Flitcroft, Johansson (Grabbi 82) — Cole, Yorke (Ostenstad 72) *Subs not used* Jansen, Kelly *Booked* Neill, Thompson
Scorer **Flitcroft 50, 90**
Report page 277

Saturday February 8
SOUTHAMPTON (h)
Won 1-0 **HT 1-0** Att **24,896** Position **10th**
Friedel — Neill, Berg, Short, Gresko — Gillespie
(Ostenstad 89), Tugay (Johansson 58), Flitcroft,
Thompson — Cole, Yorke (Taylor 63) *Subs not used*
Grabbi, Kelly
Scorer **Thompson 26**
Referee **M Riley**

Swept into the England squad for the match against
Australia on a tide of goals, Beattie dries up on the day
of the announcement, putting his one chance over the
bar as Southampton — for whom Higginbotham and
Prutton make debuts — are beaten by Thompson's
first-half goal from Gillespie's cross.

Saturday February 22
CHELSEA (a)
Won 2-1 **HT 0-0** Att **40,850** Position **9th**
Friedel — Neill, Berg, Short, Gresko — Dunn, Tugay,
Flitcroft, Johansson (Gillespie 62) — Cole (Ostenstad
83), Grabbi (Yorke 57) *Subs not used* Kelly, Taylor
Booked Gresko
Scorers **Yorke 86, Dunn 89**
Report page 86

Saturday March 1
MANCHESTER CITY (h)
Won 1-0 **HT 1-0** Att **28,647** Position **8th**
Friedel — Neill, Berg, Taylor, McEveley (Johansson ht)
— Gillespie (Todd 66), Tugay, Flitcroft, Dunn — Cole,
Ostenstad (Hakan Sukur 41) *Subs not used* Grabbi,
Kelly *Booked* Neill, Flitcroft
Scorer **Dunn 13**
Referee **S Dunn**

Dunn, still not speaking to his manager, lets his actions
do the talking by heading Blackburn's early winner.
"That's sixth place gone," Kevin Keegan says as City's
hopes of Europe continue to fade. Fowler comes
closest to salvaging a point when his first-half effort is
blocked on the line by Berg.

Saturday March 15
ARSENAL (h)
Won 2-0 **HT 1-0** Att **29,840** Position **7th**
Friedel — Taylor, Short, Berg, Gresko — Gillespie, Tugay,
Flitcroft, Duff (Johansson 69) — Yorke (Gallagher 79),
Hakan Sukur *Subs not used* Grabbi, Kelly, Douglas
Booked Tugay, Flitcroft, Duff, Hakan Sukur
Scorers **Duff 22, Tugay 52**
Referee **S Bennett**

Arsenal's 20-match unbeaten run comes to an end as
Blackburn complete a league double over the
champions, who are outfought and out-thought.
Gillespie and Tugay, the latter scoring a fine second
goal to end Arsenal's hopes, are outstanding for
Graeme Souness's side.

HENNING BERG
Defender
Born September 1, 1969,
Eidsvell, Norway
Ht 6ft 0in **Wt** 12st 7lb
Signed from Manchester United,
September 2000, £1.75m

STIG INGE BJORNEBYE
Defender
Born December 11, 1969,
Elverum, Norway
Ht 5ft 10in **Wt** 11st 9lb
Signed from Liverpool, June 2000,
£300,000

ANDREW COLE
Forward
Born October 15, 1971,
Nottingham
Ht 5ft 11in **Wt** 11st 12lb
Signed from Manchester United,
December 2001, £7.5m

JOHN CURTIS
Defender
Born September 3, 1978,
Nuneaton
Ht 5ft 10in **Wt** 11st 9lb
Signed from Manchester United,
June 2000, £2.25m

NEIL DANNS
Midfield
Born November 23, 1982,
Liverpool
Ht 5ft 11in **Wt** 11st 1lb
Signed from trainee, August 2002

JONATHAN DOUGLAS
Midfield
Born November 22, 1981,
Monaghan
Ht 5ft 10in **Wt** 12st 12lb
Signed from trainee, February
2000

DAMIEN DUFF
Midfield
Born March 2, 1979, Dublin
Ht 5ft 10in **Wt** 9st 7lb
Signed from Lourdes Celtic,
March 1996, free

DAVID DUNN
Midfield
Born December 27, 1979,
Blackburn
Ht 5ft 10in **Wt** 12st 3lb
Signed from trainee, September
1997

GARRY FLITCROFT
Midfield
Born November 6, 1972, Bolton
Ht 6ft 0in **Wt** 12st 2lb
Signed from Manchester City,
March 1996, £3.2m

BRAD FRIEDEL
Goalkeeper
Born May 18, 1971,
Lakewood, Ohio
Ht 6ft 3in **Wt** 14st 7lb
Signed from Liverpool, November
2000, free

Andrew Cole

PAUL GALLAGHER
Forward
Born August 9, 1984, Blackburn
Signed from trainee, August 2002

KEITH GILLESPIE
Midfield
Born February 18, 1975, Bangor
Ht 5ft 10in **Wt** 11st 3lb
Signed from Newcastle United, December 1998, £2.25m

CORRADO GRABBI
Forward
Born July 29, 1975, Turin
Ht 5ft 11in **Wt** 12st 12lb
Signed from Ternana, Italy, July 2001, £6.75m

VRATISLAV GRESKO
Defender
Born July 24, 1977, Bratislava
Ht 6ft 0in **Wt** 11st 3lb
Signed from Parma (loan), January 2003

HAKAN SUKUR
Forward
Born September 1, 1971, Adapazari, Turkey
Ht 6ft 2in **Wt** 12st 8lb
Signed from Parma, December 2002, free

CRAIG HIGNETT
Midfield
Born January 12, 1970, Prescot
Ht 5ft 9in **Wt** 11st 10lb
Signed from Barnsley, July 2000, £2.25m

MATT JANSEN
Forward
Born October 20, 1977, Carlisle
Ht 5ft 11in **Wt** 10st 13lb
Signed from Crystal Palace, January 1999, £4.1m

NILS-ERIC JOHANSSON
Defender
Born January 13, 1980, Stockholm
Ht 6ft 1in **Wt** 12st 7lb
Signed from Nuremberg, October 2001, £2.7m

ALAN KELLY
Goalkeeper
Born August 11, 1968, Preston
Ht 6ft 2in **Wt** 14st 3lb
Signed from Sheffield United, July 1999, £675,000

ALAN MAHON
Midfield
Born April 4, 1978, Dublin
Ht 5ft 10in **Wt** 11st 5lb
Signed from Tranmere Rovers, December 2000, £1.5m

JAMES McEVELEY
Defender
Born November 11, 1985, Liverpool
Signed from trainee, November 2002

James McEveley

Saturday March 22
NEWCASTLE UNITED (a)
Lost 1-5   HT 0-1   Att **52,106**   Position **8th**
Friedel — Taylor, Berg, Short, Gresko — Gillespie
(Dunn ht), Tugay (Grabbi 70), Flitcroft, Duff — Yorke
(Cole 63), Hakan Sukur *Subs not used* Kelly, Todd
Booked Gresko
Scorer **Duff 54**
Report page 75

Monday April 7
FULHAM (a)
Won 4-0   HT 2-0   Att **14,017**   Position **7th**
Friedel — Neill (Taylor 53), Berg, Short, Gresko — Dunn,
Tugay (Gillespie 68; Grabbi 89), Flitcroft, Duff — Cole,
Hakan Sukur *Subs not used* Kelly, Yorke *Booked* Short,
Tugay, Neill
Scorers **Dunn 37 (pen), Hakan Sukur 42, 54,
Duff 52**
Report page 207

Saturday April 12
CHARLTON ATHLETIC (h)
Won 1-0   HT 1-0   Att **27,506**   Position **7th**
Friedel — Neill, Berg, Short, Gresko — Dunn, Tugay
(Gillespie 70), Flitcroft, Duff (Grabbi 85) — Cole, Hakan
Sukur (Yorke 62) *Subs not used* Kelly, Taylor
Scorer **Duff 34**
Referee **J Winter**

A soporific afternoon is enlivened only by Duff, who
keeps his and Rovers' runs going with his fourth goal in
four games, a superbly taken effort that leaves Charlton
spiralling down the table from the fringes of the
European race.

Saturday April 19
MANCHESTER UNITED (a)
Lost 1-3   HT 1-2   Att **67,626**   Position **7th**
Friedel — Neill, Berg (Taylor 63), Short, Gresko — Dunn,
Tugay, Flitcroft, Duff (Hakan Sukur 66) — Cole, Yorke
Subs not used Kelly, Grabbi, Todd
Scorer **Berg 24**
Report page 52

Monday April 21
BOLTON WANDERERS (h)
Drew 0-0 HT 0-0 Att **28,862** Position **7th**
Friedel — Neill, Berg (Taylor 56), Short, Gresko — Dunn,
Tugay, Flitcroft, Duff — Cole, Hakan Sukur *Subs not
used* Grabbi, Yorke, Ostenstad, Kelly *Booked*
Duff, Cole
Referee **M Dean**

Bolton are much the happier team with a point from a
strangely subdued match, especially after Cole heads
the best of the few real chances horribly wide and
Mendy clears off the line from Duff as Blackburn look to
improve their Uefa Cup chances.

Saturday April 26
LEEDS UNITED (a)
Won 3-2 HT 1-1 Att **38,062** Position **7th**
Friedel — Neill, Taylor, Short (Todd 65), Gresko —
Dunn (Johansson 51), Flitcroft, Tugay, Duff — Hakan
Sukur (Yorke 61), Cole *Subs not used* Kelly, Ostenstad
Booked Cole
Scorers **Dunn 38 (pen), Cole 69, Todd 78**
Report page 220

Saturday May 3
WEST BROMWICH ALBION (h)
Drew 1-1 HT 1-0 Att **27,470** Position **7th**
Friedel — Neill, Todd, Taylor, McEveley (Johansson 71)
— Dunn, Flitcroft (Hignett 67), Tugay, Duff — Cole,
Hakan Sukur (Yorke 61) *Subs not used* Kelly, Ostenstad
Booked Cole, Todd
Scorer **Duff 11**
Referee **R Styles**

Ahead early on when Duff beats the offside trap,
Blackburn concede a fine solo equaliser to Koumas
and are dealt a potentially decisive blow to their hopes
of qualifying for Europe. Certainly, Graeme Souness is
distinctly unimpressed with his team's performance and
refuses to speak to the media afterwards.

Sunday May 11
TOTTENHAM HOTSPUR (a)
Won 4-0 HT 2-0 Att **36,036** Position **6th**
Friedel — Neill, Taylor, Todd, McEveley (Johansson 62)
— Hignett (Jansen 76), Flitcroft (Dunn ht), Tugay, Duff —
Cole, Yorke *Subs not used* Kelly, Hakan Sukur
Scorers **Yorke 5, Hignett 45, Duff 48, Cole 60**
Report page 160

LUCAS NEILL
Defender
Born March 9, 1978, Sydney
Ht 6ft 1in **Wt** 12st 0lb
Signed from Millwall, July 2001,
£1m

EGIL OSTENSTAD
Forward
Born January 2, 1972,
Haugesun, Norway
Ht 6ft 0in **Wt** 13st 0lb
Signed from Southampton, August
1999, swap

MARC SEBASTIAN PELZER
Defender
Born September 24, 1980, Trier,
Germany
Ht 6ft 1in **Wt** 12st 4lb
Signed from 1FC Kaiserslautern,
June 2002, £375,000

MARC RICHARDS
Midfield
Born July 8, 1982,
Wolverhampton
Ht 6ft 2in **Wt** 12st 8lb
Signed from trainee, August 2000

CRAIG SHORT
Defender
Born June 25, 1968, Bridlington
Ht 6ft 1in **Wt** 13st 8lb
Signed from Everton, August
1999, £1.7m

MARTIN TAYLOR
Defender
Born November 9, 1979,
Ashington
Ht 6ft 4in **Wt** 15st 0lb
Signed from trainee, August
1997

DAVID THOMPSON
Midfield
Born September 12, 1977,
Birkenhead
Ht 5ft 7in **Wt** 10st 0lb
Signed from Coventry City, August
2002, £1.5m

ANDY TODD
Defender
Born September 21, 1974, Derby
Ht 5ft 10in **Wt** 11st 10lb
Signed from Charlton Athletic,
May 2002, £750,000

TUGAY KERIMOGLU
Midfield
Born August 24, 1970, Istanbul
Ht 5ft 9in **Wt** 11st 6lb
Signed from Rangers, July 2001,
£1.3m

DWIGHT YORKE
Forward
Born November 3, 1971,
Canaan, Tobago
Ht 5ft 10in **Wt** 12st 4lb
Signed from Manchester United,
July 2002, £2m

Tugay Kerimoglu

EVERTON

PREMIERSHIP

	P	W	D	L	F	A	Pts
Man Utd	38	25	8	5	74	34	83
Arsenal	38	23	9	6	85	42	78
Newcastle	38	21	6	11	63	48	69
Chelsea	38	19	10	9	68	38	67
Liverpool	38	18	10	10	61	41	64
Blackburn	38	16	12	10	52	43	60
Everton	**38**	**17**	**8**	**13**	**48**	**49**	**59**
Southampton	38	13	13	12	43	46	52
Man City	38	15	6	17	47	54	51
Tottenham	38	14	8	16	51	62	50
Middlesbro	38	13	10	15	48	44	49
Charlton	38	14	7	17	45	56	49
Birmingham	38	13	9	16	41	49	48
Fulham	38	13	9	16	41	50	48
Leeds	38	14	5	19	58	57	47
Aston Villa	38	12	9	17	42	47	45
Bolton	38	10	14	14	41	51	44
West Ham	38	10	12	16	42	59	42
West Brom	38	6	8	24	29	65	26
Sunderland	38	4	7	27	21	65	19

FA CUP
Third round

WORTHINGTON CUP
Fourth round

Wayne Rooney, the most startling new talent of 2002-03

THE GAMES

Saturday August 17
TOTTENHAM HOTSPUR (h)
Drew 2-2   HT 1-0   Att 40,120   Position 5th
Wright — Hibbert, Weir, Stubbs, Naysmith — Gravesen,
Li Tie (Rodrigo 76), Pembridge — Radzinski (Unsworth
84), Campbell, Rooney (Alexandersson 67) *Subs not
used* Simonsen, Linderoth *Booked* Pembridge
Scorers **Pembridge 37, Radzinski 81**
Referee **N Barry**

Rooney (much more of him later) sets up Pembridge's
opener on the day that he becomes, at 16 years and
306 days, the second-youngest player to make his
Everton debut. But they need a late equaliser from
Radzinski after Spurs, with their only real efforts at
Wright's goal, punish two mistakes by the goalkeeper to
take the lead.

Saturday August 24
SUNDERLAND (a)
Won 1-0   HT 1-0   Att 37,698   Position 6th
Wright — Hibbert, Weir, Stubbs, Naysmith — Gravesen,
Li Tie (Linderoth 74), Pembridge — Radzinski,
Alexandersson (Rooney 74) — Campbell, Radzinski *Subs not used*
Rodrigo, Unsworth, Simonsen *Booked* Naysmith
Scorer **Campbell 28**
Report page 270

Wednesday August 28
BIRMINGHAM CITY (h)
Drew 1-1   HT 0-0   Att 37,197   Position 6th
Simonsen — Hibbert, Weir, Stubbs, Naysmith (Rodrigo
85) — Gravesen, Li Tie, Unsworth — Radzinski,
Campbell, Rooney *Subs not used* Gerrard,
Alexandersson, Linderoth, Carsley *Booked* Unsworth
Sent off Stubbs 49
Scorer **Cunningham 90 (og)**
Referee **E Wolstenholme**

Birmingham get their first goal of the campaign at the
third attempt, courtesy of John's penalty, after Stubbs
brings him down and is sent off for a professional foul,
but Everton conjure a bizarre last-minute equaliser
when Unsworth's shot goes in via Kenna, the post and,
finally, Cunningham.

Saturday August 31
MANCHESTER CITY (a)
Lost 1-3   HT 1-2   Att 34,835   Position 12th
Simonsen — Hibbert, Weir, Stubbs, Naysmith —
Alexandersson (Rodrigo 64), Li Tie (Linderoth 25),
Gravesen, Unsworth (Rooney 64) — Campbell, Radzinski
Subs not used Gerrard, Li Weifeng
Scorer **Unsworth 29 (pen)**
Report page 138

IT WILL PROVE, PERHAPS, TO be a defining moment in the history of Everton Football Club. The Park End scoreboard showed 81 minutes, though Tomasz Radzinski's eyes were focused elsewhere. The fourth official raised the board and, not for the only time that season, would it offer him an early departure. The figure of eight trundled off to be replaced by No 18. Enter Wayne Rooney. A football genius.

The rest, as they say, is history. Rooney, physically showing the maturity of a person years beyond his age, was about to captivate the Premiership. A cross from Thomas Gravesen was controlled gracefully by the teenager. Arsenal defenders stood off him, and, with the execution of a master, the ball, curled from 25 yards, was beyond David Seaman in the Arsenal net.

The Gunners, the Double winners, came to Goodison holding a stunning unbeaten record, but they had been undone in injury time by a kid aged just 16 years and 360 days. A star was born. The David Moyes revolution had begun.

It was a bizarre season for Everton fans, one, unusually, conducted on a level plain, radically different from those annual rollercoaster, heartstopping, battles against relegation. True, Everton still had to be Everton. The wheeze to win over billions of Chinese fans by taking on an oriental sponsor almost backfired. The club found themselves with two Chinese players in return, including Li Tie, the country's talented World Cup captain.

The other, Li Weifeng, was, some alleged, signed by mistake. He was peripheral at Goodison and finally, after suffering an injury, went home never to return.

Then, there was a sharp reminder of days gone by . . . Shrewsbury Town, a ninetieth-minute FA Cup defeat offering unprecedented humiliation at the hands of a team later shown to be the worst in the Football League when they were relegated to the Nationwide Conference.

But Everton's otherwise serene progress left little time to dwell on setbacks. Even the club's late-season scrapping of the proposed King's Dock stadium development could not detract from what really mattered. Results.

David Moyes, he of the, dare we say it, red hair, the League Managers' Association's manager of the year, is the new breed. His tough, determined approach is motivation enough to his team, a majority of whom had flopped in another life under Walter Smith.

And, of course, there was Rooney. The Duke, Roonaldo, call him what you like. An unknown outside Everton in August, the owner of three England caps by the end of March, an astonishing rise for a

Everton were impressive in disposing of Blackburn Rovers in December

boy who is only 18 in October. Rooney has an amazing affect on people. He makes defenders nervous, spectators stand up ... the anticipation is truly breathtaking whenever he gets the ball. Rooney has been the catalyst of the Goodison revival, a player who has made the scriptwriters put their red pens through the club's name in the joke-sheets. They have stopped laughing at this stock.

He was not quite a one-kid team. Radzinski's 11 goals, coupled with electric pace, also lit up this fairytale journey. It is no coincidence that his absence through injury saw Everton stagger falteringly towards the finishing line with Blackburn Rovers in hot pursuit of the final Uefa Cup slot.

Moyes pondered whether there was a place for Radzinski and Rooney in the same side, but the manager's plan to nurture the teenager carefully avoided a confrontation. Kevin Campbell's ten league goals were also vital, especially while the injury-blighted career of Duncan Ferguson reduced Moyes' options up front.

For a long time, the Champions League beckoned, sell-out signs were posted at Goodison for game after game, but then the late slide set in. The Uefa Cup would do, echoed the Gwladys Street End, but the fatigue began to show away to West Bromwich Albion, just six games from the Holy Grail. Defeats by Liverpool and Chelsea at Easter made it tough. Rooney won it against Villa, but at Fulham, Everton gave it away with two comical own goals.

A showdown with Manchester United might, twelve months ago, have been considered a death sentence. Who would have thought the prize would be a European place. Moyes sent for the boy, and the fatigued Rooney manfully stuck to it, but United were supreme and Blackburn stole sixth spot. The realisation of being so close left the faithful with only tears for souvenirs, but only for moments, as misery quickly turned into a huge celebration. The fans had seen a star born and the rebirth of their beloved blues. Everton are back.

Wednesday September 11
SOUTHAMPTON (a)
Lost 0-1 HT 0-1 Att 29,190 Position 15th
Gerrard — Hibbert, Weir, Li Weifeng, Unsworth (Rodrigo 83) — Alexandersson (Rooney 79), Li Tie, Gravesen, Pembridge — Campbell, Radzinski *Subs not used* Watson, Gemmill, Linderoth *Booked* Weir, Gravesen, Li Weifeng
Report page 126

Saturday September 14
MIDDLESBROUGH (h)
Won 2-1 HT 1-1 Att 32,240 Position 10th
Gerrard — Hibbert, Weir, Stubbs, Unsworth — Alexandersson (Rooney ht), Li Tie, Gravesen, Pembridge — Campbell, Radzinski (Carsley 85) *Subs not used* Simonsen, Li Weifeng, Linderoth *Booked* Stubbs, Rooney
Scorer **Campbell 32, 77**
Referee **M Messias**

Not for the first time, or the last, Rooney, a half-time substitute, steals the show with the sheer verve of his performance, but it is Campbell who wins the points for Everton after Nemeth, pouncing on the rebound when Gerrard parries Maccarone's shot, had given Middlesbrough the lead.

Sunday September 22
ASTON VILLA (a)
Lost 2-3 HT 0-1 Att 30,023 Position 13th
Wright — Hibbert, Weir, Stubbs, Unsworth — Rooney (Alexandersson 77), Li Tie, Gravesen, Pembridge — Campbell, Radzinski *Subs not used* Naysmith, Li Weifeng, Linderoth, Gerrard *Booked* Rooney
Scorers **Radzinski 51, Campbell 66**
Report page 224

Saturday September 28
FULHAM (h)
Won 2-0 HT 2-0 Att 34,371 Position 9th
Wright — Hibbert, Weir, Yobo, Unsworth — Carsley, Li Tie, Gravesen, Pembridge — Campbell, Radzinski *Subs not used* Stubbs, Ferguson, Naysmith, Rooney, Gerrard *Booked* Campbell, Unsworth
Scorers **Campbell 45, Gravesen 45**
Referee **S Dunn**

China meets Japan for the first time in the Premiership as Li Tie goes head to head with Inamoto in midfield, and it is China (and Everton) who triumph with two goals inside 60 seconds against Fulham just before the interval, Campbell flicking home a header and Gravesen netting from 25 yards.

Tuesday October 1
WREXHAM (a)
Worthington Cup, 2nd rnd
Won 3-0   HT 1-0   Att 13,428
Wright — Hibbert, Li Weifeng, Yobo, Unsworth —
Carsley, Li Tie (Stubbs 83), Gemmill, Naysmith —
Campbell (Ferguson 73), Radzinski (Rooney 63)
Subs not used Simonsen, McLeod *Booked* Hibbert
Scorers **Campbell 25, Rooney 83, 89**
Referee **A Kaye**

Fears of a Worthington Cup embarrassment for
Everton are eased by Campbell's opener before
Rooney, a second-half substitute, registers his first
senior goals in the closing stages, becoming the
youngest scorer in the club's history in the process.

Monday October 7
MANCHESTER UNITED (a)
Lost 0-3   HT 0-0   Att 67,629   Position 12th
Wright — Hibbert, Weir, Yobo, Unsworth — Carsley,
Li Tie, Gravesen, Pembridge — Campbell, Radzinski
(Rooney 74) *Subs not used* Gerrard, Naysmith,
Li Weifeng, Ferguson *Booked* Gravesen, Unsworth
Sent off Weir 90
Report page 44

Saturday October 19
ARSENAL (h)
Won 2-1   HT 1-1   Att 39,038   Position 9th
Wright — Hibbert, Weir, Yobo, Unsworth — Carsley
(Stubbs 90), Li Tie (Linderoth 50), Gravesen,
Pembridge — Campbell, Radzinski (Rooney 80)
Subs not used Alexandersson, Gerrard *Booked* Weir,
Pembridge, Linderoth
Scorers **Radzinski 22, Rooney 90**
Referee **U Rennie**

Remember the name? The football world goes Rooney
crazy as a spectacular last-minute winner, thundered
over Seaman and in off the underside of the bar after
a great first touch, ends Arsenal's 30-match unbeaten
league run and establishes him as the youngest scorer
in the history of the Premiership.

Sunday October 27
WEST HAM UNITED (a)
Won 1-0   HT 0-0   Att 34,117   Position 8th
Wright — Hibbert, Stubbs, Yobo, Unsworth — Carsley,
Li Tie (Pistone 90), Linderoth, Pembridge — Campbell,
Radzinski (Rooney 54) *Subs not used* Gerrard,
Alexandersson, Li Weifeng
Scorer **Carsley 70**
Report page 248

MATCH OF THE SEASON

Everton 2   Arsenal 1
Goodison Park, Saturday October 19 2002
Kevin McCarra

IT IS AS WELL WAYNE ROONEY IS SO stocky a youngster
because his work has not been completed merely by flexing his
muscles to knock over Arsenal. Those broad shoulders are being
asked to bear all the hopes of the supporters, to lift Everton's spirits
and to hoist the club back to the eminent position that was once
taken for granted. This, of course, is an entirely ridiculous and
hazardous way to treat a 16-year-old.

Yet people cannot help themselves. The fans have endured so
much that they regard Rooney as overdue reparation from the fates
for all the damage done since the late 1980s.

He is still the kid who plays street football with his mates, but
those exertions cannot be proper contests, considering the
magnitude of his talent. If eminent Arsenal could not cope during
his ten minutes on the field, what chance would his pals have?

After he had made a steeply-dropping ball nestle on his boot,
Rooney's winner from 25 yards was half-drive, half-chip and
complete masterstroke. At so uplifting a moment, it was deeply
dreary to have to bother noting that he had become the youngest
person to score a league goal in the history of both his club and of
the Premiership.

At least Rooney did not pause in solemnity and, during the
stoppage time that remained, another cunningly-flighted effort
plopped on to the roof of the net.

When he is performing like that everyone has to recite the cold
facts if they are to avoid overheated presumptions about Rooney's
future. As recently as last season, he was only dabbling in reserve-
team football, where he made four appearances without scoring. He
turns 17 on Thursday and his age will see him classified as a novice
even when he gets to the end of the three-year contract that the club
has now agreed with him.

At least Rooney is inside the portals now. It is virtually inhuman
that Goodison fans are forced to recall that Ian Rush, Robbie
Fowler, Steve McManaman and Michael Owen all reputedly
supported Everton before signing for Liverpool. The club, too, has
had a poor record in keeping hold of those who did make it on to
their books. Francis Jeffers, lambasted from the stands on Saturday,
is now at Arsenal and Michael Ball is with Rangers.

David Moyes, the Everton manager, thinks that times have
changed. "I just said to the board let me build some foundations that
aren't going to get knocked away," he said. "I understand the
reasons why that had to happen in the past, but if I want to keep
players, then the board will always support me no matter what the
offer is. Why should Everton not be trying to compete with

Radzinski blasts home Everton's first-half equaliser against Arsenal

Manchester United and Arsenal? It would be an insult to people to say that we should sell our best players to clubs such as the ones I have mentioned."

The sensible Moyes would prefer to treat Rooney as an apprentice, but in telling the truth he puts himself on the fringes of the excitable pack. "I thought Charlie Nicholas was the best 16-year-old I ever saw," the manager said. "but Rooney is better than Charlie was at that age."

Although the forward halted Arsenal's unbeaten run of 30 Barclaycard Premiership matches, the losers could still appreciate the thrill that coursed through Goodison.

Arsene Wenger's team had led through a Freddie Ljungberg goal. The lively Tomasz Radzinski equalised and Everton were never subdued, but the visitors could have scored on several occasions and, at the very close of the game, Edu was vehement that he should have been awarded a penalty kick. All the same, the dignified Arsenal manager had no recriminations when there was a tribute to

Sunday November 3
LEEDS UNITED (a)
Won 1-0   HT 0-0   Att **40,161**   Position **6th**
Wright — Hibbert, Stubbs, Yobo, Unsworth — Carsley, Li Tie (Naysmith 82), Linderoth, Pembridge — Campbell, Radzinski (Rooney 75) *Subs not used* Gerrard, Weir, Watson *Booked* Wright, Campbell, Unsworth
Scorer **Rooney 80**
Report page 213

Wednesday November 6
NEWCASTLE UNITED (a)
Worthington Cup, 3rd rnd
Drew 3-3 (aet; win 3-2 on pens) HT 1-0   Att **34,584**
Wright — Pistone, Weir, Stubbs, Unsworth — Carsley, Li Tie (Radzinski 56), Linderoth (Watson 39), Naysmith — Campbell, Rooney *Subs not used* Simonsen, Li Weifeng, McLeod *Booked* Weir, Rooney, Carsley, Watson, Pistone
Scorers **Campbell 11, Watson 85, Unsworth 112 (pen)**
Report page 69

Saturday November 9
CHARLTON ATHLETIC (h)
Won 1-0   HT 1-0   Att **37,621**   Position **4th**
Wright — Hibbert, Yobo, Stubbs (Weir 68), Unsworth — Carsley, Li Tie (Naysmith 73), Gravesen, Pembridge — Campbell, Radzinski (Rooney 73) *Subs not used* Watson, Gerrard *Booked* Gravesen, Rooney
Scorer **Radzinski 31**
Referee **R Styles**

Radzinski's goal, set up by Gravesen after he catches a hesitant Mustoe in possession, makes it four straight league wins for the first time since 1991 for Everton, although Charlton's late rally almost earns them a point, when Fish has a header cleared off the line by Hibbert.

Sunday November 17
BLACKBURN ROVERS (a)
Won 1-0   HT 1-0   Att **26,496**   Position **4th**
Wright — Hibbert, Yobo, Stubbs, Unsworth — Carsley, Li Tie (Watson 57), Gravesen, Naysmith (Rooney 81) — Campbell, Radzinski (Weir 89) *Subs not used* Pistone, Simonsen *Booked* Li Tie
Scorer **Campbell 19**
Report page 106

Saturday November 23
WEST BROMWICH ALBION (h)
Won 1-0 HT 1-0 Att 40,113 Position **3rd**
Wright — Hibbert, Yobo, Stubbs, Unsworth — Carsley,
Li Tie, Gravesen, Naysmith (Pistone 84) — Campbell,
Radzinski (Rooney 87) *Subs not used* Simonsen,
Watson, Weir *Booked* Gravesen, Li Tie
Scorer **Radzinski 35**
Referee **J Winter**

Radzinski's winner, created by the outstanding Li Tie,
means that this is Everton's best run since they last
won the title, in 1987, and have not conceded a league
goal for nearly nine hours. Albion's consolation is that
they move off the bottom despite defeat as West Ham
crash to Aston Villa.

Sunday December 1
NEWCASTLE UNITED (a)
Lost 1-2 HT 1-0 Att 51,607 Position **5th**
Wright — Hibbert, Yobo, Stubbs, Unsworth — Carsley
(Weir 24), Li Tie, Gravesen, Pembridge — Campbell,
Radzinski (Rooney 72) *Subs not used* Simonsen,
Naysmith, Gemmill *Booked* Unsworth *Sent off*
Yobo 22
Scorer **Campbell 17**
Report page 71

Wednesday December 4
CHELSEA (a)
Worthington Cup, 4th rnd
Lost 1-4 HT 0-2 Att 32,322
Wright — Pistone, Yobo, Weir, Unsworth — Gravesen,
Li Tie (Gemmill 70), Pembridge (Naysmith 36) —
Radzinski, Campbell, Rooney *Subs not used* Simonsen,
Stubbs, Hibbert *Booked* Pistone
Scorer **Naysmith 80**
Report page 82

Saturday December 7
CHELSEA (h)
Lost 1-3 HT 1-2 Att 39,396 Position **5th**
Wright — Hibbert, Yobo, Stubbs, Unsworth — Carsley,
Li Tie (Gemmill 63), Gravesen, Naysmith — Campbell,
Radzinski (Rooney 63) *Subs not used* Simonsen,
Pistone, Weir *Booked* Stubbs *Sent off* Unsworth 90
Scorer **Naysmith 43**
Referee **E Wolstenholme**

Chelsea move menacingly into second place as
Everton suffer their fourth and much the most
controversial sending-off of the season, Unsworth
tangling with Gronkjaer in the last minute. The Dane
rubs salt into their wounds by adding Chelsea's third
goal to seal Everton's first home defeat of the season.

The arrival of Wayne Rooney with a startling cameo against Arsenal

be paid to Rooney. "This boy is supposed to be 16," Wenger said in
disbelief. "He is a natural football player. Even if you were playing
on the beach — four against four — you would see that. He is not
the guy who just stands in the box and waits to score. You can put
him on the wing, you can put him in the centre, you can put him
behind the striker. He is short with a low centre of gravity and, with
that build, he reminds me a bit of [Paul] Gascoigne."

Gascoigne? Nicholas? Moyes ought to sigh with relief. With
those examples to hand, he will be able to caution Rooney about
stars for whom the acclaim was always greater than the
achievement.

EVERTON (4-4-2): R Wright — A Hibbert, J Yobo, D Weir, D Unsworth — L Carsley (sub: A Stubbs,
90min), Li Tie (sub: T Linderoth, 50), T Gravesen, M Pembridge — K Campbell, T Radzinski (sub: W
Rooney, 80). **Substitutes not used:** N Alexandersson, P Gerrard. **Booked:** Weir, Pembridge, Lin-
deroth.
ARSENAL (4-4-2): D Seaman — Lauren, S Campbell, P Cygan, A Cole — K Toure (sub: S Wiltord, 64), P
Vieira, Gilberto, F Ljungberg (sub: Edu, 85) — Kanu 6 (sub: F Jeffers, 71), T Henry. **Substitutes not
used:** O Luzhny, R Shaaban. **Booked:** Edu.
Referee: U Rennie.

THE MANAGER

David Moyes

Every club without a manager is suddenly searching for the "new David Moyes". It is not hard to see why. Moyes' boys came from behind to win eight times last season — more than any other club — a tribute to his tremendous motivational skills. Moyes is undemonstrative, a cool character with steely eyes, a no-nonsense demeanour and unafraid to make difficult decisions. He will be well aware that 2003-04 will be tougher and the success-starved fans will be looking for him to deliver. Everton's problem will be keeping him.

Chris Gill

APPEARANCES

	Prem	FAC	WC	Total
N Alexandersson	4 (3)	0 (1)	-	4 (4)
E Baardsen	1	-	-	1
K Campbell	31 (5)	-	3	34 (5)
L Carsley	21 (3)	1	2	24 (3)
N Chadwick	0 (1)	-	-	0 (1)
P Clarke	-	1	-	1
D Ferguson	0 (7)	-	0 (1)	0 (8)
S Gemmill	10 (6)	1	1 (1)	12 (7)
P Gerrard	2	-	-	2
T Gravesen	30 (3)	1	1	32 (3)
A Hibbert	23 (1)	-	1	24 (1)
T Linderoth	2 (3)	-	1	3 (3)
Li Tie	28 (1)	0 (1)	3	31 (2)
Li Weifeng	1	-	1	2
B McBride	7 (1)	-	-	7 (1)
K McLeod	-	0 (1)	-	0 (1)
G Naysmith	24 (4)	1	2 (1)	27 (5)
L Osman	0 (2)	-	-	0 (2)
M Pembridge	19 (2)	-	1	20 (2)
A Pistone	10 (5)	-	2	12 (5)
T Radzinski	27 (3)	1	2 (1)	30 (4)
J Rodrigo	0 (4)	-	-	0 (4)
W Rooney	14 (19)	1	2 (1)	17 (20)
S Simonsen	2	-	-	2
A Stubbs	34 (1)	1	1 (1)	36 (2)
D Unsworth	32 (1)	1	3	36 (1)
S Watson	14 (4)	-	0 (1)	14 (5)
D Weir	27 (4)	1	2	30 (4)
R Wright	33	1	3	37
J Yobo	22 (2)	-	2	24 (2)

Saturday December 14
BLACKBURN ROVERS (h)
Won 2-1   HT **2-1**   Att **36,578**   Position **4th**
Wright — Hibbert (Pistone 90), Yobo, Stubbs, Unsworth — Carsley, Li Tie (Weir 63), Gravesen, Naysmith — Campbell, Rooney (Radzinski 90) *Subs not used* Simonsen, Gemmill *Booked* Hibbert
Scorers **Carsley 12, Rooney 25**
Referee **G Barber**

A minor classic of non-stop attacking and chances galore goes Everton's way thanks to Rooney, whose shot against a post leads to Carsley's opener and who then thrashes home the winner as they come from behind. Blackburn deserve more reward — and certainly not the harsh dismissal of Neill for two bookable offences.

Sunday December 22
LIVERPOOL (a)
Drew 0-0   HT **0-0**   Att **44,025**   Position **4th**
Wright — Hibbert (Watson 60), Weir, Stubbs, Pistone — Carsley, Pembridge, Gravesen, Naysmith — Campbell, Radzinski (Rooney 64) *Subs not used* Li Tie, Simonsen, Gemmill *Booked* Gravesen, Weir, Campbell, Naysmith
Report page 95

Thursday December 26
BIRMINGHAM CITY (a)
Drew 1-1   HT **1-1**   Att **29,505**   Position **4th**
Wright — Yobo, Weir, Stubbs, Pistone — Carsley, Gravesen, Pembridge (Watson 64), Naysmith — Campbell, Radzinski (Rooney 64) *Subs not used* Baardsen, Li Tie, Gemmill *Booked* Weir, Gravesen
Sent off Rooney 81
Scorer **Radzinski 45**
Report page 191

Saturday December 28
BOLTON WANDERERS (h)
Drew 0-0   HT **0-0**   Att **39,480**   Position **4th**
Wright — Yobo, Weir, Stubbs, Pistone — Carsley (Alexandersson 78), Gravesen, Li Tie, Naysmith (Pembridge 78) — Campbell (Radzinski 55), Rooney *Subs not used* Baardsen, Watson *Booked* Weir
Referee **D Gallagher**

Picked to start despite his dismissal against Birmingham, Rooney turns in an attacking masterclass that contains everything but a goal. Continually thwarted by Jaaskelainen, the Bolton goalkeeper, he also hits the bar; but then so do Bolton, who lift the siege to go desperately close through Okocha's free kick.

Wednesday January 1
MANCHESTER CITY (h)
Drew 2-2   **HT 1-1**   Att **40,163**   Position **5th**
Wright — Yobo (Carsley ht), Weir, Stubbs, Naysmith
— Watson, Gravesen (Gemmill 57), Li Tie, Pembridge
— Campbell (Radzinski ht), Rooney *Subs not used*
Baardsen, McLeod *Booked* Rooney
Scorers **Watson 6, Radzinski 90**
Referee **A D'Urso** (rep **A Wiley, 15**)

With more than 300 million fans tuning in on Chinese
television (this time for the battle between Li Tie and
Sun Jihai), Everton take the lead through Watson, on his
first start of the season, go 2-1 behind and need
Radzinski's header to rescue a point in the second
minute of injury time.

Saturday January 4
SHREWSBURY TOWN (a)
FA Cup, 3rd rnd
Lost 1-2   **HT 0-1**   Att **7,800**
Wright — Clarke, Weir, Stubbs, Unsworth (McLeod 90)
— Carsley, Gravesen (Alexandersson ht), Gemmill
(Li Tie 75), Naysmith — Radzinski, Rooney *Subs not
used* Pembridge, Baardsen *Booked* Stubbs, Gravesen,
Rooney
Scorer **Alexandersson 60**
Referee **S Dunn**

Not only the undoubted shock of the round, but one of
the classic Cup upsets of all time as the third division
side — managed by Kevin Ratcliffe, the most successful
captain in Everton's history — unearth a hero in Jemson,
whose 38th-minute free kick and late header secure a
deserved triumph.

Sunday January 12
TOTTENHAM HOTSPUR (a)
Lost 3-4   **HT 1-1**   Att **36,070**   Position **6th**
Baardsen — Pistone, Yobo (Carsley 86), Stubbs,
Unsworth — Watson, Li Tie (Osman 90), Gemmill,
Naysmith — Radzinski, McBride *Subs not used*
Alexandersson, Pembridge, Said *Booked* Gemmill
Scorers **McBride 10, Watson 58, Radzinski 74**
Report page 156

PLAYER OF THE SEASON   Tomasz Radzinski

Everton won more games than they lost
when the insatiable Radzinski was in the
team. He had to work harder than most
to fend off the clamour for Rooney, and
top scored in the league with 11 goals.
The 93rd-minute stunning strike that
defeated Southampton will linger long in
the memory. Sadly, a late-season groin
injury proved crucial and his absence
almost certainly cost Everton a deserved
return to Europe. David Moyes has
hinted his team may not be able to
accommodate a spot of R and R. But he
will discard the talented, and popular,
Radzkinsi at his peril.
Chris Gill

STATS AND FACTS

- All but two of Everton's 17 Premiership victories were by a one-goal margin.

- Wayne Rooney was one of two 16-year-olds to score against a goalkeeper well over twice his age last season. Rooney fired a late winner against Arsenal, who had the 39-year-old David Seaman in goal, while James Milner, of Leeds United, beat Ed De Goey, 36, of Chelsea.

- Steve Watson's goal against Middlesbrough on March 1 meant he had scored in six out of nine away games, having netted in only one of his previous 101 on the road for Everton, Villa and Newcastle.

- The televised home match against Southampton on February 22 followed seven successive away games for the club live on television.

- Everton won more points than Arsenal between mid-October and early February – 34 to 31.

- The win away to Leeds United on November 2 was their first in 37 league visits to Elland Road.

- Everton finished above West Ham United for the first time in seven seasons.

- Everton became the first club to play 100 seasons in the top flight.

- David Moyes is a Scot who replaced a Scot (Walter Smith) at Everton and was replaced by a Scot (Craig Brown) at Preston North End.

- Everton against Aston Villa is the most-played top-flight fixture and each side has won 67 times.

- Never before in a fixture first played in 1894 has the first Merseyside derby of the campaign come so late in the season as December 22.

- Everton exceeded two goals in the league only once, and they lost that game, 4-3 away to Tottenham Hotspur.

- Apart from Everton's title triumphs of 1970, 1985 and 1987, they have not finished above Liverpool in the table since 1965.

Bill Edgar

Saturday January 18
SUNDERLAND (h)
Won 2-1 **HT 0-1** Att **37,409** Position **5th**
Wright — Pistone, Weir, Stubbs, Unsworth — Watson, Li Tie (Gravesen ht), Gemmill, Naysmith — McBride (Campbell 74), Radzinski *Subs not used* Pembridge, Yobo, Gerrard *Booked* Weir, Gemmill
Scorer **McBride 51, 57**
Referee **P Dowd**

Charity begins at home, but McBride, the American striker on loan from Columbus Crew, who sends money back to a diabetes foundation every time he scores, is happily $300 out of pocket after getting the goals that see Everton beat Sunderland after Kilbane had given Howard Wilkinson's team the lead.

Tuesday January 28
BOLTON WANDERERS (a)
Won 2-1 **HT 2-0** Att **25,119** Position **5th**
Wright — Pistone, Weir, Stubbs (Yobo 78), Unsworth — Watson, Li Tie, Gemmill, Naysmith (Pembridge 84) — McBride, Radzinski *Subs not used* Campbell, Gravesen, Gerrard *Booked* Watson
Scorer **Watson 33, 39**
Report page 241

Saturday February 1
LEEDS UNITED (h)
Won 2-0 **HT 0-0** Att **40,153** Position **5th**
Wright — Pistone, Weir, Stubbs, Unsworth — Watson, Li Tie, Gemmill, Naysmith (Campbell 73), Radzinski *Subs not used* Pembridge, Gravesen, Yobo, Gerrard
Scorers **Unsworth 55 (pen), Radzinski 67**
Referee **M Halsey**

The futures of Terry Venables and Peter Ridsdale, manager and chairman respectively of the Premiership's crisis club, are in the balance after the sale of Woodgate to Newcastle United for £9 million. But while all the media attention is on the pair, Everton quietly secure another victory to maintain their challenge for Europe.

Saturday February 8
CHARLTON ATHLETIC (a)
Lost 1-2 **HT 0-1** Att **26,623** Position **5th**
Wright — Pistone, Weir, Stubbs (Yobo 45), Unsworth (Rooney 86) — Gravesen, Li Tie, Gemmill (Campbell 90), Naysmith — McBride, Radzinski *Subs not used* Gerrard, Carsley *Booked* Li Tie
Scorer **McBride 69**
Report page 181

GOALSCORERS

	Prem	FAC	WC	Total
N Alexandersson	-	1	-	1
K Campbell	10	-	2	12
L Carsley	3	-	-	3
T Gravesen	1	-	-	1
B McBride	4	-	-	4
G Naysmith	1	-	1	2
T Radzinski	11	-	-	11
W Rooney	6	-	2	8
D Unsworth	4 (4p)	-	1 (1p)	5 (5p)
S Watson	5	-	1	6
D Weir	1	-	-	1
Own goals	1	-	-	1

Saturday February 22
SOUTHAMPTON (h)
Won 2-1 **HT 0-1** Att 36,569 Position **5th**
Wright — Pistone, Weir, Stubbs, Unsworth — Watson,
Li Tie (Gravesen 59), Gemmill, Naysmith (Rooney 65)
— McBride (Campbell 59), Radzinski *Subs not used*
Yobo, Gerrard
Scorer **Radzinski 83, 90**
Referee **D Elleray**

Ahead through the unmarked Beattie's chip,
Southampton hang on under increasing pressure
thanks to Niemi's brilliance in goal, but finally crack as
Radzinski, with a header from Rooney's cross and a
ferocious injury-time winner, sends Goodison into a
state of pandemonium.

Saturday March 1
MIDDLESBROUGH (a)
Drew 1-1 **HT 1-0** Att 32,473 Position **4th**
Wright — Pistone, Weir, Stubbs, Unsworth — Watson,
Gravesen (Rooney 79), Gemmill, Naysmith — Campbell
(McBride 65), Radzinski *Subs not used* Li Tie, Yobo,
Gerrard
Scorer **Watson 23**
Report page 169

Saturday March 15
WEST HAM UNITED (h)
Drew 0-0 **HT 0-0** Att 40,158 Position **4th**
Wright — Hibbert, Weir, Stubbs, Unsworth — Watson,
Gravesen, Gemmill (Li Tie 55), Naysmith (Campbell 55)
— McBride (Rooney 55), Radzinski *Subs not used* Yobo,
Gerrard *Booked* Hibbert, Gravesen
Referee **M Halsey**

The Goodison party to celebrate David Moyes's first
year in charge falls spectacularly flat, courtesy of a
dogged West Ham performance that restricts Everton
to just a couple of half-chances, one of which Rooney
is unable to accept. West Ham create next to nothing,
but that will not bother them as they pick up
a valuable point.

Sunday March 23
ARSENAL (a)
Lost 1-2 **HT 0-1** Att 38,042 Position **6th**
Wright — Yobo, Weir, Stubbs, Unsworth — Watson
(Ferguson 88), Gravesen, Li Tie (Gemmill 74), Pembridge
— Campbell, Rooney *Subs not used* Simonsen,
Naysmith, Carsley *Booked* Li Tie
Scorer **Rooney 56**
Report page 63

THE PLAYERS

NICLAS ALEXANDERSSON
Midfield
Born December 29, 1971,
Halmstad, Sweden
Ht 6ft 2in **Wt** 11st 8lb
Signed from Sheffield Wednesday,
July 2000, £2.5m

ESPEN BAARDSEN
Goalkeeper
Born December 7, 1977, San
Rafael, California
Ht 6ft 5in **Wt** 13st 13lb
Signed from Watford, December
2002, free

KEVIN CAMPBELL
Forward
Born February 4, 1970, Lambeth
Ht 6ft 1in **Wt** 13st 8lb
Signed from Nottingham Forest,
March 1999, £3m

LEE CARSLEY
Midfield
Born February 28, 1974,
Birmingham
Ht 5ft 10in **Wt** 11st 11lb
Signed from Coventry City,
February 2002, £1.95m

NICKY CHADWICK
Forward
Born October 26, 1982, Market
Drayton
Ht 6ft 0in **Wt** 12st 8lb
Signed from trainee, October
1999

PETER CLARKE
Defender
Born January 3, 1982, Southport
Ht 6ft 0in **Wt** 12st 0lb
Signed from trainee, January
1999

DUNCAN FERGUSON
Forward
Born December 27, 1971, Stirling
Ht 6ft 4in **Wt** 14st 6lb
Signed from Newcastle United,
August 2000, £3.75m

SCOT GEMMILL
Midfield
Born January 2, 1971, Paisley
Ht 5ft 11in **Wt** 11st 6lb
Signed from Nottingham Forest,
March 1999, £250,000

PAUL GERRARD
Goalkeeper
Born January 22, 1973, Heywood
Ht 6ft 2in **Wt** 14st 4lb
Signed from Oldham Athletic, July
1996, £1m

THOMAS GRAVESEN
Midfield
Born March 11, 1976, Vejle,
Denmark
Ht 5ft 10in **Wt** 12st 4lb
Signed from Hamburg SV, August
2000, £2.5m

Kevin Campbell

TONY HIBBERT
Defender
Born February 20, 1981, Liverpool
Ht 5ft 8in **Wt** 11st 3lb
Signed from trainee, July 1998

TOBIAS LINDEROTH
Midfield
Born April 21, 1979, Marseilles
Ht 5ft 9in **Wt** 10st 12lb
Signed from Stabaek, Norway, February 2002, £2.5m

LI TIE
Midfield
Born September 18, 1977, Liaoning, China
Ht 6ft 0in **Wt** 12st 1lb
Signed from Liaoning Bodao (loan), July 2002

LI WEIFENG
Midfield
Born January 26, 1978, Shenzhen, China
Ht 6ft 1in **Wt** 11st 0lb
Signed from Shenzhen Ping'an (loan), July 2002

BRIAN McBRIDE
Forward
Born June 19, 1972, Arlington Heights, Illinois
Ht 6ft 1in **Wt** 12st 0lb
Signed from Columbus Crew (loan), January 2003

KEVIN McLEOD
Midfield
Born September 12, 1980, Liverpool
Ht 5ft 11in **Wt** 11st 3lb
Signed from trainee, September 1998

GARY NAYSMITH
Defender
Born November 16, 1979, Edinburgh
Ht 5ft 7in **Wt** 11st 8lb
Signed from Heart of Midlothian, October 2000, £1.75m

LEON OSMAN
Midfield
Born May 17, 1981, Billinge, Merseyside
Ht 5ft 8in **Wt** 10st 7lb
Signed from trainee, August 2000

MARK PEMBRIDGE
Midfield
Born November 29, 1970, Merthyr Tydfil
Ht 5ft 8in **Wt** 12st 0lb
Signed from Sheffield Wednesday, August 1999, £800,000

ALESSANDRO PISTONE
Defender
Born July 27, 1975, Milan
Ht 5ft 11in **Wt** 12st 1lb
Signed from Newcastle United, July 2000, £3m

Gary Naysmith

Sunday April 6
NEWCASTLE UNITED (h)
Won 2-1 HT 1-1 Att 40,031 Position 5th
Wright — Yobo, Weir, Stubbs, Unsworth — Watson, Carsley, Gravesen, Pembridge (Naysmith 84) — Campbell, Rooney *Subs not used* Ferguson, Li Tie, Gemmill, Gerrard *Booked* Gravesen
Scorers **Rooney 18, Unsworth 65 (pen)**
Referee **N Barry**

With the country still swept by "Rooney-mania" after his full England debut against Turkey, the teenager heads Everton in front and it is his excellent pass that leads to the decisive penalty. Sir Bobby Robson, angry that a foul by Gravesen on Bernard goes undetected in the build-up to the winner, concedes that Newcastle are now unlikely to win the title.

Saturday April 12
WEST BROMWICH ALBION (a)
Won 2-1 HT 2-1 Att 27,039 Position 5th
Wright — Yobo, Weir, Stubbs, Unsworth — Watson (Ferguson 82), Gravesen (Gemmill 66), Carsley, Pembridge (Naysmith 75) — Campbell, Rooney *Subs not used* Gerrard, Li Tie *Booked* Gravesen, Rooney
Scorers **Weir 23, Campbell 45**
Report page 267

Saturday April 19
LIVERPOOL (h)
Lost 1-2 HT 0-1 Att 40,162 Position 6th
Wright — Yobo, Weir, Stubbs, Unsworth — Watson (Ferguson 69), Gravesen (Gemmill 76), Carsley, Naysmith — Campbell, Rooney *Subs not used* Li Tie, Alexandersson, Simonsen *Booked* Weir, Stubbs, Naysmith, Gravesen *Sent off* Weir 82, Naysmith 90
Scorer **Unsworth 58 (pen)**
Referee **P Durkin**

Everton have not finished above Liverpool since they last won the title and they are behind them again now after Murphy's delicious long-range winner. Everton finish with nine men, Weir and Naysmith both incurring second bookings, and with Rooney under investigation for an alleged spitting incident, although TV pictures seem to exonerate him.

Monday April 21
CHELSEA (a)
Lost 1-4 HT 0-1 Att 40,875 Position 6th
Wright — Yobo (Gravesen 53), Weir, Stubbs, Unsworth (Hibbert 53) — Carsley, Li Tie (Ferguson 76), Gemmill, Naysmith — Campbell, Rooney *Subs not used* Gerrard, Alexandersson *Booked* Gravesen
Scorer **Carsley 77**
Report page 88

Saturday April 26
ASTON VILLA (h)
Won 2-1 HT 0-0   Att **40,167**   Position **6th**
Wright — Hibbert, Weir, Stubbs, Unsworth (Ferguson 56)
— Watson (Osman 89), Carsley, Gravesen, Naysmith —
Campbell, Rooney (Gemmill 89) *Subs not used* Yobo,
Gerrard
Scorers **Campbell 59, Rooney 90**
Referee **G Poll**

Trailing to Allback's goal and with their Uefa Cup hopes
dimming, Everton again find a saviour in Rooney. After
Campbell's headed equaliser, the 17-year-old — who
would not have played had Radzinski been fit — hits the
winner in the third minute of stoppage time, although
Ferguson's apparent elbowing offence on Gudjonsson,
caught on camera and prompting an FA charge, takes
some of the gloss off victory.

Saturday May 3
FULHAM (a)
Lost 0-2 HT 0-2   Att **18,385**   Position **6th**
Wright — Hibbert (Watson 63), Yobo, Stubbs, Unsworth
— Carsley, Gemmill (Ferguson ht), Gravesen, Pembridge
(Pistone 63) — Rooney, Campbell *Subs not used*
Simonsen, Osman *Booked* Hibbert
Report page 208

Sunday May 11
MANCHESTER UNITED (h)
Lost 1-2 HT 1-1   Att **40,168**   Position **7th**
Wright — Hibbert, Stubbs, Yobo, Unsworth — Watson,
Gravesen (Chadwick 74), Carsley, Naysmith (Pistone 80)
— Rooney, Campbell (Ferguson 40) *Subs not used*
Simonsen, Gemmill *Booked* Gravesen, Hibbert,
Rooney, Stubbs
Scorer **Campbell 8**
Referee **M Riley**

Manchester United's post-match title celebrations add
to the angst felt by Everton, who take the lead but are
beaten by Van Nistelrooy's 44th goal of the season, a
penalty that earns him the Golden Boot, and surrender
the last Uefa Cup place. Rooney, of all people, misses a
sitter at 1-1 and walks off the pitch straight into a
club-versus-country row.

TOMASZ RADZINSKI
Forward
Born December 14, 1973,
Poznan, Poland
Ht 5ft 9in **Wt** 11st 7lb
Signed from Anderlecht, August
2001, £4.5m

JULIANO RODRIGO
Midfield
Born August 7, 1976, Santos
Ht 5ft 8in **Wt** 12st 0lb
Signed from Botafogo (loan), July
2002

WAYNE ROONEY
Forward
Born October 24, 1985, Croxteth,
Liverpool
Ht 5ft 10in **Wt** 12st 4lb
Signed from trainee, April 2002

STEVE SIMONSEN
Goalkeeper
Born April 3, 1979, South Shields
Ht 6ft 3in **Wt** 13st 2lb
Signed from Tranmere Rovers,
September 1998, £3.3m

ALAN STUBBS
Defender
Born October 6, 1971, Kirkby,
Liverpool
Ht 6ft 2in **Wt** 13st 10lb
Signed from Celtic, July 2001,
free

DAVID UNSWORTH
Defender
Born October 16, 1973, Chorley
Ht 6ft 1in **Wt** 14st 2lb
Signed from Aston Villa, August
1998, £3m

STEVE WATSON
Midfield
Born April 1, 1974,
North Shields
Ht 6ft 0in **Wt** 12st 7lb
Signed from Aston Villa, July
2000, £2.5m

DAVID WEIR
Defender
Born May 10, 1970, Falkirk
Ht 6ft 2in **Wt** 13st 7lb
Signed from Heart of Midlothian,
February 1999, £250,000

RICHARD WRIGHT
Goalkeeper
Born November 5, 1977, Ipswich
Ht 6ft 2in **Wt** 13st 0lb
Signed from Arsenal, July 2002,
£3.5m

JOSEPH YOBO
Defender
Born September 5, 1980,
Kano, Nigeria
Ht 6ft 1in **Wt** 13st 2lb
Signed from Marseilles, July 2002,
£1m (rising to £5m)

Steve Watson

SOUTHAMPTON

PREMIERSHIP

	P	W	D	L	F	A	Pts
Man Utd	38	25	8	5	74	34	83
Arsenal	38	23	9	6	85	42	78
Newcastle	38	21	6	11	63	48	69
Chelsea	38	19	10	9	68	38	67
Liverpool	38	18	10	10	61	41	64
Blackburn	38	16	12	10	52	43	60
Everton	38	17	8	13	48	49	59
Southampton	**38**	**13**	**13**	**12**	**43**	**46**	**52**
Man City	38	15	6	17	47	54	51
Tottenham	38	14	8	16	51	62	50
Middlesbro	38	13	10	15	48	44	49
Charlton	38	14	7	17	45	56	49
Birmingham	38	13	9	16	41	49	48
Fulham	38	13	9	16	41	50	48
Leeds	38	14	5	19	58	57	47
Aston Villa	38	12	9	17	42	47	45
Bolton	38	10	14	14	41	51	44
West Ham	38	10	12	16	42	59	42
West Brom	38	6	8	24	29	65	26
Sunderland	38	4	7	27	21	65	19

FA CUP
Runners-up

WORTHINGTON CUP
Third round

Brett Ormerod and James Beattie proved
a potent partnership

THE GAMES

Saturday August 17
MIDDLESBROUGH (h)
Drew 0-0   HT 0-0   Att 28,341   Position 9th
Jones — Dodd, Lundekvam, Williams, Bridge —
Fernandes (Telfer 90), A Svensson, Delap, Marsden —
Beattie, Pahars (Tessem 60) *Subs not used* M
Svensson, Moss, Ormerod
Referee **B Knight**

The sunshine may be glorious but the football is dull,
verging on overcast, with defences on top throughout at
St Mary's. Middlesbrough include Maccarone, their
£8.15 million Italian import, but he also fails to shine on
his debut.

Saturday August 24
LIVERPOOL (a)
Lost 0-3   HT 0-1   Att 43,058   Position 15th
Jones — Telfer, Lundekvam (M Svensson 44), Williams,
Bridge — Fernandes, A Svensson, Delap, Marsden —
Beattie, Pahars (Tessem 58) *Subs not used* Oakley,
Moss, Ormerod *Booked* Williams
Report page 90

Wednesday August 28
CHELSEA (h)
Drew 1-1   HT 0-0   Att 31,208   Position 16th
Jones — Telfer, M Svensson, Williams, Bridge —
Fernandes, A Svensson, Delap, Marsden — Beattie,
Pahars (Tessem 70; Ormerod 87) *Subs not used*
Oakley, Niemi, Monk *Booked* Telfer, M Svensson
Scorer **Fernandes 51**
Referee **C Foy**

Fernandes gives Southampton the lead with a
second-half header in an error-strewn match, but
Lampard — the only Englishman in the Chelsea line-up
— rescues a point with a cleverly taken equaliser ten
minutes from time.

Saturday August 31
TOTTENHAM HOTSPUR (a)
Lost 1-2   HT 1-1   Att 35,573   Position 18th
Jones — Telfer, M Svensson, Williams, Bridge —
Fernandes, A Svensson, Delap, Marsden — Beattie,
Ormerod *Subs not used* Niemi, Dodd, Oakley,
Pahars, El Khalej *Booked* Marsden *Sent off*
M Svensson 90
Scorer **Taricco 30 (og)**
Report page 150

Wednesday September 11
EVERTON (h)
Won 1-0   HT 0-0   Att 29,190   Position 17th
Jones — Dodd (Telfer 65), Lundekvam, Williams, Bridge
— Fernandes, A Svensson (Pahars 55), Delap, Marsden
— Beattie, Ormerod (Kanchelskis 55) *Subs not used*
Niemi, M Svensson *Booked* Marsden, Beattie, Pahars
Scorer **Pahars 73 (pen)**
Referee **S Bennett**

Gordon Strachan celebrates Southampton's first win
from the stand, sent there by Steve Bennett, the
referee, after a dispute over the number of coaching
staff in the technical area. Everton are far from happy
with Pahars, either. He collapses theatrically under
Weir's shoulder-to-shoulder challenge to win the
decisive penalty.

SOUTHAMPTON FANS WILL BE looking forward to the short
trip down the M27 to Portsmouth. After all, it's a handy port for the
ferry to the Continent. Such is the delicious irony of South Coast
rivalry. Pompey may be back in the top flight — but Saints are also
back in Europe, with their most successful Premiership campaign to
date in the bag.

An FA Cup Final appearance, eighth in the table and the foundation of a young, hungry team bodes well for the future. The local
paper, the Echo, may have been wide of the mark in saying that
Southampton pulled in £24 million from last season, but there is also
no doubt that, financially, Saints are well grounded.

Season ticket sales have soared as the thousands of fans who
could not get a ticket for Cardiff try to ensure they don't miss out on
Europe. And, who knows, another cup final. Looking for negatives,
the customary fear of any fan whose team finally shows signs of real
progress but is desperate not to get too carried away (ask any
Newcastle fan), is difficult to avoid.

Dave Jones, the Wolves manager and ex-Saints boss, once said
that he thought the team's name was officially Struggling
Southampton. But after a third season of jockeying for mid-table
supremacy, fans now look up the table, rather than down.

In Wayne Bridge and James Beattie, the club contributed two
players to the England squad. Chris Baird capped his remarkable
emergence at right back (Premiership starts, one: FA Cup final
starts, one) by being immediately named in the Northern Ireland
squad, while the Scandic contingent of Lundekvam, Niemi and
Michael Svensson formed an heroic central defensive trio. Before
the largely irrelevant pre-Cardiff 6-1 drubbing by Arsenal, Saints
had one of the best defensive records in the Premiership.

Southampton very rarely looked out of their depth, taking points
off every team bar Liverpool and Manchester United, but did suffer
early in the season by conceding late goals. Remarkably, nobody
scored against Saints between the 55th and 70th minute all season
— then the team conceded 11 goals in the last ten minutes. The last-
minute defeat at White Hart Lane particularly hurt supporters who
are not noted for their admiration of Glenn Hoddle.

Heads never dropped, however, a tribute to Gordon Strachan's
motivational skills and practical outlook, a philosophy that won him
many admirers in post-match interviews. Things inevitably
balanced out and Saints went on to score ten league goals in the last
ten minutes of games, coming back from 2-0 down against Fulham
and Villa with goals in the last minute. Injury time goals also
defeated Sunderland and West Ham United.

Saints hit peak form in the FA Cup third-round demolition of Tottenham

However, scoring goals was the one real negative of the season. Without Beattie and his 23 in the Premiership, the work at the back would have counted for nothing. Thankfully, he stayed free of injury and did not suffer a barren spell. With Pahars due back from injury and Ormerod maturing well, there should not be the same reliance on one player in future.

But goals from midfield remain a priority. The regular midfield four of Oakley, Marsden, Fernandes and Anders Svensson contributed six Premiership goals between them, a woeful return. Still, Beattie scored just one of the 13 Cup goals. He kept the team in the Premiership, the team took him to Cardiff — it was a fair deal. With no need to sell players to balance the books, Strachan has looked to add depth to the squad. As with the previous season, the team ran out of steam after securing enough points to stay up. Even without the distraction of the Cup, 13 points from the last 13 games was poor.

Strachan again proved his liking for lower-division players by signing David Prutton from Nottingham Forest. Like Ormerod (from Blackpool) and Danny Higginbotham (Derby County), the policy has been to sign emerging players for around £2 million. While good for the squad, the post-Final view of fans was the need to add a proven midfield playmaker who can add bite — and goals.

The financial turmoil at the likes of Leeds United only confirms the wisdom of the prudent policies of Rupert Lowe, the chairman. "We have done the groundwork and as long as we don't go buying so-called superstars who don't want to play, I'm sure we will be fine," Nick Illingsworth, chairman of Southampton Independent Supporters' Association, said. "The truth is we have crept past teams like Manchester City and Sunderland by having a strategy not of looking for quick fixes, but of making steady progress. Sometimes the perception of Saints can be annoying, but mostly we just laugh at it now."

Saturday September 14
WEST BROMWICH ALBION (a)
Lost 0-1 HT **0-0** Att **26,383** Position **17th**
Jones — Dodd (Ormerod 83), Lundekvam, Williams, Bridge — Telfer, Oakley (A Svensson 77), Delap, Marsden (El Khalej 88) — Beattie, Pahars *Subs not used* Niemi, Fernandes *Booked* Lundekvam, Williams *Sent off* Williams 85
Report page 259

Saturday September 21
CHARLTON ATHLETIC (h)
Drew 0-0 HT **0-0** Att **25,714** Position **18th**
Niemi — Telfer, Lundekvam, Williams, Bridge — Fernandes (Beattie 75), Oakley (A Svensson 68), Delap, Marsden — Pahars, Tessem *Subs not used* Jones, M Svensson, Dodd *Booked* Delap, Bridge
Referee **P Dowd**

A candidate for the worst match ever played, in which there are only two incidents of note, both in the first half. Powell heads off the Charlton line from Tessem, while at the other end, Niemi, the Finn making his debut in the Southampton goal — Jones is dropped after his blunder against West Bromwich Albion — makes a superb save from Jensen's free kick.

Saturday September 28
BOLTON WANDERERS (a)
Drew 1-1 HT **0-0** Att **22,692** Position **18th**
Niemi — Telfer, Lundekvam, M Svensson, Bridge — Fernandes, Oakley (Ormerod 75), Delap, Marsden — Tessem (Beattie 65), A Svensson *Subs not used* Jones, Dodd, Hall
Scorer **Bridge 82**
Report page 235

Wednesday October 2
TRANMERE ROVERS (h)
Worthington Cup, 2nd rnd
Won 6-1 HT **3-1** Att **16,603**
Niemi — Dodd, Lundekvam, M Svensson, Bridge — Fernandes, Oakley, A Svensson, Marsden (Kanchelskis 70) — Beattie (Tessem 60), Ormerod (Delap 78) *Subs not used* Jones, Williams
Scorers **Marsden 1, Ormerod 25, 43, 68, Fernandes 52, M Svensson 66**
Referee **P Taylor**

Tranmere, who turned a 3-0 deficit into a 4-3 win in an FA Cup tie against Southampton 18 months earlier, are given no chance of a repeat in the Worthington Cup after Marsden gets the opening goal in just 21 seconds. Ormerod is Tranmere's principal destroyer with a hat-trick.

Saturday October 5
MANCHESTER CITY (h)
Won 2-0 HT **2-0** Att **31,009** Position **13th**
Niemi — Dodd, Lundekvam, M Svensson, Bridge — Fernandes, A Svensson (Oakley 80), Delap, Marsden — Beattie (Tessem 87), Ormerod (Pahars 54) *Subs not used* Jones, Telfer *Booked* Marsden, Pahars *Sent off* Pahars 85
Scorers **Ormerod 1, 43**
Referee **M Messias**

Always in control once Ormerod has put them in front, Southampton's day is spoilt only by the sending-off of Pahars, their substitute, who gets yellow cards — both harsh — for dissent and diving. "That was relegation form," Kevin Keegan says.

Monday October 21
ASTON VILLA (a)
Won 1-0 HT 0-0 Att **25,817** Position **12th**
Niemi — Dodd, Lundekvam (Williams 73), M Svensson, Bridge — Fernandes (Telfer 90), A Svensson, Delap, Marsden — Beattie, Ormerod (Tessem 77) *Subs not used* Jones, Oakley *Booked* Delap
Scorer **Beattie 48 (pen)**
Report page 225

Sunday October 27
FULHAM (h)
Won 4-2 HT 2-2 Att **26,188** Position **10th**
Niemi — Dodd, Lundekvam, M Svensson, Bridge — Fernandes, A Svensson, Oakley, Marsden — Beattie, Ormerod (Delgado 79) *Subs not used* Jones, Telfer, Williams, Tessem *Booked* M Svensson
Scorers **Beattie 27 (pen), 42, 53, Ormerod 72**
Referee **M Halsey**

Having got off the mark for the season with a penalty in their previous match, Beattie makes up for lost time with Southampton's first league hat-trick for seven years, converting another spot kick and adding two headers as they recover from 2-0 down after 24 minutes to stun Fulham.

Saturday November 2
MANCHESTER UNITED (a)
Lost 1-2 HT 1-1 Att **67,691** Position **10th**
Niemi — Dodd, Lundekvam, M Svensson, Bridge — Fernandes, Oakley, Marsden (Delgado 88) — Beattie, Ormerod (Delap 74) *Subs not used* Jones, Hall, Telfer *Booked* Dodd
Scorer **Fernandes 18**
Report page 45

Wednesday November 6
LIVERPOOL (a)
Worthington Cup, 3rd rnd
Lost 1-3 HT 0-1 Att **35,870**
Niemi — Dodd, Lundekvam, M Svensson, Bridge — Telfer, Delap, Oakley, Marsden (Pahars 68) — Beattie, Delgado. *Subs not used* Williams, Tessem, Kanchelskis, Blayney *Booked* Marsden
Scorer **Delgado 55**
Report page 93

MATCH OF THE SEASON

Southampton 4 Fulham 2
St Mary's Stadium, Sunday October 27 2002
Peter Lansley

AS THE FINAL WHISTLE blew here yesterday, James Beattie, jumping for Antti Niemi's long punt into the wild winds of Hampshire, caught the ball and huddled it close to his chest. No one else has since been allowed near it. The satisfaction yielded from his hat-trick, which enabled Southampton to overcome a two-goal deficit and win their fourth consecutive match, was all the deeper for the forward's recent travails.

Banned from driving for 30 months and ordered to do 100 hours of community service after he was convicted of drink-driving last month, Beattie's troubled soul was barely soothed by the loss of his goalscoring touch. A week ago, you would not have considered Southampton a likely source of one of the Premiership's most prolific strike partnerships. Yet Beattie, having opened his seasonal account with the winning penalty away to Aston Villa last Monday, and Brett Ormerod, who scored the final goal in yesterday's fine entertainment, have now totalled ten goals between them.

Beattie's crime and punishment have been exacerbated by the fact that his drink-driving offence took place when he moved his car 20 yards to a new parking spot. "It's been a very difficult time," he said. "I always thought I was mentally strong and it would not affect me that much but it did. I know what I did was wrong. It was one minute of madness and I was stupid." The forward said that scoring again had helped to lift the pressure.

Gordon Strachan, the Southampton manager, enforced the maximum fine of two weeks' wages. "That's the response his team-mates have been looking for because they've been good to him," Strachan said. "But they know he's been good for them, too."

Two years ago, Beattie went on a scoring spree with ten goals in as many games, and last season struck five in five. "They tell me he goes on these daft binges," Strachan said, without any detectable irony. "He gets right noisy so I'll have to wear my ear muffs for the next fortnight. It just shows that strikers are the most important players at a club."

Beattie's heroics enabled Strachan's team to recover from a terrible start to enter the top half of the table, overtaking a Fulham side who are showing signs of tiredness after starting their season in July. Yet for a team that had conceded only one goal at home before yesterday, Southampton appeared only too eager to join in the fun and frolics that the blustery weather prompted. Fulham went two goals ahead before Ormerod induced the handball in the penalty area by Alain Goma that allowed the home side a prompt way back into the match.

Lee Clark celebrated his thirtieth birthday by opening the

Delgado shoots during Southampton's thrilling victory over Fulham

Ormerod, scorer of the final goal, hurdles a tackle by Boa Morte

Saturday November 9
BLACKBURN ROVERS (h)
Drew 1-1 HT 1-0 Att 30,059 Position 10th
Niemi — Dodd, Lundekvam, M Svensson, Bridge — Fernandes, A Svensson, Oakley, Marsden — Beattie, Ormerod (Pahars 72) *Subs not used* Jones, Telfer, Delap, Delgado
Scorer **Beattie 38 (pen)**
Referee **A Wiley**

Gordon Strachan says it is the best Southampton have played under him, Graeme Souness cannot remember a worse Blackburn display since he took charge. Wildly contrasting views, but a point apiece after Beattie's penalty is negated by Cole's fortuitous last-minute equaliser for Rovers' ten men after Tugay's dismissal. Blackburn's real hero is the outstanding Friedel in goal.

Saturday November 16
NEWCASTLE UNITED (a)
Lost 1-2 HT 1-1 Att 51,812 Position 11th
Niemi — Dodd (Telfer 69), Lundekvam, M Svensson, Bridge — Fernandes, Oakley, A Svensson (Pahars 82), Marsden — Beattie, Ormerod (Delgado 56) *Subs not used* Jones, Hall *Booked* Bridge, M Svensson, Ormerod
Scorer **Beattie 2**
Report page 70

Saturday November 23
ARSENAL (h)
Won 3-2 HT 1-1 Att 31,797 Position 9th
Niemi — Dodd, Lundekvam, M Svensson, Bridge — Fernandes (Telfer 88), Oakley, Delap, Marsden — Beattie, Delgado (Ormerod 83) *Subs not used* Jones, Williams, A Svensson *Booked* Marsden
Scorers **Beattie 45, 59 (pen), Delgado 67**
Referee **P Durkin**

Ahead through Bergkamp, Arsenal are stunned by a splendid Southampton revival launched by Beattie's 25-yard free kick. The sending-off of Campbell for a professional foul allows Beattie to net again, this time from 12 yards, and Delgado's first Premiership goal — on his first start — makes the game safe before Pires replies.

Monday December 2
WEST HAM UNITED (a)
Won 1-0 HT 0-0 Att 28,844 Position 10th
Niemi — Dodd, Lundekvam, M Svensson, Bridge — Fernandes (Telfer 90), Oakley (Ormerod 66), Delap, Marsden — Beattie, Delgado (A Svensson ht) *Subs not used* Jones, Williams *Booked* Marsden, Beattie
Scorer **Beattie 90**
Report page 250

Saturday December 7
BIRMINGHAM CITY (h)
Won 2-0 HT 0-0 Att 31,132 Position 7th
Jones — Dodd, Lundekvam, M Svensson, Bridge — Fernandes (Telfer 88), Oakley, Delap, A Svensson — Beattie, Ormerod (Tessem 79) *Subs not used* Blayney, Williams, Delgado *Booked* Delap
Scorer **Beattie 60 (pen), 82**
Referee **J Winter**

The "Beattie for England" campaign gathers pace as a penalty and a tap-in account for Birmingham and make him the Premiership's leading scorer. The spot-kick award, for handball by Purse, seems harsh, all the more so when Beattie later escapes punishment for a similar offence.

Saturday December 14
NEWCASTLE UNITED (h)
Drew 1-1 HT 0-0 Att 32,061 Position 7th
Jones — Telfer, Lundekvam, M Svensson, Bridge — Fernandes, A Svensson, Delap, Marsden — Beattie, Ormerod (Tessem 65). *Subs not used* Blayney, K Davies, Williams, Kanchelskis
Scorer **Marsden 52**
Referee **P Dowd**

The biggest crowd that Southampton have ever attracted for a home league match are treated to a thrilling contest of non-stop attacking in which Bellamy curls in Newcastle's opener and O'Brien heads against his own bar after Marsden equalises with his first league goal of the season.

Saturday December 21
LEEDS UNITED (a)
Drew 1-1 HT 0-0 Att 36,687 Position 7th
Niemi — Telfer, Lundekvam, M Svensson, Bridge — Fernandes, Oakley, Delap, Marsden (A Svensson 83) — Beattie, Ormerod (Tessem 62) *Subs not used* Jones, Williams, K Davies *Booked* Marsden
Scorer **Fernandes 89**
Report page 215

Thursday December 26
CHELSEA (a)
Drew 0-0 HT 0-0 Att 39,428 Position 9th
Niemi — Telfer, Lundekvam, M Svensson, Bridge — Fernandes, Oakley (A Svensson 90), Delap, Marsden — Beattie, Tessem (K Davies 86) *Subs not used* Jones, Williams, Ormerod *Booked* Bridge, Fernandes
Report page 83

Saturday December 28
SUNDERLAND (h)
Won 2-1 HT 0-0 Att 31,423 Position 7th
Niemi — Telfer, Lundekvam, M Svensson, Bridge — Fernandes, A Svensson (Oakley 72), Delap, Marsden — Beattie, Ormerod (Tessem 72) *Subs not used* Jones, K Davies, Williams *Booked* Telfer
Scorers **Beattie 73, Tessem 90**
Referee **M Riley**

The gloom deepens for Sunderland as the last of three headed goals, this one by Tessem from Delap's long throw, just crosses the line in the fourth minute of stoppage time to give Southampton victory. Flo had earlier cancelled out Beattie's opener.

Beattie celebrates the hat-trick that launched his remarkable season

scoring. Starting his first match since Boxing Day, after calf and Achilles injuries, Clark found space behind Southampton's midfield and his 20-yard shot, deflected off Michael Svensson, brought Fulham the lead.

Southampton's unbeaten home record looked endangered when Luis Boa Morte, a former Saint himself, slid the ball wide to Steve Marlet, who invited Steve Finnan to cross from the byline. Chris Marsden and Fabrice Fernandes both missed the ball to allow Steed Malbranque to score with ease.

Beattie's penalty was sweetly struck and, confidence soaring, he leapt to head a marvellous equaliser from Fernandes's centre three minutes before half-time. Christian Damiano, the Fulham coach, said that a long-ball approach was an easier tactic with which to adapt to the swirling winds, yet Southampton deserve credit for the manner in which they took control.

From Fernandes's free kick, Beattie completed his first senior hat-trick with a glancing header. Ormerod was slipped in by Chris Marsden to beat Edwin van der Sar but the plaudits belonged to Southampton's first hat-trick hero in seven years, since Matt Le Tissier scored a treble in Nottingham Forest's 4-3 win at The Dell in August 1995. Beattie's prize was the match ball; the champagne, surely, he will keep on ice.

SOUTHAMPTON (4-4-2): A Niemi — J Dodd, C Lundekvam, M Svensson, W Bridge — F Fernandes, A Svensson, M Oakley, C Marsden — J Beattie, B Ormerod (sub: A Delgado, 79min). **Substitutes not used:** P Jones, P Telfer, P Williams, J Tessem. **Booked** M Svensson.
FULHAM (4-1-3-2): E van der Sar — S Finnan, Z Knight (A Ouaddou 60), A Goma, R Brevett — M Djetou (sub: B Hayles 63) — S Legwinski, L Clark, S Malbranque — S Marlet, L Boa Morte. **Substitutes not used:** M Taylor, A Melville, A Stolcers. **Booked** Goma, Boa Morte.
Referee M Halsey.

THE MANAGER

Gordon Strachan

Never one to suffer fools gladly, Strachan has also proved to be one who could not be said to lack loyalty. His first signings were his old Coventry City stalwarts, Paul Telfer and Paul Williams. While neither makes headlines, neither has let the team down. In retrospect, fans will say he was too cautious in the Cup Final. He knew commitment and tackling were the only way to stop Arsenal, but should Fernandes have come on earlier? Managers go awry when they start believing their own publicity. With Strachan, you don't sense — yet — that there is any chance of that happening.

Steve Keenan

APPEARANCES

	Prem	FAC	WC	Total
C Baird	1 (2)	1	-	2 (2)
J Beattie	35 (3)	7	2	44 (3)
F Benali	2	2	-	4
W Bridge	34	4	2	40
K Davies	1 (8)	0 (4)	-	1 (12)
R Delap	22 (2)	3 (1)	1 (1)	26 (4)
A Delgado	2 (4)	-	1	3 (4)
J Dodd	13 (2)	1 (1)	2	16 (3)
T El Khalej	0 (1)	-	-	0 (1)
F Fernandes	35 (2)	5 (2)	1	41 (4)
D Higginbotham	3 (6)	1	-	4 (6)
P Jones	13 (1)	1 (1)	-	14 (2)
A Kanchelskis	0 (1)	-	0 (1)	0 (2)
C Lundekvam	33	6	2	41
C Marsden	30	6 (1)	2	38 (1)
G Monk	1	-	-	1
A Niemi	25	6	2	33
M Oakley	28 (3)	7	2	37 (3)
B Ormerod	22 (9)	5 (2)	1	28 (11)
M Pahars	5 (4)	-	0 (1)	5 (5)
D Prutton	9 (3)	-	-	9 (3)
A Svensson	26 (7)	6 (1)	1	33 (8)
M Svensson	33 (1)	7	2	42 (1)
P Telfer	26 (7)	6	1	33 (7)
J Tessem	9 (18)	2 (5)	0 (1)	11 (24)
P Williams	10 (1)	1	-	11 (1)

Wednesday January 1
TOTTENHAM HOTSPUR (h)
Won 1-0 HT 0-0 Att 31,890 Position 6th
Niemi — Telfer, Lundekvam, M Svensson, Bridge — Fernandes (K Davies 90), Oakley, Delap, Marsden — Beattie, Ormerod (Tessem ht) *Subs not used* Jones, Williams, A Svensson
Scorer **Beattie 82**
Referee **M Halsey**

Victories do not come much sweeter — or more fortunate — than this. After Sheringham and Keane, the latter squandering three clear chances, fail to reward Spurs' dominance, Beattie turns Richards, the Southampton old boy, to poach a late winner against their former manager Glenn Hoddle's team.

Saturday January 4
TOTTENHAM HOTSPUR (h)
FA Cup, 3rd rnd
Won 4-0 HT 1-0 Att 25,589
Niemi — Telfer, Lundekvam, M Svensson, Bridge — Fernandes, Oakley, Delap, Marsden (A Svensson 27) — Beattie (Ormerod 87), Tessem (K Davies 79) *Subs not used* Jones, Williams
Scorers **M Svensson 13, Tessem 50, A Svensson 56, Beattie 80**
Referee **M Dean**

Unluckily beaten in the league three days earlier, Spurs now suffer a defeat bordering on humiliation in the FA Cup as Southampton, producing what Gordon Strachan calls "the complete performance", leave them gasping. Worse for Spurs, they show little stomach for the fight as well as little ability.

Saturday January 11
MIDDLESBROUGH (a)
Drew 2-2 HT 1-0 Att 27,443 Position 5th
Niemi — Telfer, Lundekvam, M Svensson, Bridge — Fernandes, Oakley, Delap, Marsden — Beattie, Tessem (Ormerod 88) *Subs not used* Jones, Williams, K Davies, A Svensson *Booked* Marsden, Beattie
Scorer **Beattie 40, 60**
Report page 168

Saturday January 18
LIVERPOOL (h)
Lost 0-1 HT 0-1 Att 32,104 Position 8th
Niemi — Telfer, Lundekvam, M Svensson, Bridge (Delgado 80) — Fernandes, Oakley, Delap, Marsden (A Svensson 61) — Beattie, Tessem (Ormerod 61) *Subs not used* Jones, Williams *Booked* A Svensson
Referee **S Bennett**

In front of another ground record crowd, two Premiership runs are brought to a halt by Heskey's fourteenth-minute header: Southampton's nine-match unbeaten sequence and Liverpool's 11-game winless streak. An injury to Bridge also cuts short the Southampton defender's proud boast of successive full 90 minutes after 119 fixtures.

Saturday January 25
MILLWALL (h)
FA Cup, 4th rnd
Drew 1-1　**HT 0-1**　Att **23,809**
Niemi — Telfer, Williams, M Svensson, Benali —
Fernandes (K Davies 78), Oakley, A Svensson, Delap —
Beattie (Marsden 78), Ormerod (Tessem 58) *Subs not
used* Jones, Dodd *Booked* Ormerod
Scorer **Davies 88**
Referee **M Messias**

Trailing to a goal from a former Portsmouth man,
Claridge, from the seventeenth minute, Southampton's
agony lasts almost until the death before they prolong
their Cup hopes when Davies, on loan to Millwall earlier
in the season and seemingly on his way out of St
Mary's, pounces on a rebound.

Tuesday January 28
SUNDERLAND (a)
Won 1-0　**HT 0-0**　Att **34,102**　Position **6th**
Niemi — Telfer, Williams, M Svensson, Benali —
Fernandes (Dodd 70), Oakley, Delap (Tessem 36),
Marsden — Beattie (K Davies 87), A Svensson *Subs not
used* Jones, Ormerod
Scorer **Beattie 50**
Report page 275

Saturday February 1
MANCHESTER UNITED (h)
Lost 0-2　**HT 0-2**　Att **32,085**　Position **7th**
Niemi (Jones 88) — Telfer, Lundekvam, M Svensson,
Benali — Fernandes, Oakley, A Svensson, Marsden —
Beattie, Tessem (K Davies 70) *Subs not used* Williams,
Arias, Ormerod *Booked* A Svensson, Benali
Referee **P Dowd**

Everything comes in twos and a couple of beautifully
created goals win the match for United, both
goalkeepers are helped off after sustaining injuries and
Prutton and Higginbotham, the players signed by
Southampton as the transfer window slammed shut the
night before, watch as their new team are defeated.

Wednesday February 5
MILLWALL (a)
FA Cup, 4th rnd replay
Won 2-1 (aet)　**HT 1-1**　Att **10,197**
Niemi — Telfer, Lundekvam, M Svensson, Benali — A
Svensson, Oakley, Marsden, Fernandes (Ormerod 105)
— Beattie, Tessem (K Davies 65) *Subs not used* Jones,
Williams, Arias *Booked* Marsden, Beattie
Scorer **Oakley 21, 102**
Referee **M Halsey**

Given specific licence to attack, Oakley responds with
the two goals that see off Millwall at the New Den. His
opener, Oakley's first of the season, follows a
scintillating build-up and he strikes again in extra time
after Reid rewards Millwall's tenacity with an equaliser.

PLAYER OF THE SEASON　**Michael Svensson**

Strikers get the headlines and Beattie
deserved every accolade last season for
his willingess to run, challenge and make
the best of his ability. Yet while he led
from the front, Michael Svensson did so
from the back. Saints' defence was
outstanding and his part in the
opposition's downfall has been exemplary.
Lining up alongside the team's unsung
hero, Claus Lundekvam, and with Niemi
replacing Paul Jones, the trio formed a
formidable Scandinavian defensive
bulwark. Killer, as he is nicknamed, also
showed a penchant late in the season for
joining the attack, and scored four goals.
Steve Keenan

STATS AND FACTS

- Striking off James Beattie's goals last season would reduce the team's points tally by 27, from 52 to 25. When they beat West Bromwich Albion at home on March 1, it was their fifth 1-0 win via a Beattie goal in 20 league games.

- Southampton have only lost once at home in the FA Cup since 1989.

- Southampton are unbeaten in 16 home matches against West Bromwich Albion.

- The teams of all four Scottish managers in the Premiership finished in the top eight: Strachan at Southampton, Souness at Blackburn, Ferguson at Manchester United and Moyes at Everton.

- Alan Shearer has finished either top scorer or joint top scorer for his club in each of the past 12 seasons, covering spells at Southampton, Blackburn and Newcastle United.

- Saints are unbeaten in 15 home games against Fulham.

- Southampton did not score via a corner in the Premiership all season before they managed it twice in nine minutes against Fulham on March 15.

- Fulham have twice failed to win after building a two-goal lead in their past 180 matches, both times against Saints

- When Southampton played Wolves in the FA Cup it was a story of Joneses who had swapped roles. Dave Jones, the Wolves manager, used to manage Saints. Paul Jones, the Southampton goalkeeper, used to play for Wolves.

- Saints have won one of their past 37 matches away to Manchester United.

- The 78 meetings between Newcastle United and Saints Southampton have produced only seven away wins.

- Nine of Southampton's Premiership games this season featured a decisive goal in the 90th minute or stoppage time.

Bill Edgar

Saturday February 8
BLACKBURN ROVERS (a)
Lost 0-1 HT **0-1** Att **24,896** Position **9th**
Niemi — Telfer, Lundekvam, M Svensson, Higginbotham — Fernandes (Prutton 73), Oakley, Marsden, A Svensson (Ormerod 81) — Beattie, Tessem *Subs not used* Williams, K Davies, Jones *Booked* Marsden
Report page 110

Saturday February 15
NORWICH CITY (h)
FA Cup, 5th rnd
Won 2-0 HT **0-0** Att **31,103**
Niemi — Telfer, Lundekvam, M Svensson, Higginbotham — A Svensson, Oakley (Dodd 68), Delap (Fernandes 32), Marsden — Beattie (Tessem 72), Ormerod *Subs not used* Jones, Williams
Scorers **A Svensson 71, Tessem 74**
Referee **G Barber**

Even though Beattie is desperately below par after his midweek debut for England against Australia, Southampton eventually wear down Norwich through Anders Svensson and Tessem, Beattie's replacement, who scores with his first touch. Norwich's hopes finally disappear when Mackay is sent off for a second cautionary offence.

Saturday February 22
EVERTON (a)
Lost 1-2 HT **1-0** Att **36,569** Position **10th**
Niemi — Telfer, Lundekvam, M Svensson, Higginbotham — Fernandes (Dodd 70), Oakley, A Svensson (K Davies 88), Prutton — Beattie, Ormerod (Tessem 61) *Subs not used* Jones, Williams *Booked* Prutton
Scorer **Beattie 33**
Report page 122

Saturday March 1
WEST BROMWICH ALBION (h)
Won 1-0 HT **1-0** Att **31,915** Position **10th**
Niemi — Telfer, Lundekvam, M Svensson, Bridge — Fernandes (Higginbotham 90), Oakley, A Svensson (Prutton 28), Bridge — Beattie, Ormerod (Tessem 76) *Subs not used* Jones, Dodd *Booked* Bridge, Oakley
Scorer **Beattie 8**
Referee **D Gallagher**

After three successive Premiership defeats, Southampton get back on track with Beattie's thunderous early winner against an Albion team later praised by Gordon Strachan as "the gutsiest in the league". And one of the unluckiest — Telfer had taken the ball fractionally out of play in the build-up to the only goal.

GOALSCORERS

	Prem	FAC	WC	Total
J Beattie	23 (5p)	1	-	24 (5p)
W Bridge	1	-	-	1
K Davies	1	1	-	2
A Delgado	1	-	1	2
F Fernandes	3	-	1	4
C Marsden	1	1	1	3
M Oakley	-	2	-	2
B Ormerod	5	1	3	9
M Pahars	1 (p)	-	-	1 (p)
A Svensson	2	2	-	4
M Svensson	2	1	1	4
J Tessem	2	2	-	4
Own goals	1	2	-	3

Sunday March 9
WOLVERHAMPTON WANDERERS (h)
FA Cup, 6th rnd
Won 2-0   HT 0-0   Att 31,715
Niemi — Dodd, Lundekvam, M Svensson, Bridge —
Fernandes, A Svensson (Tessem 78), Oakley, Marsden
— Beattie (K Davies 90), Ormerod *Subs not used* Jones,
Williams, Higginbotham *Booked* Beattie
Scorers **Marsden 56, Butler 81 (og)**
Referee **A D'Urso**

With all the pre-match attention focused on Dave Jones,
the Wolves manager returning to Southampton for the
first time since the club discarded him in hugely
controversial circumstances, it is Marsden, a player
Jones brought to the South Coast, who eases
Southampton through to the semi-finals with a
speculative overhead kick before Butler's own goal from
Tessem's cross seals the tie.

Saturday March 15
FULHAM (a)
Drew 2-2   HT 0-1   Att 18,031   Position 9th
Niemi — Dodd, Lundekvam, M Svensson, Bridge —
Fernandes (Tessem 56), Oakley,
Telfer, Prutton (K Davies 78) — Beattie, Ormerod
Subs not used Jones, Williams
Scorers **Beattie 82, M Svensson 90**
Report page 207

Saturday March 22
ASTON VILLA (h)
Drew 2-2   HT 1-2   Att 31,888   Position 9th
Niemi — Telfer, Lundekvam, M Svensson, Bridge —
Fernandes (K Davies 81), Oakley, Tessem (Higginbotham
ht), Prutton (Baird 86) — Beattie, Ormerod *Subs not
used* Jones, Williams
Scorers **Beattie 40, Davies 90**
Referee **G Barber**

For the second week running, Southampton hit back
from 2-0 down to grab a point, although this time in
more conventional style after Niemi's heroics against
Fulham. Davies, a perpetual substitute, gets the
last-minute goal — Beattie had launched the recovery —
after Hendrie and Vassell had put Villa 2-0 up.

Saturday April 5
WEST HAM UNITED (h)
Drew 1-1   HT 1-0   Att 31,941   Position 11th
Niemi — Telfer, Lundekvam, M Svensson, Bridge —
Fernandes (A Svensson 78), Oakley, Prutton, Marsden
— Beattie, Ormerod (K Davies 67) *Subs not used* Jones,
Higginbotham, Tessem *Booked* Fernandes, Marsden,
M Svensson
Scorer **Beattie 44**
Referee **M Messias**

Strangely omitted for England's European Championship
double-header, Beattie responds with his 22nd goal of
the season in Southampton's FA Cup semi-final
warm-up, but Defoe poaches an equaliser for a
revitalised West Ham side still in the thick of the
relegation battle.

THE PLAYERS

CHRIS BAIRD
Defender
Born February 25, 1982,
Ballymena
Ht 6ft 1in **Wt** 12st 0lb
Signed from trainee, August 2001

JAMES BEATTIE
Forward
Born February 27, 1978,
Lancaster
Ht 6ft 1in **Wt** 13st 3lb
Signed from Blackburn Rovers,
July 1998, £1m

FRANCIS BENALI
Defender
Born December 30, 1968,
Southampton
Ht 5ft 10in **Wt** 11st 1lb
Signed from trainee, May 1987

WAYNE BRIDGE
Defender
Born August 5, 1980,
Southampton
Ht 5ft 10in **Wt** 11st 11lb
Signed from trainee, July 1998

KEVIN DAVIES
Forward
Born March 26, 1977, Sheffield
Ht 6ft 0in **Wt** 13st 6lb
Signed from Blackburn Rovers,
August 1999, swap

RORY DELAP
Midfield
Born July 6, 1976, Sutton
Coldfield
Ht 6ft 0in **Wt** 11st 11lb
Signed from Derby County, July
2001, £4m

AGUSTIN DELGADO
Forward
Born December 23, 1974,
Ibarra, Ecuador
Ht 6ft 3in **Wt** 14st 2lb
Signed from Necaxa, Mexico,
November 2001, £3.2m

JASON DODD
Defender
Born November 2, 1970, Bath
Ht 5ft 11in **Wt** 12st 3lb
Signed from Bath City, April 1989,
£50,000

TAHAR EL KHALEJ
(see Charlton Athletic)

Wayne Bridge

FABRICE FERNANDES
Midfield
Born October 29, 1979, Aubervilliers, France
Ht 5ft 8in **Wt** 11st 7lb
Signed from Rennes, December 2001, £1.1m

DANNY HIGGINBOTHAM
Defender
Born December 29, 1978, Manchester
Ht 6ft 2in **Wt** 12st 6lb
Signed from Derby County, January 2003, £1.5m

PAUL JONES
Goalkeeper
Born April 18, 1967, Chirk
Ht 6ft 2in **Wt** 14st 8lb
Signed from Stockport County, January 1997, £900,000

ANDREI KANCHELSKIS
Midfield
Born January 23, 1969, Kirovograd, Ukraine
Ht 5ft 10in **Wt** 13st 3lb
Signed from Manchester City, August 2002, free

CLAUS LUNDEKVAM
Defender
Born February 22, 1973, Austevoll, Norway
Ht 6ft 3in **Wt** 12st 10lb
Signed from SK Brann, September 1996, £400,000

CHRIS MARSDEN
Midfield
Born January 3, 1969, Sheffield
Ht 6ft 0in **Wt** 10st 12lb
Signed from Birmingham City, February 1999, £800,000

GARRY MONK
Defender
Born March 6, 1979, Bedford
Ht 6ft 0in **Wt** 13st 0lb
Signed from Torquay United, July 1996, nominal

ANTTI NIEMI
Goalkeeper
Born May 31, 1971, Oulu, Finland
Ht 6ft 1in **Wt** 14st 0lb
Signed from Heart of Midlothian, August 2002, £2m

MATTHEW OAKLEY
Midfield
Born August 17, 1977, Peterborough
Ht 5ft 10in **Wt** 11st 0lb
Signed from trainee, July 1995

Paul Jones

Sunday April 13
WATFORD
FA Cup, semi-final (Villa Park)
Won 2-1 **HT 1-0** Att **42,602**
Details page 332

Saturday April 19
LEEDS UNITED (h)
Won 3-2 **HT 2-0** Att **32,032** Position **8th**
Jones — Telfer, Lundekvam, M Svensson, Bridge — Fernandes, Oakley, A Svensson (Delap 89), Prutton — Beattie, Ormerod *Subs not used* Blayney, Williams, Higginbotham, Tessem
Scorers **Ormerod 31, Beattie 45, A Svensson 53**
Referee **M Halsey**

"As well as we have played this season," Gordon Strachan says as his Southampton side races into a 3-0 lead before Leeds, reduced to ten men when Smith's second booking results in the ninth sending-off of his career, recover some pride with two late goals.

Monday April 21
BIRMINGHAM CITY (a)
Lost 2-3 **HT 1-0** Att **29,115** Position **9th**
Jones — Telfer (Tessem 85), Lundekvam, M Svensson, Bridge — Fernandes (Higginbotham 76), Delap (Ormerod ht), Oakley, Prutton — Beattie, A Svensson *Subs not used* Blayney, Williams *Booked* Telfer, Bridge
Scorers **A Svensson 26, Ormerod 77**
Report page 195

Saturday April 26
CHARLTON ATHLETIC (a)
Lost 1-2 **HT 0-1** Att **25,894** Position **10th**
Jones — Monk (Tessem 66), Lundekvam, M Svensson, Bridge — Prutton, A Svensson (Fernandes 58), Oakley, Marsden — Beattie, Ormerod *Subs not used* Blayney, Williams, Higginbotham *Booked* Bridge
Scorer **Beattie 90**
Report page 184

Saturday May 3
BOLTON WANDERERS (h)
Drew 0-0 HT 0-0 Att **30,951** Position **11th**
Niemi — Telfer, M Svensson, Williams (Tessem 76),
Bridge — Fernandes, Oakley, A Svensson (Higginbotham
76), Marsden (Prutton 67) — Beattie, Ormerod *Subs not
used* Jones, A Davies *Booked* Fernandes, Ormerod,
Williams
Referee **P Dowd**

Desperately dull tea-time fare perhaps, but that will not
worry Bolton, who climb back above West Ham on goal
difference after 2½ hours in the bottom three, thanks
to a point at St Mary's earned by Jaaskelainen's
first-half save and Ormerod's awful miss after the break.

Wednesday May 7
ARSENAL (a)
Lost 1-6 HT 1-5 Att **38,052** Position **11th**
Jones — Telfer, M Svensson, Williams, Higginbotham —
Fernandes (Baird 25), A Svensson (Oakley 56), Prutton,
Bridge — Tessem, K Davies (Beattie 77) *Subs not used*
A Davies, Ormerod
Scorer **Tessem 35**
Report page 64

Sunday May 11
MANCHESTER CITY (a)
Won 1-0 HT 1-0 Att **34,957** Position **8th**
Jones — Telfer, Lundekvam, M Svensson, Bridge —
Baird, A Svensson (Tessem 65), Oakley, Prutton
(Higginbotham 80) — Beattie, Ormerod (Fernandes 90)
Subs not used Williams, Blayney *Booked* Beattie,
A Svensson, Ormerod, Baird
Scorer **M Svensson 34**
Report page 148

Saturday May 17
ARSENAL
FA Cup, Final (Cardiff)
Lost 0-1 HT 0-1 Att **73,726**
Details page 332

BRETT ORMEROD
Forward
Born October 18, 1976,
Blackburn
Ht 5ft 11in **Wt** 11st 4lb
Signed from Blackpool, December
2001, £1.75m

MARIAN PAHARS
Forward
Born August 5, 1976, Riga, Latvia
Ht 5ft 8in **Wt** 10st 9lb
Signed from Skonto Riga, March
1999, £800,000

DAVID PRUTTON
Midfield
Born September 12, 1981, Hull
Ht 5ft 10in **Wt** 11st 10lb
Signed from Nottingham Forest,
January 2003, £2.5m

ANDERS SVENSSON
Midfield
Born July 17, 1976, Gothenburg
Ht 5ft 10in **Wt** 12st 1lb
Signed from IF Elfsborg, Sweden,
June 2001, £750,000

MICHAEL SVENSSON
Defender
Born November 25, 1975,
Sweden
Ht 6ft 2in **Wt** 13st 3lb
Signed from Troyes, June 2002,
£2m

PAUL TELFER
Defender
Born October 21, 1971, Edinburgh
Ht 5ft 9in **Wt** 11st 6lb
Signed from Coventry City,
November 2001, free

JO TESSEM
Midfield
Born February 28, 1972,
Orlandet, Norway
Ht 6ft 3in **Wt** 13st 5lb
Signed from Molde, November
1999, £600,000

PAUL WILLIAMS
Defender
Born March 26, 1971,
Burton upon Trent
Ht 5ft 11in **Wt** 13st 0lb
Signed from Coventry City,
November 2001, free

Jo Tessem

MANCHESTER CITY

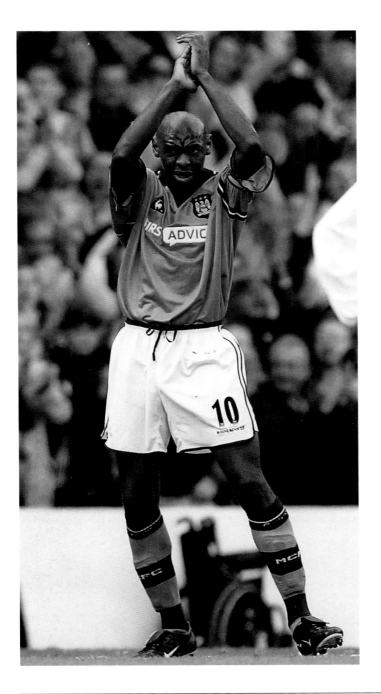

PREMIERSHIP

	P	W	D	L	F	A	Pts
Man Utd	38	25	8	5	74	34	83
Arsenal	38	23	9	6	85	42	78
Newcastle	38	21	6	11	63	48	69
Chelsea	38	19	10	9	68	38	67
Liverpool	38	18	10	10	61	41	64
Blackburn	38	16	12	10	52	43	60
Everton	38	17	8	13	48	49	59
Southampton	38	13	13	12	43	46	52
Man City	**38**	**15**	**6**	**17**	**47**	**54**	**51**
Tottenham	38	14	8	16	51	62	50
Middlesbro	38	13	10	15	48	44	49
Charlton	38	14	7	17	45	56	49
Birmingham	38	13	9	16	41	49	48
Fulham	38	13	9	16	41	50	48
Leeds	38	14	5	19	58	57	47
Aston Villa	38	12	9	17	42	47	45
Bolton	38	10	14	14	41	51	44
West Ham	38	10	12	16	42	59	42
West Brom	38	6	8	24	29	65	26
Sunderland	38	4	7	27	21	65	19

FA CUP
Third round

WORTHINGTON CUP
Third round

A fond farewell — to Maine Road and Shaun Goater

THE GAMES

Saturday August 17
LEEDS UNITED (a)
Lost 0-3   **HT 0-2**   Att **40,195**   Position **20th**
Nash — Sun (Huckerby 59), Howey (Dunne ht), Distin
— Wright-Phillips, Horlock, Foe, Jensen — Benarbia,
Berkovic (Shuker 64) — Anelka *Subs not used* Flowers,
Goater *Booked* Jensen
Report page 210

Saturday August 24
NEWCASTLE UNITED (h)
Won 1-0   **HT 1-0**   Att **34,776**   Position **12th**
Schmeichel — Sun, Howey, Distin — Wright-Phillips,
Benarbia, Foe, Berkovic (Horlock 79) — Anelka,
Huckerby *Subs not used* Nash, Dunne, Tiatto, Goater
Booked Distin
Scorer **Huckerby 36**
Referee **U Rennie**

Kevin Keegan's former team, in unfamiliar 3-5-2
formation, are almost overrun by his present one,
whose first home match on their return to the
Premiership produces a feast of attacking football
that is rewarded with Huckerby's decisive header.
Dyer, though, fails to punish them when he misses an
open goal for Newcastle.

Wednesday August 28
ASTON VILLA (a)
Lost 0-1   **HT 0-0**   Att **33,494**   Position **14th**
Schmeichel — Sun, Howey, Distin — Wright-Phillips,
Benarbia, Foe, Berkovic (Tiatto 67), Jensen — Anelka,
Huckerby (Goater 80) *Subs not used* Nash, Horlock,
Dunne *Booked* Sun, Howey, Foe
Report page 223

Saturday August 31
EVERTON (h)
Won 3-1   **HT 2-1**   Att **34,835**   Position **6th**
Schmeichel — Sun, Howey, Distin — Wright-Phillips,
Benarbia (Goater 86), Foe, Berkovic (Horlock 66),
Jensen — Anelka, Huckerby (Tiatto 79) *Subs not used*
Nash, Dunne *Booked* Benarbia *Sent off*
Wright-Phillips 28
Scorers **Radzinski 14 (og), Anelka 16, 85**
Referee **B Knight**

All change for City. Anelka is off the mark in style,
although the first goal of his 'hat-trick' is later ruled
an own goal by Radzinski, and City are deserving
winners despite playing most of the match with ten
men. Wright-Phillips's sending-off, for a foul on Naysmith
that concedes a penalty, is subsequently downgraded to
a yellow-card offence.

IT WAS AN ODD SEASON FOR Manchester City. Their large and
devoted following should have been extremely pleased with the
club's return to the Premiership. Not only did Kevin Keegan's
flamboyant side finish in a comfortable ninth position in the league
and qualify for the Uefa Cup via their disciplinary record, but they
trounced Manchester United in the final derby at Maine Road and,
arguably, were robbed of victory in the return when an over-zealous
referee penalised Nicolas Anelka for an inadvertent handball before
he squared for Shaun Goater to fire home in injury time.

But, somehow, the season was seen by many as an anticlimax.
For instance, it was City's last season at their home for 80 fitfully
successful years, but they managed to fluff their lines by scoring in
only one of their last four games at Maine Road and losing the very
last one, tamely, to Southampton. Furthermore, ninth place was
reached despite some truly dreadful results in front of their own
supporters. Miserable 3-0 defeats by Liverpool and Chelsea were
compounded by a 5-1 thrashing from Arsenal and an abject
surrender against West Bromwich Albion.

Throw in a typically embarrassing 1-0 defeat away to Wigan
Athletic in the Worthington Cup and a characteristic early exit from
the FA Cup, this time at the hands of Liverpool, and you have an
archetypal City season — albeit one not marked by relegation or
promotion (the first time City have not changed divisions since the
1997-97 season).

Off the pitch, the prolonged period of stability brought by David
Bernstein was ended abruptly when boardroom wrangling saw the
chairman ousted. Some insiders suggested that he was pushed by
Keegan, who was outraged at Bernstein's interference in the
interminable Robbie Fowler transfer saga. Bernstein's supporters
claim that his involvement ensured City were the beneficiaries of a
brilliantly executed deal, which meant that they not only deferred
much of the transfer fee until Fowler had proved his worth, but also
that Leeds United continued to pay for a large part of his salary.
Certainly, Fowler's failure to shine in City colours suggests that
Bernstein had every right to be concerned about his fitness.
However, predictions of imminent financial meltdown under John
Wardle, the new chairman, look a little hysterical. Wardle insisted
that Keegan had limited funds for any summer wheeler-dealing.

A minority of fans, however, are still uncertain about Keegan as a
manager. While the majority are pleased at the progress of the club
under his tenure, others point to the £40 million-plus he has spent
on players and insist he should have done better. There have been
several questionable signings. Players such as Lucien Mettomo,

Anelka's pace troubles Mellberg in the 3-1 win over Villa on Boxing Day

Christian Negouai and Vicente Matias Vuoso cost in excess of £6 million and have started just 26 games between them. In fact, Vuoso, the costliest of the three at £3.5 million, has yet to start a game for the first team.

It would, however, take the most cavilling of City fans to claim that Keegan has not delivered on his vows when he joined in 2001 after City had been relegated to the first division. He promised European football within five years and although City may have sneaked into the Uefa Cup via the "Boy Scout" route, it is testament to Keegan's buccaneering philosophy that City have qualified.

At the start of the season, most fans would have been ecstatic at the prospect of surviving comfortably in the Premiership and getting into Europe. By mid-October, when a series of poor results had left them third from bottom, survival was the only target. City's season was finally kick-started in November, when a thrilling display of mid-field virtuosity from Eyal Berkovic and some predatory finishing from Goater saw United dispatched 3-1.

Slowly but surely, City began to claw their way up the table, until by mid-January a top-six finish looked probable. They fell away in alarming fashion and it was not until Keegan finally conceded that his adherence to 3-5-2 was not working and switched to 4-4-2 that the slide was arrested.

Almost by accident, Keegan may have found the system that works best for his inconsistent side. David Sommeil, a £3.5 million signing during the transfer window, and the magnificent Sylvain Distin have forged a very promising centre half pairing and City have looked more solid than for a very long time. A City side managed by Keegan looking mean at the back? Whatever next?

Now, if only Anelka and Fowler could start scoring, City's first season at their splendid new 48,000-capacity City of Manchester Stadium could prove interesting indeed.

Tuesday September 10
ARSENAL (a)
Lost 1-2 HT 1-2 Att **37,878** Position **9th**
Schmeichel — Sun, Howey (Horlock 79), Distin — Wright-Phillips, Benarbia, Foe, Berkovic, Jensen — Anelka, Huckerby (Goater 59) *Subs not used* Nash, Dunne, Tiatto *Booked* Distin, Benarbia *Sent off* Benarbia 85
Scorer **Anelka 29**
Report page 55

Sunday September 15
BLACKBURN ROVERS (h)
Drew 2-2 HT 0-1 Att **34,130** Position **11th**
Schmeichel — Sun, Bischoff (Tiatto 61), Distin — Wright-Phillips, Benarbia, Foe, Berkovic, Jensen — Anelka, Shuker (Goater 61) *Subs not used* Nash, Ritchie, Horlock *Booked* Wright-Phillips, Foe, Berkovic *Sent off* Tiatto 68
Scorers **Anelka 80, Goater 90**
Referee **M Dean**

Kevin Keegan's cavaliers enhance their reputation as the great Premiership entertainers when, two goals and one man down — Tiatto, within minutes of arriving as a substitute, is sent off after launching himself into a dreadful two-footed tackle on Thompson — they rescue a point by scoring twice in the last ten minutes, Goater's equaliser arriving with only seconds remaining. Only Graeme Souness and his Blackburn team are not amused.

Saturday September 21
WEST HAM UNITED (a)
Drew 0-0 HT 0-0 Att **35,550** Position **12th**
Schmeichel — Sun, Howey, Distin — Wright-Phillips, Foe, Horlock, Jensen — Benarbia (Huckerby 83), Berkovic — Anelka *Subs not used* Nash, Bischoff, Tiatto, Shuker
Report page 247

Saturday September 28
LIVERPOOL (h)
Lost 0-3 HT 0-1 Att **35,131** Position **15th**
Schmeichel — Sun, Howey (Shuker 70), Distin — Wright-Phillips, Foe, Horlock, Berkovic, Jensen — Anelka, Huckerby (Goater 61) *Subs not used* Mettomo, Kerkar, Nash
Referee **P Durkin**

Crisis over, for Liverpool and Owen at least. After one goal, and that a penalty, in 833 minutes, the England striker destroys City with a hat-trick, punishing poor defending at a corner and then Sun's lack of pace. He later takes delight in hitting out at the "stupid people" who had written him off. Kevin Keegan had not been among them.

Tuesday October 1
CREWE ALEXANDRA (h)
Worthington Cup, 2nd rnd
Won 3-2 **HT 0-1** **Att 21,820**
Schmeichel — Sun, Howey, Mettomo (Wright-Phillips 60),
Jensen — Foe, Benarbia, Horlock, Berkovic — Anelka,
Goater (Huckerby 60) *Subs not used* Nash, Bischoff,
Vuoso
Scorers **Berkovic 69, Walker 84 (og), Huckerby 87**
Referee **R Pearson**

"We got away with it," Kevin Keegan admits after City,
behind inside 20 seconds, eventually recover to
dispatch their neighbours in an enthralling cup-tie that
produces three goals in the last six minutes, Huckerby
having the last word when he meets a cross from
Wright-Phillips.

Saturday October 5
SOUTHAMPTON (a)
Lost 0-2 **HT 0-2** **Att 31,009** Position **16th**
Schmeichel — Sun, Howey (Mettomo 37), Distin —
Wright-Phillips (Huckerby 73), Foe, Horlock, Jensen —
Benarbia, Berkovic — Anelka *Subs not used* Nash,
Goater, Kerkar *Booked* Foe, Jensen
Report page 127

Saturday October 19
CHELSEA (h)
Lost 0-3 **HT 0-0** **Att 34,953** Position **17th**
Schmeichel — Sun, Howey, Distin — Wright-Phillips,
Benarbia, Foe, Berkovic, Jensen — Anelka, Goater
(Huckerby 71) *Subs not used* Nash, Dunne, Horlock,
Vuoso *Booked* Benarbia
Referee **D Gallagher**

This is a meeting of sides in poor form and it is
Chelsea who shoot their way out of a slump. City are
on top for long spells but fail to make the most of
their chances, while Chelsea strike with three goals in
17 second-half minutes, the irrepressible Zola getting
the first two.

MATCH OF THE SEASON

Manchester City 3   Manchester United 1
Maine Road, Saturday November 9 2002
Oliver Kay

Goater's second goal secures City's victory in the last Maine Road derby

THE LAST TIME THIS HAPPENED, 13 years ago, Sir Alex
Ferguson went home and buried his head under the pillow until his
wife told him it was safe to come out. This time, there was no hiding
place, not for him and certainly not for his players. The Manchester
United manager opted for a different approach. He gave them what
he quaintly described as a "bollocking".

Publicly, he said that they had "let us down". Privately, behind
the dressing-room walls, he went farther and questioned their
desire. "At times like this, I wonder if I should open the door and let
the fans in to tell the players exactly how they feel," he said. Had he
done so, the most successful manager in British football history
would have been unlikely to escape the flak.

The emphatic defeat at the hands of Manchester City confirmed
what many have long suspected — that United, anaemic so often
over the past 18 months, badly need an injection of new blood. Has
Ferguson, at 60, got the energy to assemble a third great United
team? Moreover, will he be given the time to do so?

These are the type of questions that have not been asked of
Ferguson since the winter of discontent that followed their previous
defeat at Maine Road, in September 1989. During the glory years
that ensued, he was untouchable. No more; growing numbers of
supporters are wondering whether his decision to postpone his
retirement was the wrong one — for himself and for the club.

Anelka leaves Ferdinand in his wake during City's derby victory

This result was attributed to "lapses of concentration", but this has happened too often to United over the past year. When even habitual straight men such as Gary Neville start to play the stooge, as he did to such calamitous effect to hand Shaun Goater his first goal in the 26th minute, it is clear something serious is wrong.

Neville was by no means the worst culprit, though. That distinction fell, not for the first time, to Juan Sebastian Veron. The Argentinian, £28.1 million worth of lethargy, was lamentable, ducking out of challenges and, when the mood took him, hitting 40-yard passes that served not the slightest purpose.

On days such as this, when they were comprehensively outfought and overrun by their less illustrious neighbours, United miss Roy Keane more than ever. Whatever his faults, the captain at least strives to ensure that standards do not slip. In his absence, those standards have slipped alarmingly. Ruud van Nistelrooy, for instance, was reduced to petty acts of gamesmanship on Saturday.

United also look a soft touch physically when Keane is not there. In recent home matches against Everton and Aston Villa, they have been outmuscled in midfield and carved open in defence. The crucial difference was that City, seizing the day, took their chances.

The first came after just five minutes, Phil Neville's stray pass allowing Nicolas Anelka to sprint away from Rio Ferdinand —

Saturday October 26
BIRMINGHAM CITY (a)
Won 2-0 HT 1-0 Att 29,316 Position 16th
Nash — Dunne, Howey, Distin — Sun, Berkovic, Foe, Tiatto, Jensen (Horlock ht) — Anelka, Goater (Huckerby 90) Subs not used Flowers, Wright-Phillips, Benarbia Booked Sun, Foe
Scorers **Sun 24, Anelka 87**
Report page 188

Saturday November 2
WEST BROMWICH ALBION (a)
Won 2-1 HT 0-0 Att 27,044 Position 14th
Nash — Dunne, Howey, Distin — Sun, Berkovic, Foe, Tiatto (Horlock 86), Jensen — Anelka, Goater Subs not used Flowers, Wright-Phillips, Benarbia, Huckerby Booked Berkovic, Dunne
Scorers **Anelka 51, Goater 71**
Report page 261

Tuesday November 5
WIGAN ATHLETIC (a)
Worthington Cup, 3rd rnd
Lost 0-1 HT 0-1 Att 15,007
Nash — Dunne, Howey (Wiekens 19), Distin (Horlock 35) — Sun, Wright-Phillips, Foe, Benarbia, Jensen — Anelka, Goater (Huckerby 68) Subs not used Flowers, Vuoso Booked Horlock, Foe
Referee **M Dean**

City go the way of West Bromwich Albion in the previous round, deservedly beaten by the second division high-flyers at the JJB Stadium. Kevin Keegan loses Howey and Distin to injury in the first half and then the match to Roberts's opportunist 35th-minute strike.

Saturday November 9
MANCHESTER UNITED (h)
Won 3-1 HT 2-1 Att 34,649 Position 11th
Schmeichel — Dunne, Wiekens, Mettomo — Sun, Foe, Tiatto (Horlock 88), Jensen — Berkovic (Wright-Phillips 78) — Anelka, Goater Subs not used Nash, Benarbia, Huckerby Booked Wiekens
Scorers **Anelka 5, Goater 25, 50**
Referee **P Durkin**

Thirteen years after their previous victory in a Maine Road derby, City choose the last such fixture to re-emerge from United's shadows, Goater settling local bragging rights with a double after Solskjaer and Anelka had exchanged early goals. Sir Alex Ferguson tears into his troops in the United dressing-room, questioning their desire.

Saturday November 16
CHARLTON ATHLETIC (h)
Lost 0-1 **HT 0-0** Att **33,455** Position **12th**
Schmeichel — Sun, Dunne, Mettomo — Wright-Phillips, Foe (Horlock 47), Tiatto, Jensen — Berkovic (Benarbia 74) — Anelka, Goater (Huckerby 73) *Subs not used* Shuker, Nash
Referee **G Barber**

Manchester City's capacity to veer from the sublime to the ridiculous is well illustrated when they return to the scene of their derby delight and put in a timid display against struggling Charlton Athletic, who take the points when Bartlett meets Johansson's cross at the far post.

Saturday November 23
MIDDLESBROUGH (a)
Lost 1-3 **HT 0-0** Att **31,510** Position **16th**
Schmeichel — Sun, Dunne, Mettomo (Benarbia 86) — Wright-Phillips, Horlock, Berkovic, Tiatto, Jensen — Anelka, Goater (Huckerby 76) *Subs not used* Nash, Vuoso, Barton *Booked* Tiatto, Mettomo, Wright-Phillips *Sent off* Wright-Phillips 72
Scorer **Anelka 68**
Report page 166

Saturday November 30
BOLTON WANDERERS (h)
Won 2-0 **HT 1-0** Att **34,860** Position **12th**
Schmeichel — Dunne, Howey, Distin — Sun, Foe, Horlock, Tiatto — Berkovic — Anelka, Goater (Benarbia 81) *Subs not used* Nash, Wiekens, Wright-Phillips, Huckerby
Scorers **Howey 25, Berkovic 56**
Referee **J Winter**

With Bolton managing just two shots on goal throughout, both routinely gathered by Schmeichel, City's victory could hardly be more easily obtained. Howey heads the first, from Berkovic's free kick, and the Israeli playmaker gets his first Premiership goal from Anelka's pass.

Monday December 9
SUNDERLAND (a)
Won 3-0 **HT 1-0** Att **36,511** Position **12th**
Schmeichel — Dunne, Howey, Distin — Sun, Foe, Horlock, Tiatto — Berkovic — Anelka, Goater *Subs not used* Nash, Benarbia, Huckerby, Wiekens, Jensen *Booked* Sun, Tiatto
Scorers **Foe 44, Sun 62, Goater 86**
Report page 274

Goater punishes a mistake by Gary Neville to restore City's advantage

who, incidentally, does not look a £30 million defender. The City forward passed the ball to Goater, whose shot was spilt by Fabien Barthez into the path of Anelka, who will rarely score an easier goal.

United were level within three minutes, Ole Gunnar Solskjaer producing a tidy finish, but Gary Neville's dreadful lapse of concentration handed the initiative back to City. The full back dithered as he tried to shepherd the ball out of play, allowing Goater to score his 99th goal for City. His century came early in the second half as the excellent Eyal Berkovic set up the Bermudan to make it 3-1, a lead that City fully deserved, even if Solskjaer and John O'Shea, in particular, should have reduced the arrears during a belated siege on the home goal.

The man who kept United at bay during those final minutes was Peter Schmeichel, taking great delight in repelling his former club with a series of excellent saves. "Don't try to get me talking about United," he said. "They've suffered enough. They'll just want to go home and forget about it."

MANCHESTER CITY (3-4-1-2): P Schmeichel — R Dunne, G Wiekens, L Mettomo — Sun Jihai, M-V Foe, D Tiatto (sub: K Horlock, 88min), N Jensen — E Berkovic (sub: S Wright-Phillips, 78) — N Anelka, S Goater. **Substitutes not used:** C Nash, A Benarbia, D Huckerby. **Booked:** Wiekens.
MANCHESTER UNITED (4-3-2-1): F Barthez — G Neville (sub: J O'Shea, 62), R Ferdinand, L Blanc, M Silvestre — O G Solskjaer, P Neville, J S Veron (sub: D Forlan, 62), R Giggs — P Scholes — R van Nistelrooy. **Substitutes not used:** Ricardo, D May, Q Fortune. **Booked:** Solskjaer, P Neville.
Referee: P Durkin

THE MANAGER

Kevin Keegan

Obviously, Kevin Keegan *is* City these days — the little chap with the huge charisma cannot help but blot out everything else. He may still exhibit questionable judgment in the transfer market (will Robbie Fowler ever recover his form?) and his tactics are often inexplicable (when will City learn to defend at corners?) But the club have prospered under his guidance. If City do finally end their 27-year trophy drought while Keegan is at the helm, then the esteem in which he is held at Newcastle United will suddenly seem like little more than a minor crush.

Paul Connolly

APPEARANCES

	Prem	FAC	WC	Total
N Anelka	38	1	2	41
J Barton	7	-	-	7
D Belmadi	2 (6)	-	-	2 (6)
A Benarbia	21 (12)	1	2	24 (12)
E Berkovic	27	0 (1)	1	28 (1)
M Bischoff	0 (1)	-	-	0 (1)
S Distin	34	1	1	36
R Dunne	24 (1)	-	1	25 (1)
M-V Foe	35	1	2	38
R Fowler	12 (1)	-	-	12 (1)
S Goater	14 (12)	0 (1)	2	16 (13)
K Horlock	22 (8)	1	1 (1)	24 (9)
S Howey	24	-	2	26
D Huckerby	6 (10)	0 (1)	0 (2)	6 (13)
N Jensen	32 (1)	1	2	35 (1)
S Jordan	0 (1)	-	-	0 (1)
J Macken	0 (5)	-	-	0 (5)
L Mettomo	3 (1)	1	1	5 (1)
C Nash	9	-	1	10
P Schmeichel	29	1	1	31
C Shuker	1 (2)	-	-	1 (2)
D Sommeil	14	-	-	14
Sun Jihai	25 (3)	1	2	28 (3)
D Tiatto	10 (3)	-	-	10 (3)
G Wiekens	5 (1)	1	0 (1)	6 (2)
S Wright-Phillips	23 (8)	1	1 (1)	25 (9)

Saturday December 14
CHARLTON ATHLETIC (a)
Drew 2-2 **HT 0-0** Att **26,434** Position **12th**
Schmeichel — Dunne, Howey (Benarbia 73), Distin — Sun, Foe, Horlock, Tiatto — Berkovic — Anelka, Goater
Subs not used Nash, Jensen, Wiekens, Huckerby
Booked Horlock
Scorer **Foe 73, 87**
Report page 178

Monday December 23
TOTTENHAM HOTSPUR (h)
Lost 2-3 **HT 1-1** Att **34,563** Position **12th**
Schmeichel — Dunne, Howey, Distin — Sun (Benarbia 58), Foe, Horlock, Berkovic, Tiatto — Anelka, Goater (Huckerby 84) *Subs not used* Wiekens, Jensen, Nash
Booked Foe, Tiatto
Scorers **Howey 29, Benarbia 90**
Referee **J Winter**

Howey gets the ball rolling with a header, only for Tottenham to reply with three similar efforts of their own. The visiting team can afford to admire Benarbia's beautiful late reply, the goal of the match — and to regret the stupidity that sees Ziege dismissed in the last minute for his second offence of kicking the ball away in quick succession.

Thursday December 26
ASTON VILLA (h)
Won 3-1 **HT 1-1** Att **33,991** Position **11th**
Schmeichel — Dunne, Howey, Distin — Wright-Phillips (Benarbia 65), Foe, Horlock, Berkovic, Tiatto (Jensen ht) — Anelka, Goater (Huckerby 73) *Subs not used* Wiekens, Nash
Scorers **Foe 15, 80, Benarbia 78**
Referee **M Halsey**

Rarely can a substitute have made such an impact. With City and Villa locked at 1-1, Benarbia — a regular Maine Road bench-warmer for two months — arrives to hit the bar, put City in front with a brilliant diving header and finally set up Foe for his second, and City's third, goal.

Saturday December 28
FULHAM (a)
Won 1-0 **HT 0-0** Att **17,937** Position **9th**
Schmeichel — Dunne, Howey, Distin, Jensen — Horlock — Benarbia (Wiekens 86), Foe, Berkovic (Sun 35) — Anelka, Huckerby (Wright-Phillips 68) *Subs not used* Nash, Goater *Booked* Jensen
Scorer **Anelka 84**
Report page 205

Wednesday January 1
EVERTON (a)
Drew 2-2   HT 1-1   Att **40,163**   Position **10th**
Schmeichel — Dunne, Howey, Distin — Sun, Horlock,
Foe, Benarbia, Jensen — Anelka (Huckerby 82),
Wright-Phillips *Subs not used* Nash, Wiekens, Goater,
Mettomo *Booked* Horlock, Jensen
Scorers **Anelka 33, Foe 82**
Report page 120

Sunday January 5
LIVERPOOL (h)
FA Cup, 3rd rnd
Lost 0-1   HT 0-0   Att **28,586**
Schmeichel — Mettomo (Berkovic 40), Wiekens,
Distin — Sun (Goater 70), Horlock, Foe, Benarbia
(Huckerby 85), Jensen — Wright-Phillips — Anelka
Subs not used Nash, Ritchie *Booked* Distin, Berkovic
Referee **U Rennie**

What many thought would be the tie of the round is
instead a drab, uneventful let-down, settled by a far
from convincing penalty, awarded when Foe is
penalised for blocking Smicer's cross with his hand.
Anelka, looking to make a point against the club that
let him go, is one of several players who never get into
their stride.

Saturday January 11
LEEDS UNITED (h)
Won 2-1   HT 1-0   Att **34,884**   Position **8th**
Schmeichel — Dunne, Howey, Distin — Sun, Horlock,
Foe, Jensen — Berkovic (Benarbia 84) — Anelka, Goater
(Wright-Phillips 79) *Subs not used* Nash, Wiekens,
Huckerby
Scorers **Goater 29, Jensen 50**
Referee **R Styles**

Kevin Keegan is dreaming of Europe again after a
victory that ends Leeds's mini-revival in emphatic style,
despite the closeness of the scoreline. Goater's opener
is followed by a stunning volley from Jensen, a
goal-of-the-season contender, before Kewell's late
consolation effort.

PLAYER OF THE SEASON   Sylvain Distin

It may seem strange after a season in
which City conceded 54 Premiership
goals (only six teams conceded more)
to nominate a defender as the player
of the season, but Sylvain Distin was
outstanding. In Kevin Keegan's
three-man defence he was often seen
marauding upfield, drifting past tackle
after tackle before delivering a perfect
pass to Nicolas Anelka, his compatriot,
but it was his dominance in the flat
back four that so impressed. Distin is
a truly imperious centre half — "Dave
Watson with skill", as one City wag
suggested.
Paul Connolly

STATS AND FACTS

- Since April 1998 there have been only two instances of the away team scoring four times in the first 40 minutes of a Premiership game — both times achieved by Arsenal . . . and both times against Manchester City.

- Neil Clement, the West Bromwich Albion defender, scored three goals this season, including the matches at home and away to City. The only time in his career that he has scored twice in a game also came against City.

- In September, when they were beaten 3-0, City suffered a tenth home defeat to Liverpool by at least a three-goal margin since 1976.

- Manchester City have not won in 22 games away to Manchester United.

- Manchester City's average attendance in 2002-03 of 34,564 was their highest since 1979-80.

- In the autumn, City did not manage a goal in four successive league games (against West Ham, Liverpool, Southampton and Chelsea). It was their first such run of blanks in five years.

- Last season was only the sixth since 1966 that City and Bolton Wanderers have been in the same division.

- Manchester City have scored four times in their 12 Premiership games against Arsenal.

- City's 2-1 win at Anfield in May was only their third in their past 25 meetings with Liverpool.

Bill Edgar

GOALSCORERS

	Prem	FAC	WC	Total
N Anelka	14 (1p)	-	-	14 (1p)
J Barton	1	-	-	1
A Benarbia	3	-	-	3
E Berkovic	1	-	1	2
M-V Foe	9	-	-	9
R Fowler	2	-	-	2
S Goater	7	-	-	7
S Howey	2	-	-	2
D Huckerby	1	-	1	2
N Jensen	1	-	-	1
Sun Jihai	2	-	-	2
D Sommeil	1	-	-	1
S Wright-Phillips	1	-	-	1
Own goals	2	-	1	3

Saturday January 18
NEWCASTLE UNITED (a)
Lost 0-2 **HT 0-1** Att **52,152** Position **10th**
Nash — Dunne, Howey, Distin — Sun (Macken 70), Horlock, Foe, Benarbia, Jensen — Anelka, Goater (Belmadi 60) Subs not used Murphy, Wiekens, Ritchie
Booked Sun
Report page 73

Wednesday January 29
FULHAM (h)
Won 4-1 **HT 1-1** Att **33,260** Position **9th**
Nash — Sommeil, Howey, Distin — Dunne, Foe, Horlock, Benarbia (Wright-Phillips 70), Jensen — Anelka (Goater 87), Belmadi Subs not used Weaver, Sun, Huckerby
Booked Foe, Jensen, Sommeil
Scorers **Anelka 21, Benarbia 47, Foe 61, Wright-Phillips 70**
Referee **S Bennett**

With Fowler having done a U-turn and about to put pen to paper on his on-off transfer from Leeds United, City show that they already have plenty of firepower in their ranks, taking Malbranque's early strike for Fulham as a signal to attack. Wright-Phillips completes a facile win just 35 seconds after his introduction as a substitute.

Saturday February 1
WEST BROMWICH ALBION (h)
Lost 1-2 **HT 1-1** Att **34,765** Position **10th**
Nash — Sommeil, Howey, Distin — Dunne (Wright-Phillips ht), Foe, Horlock, Benarbia (Belmadi 67), Jensen (Goater 80) — Anelka, Fowler Subs not used Weaver, Sun Booked Distin
Scorer **Gilchrist 22 (og)**
Referee **N Barry**

Kevin Keegan unveils his "dream team" of Anelka and Fowler up front, but it immediately turns into a nightmare as struggling Albion secure a deserved victory, despite the dismissal of Roberts for using his elbow in an off-the-ball tangle with Sommeil, and despite Gilchrist's own goal. Clement and Moore strike for Gary Megson's team at set-pieces.

Sunday February 9
MANCHESTER UNITED (a)
Drew 1-1 **HT 0-1** Att **67,646** Position **10th**
Nash — Sommeil, Howey, Distin — Sun, Foe, Horlock (Wright-Phillips 66), Jensen — Berkovic (Benarbia 86) — Anelka, Fowler (Goater 86) Subs not used Dunne, Stuhr-Ellegaard Booked Foe
Scorer **Goater 86**
Report page 49

Saturday February 22
ARSENAL (h)
Lost 1-5 **HT 0-4** Att **34,960** Position **11th**
Nash — Dunne (Wright-Phillips ht), Howey, Sommeil —
Sun, Belmadi (Benarbia 65), Foe, Berkovic, Jensen —
Anelka, Fowler *Subs not used* Horlock, Goater, Weaver
Scorer **Anelka 87**
Referee **P Durkin**

Arsenal are "on another planet", Kevin Keegan says
after watching them put four goals past his bemused
side in the first 19 minutes. The leaders are aided by
some shambolic defending, which sees Dunne replaced
at half-time "for his own protection". Vieira adds a fifth
before Anelka's late reply.

Saturday March 1
BLACKBURN ROVERS (a)
Lost 0-1 **HT 0-1** Att **28,647** Position **11th**
Nash — Sommeil, Wiekens (Goater 82), Distin — Sun
(Wright-Phillips 59), Horlock, Foe, Berkovic (Benarbia ht),
Jensen — Anelka, Fowler *Subs not used* Weaver,
Bischoff
Report page 110

Sunday March 16
BIRMINGHAM CITY (h)
Won 1-0 **HT 0-0** Att **34,596** Position **12th**
Schmeichel — Sommeil, Wiekens, Distin —
Wright-Phillips, Foe, Horlock, Benarbia, Jensen —
Anelka, Fowler (Sun 81) *Subs not used* Nash, Dunne,
Belmadi, Goater *Booked* Jensen, Wiekens *Sent off*
Jensen 79
Scorer **Fowler 72**
Referee **M Messias**

A drab game is settled by one moment of undoubted
class as Fowler opens his Manchester City account with
an expert volley from Benarbia's cross. Sadly for
Horsfield, the Birmingham substitute, when presented
with a much easier opportunity to equalise, he is guilty
of an embarrassing air shot. Jensen is sent off for two
bookings.

Saturday March 22
CHELSEA (a)
Lost 0-5 **HT 0-2** Att **41,105** Position **12th**
Schmeichel — Sommeil, Wiekens, Distin —
Wright-Phillips (Sun 63), Foe, Horlock (Belmadi 58),
Benarbia, Jensen — Anelka, Fowler (Goater ht) *Subs not
used* Nash, Dunne *Booked* Sun, Distin, Benarbia
Sent off Sun 90
Report page 86

NICOLAS ANELKA
Forward
Born March 14, 1979, Versailles
Ht 6ft 0in **Wt** 12st 3lb
Signed from Paris Saint-Germain,
July 2002, £13m

JOEY BARTON
Midfield
Born September 2, 1982, Huyton
Ht 5ft 9in **Wt** 11st 0lb
Signed from trainee, August
2001

DJAMEL BELMADI
Midfield
Born March 27, 1976,
Champigny-sur-Marne, France
Ht 5ft 8in **Wt** 10st 7lb
Signed from Marseilles (loan),
January 2003

ALI BENARBIA
Midfield
Born October 8, 1968,
Oran, Algeria
Ht 5ft 7in **Wt** 10st 7lb
Signed from Paris Saint-Germain,
September 2001, free

EYAL BERKOVIC
Midfield
Born April 2, 1972, Haifa
Ht 5ft 7in **Wt** 10st 6lb
Signed from Celtic, August 2001,
£1.5m

MIKKEL BISCHOFF
Defender
Born February 3, 1982, Denmark
Ht 6ft 3in **Wt** 13st 4lb
Signed from AB Copenhagen, July
2002, £750,000

SYLVAIN DISTIN
Defender
Born December 16, 1977, Paris
Ht 6ft 4in **Wt** 13st 10lb
Signed from Newcastle United,
May 2002, £4m

RICHARD DUNNE
Defender
Born September 21, 1979, Dublin
Ht 6ft 1in **Wt** 14st 0lb
Signed from Everton, October
2000, £3m

Ali Benarbia

MARC-VIVIEN FOE
Midfield
Born May 1, 1975, Nkolo,
Cameroon **Died** June 26, 2003
Signed from Lyons (loan), July
2003
Obituaries, page 389

ROBBIE FOWLER
Forward
Born April 9, 1975,
Toxteth, Liverpool
Ht 5ft 11in **Wt** 11st 10lb
Signed from Leeds United,
January 2003, £6m

SHAUN GOATER
Forward
Born February 25, 1970,
Hamilton, Bermuda
Ht 6ft 1in **Wt** 12st 0lb
Signed from Bristol City, March
1998, £400,000

KEVIN HORLOCK
Midfield
Born November 1, 1972, Erith
Ht 6ft 0in **Wt** 12st 0lb
Signed from Swindon Town,
January 1997, £1.25m

STEVE HOWEY
Defender
Born October 26, 1971,
Sunderland
Ht 6ft 2in **Wt** 11st 12lb
Signed from Newcastle United,
August 2000, £2m

DARREN HUCKERBY
Forward
Born April 23, 1976, Nottingham
Ht 5ft 10in **Wt** 11st 12lb
Signed from Leeds United,
December 2000, £2.25m

NICLAS JENSEN
Defender
Born August 17, 1974,
Copenhagen
Ht 5ft 11in **Wt** 12st 3lb
Signed from FC Copenhagen,
January 2002, £700,000

STEPHEN JORDAN
Midfield
Born March 6, 1982, Warrington
Ht 6ft 0in **Wt** 11st 0lb
Signed from trainee, June 2000

JON MACKEN
Forward
Born September 7, 1977,
Manchester
Ht 5ft 10in **Wt** 12st 8lb
Signed from Preston North End,
March 2002, £4m

Robbie Fowler

Saturday April 5
BOLTON WANDERERS (a)
Lost 0-2 HT 0-1 Att 26,949 Position 12th
Schmeichel — Dunne, Wiekens (Benarbia 69),
Sommeil — Wright-Phillips, Berkovic, Barton, Horlock
(Jordan 69), Distin — Anelka, Fowler (Macken 69)
Subs not used Goater, Nash *Booked* Distin, Horlock,
Dunne, Schmeichel, Wiekens
Report page 243

Saturday April 12
MIDDLESBROUGH (h)
Drew 0-0 HT 0-0 Att 34,793 Position 12th
Schmeichel — Dunne, Sommeil, Distin, Jensen —
Wright-Phillips, Foe, Barton — Berkovic (Benarbia ht) —
Anelka (Goater 63), Fowler (Macken 63) *Subs not used*
Nash, Sun
Referee **A D'Urso**

At least Schmeichel is able to celebrate the
announcement of his impending retirement with a
clean sheet as City and Middlesbrough complete a
desperately dull draw. "Not a classic," Kevin Keegan,
who replaces his £19 million dream pairing of Anelka
and Fowler in the second half, says with untypical
understatement.

Friday April 18
TOTTENHAM HOTSPUR (a)
Won 2-0 HT 2-0 Att 36,075 Position 12th
Schmeichel — Dunne, Sommeil, Distin, Jensen —
Benarbia, Foe, Barton, Wright-Phillips — Anelka, Fowler
(Macken 80) *Subs not used* Nash, Sun, Horlock, Goater
Booked Wright-Phillips, Dunne, Barton
Scorers **Sommeil 3, Barton 21**
Report page 159

Monday April 21
SUNDERLAND (h)
Won 3-0 HT 2-0 Att 34,357 Position 10th
Schmeichel — Dunne (Belmadi 40), Sommeil, Distin,
Jensen — Foe, Benarbia, Barton, Wright-Phillips —
Anelka, Fowler *Subs not used* Nash, Macken,
Bischoff, Sun
Scorers **Foe 36, 80, Fowler 38**
Referee **G Barber**

City move back into the top half of the table when
Foe's brace sandwiches a clever lob by Fowler and
inflicts a twelfth successive league defeat on
Sunderland, who are heading for all sorts of unwanted
records.

Sunday April 27
WEST HAM UNITED (h)
Lost 0-1 **HT 0-0** Att **34,815** Position **11th**
Schmeichel — Dunne, Distin, Sommeil, Jensen (Goater
87) — Benarbia (Macken 71), Barton, Foe, Wright-Phillips
— Anelka, Fowler (Belmadi 71) *Subs not used* Nash,
Bischoff *Booked* Sommeil
Referee **R Styles**

Kevin Keegan promises no favours for Trevor Brooking,
his friend and former England room-mate, who has
taken charge for West Ham United's last three games
while Glenn Roeder recovers in hospital. But City have
no answer to the 81st-minute winner from Kanoute,
scored from a couple of inches, that keeps West
Ham's survival hopes alive as they close the gap on
Bolton.

Saturday May 3
LIVERPOOL (a)
Won 2-1 **HT 0-0** Att **44,220** Position **8th**
Schmeichel — Dunne, Sommeil, Distin, Jensen —
Wright-Phillips, Barton, Horlock, Benarbia — Fowler,
Anelka *Subs not used* Macken, Sun, Nash, Bischoff,
Belmadi *Booked* Horlock, Benarbia, Dunne
Scorer **Anelka 74 (pen), 90**
Report page 100

Sunday May 11
SOUTHAMPTON (h)
Lost 0-1 **HT 0-1** Att **34,957** Position **9th**
Schmeichel — Dunne (Horlock 82), Sommeil, Distin,
Jensen — Foe, Barton (Belmadi 70), Wright-Phillips,
Benarbia — Anelka, Goater (Fowler 63) *Subs not used*
Nash, Wiekens *Booked* Distin, Dunne, Barton
Referee **M Dean**

Almost predictably, City bid farewell to Maine Road,
their home for 80 years — as well as to Schmeichel
and Goater — with a last-day defeat to go with the
expected tears, Southampton ruining the Blue Moon
party when Michael Svensson heads the last goal at the
ground for a side six days away from a date with Arsenal
in the Cup Final.

LUCIEN METTOMO
Defender
Born April 19, 1977,
Douala, Cameroon
Ht 6ft 0in **Wt** 12st 7lb
Signed from St Etienne, October
2001, £1.2m

CARLO NASH
Goalkeeper
Born September 13, 1973,
Bolton
Ht 6ft 5in **Wt** 14st 1lb
Signed from Stockport County,
January 2001, £100,000

PETER SCHMEICHEL
Goalkeeper
Born November 18, 1963,
Gladsaxe, Denmark
Ht 6ft 4in **Wt** 16st 1lb
Signed from Aston Villa, July
2002, free

CHRIS SHUKER
Midfield
Born May 9, 1982, Liverpool
Ht 5ft 5in **Wt** 10st 1lb
Signed from trainee, September
1999

DAVID SOMMEIL
Defender
Born August 10, 1974,
Guadeloupe
Ht 5ft 11in **Wt** 11st 6lb
Signed from Bordeaux,
January 2003, £3.5m

SUN JIHAI
Defender
Born September 30, 1977,
Dalian, China
Ht 5ft 10in **Wt** 10st 12lb
Signed from Crystal Palace,
February 2002, £2m

DANNY TIATTO
Midfield
Born May 22, 1973, Melbourne
Ht 5ft 7in **Wt** 12st 0lb
Signed from FC Baden,
Switzerland, July 1998, £300,000

GERARD WIEKENS
Defender
Born February 25, 1973,
Tolhuiswyk, Holland
Ht 6ft 0in **Wt** 13st 4lb
Signed from SC Veendam,
Holland, July 1997, £500,000

SHAUN WRIGHT-PHILLIPS
Midfield
Born October 25, 1981,
Greenwich
Ht 5ft 6in **Wt** 10st 1lb
Signed from trainee, October
1998

Shaun Wright-Phillips

TOTTENHAM HOTSPUR

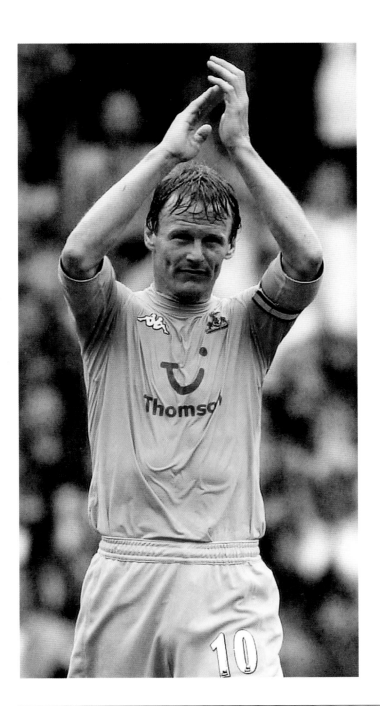

PREMIERSHIP

	P	W	D	L	F	A	Pts
Man Utd	38	25	8	5	74	34	83
Arsenal	38	23	9	6	85	42	78
Newcastle	38	21	6	11	63	48	69
Chelsea	38	19	10	9	68	38	67
Liverpool	38	18	10	10	61	41	64
Blackburn	38	16	12	10	52	43	60
Everton	38	17	8	13	48	49	59
Southampton	38	13	13	12	43	46	52
Man City	38	15	6	17	47	54	51
Tottenham	**38**	**14**	**8**	**16**	**51**	**62**	**50**
Middlesbro	38	13	10	15	48	44	49
Charlton	38	14	7	17	45	56	49
Birmingham	38	13	9	16	41	49	48
Fulham	38	13	9	16	41	50	48
Leeds	38	14	5	19	58	57	47
Aston Villa	38	12	9	17	42	47	45
Bolton	38	10	14	14	41	51	44
West Ham	38	10	12	16	42	59	42
West Brom	38	6	8	24	29	65	26
Sunderland	38	4	7	27	21	65	19

FA CUP
Third round

WORTHINGTON CUP
Third round

Teddy Sheringham says a fond farewell to White Hart Lane

THE GAMES

Saturday August 17
EVERTON (a)
Drew 2-2   **HT 0-1**   Att **40,120**   Position **6th**
Keller — Carr (Thatcher 45), Richards, Gardner, Taricco
— Davies, Redknapp, Bunjevcevic, Etherington — Iversen
(Acimovic 84), Sheringham (Ferdinand 72) *Subs not
used* Sullivan, Perry *Booked* Davies
Scorers **Etherington 63, Ferdinand 74**
Report page 114

Saturday August 24
ASTON VILLA (h)
Won 1-0   **HT 1-0**   Att **35,384**   Position **8th**
Keller — Taricco, Richards, Gardner, Ziege (Thatcher
67) — Davies, Redknapp, Acimovic, Etherington
(Bunjevcevic 61) — Ferdinand (Doherty 82),
Sheringham *Subs not used* Sullivan, Rebrov *Booked*
Bunjevcevic, Ziege
Scorer **Redknapp 26**
Referee **C Wilkes**

Flattered by their opening-day draw at Goodison Park,
Spurs ride their luck again when Redknapp, on his first
appearance at White Hart Lane after switching from
Liverpool, sends the winning goal past Enckelman from
20 yards with the Aston Villa goalkeeper grounded and
hurt. Villa have the better chances; Spurs have the
points.

Tuesday August 27
CHARLTON ATHLETIC (a)
Won 1-0   **HT 1-0**   Att **26,461**   Position **2nd**
Keller — Taricco, Richards, Gardner, Ziege — Davies,
Redknapp, Bunjevcevic, Etherington — Doherty
(Ferdinand 79), Sheringham *Subs not used*
Hirschfeld, Rebrov, Thatcher, Acimovic *Booked* Davies,
Bunjevcevic
Scorer **Davies 8**
Report page 174

Saturday August 31
SOUTHAMPTON (h)
Won 2-1   **HT 1-1**   Att **35,573**   Position **1st**
Keller — Taricco (Bunjevcevic 71), Richards, Doherty,
Thatcher — Davies, Redknapp, Acimovic (Blondel 80),
Etherington — Ferdinand (Iversen 64), Sheringham
Subs not used Hirschfeld, Perry *Booked* Richards,
Redknapp, Ferdinand
Scorers **Ferdinand 10, Sheringham 90 (pen)**
Referee **M Dean**

Spurs have enjoyed few such days as this in recent
seasons, with Keane paraded before the match after
his £7 million move from Leeds United and
Sheringham converting a last-minute penalty —
conceded by Michael Svensson, who blocks Iversen's
volley with his arm and is sent off — to put Glenn
Hoddle's team on top of the table.

IT WAS THE WATERSHED THAT Tottenham Hotspur
supporters dreaded. Twenty-five months after the return of the
prodigal son, the first chants of "We want Hoddle out" crept into the
air at White Hart Lane as Blackburn Rovers coasted to a 4-0 victory.
The dissenters were soon shouted down by fans who realised that
the manager was sandwiched between an underspending board and
underperforming players for much of another woeful season.

Of the nine clubs that have been in the Premiership since its
inception, only Spurs and Southampton have not finished in the top
six. The two defeats at St Mary's Stadium suggested that Southampton are closer to ending that run, and this after Hoddle opted to
pursue glory in North London rather than on the South Coast.

His dream was becoming a nightmare by the end of the season.
The defeat to Blackburn left Spurs with seven points from their final
ten matches, but the real damage was done a month before that run
began. The failure to make any meaningful signings in the January
transfer window meant Spurs tackled the push for Europe with a
near-identical group of ageing players to that which had faltered
when similarly placed in the previous season.

Worse still, Les Ferdinand, Stephen Clemence and Tim
Sherwood left the club, while Sergei Rebrov was loaned out to
Fenerbahçe without having the chance to show if he could form a
partnership with Robbie Keane. In came Kazuyuki Toda and an
accompanying flood of merchandising — another case of lagging
behind Arsenal after their recruitment of Junichi Inamoto, Toda's
Japan team-mate, in 2001. Enic, the club's owning company, may
have had limited resources, but the departures shaved thousands off
the wage bill that could at least have financed one or two more loan
signings. If Bolton Wanderers can do it, why not Spurs? Hoddle said
the policy should be judged at the end of the season, when European
qualification would entice better players than those on offer in
January. The verdict was not that long in coming.

The folly of the gamble was exposed when Keane, a testimony to
the importance of investment, sustained two injuries near to the
closure of the transfer window. With Steffen Iversen ruled out
because of a long-term back injury, the game but limited Gary
Doherty partnered Teddy Sheringham. The attack's impotence was
demonstrated when Spurs failed to defeat a Fulham side reduced to
ten men in the first half at White Hart Lane. Ferdinand added insult
to the injuries in the next game, when he scored in West Ham
United's 2-0 victory. The moment had passed and Tottenham had
not seized it. Before the draw with Fulham they were six points off
the final Champions League place with a game in hand and a

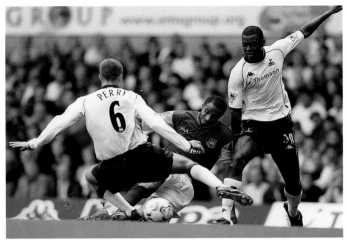

Spurs enjoyed copious luck early in the season, as West Ham discovered

seemingly straightforward run-in. There was, however, already a sense that the past would catch up with them.

Victory over Southampton on August 31 put Spurs top of the table but was typical of the fortune enjoyed in the early matches; a last-minute penalty earned full points from an evenly-matched game. Spurs also had to rely upon the superb form of Kasey Keller to a worrying extent in the opening matches. The goalkeeper was criticised later in the season — rashly conceding the penalty that costs victory against Arsenal is not the best way to curry favour in N17 — but he was not helped by the frequent chaos in front of him. That Dean Richards was limited to 27 appearances by injury was particularly damaging.

Keller was not alone in faltering after a good start. Simon Davies often became lost in an ineffective midfield that lacked a ball-winner and the nous to keep it once it was won. Jamie Redknapp was sorely missed in that regard after he broke a toe in December. To get 17 appearances out of him was more than many expected and it was no surprise that he and Darren Anderton started just one game together; it was a pairing to strike fear into the heart of any physio.

Faults ran through the team and widened as the season progressed as players Spurs looked to for inspiration disappointed. The decision not to award Sheringham a mutually agreeable contract was painful but justified as the 37-year-old forward's influence was increasingly negligible. The same could be said of Anderton and Stephen Carr, who was a shadow of the player who used to terrorise left backs. Reputations, however, count for little. Just ask West Ham. Tottenham's laughter at their relegation on the final day was nervous, for a season of struggle in 2003-04 seemed equally likely then as one in which the path to Europe could be found. The club has found itself at another crossroads and the glory glory years seem as distant as ever.

Wednesday September 11
FULHAM (a)
Lost 2-3 **HT 2-0** Att **16,757** Position **2nd**
Keller — Perry (Doherty 80), Richards, Gardner, Thatcher — Davies, Bunjevcevic, Acimovic (Ziege 72), Etherington (Iversen 84) — Ferdinand, Sheringham
Subs not used Hirschfeld, Keane *Booked* Thatcher
Scorers **Richards 36, Sheringham 44**
Report page 200

Sunday September 15
WEST HAM UNITED (h)
Won 3-2 **HT 0-0** Att **36,005** Position **2nd**
Keller — Taricco (Thatcher ht), Perry (Doherty 32), Gardner, Ziege — Davies, Redknapp, Bunjevcevic, Etherington (Iversen 85) — Keane, Sheringham *Subs not used* Hirschfeld, Acimovic *Booked* Redknapp, Bunjevcevic
Scorers **Davies 62, Sheringham 72 (pen), Gardner 89**
Referee **U Rennie**

West Ham twice come from behind in a match that springs into life after the break, the second time having been reduced to ten men through Pearce's dismissal for a foul on Keane, whose skill shines through on his debut. Spurs have the last word, however, when Gardner's shot takes a deflection off Breen to beat James in the West Ham goal.

Saturday September 21
MANCHESTER UNITED (a)
Lost 0-1 **HT 0-0** Att **67,611** Position **3rd**
Keller — Davies, Richards, Doherty, Thatcher — Iversen (Ferdinand 76), Redknapp, Bunjevcevic, Etherington — Keane, Sheringham (Acimovic 85)
Subs not used Hirschfeld, Ricketts, Henry *Booked* Richards
Report page 43

Saturday September 28
MIDDLESBROUGH (h)
Lost 0-3 **HT 0-1** Att **36,082** Position **6th**
Keller — Davies, Richards, Thatcher, Ziege (Doherty 12) — Iversen (Acimovic 67), Bunjevcevic, Redknapp, Etherington — Ferdinand (Sheringham ht), Keane *Subs not used* Hirschfeld, Ricketts *Booked* Davies
Referee **G Poll**

Inspired by Boksic and Maccarone, the newly recruited Italian forward poaching the first goal and setting up two more for Geremi and Job, Middlesbrough produce a magnificent display to overpower an understrength Spurs side who produce, according to Glenn Hoddle, "the worst performance since I became manager".

Tuesday October 1
CARDIFF CITY (h)
Worthington Cup, 2nd rnd
Won 1-0   HT 1-0   Att 23,723
Keller — Taricco (Doherty 66), Richards, Bunjevcevic,
Thatcher — Davies, Freund (Iversen 86), Acimovic,
Etherington — Keane (Ferdinand 89), Sheringham
Subs not used Hirschfeld, Blondel *Booked* Richards,
Thatcher
Scorer **Sheringham 30**
Referee **S Mathieson**

Cardiff bring to White Hart Lane an unbeaten away
record in all competitions under Lennie Lawrence that
stretches back to February, but despite the closeness
of the scoreline the second division side are well
beaten by last season's losing finalists. Freund, in his
first game since January, sets up the first-half winner for
Sheringham.

Sunday October 6
BLACKBURN ROVERS (a)
Won 2-1   HT 1-0   Att 26,203   Position 4th
Keller — Taricco (Perry 69), Richards, Bunjevcevic,
Thatcher — Davies, Freund, Redknapp, Acimovic
(Iversen 69) — Keane, Sheringham *Subs not used*
Hirschfeld, Ferdinand, Doherty
Scorers **Keane 6, Redknapp 89**
Report page 104

Sunday October 20
BOLTON WANDERERS (h)
Won 3-1   HT 0-0   Att 35,909   Position 3rd
Keller — Carr, Richards, Perry, Bunjevcevic — Davies,
Redknapp, Freund, Etherington (Poyet 70) — Keane,
Sheringham *Subs not used* Hirschfeld, Doherty, Iversen,
Acimovic
Scorers **Keane 58, 74, Davies 90**
Referee **P Durkin**

"It's looking very bleak," Sam Allardyce confesses after
his Bolton team are returned to the foot of the table,
well beaten by a Tottenham side whose fluency is
rewarded with Keane's display of goal-poaching, a
precise late finish from Davies and a move back up to
third place.

MATCH OF THE SEASON

Tottenham Hotspur 4   Everton 3
White Hart Lane, Sunday January 12 2003
Nick Szczepanik

A goal from the exultant Poyet preceded Keane's hat-trick against Everton

A SECOND-HALF HAT-TRICK by Robbie Keane, his first in the Barclaycard Premiership, settled an exciting encounter at White Hart Lane yesterday, bringing an emphatic end to a run of three defeats for Tottenham Hotspur and taking them up to eighth place, only a point behind Everton. "It was nice to see the first one go in and the rest came after that," the Ireland forward said. "It was tough. Everton worked very hard and we rode our luck at times, but we got the three points."

Only just. After going out of the FA Cup last week, both sides were supposedly concentrating on the league, but neither was concentrating very hard — three times a team took the lead only to surrender it again within minutes. The biggest surprise was that Spurs held out after Keane's third to record their first win in five games. "We will analyse the way we kept giving the lead away and not only in today's game," Glenn Hoddle, the Tottenham manager, said. "There is a pattern to the way we are conceding and we have to put that right."

Everton also need to look at their rearguard after what David Moyes, the manager, described as their worst defensive performance of the season, but, despite a run of only one win in nine games, he refused to panic. "It was a marked improvement from Shrewsbury last week," he said. "We played well at times, created chances and were more enterprising than we have been. I would be worried if we were fifth bottom of the league, but we're sixth from top."

Hoddle left out four of the team beaten 4-0 away to Southampton last weekend, but his reshaped side was behind after only ten minutes. Brian McBride, the United States forward, on his debut for Everton on a three-month loan from Columbus Crew, ran on to Scot Gemmill's pass to beat Kasey Keller, his room-mate at last year's World Cup, with a low right-foot shot.

Everton did not have much time to savour their lead. Only four minutes later, Gustavo Poyet's forehead made just enough contact with Simon Davies's forward nod to take the ball inside the right-hand post of Espen Baardsen, the former Tottenham goalkeeper, who was playing after Richard Wright hurt a knee in the warm-up.

Hoddle administered what he termed "an old-fashioned rollicking" at half-time. It seemed to have worked five minutes into the second period as Everton looked in vain for a flag as Darren Anderton's long, high pass reached Keane, who rounded Baardsen to put the ball into the empty net. Tottenham, though, repeated Everton's first-half failure to hold their advantage, Steffen Iversen's

Saturday October 26
LIVERPOOL (a)
Lost 1-2 HT 0-0 Att 44,084 Position 5th
Keller — Carr, Richards, Perry, Bunjevcevic — Davies, Redknapp (Etherington 90), Freund, Poyet (Acimovic 79) — Keane, Sheringham (Ferdinand 75) *Subs not used* Hirschfeld, Gardner *Booked* Carr, Richards, Redknapp, Freund
Scorer **Richards 82**
Report page 92

Sunday November 3
CHELSEA (h)
Drew 0-0 HT 0-0 Att 36,049 Position 5th
Keller — Carr, Richards, Perry, Bunjevcevic — Davies, Redknapp, Freund, Poyet (Acimovic 79) — Keane, Sheringham (Ferdinand 89) *Subs not used* Hirschfeld, Etherington, Gardner *Booked* Keller, Sheringham, Acimovic
Referee **R Styles**

Spurs' league jinx against Chelsea is extended to 25 matches without a victory, dating back to 1990, as Cudicini denies them with a string of excellent saves in a generally low-key derby. The visiting team almost pull off an undeserved triumph when Melchiot heads against a post.

Wednesday November 6
BURNLEY (a)
Worthington Cup, 3rd rnd
Lost 1-2 HT 1-0 Att 13,512
Keller — Carr, Perry, Gardner, Bunjevcevic — Davies, Clemence, Poyet, Etherington (Anderton 59) — Ferdinand (Keane ht), Iversen (Doherty 82) *Subs not used* Hirschfeld, Acimovic *Booked* Carr, Bunjevcevic
Scorer **Poyet 17**
Referee **D Gallagher**

The runners-up in 2002 are one of seven Barclaycard Premiership sides eliminated on a night of shocks — and they have only themselves to blame, taking the lead through Poyet's header and missing a string of chances after Burnley score twice in four second-half minutes. Keane, who fluffs two sitters, is the biggest culprit.

Sunday November 10
SUNDERLAND (a)
Lost 0-2 HT 0-0 Att 40,024 Position 8th
Keller — Carr, Richards, Perry, Thatcher (Iversen 90) — Davies, Anderton, Freund (Acimovic 79), Poyet (Bunjevcevic 65) — Keane, Sheringham *Subs not used* Hirschfeld, Doherty *Booked* Davies, Perry
Report page 273

Saturday November 16
ARSENAL (a)
Lost 0-3 HT **0-1** Att **38,152** Position **9th**
Keller — Carr, Richards, King, Bunjevcevic — Davies,
Redknapp (Iversen 65), Freund, Etherington
(Poyet ht) — Keane, Sheringham (Anderton 65)
Subs not used Hirschfeld, Perry *Booked* Davies, Poyet
Sent off Davies 27
Report page 58

Sunday November 24
LEEDS UNITED (h)
Won 2-0 HT **2-0** Att **35,718** Position **7th**
Keller — King, Richards, Bunjevcevic — Carr, Anderton
(Redknapp 77), Freund, Ziege (Davies 79) — Poyet
(Iversen 90) — Keane, Sheringham *Subs not used*
Hirschfeld, Perry *Booked* Poyet, Ziege, Bunjevcevic
Scorers **Sheringham 12, Keane 41**
Referee **S Bennett**

It is getting worse by the minute for Terry Venables. He
returns to White Hart Lane, loses Barmby to injury in the
warm-up, the match to well-taken goals from
Sheringham and Keane, and sees the names of seven
of his Leeds players end up in Steve Bennett's
notebook to incur an FA fine.

Saturday November 30
BIRMINGHAM CITY (a)
Drew 1-1 HT **0-0** Att **29,505** Position **7th**
Keller — King, Richards, Bunjevcevic — Carr, Anderton
(Redknapp 79), Freund, Poyet (Acimovic 85), Ziege —
Sheringham — Keane (Iversen 75) *Subs not used*
Hirschfeld, Perry
Scorer **Sheringham 55**
Report page 190

Sunday December 8
WEST BROMWICH ALBION (h)
Won 3-1 HT **2-0** Att **35,958** Position **7th**
Keller — King (Iversen 64), Richards, Perry — Carr,
Davies, Redknapp, Anderton, Ziege — Keane,
Sheringham (Poyet 84) *Subs not used* Hirschfeld,
Ferdinand, Doherty *Booked* Ziege, Keller
Scorers **Ziege 3, Keane 30, Poyet 80**
Referee **A Wiley**

West Brom's dismal luck — and dreadful finishing —
cost them dear again as Spurs, who are fortunate not
to have Keller sent off for a wild challenge on Dobie,
take their chances while the visiting team do not.
Clement gives Albion hope when he pulls the deficit
back to 2-1, but Poyet finishes them off.

Keane's tricks of the trade were enough to outscore Everton in a thriller

error allowing Steve Watson to sweep the loose ball in from six
yards. Ten more minutes and Everton were behind again when
Keane evaded a hasty challenge from Joseph Yobo, turned and fired
low past Baardsen from 20 yards, but it didn't last. After 64 minutes
Watson set up Radzinski, who drove the ball low past Keller with his
left foot.

Eight minutes from time, however, Keane settled the match.
Stubbs misjudged the bounce of a goal kick and Keane fastened on
to the ball, swept past Yobo's attempt to intercept and slipped the
ball past Baardsen.

"That has been waiting to happen," Hoddle said. "He's had the
chances, but today he was clinical — a magnificent hat-trick, a great
exhibition of finishing. There have been stupid reports that there is
something wrong with our spirit, but you can't perform like that and
keep coming back when you've just lost three games if you haven't
got team spirit."

TOTTENHAM HOTSPUR (3-4-1-2): K Keller — G Doherty, C Perry, L King — S Carr, D Anderton,
G Bunjevcevic, G Poyet, S Davies — R Keane, S Iversen (sub: M Acimovic, 80min). **Substitutes not
used:** N Sullivan, M Taricco, J Blondel, A Gardner. **Booked:** Doherty.

EVERTON (4-4-2): E Baardsen — A Pistone, J Yobo 6 (sub: L Carsley, 86), A Stubbs, D Unsworth
— S Watson, Li Tie (sub: L Osman, 90), S Gemmill, G Naysmith — T Radzinski 7, B McBride.
Substitutes not used: N Alexandersson, M Pembridge, I Said. **Booked:** Gemmill.
Referee: S Dunn.

THE MANAGER

Glenn Hoddle

Injuries and a lack of investment undermined Glenn Hoddle's efforts but did not explain why the team regularly failed to respond to him. The manner of defeat to Southampton in the FA Cup and at home to Middlesbrough and Manchester City lent credence to the allegations by Tim Sherwood and Steffen Freund that team spirit was crumbling. Some of Hoddle's decisions certainly betrayed a perceived eccentricity. The freezing out of Sergei Rebrov and the misplaced faith in Goran Bunjevcevic were baffling. Hoddle's second full season in charge may have matched his first in terms of points, but it was far more disappointing.

Phil Myers

APPEARANCES

	Prem	FAC	WC	Total
M Acimovic	4 (13)	-	1	5 (13)
D Anderton	18 (2)	0 (1)	0 (1)	18 (4)
J Blondel	0 (1)	-	-	0 (1)
G Bunjevcevic	31 (4)	-	2	33 (4)
S Carr	30	1	1	32
S Clemence	-	-	1	1
S Davies	33 (3)	1	2	36 (3)
G Doherty	7 (8)	0 (1)	0 (2)	7 (11)
M Etherington	15 (8)	-	2	17 (8)
L Ferdinand	4 (7)	-	1 (1)	5 (8)
S Freund	13 (4)	1	1	15 (4)
A Gardner	11 (1)	-	1	12 (1)
S Iversen	8 (11)	0 (1)	1 (1)	9 (13)
R Keane	29	1	1 (1)	31 (1)
K Keller	38	1	2	41
L King	25	1	-	26
C Perry	15 (3)	1	1	17 (3)
G Poyet	22 (6)	1	1	24 (6)
J Redknapp	14 (3)	-	-	14 (3)
D Richards	26	0	1	27
T Sheringham	34 (2)	1	1	36 (2)
J Slabber	0 (1)	-	-	0 (1)
M Taricco	21	1	1	23
B Thatcher	8 (4)	1	1	10 (4)
K Toda	2 (2)	-	-	2 (2)
C Ziege	10 (2)	-	-	10 (2)

Sunday December 15
ARSENAL (h)
Drew 1-1 HT 1-1 Att **36,076** Position **7th**
Keller — King, Richards, Bunjevcevic — Carr, Anderton (Davies 70), Freund, Ziege — Poyet — Keane, Sheringham *Subs not used* Hirschfeld, Perry, Iversen, Clemence *Booked* Keller, Sheringham, Freund
Scorer **Ziege 11**
Referee **N Barry**

What Glenn Hoddle describes as Spurs' best performance of the season still brings them only a point as Cole denies them with two goalline clearances after Ziege's brilliant free kick opener. Pires equalises from the spot for Arsenal when Keller brings down Henry on the stroke of half-time.

Monday December 23
MANCHESTER CITY (a)
Won 3-2 HT 1-1 Att **34,563** Position **7th**
Keller — Perry, Richards, King — Carr, Davies, Freund, Anderton, Ziege — Keane, Iversen (Poyet 71) *Subs not used* Bunjevcevic, Thatcher, Clemence, Sullivan *Booked* Perry, Ziege, Freund *Sent off* Ziege 86
Scorers **Perry 38, Davies 48, Poyet 84**
Report page 143

Thursday December 26
CHARLTON ATHLETIC (h)
Drew 2-2 HT 0-1 Att **36,043** Position **7th**
Keller — Perry, King, Bunjevcevic — Carr, Anderton (Davies ht), Freund (Iversen 60), Poyet, Ziege — Keane, Sheringham (Ferdinand 60) *Subs not used* Sullivan, Taricco *Booked* Ziege, Freund *Sent off* Ziege 90
Scorers **Keane 68, Iversen 87**
Referee **A D'Urso**

Euell's double, both created in part by Lisbie, seems to have won the match for Charlton, but Spurs storm back through Iversen, who heads down for Keane to volley in and equalises himself three minutes from time. Spurs' relief is diluted when Ziege is sent off for the second successive match, for fouls on Lisbie and Parker, the second caution appearing particularly harsh.

Sunday December 29
NEWCASTLE UNITED (a)
Lost 1-2 HT 0-1 Att 52,145 Position **8th**
Keller — Carr, Perry, King, Taricco — Poyet (Sheringham 68), Freund, Bunjevcevic — Davies — Keane (Acimovic 79), Iversen (Ferdinand 68) *Subs not used* Sullivan, Thatcher *Booked* Perry, Freund
Scorer **Dabizas 73 (og)**
Report page 72

Wednesday January 1
SOUTHAMPTON (a)
Lost 0-1 HT 0-1 Att 31,890 Position **9th**
Keller — Perry, Richards, King — Carr, Freund, Bunjevcevic (Poyet 67), Taricco (Anderton 67) — Sheringham — Keane, Iversen (Acimovic 87) *Subs not used* Sullivan, Thatcher
Report page 131

Saturday January 4
SOUTHAMPTON (a)
FA Cup, 3rd rnd
Lost 0-4 HT 0-1 Att 25,589
Keller — Perry (Anderton ht), King, Thatcher — Carr, Davies (Doherty 74), Freund (Iversen 58), Poyet, Taricco — Keane, Sheringham *Subs not used* Sullivan, Bunjevcevic
Report page 131

Sunday January 12
EVERTON (h)
Won 4-3 HT 1-1 Att 36,070 Position **8th**
Keller — Doherty, Perry, King — Carr, Anderton, Bunjevcevic, Poyet, Davies — Keane, Iversen (Acimovic 80) *Subs not used* Sullivan, Taricco, Blondel, Gardner *Booked* Doherty
Scorers **Poyet 14, Keane 50, 68, 83**
Referee **S Dunn**

Everton, ahead through McBride's debut goal, are destroyed by Keane in an error-strewn but thrilling encounter. The Ireland striker plunders his first Premiership hat-trick to keep David Moyes's Rooney-less team at arm's length, although they twice pull level in the second half.

Of the few memories to savour from Tottenham Hotspur's 2002-03 season, Robbie Keane created the majority. From the sublime of his sweet half-volley against Leeds United at White Hart Lane in November, to the ridiculous and his cheeky dispossession of Andy Marriott, the Birmingham City goalkeeper, in April, the forward was a constant inspiration. However, Keane's crowning glory in a season in which he scored 13 goals in 32 appearances was almost single-handedly earning a 4-3 victory at home to Everton in January with a hat-trick. The 23-year-old's finishing still needs some work, but his inventive runs showed that Spurs had landed a bargain — and a rare talent — for their £7 million.

Phil Myers

STATS AND FACTS

● Spurs crumble when visiting the leading clubs. They have not won in the league in nine games at Anfield; nor in ten games at Highbury, in 13 games at Stamford Bridge and in 13 games at Old Trafford.

● They finished above Aston Villa in the Premiership for the first time in eight seasons.

● Robbie Keane is the only Spurs player to have scored more than once in a game in their past 72 Premiership matches.

● Spurs have not finished in either the top six or the bottom six for 13 seasons.

● Only two of their last 15 home league games of the season were played on a Saturday.

Bill Edgar

Saturday January 18
ASTON VILLA (a)
Won 1-0   HT 0-0   Att 38,576   Position 7th
Keller — Carr, King, Richards, Taricco — Davies, Bunjevcevic, Anderton, Poyet (Freund 81) — Keane, Sheringham *Subs not used* Sullivan, Perry, Iversen, Acimovic *Booked* Bunjevcevic, Keane, Anderton
Scorer **Sheringham 69**
Report page 229

Wednesday January 29
NEWCASTLE UNITED (h)
Lost 0-1   HT 0-0   Att 36,084   Position 8th
Keller — Carr, Richards, Gardner, King — Davies, Bunjevcevic, Anderton, Poyet — Keane (Doherty 37), Sheringham *Subs not used* Sullivan, Taricco, Acimovic, Freund
Referee **D Elleray**

On the day that Sherwood and Rebrov follow Ferdinand through the White Hart Lane exit, Tottenham, having had a goal by Poyet wrongly disallowed for offside, suffer another blow when a last-minute goal by Jenas, following up when Keller parries Bellamy's shot, gives Newcastle victory and takes them above Manchester United into second position.

Saturday February 1
CHELSEA (a)
Drew 1-1   HT 1-1   Att 41,384   Position 9th
Keller — Carr, Gardner (Doherty 37), King, Taricco — Davies, Bunjevcevic, Anderton, Poyet — Iversen (Etherington 80), Sheringham *Subs not used* Sullivan, Acimovic, Freund *Booked* Taricco
Scorer **Sheringham 18**
Report page 85

Saturday February 8
SUNDERLAND (h)
Won 4-1   HT 2-1   Att 36,075   Position 7th
Keller — Carr, Richards, King, Taricco — Bunjevcevic (Freund 76) — Davies, Poyet (Etherington 73), Anderton — Keane (Doherty 21), Sheringham *Subs not used* Sullivan, Acimovic
Scorers **Poyet 14, Doherty 45, Davies 67, Sheringham 84**
Referee **R Styles**

Tottenham's biggest win of the season — and Sunderland's heaviest defeat — is set up on the stroke of half-time, when Doherty's header puts the home side 2-1 up to end Sunderland's resistance, and confirmed by the 300th goal of Sheringham's career: cue the unveiling of the celebratory T-shirt.

GOALSCORERS

	Prem	FAC	WC	Total
S Davies	5	-	-	5
G Doherty	1	-	-	1
M Etherington	1	-	-	1
L Ferdinand	2	-	-	2
A Gardner	1	-	-	1
S Iversen	1	-	-	1
R Keane	13	-	-	13
C Perry	1	-	-	1
G Poyet	5	-	1	6
J Redknapp	3	-	-	3
D Richards	2	-	-	2
T Sheringham	12 (3p)	-	1	13 (3p)
M Taricco	1	-	-	1
C Ziege	2	-	-	2
Own goals	1	-	-	1

Monday February 24
FULHAM (h)
Drew 1-1   HT 1-1   Att 34,704   Position 8th
Keller — Carr, Richards, King, Taricco — Bunjevcevic —
Davies, Poyet (Acimovic 35; Etherington 84),
Anderton — Doherty, Sheringham *Subs not used*
Sullivan, Thatcher, Toda *Booked* Richards, Anderton
Sent off Anderton 73
Scorer **Sheringham 40 (pen)**
Referee **G Barber**

When Anderton is sent off and labelled a "hatchet man"
in the morning newspapers, you know it has been a
strange night. And it is. Highlights include Fulham losing
two players to injury and Taylor, their goalkeeper, to a
debatable red card in the first half, with Spurs
contributing King's own goal and Acimovic's claim to the
"worst miss ever", as well as Anderton's dismissal for
two yellow cards.

Saturday March 1
WEST HAM UNITED (a)
Lost 0-2   HT 0-1   Att 35,049   Position 9th
Keller — Carr, Richards, King, Taricco — Davies,
Bunjevcevic (Thatcher ht), Anderton, Etherington
(Acimovic 76) — Sheringham — Doherty (Freund 66)
Subs not used Sullivan, Toda *Booked* Taricco, Davies
Report page 254

Sunday March 16
LIVERPOOL (h)
Lost 2-3   HT 0-0   Att 36,077   Position 10th
Keller — Carr, King, Thatcher, Taricco (Freund 69) —
Davies, Bunjevcevic, Poyet, Etherington — Doherty
(Slabber 78), Sheringham *Subs not used* Sullivan,
Acimovic, Toda *Booked* Taricco
Scorers **Taricco 49, Sheringham 87**
Referee **U Rennie**

Gerard Houllier accuses Taricco of trying to get Diouf
sent off, but that is the only thing that rankles with the
Liverpool manager after a sparkling display by Gerrard
paves the way for victory. The England midfield player
sets up goals for Owen and Heskey before adding a fine
third himself, Spurs opening and closing the scoring to
no avail.

Monday March 24
BOLTON WANDERERS (a)
Lost 0-1   HT 0-0   Att 23,084   Position 10th
Keller — Carr, King, Thatcher (Doherty 21), Taricco —
Davies, Bunjevcevic, Poyet, Anderton (Etherington
87) — Keane, Sheringham *Subs not used* Slabber,
Toda, Sullivan *Booked* Doherty
Report page 242

THE PLAYERS

MILENKO ACIMOVIC
Midfield
Born February 15, 1977,
Ljubljana, Slovenia
Ht 6ft 1in **Wt** 13st 0lb
Signed from Red Star Belgrade,
May 2002, free

DARREN ANDERTON
Midfield
Born March 3, 1972,
Southampton
Ht 6ft 1in **Wt** 12st 11lb
Signed from Portsmouth, June
1992, £1.75m

JONATHAN BLONDEL
Midfield
Born May 3, 1984,
Ypres, Belgium
Ht 5ft 8in **Wt** 10st 9lb
Signed from Excelsior Mouscron,
July 2002, undisclosed

GORAN BUNJEVCEVIC
Midfield
Born February 17, 1973,
Karlovac, Croatia
Ht 6ft 2in **Wt** 11st 11lb
Signed from Red Star Belgrade,
July 2001, £1.4m

STEPHEN CARR
Defender
Born August 29, 1976, Dublin
Ht 5ft 9in **Wt** 12st 4lb
Signed from trainee, September
1993

STEPHEN CLEMENCE
(see Birmingham City)

SIMON DAVIES
Midfield
Born October 23, 1979,
Haverfordwest
Ht 5ft 10in **Wt** 11st 4lb
Signed from Peterborough United,
January 2000, £700,000

GARY DOHERTY
Defender
Born January 31, 1980, Donegal
Ht 6ft 1in **Wt** 13st 6lb
Signed from Luton Town, April
2000, £1m

Simon Davies

MATTHEW ETHERINGTON
Midfield
Born August 14, 1981, Truro
Ht 5ft 10in **Wt** 10st 12lb
Signed from Peterborough United, January 2000, £500,000

LES FERDINAND
(see West Ham United)

STEFFEN FREUND
Midfield
Born January 19, 1970, Brandenburg, Germany
Ht 5ft 11in **Wt** 12st 6lb
Signed from Borussia Dortmund, December 1998, £750,000

ANTHONY GARDNER
Defender
Born September 10, 1980, Stafford
Ht 6ft 5in **Wt** 13st 8lb
Signed from Port Vale, January 2000, £1m

STEFFEN IVERSEN
Forward
Born October 11, 1976, Oslo
Ht 6ft 1in **Wt** 12st 7lb
Signed from Rosenborg, December 1996, £2.7m

ROBBIE KEANE
Forward
Born July 8, 1980, Dublin
Ht 5ft 9in **Wt** 11st 10lb
Signed from Leeds United, August 2002, £7m

KASEY KELLER
Goalkeeper
Born November 29, 1969, Washington, United States
Ht 6ft 1in **Wt** 13st 12lb
Signed from Rayo Vallecano, August 2001, free

LEDLEY KING
Defender
Born December 10, 1980, Bow
Ht 6ft 2in **Wt** 14st 5lb
Signed from trainee, July 1998

CHRIS PERRY
Defender
Born April 26, 1973, Carshalton
Ht 5ft 8in **Wt** 10st 12lb
Signed from Wimbledon, July 1999, £4m

Kasey Keller

Saturday April 5
BIRMINGHAM CITY (h)
Won 2-1 **HT 1-0** Att **36,058** Position **8th**
Keller — Carr, Perry, King, Taricco (Etherington 84) — Davies, Bunjevcevic, Poyet, Anderton — Sheringham — Keane *Subs not used* Sullivan, Doherty, Acimovic, Toda *Booked* Bunjevcevic
Scorers **Keane 7, Poyet 88**
Referee **D Elleray**

Having waited many years to make his Premiership debut, Marriott finally lines up between the posts for Birmingham . . . and within seven minutes concedes the most bizarre goal of his career, when he fails to spot Keane lurking behind him as he puts the ball down in order to make a clearance, allowing the cunning Irishman to score the opener. Poyet volleys a late and decidedly flattering winner for Spurs.

Saturday April 12
LEEDS UNITED (a)
Drew 2-2 **HT 2-1** Att **39,560** Position **8th**
Keller — Carr, King, Gardner, Taricco — Davies, Bunjevcevic, Poyet (Etherington 87), Anderton — Sheringham — Keane *Subs not used* Sullivan, Perry, Acimovic, Toda *Booked* Keller, Gardner
Scorers **Sheringham 37, Keane 39**
Report page 219

Friday April 18
MANCHESTER CITY (h)
Lost 0-2 **HT 0-2** Att **36,075** Position **8th**
Keller — Carr, King, Gardner, Taricco (Perry ht) — Davies, Bunjevcevic (Toda ht), Poyet (Acimovic 71), Anderton — Keane, Sheringham *Subs not used* Sullivan, Iversen *Booked* Carr, Poyet
Referee **M Riley**

Glenn Hoddle apologises to Spurs fans after a miserable display all but ends their Uefa Cup hopes. City have already gone close twice when Sommeil puts them ahead in the third minute and they are never really threatened once Barton doubles the lead with his first senior goal.

Monday April 21
WEST BROMWICH ALBION (a)
Won 3-2 **HT 1-1** Att **26,899** Position **8th**
Keller — Carr, Richards (Perry 83), King, Gardner — Davies, Bunjevcevic, Toda (Poyet ht), Etherington — Sheringham — Keane *Subs not used* Sullivan, Iversen, Acimovic *Booked* Richards, Gardner
Scorers **Keane 45, 85, Sheringham 63**
Report page 267

Sunday April 27
MANCHESTER UNITED (h)
Lost 0-2   HT 0-0   Att **36,073**   Position **8th**
Keller — Carr, Richards (Gardner 31), King, Taricco —
Davies, Toda (Bunjevcevic 79), Poyet, Etherington
(Iversen 79) — Keane, Sheringham *Subs not used*
Sullivan, Acimovic
Referee **J Winter**

Spurs are unable to give their North London rivals a
championship hand as United — for whom Beckham is
back but Barthez is dropped — take full advantage of
Arsenal's draw away to Bolton by winning at White Hart
Lane and extending their lead to five points. Keller's
fine form forces United to wait 69 minutes for a
breakthrough, Van Nistelrooy adding a second — his
fortieth goal of the season — at the death.

Saturday May 3
MIDDLESBROUGH (a)
Lost 1-5   HT 0-3   Att **30,230**   Position **9th**
Keller — King, Perry, Gardner — Bunjevcevic — Carr,
Davies, Poyet (Redknapp ht), Taricco — Sheringham
(Etherington ht), Keane *Subs not used* Acimovic,
Yeates, Burch *Booked* Bunjevcevic, Poyet
Scorer **Redknapp 60**
Report page 172

Sunday May 11
BLACKBURN ROVERS (h)
Lost 0-4   HT 0-2   Att **36,036**   Position **10th**
Keller — Carr, Perry, King, Taricco (Ziege 60) — Davies,
Poyet, Redknapp (Toda 69), Etherington — Keane,
Sheringham *Subs not used* Sullivan, Bunjevcevic,
Acimovic *Booked* Taricco *Sent off* Poyet 31
Referee **A D'Urso**

A rout against ten men, once Poyet is dismissed for a
two-footed tackle on Flitcroft, gives Blackburn the Uefa
Cup place that Spurs once aspired to. For Tottenham's
fans, there is the chance to cheer Sheringham's farewell
performance and jeer the manager who surprisingly
decided to let him go.

GUSTAVO POYET
Midfield
Born November 15, 1967,
Montevideo
Ht 6ft 1in **Wt** 13st 0lb
Signed from Chelsea, July 2001,
£2m

JAMIE REDKNAPP
Midfield
Born June 25, 1973,
Barton-on-Sea
Ht 6ft 0in **Wt** 13st 4lb
Signed from Liverpool, April 2002,
free

DEAN RICHARDS
Defender
Born June 9, 1974, Bradford
Ht 6ft 2in **Wt** 13st 12lb
Signed from Southampton,
September 2001, £8.1m

TEDDY SHERINGHAM
Forward
Born April 2, 1966,
Highams Park
Ht 6ft 0in **Wt** 12st 5lb
Signed from Manchester United,
May 2001, free

JAMIE SLABBER
Forward
Born December 31, 1984,
Enfield
Signed from trainee, August
2001

MAURICIO TARICCO
Defender
Born March 10, 1973,
Buenos Aires
Ht 5ft 9in **Wt** 11st 7lb
Signed from Ipswich Town,
December 1998, £1.8m

BEN THATCHER
Defender
Born November 30, 1975,
Swindon
Ht 5ft 10in **Wt** 12st 6lb
Signed from Wimbledon, July
2000, £5m

KAZUYUKI TODA
Midfield
Born December 30, 1977, Tokyo
Ht 5ft 10in **Wt** 10st 10lb
Signed from Shimizu S-Pulse
(loan), January 2003

CHRISTIAN ZIEGE
Defender
Born February 1, 1972, Berlin
Ht 6ft 2in **Wt** 12st 13lb
Signed from Liverpool, August
2001, £4m

Dean Richards

MIDDLESBROUGH

PREMIERSHIP

	P	W	D	L	F	A	Pts
Man Utd	38	25	8	5	74	34	83
Arsenal	38	23	9	6	85	42	78
Newcastle	38	21	6	11	63	48	69
Chelsea	38	19	10	9	68	38	67
Liverpool	38	18	10	10	61	41	64
Blackburn	38	16	12	10	52	43	60
Everton	38	17	8	13	48	49	59
Southampton	38	13	13	12	43	46	52
Man City	38	15	6	17	47	54	51
Tottenham	38	14	8	16	51	62	50
Middlesbro	**38**	**13**	**10**	**15**	**48**	**44**	**49**
Charlton	38	14	7	17	45	56	49
Birmingham	38	13	9	16	41	49	48
Fulham	38	13	9	16	41	50	48
Leeds	38	14	5	19	58	57	47
Aston Villa	38	12	9	17	42	47	45
Bolton	38	10	14	14	41	51	44
West Ham	38	10	12	16	42	59	42
West Brom	38	6	8	24	29	65	26
Sunderland	38	4	7	27	21	65	19

FA CUP
Third round

WORTHINGTON CUP
Third round

Gareth Southgate was a rock of reliability at the back

THE GAMES

Saturday August 17
SOUTHAMPTON (a)
Drew 0-0 HT 0-0 Att 28,341 Position 8th
Schwarzer — Stockdale, Ehiogu, Southgate, Murphy
(Cooper 15) — Geremi, Boateng, Greening, Marinelli
— Maccarone (Boksic 76), Whelan (Nemeth ht)
Subs not used Crossley, Wilson
Report page 126

Saturday August 24
FULHAM (h)
Drew 2-2 HT 1-0 Att 28,588 Position 13th
Schwarzer — Stockdale, Ehiogu, Southgate, Cooper
— Greening, Boateng, Geremi, Marinelli (Wilson 84)
— Boksic (Job 79), Maccarone (Whelan 84) *Subs not
used* Crossley, Gavin *Booked* Ehiogu, Geremi, Marinelli,
Wilson
Scorer Maccarone 32, 51
Referee M Dean

The Premiership season is only a week old and already
a claim to the most dramatic finish of the campaign
has been staked. Cruising to victory on the back of
Maccarone's double, Middlesbrough concede a
scrambled goal to Davis in the 89th minute and,
precisely 48 seconds later, another to Sava, the
Fulham substitute.

Saturday August 31
BLACKBURN ROVERS (h)
Won 1-0 HT 0-0 Att 28,270 Position 9th
Schwarzer — Stockdale, Ehiogu, Southgate, Queudrue
— Greening, Boateng, Geremi, Marinelli (Cooper ht) —
Boksic, Maccarone (Job 79) *Subs not used* Crossley,
Wilson, Whelan *Booked* Stockdale, Geremi, Boateng
Scorer Job 90
Referee M Halsey

The introduction of Job for Middlesbrough, at
Maccarone's expense, is roundly booed, but fans
change their tune when the substitute pounces on
Johansson's error to grab a last-minute winner.
Blackburn, on top for long periods but frustrated by
Schwarzer, are left bemoaning their luck.

Tuesday September 3
MANCHESTER UNITED (a)
Lost 0-1 HT 0-1 Att 67,464 Position 10th
Schwarzer — Stockdale, Cooper, Ehiogu, Southgate,
Queudrue (Marinelli 72) — Geremi, Boateng, Greening
— Maccarone (Whelan 72), Job *Subs not used*
Crossley, Gavin, Wilson *Booked* Ehiogu, Southgate
Report page 42

WHO WOULD HAVE THOUGHT IT? Another rollercoaster
season at the Riverside. After an erratic start, Middlesbrough found
themselves third in the Premiership, prompting praise from Sir Alex
himself and press talk of possible European qualification, even if
Steve McClaren wrote off their chances as early as December after
they were deservedly beaten away to West Bromwich Albion.

Middlesbrough were the Premiership's biggest pre-season
spenders and the new signings all grabbed their share of the
headlines over the long winter months. The Gang Of Four (George
Boateng, Geremi, Juninho and Massimo Maccarone) were primed
to take centre stage in the opening game of the season, but
McClaren's tactics had to be rethought at short notice after
Juninho's pre-season knee injury. It was to be another seven months
before the Brazilian made a first-team appearance.

The rollercoaster continued its downward course as
Middlesbrough lost eight consecutive away games in a three-month
period, failing to get on the scoresheet in any of them. The
rumblings of discontent threatened to spill over when, the week
after the last of these defeats, they capitulated 5-2 at the Riverside
against Aston Villa. By this time, they were looking over their
shoulder at the trapdoor. Salvation quickly followed with a
long-awaited away goal and point — at Anfield of all places —
quickly followed by a 3-1 win away to Sunderland. Middlesbrough
and McClaren were off the hook and the rollercoaster started a
tentative climb. However, their woeful record on their travels ruined
a potentially glorious season and it is the lack of ambition when
away from Teesside that needs to be addressed.

The draw at Anfield was indeed a turning point. Middlesbrough
went on a run of eight matches unbeaten and the long-awaited
return of Juninho gave the club and fans a massive boost. Such was
the anticipation that 19,450 turned up the week before to watch him
in a reserve game and he immediately showed what might have
been achieved had he been available from the beginning of the
season. Even though the Brazilian's pace is not what it was, his mere
presence on the field transmits a tangible feel-good factor among
fans. This in itself must carry a knock-on effect to the spirit of his
team-mates.

With what looked like a not-too-difficult series of opponents to
end the season, Middlesbrough were again being touted as
contenders for their first European campaign. Not for the first time,
though, McClaren showed great maturity and wisdom in refusing to
get involved in such talk.

Of the transfer window signings (Michael Ricketts, Malcolm

MIDDLESBROUGH

PREMIERSHIP

	P	W	D	L	F	A	Pts
Man Utd	38	25	8	5	74	34	83
Arsenal	38	23	9	6	85	42	78
Newcastle	38	21	6	11	63	48	69
Chelsea	38	19	10	9	68	38	67
Liverpool	38	18	10	10	61	41	64
Blackburn	38	16	12	10	52	43	60
Everton	38	17	8	13	48	49	59
Southampton	38	13	13	12	43	46	52
Man City	38	15	6	17	47	54	51
Tottenham	38	14	8	16	51	62	50
Middlesbro	**38**	**13**	**10**	**15**	**48**	**44**	**49**
Charlton	38	14	7	17	45	56	49
Birmingham	38	13	9	16	41	49	48
Fulham	38	13	9	16	41	50	48
Leeds	38	14	5	19	58	57	47
Aston Villa	38	12	9	17	42	47	45
Bolton	38	10	14	14	41	51	44
West Ham	38	10	12	16	42	59	42
West Brom	38	6	8	24	29	65	26
Sunderland	38	4	7	27	21	65	19

FA CUP
Third round

WORTHINGTON CUP
Third round

Gareth Southgate was a rock of reliability at the back

THE GAMES

Shaun Keogh

Saturday August 17
SOUTHAMPTON (a)
Drew 0-0 HT 0-0 Att **28,341** Position **8th**
Schwarzer — Stockdale, Ehiogu, Southgate, Murphy
(Cooper 15) — Geremi, Boateng, Greening, Marinelli
— Maccarone (Boksic 76), Whelan (Nemeth ht)
Subs not used Crossley, Wilson
Report page 126

Saturday August 24
FULHAM (h)
Drew 2-2 HT 1-0 Att **28,588** Position **13th**
Schwarzer — Stockdale, Ehiogu, Southgate, Cooper
— Greening, Boateng, Geremi, Marinelli (Wilson 84)
— Boksic (Job 79), Maccarone (Whelan 84) *Subs not
used* Crossley, Gavin *Booked* Ehiogu, Geremi, Marinelli,
Wilson
Scorer Maccarone 32, 51
Referee **M Dean**

The Premiership season is only a week old and already
a claim to the most dramatic finish of the campaign
has been staked. Cruising to victory on the back of
Maccarone's double, Middlesbrough concede a
scrambled goal to Davis in the 89th minute and,
precisely 48 seconds later, another to Sava, the
Fulham substitute.

Saturday August 31
BLACKBURN ROVERS (h)
Won 1-0 HT 0-0 Att **28,270** Position **9th**
Schwarzer — Stockdale, Ehiogu, Southgate, Queudrue
— Greening, Boateng, Geremi, Marinelli (Cooper ht) —
Boksic, Maccarone (Job 79) *Subs not used* Crossley,
Wilson, Whelan *Booked* Stockdale, Geremi, Boateng
Scorer Job 90
Referee **M Halsey**

The introduction of Job for Middlesbrough, at
Maccarone's expense, is roundly booed, but fans
change their tune when the substitute pounces on
Johansson's error to grab a last-minute winner.
Blackburn, on top for long periods but frustrated by
Schwarzer, are left bemoaning their luck.

Tuesday September 3
MANCHESTER UNITED (a)
Lost 0-1 HT 0-1 Att **67,464** Position **10th**
Schwarzer — Stockdale, Cooper, Ehiogu, Southgate,
Queudrue (Marinelli 72) — Geremi, Boateng, Greening
— Maccarone (Whelan 72), Job *Subs not used*
Crossley, Gavin, Wilson *Booked* Ehiogu, Southgate
Report page 42

WHO WOULD HAVE THOUGHT IT? Another rollercoaster
season at the Riverside. After an erratic start, Middlesbrough found
themselves third in the Premiership, prompting praise from Sir Alex
himself and press talk of possible European qualification, even if
Steve McClaren wrote off their chances as early as December after
they were deservedly beaten away to West Bromwich Albion.

Middlesbrough were the Premiership's biggest pre-season
spenders and the new signings all grabbed their share of the
headlines over the long winter months. The Gang Of Four (George
Boateng, Geremi, Juninho and Massimo Maccarone) were primed
to take centre stage in the opening game of the season, but
McClaren's tactics had to be rethought at short notice after
Juninho's pre-season knee injury. It was to be another seven months
before the Brazilian made a first-team appearance.

The rollercoaster continued its downward course as
Middlesbrough lost eight consecutive away games in a three-month
period, failing to get on the scoresheet in any of them. The
rumblings of discontent threatened to spill over when, the week
after the last of these defeats, they capitulated 5-2 at the Riverside
against Aston Villa. By this time, they were looking over their
shoulder at the trapdoor. Salvation quickly followed with a
long-awaited away goal and point — at Anfield of all places —
quickly followed by a 3-1 win away to Sunderland. Middlesbrough
and McClaren were off the hook and the rollercoaster started a
tentative climb. However, their woeful record on their travels ruined
a potentially glorious season and it is the lack of ambition when
away from Teesside that needs to be addressed.

The draw at Anfield was indeed a turning point. Middlesbrough
went on a run of eight matches unbeaten and the long-awaited
return of Juninho gave the club and fans a massive boost. Such was
the anticipation that 19,450 turned up the week before to watch him
in a reserve game and he immediately showed what might have
been achieved had he been available from the beginning of the
season. Even though the Brazilian's pace is not what it was, his mere
presence on the field transmits a tangible feel-good factor among
fans. This in itself must carry a knock-on effect to the spirit of his
team-mates.

With what looked like a not-too-difficult series of opponents to
end the season, Middlesbrough were again being touted as
contenders for their first European campaign. Not for the first time,
though, McClaren showed great maturity and wisdom in refusing to
get involved in such talk.

Of the transfer window signings (Michael Ricketts, Malcolm

Victory over Liverpool showed that Middlesbrough could mix it with the best

Christie and Chris Riggott), only Ricketts failed to impress. Apparently unfit, off the pace and virtually invisible from the outset, he only seemed to play with any fire when he came on against Bolton Wanderers, his former team, in the last game of the season, but his first goal for the club was of scant consolation.

And yet, notwithstanding their performances in most of the final six games of the season, Middlesbrough do have a lot to shout about. The defensive partnership of Ugo Ehiogu and Gareth Southgate brings back memories for older fans of the equally solid pairing in the 1970s of Stuart Boam and Willie Maddren, while Jonathan Greening, for so long the target of fan abuse, is maturing into a fine player and Geremi, on loan from Real Madrid, brought some pace and power to midfield.

Some may say that the most disappointing player was Maccarone, but this was due to the fact that the £8.15 million signing started so well that he raised expectations too high. At 23, he still has much to learn about playing through English winters and the pace of the Premiership.

Despite some notable victories and outstanding performances against top-five finishers such as Manchester United, Newcastle United and Liverpool, Middlesbrough lacked bite and ambition against some of their co-habitees of mid-table. Even though they ended the season with a number of substandard displays, any fan will tell you that mid-table in the Premiership is quite an achievement for this club.

McClaren and his assistant, Bill Beswick, have built a solid platform to take the club to the next phase of development. This can be measured by the fact that, for the second season in succession, Middlesbrough have not been involved in a relegation dogfight. That alone is a sign of significant progress for this ambitious club.

Tuesday September 10
SUNDERLAND (h)
Won 3-0 **HT 2-0** Att **32,155** Position **4th**
Schwarzer — Ehiogu, Southgate, Cooper — Stockdale, Geremi, Greening, Queudrue — Job (Wilson 86) — Maccarone, Nemeth (Whelan 88) *Subs not used* Crossley, Boksic, Marinelli *Booked* Stockdale, Greening, Queudrue
Scorers **Nemeth 17, 66, Maccarone 37**
Referee **A Wiley**

An error by Sorensen in the Sunderland goal sees Maccarone set up Nemeth for the opener and the same pair combine again later, Maccarone heading No 2 in between as Middlesbrough romp to a decisive derby victory.

Saturday September 14
EVERTON (a)
Lost 1-2 **HT 1-1** Att **32,240** Position **8th**
Schwarzer — Ehiogu, Southgate (Whelan 74), Cooper — Stockdale, Geremi, Greening, Queudrue — Job (Boksic 81) — Maccarone (Marinelli 81), Nemeth *Subs not used* Crossley, Wilson *Booked* Schwarzer
Scorer **Nemeth 10**
Report page 115

Saturday September 21
BIRMINGHAM CITY (h)
Won 1-0 **HT 1-0** Att **29,869** Position **6th**
Schwarzer — Ehiogu, Cooper, Vidmar — Stockdale, Geremi, Boateng, Queudrue — Job (Wilkshire 76) — Maccarone, Nemeth (Boksic 63) *Subs not used* Marinelli, Crossley, Whelan *Booked* Greening, Maccarone, Boksic
Scorer **Queudrue 29**
Referee **A D'Urso**

It takes a delightful free kick temporarily to illuminate a drab contest, Queudrue finding the top corner with a sublime left-foot shot and leaving Steve Bruce, the Birmingham manager, to complain about the four yellow cards shown to his team out of the seven flourished by Andy D'Urso.

Saturday September 28
TOTTENHAM HOTSPUR (a)
Won 3-0 **HT 1-0** Att **36,082** Position **3rd**
Schwarzer — Stockdale, Ehiogu, Southgate, Queudrue — Geremi, Boateng (Wilkshire 84), Greening — Job — Maccarone, Boksic *Subs not used* Crossley, Cooper, Wilson, Marinelli *Booked* Queudrue
Scorers **Maccarone 32, Geremi 55, Job 58**
Report page 151

Tuesday October 1
BRENTFORD (a)

Worthington Cup, 2nd rnd

Won 4-1 HT 2-0   Att 7,558

Crossley — Parnaby, Vidmar, Gavin, Cooper — Wilkshire, Wilson, Johnston, Marinelli — Whelan (Dove 83), Windass (Downing ht) *Subs not used* Russell, Close, Davies *Booked* Wilson

Scorers **Marinelli 18, Whelan 20, Wilson 75, Downing 76**

Referee **K Hill**

Steve McClaren follows the accepted Premiership pattern by making changes — no fewer than 11 of them — for the visit to West London, and Marinelli grabs his chance by scoring the first and making the next two against second division opposition, who are 4-0 down before Sonko's reply.

Saturday October 5

BOLTON WANDERERS (h)

Won 2-0   HT 1-0   Att 31,005   Position 3rd

Schwarzer — Stockdale (Cooper 81), Ehiogu, Southgate, Queudrue — Geremi, Boateng, Greening — Job — Maccarone (Whelan 90), Boksic (Nemeth 72) *Subs not used* Crossley, Marinelli

Scorers **Ehiogu 23, Geremi 69**

Referee **C Wilkes**

Ehiogu has plenty to celebrate after scoring the opening goal against Bolton and being named the next day in England's squad for the European Championship qualifying matches against Slovakia and Macedonia. Geremi completes a comfortable win against opponents who slip back into the bottom three.

Sunday October 20

CHARLTON ATHLETIC (a)

Lost 0-1   HT 0-1   Att 26,271   Position 5th

Schwarzer — Stockdale (Cooper 68), Ehiogu, Southgate, Queudrue — Geremi, Boateng, Greening — Job — Maccarone (Marinelli 68), Nemeth (Whelan 68) *Subs not used* Crossley, Wilkshire *Booked* Stockdale, Boateng, Whelan

Report page 176

MATCH OF THE SEASON

Tottenham Hotspur 0   Middlesbrough 3
White Hart Lane, Saturday September 28 2003
Keith Pike

Maccarone gets the first of Middlesbrough's three goals in the rout of Spurs

IT WAS DEPRESSING ENOUGH already, but as Glenn Hoddle had all but completed his inquest into Tottenham Hotspur's home defeat, someone mentioned injuries. Bad mistake. Half an hour later it was as if the cast of *Casualty* had been in a head-on crash with their rivals on *A & E* on the outskirts of Holby City. Even the reporters were staggering from the press room with their laptops strung up to intravenous drips.

Hoddle must sometimes feel like a wartime correspondent himself. Every Saturday he counts his team out, but when he counts them back in again there are a couple missing. No sooner had his list of 13 first-team players *hors de combat* been reduced to 12 with the recovery of Christian Ziege than it was back up to 13 (Ziege again, obviously), then 14 (Kasey Keller) and possibly 15 (Jamie Redknapp, like the goalkeeper, finished hobbling). Hoddle would like to prise

Maccarone celebrates after showing why McClaren paid £8.15 million for him

Fifa's transfer window back open; he would undoubtedly break his wrists in the process.

But at least the Tottenham manager was not using his predicament to excuse what he described as their worst performance in 53 games under him. Middlesbrough, he recognised, would have been a match for any side in the Premiership.

Their transformation from dull, predictable makeweights into one of the most attractive teams has been dramatic. A year ago, after a 3-1 home defeat by Southampton, Steve McClaren's first season in charge had already been condemned to a relegation battle. Now there are realistic hopes of a top-six finish and Europe. "We have recruited younger legs and it shows," McClaren said, "but the biggest difference is in our quality."

Among the fresh legs are those belonging to Massimo

Saturday October 26
LEEDS UNITED (h)
Drew 2-2   HT 1-1   Att **34,723**   Position **6th**
Schwarzer — Parnaby, Ehiogu, Southgate, Queudrue — Geremi, Boateng, Greening — Job — Maccarone, Boksic (Nemeth 61) *Subs not used* Crossley, Marinelli, Whelan, Cooper *Booked* Southgate, Greening, Queudrue *Sent off* Queudrue 90
Scorers **Job 25, Southgate 83**
Referee **R Styles**

A tempestuous affair in which matters of discipline — Smith and Queudrue both see red (Smith harshly) and the match culminates in an unpleasant spat between Boateng and Barmby — overshadow a pulsating contest, Middlesbrough twice coming from behind to earn a point and stay in the top six.

Monday November 4
NEWCASTLE UNITED (a)
Lost 0-2   HT 0-1   Att **51,558**   Position **9th**
Schwarzer — Parnaby, Ehiogu, Southgate, Queudrue — Geremi, Boateng, Greening — Job — Maccarone, Nemeth (Marinelli 70) *Subs not used* Crossley, Cooper, Vidmar, Wilkshire *Booked* Ehiogu, Queudrue *Sent off* Queudrue 90
Report page 69

Wednesday November 6
IPSWICH TOWN (a)
Worthington Cup, 4th rnd
Lost 1-3   HT 0-3   Att **14,417**
Crossley — Stockdale (Dove 78), Cooper, Davies, Vidmar, Queudrue — Wilson, Wilkshire, Johnston — Nemeth (Close 66), Marinelli (Cade 66) *Subs not used* Gulliver, Russell *Booked* Vidmar, Wilson
Scorer **Queudrue 88**
Referee **E Wolstenholme**

Middlesbrough's reserves and youngsters this time find the task of taking on Nationwide League opposition in the Worthington Cup too demanding, an Ipswich side that has been quickly revived by Joe Royle's appointment as manager settling the tie with three first-half goals. At least Queudrue, sent off in the previous two matches, makes his name in the right way with a consolation goal.

Saturday November 9
LIVERPOOL (h)
Won 1-0   HT 0-0   Att **34,747**   Position **6th**
Schwarzer — Parnaby, Ehiogu, Southgate, Vidmar — Geremi, Boateng, Greening — Job — Maccarone (Boksic 70), Nemeth (Wilkshire 86) *Subs not used* Crossley, Cooper, Wilson *Booked* Boksic
Scorer **Southgate 82**
Referee **M Halsey**

The last unbeaten record in England finally goes as Liverpool, after seven straight Premiership victories, hand victory to Middlesbrough when, under pressure from Boksic, Dudek drops Nemeth's cross at the feet of a grateful Southgate. Steve McClaren's team, though, deserve victory for their greater enterprise.

Saturday November 16
CHELSEA (a)
Lost 0-1 HT 0-0 Att **39,064** Position **7th**
Schwarzer — Parnaby (Queudrue 67), Ehiogu,
Southgate, Vidmar — Geremi, Boateng, Greening — Job
— Maccarone (Whelan 71), Nemeth (Boksic 71) *Subs
not used* Crossley, Wilkshire *Booked* Boateng
Report page 81

Saturday November 23
MANCHESTER CITY (h)
Won 3-1 HT 0-0 Att **31,510** Position **6th**
Schwarzer — Parnaby, Southgate, Ehiogu, Vidmar —
Geremi, Job, Boateng, Greening — Boksic (Whelan 84),
Maccarone *Subs not used* Crossley, Nemeth, Cooper,
Wilkshire
Scorers **Ehiogu 53, Boksic 62, Geremi 84**
Referee **N Barry**

Geremi proves the main difference as his crosses pave
the way for headers by Ehiogu and Boksic. He then
snuffs out a Manchester City revival, sparked by
Anelka's goal, by scoring Middlesbrough's third himself.
City have Wright-Phillips dismissed for two cautions, the
second after a bad foul on Greening.

Saturday November 30
WEST BROMWICH ALBION (a)
Lost 0-1 HT 0-0 Att **27,029** Position **6th**
Schwarzer — Parnaby (Cooper 62), Ehiogu, Southgate,
Vidmar — Geremi, Boateng, Greening — Job — Boksic
(Nemeth 76), Maccarone (Whelan 74) *Subs not used*
Wilkshire, Jones *Booked* Ehiogu
Report page 262

Saturday December 7
WEST HAM UNITED (h)
Drew 2-2 HT 0-0 Att **28,283** Position **8th**
Schwarzer — Ehiogu, Southgate, Vidmar (Nemeth ht) —
Parnaby, Boateng, Greening, Queudrue — Geremi —
Boksic (Whelan 86), Maccarone (Wilkshire 89) *Subs
not used* Crossley, Wilson *Booked* Parnaby
Scorers **Nemeth 58, Ehiogu 88**
Referee **G Poll**

Cole, entrusted with the West Ham United captaincy
at 21 in Di Canio's absence, leads from the front with
the opening goal and Pearce, an emergency striker,
also scores for the visiting team, but the bottom club
are twice unable to protect the lead, Nemeth and
Ehiogu — the latter heading in with just two minutes
remaining — earning Middlesbrough a point on a
freezing afternoon.

The wily Boksic proved a real handful for the Tottenham defence

Maccarone and the Italian used them to devastating effect, poking
in Middlesbrough's opener and unleashing the second-half rapier
thrusts that produced goals for Geremi and Joseph-Desire Job. The
three goalscorers, as well as George Boateng and Jonathan
Greening, excelled, but it was the wily veteran, Alen Boksic, who
stole the show with a mesmeric display of hard graft, link play and
party pieces.

"We have set ourselves a standard today," McClaren said. It may
be hard to match.

TOTTENHAM HOTSPUR (4-4-2): K Keller — S Davies, D Richards, B Thatcher, C Ziege (sub:
G Doherty, 12min) — S Iversen (sub: M Acimovic, 67), G Bunjevcevic, J Redknapp, M Etherington
— L Ferdinand (sub: T Sheringham, 46), R Keane. **Substitutes not used:** L Hirschfeld, R Ricketts.
Booked: Davies.

MIDDLESBROUGH (4-3-1-2): M Schwarzer — R Stockdale, U Ehiogu, G Southgate, F Queudrue
— Geremi, G Boateng (sub: L Wilkshire, 84), J Greening — J-D Job — M Maccarone, A Boksic.
Substitutes not used: M Crossley, C Cooper, M Wilson, C Marinelli. **Booked:** Queudrue.
Referee: G Poll.

THE MANAGER

Steve McClaren

Such is the respect that Steve McClaren enjoys, it is easy to forget that he is only two seasons into his first managerial appointment. All the more credit to him, then, that he is able to attract players such as Geremi and Juninho, a World Cup winner, to the Riverside. For a rookie manager, it can be argued that he has exceeded all expectations by not only attracting these and other quality players, but also in having the coaching skills to blend them together.

Shaun Keogh

APPEARANCES

	Prem	FAC	WC	Total
G Boateng	28	-	-	28
A Boksic	13 (5)	0 (1)	-	13 (6)
J Cade	-	-	0 (1)	0 (1)
M Christie	11 (1)	-	-	11 (1)
B Close	-	-	0 (1)	0 (1)
C Cooper	14 (6)	0 (1)	2	16 (7)
M Crossley	-	-	2	2
A Davies	1	-	1	2
Doriva	3 (2)	-	-	3 (2)
C Dove	-	-	0 (2)	0 (2)
S Downing	0 (2)	-	0 (1)	0 (3)
U Ehiogu	31 (1)	-	-	31 (1)
J Eustace	0 (1)	-	-	0 (1)
J Gavin	-	-	1	1
Geremi	33	1	-	34
J Greening	38	1	-	39
J-D Job	22 (6)	1	-	23 (6)
A Johnston	-	-	2	2
Juninho	9 (1)	-	-	9 (1)
M Maccarone	26 (8)	-	-	26 (8)
C Marinelli	3 (4)	-	2	5 (4)
D Murphy	4 (4)	-	-	4 (4)
S Nemeth	15 (13)	1	1	17 (13)
S Parnaby	21	1	1	23
F Queudrue	29 (2)	1	1	31 (2)
M Ricketts	5 (4)	-	-	5 (4)
C Riggott	4 (1)	-	-	4 (1)
M Schwarzer	38	1	-	39
G Southgate	36	1	-	37
R Stockdale	12 (2)	-	1	13 (2)
A Vidmar	9 (3)	1	2	12 (3)
N Whelan	2 (12)	0 (1)	1	3 (13)
L Wilkshire	7 (7)	-	2	9 (7)
M Wilson	4 (3)	1	2	7 (3)
D Windass	0 (2)	1	1	2 (2)

Saturday December 14
CHELSEA (h)
Drew 1-1 HT **1-1** Att **29,160** Position **9th**
Schwarzer — Parnaby, Ehiogu, Southgate, Queudrue — Geremi, Boateng, Greening — Nemeth — Boksic, Maccarone (Whelan ht) *Subs not used* Vidmar, Wilson, Crossley, Wilkshire
Scorer **Geremi 32**
Referee **M Messias**

Chelsea need a win to go top, but have to settle for a single point when Terry stabs home from close range after Geremi's splendid free kick had put Middlesbrough ahead. Fortunate when Petit is harshly penalised on that occasion, Middlesbrough's luck turns when Nemeth has a winning goal wrongly disallowed for offside.

Saturday December 21
ARSENAL (a)
Lost 0-2 HT **0-1** Att **38,003** Position **9th**
Schwarzer — Parnaby, Ehiogu, Southgate, Queudrue — Geremi, Boateng (Job 24), Wilkshire, Greening — Boksic (Windass 69), Nemeth (Vidmar 77) *Subs not used* Maccarone, Crossley *Booked* Greening, Queudrue, Wilkshire *Sent off* Wilkshire 73
Report page 59

Thursday December 26
MANCHESTER UNITED (h)
Won 3-1 HT **1-0** Att **34,673** Position **8th**
Schwarzer — Parnaby, Ehiogu, Southgate, Queudrue — Geremi, Wilson, Greening — Job — Boksic (Wilkshire 64), Nemeth (Maccarone 83) *Subs not used* Vidmar, Windass, Crossley *Booked* Job
Scorers **Boksic 44, Nemeth 48, Job 85**
Referee **G Barber**

Keane, out since August, and Ferdinand, who has missed ten matches, return for Manchester United, but despite a goal from Giggs on the hour they suffer their first Boxing Day defeat since 1989 as Middlesbrough, getting back to their early-season form, secure their first victory over Steve McClaren's old club at the Riverside Stadium.

Saturday December 28
ASTON VILLA (a)
Lost 0-1 HT **0-1** Att **33,637** Position **10th**
Schwarzer — Parnaby (Maccarone 88), Ehiogu, Southgate, Queudrue — Geremi, Wilson, Greening, Wilkshire (Vidmar 57) — Nemeth (Whelan 57), Job *Subs not used* Crossley, Windass *Booked* Whelan, Wilson *Sent off* Wilson 27
Report page 228

Wednesday January 1
BLACKBURN ROVERS (a)
Lost 0-1   **HT 0-0**   Att **23,413**   Position **12th**
Schwarzer — Parnaby, Ehiogu (Vidmar 8), Southgate,
Queudrue — Geremi, Wilson, Greening — Job (Windass
78) — Boksic, Maccarone (Nemeth 72) *Subs not used*
Crossley, Wilkshire
Report page 108

Saturday January 4
CHELSEA (a)
FA Cup, 3rd rnd
Lost 0-1   **HT 0-1**   Att **29,796**
Schwarzer — Parnaby, Vidmar, Southgate,
Queudrue — Job (Whelan ht), Geremi, Wilson (Cooper
21), Greening, Nemeth — Windass (Boksic 81) *Subs
not used* Crossley, Maccarone *Booked* Cooper, Vidmar,
Windass
Report page 84

Saturday January 11
SOUTHAMPTON (h)
Drew 2-2   **HT 0-1**   Att **27,443**   Position **11th**
Schwarzer — Parnaby, Vidmar, Southgate, Queudrue —
Geremi, Wilkshire, Greening — Job (Whelan ht) —
Boksic (Maccarone 70), Nemeth (Murphy 70) *Subs not
used* Crossley, Cooper
Scorers **Whelan 73, Maccarone 82 (pen)**
Referee **D Elleray**

Two more superb finishes from Beattie, surely now
England-bound, put Southampton in the driving seat,
only for Middlesbrough to fight back in a Riverside
thriller, Whelan netting with a stunning lob-volley and
Maccarone converting a contentious penalty, Telfer
having been adjudged by David Elleray to have brought
down Wilkshire.

Sunday January 19
FULHAM (a)
Lost 0-1   **HT 0-1**   Att **14,253**   Position **12th**
Schwarzer — Parnaby, Southgate, Vidmar, Queudrue —
Greening, Wilson, Geremi, Wilkshire (Job ht) — Whelan
(Nemeth 64), Maccarone *Subs not used* Crossley,
Boksic, Cooper *Booked* Southgate
Report page 205

When Geremi made his Middlesbrough debut in the opening game of the season, away to Southampton, he was described as "solid rather than spectacular". If he had read this comment, he may have thought to himself: "And the problem is?" Solid rather than spectacular sums up Geremi's contribution to Steve McClaren's midfield powerhouse last season and if all of the squad had managed that, the club may have won something. Geremi's influence on this side after being signed on loan from Real Madrid became apparent from the moment he was not on the team-sheet. Injury kept him out of the final five games, four of which were lost.

Shaun Keogh

STATS AND FACTS

● Juninho scored in successive games for Middlesbrough, three years apart and both against Everton. The goals came in May 2000 and on March 1, 2003.

● The past nine wins against Chelsea have all come at home.

● Franck Queudrue, the Middlesbrough left back, was sent off three times in the Premiership this season; Christian Ziege, the former Middlesbrough left back who is now at Tottenham Hotspur, was dismissed twice.

● The past six meetings with Fulham have produced just four goals.

● Middlesbrough have lost only one of their past 28 home games against West Bromwich Albion.

Bill Edgar

GOALSCORERS

	Prem	FAC	WC	Total
A Boksic	2	-	-	2
M Christie	4	-	-	4
S Downing	-	-	1	1
U Ehiogu	3	-	-	3
Geremi	7	-	-	7
J Greening	2	-	-	2
J-D Job	4	-	-	4
Juninho	3	-	-	3
M Maccarone	9 (2p)	-	-	9 (2p)
C Marinelli	-	-	1	1
S Nemeth	7	-	-	7
F Queudrue	1	-	1	2
M Ricketts	1	-	-	1
C Riggott	2	-	-	2
G Southgate	2	-	-	2
N Whelan	1	-	1	2
M Wilson	-	-	1	1

Tuesday January 28
ASTON VILLA (h)
Lost 2-5 **HT 2-2** Att **27,546** Position **14th**
Schwarzer — Parnaby, Davies, Vidmar, Queudrue — Geremi, Boateng, Greening — Job (Murphy 69) — Maccarone, Nemeth *Subs not used* Downing, Crossley, Cooper, Wilkshire *Booked* Boateng
Scorers **Maccarone 33, Greening 35**
Referee **D Gallagher**

The team with the last unbeaten home record in the Premiership versus the only side not to have won away: in other words, a Middlesbrough banker. Except that Villa, having squandered a 2-0 lead in the first half — when Gudjonsson marks his debut with a 30-yard free kick through Schwarzer's hands — hit three more after the break, this time without reply.

Saturday February 8
LIVERPOOL (a)
Drew 1-1 **HT 1-0** Att **42,247** Position **14th**
Schwarzer — Riggott, Southgate, Cooper — Stockdale, Geremi, Boateng, Greening, Murphy — Ricketts, Job (Christie ht; Eustace 86) *Subs not used* Nemeth, Maccarone, Crossley *Booked* Eustace, Riggott
Scorer **Geremi 38**
Report page 97

Saturday February 22
SUNDERLAND (a)
Won 3-1 **HT 2-0** Att **42,134** Position **13th**
Schwarzer — Riggott, Southgate, Cooper — Parnaby, Geremi, Boateng, Greening, Queudrue (Murphy 76) — Ricketts, Christie (Nemeth 82) *Subs not used* Crossley, Job, Maccarone *Booked* Queudrue
Scorers **Riggott 21, 28, Christie 59**
Report page 278

Saturday March 1
EVERTON (h)
Drew 1-1 **HT 0-1** Att **32,473** Position **13th**
Schwarzer — Riggott (Ehiogu ht), Southgate, Cooper (Juninho ht) — Parnaby, Geremi, Boateng, Greening, Queudrue — Ricketts, Christie (Maccarone ht) *Subs not used* Nemeth, Crossley
Scorer **Juninho 74**
Referee **U Rennie**

His previous match was the World Cup final, his last game for Middlesbrough almost three years ago, but Juninho is fit and back to cement his place in Teesside hearts, cancelling out Watson's opener on his return. Everton would have spoilt the party had Southgate's last-ditch tackle not robbed Rooney of a late winner.

Wednesday March 5
NEWCASTLE UNITED (h)
Won 1-0   HT 0-0   Att 34,814   Position 11th
Schwarzer — Parnaby, Ehiogu, Southgate, Queudrue —
Geremi, Boateng, Greening — Juninho — Ricketts,
Maccarone (Murphy 80) *Subs not used* Nemeth, Job,
Doriva, Crossley
Scorer **Geremi 62**
Referee **A D'Urso**

Sir Bobby Robson, still fuming over the postponement
of the original fixture, is less than amused when
Middlesbrough win the rearranged match thanks to
Geremi's header. A record Riverside crowd sees the
home side keep a clean sheet for the first time since
November 9 and Newcastle fail to score for the first
time in 23 games.

Saturday March 15
LEEDS UNITED (a)
Won 3-2   HT 2-1   Att 39,073   Position 11th
Schwarzer — Parnaby (Cooper 41), Ehiogu, Southgate,
Murphy — Geremi, Boateng, Greening — Juninho —
Maccarone (Ricketts 80), Christie (Nemeth 85) *Subs
not used* Jones, Job *Booked* Maccarone, Juninho
Scorers **Maccarone 36 (pen), Juninho 45,**
Geremi 64
Report page 219

Saturday March 22
CHARLTON ATHLETIC (h)
Drew 1-1   HT 0-1   Att 29,080   Position 11th
Schwarzer — Cooper, Ehiogu, Southgate, Murphy
(Queudrue ht) — Geremi, Boateng, Greening — Juninho
— Maccarone (Ricketts ht), Christie (Nemeth 76) *Subs
not used* Stockdale, Jones *Booked* Ricketts
Scorer **Christie 57**
Referee **M Dean**

A fine contest between European hopefuls swings
Charlton's way when Lisbie, guilty of a bad miss earlier,
sets up Johansson for the opening goal, but Steve
McClaren's substitutions change the match and Christie
gets a deserved equaliser from Queudrue's cross,
although Konchesky hits the Middlesbrough bar with
almost the last kick.

THE PLAYERS

GEORGE BOATENG
Midfield
Born September 5, 1975,
Nkawkaw, Ghana
Ht 5ft 9in **Wt** 11st 7lb
Signed from Aston Villa, August
2002, £5m

ALEN BOKSIC
Forward
Born January 31, 1970,
Makarska, Croatia
Ht 6ft 1in **Wt** 12st 8lb
Signed from Lazio, August 2000,
£2.5m

JAMIE CADE
Forward
Born January 15, 1984, Durham
Ht 5ft 8in **Wt** 10st 10lb
Signed from trainee, November
2002

MALCOLM CHRISTIE
Forward
Born April 11, 1979,
Stamford
Ht 5ft 6in **Wt** 11st 4lb
Signed from Derby County,
January 2003, £3m

BRIAN CLOSE
Defender
Born January 27, 1982, Dublin
Ht 5ft 10in **Wt** 12st 3lb
Signed from trainee, October
2002

COLIN COOPER
Defender
Born February 28, 1967,
Sedgefield
Ht 5ft 10in **Wt** 11st 9lb
Signed from Nottingham Forest,
August 1998, £2.5m

MARK CROSSLEY
Goalkeeper
Born June 16, 1969, Barnsley
Ht 6ft 0in **Wt** 16st 0lb

Signed from Nottingham Forest,
July 2000, free

ANDREW DAVIES
Defender
Born December 17, 1984,
Stockton-on-Tees
Ht 6ft 1in **Wt** 13st 1lb
Signed from trainee, October
2002

DORIVA
Midfield
Born May 28, 1972,
Maranhao, Brazil
Ht 5ft 6in **Wt** 11st 5lb
Signed from Celta Vigo (loan),
January 2003

CRAIG DOVE
Midfield
Born August 6, 1983, Hartlepool
Ht 5ft 8in **Wt** 11st 0lb
Signed from trainee, October
2002

STEWART DOWNING
Midfield
Born July 22, 1984,
Middlesbrough
Ht 5ft 11in **Wt** 10st 6lb
Signed from trainee, September
2001

Malcolm Christie

UGO EHIOGU
Defender
Born November 3, 1972, Hackney
Ht 6ft 2in **Wt** 14st 10lb
Signed from Aston Villa, October 2000, £8m

JOHN EUSTACE
Midfield
Born November 3, 1979, Solihull
Ht 5ft 10in **Wt** 11st 12lb
Signed from Coventry City (loan), January 2003

JASON GAVIN
Defender
Born March 14, 1980, Dublin
Ht 6ft 1in **Wt** 12st 7lb
Signed from trainee, March 1997

GEREMI
Midfield
Born December 20, 1978, Baffoussam, Cameroon
Ht 5ft 9in **Wt** 12st 6lb
Signed from Real Madrid (loan), July 2002

JONATHAN GREENING
Midfield
Born January 2, 1979, Scarborough
Ht 5ft 11in **Wt** 11st 7lb
Signed from Manchester United, August 2001, £2m

JOSEPH-DESIRE JOB
Forward
Born December 1, 1977, Lyons
Ht 5ft 10in **Wt** 11st 3lb
Signed from Lens, August 2000, £3m

ALLAN JOHNSTON
Midfield
Born December 14, 1973, Glasgow

Ht 5ft 9in **Wt** 11st 0lb
Signed from Rangers, September 2001, £1m

JUNINHO
Midfield
Born February 22, 1973, Sao Paulo
Ht 5ft 5in **Wt** 9st 6lb
Signed from Atletico Madrid, August 2002, £6m

MASSIMO MACCARONE
Forward
Born September 6, 1979, Galliate, Italy
Ht 5ft 9in **Wt** 11st 5lb
Signed from Empoli, July 2002, £8.15m

CARLOS MARINELLI
Midfield
Born March 14, 1982, Buenos Aires
Ht 5ft 8in **Wt** 11st 6lb
Signed from Boca Juniors, October 1999, £1.5m

DAVID MURPHY
Defender
Born June 1, 1984, Hartlepool
Ht 6ft 1in **Wt** 12st 5lb
Signed from trainee, August 2001

SZILARD NEMETH
Forward
Born September 14, 1972, Komarno, Slovakia
Ht 5ft 10in **Wt** 10st 10lb
Signed from Inter Bratislava, July 2001, free

STUART PARNABY
Defender
Born July 19, 1982, Durham
Ht 5ft 11in **Wt** 11st 0lb
Signed from trainee, August 2000

Saturday April 5
WEST BROMWICH ALBION (h)
Won 3-0 HT 1-0 Att **30,187** Position **10th**
Schwarzer — Cooper, Ehiogu, Southgate, Queudrue — Geremi, Doriva, Greening — Juninho (Stockdale 90) — Christie (Nemeth 69), Job (Maccarone 69) *Subs not used* Jones, Wilkshire
Scorers Christie 36, Greening 76, Nemeth 87
Referee **M Halsey**

The game is almost up now for West Brom, who are 14 points adrift of safety with six matches to go after being well beaten at the Riverside. Christie gets Middlesbrough's first, with the consistently excellent Juninho creating second-half strikes for Greening and Nemeth before the Brazilian withdraws to a standing ovation.

Saturday April 12
MANCHESTER CITY (a)
Drew 0-0 HT 0-0 Att **34,793** Position **9th**
Schwarzer — Cooper, Ehiogu, Southgate, Queudrue — Geremi (Wilkshire 88), Doriva, Greening — Juninho — Christie, Job (Nemeth 59) *Subs not used* Jones, Stockdale, Maccarone *Booked* Ehiogu
Report page 147

Saturday April 19
ARSENAL (h)
Lost 0-2 HT 0-0 Att **34,724** Position **10th**
Schwarzer — Cooper, Ehiogu, Southgate — Greening, Boateng, Doriva (Wilkshire 71), Nemeth — Juninho (Maccarone 83) — Christie (Job 85) *Subs not used* Stockdale, Jones
Referee **D Elleray**

With Parlour outstanding in his first match as captain of the champions, Arsenal keep pace with Manchester United as Henry sets up Wiltord's opener and then curls in a trademark free kick to register his 110th goal on his 200th appearance for the club. Juninho, of all people, skies Middlesbrough's only real chance over the bar.

Monday April 21
WEST HAM UNITED (a)
Lost 0-1 **HT 0-0** **Att 35,019** Position **11th**
Schwarzer — Cooper, Ehiogu, Southgate, Queudrue (Stockdale 53) — Wilkshire, Boateng, Greening — Juninho (Job ht) — Christie (Ricketts 72), Maccarone
Subs not used Jones, Doriva *Booked* Greening, Queudrue
Report page 255

Saturday April 26
BIRMINGHAM CITY (a)
Lost 0-3 **HT 0-2** **Att 28,821** Position **13th**
Schwarzer — Ehiogu, Southgate, Cooper (Doriva ht) — Parnaby, Boateng, Greening, Queudrue — Job (Maccarone 78) — Christie, Ricketts (Nemeth 67)
Subs not used Jones, Stockdale *Booked* Boateng, Maccarone
Report page 196

Saturday May 3
TOTTENHAM HOTSPUR (h)
Won 5-1 **HT 3-0** **Att 30,230** Position **10th**
Schwarzer — Stockdale, Ehiogu (Riggott 11), Southgate, Queudrue — Wilkshire (Downing 77), Boateng, Greening — Juninho — Christie (Maccarone ht), Nemeth *Subs not used* Jones, Doriva
Scorers **Christie 23, Juninho 26, Nemeth 28, Maccarone 51, 75**
Referee **U Rennie**

Already ahead through Christie, Middlesbrough romp to their biggest win of the season once Perry is sent off for bringing down Nemeth and a penalty is awarded, although the foul takes place outside the area. Juninho scores after Keller saves his initial spot kick and only Redknapp's goal on his return from injury eases Tottenham's misery.

Sunday May 11
BOLTON WANDERERS (a)
Lost 1-2 **HT 0-2** **Att 27,241** Position **17th**
Schwarzer — Parnaby, Riggott, Southgate, Queudrue — Wilkshire, Boateng, Greening (Downing ht) — Juninho — Maccarone (Ricketts ht), Christie (Doriva ht)
Subs not used Davies, Crossley *Booked* Greening, Queudrue
Scorer **Ricketts 61**
Report page 244

FRANCK QUEUDRUE
Defender
Born August 27, 1978, Paris
Ht 6ft 1in **Wt** 12st 7lb
Signed from Lens, October 2001, £2.5m

MICHAEL RICKETTS
Forward
Born December 4, 1978, Birmingham
Ht 6ft 2in **Wt** 11st 12lb
Signed from Bolton Wanderers, January 2003, £3.5m

CHRIS RIGGOTT
Defender
Born September 1, 1980, Derby
Ht 6ft 3in **Wt** 12st 2lb
Signed from Derby County, January 2000, £2m

MARK SCHWARZER
Goalkeeper
Born October 6, 1972, Sydney
Ht 6ft 5in **Wt** 13st 6lb
Signed from Bradford City, February 1997, £1.5m

GARETH SOUTHGATE
Defender
Born September 3, 1970, Watford
Ht 6ft 0in **Wt** 12st 8lb
Signed from Aston Villa, July 2001, £6.5m

ROBBIE STOCKDALE
Defender
Born November 30, 1979, Redcar
Ht 5ft 11in **Wt** 11st 3lb
Signed from trainee, July 1998

TONY VIDMAR
Defender
Born April 15, 1969, Adelaide
Ht 6ft 1in **Wt** 12st 13lb
Signed from Rangers, September 2002, free

NOEL WHELAN
Forward
Born December 30, 1974, Leeds
Ht 6ft 2in **Wt** 12st 3lb
Signed from Coventry City, August 2000, £2.2m

LUKE WILKSHIRE
Midfield
Born October 2, 1981, Wollongong, Australia
Ht 5ft 9in **Wt** 11st 5lb
Signed from trainee, August 1988

MARK WILSON
Midfield
Born February 9, 1979, Scunthorpe
Ht 5ft 11in **Wt** 13st 0lb
Signed from Manchester United, August 2001, £1.5m

DEAN WINDASS
Forward
Born April 1, 1969, Hull
Ht 5ft 10in **Wt** 12st 6lb
Signed from Bradford City, March 2001, £600,000

Mark Schwarzer

CHARLTON ATHLETIC

PREMIERSHIP

	P	W	D	L	F	A	Pts
Man Utd	38	25	8	5	74	34	83
Arsenal	38	23	9	6	85	42	78
Newcastle	38	21	6	11	63	48	69
Chelsea	38	19	10	9	68	38	67
Liverpool	38	18	10	10	61	41	64
Blackburn	38	16	12	10	52	43	60
Everton	38	17	8	13	48	49	59
Southampton	38	13	13	12	43	46	52
Man City	38	15	6	17	47	54	51
Tottenham	38	14	8	16	51	62	50
Middlesbro	38	13	10	15	48	44	49
Charlton	**38**	**14**	**7**	**17**	**45**	**56**	**49**
Birmingham	38	13	9	16	41	49	48
Fulham	38	13	9	16	41	50	48
Leeds	38	14	5	19	58	57	47
Aston Villa	38	12	9	17	42	47	45
Bolton	38	10	14	14	41	51	44
West Ham	38	10	12	16	42	59	42
West Brom	38	6	8	24	29	65	26
Sunderland	38	4	7	27	21	65	19

FA CUP
Fourth round

WORTHINGTON CUP
Second round

Claus Jensen, Charlton's great Dane and midfield mainstay

THE GAMES

　　　　　　　　　　　Nigel Williamson

Saturday August 17
CHELSEA (h)
Lost 2-3 HT 2-1 Att 25,640 Position 17th
Kiely — Young, Rowett, Rufus, Powell — Stuart,
Bart-Williams (Kishishev 58), Jensen, Konchesky — Euell
(Svensson 85), Johansson (Lisbie 79) *Subs not used*
Rachubka, Fortune *Sent off* Konchesky 26
Scorers **Konchesky 7, Rufus 33**
Referee **G Barber**

Half an hour into the season and Charlton are leading
Chelsea 2-0, but by then Konchesky, the scorer of their
opening goal, has been harshly sent off after an aerial
challenge on De Lucas and they are swept aside by
Chelsea's late revival, culminating in Lampard's
89th-minute winner.

Saturday August 24
BOLTON WANDERERS (a)
Won 2-1 HT 1-1 Att 21,753 Position 11th
Kiely — Young, Rowett (Brown 6), Rufus, Powell — Stuart
(Lisbie 73), Bart-Williams, Jensen, Konchesky — Euell,
Johansson (Svensson 82) *Subs not used* Kishishev,
Rachubka *Booked* Euell
Scorers **Bart-Williams 26 (pen), Euell 71**
Referee **M Messias**
Report page 234

Tuesday August 27
TOTTENHAM HOTSPUR (h)
Lost 0-1 HT 0-1 Att 26,461 Position 11th
Kiely — Young, Fortune (Brown 71), Rufus, Powell —
Kishishev (Robinson 65), Bart-Williams, Jensen,
Konchesky — Euell, Johansson (Svensson 55) *Subs not
used* Lisbie, Rachubka *Booked* Konchesky
Referee **A Wiley**

Unbeaten in ten London derbies last season, Charlton
have now lost two in 11 days. They fail to break down a
stubborn defence after Simon Davies gives the visiting
team an early lead with a well-taken goal, Spurs moving
to second in the table. Only Arsenal are above them, on
goal difference.

Saturday August 31
WEST HAM UNITED (a)
Won 2-0 HT 2-0 Att 32,424 Position 5th
Kiely — Young, Fortune, Rufus, Powell — Kishishev,
Bart-Williams, Jensen, Robinson (Johansson 87) — Euell,
Svensson (Bartlett 79) *Subs not used* Rachubka, Brown,
Fish *Booked* Rufus
Scorers **Jensen 4, Fortune 44**
Referee **J Winter**
Report page 246

IT IS AMAZING THE DRAMA that can lie behind the statistics.
Look at the table and Charlton's twelfth place appears a safe and
solid achievement — a comfortable position reflecting a steady if
unexciting season of respectable consistency.

And yet at no time during the campaign did it ever seem like
that, as Charlton's fortunes vacillated wildly to produce some of the
best and worst runs in the club's Premiership history. It was a season
of three vastly contrasting halves — as I hope Alan Curbishley
would never say — with all of the success squeezed into the middle.

Two months in, with the team rock bottom and still awaiting the
first home win, even the official website conceded that a dogged
struggle to avoid relegation appeared to be the best the club could
hope for. For the first time in a decade, a section of the crowd was
suggesting that Curbishley should consider his future after a
comically inept performance against Oxford United in the
Worthington Cup. The sale of the highly popular Mark Kinsella to
Aston Villa further upset the fans.

Yet by February, all had been forgiven. After just a single defeat
in 15 matches, Charlton found themselves improbably cast as the
league's "form" team. A club Premiership record of five straight wins
put them in seventh place and produced talk of European football at
The Valley. Could they push on for a top six place? Or, with survival
achieved almost three months early, would they fall away as they
had done in the previous campaign?

Sadly, it was the latter. The last ten games produced eight
defeats, a miserable four points and just six goals. To fail to reach
even 50 points, when 45 had been bagged with more than a quarter
of the season to go, was bitterly disappointing. A pro-rata return
would have given them a total of 60 points and the prospect of
taking the last Uefa Cup place from Blackburn Rovers. Instead, they
suffered a loss of form so dismal that, had the season gone on a
month longer, Charlton would have found themselves struggling to
stay out of the relegation zone.

During the team's earlier successful run, the engine was an
industrious and talented midfield in which Scott Parker, Claus
Jensen and Jason Euell were outstanding. Dean Kiely had another
excellent season in goal, but injuries at times played havoc with the
stability of the defence. Gary Rowett looked the part when fit, but
was sidelined for much of the time. Richard Rufus and Mark Fish
also had injuries and, with all three central defenders out, at one
point a makeshift pairing of full back Luke Young and the
improving but inexperienced Jonathan Fortune found themselves
attempting to tame a rampant Ruud Van Nistelrooy. Predictably, he

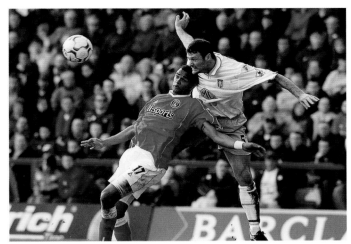

Shaun Bartlett is beaten in the air by Alpay in the 3-0 win over Villa in February

exposed the squad's lack of depth by scoring the easiest hat-trick of his career. Up front, the team suffered from a lack of firepower. Euell scored most of his goals from midfield and the combined talents of Shaun Bartlett, Jonatan Johansson, Matthias Svensson and Kevin Lisbie — international strikers all — managed only 11 league goals between them.

Yet despite the inconsistencies and the lack of depth in the squad, after three consecutive seasons in the Premiership Charlton are routinely held up as a model of how smaller clubs can survive at the top. In a season that saw them celebrating the tenth anniversary of the return to The Valley, the likes of Fulham must have been casting envious glances. Charlton have everything Mohamed Al Fayed's millions have failed to buy — shrewd management, an established position in the Premiership and a place to call home.

And yet, is Charlton's place really so secure? There is the cautionary experience of clubs such as Leicester City and West Ham United, who believed that they were established in the top flight. But Charlton's problem has never been a classy squad of overpaid players grown too big for their boots. Instead, it is a lack of ambition that remains a greater threat. At the start of each season, the club's primary aim is to secure Premiership survival. That is fair enough, but the outcome has been that, for the past two seasons, when that objective has been achieved with time to spare, the team has shut down and Curbishley has been unable to motivate them to press on.

The reduced financial circumstances of the game that has shifted the emphasis back on to coaching prowess, value-for-money deals and the development of youth-team players, should work to the benefit of a club such as Charlton. Yet whether they can ever rise above mid-table status depends on the manager's ability to inject a self-belief that they really are good enough to break into the top six.

At the moment, that confidence is still glaringly lacking.

Wednesday September 11
ASTON VILLA (a)
Lost 0-2   HT 0-0   Att 26,483   Position 10th
Kiely — Young, Fortune, Rufus, Powell — Kishishev (Brown 69), Bart-Williams (Bartlett 76), Jensen, Robinson — Euell, Svensson (Johansson 86) *Subs not used* Rachubka, Fish *Booked* Robinson
Referee **G Poll**
Report page 223

Saturday September 14
ARSENAL (h)
Lost 0-3   HT 0-1   Att 26,080   Position 14th
Kiely — Young, Fortune, Rufus, Powell — Robinson, Bart-Williams (Kishishev 74), Jensen, Johansson (Blomqvist 68) — Euell (Svensson 74), Lisbie *Subs not used* Rachubka, Fish
Referee **S Dunn**

Henry's sweet strike puts awesome Arsenal on the record trail as they break Manchester City's 1937 mark of scoring in 44 successive top-flight games and their own club record of 26 league matches without defeat. Wiltord's goal and Edu's header are merely the icing on the cake.

Saturday September 21
SOUTHAMPTON (a)
Drew 0-0   HT 0-0   Att 25,714   Position 14th
Kiely — Young, Fortune, Rufus, Powell — Robinson (Lisbie 85), Bart-Williams, Jensen, Konchesky — Euell, Johansson (Bartlett ht) *Subs not used* Rachubka, Fish, Kishishev *Booked* Euell
Referee **P Dowd**
Report page 127

Saturday September 28
MANCHESTER UNITED (h)
Lost 1-3   HT 1-0   Att 26,630   Position 19th
Kiely — Young — Fortune, Rufus, Powell — Robinson, Mustoe (Kishishev 87), Jensen, Konchesky — Euell, Bartlett *Subs not used* Rachubka, Fish, Svensson *Booked* Robinson, Mustoe
Scorer **Jensen 43**
Referee **D Gallagher**

Charlton take the lead just before half-time through Jensen's excellent finish, but after that it is the Ryan Giggs Show as the Manchester United winger takes them apart, setting up goals for Scholes and Van Nistelrooy as well as putting his side ahead in between times.

Tuesday October 1
OXFORD UNITED (h)
Worthington Cup, 2nd rnd
Drew 0-0 (aet; Oxford win 6-5 on pens)
HT 0-0   Att **9,464**
Kiely — Fortune, Fish (Brown 95), Rufus — Kishishev,
Euell, Mustoe (Robinson ht), Jensen, Konchesky —
Johansson, Bartlett (Svensson 68) *Subs not used*
Rachubka, Bart-Williams *Booked* Fortune
Referee **P Joslin**

Charlton's fifth successive home defeat sees them
humbled by third division opposition as they become
the first Premiership side to be eliminated from the
Worthington Cup. Kishishev is the fourth Charlton player
to miss in a protracted shoot-out, Jefferson Louis
converting the eighteenth and final kick.

Sunday October 6
FULHAM (a)
Lost 0-1   HT 0-1   Att 14,775   Position 19th
Kiely — Young (Johansson 82), Fish, Rufus, Powell —
Robinson, Mustoe, Jensen, Konchesky (Lisbie 66) —
Euell, Bartlett *Subs not used* Rachubka, Kishishev,
Fortune *Booked* Rufus, Euell
Report page 201

Sunday October 20
MIDDLESBROUGH (h)
Won 1-0   HT 1-0   Att 26,271   Position 15th
Kiely — Rufus, Rowett, Fish — Robinson, Mustoe (Young
78), Parker (Kishishev 78), Jensen, Powell — Euell,
Bartlett *Subs not used* Rachubka, Johansson, Fortune
Booked Bartlett
Scorer **Euell 5**
Referee **N Barry**

Sent to the bottom of the table the previous day, and
with Alan Curbishley admitting that he fears for his job,
Charlton start their recovery with Euell's early header,
bringing an end to Middlesbrough's good form and
breaking their own desperate sequence of home
defeats.

MATCH OF THE SEASON

Charlton Athletic 2   Liverpool 0
The Valley, Saturday December 7 2002
Keith Pike

Paul Konchesky celebrates his goal against Liverpool

ALAN CURBISHLEY WILL HAVE to remind himself to be more careful the next time he drives to work. As the Charlton Athletic manager arrived at The Valley on Thursday, he almost lost control of the car when he heard on the radio that Port Vale had become the latest club to be forced into administration. Two days later he found Liverpool, metaphorically at least, stuck in reverse and careering towards him down the Barclaycard Premiership at high speed. Gerard Houllier's team, it seems, were an accident waiting to happen.

Quite how the Merseyside club, in five short and traumatic weeks, have turned a seven-point advantage at the top of the table into a four-point deficit is a mystery that only Houllier and Jerzy Dudek could solve. "Now is not the time to be throwing teacups at them," the Liverpool manager reasoned. But if not now, after they have taken just one point from five matches, then when? His deposed goalkeeper would probably find flying crockery easier to handle than routine back-headers. But neither the short-term problems of Houllier's team nor the deep-rooted malaise of impoverished Nationwide League clubs is Curbishley's concern.

Little more than a decade ago, Charlton Athletic were homeless, playing in front of 4,000 people and flirting with extinction. Now here they were, celebrating the tenth anniversary of their return from exile, with more than 26,000 — a record for their lovingly restored ground — cheering them to a fourth consecutive Premiership win, another club first, as the potential champions were being beaten. "There are clubs like Port Vale in despair, but their fans should look at us and see what can be done," Curbishley said. "Perhaps we are an inspiration."

They are certainly that. It is hard to think of another ground where the directors would get a standing ovation. Elland Road? Upton Park? Perhaps not. But then Charlton fans recognise how well-served they have been, especially by Curbishley. And he assured them that his job is not yet complete.

"We're solvent, we haven't got the millions of pounds of debt that other clubs have and if we can stay up this season, we can only get stronger," he said. "Well-run clubs like ourselves will have the chance to become really big Premiership clubs. That has got to be our aim. Ten years ago I had to sell Robert Lee and Anthony Barness to help get us back here. This time [when the transfer window opens next month], I don't have to sell anybody. I can take a lot of pride in what has been achieved here."

It was one of the players nurtured by Curbishley who scored the goal that finally killed off Liverpool. "I joined the club at 13 and we

Saturday October 26
NEWCASTLE UNITED (a)
Lost 1-2 HT 1-1 Att **51,670** Position **17th**
Kiely — Rufus, Rowett, Fish — Young (Kishishev 79), Mustoe, Parker (Johansson 83), Jensen, Robinson (Blomqvist 72) — Euell, Bartlett Subs not used Rachubka, Fortune Booked Rufus
Scorer **Bartlett 30**
Report page 69

Sunday November 3
SUNDERLAND (h)
Drew 1-1 HT 0-1 Att **26,284** Position **16th**
Kiely — Rowett, Rufus, Fish — Robinson (Johansson 90), Mustoe, Parker (Kishishev 85), Powell — Jensen — Euell, Bartlett (Lisbie 73) Subs not used Young, Roberts Booked Parker
Scorer **Rowett 77**
Referee **D Gallagher**

Ahead through Flo's low shot and denied a second goal when Parker clears off the line from Phillips, Sunderland are unable to hold on to a lead for the second match running, Rowett sliding in to secure a deserved point for Charlton with his first goal for the club.

Saturday November 9
EVERTON (a)
Lost 0-1 HT 0-1 Att **37,621** Position **16th**
Kiely — Fish, Rufus, Fortune — Kishishev (Johansson 75), Mustoe (Konchesky 55), Parker, Jensen, Powell — Euell (Bartlett 75), Lisbie Subs not used Young, Roberts Booked Rufus, Fortune, Fish
Report page 117

Saturday November 16
MANCHESTER CITY (a)
Won 1-0 HT 0-0 Att **33,455** Position **16th**
Kiely — Rowett, Rufus, Fish — Young, Kishishev, Parker (Konchesky 90), Powell — Euell — Johansson, Bartlett (Lisbie 86) Subs not used Fortune, Bart-Williams, Rachubka Booked Young, Rufus, Kishishev, Parker
Scorer **Bartlett 79**
Report page 142

Sunday November 24
BLACKBURN ROVERS (h)
Won 3-1   HT 0-0   Att 6,152   Position 15th
Kiely — Rufus, Fortune (Konchesky ht), Fish — Young,
Kishishev, Parker, Powell — Euell — Bartlett, Lisbie
(Bart-Williams 86) *Subs not used* Rachubka, Brown,
Svensson *Booked* Euell, Lisbie
Scorers **Konchesky 59, Rufus 74, Euell 90**
Referee **U Rennie**

Charlton need an early slice of Fortune, who goes
unpunished for a clear penalty-area foul on Cole, before
shooting down Blackburn. Konchesky's fine free kick
gives them the lead and, after Thompson's rapid
equaliser, Rufus's header and Euell's late third continue
Charlton's revival.

Sunday December 1
LEEDS UNITED (a)
Won 2-1   HT 0-1   Att 35,537   Position 12th
Kiely — Young, Rowett, Fish (Fortune 20) — Kishishev
(Jensen 75), Parker, Konchesky, Powell — Euell — Lisbie,
Bartlett (Svensson 90) *Subs not used* Roberts,
Bart-Williams *Booked* Parker
Scorers **Lisbie 80, Parker 90**
Report page 214

Saturday December 7
LIVERPOOL (h)
Won 2-0   HT 1-0   Att 26,694   Position 11th
Kiely — Rowett, Rufus, Fish — Kishishev (Young 79),
Parker (Jensen 68), Konchesky, Powell — Euell — Lisbie,
Bartlett (Svensson 86) *Subs not used* Roberts, Fortune
Booked Konchesky, Euell, Svensson
Scorers **Euell 36, Konchesky 78**
Referee **M Riley**

Charlton celebrate the tenth anniversary of their return
to The Valley with a fourth straight Premiership win —
the best run in their history — in front of a packed
house. Kirkland, finally summoned to keep goal in place
of the hapless Dudek, is blameless as Liverpool's dismal
run continues.

Saturday December 14
MANCHESTER CITY (h)
Drew 2-2   HT 0-0   Att 26,434   Position 11th
Kiely — Rowett, Rufus, Fish — Young, Parker, Kishishev
(Jensen ht), Powell (Konchesky 90) — Euell — Lisbie,
Bartlett *Subs not used* Rachubka, Svensson, Fortune
Booked Euell, Parker
Scorers **Euell 51 (pen), Jensen 63**
Referee **D Pugh**

Ahead 2-0 with more than an hour gone, Charlton blow
a golden chance when Lisbie misses a sitter. City then
hit back with two goals from Foe, the second three
minutes from time, and might have won had the referee
not failed to punish Rufus's foul on Anelka with a
penalty.

Heads first: Charlton were superior to Liverpool in every department

have some good youngsters who have come through the ranks,"
Paul Konchesky said. His superbly executed 78th-minute lob,
though, was the product of instinctive ability rather than coaching.

Jason Euell, who opened the scoring from close range in the first
half, was honest enough to admit that Charlton "got the rub of the
green" against a Liverpool team who, for all that they lacked
composure in central defence and the killer instinct in attack,
created more chances, and better chances. "I'm sure they'll turn it
round and be challenging for the title," Euell said, "but at the
moment we just don't think we're going to lose."

Liverpool, by contrast, have forgotten how to win. Chris
Kirkland, Dudek's replacement, was brave and exemplary, while
Dean Kiely saved brilliantly from El-Hadji Diouf just before half-
time. But the finishing of Milan Baros, Danny Murphy and,
especially, a subdued Michael Owen betrayed a team short of
confidence as much as good fortune. "Maybe it is time to be more
composed in front of goal," Houllier said. "We need a scrappy 1-0
win." Maybe he needs to get the teacups out first.

CHARLTON ATHLETIC (4-4-2): D Kiely — R Rufus, G Rowett, M Fish, R Kishishev (sub: L Young,
79min) — S Parker (sub: C Jensen, 68), J Euell, P Konchesky, C Powell — K Lisbie, S Bartlett (sub:
M Svensson, 87). **Substitutes not used:** B Roberts, J Fortune. **Booked:** Euell, Konchesky,
Svensson.

LIVERPOOL (4-4-2): C Kirkland — J Carragher, S Henchoz, S Hyypia, D Traore (sub: M Baros, 60) —
D Murphy, D Hamann, S Gerrard, E Heskey (sub: J A Riise, 36) — E-H Diouf, M Owen. **Substitutes not
used:** J Dudek, V Smicer, S Diao. **Booked:** Traore, Henchoz.
Referee: M Riley.

THE MANAGER

Alan Curbishley

His name continued to come up whenever any big job fell vacant, so he must have been doing something right. In fact, Curbishley called most of it right most of the time throughout the season. He kept his head during the bad runs and he kept his feet on the ground during the good times. His tactics were shrewd and his man-management admirable — at least until the final furlong. Then, with survival secured, he was powerless to arrest the players' complacency and unable to instil the ambition to go the extra mile.

Nigel Williamson

APPEARANCES

	Prem	FAC	WC	Total
S Bartlett	25 (6)	2	1	28 (6)
C Bart-Williams	7 (6)	1 (1)	-	8 (7)
J Blomqvist	0 (3)	1	-	1 (3)
S Brown	0 (3)	-	0 (1)	0 (4)
J Campbell-Ryce	0 (1)	-	-	0 (1)
T El Khalej	2 (1)	-	-	2 (1)
J Euell	35 (1)	2	1	38 (1)
M Fish	23	1	1	25
J Fortune	22 (4)	1 (1)	1	24 (5)
C Jensen	32 (3)	1	1	34 (3)
J Johansson	10 (21)	2	1	13 (21)
D Kiely	38	2	1	41
R Kishishev	27 (7)	2	1	30 (7)
P Konchesky	17 (13)	2	1	20 (13)
K Lisbie	24 (8)	0 (1)	-	24 (9)
R Mustoe	6	-	1	7
S Parker	28	1	-	29
C Powell	35 (2)	-	-	35 (2)
B Roberts	0 (1)	-	-	0 (1)
J Robinson	10 (3)	-	0 (1)	10 (4)
G Rowett	12	-	-	12
R Rufus	29 (1)	2	1	32 (1)
O Sankofa	0 (1)	-	-	0 (1)
G Stuart	3 (1)	-	-	3 (1)
M Svensson	4 (11)	0 (2)	0 (1)	4 (14)
L Young	29 (3)	2	-	31 (3)

Saturday December 21
BIRMINGHAM CITY (a)
Drew 1-1 HT 1-0 Att 28,837 Position 10th
Kiely — Young, Rowett, Fish, Powell — Kishishev (Bart-Williams 73), Jensen, Parker, Konchesky — Lisbie, Bartlett (Johansson 69) *Subs not used* Blomqvist, Rachubka, Fortune *Booked* Young, Rowett, Jensen, Konchesky, Parker
Scorer **Jensen 37**
Report page 191

Saturday December 26
TOTTENHAM HOTSPUR (a)
Drew 2-2 HT 1-0 Att 36,043 Position 12th
Kiely — Rowett, Fish (Konchesky 73), Rufus — Young, Parker, Jensen (Kishishev 81), Euell, Powell — Lisbie, Bartlett (Fortune 88) *Subs not used* Johansson, Roberts *Booked* Rufus
Scorer **Euell 14, 49**
Report page 155

Saturday December 28
WEST BROMWICH ALBION (h)
Won 1-0 HT 1-0 Att 26,196 Position 12th
Kiely — Fish (Fortune 53), Rowett, Rufus — Young, Euell, Jensen, Parker (Bart-Williams 80), Powell — Lisbie, Bartlett (Johansson 66) *Subs not used* Roberts, Konchesky *Booked* Lisbie, Parker
Scorer **Lisbie 6**
Referee **S Dunn**

Lisbie rises above Hoult to head in an early corner and Charlton hang on to extend their unbeaten league run to eight matches. But they need several slices of luck, especially when Koumas hits a post from a free kick and Dichio raps the bar in stoppage time.

Saturday January 4
EXETER CITY (h)
FA Cup, 3rd rnd
Won 3-1 HT 1-0 Att 18,107
Kiely — Young, Fortune, Rufus, Konchesky — Kishishev, Bart-Williams, Euell, Blomqvist (Lisbie 76) — Johansson (Svensson 76), Bartlett *Subs not used* Rachubka, Fish, Jensen *Booked* Bartlett
Scorers **Johansson 25, 61, Euell 72 (pen)**
Referee **P Dowd**

Injured or out of form since August, Johansson puts what he describes as "the worst season of my career" behind him with his first goals of the campaign, both spectacular overhead kicks, to see off third-division opposition. The Sweden striker also earns the penalty that finally kills off Exeter's challenge.

Saturday January 11
CHELSEA (a)
Lost 1-4   HT 1-3   Att **37,284**   Position **14th**
Kiely — Young, Rufus, Fish, Powell (Bartlett ht) —
Kishishev (Johansson ht), Parker, Jensen, Konchesky —
Lisbie (Fortune 65), Euell *Subs not used* Rachubka,
Bart-Williams *Booked* Powell, Konchesky, Parker
Scorer **Euell 42 (pen)**
Report page 84

Saturday January 18
BOLTON WANDERERS (h)
Drew 1-1   HT 0-0   Att **26,057**   Position **13th**
Kiely — Young (Konchesky 56), Rufus, Fish, Powell —
Kishishev, Parker, Euell, Jensen (Johansson 88) — Lisbie,
Bartlett (Svensson 88) *Subs not used* Rachubka,
Fortune
Scorer **Fish 47**
Referee **D Elleray**

The Green, Green Grass of Home blasts out over the
Tannoy to welcome back Charlton from the sands of
Stamford Bridge, but Djorkaeff takes to the air to grab a
point for Bolton with a brilliant overhead kick to cancel
out the lead given to Charlton by Fish, their former
Bolton defender.

Wednesday January 22
WEST HAM UNITED (h)
Won 4-2   HT 2-1   Att **26,340**   Position **11th**
Kiely — Fish, Rufus, Fortune — Kishishev, Euell, Parker,
Jensen (Svensson 87), Powell — Lisbie (Konchesky 71),
Bartlett (Johansson 83) *Subs not used* Rachubka,
Bart-Williams *Booked* Kishishev, Parker
Scorers **Jensen 42, Parker 45, 52, Kishishev 90**
Referee **E Wolstenholme**

Despite the arrival of Ferdinand, on loan from Spurs, to
boost their attack and despite the gift of two own goals,
West Ham slump to another defeat as Charlton, with
Jensen's 25-yard free kick the pick of their goals,
triumph in a fixture originally scheduled for a rainy New
Year's Day.

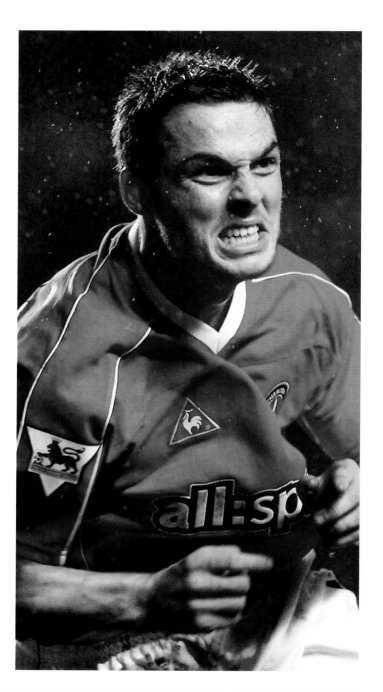

It surely wasn't coincidence that Charlton's first home win, at the fifth attempt, came with Scott Parker's first start of the season after injury. Terrier-like in the tackle, he also displayed great skill on the ball. The linchpin of most of the team's victories, he should have got more goals, but those he did score tended to be either spectacular or vital, such as his jinking run against Southampton or his last-minute winner against Leeds United. His tally of yellow cards was disappointing, but misleading, for he is a fully-committed player rather than a dirty one, and his call up to the England squad was just reward.

Nigel Williamson

STATS AND FACTS

● Charlton benefited from three own goals away to Sunderland, but just ten days earlier they had scored two own goals themselves in their win over West Ham United.

● Until November 2002, Charlton had not won more than two games in a row in the top flight since 1986.

● In two years up to early February 2003, Charlton won the same number of league points at home as away — 49.

● Charlton have lost eight of their past 12 home matches against Leeds United.

● And have won just one of their past 21 games away to Manchester United.

● Claus Jensen completed 150 successive Premiership matches without a booking against Southampton in April.

Bill Edgar

Sunday January 26
FULHAM (a)
FA Cup, 4th rnd
Lost 0-3   HT 0-0   Att 12,203
Kiely — Young (Fortune 72), Rufus, Fish, Konchesky — Kishishev, Parker (Svensson 77), Euell (Bart-Williams 72), Jensen — Johansson, Bartlett *Subs not used* Rachubka, Powell *Booked* Young, Jensen, Konchesky *Sent off* Fish 86
Report page 205

Wednesday January 29
WEST BROMWICH ALBION (a)
Won 1-0   HT 0-0   Att 26,113   Position 10th
Kiely — Fish, Rufus, Fortune — Kishishev, Euell, Parker, Jensen (Konchesky 79), Powell — Bartlett, Lisbie (Johansson 85) *Subs not used* Rachubka, Bart-Williams, El Khalej *Booked* Powell, Parker
Scorer **Bartlett 60**
Report page 265

Saturday February 1
SUNDERLAND (a)
Won 3-1   HT 3-0   Att 36,042   Position 8th
Kiely — Fish, Rufus, Fortune, Powell — Kishishev, Parker (Bart-Williams 90), Euell, Jensen (Konchesky 82) — Bartlett, Lisbie (Johansson 75) *Subs not used* Rachuba, El Khalej *Booked* Fish
Scorers **Wright 24 (og), Proctor 29 (og), 32 (og)**
Report page 277

Saturday February 8
EVERTON (h)
Won 2-1   HT 1-0   Att 26,623   Position 8th
Kiely — Fish, Rufus, Fortune, Powell — Kishishev, Parker, Euell, Jensen (Konchesky 87) — Bartlett (Johansson 67), Lisbie *Subs not used* Rachubka, Bart-Williams, El Khalej
Scorers **Kishishev 19, Lisbie 83**
Referee **J Winter**

Having selected them for the England squad to face Australia in four days' time, Sven-Goran Eriksson goes to The Valley to monitor Parker and Konchesky, of Charlton, but leaves before Rooney, back from a ban, takes the field as an Everton substitute. Lisbie wins the battle of the European hopefuls seven minutes from time.

GOALSCORERS

	Prem	FAC	WC	Total
S Bartlett	4	-	-	4
C Bart-Williams	1 (p)	-	-	1 (p)
J Euell	10 (3p)	1 (p)	-	11 (4p)
M Fish	1	-	-	1
J Fortune	1	-	-	1
C Jensen	6	-	-	6
J Johansson	3	2	-	5
R Kishishev	2	-	-	2
P Konchesky	3	-	-	3
K Lisbie	4	-	-	4
S Parker	4	-	-	4
G Rowett	1	-	-	1
R Rufus	2	-	-	2
Own goals	3	-	-	3

Saturday February 22
ASTON VILLA (h)
Won 3-0 **HT 0-0** Att **26,257** Position **6th**
Kiely — Young, El Khalej, Fortune, Powell — Kishishev, Parker (Bart-Williams 89), Euell, Jensen — Bartlett (Svensson 88), Lisbie (Johansson 84) *Subs not used* Rachubka, Turner *Booked* Kishishev, Bartlett
Scorers **Euell 51, Johansson 87, 90**
Referee **P Dowd**

Alpay is booed by his own supporters on his return to the Villa side, Kinsella cheered by Charlton fans on his return to The Valley. But there the oddities end, Parker's excellence and two late goals by Johansson, the substitute, helping Charlton to a club record fifth straight Premiership victory.

Sunday March 2
ARSENAL (a)
Lost 0-2 **HT 0-2** Att **38,015** Position **6th**
Kiely — Young, Fish, Fortune, Powell (Konchesky 79) — Kishishev, Parker (Svensson 88), Euell, Jensen — Bartlett (Johansson 59), Lisbie *Subs not used* Roberts, El Khalej
Report page 62

Saturday March 15
NEWCASTLE UNITED (h)
Lost 0-2 **HT 0-1** Att **26,728** Position **8th**
Kiely — Young (Konchesky 74), Fish (Rufus 59), Fortune, Powell — Kishishev, Parker, Euell, Jensen — Bartlett (Lisbie 59), Johansson *Subs not used* Roberts, El Khalej
Booked Young
Referee **S Dunn**

Even as Shearer puts away the penalty that sets his side en route for victory, the headlines suggesting his possible return to England duty are being written. Shearer, though, has a rethink overnight and finally confirms his international retirement, with Newcastle — after Bellamy's pace has undone Charlton — still on the heels of the Premiership leaders.

SHAUN BARTLETT
Forward
Born October 31, 1972, Cape Town
Ht 6ft 1in **Wt** 12st 4lb
Signed from FC Zurich, November 2000, £2m

CHRIS BART-WILLIAMS
Midfield
Born June 16, 1974, Freetown, Sierra Leone
Ht 5ft 11in **Wt** 11st 6lb
Signed from Nottingham Forest, December 2001, free

JESPER BLOMQVIST
Midfield
Born February 5, 1974, Umea, Sweden
Ht 5ft 9in **Wt** 11st 6lb
Signed from Everton, August 2002, free

STEVE BROWN
Defender
Born May 13, 1972, Brighton
Ht 6ft 1in **Wt** 13st 10lb
Signed from trainee, July 1990

JAMAL CAMPBELL-RYCE
Midfield
Born April 6, 1983, Lambeth
Signed from trainee, August 2001

TAHAR EL KHALEJ
Defender
Born June 16, 1968, Marrakesh
Ht 6ft 3in **Wt** 13st 8lb
Signed from Southampton, January 2002, free

JASON EUELL
Forward
Born February 6, 1977, Lambeth
Ht 6ft 0in **Wt** 12st 7lb
Signed from Wimbledon, July 2001, £4.75m

MARK FISH
Defender
Born March 14, 1974, Cape Town
Ht 6ft 3in **Wt** 13st 2lb
Signed from Bolton Wanderers, November 2000, £700,000

Shaun Bartlett

JON FORTUNE
Defender
Born August 23, 1980, Islington
Ht 6ft 2in **Wt** 11st 4lb
Signed from trainee, July 1988

CLAUS JENSEN
Midfield
Born April 29, 1977, Nykobing, Denmark
Ht 5ft 11in **Wt** 12st 6lb
Signed from Bolton Wanderers, July 2000, £4m

JONATAN JOHANSSON
Forward
Born August 16, 1975, Stockholm
Ht 6ft 1in **Wt** 12st 8lb
Signed from Rangers, August 2000, £3.25m

DEAN KIELY
Goalkeeper
Born October 10, 1970, Salford
Ht 6ft 1in **Wt** 13st 5lb
Signed from Bury, May 1999, £1m

RADOSTIN KISHISHEV
Midfield
Born July 30, 1974, Bourgas, Bulgaria
Ht 5ft 10in **Wt** 12st 4lb
Signed from Litex Lovech, Bulgaria, August 2000, £300,000

PAUL KONCHESKY
Midfield
Born May 15, 1981, Barking
Ht 5ft 10in **Wt** 10st 12lb
Signed from trainee, May 1998

KEVIN LISBIE
Forward
Born October 17, 1978, Hackney
Ht 5ft 8in **Wt** 10st 12lb
Signed from trainee, May 1996

ROBBIE MUSTOE
Midfield
Born August 28, 1968, Oxford
Ht 5ft 11in **Wt** 11st 12lb
Signed from Middlesbrough, August 2002, free

Kevin Lisbie

Saturday March 22
MIDDLESBROUGH (a)
Drew 1-1 HT 1-0 Att 29,080 Position 7th
Kiely — Fish, Rufus, Fortune, Konchesky — Stuart (Powell 42), Kishishev, Jensen (Young 75), Euell — Johansson (Bartlett 85), Lisbie *Subs not used* Rachubka, El Khalej *Booked* Rufus, Lisbie
Scorer **Johansson 26**
Report page 170

Saturday April 5
LEEDS UNITED (h)
Lost 1-6 HT 1-3 Att 26,274 Position 9th
Kiely — Young, Fish, Rufus, Konchesky (El Khalej 65) — Kishishev (Powell ht), Parker, Jensen — Euell — Johansson, Lisbie (Svensson ht) *Subs not used* Rachubka, Robinson *Booked* Kiely, Svensson
Scorer **Euell 45 (pen)**
Referee **E Wolstenholme**

Peter Reid makes five changes and is rewarded with a Leeds performance that makes a mockery of their struggles under Terry Venables. Kewell begins and ends the rout of Charlton, Viduka claims a hat-trick, but Smith is the star of the show, having a hand in five of their six goals. Alan Curbishley, meanwhile, cancels Charlton's Sunday off.

Saturday April 12
BLACKBURN ROVERS (a)
Lost 0-1 HT 0-1 Att 27,506 Position 10th
Kiely — Young, Rufus, Fortune, Powell — Robinson (Johansson 63), Parker, Kishishev (Blomqvist 77), Konchesky — Svensson, Lisbie (Campbell-Ryce 86) *Subs not used* El Khalej, Roberts
Report page 111

Saturday April 19
BIRMINGHAM CITY (h)
Lost 0-2 HT 0-1 Att 25,732 Position 11th
Kiely — Young, El Khalej (Konchesky 82), Fortune, Powell — Kishishev (Robinson ht), Parker, Euell, Jensen — Svensson (Lisbie ht), Johansson *Subs not used* Roberts, Blomqvist *Booked* Svensson, Parker
Referee **N Barry**

Fortunately for them, bearing in mind their dismal form, Charlton are already safe and Birmingham edge closer to joining them thanks to Dugarry's clever near-post finish and a penalty won and converted by Savage. "An absolute embarrassment," Alan Curbishley says of his side.

Monday April 21
LIVERPOOL (a)
Lost 1-2 **HT 0-0** Att **42,010** Position **12th**
Kiely — Young, Rufus, Fortune, Powell — Kishishev, Parker (Robinson 83), Jensen, Konchesky — Lisbie (Johansson 90), Bartlett (Euell 77) *Subs not used* Roberts, Bart-Williams *Booked* Fortune
Scorer **Bartlett 47**
Report page 100

Saturday April 26
SOUTHAMPTON (h)
Won 2-1 **HT 1-0** Att **25,894** Position **9th**
Kiely — Kishishev, Young, Fortune, Powell — Lisbie, Jensen, Parker, Konchesky — Euell, Bartlett *Subs not used* Roberts, Stuart, Bart-Williams, Johansson, Sankofa *Booked* Bartlett
Scorers **Parker 32, Lisbie 50**
Referee **A Wiley**

Charlton end their dismal run (one point out of 21) after Parker's fine solo goal puts them on the way to victory over the distracted FA Cup finalists. Beattie's last-minute volley sees him edge ahead in his race with Henry, the Arsenal striker, with his 23rd Premiership goal of the season.

Saturday May 3
MANCHESTER UNITED (a)
Lost 1-4 **HT 1-3** Att **67,621** Position **12th**
Kiely — Kishishev (Sankofa 73), Young, Fortune, Powell — Lisbie (Johansson 84), Jensen, Parker, Konchesky — Bartlett, Euell (Bart-Williams 78) *Subs not used* Stuart, Rachubka *Booked* Fortune
Scorer **Jensen 13**
Report page 52

Sunday May 11
FULHAM (h)
Lost 0-1 **HT 0-1** Att **26,108** Position **12th**
Kiely — Kishishev, Young, Fortune, Powell (Stuart 82) — Lisbie, Parker, Jensen (Johansson 82), Konchesky — Bartlett (Roberts 32), Euell *Subs not used* Bart-Williams, Sankofa *Booked* Young, Euell, Kishishev
Sent off Kiely 31
Referee **D Gallagher**

A tale of two penalties. Kiely is sent off for clattering into Saha, who beats Roberts, Kiely's replacement, from the spot, but Taylor saves Euell's effort in the second half. Fulham's first away league win since September enhances Chris Coleman's claims for the manager's post.

SCOTT PARKER
Midfield
Born October 13, 1980, Lambeth
Ht 5ft 7in **Wt** 10st 7lb
Signed from trainee, October 1997

CHRIS POWELL
Defender
Born September 8, 1969, Lambeth
Ht 5ft 10in **Wt** 11st 7lb
Signed from Derby County, July 1998, £825,000

BEN ROBERTS
Goalkeeper
Born June 22, 1975, Bishop Auckland
Ht 6ft 1in **Wt** 13st 0lb
Signed from Middlesbrough, July 2000, free

JOHN ROBINSON
Midfield
Born August 29, 1971, Bulawayo
Ht 5ft 10in **Wt** 11st 7lb
Signed from Brighton and Hove Albion, September 1992, £75,000

GARY ROWETT
Defender
Born March 6, 1974, Bromsgrove
Ht 6ft 0in **Wt** 12st 10lb
Signed from Leicester City, May 2002, £2.5m

RICHARD RUFUS
Defender
Born January 12, 1975, Lewisham
Ht 6ft 1in **Wt** 11st 10lb
Signed from trainee, July 1993

OSEI SANKOFA
Defender
Born March 19, 1985, Streatham
Signed from trainee, August 2002

GRAHAM STUART
Midfield
Born October 24, 1970, Tooting
Ht 5ft 9in **Wt** 11st 10lb
Signed from Sheffield United, March 1999, £1.1m

MATHIAS SVENSSON
Forward
Born September 24, 1974, Boras, Sweden
Ht 6ft 0in **Wt** 12st 4lb
Signed from Crystal Palace, January 2000, £600,000

LUKE YOUNG
Defender
Born July 19, 1979, Harlow
Ht 6ft 0in **Wt** 12st 4lb
Signed from Tottenham Hotspur, July 2001, £3m

Luke Young

BIRMINGHAM CITY

PREMIERSHIP

	P	W	D	L	F	A	Pts
Man Utd	38	25	8	5	74	34	83
Arsenal	38	23	9	6	85	42	78
Newcastle	38	21	6	11	63	48	69
Chelsea	38	19	10	9	68	38	67
Liverpool	38	18	10	10	61	41	64
Blackburn	38	16	12	10	52	43	60
Everton	38	17	8	13	48	49	59
Southampton	38	13	13	12	43	46	52
Man City	38	15	6	17	47	54	51
Tottenham	38	14	8	16	51	62	50
Middlesbro	38	13	10	15	48	44	49
Charlton	38	14	7	17	45	56	49
Birmingham	**38**	**13**	**9**	**16**	**41**	**49**	**48**
Fulham	38	13	9	16	41	50	48
Leeds	38	14	5	19	58	57	47
Aston Villa	38	12	9	17	42	47	45
Bolton	38	10	14	14	41	51	44
West Ham	38	10	12	16	42	59	42
West Brom	38	6	8	24	29	65	26
Sunderland	38	4	7	27	21	65	19

FA CUP
Third round

WORTHINGTON CUP
Third round

Robbie Savage proved to be an inspired signing by Steve Bruce

THE GAMES

Tim Austin

Sunday August 18
ARSENAL (a)
Lost 0-2 HT 0-2 Att 38,018 Position 18th
Vaesen — Kenna, Tebily (Carter 60), Cunningham,
Purse, Grainger — D Johnson, Cisse, Hughes —
Horsfield (Lazaridis 71), John *Subs not used* Mooney,
Bennett, M Johnson *Booked* Purse, Cisse *Sent off*
Cisse 74
Report page 54

Saturday August 24
BLACKBURN ROVERS (h)
Lost 0-1 HT 0-1 Att 28,563 Position 19th
Vaesen — Tebily, Cunningham, Purse, Grainger
(Lazaridis 82) — D Johnson, Cisse, Hughes, Carter —
Horsfield (Mooney 85), John *Subs not used* Bennett,
M Johnson, Eaden *Booked* Purse
Referee **D Gallagher**

Top-flight football returns to St Andrew's after 16 years
and old wounds are immediately reopened as
Yorke, a former Aston Villa man, scores the early goal
that condemns Birmingham to defeat. Blackburn miss
several chances to build on their lead and end up
grateful for the athleticism of Friedel in goal.

Wednesday August 28
EVERTON (a)
Drew 1-1 HT 0-0 Att 37,197 Position 17th
Vaesen — Tebily (Kenna 35), Cunningham, Purse,
Grainger — D Johnson, Cisse, Savage, Hughes (Carter
70) — Horsfield (Morrison 80), John *Subs not used*
Bennett, Mooney *Booked* Johnson, Hughes, Savage
Scorer **John 50 (pen)**
Report page 114

Saturday August 31
LEEDS UNITED (h)
Won 2-1 HT 1-0 Att 27,164 Position 14th
Vaesen — Kenna, Cunningham, Purse, Grainger —
Devlin (Hughes 83), Savage, Cisse, D Johnson —
Morrison (Horsfield 74), John (Lazaridis 90) *Subs
not used* Bennett, M Johnson *Booked* Grainger,
D Johnson, Devlin
Scorers **Devlin 32, D Johnson 58**
Referee **P Durkin**

Leeds hit the woodwork twice and conjure an excellent
equaliser from Bowyer, but can have no complaints
about defeat as Birmingham get their season up and
running with a fine all-round display capped by
long-range strikes from Devlin and Damien Johnson
that secure their first victory.

WELL, WASN'T THAT A SEASON? Birmingham City fans are hardly noted for their optimism, but to have finished thirteenth in the club's first crack at the Premiership, as top team in the Midlands for the first time in nearly 100 years, to have ended above Aston Villa for the first time since 1958-59 — as well as beating them home and away with a 5-0 aggregate — left everyone connected with St Andrew's in a state of euphoria bordering on delirium.

The key to this extraordinary state of affairs lies in the phrase "everyone connected with St Andrew's". From the board, brilliantly led by David Gold, through the management team of Steve Bruce, John Benson and Mark Bowen, through virtually the entire playing staff to the vast, roaring, boisterous and humorous band of some of the most passionate and loyal supporters in the country, everyone does seem to be pulling in the same direction.

Mind you, at the start of the season, with the team newly promoted via the play-offs and almost every national newspaper tipping the Blues for an instant return to the Nationwide League, things looked very different. Despite astute summer signings in Robbie Savage, Kenny Cunningham, Clinton Morrison, Aliou Cisse and Jovan Kirovski, apprehension was the name of the game. This mood was exacerbated by two opening defeats (a 2-0 massacre at Highbury that could have been six or seven, followed by a 1-0 home defeat by Blackburn Rovers), but draws away to Everton and Liverpool either side of the first Premiership win, 2-1 at home to Leeds United, began to instil a little belief.

Then came the first dose of euphoria, the famous 3-0 win at a cauldron-like St Andrew's, the night of the great Enckelman blunder (no wonder so many Blues fans voted for him as their player of the season) — the night when the first serious grains of self-belief began to permeate the club.

Autumn progressed into an attritional winter. Decent results alternated with downright poor ones, but another worrying factor was emerging: injuries (especially to key defenders) were stretching the squad to breaking point. In the final game of the year, at Old Trafford of all places, Blues ended with Geoff Horsfield at centre back and Paul Devlin at right back.

The turning point of the season had arrived — and Bruce and the board emerged from it triumphantly. During the January transfer window, the board backed their manager's shopping spree, thereby transforming the season and possibly the future of Birmingham City for years to come. In those four weeks Bruce signed six players: Matthew Upson (a steal from Arsenal), Stephen Clemence from Spurs and Jamie Clapham from Ipswich Town, all on long-term

The Dugarry-inspired win over Liverpool in February boosted confidence

contracts; and Christophe Dugarry, the France World Cup-winning striker from Bordeaux, Pietr Swierczewski and Ferdinand Coly, all on six-month loans.

If the last two did not make it, the other four most certainly did, spectacularly so in the case of Dugarry, arguably the finest footballer ever to wear the Birmingham shirt. David Gold, a director, summed up the French genius's panache and levels of commitment: "He has proved he not only has the skill of an angel, he will go in where angels fear to tread."

Despite a ten-game run without a win during that injury-ravaged spell, the new arrivals were bedding in well and perhaps the key result of the season was the 2-1 home win over Liverpool on February 23. This was followed by the second triumph over Villa on an ill-tempered Monday night that saw two Villa players sent off, and thereafter both the results and the team's football — inspired by Dugarry's brilliance — began to flow. A 2-0 win away to Charlton Athletic was probably the best footballing performance of the season and, with two games to go, Middlesbrough were hammered 3-0 at St Andrew's to ensure Premiership survival. "We are Premier League," the massed ranks on the Tilton chorused. "Now you're going to believe us."

Everyone in the Midlands now has to believe it, but will the rest of the country (especially the curmudgeonly Desmond Lynam and his glory-boy panellists) now acknowledge that Birmingham City are back and that Bruce is clearly among the top British managers of his generation?

The 2003-04 season should spell consolidation, particularly if it proves that Bruce has spent as wisely in the summer, as he has done previously, and if everyone at the club continues to pull together.

Where all you love, you've been dreaming of, will be there at the end of the road ...

Wednesday September 11
LIVERPOOL (a)
Drew 2-2 HT 0-1 Att 43,113 Position 15th
Vaesen — Kenna, Cunningham, Purse, Grainger — Devlin, Hughes (Horsfield 73), Savage, D Johnson (Lazaridis 73) — Morrison, John (Carter 73) *Subs not used* Bennett, Eaden *Booked* Savage
Scorer **Morrison 61, 90**
Report page 90

Monday September 16
ASTON VILLA (h)
Won 3-0 HT 1-0 Att 29,505 Position 9th
Vaesen — Kenna, Cunningham, Purse, Grainger — Devlin (Powell 79), Cisse, Savage (Hughes 87), D Johnson — Morrison (Horsfield 68), John *Subs not used* Bennett, Lazaridis *Booked* Purse, Grainger, Cisse
Scorers **Morrison 31, Enckelman 77 (og), Horsfield 83**
Referee **D Elleray**

Enckelman emerges as both hero and villain as hostilities are resumed between bitter rivals. The goalkeeper lets Mellberg's throw-in creep under his foot for a bizarre own goal (although television replays suggest that it should not have stood as he did not get a touch), then refuses to react to the baiting of Blues fans who disgrace themselves and their club by invading the pitch at each goal to taunt him.

Saturday September 21
MIDDLESBROUGH (a)
Lost 0-1 HT 0-1 Att 29,869 Position 10th
Vaesen — Kenna (Kirovski 81), Cunningham, Purse, Grainger (Lazaridis ht) — Devlin, Cisse, Savage, D Johnson — Morrison, John (Horsfield 66) *Subs not used* Bennett, Powell *Booked* Purse, Cisse, Savage
Report page 163

Saturday September 28
NEWCASTLE UNITED (h)
Lost 0-2 HT 0-1 Att 29,072 Position 14th
Vaesen — Kenna, Cunningham, Purse (Powell 79), Carter (Kirovski 68) — Devlin, Cisse, Savage, D Johnson — Morrison, John (Horsfield 79) *Subs not used* Bennett, Lazaridis *Booked* Purse, Cisse, Savage
Referee **S Bennett**

A teatime kick-off fails to sharpen Birmingham's appetite for the fray and Steve Bruce admits that they are deservedly beaten by a Newcastle side with a midweek trip to Turin on their minds. Shearer's dummy sets up the first goal for Solano and Ameobi makes sure in the last minute.

Wednesday October 2
LEYTON ORIENT (a)
Worthington Cup, 2nd rnd
Won 3-2 HT 2-0 Att 3,615
Bennett — Kenna, Vickers, Purse, Sadler — Kirovski (D Johnson 71), Powell, Woodhouse, Lazaridis — Horsfield, John (Fagan 77) Subs not used Vaesen, Morrison, Carter Booked Sadler
Scorer **John 16, 27, 77**
Referee **A Bates**

Eight first-team regulars are rested by Steve Bruce, but one who isn't makes all the difference, John's pace and finishing power proving too much for a brave Nationwide League third division side who twice pull back to only one goal behind in the second half, through Nugent and Ibehere.

Saturday October 5
WEST HAM UNITED (a)
Won 2-1 HT 2-1 Att 35,010 Position 12th
Vaesen — Kenna, Cunningham, Purse, D Johnson — Devlin, Cisse, Savage, Lazaridis (Powell 84) — Morrison, John (Horsfield 83) Subs not used Bennett, Vickers, Kirovski Booked Cisse
Scorer **John 4, 43**
Report page 248

Saturday October 19
WEST BROMWICH ALBION (a)
Drew 1-1 HT 0-0 Att 27,021 Position 12th
Vaesen — Kenna, Vickers (Hughes 90), Tebily, Carter — Devlin (Horsfield 66), Powell, Savage, Lazaridis — Morrison, John (Woodhouse 85) Subs not used Bennett, Kirovski Booked Tebily, John Sent off Tebily 82
Scorer **Moore 86 (og)**
Report page 260

Saturday October 26
MANCHESTER CITY (h)
Lost 0-2 HT 0-1 Att 29,316 Position 13th
Vaesen — Kenna (Hughes 79), Tebily, Purse, Powell (Kirovski 87) — Devlin (Horsfield 63), Cisse, Savage, Lazaridis — Morrison, John Subs not used Bennett, Carter Booked Tebily, Purse
Referee **S Bennett**

After three successive league defeats, Kevin Keegan leaves out a handful of flair players and introduces more steel to his Manchester City side. He is rewarded with a comfortable victory. "Our big players did not perform," Steve Bruce, the Birmingham manager, admits.

MATCH OF THE SEASON

Birmingham City 3   Aston Villa 0
St Andrew's, Monday September 16 2002
Rick Broadbent

FRANK WORTHINGTON ONCE recalled seeing Mark Dennis, his Birmingham City team-mate at the time, standing outside a supermarket taking aim at passing cars with a .22 air rifle. After an enduring intermission, the second club of the second city have set their sights on more worthy goals, while Aston Villa continue to shoot themselves in the foot.

An extraordinary mistake by Peter Enckelman ensured that the spoils went to Birmingham in the first top-flight derby between the clubs for 16 years, but the victory was well-earned. Steve Bruce's team are unbeaten in four matches and will believe that their aspirations should not stop at avoiding relegation.

It was a night of red-raw feelings at St Andrew's. To outsiders, this may have been a parochial affair and a battle of the mediocre. Hope and glory have long disappeared from the West Midlands wasteland, but hype and some typically gory exchanges ensured that the match was played out against a backdrop of thunderclaps. From Robbie Savage, patrolling the turf like one of Pavlov's dogs at bell-ringing practice, to the vitriol dripping from the terraces, this was always going to be a match in which emotion rode roughshod over the textbook.

If Enckelman's place in West Midlands folklore is assured, Bruce is rapidly earning himself hero status in Small Heath. From a club that perennially failed to justify their billing under Trevor Francis, Birmingham now have a solid team founded on the energy of Savage, who suffered a suspected broken rib, and pace of Paul Devlin and Damien Johnson.

"Steve Bruce has transformed this club," Geoff Horsfield, who compounded Villa's misery by scoring with a low drive late on, said. "There was a lot of unrest before he came in but you could see the impact straightaway. Everybody is willing to fight for each other now and everybody is smiling."

Villa felt hard-done-by. Darius Vassell had an effort chalked off for offside when they were dominant and Graham Taylor, the manager, cast serious doubt on the validity of Enckelman's gaffe after 78 minutes. The goalkeeper tried to control a throw-in, let the ball roll under his foot and watched in disbelief as it ran over the line. "It affected everyone," Taylor said. "But I say players have 24 hours to sulk and be miserable."

It was a sour night all round for Villa. Birmingham fans invaded the pitch after each goal, goaded Enckelman to his face and there were unconfirmed reports that Steve Staunton had been punched by a supporter. "It was always going to be different," Taylor said, admitting that he expected a backlash from Villa's beleaguered

John leads the line in the historic victory over Aston Villa at St Andrew's

faithful. The bitterness of the rivalry is nothing new. In 1980, when hooliganism was baring its teeth, Birmingham reasoned that a parachute display by the Royal Marines would distract the troublemakers. Cloud cover jeopardised the event, but you could hardly blame the Paras. Nobody drops in to St Andrew's on derby day without a full appreciation of the consequences.

The freefall of Midlands football has continued since that time. Birmingham went into the third division and receivership, while Villa are now a pallid shroud of the team that once ruled Europe. Taylor, once the doyen of the Holte End, is struggling to rekindle fading glories and the £7 million investment in Peter Crouch and Marcus Allback has not removed the banners lamenting a lack of ambition.

By contrast, Birmingham's pessimism has been replaced by burgeoning belief and they took the game to Villa. Devlin was the first to light the powder keg, cutting in from the right flank to curl a 20-yard drive into Enckelman's midriff. Then Clinton Morrison played an astute ball into the penalty area that Aliou Cisse lifted over the bar. Birmingham's tails were up. They stormed forward, like a boxer looking for the knockout punch, while Villa adopted a

Saturday November 2
BOLTON WANDERERS (h)
Won 3-1   HT 0-0   Att 27,224   Position 12th
Vaesen — Kenna, Cunningham, Purse, Sadler — Devlin, Cisse, Savage (Hughes 84), Lazaridis (Horsfield 60) — Morrison, John (Powell 77) *Subs not used* Bennett, Kirovski *Booked* Cisse, Morrison
Scorers Purse 61, Savage 73, Horsfield 83
Referee **C Foy**

Aided by the dismissal of Gardner for a second bookable offence, which replays show to be extremely harsh — and which prompt an angry Sam Allardyce to lambast the referee — Birmingham surf through the downpour for a deserved victory over Bolton, Savage confirming his St Andrew's cult status with his first goal for the club.

Tuesday November 5
PRESTON NORTH END (h)
Worthington Cup, 3rd rnd
Lost 0-2   HT 0-0   Att 12,241
Bennett — Hutchinson, Tebily, Cunningham, Sadler (Fagan ht) — Hughes, Powell, Carter (Kirovski 63), Lazaridis — Horsfield, Morrison *Subs not used* Vaesen, Devlin, John *Booked* Powell *Sent off* Horsfield 28
Referee **G Poll**

Forced to play with ten men for more than an hour after Horsfield elbows Alexander — off the ball, but right in front of the referee — a weakened Birmingham side depart the Worthington Cup with no cause for complaint after second-half goals by Fuller and Powell for the first division side.

Saturday November 9
CHELSEA (a)
Lost 0-3   HT 0-3   Att 35,237   Position 14th
Vaesen — Tebily, Cunningham, Purse, Kenna — Devlin, Cisse, Savage, Powell (Lazaridis 43) — Morrison (Horsfield 63), John (Hughes 74) *Subs not used* Bennett, Kirovski *Booked* Powell
Report page 81

Sunday November 17
FULHAM (h)
Drew 0-0   HT 0-0   Att 26,164   Position 15th
Vaesen — Tebily (Hughes 75), Cunningham, Purse, Kenna — Devlin, Cisse, Savage (Kirovski 81), Lazaridis — Horsfield, John (Morrison 75) *Subs not used* Bennett, Powell *Booked* Savage, Devlin
Referee **M Messias**

Failure to beat nine men must count as two points lost for Birmingham. Brevett is the first to go, for handling Purse's header on the line — Van der Sar saves John's spot kick — then Marlet follows for a retaliatory kick at Savage, leaving Jean Tigana, the Fulham manager, in a rage.

Saturday November 23
SUNDERLAND (a)
Won 1-0   HT 0-0   Att **38,803**   Position **13th**
Vaesen — Tebily, Cunningham, Purse, Kenna — Devlin
(D Johnson 84), Cisse, Savage (Powell 60; Hughes 84),
Lazaridis — Morrison, John *Subs not used* Bennett,
Kirovski *Booked* Tebily, Cisse, Savage
Scorer **Morrison 89**
Report page 273

Saturday November 30
TOTTENHAM HOTSPUR (h)
Drew 1-1   HT 0-0   Att **29,505**   Position **11th**
Vaesen — Tebily, Cunningham, Purse, Kenna — Devlin
(D Johnson 63), Cisse, Savage, Lazaridis (Kirovski 90)
— Morrison, John (Hughes 83) *Subs not used* Bennett,
Hutchinson *Booked* Cisse
Scorer **Kenna 68**
Referee **E Wolstenholme**

Perhaps the unlikeliest strike of the season earns
another precious point for Birmingham. After
Sheringham pounces to give Spurs the lead, Vaesen
failing to hold Ziege's shot, Kenna cuts in from the left
and, with the aid of a deflection, registers his first
Premiership goal since Blackburn's 1994-95
title-winning campaign.

Saturday December 7
SOUTHAMPTON (a)
Lost 0-2   HT 0-0   Att **31,132**   Position **13th**
Vaesen — Tebily, Cunningham, Purse, Kenna —
D Johnson (Carter 70), Cisse (Fagan 81), Hughes
(Kirovski 81), Lazaridis — Morrison, John *Subs not used*
Bennett, Hutchinson *Booked* Johnson, Morrison
Report page 130

Sunday December 15
FULHAM (a)
Won 1-0   HT 1-0   Att **14,962**   Position **13th**
Vaesen — Tebily, Cunningham, Purse, Kenna — Savage,
Cisse, Kirovski (Powell 73), D Johnson (Woodhouse 75)
— Horsfield (Hughes 79), Morrison *Subs not used*
Bennett, Fagan *Booked* Tebily, Purse, Johnson, Cisse,
Horsfield, Powell, Kirovski *Sent off* Purse 70
Scorer **Kirovski 7**
Report page 204

Savage encourages Birmingham fans to join in the celebrations

rope-a-dope policy. Birmingham were sharper and more committed.
The goal they threatened arrived after 30 minutes. Devlin's cross
eluded the statue-like Villa defence and landed at Savage's feet. He
failed to control it, but the ball broke to Morrison and he shot home
from ten yards.

Belatedly, Villa emerged from their shells. Ulises De La Cruz
crashed a 30-yard drive against the crossbar and Taylor seized the
initiative by throwing on Vassell and Dion Dublin. Suddenly, Villa
were the antithesis of their earlier selves. Jlloyd Samuel wrought
havoc down the left and rippled the side-netting with a rasping
drive. Vassell thought he had equalised with a neat finish. The goal
was disallowed and Taylor, a decent man caught up in the
atmosphere, berated the assistant referee.

The midfield became a minefield. Yet with Villa's pressure
mounting and an equaliser looming, Enckelman undid all the good
work. "We had a bit of luck but it's testament to our improvement,"
Bruce said. He was right on both counts.

BIRMINGHAM CITY (4-4-2): N Vaesen — J Kenna, K Cunningham, D Purse, M Grainger — P Devlin
(sub: D Powell, 79min), A Cisse, R Savage (sub: B Hughes, 86), D Johnson — C Morrison
(sub: G Horsfield, 68), S John. **Substitutes not used:** I Bennett, S Lazaridis. **Booked:** Purse, Grainger,
Cisse.
ASTON VILLA (3-5-2): P Enckelman — O Mellberg, Alpay, S Staunton — U De La Cruz, M Kinsella,
R Johnsen, G Barry, J Samuel — M Allback (sub: D Dublin, 46), J P Angel (sub: D Vassell, 46).
Substitutes not used: S Postma, L Hendrie, S Moore. **Booked:** Barry, Staunton, Alpay.
Referee: D Elleray.

THE MANAGER

Steve Bruce

Steve Bruce is quite simply a winner. He was as a player, he is now as a manager. To have taken Birmingham from a moderate first division side (twelfth when he arrived in December 2001), through the play-off final triumph at the Millennium Stadium only five months later and now to have led them to Premiership respectability, all in a year and a half, is the work of a miracle man. His transfer dealings are superb, he loves it at Brum, he has signed a new five-year deal. He is the club's present and its future.

Tim Austin

APPEARANCES

	Prem	FAC	WC	Total
I Bennett	10	-	2	12
D Carter	3 (9)	-	1	4 (9)
A Cisse	21	-	-	21
J Clapham	16	-	-	16
S Clemence	15	-	-	15
F Coly	1	1	-	2
K Cunningham	31	-	1	32
P Devlin	20 (12)	1	-	21 (12)
C Dugarry	16	-	-	16
C Fagan	0 (1)	0 (1)	0 (2)	0 (4)
M Grainger	8 (1)	1	-	9 (1)
G Horsfield	15 (16)	-	2	17 (16)
B Hughes	10 (12)	0 (1)	1	11 (13)
J Hutchinson	1	1	1	3
S John	20 (10)	0 (1)	1	21 (11)
D Johnson	28 (2)	1	0 (1)	29 (3)
M Johnson	5 (1)	-	-	5 (1)
J Kenna	36 (1)	1	1	38 (1)
J Kirovski	5 (12)	1	1 (1)	7 (13)
S Lazaridis	17 (13)	-	2	19 (13)
A Marriott	1	-	-	1
T Mooney	0 (1)	-	-	0 (1)
C Morrison	24 (4)	1	1	26 (4)
D Powell	3 (8)	1	2	6 (8)
D Purse	19 (1)	-	1	20 (1)
M Sadler	2	-	2	4
R Savage	33	1	-	34
P Swierczewski	0 (1)	-	-	0 (1)
O Tebily	12	-	1	13
M Upson	14	-	-	14
N Vaesen	27	1	-	28
S Vickers	5	-	1	6
C Woodhouse	0 (3)	-	1	1 (3)

Saturday December 21
CHARLTON ATHLETIC (h)
Drew 1-1 HT 0-1 Att 28,837 Position 13th
Vaesen — Tebily, Cunningham, Vickers, Kenna (Lazaridis 59) — Kirovski, Cisse, Savage, D Johnson (Devlin 59) — Horsfield, Morrison *Subs not used* Bennett, Hughes, Woodhouse *Booked* Tebily, Cisse, Savage, Morrison *Sent off* Horsfield 54
Scorer Devlin 67 (pen)
Referee R Styles

Jensen is the player on whom Charlton's fortunes hang. He gives them the lead after a slalom run but concedes the penalty from which Devlin equalises by holding Cisse. By then, Birmingham are down to ten men, Horsfield seeing red for the second time this season after a crude challenge on Young.

Thursday December 26
EVERTON (h)
Drew 1-1 HT 1-1 Att 29,505 Position 13th
Vaesen — Kenna, Cunningham, Vickers, M Johnson — Devlin, Cisse, Savage, D Johnson (Lazaridis 42) — Horsfield (Hughes 74), Kirovski (Morrison 60) *Subs not used* Bennett, Powell *Booked* Morrison
Scorer Kirovski 45
Referee D Elleray

The outcome is decided in 60 seconds just before half-time, Kirovski's header cancelling out Radzinski's opener, but the real talking point is Rooney's 81st-minute dismissal for a challenge that leaves Vickers needing eight stitches in his ankle, making Everton's teenaged star the youngest player to see red in the Premiership.

Saturday December 28
MANCHESTER UNITED (a)
Lost 0-2 HT 0-1 Att 67,640 Position 15th
Vaesen — Kenna, Cunningham (Powell 63), M Johnson, Sadler (Woodhouse 68) — Devlin, Cisse, Savage, Lazaridis (Horsfield 51) — Morrison, Kirovski *Subs not used* Bennett, Hughes *Booked* Kenna, Cisse
Report page 48

Wednesday January 1
LEEDS UNITED (a)
Lost 0-2   **HT 0-1**   Att **40,034**   Position **15th**
Vaesen — Kenna, Hutchinson, M Johnson (Horsfield 63),
Grainger (Powell 70) — Devlin, Cisse, Savage, D Johnson
— Morrison, Kirovski *Subs not used* Bennett, Hughes,
Woodhouse *Booked* Grainger, Savage
Report page 216

Sunday January 5
FULHAM (a)
FA Cup, 3rd rnd
Lost 1-3   **HT 0-2**   Att **9,203**
Vaesen — Coly, Kenna, Hutchinson, Grainger — Devlin
(Hughes 69), Powell, Savage, D Johnson — Morrison
(Fagan ht), Kirovski (John ht) *Subs not used* Bennett,
Woodhouse *Booked* Savage, Devlin
Scorer **John 90**
Report page 205

Sunday January 12
ARSENAL (h)
Lost 0-4   **HT 0-2**   Att **29,505**   Position **15th**
Vaesen — Coly (Grainger 68), Vickers, M Johnson,
Kenna — D Johnson, Savage, Clemence (Devlin 68),
Clapham — Dugarry (Kirovski 85), John *Subs not used*
Bennett, Hutchinson *Booked* D Johnson, Coly
Referee **S Bennett**

Floodlight failure forces a packed St Andrew's to wait
an extra half an hour to see four newcomers make
their Premiership debuts for Birmingham — and then
see Arsenal turn on the power with an awesome display
featuring two goals from Henry, the second taking him
to the 100-goal mark for the club.

Saturday January 18
BLACKBURN ROVERS (a)
Drew 1-1   **HT 0-1**   Att **23,331**   Position **15th**
Bennett — Kenna (John 74), Vickers (Devlin 35), M
Johnson (Kirovski 64), Clapham — D Johnson, Cisse,
Savage, Lararidis — Morrison, Dugarry *Subs not used*
Coly, Vaesen *Booked* Lazaridis, Dugarry, Clapham
Scorer **John 83**
Report page 108

PLAYER OF THE SEASON   **Kenny Cunningham**

Robbie Savage was almost unanimously the fans' choice for his huge commitment, his workrate, his enthusiasm, his willingness to play through pain and his inspiration to his team-mates. Christophe Dugarry was also immense. The Frenchman's ability to bring the best from his colleagues was awesome, as was his trickery and skill and, when they mattered most, his goals. But perhaps the best of the lot — the steadiest voice, the calming influence, the experienced anchor at the heart of the defence — was the Ireland captain, Blues' utterly consistent centre back, Kenny Cunningham.

Tim Austin

STATS AND FACTS

● Birmingham had not played in East London for eight years but then appeared there twice in four days in October, facing Leyton Orient in the Worthington Cup and West Ham United in the Premiership.

● Between early October and early April they scored only four first-half goals in 25 games in all competitions.

● Successive top-flight games staged at St Andrew's drew 6,234 (against Arsenal in May 1986) and 28,563 (against Blackburn Rovers in August 2002).

● Birmingham gained their first win over Liverpool in 21 attempts in February.

● Christophe Dugarry scored in none of his first ten games, but netted in each of the next four.

Bill Edgar

Saturday February 1
BOLTON WANDERERS (a)
Lost 2-4 HT 1-1 Att **24,288** Position **16th**
Bennett — Kenna, Cunningham, Upson, Clapham — Devlin (Kirovski 73), Savage, Clemence, Lazaridis — Morrison, Dugarry (John 67) *Subs not used* Vaesen, M Johnson, Swierczewski *Booked* Dugarry, Morrison
Scorers **Savage 44, Morrison 60**
Report page 241

Tuesday February 4
MANCHESTER UNITED (h)
Lost 0-1 HT 0-0 Att **29,475** Position **16th**
Vaesen — Kenna (Devlin 84), Cunningham, Upson, Clapham — D Johnson, Savage, Clemence — Morrison (Kirovski 78), Dugarry — John (Lazaridis 63) *Subs not used* Swierczewski, Bennett *Booked* Clemence
Referee **S Dunn**

United capitalise on their game in hand to close the gap on Arsenal to three points, Van Nistelrooy settling an undistinguished affair when his shot on the turn is deflected past the recalled Vaesen by Cunningham, his Birmingham team-mate. Dugarry's header had previously been cleared off the United line by Veron, but Scholes also hit the woodwork.

Saturday February 8
CHELSEA (h)
Lost 1-3 HT 0-1 Att **29,475** Position **16th**
Vaesen — Kenna (Swierczewski 52), Cunningham, Upson, Clapham — Clemence — Horsfield (Morrison 65), D Johnson, Savage, Lazaridis — Dugarry (Devlin 79) *Subs not used* Bennett, John *Booked* Johnson
Scorer **Savage 87 (pen)**
Referee **M Halsey**

Denied the goal that their early pressure merits, Cudicini excelling in goal once again, Birmingham are punished by the limping Zola, who uses his "good" leg to put Chelsea ahead just before half-time. Gudjohnsen and Hasselbaink make the game safe for the visiting team before Savage replies, like Hasselbaink from the penalty spot.

GOALSCORERS

	Prem	FAC	WC	Total
S Clemence	2	-	-	2
P Devlin	3 (2p)	-	-	3 (2p)
C Dugarry	5	-	-	5
G Horsfield	5	-	-	5
B Hughes	2	-	-	2
S John	5 (1p)	1	3	9 (1p)
D Johnson	1	-	-	1
J Kenna	1	-	-	1
J Kirovski	2	-	-	2
S Lazaridis	2	-	-	2
C Morrison	6	-	-	6
D Purse	1	-	-	1
R Savage	4 (2p)	-	-	4 (2p)
Own goals	2	-	-	2

Sunday February 23
LIVERPOOL (h)
Won 2-1 HT 1-0 Att **29,449** Position **16th**
Vaesen — Kenna, Cunningham, Upson, Clapham —
D Johnson, Savage, Clemence (Carter 79), Lazaridis —
Morrison (Devlin 88), Dugarry (Horsfield 82) *Subs not
used* Bennett, John *Booked* Dugarry, Upson
Scorers **Clemence 34, Morrison 68**
Referee **C Wilkes**

Birmingham's determination is too much for Liverpool,
their win taking them six points clear of the relegation
zone while Gerard Houllier's side are now five points off
the Champions League pace. Clemence gets the ball
rolling with a header — his first goal for Blues — against
the club where his father made his name, Owen coming
off the bench to halve the deficit.

Monday March 3
ASTON VILLA (a)
Won 2-0 HT 0-0 Att **42,602** Position **16th**
Vaesen — Kenna, Cunningham, Upson, Clapham —
D Johnson, Savage (Carter 84), Clemence, Lazaridis
(Devlin 74) — Morrison (Horsfield 72), Dugarry *Subs not
used* Bennett, John *Booked* Cunningham, Devlin
Scorers **Lazaridis 74, Horsfield 77**
Report page 231

Sunday March 16
MANCHESTER CITY (a)
Lost 0-1 HT 0-0 Att **34,596** Position **16th**
Bennett — Kenna (Devlin 75), Cunningham, Upson,
Clapham — D Johnson (John 84), Savage, Clemence,
Lazaridis — Morrison (Horsfield 59), Dugarry *Subs not
used* Carter, Marriott *Booked* Savage
Report page 146

Saturday March 22
WEST BROMWICH ALBION (h)
Won 1-0 HT 0-0 Att **29,449** Position **15th**
Bennett — Kenna (Carter 67), Cunningham, Upson,
Clapham — Devlin, Savage, Clemence (John 78),
D Johnson — Morrison (Horsfield 56), Dugarry *Subs not
used* Marriott, M Johnson
Scorer **Horsfield 90**
Referee **P Durkin**

The villain of the piece six days earlier with his air shot
against Manchester City, Horsfield is now the toast of
St Andrew's as he heads the only goal in the fourth
minute of stoppage time to send their luckless
neighbours one step nearer the Nationwide League
precipice.

THE PLAYERS

IAN BENNETT
Goalkeeper
Born October 10, 1971, Worksop
Ht 6ft 0in **Wt** 13st 1lb
Signed from Peterborough United,
December 1993, £325,000

DARREN CARTER
Defender
Born December 18, 1983, Solihull
Ht 6ft 2in **Wt** 12st 3lb
Signed from trainee, August 2001

ALIOU CISSE
Midfield
Born March 24, 1976,
Zinguinchor, Senegal
Ht 6ft 0in **Wt** 11st 5lb
Signed from Montpellier, July
2002, £1.5m

JAMIE CLAPHAM
Defender
Born December 7, 1975, Lincoln
Ht 5ft 10in **Wt** 10st 8lb
Signed from Ipswich Town,
January 2003, £1.3m

STEPHEN CLEMENCE
Midfield
Born March 31, 1978, Liverpool
Ht 5ft 11in **Wt** 11st 7lb
Signed from Tottenham Hotspur,
January 2003, £250,000

FERDINAND COLY
Defender
Born September 10, 1973,
Dakar, Senegal
Ht 5ft 10in **Wt** 12st 10lb
Signed from Lens (loan), January
2003

KENNY CUNNINGHAM
Defender
Born June 28, 1971, Dublin
Ht 5ft 11in **Wt** 11st 4lb
Signed from Wimbledon, July
2003, free

PAUL DEVLIN
Midfield
Born April 14, 1972, Birmingham
Ht 5ft 8in **Wt** 11st 1lb
Signed from Sheffield United,
February 2002, £200,000

CHRISTOPHE DUGARRY
Forward
Born March 24, 1972, Bordeaux
Ht 6ft 2in **Wt** 12st 4lb
Signed from Bordeaux, January
2003, free

CRAIG FAGAN
Forward
Born December 11, 1982,
Birmingham
Ht 5ft 11in **Wt** 11st 1lb
Signed from trainee, August 2001

Jamie Clapham

MARTIN GRAINGER
Defender
Born August 23, 1972, Enfield
Ht 5ft 10in **Wt** 12st 10lb
Signed from Brentford, March
1996, £400,000

GEOFF HORSFIELD
Forward
Born November 1, 1973, Barnsley
Ht 6ft 1in **Wt** 11st 7lb
Signed from Fulham, July 2000,
£2.25m

BRYAN HUGHES
Midfield
Born June 19, 1976, Liverpool
Ht 5ft 10in **Wt** 11st 2lb
Signed from Wrexham, March
1997, £750,000

JONATHAN HUTCHINSON
Midfield
Born April 2, 1982, Middlesbrough
Ht 5ft 11in **Wt** 11st 11lb
Signed from trainee, July 2000

STERN JOHN
Forward
Born October 30, 1976,
Tunapuna, Trinidad
Ht 5ft 11in **Wt** 13st 2lb
Signed from Nottingham Forest,
February 2002, free

DAMIEN JOHNSON
Midfield
Born November 18, 1978,
Lisburn
Ht 5ft 9in **Wt** 11st 7lb
Signed from Blackburn Rovers,
March 2002, £100,000

MICHAEL JOHNSON
Defender
Born July 4, 1973, Nottingham
Ht 5ft 11in **Wt** 12st 8lb
Signed from Notts County,
September 1995, £225,000

JEFF KENNA
Defender
Born August 27, 1907, Dublin
Ht 5ft 11in **Wt** 12st 2lb
Signed from Blackburn Rovers,
December 2001, free

JOVAN KIROVSKI
Forward
Born March 18, 1976,
Escondido, California
Ht 6ft 1in **Wt** 12st 4lb
Signed from Crystal Palace,
August 2002, free

STAN LAZARIDIS
Midfield
Born August 16, 1972,
Perth, Australia
Ht 5ft 9in **Wt** 11st 12lb
Signed from West Ham United,
July 1999, £1.6m

ANDREW MARRIOTT
Goalkeeper
Born October 11, 1970,
Sutton-in-Ashfield
Ht 6ft 1in **Wt** 12st 6lb
Signed from Barnsley, March
2003, nominal

TOMMY MOONEY
Forward
Born August 11, 1971,
Billingham
Ht 5ft 10in **Wt** 12st 6lb
Signed from Watford, July 2001,
free

CLINTON MORRISON
Forward
Born May 14, 1979, Tooting
Ht 6ft 1in **Wt** 11st 2lb
Signed from Crystal Palace, July
2002, £4.25m

Saturday April 5
TOTTENHAM HOTSPUR (a)
Lost 1-2 HT 0-1 Att **36,058** Position **17th**
Marriott — Kenna (Carter 90), Cunningham, Upson,
Clapham — Devlin, D Johnson, Clemence, Dugarry
(Kirovski 86) — Horsfield, John (Lazaridis 56) *Subs not
used* Davies, M Johnson *Booked* John
Scorer **Devlin 77 (pen)**
Report page 159

Saturday April 12
SUNDERLAND (h)
Won 2-0 HT 1-0 Att **29,132** Position **16th**
Bennett — Kenna, Cunningham, Upson, Clapham —
Devlin (Carter 79), Hughes (Kirovski 84), Clemence,
Lazaridis — Horsfield, Dugarry (John 64) *Subs not used*
Marriott, Purse
Scorers **Hughes 43, Dugarry 60**
Referee **P Dowd**

Sunderland are finally put out of their misery at St
Andrew's, where a club record tenth straight league
defeat confirms the relegation that has looked certain
all season. They also incur their first red card of the
campaign, Stewart kicking out at John in frustration
after Dugarry's header, his first goal for Birmingham,
seals their fate.

Saturday April 19
CHARLTON ATHLETIC (a)
Won 2-0 HT 1-0 Att **25,732** Position **15th**
Bennett — Kenna, Cunningham, Upson, Clapham —
D Johnson (Purse 90), Savage, Clemence, Hughes —
Horsfield (Devlin 87), Dugarry (John 68) *Subs not used*
Marriott, Lazaridis *Booked* Clemence
Scorers **Dugarry 20, Savage 55 (pen)**
Report page 183

Monday April 21
SOUTHAMPTON (h)
Won 3-2 HT 0-1 Att **29,115** Position **13th**
Bennett — Kenna (Devlin 65), Cunningham, Upson,
Clapham — D Johnson (John 79), Savage, Clemence
(Lazaridis 54) — Horsfield, Dugarry *Subs not
used* Marriott, Purse
Scorers **Dugarry 75, 82, Hughes 79**
Referee **S Bennett**

Twice behind to the Cup finalists, Birmingham draw on
Dugarry's brilliance to win a thrilling match and move to
within one point of safety. "He is the best player the
club has ever had," Steve Bruce says of the former
France striker, who scores with a curling free kick and a
header, either side of a neat volley from Hughes.

Saturday April 26
MIDDLESBROUGH (h)
Won 3-0 **HT 2-0** Att **28,821** Position **12th**
Bennett — Kenna, Cunningham, Upson, Clapham —
D Johnson, Savage, Clemence, Hughes (Lazaridis 70)
— Horsfield (Devlin 75), Dugarry (John 81) *Subs not
used* Marriott, Purse *Booked* Hughes
Scorers **Dugarry 18, Clemence 40, Lazaridis 80**
Referee **M Dean**

Finally the celebrations can begin as Birmingham secure
their Premiership place with two matches to spare, set
on their way once again by Dugarry. Clever thigh control
precedes his opener and he wins the free kick for
Clemence to double the lead against a woeful
Middlesbrough side who offer little in response.

Saturday May 3
NEWCASTLE UNITED (a)
Lost 0-1 **HT 0-1** Att **52,146** Position **13th**
Bennett — Kenna (M Johnson ht), Purse, Upson,
Clapham — D Johnson, Savage (Lazaridis 70),
Clemence, Hughes — Horsfield, Dugarry (John 79)
Subs not used Marriott, Devlin *Booked* Hughes, Dugarry
Sent off Upson 41
Report page 76

Sunday May 11
WEST HAM UNITED (h)
Drew 2-2 **HT 0-0** Att **29,505** Position **13th**
Bennett — Kenna (Devlin 73), Purse, Upson, Clapham
— D Johnson, Savage, Clemence, Lazaridis (Hughes 73)
— Horsfield, Dugarry (John 63) *Subs not used* Marriott,
M Johnson *Booked* Savage, Clemence
Scorers **Horsfield 80, John 88**
Referee **G Poll**

Bottom at Christmas, down in May: the bubble finally
bursts for West Ham as relegation is confirmed. They
fail to beat Birmingham — whose joy at finishing above
Aston Villa is as heartfelt as West Ham's tears — but,
with Bolton also winning, even that would not have been
enough to save them.

DARRYL POWELL
Midfield
Born January 15, 1971,
Lambeth
Ht 6ft 0in **Wt** 12st 3lb
Signed from Derby County,
September 2002, free

DARREN PURSE
Defender
Born February 14, 1977,
London
Ht 6ft 2in **Wt** 13st 1lb
Signed from Oxford United,
February 1998, £700,000

MATHEW SADLER
Defender
Born February 26, 1985,
Solihull
Ht 5ft 11in **Wt** 11st 5lb
Signed from trainee, October
2002

ROBBIE SAVAGE
Midfield
Born October 18, 1974,
Wrexham
Ht 5ft 11in **Wt** 10st 8lb
Signed from Leicester City, May
2002, £1.25m

PIOTR SWIERCZEWSKI
Midfield
Born April 8, 1972, Mowyn Sacz,
Poland
Ht 6ft 0in **Wt** 11st 10lb
Signed from Marseilles (loan),
January 2003

OLIVIER TEBILY
Defender
Born December 19, 1975,
Abidjan, Ivory Coast
Ht 6ft 0in **Wt** 13st 3lb
Signed from Celtic, March 2002,
£700,000

MATTHEW UPSON
Defender
Born April 18, 1979, Stowmarket
Ht 6ft 1in **Wt** 11st 5lb
Signed from Arsenal, January
2003, £1m

NICO VAESEN
Goalkeeper
Born September 28, 1969, Ghent
Ht 6ft 3in **Wt** 12st 8lb
Signed from Huddersfield Town,
June 2001, £800,000

STEVE VICKERS
Defender
Born October 13, 1967,
Bishop Auckland
Ht 6ft 1in **Wt** 12st 12lb
Signed from Middlesbrough,
November 2001, £400,000

CURTIS WOODHOUSE
Midfield
Born April 17, 1980, Beverley
Ht 5ft 8in **Wt** 11st 6lb
Signed from Sheffield United,
February 2001, £1m

Matthew Upson

FULHAM

PREMIERSHIP

	P	W	D	L	F	A	Pts
Man Utd	38	25	8	5	74	34	83
Arsenal	38	23	9	6	85	42	78
Newcastle	38	21	6	11	63	48	69
Chelsea	38	19	10	9	68	38	67
Liverpool	38	18	10	10	61	41	64
Blackburn	38	16	12	10	52	43	60
Everton	38	17	8	13	48	49	59
Southampton	38	13	13	12	43	46	52
Man City	38	15	6	17	47	54	51
Tottenham	38	14	8	16	51	62	50
Middlesbro	38	13	10	15	48	44	49
Charlton	38	14	7	17	45	56	49
Birmingham	38	13	9	16	41	49	48
Fulham	**38**	**13**	**9**	**16**	**41**	**50**	**48**
Leeds	38	14	5	19	58	57	47
Aston Villa	38	12	9	17	42	47	45
Bolton	38	10	14	14	41	51	44
West Ham	38	10	12	16	42	59	42
West Brom	38	6	8	24	29	65	26
Sunderland	38	4	7	27	21	65	19

FA CUP
Fifth round

WORTHINGTON CUP
Fourth round

UEFA CUP
Third round

**Chris Coleman won the board's backing
to replace Jean Tigana**

THE GAMES

Saturday July 6
FC HAKA (h)
InterToto Cup, 2nd rnd, 1st leg
Drew 0-0   HT 0-0   Att 7,908
Taylor — Ouaddou, Melville, Goma, Harley — Marlet (Boa
Morte 71), Davis, Collins, Malbranque (Goldbaek 79)
— Sava (Hayles 61), Saha *Subs not used* Hahnemann,
Knight, Hudson, Legwinski *Booked* Malbranque
Referee **L Gadosi (Slovakia)**

Lleyton Hewitt has yet to win the men's singles at
Wimbledon as Fulham launch the new season and
immediately run into a goalkeeper in top form, Slawuta
repelling all that Jean Tigana's side can throw at them.

Sunday July 14
FC HAKA (a)
InterToto Cup, 2nd rnd, 2nd leg
Drew 1-1 (win on away goals)   HT 0-0   Att 3,500
Taylor — Ouaddou, Melville, Goma, Harley — Legwinski
(Boa Morte 57), Davis, Malbranque (Goldbaek 89),
Collins (Knight 79) — Saha, Marlet *Subs not used*
Van der Sar, Sava, Hayles, Stolcers *Booked* Goma,
Boa Morte
Scorer **Marlet 47**
Referee **E Laursen (Denmark)**

A goal early in the second half from Marlet, who runs on
to a long clearance from Taylor, is enough to take
Fulham through, despite an equaliser from Ristila with
almost 25 minutes to go. A successful day is completed
with the signing of Inamoto from Arsenal.

Saturday July 20
EGALEO (h)
InterToto Cup, 3rd rnd, 1st leg
Won 1-0   HT 0-0   Att 5,199
Van der Sar — Ouaddou (Saha ht), Knight, Goma, Harley
— Malbranque (Hayles 66), Davis, Collins, Boa Morte —
Marlet, Sava (Legwinski ht) *Subs not used* Herrera,
Melville, Goldbaek, Stolcers
Scorer **Saha 78**
Referee **J ver Ecke (Belgium)**

With his new-born son present in the stands, Saha
indulges in a little showing-off with the second-half
goal that gives Fulham a narrow advantage over their
Greek opponents.

Saturday July 27
EGALEO (a)
InterToto Cup, 3rd rnd, 2nd leg
Drew 1-1 (win 2-1 on agg)   HT 1-1   Att 4,339
Van der Sar — Ouaddou, Melville, Goma, Harley —
Malbranque (Stolcers 85), Davis, Legwinski (Goldbaek
70), Boa Morte — Saha, Marlet (Hayles 71) *Subs not
used* Herrera, Collins, Sava, Knight
Scorer **Marlet 34**
Referee **R Bossen (the Netherlands)**

Behind after 24 minutes to a goal from Chloros, Fulham
are again indebted to Marlet for the strike that puts
them through on away soil.

Wednesday July 31
SOCHAUX (h)
InterToto Cup, semi-final, 1st leg
Won 1-0   HT 0-0   Att 4,599
Van der Sar — Ouaddou (Knight 63), Melville, Goma,
Brevett — Boa Morte, Davis, Legwinski (Inamoto ht),
Malbranque (Hayles 68) — Saha, Marlet *Subs not used*
Herrera, Collins, Harley, Sava *Booked* Davis, Marlet
Scorer **Davis 90**
Referee **S Corpodean (Romania)**

IT WAS SUPPOSED TO BE THE BIGGEST match in Fulham's
history, but the size of the attendance was simply embarrassing. The
Uefa Cup tie against Hajduk Split in October encapsulated
Fulham's season — one of magnificent triumphs marred by protest
and broken promises.

Fewer than 10,000 turned up for this historic game after the club
announced that it was considering jettisoning plans to redevelop
Craven Cottage. Fortunately for Fulham, "technical problems" at
the turnstiles meant that the attendance did not become public
knowledge for a few days. Five years earlier, Fulham had managed
to attract a bigger crowd for their third division match against
Wigan Athletic. But how on earth could the glories of Europe have
been eclipsed by a fixture in football's basement?

Diehard supporters who had campaigned for two decades to keep
Fulham in Fulham were not happy and showed as much by boycott-
ing the start of the European campaign. While the board
was insisting that a return to the Cottage was still "preferred", it
failed to mention that an option to sell the ground had already been
secretly negotiated. The silverware won in August — in the form of
the InterToto Cup — soon tarnished and by the end of the season
the volte-face was complete. The belief that the intense rivalry with
Chelsea would prevent them from ever sharing a ground
disappeared with the news that the clubs were in talks over just such
a proposal.

The future of Craven Cottage is for many fans inextricably linked
with the future of Fulham Football Club. And when it was revealed
that the club might not return to its historic home, the season was
spoilt. But while some fans were in revolt, others were just grateful
to be in the Premiership — an inconceivable notion five years
earlier.

And there was much to enjoy. Among the season's most notable
scalps were Tottenham Hotspur, Newcastle United, Leeds United
and Liverpool. It was not the humiliating 10-0 scoreline that
Liverpool had once inflicted upon Fulham, but it was a victory
nonetheless. Points taken from Chelsea and Manchester United
were also well deserved and well received.

The star of many of these performances was the one player to
pre-date the Mohamed Al Fayed era. Sean Davis, a home-grown
player, had the spirit, determination and talent to take control of
games. When injury or suspension kept him out of the side, loan
signings such as Martin Djetou and Pierre Wome could not
compete. And for every win there was a performance that lacked
passion. Having briefly topped the Barclaycard Premiership, the

Fulham go top of the first Premiership table with a heavy defeat of Bolton

early-season promise gave way to a flirtation with relegation. As the club tumbled down the table, the FA Cup was a welcome distraction that could so easily have saved the season. With Birmingham City and Charlton Athletic dispatched and with several first-division clubs bobbing about in the draw, it looked as if Fulham might go one better than the previous season's semi-final against Chelsea. Defeat away to Burnley reflected the general malaise. A season of much promise but little reward.

There was no easy way out. Jean Tigana had nowhere to turn because the money had dried up as Fulham attempted to wrest control of their increasing debts. Even the half-time entertainment, the skimpily clad Cravenettes, disappeared.

It culminated in the sale of Rufus Brevett to West Ham United, their relegation rivals. With just a few months left on the 33-year-old full back's contract, the undisclosed sum must have been paltry. But with Jon Harley eager to step into Brevett's very large boots, Fulham's problems weren't at the back but in front of goal.

The forward line was ravaged by injury and the team were having to rely on Steve Marlet. After two seasons and only ten league goals, he was retailing at more than a million pounds a strike. These are the sort of figures that a shopkeeper understands. Someone had to pay — the fans in frustration, the manager with his job.

But while West Ham merely believed they were too good to go down, Fulham actually proved it. Performances improved remarkably when Chris Coleman took control of the team. Was the renaissance simply "new manager syndrome", or does the Welshman — who is popular with fans and players alike — have what it takes? Success and failure may rest on who Coleman can persuade to stay at the club and, crucially, whom he can afford to keep.

After Legwinski has hit the bar with a header and then missed an open goal from two yards, Davis shows Fulham's strikers how to do it with a goal two minutes into stoppage time in the first match at their adopted Loftus Road home.

Wednesday August 7
SOCHAUX (a)
InterToto Cup, semi-final, 2nd leg
Won 2-0 (win 3-0 on agg) HT 0-0 Att **11,000**
Van der Sar — Ouaddou, Melville, Goma, Brevett — Legwinski, Davis, Malbranque (Inamoto 58), Boa Morte (Collins 72) — Saha (Hayles 68), Marlet *Subs not used* Herrera, Knight, Sava, Lewis *Booked* Brevett
Scorers **Legwinski 64, Hayles 72**
Referee **M Wack (Germany)**

With five Frenchmen on the pitch, Fulham feel at home as second-half goals from Legwinski — a header — and Hayles take them through to one of the three InterToto Cup finals and two matches from a coveted place in the Uefa Cup itself.

Tuesday August 13
BOLOGNA (a)
InterToto Cup, final, 1st leg
Drew 2-2 HT 0-0 Att **23,000**
Van der Sar — Ouaddou, Melville, Goma, Brevett — Legwinski, Davis, Malbranque (Inamoto 60), Boa Morte — Hayles (Saha 60), Marlet *Subs not used* Collins, Knight, Leacock, Sava *Booked* Ouaddou, Boa Morte, Legwinski
Scorers **Inamoto 62, Legwinski 85**
Referee **I Gonzalez Eduardo (Spain)**

Fulham are put on the spot by Davis and Ouaddou, who concede second-half penalties — put away by Signori — only for Inamoto, with a brilliant strike two minutes after his introduction as a substitute, and Legwinski, with a firm late drive, to give them the advantage.

Saturday August 17
BOLTON WANDERERS (h)
Won 4-1 HT 3-1 Att **16,338** Position **1st**
Van der Sar — Finnan, Melville, Goma, Brevett — Legwinski, Davis, Malbranque (Inamoto 69), Boa Morte — Saha (Sava 78), Marlet *Subs not used* Taylor, Collins, Ouaddou *Booked* Melville
Scorers **Saha 11 (pen), Legwinski 33, 79, Marlet 38 (pen)**
Referee **A Wiley**

Seven matches already under their belt, Fulham are far too slick and settled against Bolton and finish the day top of the nascent Premiership table, despite conceding the first goal of the campaign. Bolton's opener, a penalty, is soon wiped out by two spot-kicks during a comprehensive victory.

Saturday August 24
MIDDLESBROUGH (a)
Drew 2-2 HT 0-1 Att **28,588** Position **3rd**
Van der Sar — Finnan, Melville, Goma, Brevett — Legwinski, Davis, Malbranque (Inamoto 60), Boa Morte — Saha, Marlet (Sava 61) *Subs not used* Taylor, Ouaddou, Collins *Booked* Malbranque, Brevett, Finnan
Scorers **Davis 90, Sava 90**
Report page 162

Tuesday August 27
BOLOGNA (h)
InterToto Cup, final, 2nd leg
Won 3-1 (win 5-3 on agg) HT 1-1 Att **13,756**
Van der Sar — Finnan, Knight, Goma, Brevett — Legwinski, Davis (Collins 74), Inamoto (Malbranque 72),

Boa Morte — Sava, Marlet (Saha 72) *Subs not used*
Taylor, Melville, Hayles, Ouaddou *Booked* Legwinski,
Finnan
Scorer **Inamoto 12, 47, 50**
Referee **M Busacca (Switzerland)**

Having emerged into the World Cup daylight after a year
in the shadows at Highbury, Inamoto lays claim to being
the brightest star on Fulham's horizon with a superb
hat-trick that wins one of the three InterToto Cup finals
and earns a place in the Uefa Cup for the first time in
the club's history.

Saturday August 31
WEST BROMWICH ALBION (a)
Lost 0-1   HT 0-0   Att 25,461   Position 13th
Van der Sar — Finnan, Melville (Knight 60), Goma,
Brevett — Davis — Legwinski, Inamoto (Malbranque 60),
Boa Morte — Sava (Saha 60), Marlet *Subs not used*
Taylor, Hayles *Booked* Finnan, Boa Morte, Legwinski,
Davis
Report page 258

Wednesday September 11
TOTTENHAM HOTSPUR (h)
Won 3-2   HT 0-2   Att 16,757   Position 8th
Van der Sar — Finnan, Knight, Goma, Wome (Collins 80)
— Legwinski, Davis, Inamoto, Boa Morte (Malbranque ht)
— Sava, Saha (Hayles 20) *Subs not used* Taylor, Melville
Scorers **Inamoto 68, Malbranque 84 (pen),
Legwinski 90**
Referee **M Halsey**

Hoping to regain pole position in the Premiership, Spurs
are 2-0 up and cruising at half-time before being
stunned by the ferocity of Fulham's fightback. The home
side level when Gardner's challenge on Hayles is
contentiously ruled worthy of a penalty and Legwinski
hits the winner in the fourth minute of stoppage time.

Saturday September 14
SUNDERLAND (a)
Won 3-0   HT 1-0   Att 35,432   Position 5th
Van der Sar — Ouaddou, Knight, Goma, Brevett —
Legwinski, Davis, Malbranque — Inamoto (Collins 85) —
Hayles (Sava 76), Marlet *Subs not used* Taylor, Melville,
Stolcers *Booked* Hayles, Brevett
Scorers **Inamoto 34, Hayles 54, Marlet 78**
Report page 271

Thursday September 19
HAJDUK SPLIT (a)
Uefa Cup, 1st rnd, 1st leg
Won 1-0   HT 0-0   Att 25,000
Van der Sar — Ouaddou, Melville, Goma, Brevett (Wome
63) — Legwinski, Davis, Malbranque — Inamoto (Clark
78) — Hayles, Marlet (Sava 82) *Subs not used* Taylor,
Collins, Knight, Stolcers
Scorer **Malbranque 50**
Referee **F Carmona Mendez (Spain)**

Goran Ivanisevic is among the Croatian supporters
willing on Hajduk, who lay siege to Van der Sar's goal for
half an hour, but Fulham slowly get on top and score a
deserved winner when Marlet sets up Malbranque. The
match is soured, though, by racial abuse aimed at
Fulham's black players from the terraces.

Monday September 23
CHELSEA (h)
Drew 0-0   HT 0-0   Att 16,503   Position 6th
Van der Sar — Ouaddou, Knight, Goma, Wome —
Legwinski, Davis, Inamoto (Boa Morte 63), Malbranque

MATCH OF THE SEASON

Fulham 1   Manchester United 1
Loftus Road, Saturday October 19 2002
Alyson Rudd

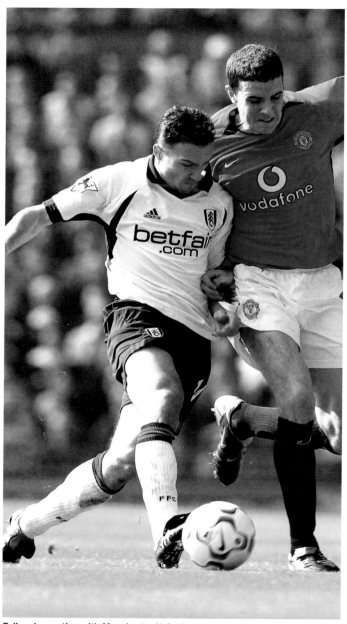

Fulham's meeting with Manchester United was a case of little and large

Honours are even as Fulham go head to head with United at Loftus Road

WHEN FULHAM REACHED THE Barclaycard Premiership, Jean Tigana promised that he would not compromise the team's style. If scrapping was the only way to stay up, the message seemed, then he would rather not be there. He was almost undone last season. The big clubs tore into Fulham, and in reply Fulham failed to tear into the smaller ones.

This time it is a bit different. Fulham are scoring a little more freely and are far more difficult to beat. They have proved that the big clubs can no longer treat them with contempt. Fulham kept the ball better than United, who looked more threatening in the final third. It was an equal contest with a pulsating second half.

"We definitely should have won that," Zat Knight, the Fulham defender, said. Knight doubts that clubs fear United the way they used to. Just a glance at their substitutes' bench must have filled the home fans with glee. It was uninspiring for such a massive operation. Fulham's bench boasted class, pace and experience. The United bench told a sorry tale of lack of depth.

United salvaged a point courtesy of some gamesmanship. Fulham's least obvious penalty appeal was the one Mike Dean chose to award. Fabien Barthez, miffed perhaps that Laurent Blanc was judged to have brought down Steve Marlet, or possibly sensing that three points were about to slip away, dawdled as Steed Malbranque prepared. Malbranque's body language said it all. Should he take the

— Hayles, Marlet *Subs not used* Herrera, Melville, Clark, Sava *Booked* Ouaddou
Referee **P Durkin**

The appearance on the Chelsea bench of Bogarde, last seen near the first team on Boxing Day 2000, promises an unusually entertaining night, but that is as interesting as the West London derby gets. Cudicini's save from Inamoto is the one real time a goal threatens.

Saturday September 28
EVERTON (a)
Lost 0-2 **HT 0-2** **Att 34,371** **Position 8th**
Van der Sar — Finnan, Knight, Goma (Melville 27), Wome — Legwinski, Davis, Inamoto (Boa Morte 55), Malbranque — Hayles (Sava 60), Marlet *Subs not used* Clark, Taylor *Booked* Melville, Hayles, Wome
Report page 115

Thursday October 3
HAJDUK SPLIT (h)
Uefa Cup, 1st rnd, 2nd leg
Drew 2-2 (win 3-2 on agg) **HT 2-2** **Att 9,162**
Van der Sar — Ouaddou, Melville, Knight, Brevett — Legwinski, Davis, Malbranque, Boa Morte (Inamoto 67) — Sava (Hayles 74), Marlet *Subs not used* Taylor, Clark, Collins, Wome, Leacock *Booked* Melville, Brevett
Scorers **Marlet 20, Malbranque 44 (pen)**
Referee **S Farina (Italy)**

Trailing twice, Fulham are inspired by Malbranque, who makes an equaliser for Marlet and scores the second with a twice-taken penalty. But it needs Inamoto's last-ditch clearance off the line to take them through.

Sunday October 6
CHARLTON ATHLETIC (h)
Won 1-0 **HT 1-0** **Att 14,775** **Position 5th**
Van der Sar — Ouaddou, Melville, Knight, Brevett — Legwinski, Davis (Wome 66), Malbranque, Boa Morte (Inamoto 62) — Sava (Hayles 73), Marlet *Subs not used* Taylor, Collins *Booked* Brevett
Scorer **Sava 36**
Referee **J Winter**

A drab game, a so-so goal . . . but a legend is made nonetheless as Sava marks his winner by reaching into his sock for the Zorro mask that is to become the Argentinian's trademark celebration.

Saturday October 19
MANCHESTER UNITED (h)
Drew 1-1 **HT 1-0** **Att 14,775** **Position 7th**
Van der Sar — Ouaddou, Knight, Goma, Brevett — Finnan, Davis, Legwinski, Malbranque — Sava (Hayles 79), Marlet *Subs not used* Taylor, Inamoto, Collins, Boa Morte *Booked* Marlet
Scorer **Marlet 35**
Referee **M Dean**

Professionalism, gamesmanship or downright cheating? The debate is sparked by Barthez's post-kicking delaying tactics before saving Malbranque's 71st-minute penalty. Nine minutes earlier, Solskjaer had cancelled out the Fulham striker's first-half opener. Barthez is booked for his pains — not a bad trade-off for United.

Wednesday October 23
WEST HAM UNITED (h)
Lost 0-1 **HT 0-0** **Att 15,858** **Position 8th**
Van der Sar — Finnan, Melville, Knight, Wome — Malbranque, Legwinski, Inamoto (Djetou ht), Boa Morte (Stolcers 77) — Marlet, Hayles *Subs not used* Taylor, Collins, Ouaddou *Booked* Marlet, Boa Morte *Sent off* Knight 88
Referee **R Styles**

Fulham's first defeat at their adopted home is inflicted in the dying seconds, when Knight cuts down Defoe and is sent off for a professional foul before Di Canio coolly claims West Ham's third successive away win, from the penalty spot, and is involved in an argument with home supporters as he leaves the pitch.

Sunday October 27
SOUTHAMPTON (a)
Lost 2-4 HT 2-2 Att 26,188 Position 11th
Van der Sar — Finnan, Knight (Ouaddou 60), Goma, Brevett — Djetou (Hayles 63) — Legwinski, Clark, Malbranque — Marlet, Boa Morte *Subs not used* Taylor, Melville, Stolcers *Booked* Goma, Boa Morte
Scorers **Clark 15, Malbranque 24**
Report page 128

Thursday October 31
DYNAMO ZAGREB (a)
Uefa Cup, 2nd rnd, 1st leg
Won 3-0 HT 1-0 Att 30,000
Van der Sar — Ouaddou, Melville, Goma, Brevett — Finnan, Djetou (Inamoto 59), Legwinski, Malbranque — Marlet (Hayles 65), Boa Morte (Stolcers 71) *Subs not used* Taylor, Clark, Knight, Wome *Booked* Finnan
Scorers **Boa Morte 35, Marlet 59, Hayles 77**
Referee **E Iturralde Gonzalez (Spain)**

Unbeaten in six European matches on their travels, Fulham produce a template for the perfect away performance. Clearly frightened by Boa Morte's pace, Dynamo are reduced to ten men when Polovanec brings him down in the 32nd minute and the path is cleared for a rout.

Sunday November 3
ARSENAL (h)
Lost 0-1 HT 0-1 Att 18,800 Position 11th
Van der Sar — Ouaddou, Melville, Goma, Brevett — Finnan, Djetou (Inamoto 53), Legwinski, Malbranque (Hayles 53) — Marlet, Boa Morte *Subs not used* Taylor, Clark, Knight *Booked* Djetou
Referee **J Winter**

"Winter of discontent" headlines are all the rage as the referee turns down two seemingly certain penalties, Campbell the offender and Boa Morte the victim each time, while Marlet's sliced own goal from Henry's corner allows Arsenal to end an unimagined run of four successive defeats, albeit in less than championship style.

Wednesday November 6
BURY (h)
Worthington Cup, 3rd rnd
Won 3-1 HT 1-0 Att 6,700
Taylor — Finnan (Djetou 64), Ouaddou, Melville (Hudson 79), Wome — Goldbaek, Clark, Collins, Inamoto (Sava ht) — Hayles, Stolcers *Subs not used* Herrera, Boa Morte
Scorers **Stolcers 40, 53, Clark 73**
Referee **D Pugh**

On the night that seven Premiership "giants" depart the Worthington Cup, Fulham's depleted selection still has too many guns for Bury, Stolcers getting his first goals for nearly two years.

Saturday November 9
ASTON VILLA (a)
Lost 1-3 HT 0-1 Att 29,563 Position 12th
Van der Sar — Ouaddou (Stolcers 72), Melville, Goma, Brevett — Finnan, Djetou (Inamoto 64), Legwinski, Malbranque — Marlet, Boa Morte (Sava 78) *Subs not used* Taylor, Knight *Booked* Melville, Boa Morte
Scorer **Boa Morte 51**
Report page 226

Sava, Fulham's Argentine striker, takes on the United defence

penalty even though Barthez was stood next to his post as if waiting for a bus? Or would Malbranque be booked if he did? He chose to be a gentleman, waited until Barthez had been cautioned and promptly played, literally, into the France keeper's hands. "He was too sporting," Sean Davis said. It was his first penalty miss for Fulham.

Marlet had given Fulham the lead after United had been sloppy in possession in midfield. In the second half, Fulham returned the compliment with Knight and Abdeslam Ouaddou engaging in a spot of slapstick to allow Ole Gunnar Solskjaer to nip in to equalise.

United seemed distracted in the first half. Sir Alex Ferguson, their manager, chose to call this "the comfort zone". Paul Scholes had a good excuse, because he must win the week's award for most moved player. He shifted around the pitch for England and for United, too, played up front, in central midfield and wide left.

Once bitten, United snarl and are at their most dangerous, but Fulham steadily passed and probed. They face Arsenal next month, their real test because Arsene Wenger's side thoroughly outclassed them home and away last season. That the players felt able to swagger a little after this probably says most about United.

FULHAM (4-4-2): E van der Sar — A Ouaddou, Z Knight, A Goma, R Brevett — S Finnan, S Davis, S Legwinski, S Malbranque — F Sava (sub: B Hayles, 79min), S Marlet. **Substitutes not used:** M Taylor, J Inamoto, J Collins, L Boa Morte.
MANCHESTER UNITED (4-4-1-1): F Barthez — G Neville, J O'Shea, L Blanc, M Silvestre (sub: D Forlan, 80) — D Beckham, P Neville (sub: Q Fortune, 59), J S Veron, R Giggs — P Scholes — O G Solskjaer. **Substitutes not used:** Ricardo, D May, K Richardson. **Booked:** Blanc, Beckham, Barthez.
Referee: M Dean.

THE MANAGER

Jean Tigana

Fulham's run of 11 straight wins when Jean Tigana took charge in 2000 was no fluke. With only slight tinkering, he transformed the rather lacklustre squad he inherited. His strength was to extract the very best from existing players who many thought would never cut it at a higher level. But an horrendous error in the transfer market sullied his reputation. Spending £11.5 million on Steve Marlet rightly cost him his job. The chairman was understandably disappointed with his investment. The multimillion-pound signing of Edwin van der Sar was also wasteful with an accomplished keeper, Maik Taylor, already in situ. Everyone can make mistakes, but not when they cost that much.

Tim Miller

APPEARANCES

	Prem	FAC	WC	Euro	Total
L Boa Morte	25 (4)	2	0 (1)	10 (3)	37 (8)
R Brevett	20	-	-	10	30
L Clark	9 (2)	-	2	1 (1)	12 (3)
J Collins	0 (5)	0 (1)	2	3 (2)	5 (8)
S Davis	28	4	0 (1)	12	44 (1)
M Djetou	22 (3)	4	1 (1)	3 (1)	30 (5)
S Finnan	32	3	1	5	41
B Goldbaek	8 (2)	2 (1)	1	2 (4)	13 (7)
A Goma	29	3	-	13	45
E Hammond	3 (7)	-	-	-	3 (7)
J Harley	11	4	-	4	19
B Hayles	4 (10)	-	1	2 (7)	7 (17)
M Herrera	1 (1)	-	-	-	1 (1)
M Hudson	-	-	0 (1)	-	0 (1)
J Inamoto	9 (10)	1 (1)	2	3 (7)	15 (18)
Z Knight	12 (5)	0 (1)	1	3 (2)	16 (8)
D Leacock	-	-	1	-	1
S Legwinski	33 (2)	3	-	10 (2)	46 (4)
S Malbranque	35 (2)	4	-	12 (2)	51 (4)
S Marlet	28	1 (1)	-	13 (1)	42 (2)
A Melville	24 (2)	3	1	12	40 (2)
A Ouaddou	9 (4)	0 (1)	2	10	21 (5)
L Saha	13 (4)	3	-	5 (3)	21 (7)
F Sava	13 (7)	3 (1)	1 (1)	6 (1)	23 (10)
A Stolcers	0 (5)	-	2	0 (2)	2 (7)
M Taylor	18 (1)	4	2	3	27 (1)
E van der Sar	19	-	-	11	30
C Willock	0 (2)	-	-	-	0 (2)
P Wome	13 (1)	0 (1)	2	1 (1)	16 (3)

Thursday November 14
DYNAMO ZAGREB (h)
Uefa Cup, 2nd rnd, 2nd leg
Won 2-1 (win 5-1 on agg) HT 0-0 Att **7,700**
Van der Sar — Finnan, Melville, Goma, Brevett — Goldbaek, Clark (Djetou 73), Legwinski, Inamoto (Malbranque 64) — Sava (Marlet 60), Boa Morte *Subs not used* Taylor, Ouaddou, Wome, Stolcers
Scorers **Malbranque 89, Boa Morte 90**
Referee L Duhamel (France)

Trailing to Olic's 52nd-minute header, Fulham save face — and their unbeaten European record — when Malbranque, a substitute, levels with a minute to go and still finds time to create the winner for Boa Morte.

Sunday November 17
BIRMINGHAM CITY (a)
Drew 0-0 HT 0-0 Att **26,164** Position **13th**
Van der Sar — Finnan, Melville, Goma, Brevett — Goldbaek (Inamoto 85), Clark, Legwinski (Djetou 60), Malbranque — Marlet, Boa Morte (Knight 71) *Subs not used* Taylor, Sava *Booked* Finnan *Sent off* Brevett 37, Marlet 79
Report page 189

Saturday November 23
LIVERPOOL (h)
Won 3-2 HT 2-0 Att **18,144** Position **12th**
Van der Sar — Finnan, Knight, Goma, Brevett — Goldbaek (Clark 90), Djetou, Davis, Malbranque — Sava (Inamoto 75), Marlet *Subs not used* Taylor, Wome, Stolcers *Booked* Goma, Brevett *Sent off* Goma 70
Scorers **Sava 5, 68, Davis 38**
Referee **G Poll**

Dudek's early handling error presents Fulham with their opener and Sava effectively decides the match on his own by deflecting Davis's shot past the Liverpool goalkeeper in between his two orthodox strikes. Baros pulls it back to 3-2 with four minutes to go, but Fulham's ten men hold on.

Tuesday November 26
HERTHA BERLIN (a)
Uefa Cup, 3rd rnd, 1st leg
Lost 2-1 HT 0-1 Att **14,477**
Van der Sar — Finnan, Melville, Goma, Brevett — Goldbaek (Boa Morte ht), Davis, Djetou, Malbranque (Inamoto 79) — Sava, Marlet *Subs not used* Taylor, Clark, Knight, Wome, Stolcers
Scorer **Marlet 53**
Referee D van Egmond (the Netherlands)

Fulham's first European defeat is definitely a case of unlucky thirteenth, Sava slicing in the decisive own goal after Marlet had cancelled out the opener from Beinlich, once of Aston Villa, who heads in from a corner.

Saturday November 30
BLACKBURN ROVERS (a)
Lost 1-2 HT 0-1 Att **21,096** Position **13th**
Van der Sar — Finnan, Melville, Goma, Brevett — Legwinski, Clark (Inamoto 59), Davis, Malbranque — Boa Morte, Marlet *Subs not used* Taylor, Sava, Djetou, Goldbaek *Booked* Finnan, Davis
Scorer **Marlet 60**
Report page 106

Wednesday December 4
WIGAN ATHLETIC (a)
Worthington Cup, 4th rnd
Lost 1-2 HT 0-2 Att **7,615**
Taylor — Leacock, Ouaddou, Knight (Davis ht), Wome — Inamoto, Clark, Djetou, Collins — Sava (Boa Morte ht),

Stolcers *Subs not used* Herrera, Goldbaek, Hudson
Booked Inamoto, Ouaddou
Scorer **Boa Morte 86**
Referee **M Halsey**

The second division leaders claim their third
Premiership scalp, after West Brom and Manchester
City, when Ellington punishes Fulham's shambolic
first-half defensive display. Having made ten changes to
his team, Jean Tigana can do little to rectify matters.

Saturday December 7
LEEDS UNITED (h)
Won 1-0   HT 1-0   Att **17,494**   Position **12th**
Van der Sar — Finnan, Melville, Djetou, Brevett —
Goldbaek, Davis, Legwinski, Wome — Boa Morte,
Malbranque *Subs not used* Taylor, Inamoto, Knight,
Willock, Stolcers *Booked* Davis, Legwinski, Wome
Scorer **Djetou 10**
Referee **P Durkin**

With four frontline strikers missing, Fulham are happy
enough to find a winner from Djetou, the centre half,
who heads his first goal for the club from Wome's
corner. It is Leeds's fourth successive league defeat and
Robinson prevents a heavier one with an outstanding
display in goal.

Thursday December 12
HERTHA BERLIN (h)
Uefa Cup, 3rd rnd, 2nd leg
Drew 0-0 (lose 2-1 on agg)   HT 0-0   Att **15,161**
Taylor — Finnan, Melville, Goma, Brevett (Goldbaek 71)
— Malbranque, Davis (Inamoto 62), Djetou (Legwinski
ht), Wome — Marlet, Boa Morte *Subs not used* Clark,
Knight, Herrera, Willock *Booked* Goma, Inamoto
Referee **P Collina (Italy)**

The better side throughout the second leg, Fulham go
out through a combination of poor finishing and a
masterly display by Kiraly, the Hungary keeper in baggy
tracksuit bottoms in the Hertha Berlin goal.

Sunday December 15
BIRMINGHAM CITY (h)
Lost 0-1   HT 0-1   Att **14,962**   Position **14th**
Van der Sar — Finnan, Melville (Clark 65), Goma, Brevett
— Legwinski, Davis, Djetou, Wome (Inamoto ht; Willock
51) — Boa Morte, Malbranque *Subs not used* Taylor,
Goldbaek *Booked* Malbranque, Brevett, Clark
Referee **A D'Urso**

Birmingham face a £25,000 fine after incurring seven of
the ten yellow cards brandished by Andy D'Urso, two of
them (plus the subsequent red one) being shown to
Purse, but they will think it a price worth paying for the
three points gained by Kirovski's early winner.

Saturday December 21
NEWCASTLE UNITED (a)
Lost 0-2   HT 0-1   Att **51,576**   Position **14th**
Van der Sar (Taylor 62) — Djetou, Melville, Goma,
Brevett — Goldbaek, Davis, Legwinski, Wome — Marlet,
Malbranque (Willock 77) *Subs not used* Collins, Knight,
Stolcers *Booked* Van der Sar, Brevett *Sent off* Wome 66
Report page 71

Thursday December 26
WEST HAM UNITED (a)
Drew 1-1   HT 0-0   Att **35,025**   Position **15th**
Taylor — Finnan, Melville, Goma, Brevett — Malbranque
(Goldbaek 78), Davis, Legwinski (Djetou 65), Wome —
Sava (Hammond 89), Marlet *Subs not used* Herrera,
Knight *Booked* Legwinski
Scorer **Sava 49**
Report page 251

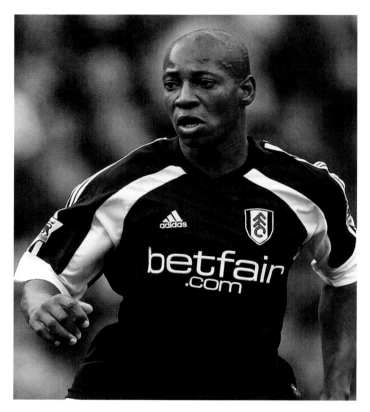

For every exciting attribute that Luis Boa
Morte boasts, critics will point to a frustrating
failure. Electric pace, but he cannot pass.
Breathtaking ball skills, but zero composure.
Passion coupled with appalling temperament.
But despite his weaknesses, his contribution
is immense. He can terrorise any defence in
the Premiership, as he proved when Sol
Campbell upended him in the penalty area
three times in a single match. As well as his
goals and the excitement he injects into a
game, he makes another contribution:
generating bookings, dismissals, free kicks
and penalties. Boa Morte's trickery secures
crucial points for Fulham.
Tim Miller

STATS AND FACTS

- Based on average attendances, Fulham had 2.87 points per thousand fans last season (48 points; 16,707 fans), the best ratio in the Premiership.

- Fulham's Premiership games featured 12 converted penalties, yet there had only been one in the previous season.

- Two strikers scored decisive own goals in November: Steve Marlet in the 1-0 home defeat by Arsenal and Facundo Sava in the 2-1 loss away to Hertha Berlin.

- Fulham's win over Liverpool was their first in 16 attempts.

- They have twice failed to win after building a two-goal lead in their past 180 matches, both times against Southampton.

- Fulham twice conceded a hat-trick in a pay-per-view match away from home this season: against Southampton (James Beattie) and Manchester United (Ruud van Nistelrooy).

- Fulham have not beaten Manchester United in their past 17 attempts.

- After going 347 matches without overcoming a two-goal deficit, dating back to 1996, Fulham did so twice in four games, drawing 2-2 away to Middlesbrough and beating Tottenham Hotspur 3-2 at home.

- Fulham have not won on their past 15 visits to Southampton.

- Between November and April Fulham scored four own goals (by Alain Goma, Steve Marlet, Rufus Brevett and Facundo Sava) and also benefited from four own goals by their opponents.

- Chris Coleman became only the second Welsh manager in the Premiership's 11-year history (Peter Shreeves, once of Sheffield Wednesday, was born in Neath).

Bill Edgar

GOALSCORERS

	Prem	FAC	WC	Euro	Total
L Boa Morte	2	-	1	2	5
L Clark	2	-	1	-	3
S Davis	3	-	-	1	4
M Djetou	1	-	-	-	1
B Goldbaek	-	1	-	-	1
J Harley	1	-	-	-	1
B Hayles	1	-	-	2	3
J Inamoto	2	-	-	4	6
S Legwinski	4	-	-	2	6
S Malbranque	6 (3p)	4 (2p)	-	3 (1p)	13 (6p)
S Marlet	4 (1p)	-	-	5	9 (1p)
L Saha	5 (2p)	1	-	1	7 (2p)
F Sava	5	1	-	-	6
A Stolcers	-	-	2	-	2
P Wome	1	-	-	-	1
Own goals	4	-	-	-	4

Saturday December 28
MANCHESTER CITY (h)
Lost 0-1 HT 0-0 Att **17,937** Position **16th**
Taylor — Finnan, Knight, Goma, Brevett — Goldbaek, Davis, Djetou (Legwinski 63), Malbranque (Hammond 76) — Sava, Marlet *Subs not used* Melville, Herrera, Wome
Referee **P Durkin**

Another defeat for Fulham but, more worryingly, doubts over whether the club will ever return to Craven Cottage mount as it is announced that a £100 million stadium redevelopment has been scrapped. Schmeichel's excellence and Anelka's 84th-minute goal earn the points for City.

Sunday January 5
BIRMINGHAM CITY (h)
FA Cup, 3rd rnd
Won 3-1 HT 2-0 Att **9,203**
Taylor — Finnan, Djetou, Goma, Harley — Goldbaek, Davis, Legwinski (Collins 76), Malbranque — Sava, Saha *Subs not used* Herrera, Melville, Willock, Hammond
Scorers **Sava 10, Goldbaek 23, Saha 46**
Referee **N Barry**

After the two league meetings had provoked much bad blood, an FA Cup tie produces a contest too one-sided to rouse passions, either on the pitch or among a poor crowd. Birmingham, with Dugarry, their new loan signing, unavailable, exit without a whimper.

Saturday January 11
BOLTON WANDERERS (a)
Drew 0-0 HT 0-0 Att **25,156** Position **16th**
Taylor — Finnan, Djetou, Goma, Brevett — Goldbaek, Davis, Legwinski, Malbranque — Sava (Boa Morte 65), Saha *Subs not used* Herrera, Melville, Collins, Hammond
Booked Sava, Finnan
Report page 240

Sunday January 19
MIDDLESBROUGH (h)
Won 1-0 HT 1-0 Att **14,253** Position **15th**
Taylor — Finnan, Djetou, Goma, Brevett — Goldbaek, Davis, Legwinski, Malbranque — Sava (Boa Morte 89), Marlet *Subs not used* Herrera, Melville, Collins, Hammond
Scorer **Davis 39**
Referee **M Halsey**

With around 200 protesters outside the ground demanding Fulham's return to Craven Cottage, Davis's neat finish in a dreary first half is followed by a goalless but much more exciting second period, after which Middlesbrough's dire away form prompts condemnation of his own team by Steve McClaren.

Sunday January 26
CHARLTON ATHLETIC (h)
FA Cup, 4th rnd
Won 3-0 HT 0-0 Att **12,203**
Taylor — Djetou (Knight 85), Melville, Goma, Harley — Malbranque (Goldbaek 88), Davis, Legwinski, Boa Morte — Sava, Marlet *Subs not used* Herrera, Inamoto, Hammond
Scorer **Malbranque 59, 65 (pen), 87 (pen)**
Referee **P Durkin**

The Englishmen trying to catch Sven-Goran Eriksson's eye are upstaged by a Frenchman, Malbranque settling this tie with a hat-trick. The last two are penalties, conceded by Young and Fish, with Fish paying for his foul on Sava with a red card as Charlton exit ingloriously.

Wednesday January 29
MANCHESTER CITY (a)
Lost 1-4 HT 1-1 Att 33,260 Position 15th
Taylor — Finnan, Djetou, Goma, Brevett — Legwinski —
Goldbaek, Davis, Malbranque — Marlet, Boa Morte *Subs
not used* Herrera, Melville, Inamoto, Sava, Harley
Booked Boa Morte
Scorer **Malbranque 2**
Report page 145

Saturday February 1
ARSENAL (a)
Lost 1-2 HT 1-1 Att 38,050 Position 15th
Taylor — Finnan, Djetou, Goma, Harley — Legwinski
(Melville 10) — Malbranque, Davis, Boa Morte — Marlet,
Sava (Saha 69) *Subs not used* Goldbaek, Herrera,
Wome *Booked* Melville
Scorer **Malbranque 29**
Report page 61

Saturday February 8
ASTON VILLA (h)
Won 2-1 HT 2-1 Att 17,092 Position 15th
Taylor — Finnan, Melville, Goma, Harley — Malbranque,
Djetou, Davis, Boa Morte (Goldbaek 82) — Saha (Sava
87), Marlet (Knight 70) *Subs not used* Herrera, Inamoto
Booked Melville
Scorers **Malbranque 14 (pen), Harley 36**
Referee **S Dunn**

Barry (three goals in three games) and Malbranque (six
in four) keep their scoring streaks going, but it is a first
goal for the club — a spectacular, swerving, 35-yard
strike from Harley — that allows Fulham to come from
behind and edge out improving Villa.

Sunday February 16
BURNLEY (h)
FA Cup, 5th rnd
Drew 1-1 HT 1-1 Att 13,062
Taylor — Finnan, Melville, Goma, Harley — Goldbaek
(Marlet ht), Djetou, Davis, Malbranque — Saha, Sava
(Inamoto 72) *Subs not used* Herrera, Ouaddou, Wome
Scorer **Malbranque 45**
Referee **G Poll**

Having disposed of two Premiership teams in the FA
Cup, Fulham find Burnley, from the Nationwide League,
a far harder proposition, especially after Alan Moore
gives the visiting team the lead. They need Malbranque,
with an expert volley just before half time, to keep their
— and his — run going.

Wednesday February 19
WEST BROMWICH ALBION (h)
Won 3-0 HT 0-0 Att 15,799 Position 14th
Taylor — Finnan, Melville, Goma (Ouaddou 44), Wome —
Marlet, Djetou, Inamoto, Malbranque (Stolcers 90) —
Saha, Sava *Subs not used* Herrera, Goldbaek, Leacock
Booked Djetou
Scorers **Saha 72, Wome 74, Malbranque 76 (pen)**
Referee **U Rennie**

Albion are bewitched by more Malbranque magic. After
Hughes misses easily the best early chance, the
Frenchman tees up Saha for the opener, rolls a free
kick into Wome's path for No 2 and finally converts a
penalty for the third, all in the space of four dramatic
minutes.

Monday February 24
TOTTENHAM HOTSPUR (a)
Drew 1-1 HT 1-1 Att 34,704 Position 15th
Taylor — Finnan, Ouaddou, Djetou (Knight 13), Wome —
Malbranque, Legwinski, Davis, Boa Morte — Sava
(Herrera 39), Marlet (Saha 18) *Subs not used* Inamoto,

LUIS BOA MORTE
Midfield
Born August 4, 1977, Lisbon
Ht 5ft 10in **Wt** 11st 5lb
Signed from Southampton, July
2000, £1.7m

RUFUS BREVETT
(see West Ham United)

LEE CLARK
Midfield
Born October 27, 1972,
Wallsend
Ht 5ft 8in **Wt** 11st 7lb
Signed from Sunderland, July
1999, £3m

JOHN COLLINS
Midfield
Born January 31, 1968,
Galashiels
Ht 5ft 7in **Wt** 10st 10lb
Signed from Everton, July 2000,
£2m

SEAN DAVIS
Midfield
Born September 20, 1979,
Clapham
Ht 5ft 10in **Wt** 12st 0lb
Signed from trainee, July 1998

MARTIN DJETOU
Defender
Born December 15, 1972,
Abidjan, Ivory Coast
Ht 6ft 2in **Wt** 12st 6lb
Signed from Parma (loan), July
2002

STEVE FINNAN
Defender
Born April 20, 1976, Limerick
Ht 5ft 10in **Wt** 11st 6lb
Signed from Notts County,
November 1998, £600,000

BJARNE GOLDBAEK
Midfield
Born October 6, 1968,
Nykobing, Denmark
Ht 5ft 10in **Wt** 12st 4lb
Signed from Chelsea, January
2000, £500,000

ALAIN GOMA
Defender
Born October 5, 1972,
Sault, France
Ht 6ft 0in **Wt** 13st 0lb
Signed from Newcastle United,
March 2001, £4m

ELVIS HAMMOND
Forward
Born October 6, 1980,
Accra, Ghana
Ht 5ft 10in **Wt** 10st 10lb
Signed from trainee, July 1999

Lee Clark

JON HARLEY
Defender
Born September 26, 1979, Maidstone
Ht 5ft 9in **Wt** 10st 3lb
Signed from Chelsea, August 2001, £3.5m

BARRY HAYLES
Forward
Born May 17, 1972, Lambeth
Ht 5ft 9in **Wt** 13st 0lb
Signed from Bristol Rovers, November 1998, £2.1m

MARTIN HERRERA
Goalkeeper
Born September 13, 1970, Cordoba
Ht 6ft 2in **Wt** 11st 8lb
Signed from Alaves, July 2002, free

MARK HUDSON
Defender
Born March 30, 1982, Guildford
Ht 6ft 3in **Wt** 12st 5lb
Signed from trainee, August 2000

JUNICHI INAMOTO
Midfield
Born September 18, 1979, Kagashima, Japan
Ht 5ft 11in **Wt** 11st 13lb
Signed from Arsenal (loan), July 2002

ZAT KNIGHT
Defender
Born May 2, 1980, Solihull
Ht 6ft 6in **Wt** 13st 8lb
Signed from Rushall Olympic, February 1999, free

DEAN LEACOCK
Defender
Born June 10, 1984, Croydon
Ht 12ft 2in **Wt** 6st 2lb
Signed from trainee, August 2001

SYLVAIN LEGWINSKI
Midfield
Born October 6, 1973, Clermont-Ferrand, France
Ht 6ft 3in **Wt** 11st 7lb
Signed from Bordeaux, August 2001, £3.5m

STEED MALBRANQUE
Midfield
Born January 6, 1980, Mouscron, Belgium
Ht 5ft 8in **Wt** 11st 7lb
Signed from Lyons, August 2001, £5m

STEVE MARLET
Forward
Born January 10, 1974, Pithiviers, France
Ht 5ft 11in **Wt** 11st 5lb
Signed from Lyons, September 2001, £13.5m

Barry Hayles

Harley *Booked* Boa Morte, Wome *Sent off* Taylor 39
Scorer **King 15 (og)**
Report page 158

Wednesday February 26
BURNLEY (a)
FA Cup, 5th rnd replay
Lost 0-3   HT 0-2   Att 11,635
Taylor — Finnan, Djetou, Melville, Harley — Malbranque (Wome 57), Legwinski, Davis, Boa Morte (Sava 39) — Inamoto — Saha (Ouaddou 57) *Subs not used* Herrera, Stolcers *Booked* Legwinski *Sent off* Davis 49
Referee **P Dowd**

Another match, another dismissal: having turned down the chance to put back the fixture for a week, Fulham exit the FA Cup in their second match in 48 hours, with a quarter-final against Watford up for grabs, well beaten by Burnley. To add to Jean Tigana's chagrin, Davis is sent off for a reckless challenge on Grant.

Saturday March 1
SUNDERLAND (h)
Won 1-0   HT 0-0   Att 16,286   Position 12th
Taylor — Finnan, Djetou, Melville, Harley — Malbranque (Stolcers 70), Legwinski, Inamoto (Ouaddou 60), Wome — Saha, Sava (Hammond 73) *Subs not used* Herrera, Leacock *Booked* Harley
Scorer **Saha 85**
Referee **E Wolstenholme**

Sunderland must know the game is up now. The better side, they create chances for Kilbane, Flo and Phillips, miss the lot and see a point snatched from them five minutes from time when Saha meets a cross from Stolcers as Fulham complete their third match in six days. Nine days later, Howard Wilkinson is dismissed.

Saturday March 15
SOUTHAMPTON (h)
Drew 2-2   HT 1-0   Att 18,031   Position 12th
Herrera — Ouaddou, Melville, Goma, Harley — Malbranque, Legwinski, Djetou, Wome (Inamoto ht; Stolcers 84) — Saha, Marlet *Subs not used* Thompson, Sava, Leacock *Booked* Wome
Scorers **Saha 44, M Svensson 52 (og)**
Referee **P Durkin**

Speculation over Jean Tigana's future increases, but the Fulham manager has to take a back seat to the Southampton goalkeeper as Niemi steals the show. A couple of brilliant saves cannot prevent Fulham going 2-0 up, but after Beattie's header halves the deficit, Niemi goes up for a last-ditch corner and creates the equaliser for Michael Svensson — scorer earlier of an own goal — when he volleys against the bar.

Saturday March 22
MANCHESTER UNITED (a)
Lost 0-3   HT 0-1   Att 67,706   Position 13th
Taylor — Ouaddou, Melville, Knight, Harley — Malbranque, Legwinski, Djetou, Boa Morte — Saha, Marlet *Subs not used* Herrera, Inamoto, Clark, Sava, Wome *Booked* Melville
Report page 51

Monday April 7
BLACKBURN ROVERS (h)
Lost 0-4   HT 0-2   Att 14,017   Position 13th
Taylor — Finnan, Knight, Goma, Harley — Malbranque, Clark (Legwinski 61), Djetou, Boa Morte — Saha, Marlet (Hammond 61) *Subs not used* Herrera, Melville, Sava
Referee **G Poll**

In the first match since he was told that Fulham would not be renewing his contract in the summer, Jean

Tigana sees his side produce what he describes as the worst performance in his time at the club. Hakan Sukur takes most advantage for Blackburn, who score four times in 19 minutes either side of the interval.

Saturday April 12
LIVERPOOL (a)
Lost 0-2 **HT 0-1** Att **42,120** Position **15th**
Taylor — Finnan, Melville, Djetou, Wome (Ouaddou 57) — Davis, Legwinski — Marlet (Sava 78), Malbranque, Boa Morte (Hammond 67) — Saha *Subs not used* Herrera, Clark *Booked* Boa Morte, Wome
Report page 99

Saturday April 19
NEWCASTLE UNITED (h)
Won 2-1 **HT 0-1** Att **17,900** Position **14th**
Taylor — Finnan, Melville, Djetou, Harley — Malbranque (Hayles 79), Legwinski, Clark, Davis, Boa Morte (Collins 90) — Saha (Hammond 17) *Subs not used* Herrera, Knight *Booked* Finnan
Scorers **Legwinski 69, Clark 86**
Referee **D Gallagher**

Two days earlier, Jean Tigana's status had changed from serving notice to sacked and Fulham profit immediately when a side now in the temporary care of Chris Coleman come from behind to beat Newcastle thanks to Legwinski's long-range special and Clark's late winner. Newcastle have Griffin sent off for two cautions.

Tuesday April 22
LEEDS UNITED (a)
Lost 0-2 **HT 0-1** Att **37,220** Position **16th**
Taylor — Finnan, Melville, Djetou (Knight 9), Harley — Inamoto (Hayles ht), Legwinski, Davis, Boa Morte — Clark — Hammond *Subs not used* Herrera, Sava, Collins *Booked* Hayles, Boa Morte
Report page 220

Saturday April 26
CHELSEA (a)
Drew 1-1 **HT 0-1** Att **40,792** Position **15th**
Taylor — Finnan, Melville, Goma, Harley — Malbranque (Hayles 83), Davis — Legwinski, Clark, Boa Morte (Collins 83) — Hammond *Subs not used* Van der Sar, Knight, Sava *Booked* Boa Morte, Clark
Scorer **Boa Morte 66**
Report page 88

Saturday May 3
EVERTON (h)
Won 2-0 **HT 2-0** Att **18,385** Position **15th**
Taylor — Finnan, Melville, Goma, Harley — Legwinski, Davis — Malbranque (Hayles 87), Clark, Boa Morte — Hammond (Saha 69) *Subs not used* Van der Sar, Knight, Collins *Booked* Hayles
Scorers **Stubbs 34 (og), Wright 43 (og)**
Referee **G Barber**

Fulham secure their Premiership safety as Everton self-destruct, Stubbs lobbing his own goalkeeper, who then fumbles in Malbranque's free kick at the near post. The clamour for Chris Coleman to be given the Fulham manager's job on a permanent basis increases.

Sunday May 11
CHARLTON ATHLETIC (a)
Won 1-0 **HT 1-0** Att **26,108** Position **14th**
Taylor — Finnan, Melville, Goma, Harley — Legwinski, Davis (Hayles 82) — Malbranque, Clark, Boa Morte (Collins 88) — Saha (Hammond 90) *Subs not used* Van der Sar, Djetou *Booked* Legwinski, Malbranque, Harley
Scorer **Saha 33 (pen)**
Report page 184

ANDY MELVILLE
Defender
Born November 29, 1968, Swansea
Ht 6ft 0in **Wt** 13st 10lb
Signed from Sunderland, July 1999, free

ABDESLAM OUADDOU
Defender
Born November 1, 1978, Morocco
Ht 6ft 3in **Wt** 12st 5lb
Signed from Nancy, France, August 2001, £2m

LOUIS SAHA
Forward
Born August 8, 1978, Paris
Ht 5ft 11in **Wt** 11st 10lb
Signed from Metz, June 2000, £2.1m

FACUNDO SAVA
Forward
Born July 3, 1974, Ituzaingo, Argentina
Ht 6ft 1in **Wt** 13st 1lb
Signed from Gimnasia y Esgrima La Plata, Argentina, May 2202, £2m

ANDREJS STOLCERS
Midfield
Born July 8, 1974, Latvia
Ht 5ft 10in **Wt** 11st 4lb
Signed from Shakhtar Donetsk, December 2000, £2m

MAIK TAYLOR
Goalkeeper
Born September 4, 1971, Hildesheim, Germany
Ht 6ft 4in **Wt** 14st 2lb
Signed from Southampton, November 1997, £800,000

EDWIN VAN DER SAR
Goalkeeper
Born October 29, ,1970, Leiden, the Netherlands
Ht 6ft 5in **Wt** 13st 6lb
Signed from Juventus, August 2001, £5m

CALUM WILLOCK
Forward
Born October 29, 1981, London
Ht 5ft 11in **Wt** 12st 7lb
Signed from trainee, July 2000

PIERRE WOME
Defender
Born March 26, 1979, Douala, Cameroon
Ht 5ft 8in **Wt** 12st 2lb
Signed from Bologna (loan), August 2002

Edwin van der Sar

LEEDS UNITED

PREMIERSHIP

	P	W	D	L	F	A	Pts
Man Utd	38	25	8	5	74	34	83
Arsenal	38	23	9	6	85	42	78
Newcastle	38	21	6	11	63	48	69
Chelsea	38	19	10	9	68	38	67
Liverpool	38	18	10	10	61	41	64
Blackburn	38	16	12	10	52	43	60
Everton	38	17	8	13	48	49	59
Southampton	38	13	13	12	43	46	52
Man City	38	15	6	17	47	54	51
Tottenham	38	14	8	16	51	62	50
Middlesbro	38	13	10	15	48	44	49
Charlton	38	14	7	17	45	56	49
Birmingham	38	13	9	16	41	49	48
Fulham	38	13	9	16	41	50	48
Leeds	**38**	**14**	**5**	**19**	**58**	**57**	**47**
Aston Villa	38	12	9	17	42	47	45
Bolton	38	10	14	14	41	51	44
West Ham	38	10	12	16	42	59	42
West Brom	38	6	8	24	29	65	26
Sunderland	38	4	7	27	21	65	19

FA CUP
Quarter-finals

WORTHINGTON CUP
Third round

UEFA CUP
Third round

Peter Ridsdale found that it was time to go

THE GAMES

Saturday August 17
MANCHESTER CITY (h)
Won 3-0   **HT 2-0**   Att **40,195**   Position **2nd**
Robinson — Mills, Radebe, Matteo, Harte — Bowyer,
Bakke, Barmby (Seth Johnson 78) — Smith, Viduka
(Keane 70), Kewell *Subs not used* Kelly, Martyn,
Dacourt *Booked* Bowyer
Scorers **Barmby 15, Viduka 45, Keane 80**
Referee **G Poll**

Life after O'Leary and Ferdinand begins with a flourish
for Leeds, who open the campaign with a decisive — if
flattering — victory as Terry Venables gets the better of
Kevin Keegan and Manchester City in the first of dozens
of meetings between former England managers in the
Premiership.

Saturday August 24
WEST BROMWICH ALBION (a)
Won 3-1   **HT 1-0**   Att **26,618**   Position **1st**
Robinson — Mills, Woodgate (Radebe 61), Matteo,
Harte — Bowyer, Bakke, Barmby — Smith, Viduka,
Kewell (Keane 83) *Subs not used* Martyn, Kelly,
Dacourt *Booked* Woodgate
Scorers **Kewell 39, Bowyer 52, Viduka 70**
Report page 258

Wednesday August 28
SUNDERLAND (h)
Lost 0-1   **HT 0-0**   Att **39,929**   Position **4th**
Robinson — Mills, Radebe, Matteo, Harte — Bowyer,
Bakke (Dacourt 55), Barmby (Keane 55) — Smith,
Viduka, Kewell *Subs not used* Kelly, Martyn, Woodgate
Booked Bowyer, Dacourt
Referee **M Halsey**

Top of the table as they take the pitch, Leeds are
booed off it after Phillips heads down for McAteer to
hit the only goal, 28 seconds into the second half, for
Sunderland's first win at Elland Road in 41 years.
Leeds are denied a clear late penalty when Gray
barges Viduka over.

Saturday August 31
BIRMINGHAM CITY (a)
Lost 1-2   **HT 0-1**   Att **27,164**   Position **4th**
Robinson — Mills, Woodgate, Matteo, Harte — Bowyer,
Bakke (Dacourt 60), Barmby — Smith, Kewell — Viduka
Subs not used Martyn, Kelly, Wilcox, Duberry *Booked*
Bowyer, Bakke, Viduka
Scorer **Bowyer 50**
Report page 186

Wednesday September 11
NEWCASTLE UNITED (a)
Won 2-0   **HT 1-0**   Att **51,730**   Position **3rd**
Robinson — Mills, Woodgate, Matteo, Harte — Smith,
Dacourt, Bowyer, Barmby — Viduka (Bakke 85), Kewell
Subs not used Martyn, Kelly, Radebe, Okon *Booked*
Mills, Smith
Scorers **Viduka 5, Smith 87**
Report page 67

THE MOST ENDURING IMAGE from a season of fractured hopes
was that of Peter Ridsdale admitting that he had chased a dream as
he sat beside an increasingly gnarled Terry Venables at an Elland
Road press conference. It was as close as the erstwhile chairman
came to removing his head from the sand, but he was still
maintaining a Canute-like stance as he exited the club, broken by a
thousand soundbites and a £79 million debt, the field of dreams long
since despoiled by the feet of departing heroes.

Ridsdale was not the first scapegoat of the *annus horribilis* as
supporters struggled to understand the club's bathetic descent from
high expectations to low farce. Venables, the manager who had
breezed into the club with a pink shirt and permatan the previous
summer, was sacked in March. He cast around for excuses, wondering whether his friendship with George Graham may have been
held against him by fans, but the truth was less sinister. Leeds were
in freefall and Venables's cover of tactical genius had been blown.

The grim reality was that, even after all the sales, Leeds had a
squad that included nine of those who had started the second leg of
the European Cup semi-final two years earlier. But from the heady
swagger of audacious victories over AC Milan and Lazio, Leeds were
reduced to a pallid shroud, lapsing into self-pity, denial and, ultimately, relegation trouble. By the end of a torturous campaign, the blame
culture was deeply embedded.

It was as if the trauma of the previous three years, from the
murders of two fans in Istanbul to the trials of Lee Bowyer and
Jonathan Woodgate, complete with all the attendant bile and
prejudice, had finally taken its toll. This was more than just a bad
season; it was a damning indictment of Ridsdale's tainted love. The
late victory away to Arsenal that ensured survival and denied the
Gunners the championship was merely a nostalgic nod to better
days and it was hard to see Leeds recovering for many years.

None but the most prescient could have foretold the disasters
that lay ahead in August. Leeds won their opening two games and,
despite a couple of defeats, recovered to beat Manchester United
and Newcastle United.

Thereafter the season plunged into disappointment and despair.
Woodgate, Bowyer, Robbie Keane, Robbie Fowler and Olivier
Dacourt all followed Rio Ferdinand out. Venables plundered the
departure lounge for mitigating circumstances, but only Ferdinand,
Woodgate and Dacourt were truly missed. Of that triumvirate,
Ferdinand was intent on leaving, while Dacourt, the midfield
linchpin, had been recklessly discarded by Venables.

Everywhere Leeds looked they encountered problems. Bowyer

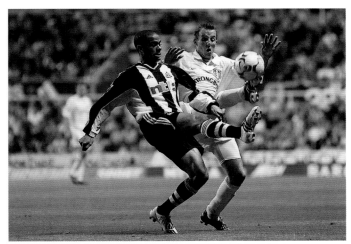

Victory at St James' Park in September was a misleading portent

refused to accept an apology from Ridsdale over comments made regarding his character and sought a move. The air was thick with irony as Bowyer invoked a point of principle and support for him waned as his lung-busting surges from midfield were replaced by demob apathy. One of the most important players of Leeds' recent past ended the season struggling to get into a West Ham United side bound for the Nationwide League.

Woodgate, by contrast, left against his will as the full scale of Leeds's myopic gamble became clear. Failure to reach the Champions League in successive seasons meant the dream faded, but still money was frittered away by boardroom fantasists. Only the outcry that followed the sale of Woodgate, one of "the untouchables", made the board appreciate the fallout from their hopeful punt.

It did not stop there. David Batty, probably the most popular player at the club post-Revie, threatened to sue Ridsdale for comments made regarding his fitness. Venables's refusal to let Batty play with the reserves meant the midfielder became a *cause celebre*, but the saga faded to footnote status when he struggled to make an impression under the more responsive Reid.

Whatever the rights and wrongs of the Batty issue, it was just another mess for a club that was imploding. That Sheffield United put them out of both domestic cup competitions was evidence of the decline, while defeat in the Uefa Cup was accompanied by the gruesome sights of the luckless Michael Bridges succumbing to another injury and the ghoulish Bowyer stamping on a Spanish head.

After three managers in ten years, Leeds had had three in ten months, Reid's eight-game rescue mission gaining him the job on a permanent basis. Ridsdale, Venables, Bowyer, Woodgate and O'Leary had all played their parts in killing hopes and ensuring that Leeds finished the season chasing shadows of former glories. The beastly team was back in what Dickens called the "beastly city".

Saturday September 14
MANCHESTER UNITED (h)
Won 1-0   HT 0-0   Att 39,622   Position 2nd
Robinson — Mills, Woodgate, Matteo (Radebe ht), Harte — Smith, Dacourt, Bowyer, Barmby (Bakke ht) — Viduka (McPhail 72), Kewell *Subs not used* Kelly, Martyn *Booked* Harte, Smith
Scorer **Kewell 67**
Referee **J Winter**

Manchester United's worst Premiership start is confirmed when Kewell's header sends Leeds back to the top of the table, if only for three hours. Ferdinand is upstaged by Woodgate on his much-hyped return to Elland Road and both Beckham (for an apparent elbowing offence on Bowyer) and Barthez (for tossing a water bottle into the crowd) come under severe media scrutiny.

Thursday September 19
METALURG ZAPORIZHZHYA (h)
Uefa Cup, 1st rnd, 1st leg
Won 1-0   HT 0-0   Att 30,000
Robinson — Kelly, Woodgate, Radebe, Harte — Bowyer, Bakke, Dacourt (McPhail 65), Kewell — Viduka (Bridges 65), Smith *Subs not used* Martyn, Mills, Okon, Burns, McMaster *Booked* Dacourt
Scorer **Smith 80**
Referee **M Vuoreia (Finland)**

They may not have been able to pronounce the name of their opponents, but Leeds are able to beat the Ukrainians thanks to the arrival of Bridges for the forward's first match in two injury-filled, frustrating years. Fifteen minutes after his arrival, the substitute powers to the byline and crosses for Smith to score the only goal.

Sunday September 22
BLACKBURN ROVERS (a)
Lost 0-1   HT 0-1   Att 25,415   Position 5th
Robinson — Mills, Woodgate, Radebe, Harte (Kelly 64) — Bowyer, Bakke, Dacourt (McPhail 64), Barmby — Viduka (McMaster 64), Smith *Subs not used* Okon, Martyn *Booked* Barmby, Smith
Report page 103

Saturday September 28
ARSENAL (h)
Lost 1-4   HT 0-2   Att 40,199   Position 7th
Robinson — Kelly, Radebe (Duberry 90), Matteo, Mills — Bowyer, Dacourt (McPhail ht), Bakke — Smith, Kewell — Viduka *Subs not used* Martyn, Harte, Barmby *Booked* Bowyer, Bakke, Smith, Dacourt
Scorer **Kewell 84**
Referee **A Wiley**

The records continue to tumble to Arsenal: 47 league matches with a goal and 23 away games without defeat, plus a share of Manchester United's mark of 29 Premiership matches unbeaten. Kelly's error precedes Kanu's opener, and it is downhill for Leeds after that.

Thursday October 3
METALURG ZAPORIZHZHYA (a)
Uefa Cup, 2nd rnd, 2nd leg
Drew 1-1 (win 2-1 on agg)   HT 0-1   Att 7,000
Robinson — Kelly, Mills, Matteo (Duberry 90), Harte
— Bakke, McPhail — Barmby — Bowyer, Smith, Kewell
Subs not used Martyn, Viduka, Okon, Burns, Dacourt,
McMaster
Scorer **Barmby 77**
Referee **M Bosat (Turkey)**

Viduka is dropped for the first time in his Leeds career,
but after Modebadze's header levels the tie on
aggregate, Barmby gets the goal that takes Leeds
through to the third round. Terry Venables is full of
praise for the outstanding performance of McPhail in
midfield.

Sunday October 6
ASTON VILLA (a)
Drew 0-0   HT 0-0   Att 33,505   Position 9th
Robinson — Mills, Woodgate, Matteo, Harte — Barmby,
McPhail (Viduka 67), Bakke — Bowyer, Smith, Kewell
Subs not used Martyn, Kelly, McMaster, Lucic
Booked Mills
Report page 225

Saturday October 19
LIVERPOOL (h)
Lost 0-1   HT 0-0   Att 40,187   Position 10th
Robinson — Mills, Woodgate, Lucic, Harte — Bowyer,
McPhail (Dacourt 75), Bakke — Barmby — Smith (Viduka
56), Kewell *Subs not used* Duberry, Kelly, Martyn
Booked Harte
Referee **S Dunn**

With Everton beating Arsenal, Liverpool go top for the
first time this season with a winner manufactured in
Senegal, Diouf setting up Diao in the 66th minute. After
a third home league defeat, the Elland Road crowd
begins to turn on Terry Venables, with chants for his
predecessor, David O'Leary.

Saturday October 26
MIDDLESBROUGH (a)
Drew 2-2   HT 1-1   Att 34,723   Position 10th
Robinson — Mills, Woodgate, Radebe, Lucic — Bowyer,
McPhail (Bakke 82), Barmby — Kewell — Viduka
(Bridges 82), Smith *Subs not used* Martyn, Kelly,
Dacourt *Booked* Smith, Viduka *Sent off* Smith 76
Scorers **Viduka 11 (pen), Bowyer 56**
Report page 165

Thursday October 31
HAPOEL TEL-AVIV (h)
Uefa Cup, 2nd rnd, 1st leg
Won 1-0   HT 0-0   Att 31,867
Robinson — Kelly, Woodgate, Radebe, Harte — Bakke,
Dacourt (McPhail 65), Barmby (Bridges 70) —
Kewell — Viduka (Mills 90), Smith *Subs not used*
Martyn, Duberry, McMaster, Singh *Booked* Radebe,
Bakke, Smith
Scorer **Kewell 82**
Referee **J van Hulten (the Netherlands)**

A first victory in seven matches eases the pressure at
Elland Road, though Leeds leave it late before Kewell
runs on to Smith's overhead kick and volleys in
emphatically against the team that eliminated Chelsea
the previous season.

MATCH OF THE SEASON

Hapoel Tel-Aviv 1   Leeds United 4
The Artemio Franchi Stadium, Thursday November 14 2002
Rick Broadbent in Florence

Alan Smith celebrates his four-goal solo demolition of Hapoel Tel-Aviv

LOVE HIM OR LOATHE him, you cannot ignore Alan Smith. Branded a "foul-mouthed thug" and a "provocateur" by Hapoel Tel-Aviv's players in the build-up to this game, the striker responded by scoring four times as Leeds United cantered into the Uefa Cup third round. You could almost taste his revenge.

Hapoel's pre-match assault on Smith's character was always fraught with danger. A maelstrom of passion and purpose with a peroxide rinse, he is one player who does not need additional motivation. By the end of this battle on neutral ground, it was Hapoel who were rewriting the book of cynicism, indulging in dives and petulant swipes at their nemesis. Josef Abukasis earned the red card that his frustration had rendered inevitable after picking up a second booking for dissent and only ambivalent officiating by the Austrian referee saved others from following suit.

Smith wallowed in his success. Although Hapoel's harping had been unwarranted, he knows that he is sometimes his own worst enemy. But when the raw rage is kept bubbling beneath the surface, he is indispensable. Having never scored a hat-trick for Leeds, this was sweet vindication.

Smith had been sufficiently concerned by Hapoel's comments to call a meeting with Peter Ridsdale, the Leeds chairman. "I wanted to know that if something did happen then I would have the full backing of the club," he said, explaining the thumbs-up he raised to the directors' box at full time. "It was just about my discipline and the chairman and gaffer [Terry Venables] told me not to let it wind me up. There is no better way to show them."

It had all started ominously, though, with Leeds conceding a goal after only 70 seconds. Shorn of three quarters of their regular back four, one wondered how they would settle against a side that had exhibited an adventurous streak in the first leg. Abukasis's unerring 25-yard free kick plucked at their nerves. For half an hour, Leeds struggled. They passed and probed but created little, while the rusty limbs of the makeshift pairing of Michael Duberry and Lucas Radebe wavered on the edge of further embarrassment.

Cue Smith. His first strike sent his team-mates smiling into the comfort zone and, with Hapoel now needing to score three, the pressure lifted.

Harry Kewell stuttered towards his true ability and Ian Harte, so often the brunt of terrace angst, had an assured game. Venables could even blood two of the club's promising youngsters. Matthew Kilgallon and Frazer Richardson made their debuts, although the injury sustained by the indomitable Radebe is a concern.

Leeds had other problems in the opening stages. Even without

Report page 249

Sunday November 3
EVERTON (h)
Lost 0-1 **HT 0-0** Att **40,161** Position **13th**
Robinson — Mills, Woodgate, Radebe, Lucic (Harte ht) — Bowyer, Bakke, Barmby — Smith (McMaster 81), Viduka (Bridges 68), Kewell *Subs not used* Martyn, Kelly *Booked* Bowyer, Barmby, Lucic
Referee **N Barry**

Rooney, the Boy Wonder, having just turned 17, celebrates with another superb strike, beating Bakke and Radebe before firing past Robinson within five minutes of his introduction to Everton's attack. It is the only goal, though Robinson's agility stands between Leeds and a heavier defeat.

Wednesday November 6
SHEFFIELD UNITED (a)
Worthington Cup, 3rd rnd
Lost 1-2 **HT 1-0** Att **26,663**
Robinson — Mills, Woodgate (Duberry 63), Lucic, Harte — Barmby, Bakke (McPhail 70), Bowyer, Wilcox (Bridges 77) — Viduka, Kewell *Subs not used* Martyn, Kelly *Booked* Mills, Kewell
Scorer **Yates 24 (og)**
Referee **J Winter**

Seemingly easing through to the fourth round courtesy of Yates's own goal, Leeds are stunned by two goals in the four minutes of stoppage time allowed, from Jagielka and Ndlovu. Mounted police are deployed as the celebrations of their Yorkshire rivals threaten to run out of control.

Sunday November 10
WEST HAM UNITED (a)
Won 4-3 **HT 4-1** Att **33,297** Position **10th**
Robinson — Kelly, Lucic, Radebe, Harte — Barmby, Bowyer, Bakke, Wilcox (Milner 85) — Viduka (Bridges 77), Kewell (McPhail 90) *Subs not used* Martyn, Duberry *Booked* Bowyer, Bakke, Viduka
Scorers **Barmby 11, Kewell 28, 41, Viduka 45**
Report page 249

Thursday November 14
HAPOEL TEL-AVIV (a*)
Uefa Cup, 2nd rnd, 2nd leg
Won 4-1 (win 5-1 on agg) **HT 1-1** Att **3,000**
(*in Florence)
Robinson — Kelly (Richardson 65), Duberry, Radebe (Kilgallon 62), Harte — Barmby, Bakke (McPhail 55), Bowyer, Wilcox — Smith, Kewell *Subs not used* Martyn, Bridges, Burns, McMaster *Booked* Barmby, Wilcox
Scorer **Smith 30, 54, 62, 83**
Referee **F Stuchlik (Austria)**

Even the Israeli side have to admit that Smith can be a devastating finisher, as his four-goal haul — the first hat-trick of his Leeds career — turns a potentially fraught evening on neutral soil in Florence into a stroll.

Sunday November 17
BOLTON WANDERERS (h)
Lost 2-4 HT 1-1 Att 36,627 Position 10th
Robinson — Kelly, Woodgate, Lucic (Duberry 80), Wilcox — Barmby, McPhail (Milner 67), Burns, Kewell — Smith, Viduka *Subs not used* Martyn, Bridges, Richardson
Booked Kewell, Burns
Scorers **Smith 4, Kewell 84**
Referee **A Wiley**

Chants of "Venables out" greet this defeat to the Premiership's bottom club, the fifth at home for Leeds in the league. Twice behind, a weakened team finally have no answer when Bolton score twice in stoppage time, through a penalty by Ricketts and the goal of the game from Pedersen, who nets with a sumptuous volley.

Sunday November 24
TOTTENHAM HOTSPUR (a)
Lost 0-2 HT 0-2 Att 35,718 Position 14th
Robinson — Woodgate, Bakke, Lucic — Kelly, Bowyer, McPhail, Burns (Viduka 37; Milner 82), Wilcox — Kewell, Smith *Subs not used* Martyn, Duberry, Richardson
Booked Bakke, Wilcox, Burns, Kewell, McPhail, Smith, Bowyer
Report page 154

Thursday November 28
MALAGA (a)
Uefa Cup, 3rd rnd, 1st leg
Drew 0-0 HT 0-0 Att 35,000
Robinson — Kelly, Woodgate, Duberry, Harte — Bowyer, Bakke, McPhail, Wilcox — Smith, Kewell *Subs not used* Burns, Martyn, Richardson, Bridges, Kilgallon, Okon
Booked Smith
Referee **O Trentalange (Italy)**

Smith and Kewell miss the best chances to round off in style a solid display in which Woodgate is outstanding, but Smith is also lucky that, having been booked for a foul on Romero, he escapes further punishment for a lunging challenge on Contreras, the Malaga goalkeeper.

Sunday December 1
CHARLTON ATHLETIC (h)
Lost 1-2 HT 1-0 Att 35,537 Position 16th
Robinson — Kelly, Woodgate, Duberry, Harte — Bowyer (Fowler 81), Bakke, McPhail (Bridges 81), Wilcox — Smith, Kewell *Subs not used* Martyn, Lucic, Mills
Booked Wilcox
Scorer **Kewell 42**
Referee **A D'Urso**

Ahead through Kewell's stunning finish, Leeds are condemned to their fifth successive home league defeat when Lisbie's first goal of the season, ten minutes from time, is followed by Parker's in the last few seconds past a slalom run past three defenders. Charlton are buoyant; Leeds are in their lowest position since November 1996.

Saturday December 7
FULHAM (a)
Lost 0-1 HT 0-1 Att 17,494 Position 16th
Robinson — Kelly, Woodgate, Duberry, Harte (Mills 73) — Bakke, Okon, McPhail (Milner 57), Wilcox — Smith (Fowler ht), Bridges *Subs not used* Martyn, Lucic
Booked Bakke, Fowler, Woodgate, Wilcox
Report page 204

Pini Balili, the striker who had been so effective at Elland Road, Hapoel carved Leeds apart on several occasions. Omri Affek rattled the bar with a left-foot drive with the score at 1-1 and Duberry looked like a man who had not started a game since March.

Abukasis was the catalyst for Hapoel's best work with his thoughtful use of the ball and surging breaks, but by the end he had departed, Leeds were rampant and Venables heaped praise on his hero for the turnaround. "We know he has got to look at certain areas, but he has and sometimes your reputation can go ahead of you," he said.

"To see Alan score four was wonderful, but he has got to deliver performances like that on a consistent basis." Equally pleasing was the way that Leeds reacted after conceding such an early goal. "So many teams could have dropped their heads, but the way they responded was great," Venables said. "I keep saying our performances have been getting better. People have doubted that, but we have an excellent spirit here." Eight goals in two games and the fact that a string of first-teamers were absent last night should fuel such optimism.

Inevitably it was Smith who changed the atmosphere in Fiorentina's sparsely populated stadium. A neat one-two with Bakke saw him burst into the penalty area and his low, angled drive crashed in off a post. Leeds were as good as home. An Exocet by Harte against the bar suggested that there was more to come; Smith delivered. After 56 minutes he scored a goal that highlighted the tenacity that makes him such a favourite of Sven-Goran Eriksson, the England head coach. With Shavit Elimelech, the goalkeeper, favourite to reach a ball close to the byline, Smith chased what seemed a lost cause and prodded the ball goalwards. It spun inches over the line before it was hacked away. Seven minutes later, Smith completed his hat-trick. Kewell floated a delicious ball across the box and, although Elimelech parried Smith's header, the 22-year-old nonchalantly stabbed home the rebound.

The 2,000 travelling fans lapped it all up, embracing their cult hero by chanting his name throughout. Smith, however, was not finished and he nodded home a fourth. In one game he had scored more times than he had managed all season and delivered the perfect riposte to Hapoel's dissenters.

HAPOEL TEL-AVIV (4-4-2): S Elimelech — R Halis, A Domb, S Gershon, Y Hillel —O Affek (sub: B Luz, 46min), J Abukasis, G Halmai, S Toema — S Clescenko (sub: K Udi, 46), A Knafo (sub: P Balili, 62). **Substitutes not used:** G Salem, K Saban, A Halfon, S Abutbul. **Booked:** Abukasis. **Sent off:** Abukasis.
LEEDS UNITED (4-4-2): P Robinson — G Kelly (sub: F Richardson, 65), L Radebe (sub: M Kilgallon, 62), M Duberry, I Harte — N Barmby, L Bowyer, E Bakke (sub: S McPhail, 55), J Wilcox — A Smith, H Kewell. **Substitutes not used:** N Martyn, M Bridges, J Burns. **Booked:** Wilcox.
Referee: F Stuchlik (Austria).

THE MANAGER

Terry Venables

Did he have the rug pulled from under his feet or was his cover of tactical guru finally blown? The debate continues but there are grains of truth in both schools of thought. Venables lost a string of first-team players as Leeds's financial mismanagement extended to rented goldfish, but the rump of the squad should have been too good to become embroiled in a relegation battle. "It didn't look like this in the brochure," Venables said, but the Leeds supporters might have said the same thing, having been sold the idea that the Cockney charmer would take the club back into the Champions League.

Rick Broadbent

APPEARANCES

	Prem	FAC	WC	Euro	Total
E Bakke	31 (3)	3 (1)	1	6	41 (4)
N Barmby	16 (3)	0 (2)	1	3	20 (5)
L Bowyer	15	-	1	5	21
R Bravo	5	1	-	-	6
M Bridges	1 (4)	-	0 (1)	1 (2)	2 (7)
J Burns	2	-	-	-	2
O Dacourt	4 (3)	-	-	2	6 (3)
M Duberry	11 (3)	1 (1)	0 (1)	3 (1)	15 (6)
R Fowler	2 (6)	0 (1)	-	0 (1)	2 (8)
I Harte	24 (3)	3	1	5	33 (3)
Seth Johnson	3 (6)	3 (1)	-	-	6 (7)
Simon Johnson	1 (3)	-	-	-	1 (3)
R Keane	0 (3)	-	-	-	0 (3)
G Kelly	24 (1)	4	-	6	34 (1)
H Kewell	31	4	1	5	41
M Kilgallon	0 (2)	-	-	0 (1)	0 (3)
T Lucic	16 (1)	2 (1)	1	-	19 (2)
D Matteo	20	3	-	1	24
J McMaster	0 (4)	-	-	-	0 (4)
S McPhail	7 (6)	-	0 (1)	2 (3)	9 (10)
D Mills	32 (1)	4	1	2 (1)	39 (2)
J Milner	1 (17)	0 (4)	-	-	1 (21)
P Okon	15	5	-	1	21
P Robinson	38	5	1	6	50
L Radebe	16 (3)	4	-	3	23 (3)
F Richardson	-	-	-	0 (1)	0 (1)
A Smith	33	4	-	6	43
M Viduka	29 (4)	4	1	2	36 (4)
J Wilcox	23 (2)	4	1	3	31 (2)
J Woodgate	18	1	1	4	24

Thursday December 12
MALAGA (h)
Uefa Cup, 3rd rnd, 2nd leg
Lost 1-2 (lose 1-2 on agg) **HT 1-1** Att **34,123**
Robinson — Mills, Woodgate, Duberry, Kelly — Bowyer, Bakke, Okon, Wilcox — Smith, Bridges (Fowler 9) *Subs not used* Martyn, Harte, Radebe, McPhail, Seth Johnson, Kilgallon *Booked* Bowyer, Smith
Scorer **Bakke 23**
Referee **M Busacca (Switzerland)**

Was this Leeds's nadir? Disgraced by the actions of a supporter, who runs on to the pitch and confronts Terry Venables in the dugout, and by Bowyer's stamp on Gerardo's head, having already been deprived of Bridges when the ill-fated forward ruptures his Achilles tendon, they are finally eliminated by a double from Dely Valdes, the Malaga man's winner coming ten minutes from time.

Monday December 16
BOLTON WANDERERS (a)
Won 3-0 **HT 2-0** Att **23,378** Position **16th**
Robinson — Mills, Woodgate, Lucic, Harte — Kelly, Bakke, Okon, Wilcox — Kewell — Fowler (Seth Johnson 79) *Subs not used* Martyn, Bowyer, Duberry, Milner *Booked* Mills, Harte, Okon
Scorers **Mills 12, Fowler 16, Wilcox 75**
Report page 238

Saturday December 21
SOUTHAMPTON (h)
Drew 1-1 **HT 0-0** Att **36,687** Position **16th**
Robinson — Mills, Woodgate, Lucic, Harte — Kelly, Smith, Okon, Wilcox — Fowler (Viduka 53), Kewell *Subs not used* Martyn, Seth Johnson, Duberry, Milner
Scorer **Kewell 73**
Referee **C Foy**

Though they are denied a rare home win by a freak late goal, a 40-yard free kick from Fernandes bouncing past Robinson in the 89th minute, Leeds can have no real complaints. Both sides hit the woodwork, but Southampton have strong claims for a penalty turned down while a goal by Marsden is wrongly ruled out for offside.

Thursday December 26
SUNDERLAND (a)
Won 2-1 **HT 0-1** Att **44,029** Position **14th**
Robinson — Kelly, Mills, Lucic, Harte (Duberry 59) — Smith (Milner 36), Bakke, Okon, Wilcox — Viduka (Fowler 77), Kewell *Subs not used* Martyn, Seth Johnson *Booked* Viduka
Scorers **Milner 51, Fowler 80 (pen)**
Report page 275

Saturday December 28
CHELSEA (h)
Won 2-0   HT 2-0   Att **40,122**   Position **13th**
Robinson — Kelly, Mills, Woodgate, Lucic — Smith,
Bakke (Seth Johnson 80), Okon, Wilcox — Viduka
(Fowler 83), Kewell (Milner 31) *Subs not used* Martyn,
Duberry *Booked* Smith, Okon
Scorers **Woodgate 30, Milner 45**
Referee **G Barber**

Chelsea's 11-match unbeaten league run is ended
emphatically as Claudio Ranieri makes it 13 team
changes in two games and sees his side well beaten.
The outstanding Woodgate heads the opener, but all
the talk is about Milner, the 16-year-old Leeds
substitute, who caps a wonderfully mature display with a
brilliant second.

Wednesday January 1
BIRMINGHAM CITY (h)
Won 2-0   HT 1-0   Att **40,034**   Position **11th**
Robinson — Kelly, Mills, Woodgate, Harte — Smith,
Bakke (Milner 73), Okon, Wilcox — Viduka, Kewell
Subs not used Martyn, Seth Johnson, Duberry, Fowler
Booked Smith
Scorers **Bakke 6, Viduka 67**
Referee **P Dowd**

The Leeds revival continues with headers from Bakke
and Viduka against a weakened Birmingham side who
have reasonable claims for two penalties (for fouls on
Devlin and Morrison) rejected. Terry Venables later
dismisses speculation that Fowler is about to be
transferred.

Saturday January 4
SCUNTHORPE UNITED (a)
FA Cup, 3rd rnd
Won 2-0   HT 1-0   Att **8,329**
Robinson — Kelly, Mills, Woodgate, Matteo — Smith,
Bakke (Milner 78), Okon, Wilcox (Seth Johnson 86) —
Viduka, Kewell (Fowler 84) *Subs not used* Martyn,
Harte
Scorers **Viduka 32 (pen), Bakke 68**
Referee **A Wiley**

Leeds refuse to go the way of Everton, who are beaten
by Shrewsbury Town on the same afternoon, although
it is against the run of play when Viduka's penalty puts
them ahead. Bakke, who earns the spot kick, later
profits from Viduka's persistence to kill brave
Scunthorpe off.

Saturday January 11
MANCHESTER CITY (a)
Lost 1-2   HT 0-1   Att **34,884**   Position **12th**
Robinson — Kelly, Mills, Woodgate, Matteo — Smith
(Milner 61), Bakke (Fowler 72), Okon, Wilcox — Viduka
(Seth Johnson 72), Kewell *Subs not used* Martyn, Lucic
Booked Mills, Matteo Kewell, Johnson
Scorer **Kewell 90**
Report page 144

PLAYER OF THE SEASON   Harry Kewell

Reports in Australia claimed that Kewell
and Mark Viduka, his Socceroo sidekick,
did not speak off the pitch, but there were
few signs of any communication problems
on it. After disappointing the previous year,
Kewell returned to something like his
mercurial best. Whether as a front-line
striker under Venables or as a fleet-footed
winger under Reid, Kewell was the shining
light in the immutable gloom. Possibly
the greatest natural talent ever to play for
the club, Kewell scored memorable
goals against Manchester United,
Arsenal and England in a season of
rejuvenation.
Rick Broadbent

STATS AND FACTS

● Having already provided the first goal in the reigns of Glenn Hoddle (against Moldova) and Sven-Goran Eriksson (against Spain) for England, Nick Barmby was the first scorer of the Terry Venables era at Leeds United (against Manchester City).

● Leeds's defeat by Everton on November 2 was their first in 37 league games at home to the Merseyside club, dating back to 1951.

● Leeds played only once on a Saturday at 3pm between the opening day of the season and December 7.

● Leeds went 20 matches without a draw until their Uefa Cup match against Metalurg Zaporizhzhya finished 1-1.

● Alan Smith has been dismissed eight times in his career. Alan Smith, the former Arsenal striker, was never sent off and booked once.

● Tottenham Hotspur like years that end in a 1, and Leeds decline in seasons that end with a 3. Having slumped from being champions in 1992 to finishing seventeenth in 1993, their fifth place in 2002 has deteriorated to fifteenth in 2003.

● Alan Smith was sent off twice this season at St Mary's Stadium — for Leeds against Southampton and for England against Macedonia.

● Despite finishing sixth from bottom, Leeds scored 11 more away goals than in the previous season, when they finished in fifth place.

● Arsenal beat Sunderland at Highbury in October to end Peter Reid's reign as manager of the North East club, but Reid gained revenge when his Leeds United side won at Highbury in May to end Arsenal's title challenge.

Bill Edgar

GOALSCORERS

	Prem	FAC	WC	Euro	Total
E Bakke	1	2	-	1	4
N Barmby	4	-	-	1	5
L Bowyer	3	-	-	-	3
R Fowler	2 (1p)	-	-	-	2 (1p)
I Harte	2 (1p)	-	-	-	2 (1p)
Seth Johnson	1	1	-	-	2
R Keane	1	-	-	-	1
G Kelly	-	1	-	-	1
H Kewell	14	-	-	1	15
T Lucic	1	-	-	-	1
D Mills	1	-	-	-	1
J Milner	2	-	-	-	2
A Smith	3	1	-	5	9
M Viduka	20 (3p)	2 (1p)	-	-	22 (4p)
J Wilcox	1	-	-	-	1
J Woodgate	1	-	-	-	1
Own goals	1	-	1	-	2

Saturday January 18
WEST BROMWICH ALBION (h)
Drew 0-0   HT 0-0   Att **39,708**   Position **11th**
Robinson — Kelly, Radebe, Matteo, Lucic — Bakke (Seth Johnson 69), Okon (Fowler 78), Wilcox (Milner 69) — Smith, Kewell — Viduka *Subs not used* Martyn, Mills
Booked Smith
Referee **U Rennie**

Fowler is back in the Leeds ranks after the plug is pulled on his £7 million move to Maine Road, but that is all there is to cheer fans in a sterile contest. Albion are reduced to ten men by the dismissal of Johnson after his protests at the failure to punish Radebe's handball with a penalty.

Saturday January 25
GILLINGHAM (a)
FA Cup, 4th rnd
Drew 1-1   HT 0-0   Att **11,093**
Robinson — Kelly, Radebe, Matteo, Lucic — Bakke, Smith, Okon, Wilcox — Viduka, Kewell *Subs not used* Martyn, Harte, Duberry, Fowler, Milner *Booked* Matteo
Sent off Viduka 81
Scorer **Smith 49**
Referee **N Barry**

Sven-Goran Eriksson travels to Kent to run the rule over Leeds's three Australians before England's forthcoming friendly at Upton Park and sees one of them — Viduka — sent off for an elbow-first challenge on Hessenthaler, the Gillingham player-manager. Almost immediately, Sidibe cancels out Smith's excellent free kick opener to force a replay.

Tuesday January 28
CHELSEA (a)
Lost 2-3   HT 1-0   Att **39,738**   Position **13th**
Robinson — Kelly, Matteo, Mills, Lucic — Smith, Bakke, Okon (Seth Johnson 68), Wilcox — Viduka (Milner 80), Kewell *Subs not used* Martyn, Harte, Radebe
Booked Bakke
Scorers **Kewell 18, Lucic 66**
Report page 85

Saturday February 1
EVERTON (a)
Lost 0-2   HT 0-0   Att **40,153**   Position **13th**
Robinson — Kelly, Matteo (Radebe 71), Mills, Lucic (Harte ht) — Smith, Bakke (Milner 79), Okon, Wilcox — Viduka, Kewell *Subs not used* Martyn, Seth Johnson
Booked Bakke
Report page 121

Tuesday, February 4
GILLINGHAM (h)
FA Cup, 4th rnd replay
Won 2-1   HT 1-0   Att **29,359**
Robinson — Mills, Radebe (Duberry 32), Matteo (Milner 76), Harte — Okon — Kelly, Seth Johnson, Wilcox — Bakke, Viduka *Subs not used* Martyn, Burns, Simon Johnson
Scorers **Viduka 11, Bakke 58**
Referee **M Dean**

A better day for troubled Leeds, with Smith's signature on a new contract followed by victory over Gillingham, although there is a nervy ending when Ipoua scores with four minutes to go and Hessenthaler misses a decent chance soon afterwards. A small number among a poor crowd continue their anti-board protests after the match.

Saturday February 8
WEST HAM UNITED (h)
Won 1-0   HT 1-0   Att 40,126   Position 13th
Robinson — Mills, Duberry, Matteo (Kilgallon 90), Bravo — Kelly, Okon, Seth Johnson, Wilcox — Bakke (McMaster 90), Milner *Subs not used* Martyn, Harte, Barmby *Booked* Okon, Bravo
Scorer **Johnson 20**
Referee **D Gallagher**

Leeds are without a recognised target man, but their supporters have a recognisable target for their vitriol: the returning Bowyer. They win thanks to a deflected goal from Johnson, his first for the club, and are aided by a typical West Ham implosion, Kanoute getting himself sent off for a retaliatory slap of the scorer's face.

Sunday February 16
CRYSTAL PALACE (a)
FA Cup, 5th rnd
Won 2-1   HT 1-1   Att 24,512
Robinson — Mills, Duberry, Radebe, Harte — Kelly, Okon (Milner 59), Seth Johnson, Wilcox — Smith (Lucic 85), Kewell (Barmby 75) *Subs not used* Martyn, Kilgallon *Booked* Kewell, Johnson, Duberry
Scorers **Kelly 33, Kewell 73**
Referee **D Gallagher**

As good as their goals are, Kelly hitting the target for the first time in six years with a quickly taken free kick and Kewell finishing a fine run with a vicious shot, Leeds need a huge slice of luck when, after Gray's equaliser, Black's close-range shot goes over the line off Duberry's arm before being cleared, only for Palace to be denied either the goal they merit or the consolation prize of a penalty.

Saturday February 22
NEWCASTLE UNITED (h)
Lost 0-3   HT 0-1   Att 40,025   Position 14th
Robinson — Mills, Duberry, Radebe (Lucic 72), Bravo — Kelly, Okon (Barmby 71), Seth Johnson, Wilcox (Milner ht) — Smith, Kewell *Subs not used* Martyn, Harte
Referee **A Wiley**

Newcastle order Woodgate, their recent recruit from troubled Leeds, to stay away from Elland Road and it is a wise move as a heavy home defeat fuels supporters' anger. Dyer's all-action display is rewarded with Newcastle's opening two goals, his first of the season in the league.

Wednesday March 5
MANCHESTER UNITED (a)
Lost 1-2   HT 0-1   Att 67,135   Position 15th
Robinson — Mills, Radebe, Lucic, Harte — Kelly, Okon, Seth Johnson, Bravo (McPhail 86) — Barmby (Milner 86) — Viduka *Subs not used* Cansdell-Sherriff, Kilgallon, Martyn *Booked* Smith
Scorer **Viduka 64**
Report page 50

THE PLAYERS

EIRIK BAKKE
Midfield
Born September 13, 1977, Sogndal, Norway
Ht 6ft 2in **Wt** 12st 9lb
Signed from Sogndal, July 1999, £1m

NICK BARMBY
Midfield
Born February 11, 1974, Hull
Ht 5ft 7in **Wt** 11st 3lb
Signed from Liverpool, August 2002, £2.75m

LEE BOWYER
(see West Ham United)

RAUL BRAVO
Defender
Born April 14, 1981, Gandia, Spain
Ht 5ft 9in **Wt** 11st 2lb
Signed from Real Madrid (loan), January 2003

MICHAEL BRIDGES
Forward
Born August 5, 1978, North Shields
Ht 6ft 1in **Wt** 12st 5lb
Signed from Sunderland, July 1999, £5m

JACOB BURNS
Midfield
Born April 21, 1978, Sydney
Ht 5ft 10in **Wt** 11st 11lb
Signed from Parramatta Power, Australia, August 2000, £250,000

OLIVIER DACOURT
Midfield
Born September 25, 1974, Montreuil-sous-Bois, France
Ht 5ft 9in **Wt** 11st 12lb
Signed from Lens, May 2000, £7.2m

MICHAEL DUBERRY
Defender
Born October 14, 1975, Enfield
Ht 6ft 1in **Wt** 13st 6lb
Signed from Chelsea, July 1999, £4m

ROBBIE FOWLER
(see Manchester City)

IAN HARTE
Defender
Born August 31, 1977, Drogheda
Ht 5ft 10in **Wt** 11st 8lb
Signed from trainee, December 1995

SETH JOHNSON
Midfield
Born March 12, 1979, Birmingham
Ht 5ft 10in **Wt** 11st 0lb
Signed from Derby County, October 2001, £7m

Nick Barmby

SIMON JOHNSON
Forward
Born March 9, 1983,
West Bromwich
Ht 5ft 9in **Wt** 11st 12lb
Signed from trainee, August 2002

ROBBIE KEANE
(see Tottenham Hotspur)

GARY KELLY
Defender
Born July 9, 1974, Drogheda
Ht 5ft 8in **Wt** 11st 8lb
Signed from Home Farm,
September 1991, free

HARRY KEWELL
Forward
Born September 22, 1978,
Sydney
Ht 5ft 11in **Wt** 11st 10lb
Signed from New South Wales
Academy, December 1995, free

MATTHEW KILGALLON
Defender
Born January 8, 1984, York
Ht 6ft 1in **Wt** 12st 4lb
Signed from trainee,
August 2002

TEDDY LUCIC
Defender
Born April 15, 1973,
Gothenburg
Ht 6ft 2in **Wt** 11st 9lb
Signed from AIK Solna (loan),
August 2002

DOMINIC MATTEO
Defender
Born April 24, 1974, Dumfries
Ht 6ft 1in **Wt** 11st 12lb
Signed from Liverpool, August
2000, £4.75m

JAMIE McMASTER
Midfield
Born November 29, 1982,
Sydney
Ht 5ft 10in **Wt** 11st 8lb
Signed from New South Wales
Academy, November 2002, free

STEPHEN McPHAIL
Midfield
Born December 9, 1979,
Westminster
Ht 5ft 10in **Wt** 12st 0lb
Signed from trainee, December
1996

DANNY MILLS
Defender
Born May 18, 1977, Norwich
Ht 5ft 11in **Wt** 11st 9lb
Signed from Charlton Athletic,
July 1999, £4m

Gary Kelly

Sunday March 9
SHEFFIELD UNITED (a)
FA Cup, 6th rnd
Lost 0-1 HT **0-0** Att **24,633**
Robinson — Mills, Radebe, Lucic, Harte (Milner 81)
— Smith, Seth Johnson, Okon (Barmby 81), Bravo
— Viduka, Kewell (Bakke ht) *Subs not used* Martyn,
Kilgallon *Booked* Mills, Radebe, Harte, Johnson
Referee **S Bennett**

"This is my finest hour," Neil Warnock proclaims after
his Sheffield United side eliminate their Yorkshire
neighbours from cup competition for the second time
this season, Kabba scoring the only goal of a scrappy
affair after Kewell blasts an easier chance over the bar
in the first half.

Saturday March 15
MIDDLESBROUGH (h)
Lost 2-3 HT **1-2** Att **39,073** Position **15th**
Richardson — Mills, Lucic, Radebe, Bravo — Barmby
(Milner 68), Okon, Bakke, Wilcox — Viduka, Smith
Subs not used Martyn, Harte, McMaster, Kilgallon
Booked Mills, Radebe, Okon
Scorer **Viduka 24, 76**
Referee **D Elleray**

Mistakes by Schwarzer in the Middlesbrough goal
present Viduka with two gifts, but the quality of the
finishing by Juninho and Geremi, who score with
delicious shots from outside the area, mean that Leeds
are chasing the game once Maccarone has equalised
from the penalty spot. Five days later, Terry Venables is
out of a job.

Sunday March 23
LIVERPOOL (a)
Lost 1-3 HT **1-2** Att **43,021** Position **16th**
Robinson — Mills, Lucic, Radebe, Bravo (Harte ht)
— Barmby (Milner ht), Okon (McMaster 78), Bakke,
Wilcox — Viduka, Smith *Subs not used* Batty, Martyn
Booked Bakke
Scorer **Viduka 44**
Report page 99

Saturday April 5
CHARLTON ATHLETIC (a)
Won 6-1 HT **3-1** Att **26,274** Position **14th**
Robinson — Mills, Radebe, Duberry, Harte — Kelly,
Matteo, Bakke (Milner 85), Kewell (Wilcox 80) — Viduka,
Smith (Simon Johnson 78) *Subs not used* Martyn,
Barmby *Booked* Matteo
Scorers **Kewell 12, 76, Harte 34 (pen),**
Viduka 42, 53, 56 (pen)
Report page 183

Saturday April 12
TOTTENHAM HOTSPUR (h)
Drew 2-2 HT **1-2** Att **39,560** Position **13th**
Robinson — Mills (Milner 63), Radebe, Bakke, Harte
(Wilcox 74) — Kelly, Matteo, Bakke, Kewell — Viduka,
Smith *Subs not used* Martyn, Barmby, Simon Johnson
Booked Bakke
Scorer **Viduka 31, 76 (pen)**
Referee **R Styles**

Leeds are well on top before Viduka gives them the
lead in the third match of Peter Reid's initial eight-game
tenure, his first at Elland Road. But they are behind and
struggling before the Australian gets his second from
the penalty spot after Keller's rash challenge on Kewell.
Leeds move one point and one place nearer safety, at
the same time damaging Tottenham's fading challenge
for a Uefa Cup place.

Saturday April 19
SOUTHAMPTON (a)
Lost 2-3   HT 0-2   Att 32,032   Position 16th
Robinson — Kelly, Mills (Barmby 56), Duberry, Harte
— Kewell, Matteo, Bakke, Wilcox — Viduka, Smith
Subs not used Martyn, Milner, Bravo, Simon Johnson
Booked Mills, Bakke, Viduka, Smith *Sent off* Smith 61
Scorers **Kewell 80, Barmby 90**
Report page 135

Tuesday April 22
FULHAM (h)
Won 2-0   HT 1-0   Att 37,220   Position 15th
Robinson — Mills, Duberry, Matteo, Harte — Kewell,
Kelly, Bakke, Wilcox — Viduka, Smith *Subs not used*
Martyn, Bravo, Barmby, Kilgallon, Simon Johnson
Scorer **Viduka 4, 49**
Referee **N Barry**

Leeds and Fulham swap positions near the basement,
but it is more than just Viduka's finishing — an
unmarked header and a goal on the follow-up — that is
the difference between the sides. Fulham are very poor
and it is they of the struggling teams who look most
likely to be dragged down into the bottom three with
three matches to go.

Saturday April 26
BLACKBURN ROVERS (h)
Lost 2-3   HT 1-1   Att 38,062   Position 16th
Robinson — Mills, Duberry, Matteo, Harte — Kelly, Bakke
(Simon Johnson 72), Wilcox — Kewell, Viduka, Smith
Subs not used Martyn, Radebe, Bravo, Barmby
Booked Duberry, Matteo
Scorers **Viduka 21, Smith 90**
Referee **P Durkin**

Leeds still cannot get clear of trouble, taking the lead
against Blackburn but finding themselves 3-1 down —
Todd getting Rovers' third, his first for the club — before
Smith's consolation. A tackle by Mills that goes
unpunished but leaves Gresko nursing three broken
bones in his foot angers the visiting camp.

Sunday May 4
ARSENAL (a)
Won 3-2   HT 1-1   Att 38,127   Position 16th
Robinson — Mills, Radebe, Duberry, Harte — Kelly,
Bakke, Matteo, Wilcox — Viduka, Kewell (Simon Johnson
80) *Subs not used* Martyn, Bravo, Barmby, Milner
Booked Viduka
Scorers **Kewell 5, Cole 48 (og), Viduka 88**
Report page 64

Sunday May 11
ASTON VILLA (h)
Won 3-1   HT 1-1   Att 40,205   Position 15th
Robinson — Mills (Barmby 70), Radebe, Duberry, Harte
— Kelly, Bakke (McPhail ht), Matteo (Kilgallon 87),
Wilcox — Viduka, Simon Johnson *Subs not used*
Martyn, Burns
Scorers **Harte 8, Barmby 81, Viduka 90**
Referee **M Halsey**

Viduka's fourteenth goal in ten league games adds a
gloss finish to a poor season for Leeds, who are slightly
flattered by their victory over a Villa side who also have
little to celebrate, though Gudjonsson will remember his
stunning first-half equaliser.

JAMES MILNER
Defender
Born January 4, 1986, Leeds
Ht 6ft 1in **Wt** 12st 2lb
Signed from trainee,
August 2001

PAUL OKON
Midfield
Born April 5, 1972, Sydney
Ht 5ft 11in **Wt** 11st 12lb
Signed from Watford, August
2002, free

LUCAS RADEBE
Defender
Born April 12, 1969,
Johannesburg
Ht 6ft 1in **Wt** 11st 9lb
Signed from Kaizer Chiefs,
South Africa, September 1994,
£250,000

PAUL ROBINSON
Goalkeeper
Born October 15, 1979,
Beverley
Ht 6ft 5in **Wt** 14st 7lb
Signed from trainee,
August 1997

FRAZER RICHARDSON
Defender
Born October 29, 1982,
Rotherham
Ht 5ft 11in **Wt** 11st 12lb
Signed from trainee,
August 2001

ALAN SMITH
Forward
Born October 28, 1980,
Rothwell
Ht 5ft 9in **Wt** 11st 10lb
Signed from trainee, March 1998

MARK VIDUKA
Forward
Born October 9, 1975,
Melbourne
Ht 6ft 2in **Wt** 13st 9lb
Signed from Celtic, July 2000,
£6m

JASON WILCOX
Midfield
Born July 15, 1971, Bolton
Ht 5ft 11in **Wt** 11st 10lb
Signed from Blackburn Rovers,
December 1999, £3m

JONATHAN WOODGATE
(see Newcastle United)

Mark Viduka

ASTON VILLA

PREMIERSHIP

	P	W	D	L	F	A	Pts
Man Utd	38	25	8	5	74	34	83
Arsenal	38	23	9	6	85	42	78
Newcastle	38	21	6	11	63	48	69
Chelsea	38	19	10	9	68	38	67
Liverpool	38	18	10	10	61	41	64
Blackburn	38	16	12	10	52	43	60
Everton	38	17	8	13	48	49	59
Southampton	38	13	13	12	43	46	52
Man City	38	15	6	17	47	54	51
Tottenham	38	14	8	16	51	62	50
Middlesbro	38	13	10	15	48	44	49
Charlton	38	14	7	17	45	56	49
Birmingham	38	13	9	16	41	49	48
Fulham	38	13	9	16	41	50	48
Leeds	38	14	5	19	58	57	47
Aston Villa	**38**	**12**	**9**	**17**	**42**	**47**	**45**
Bolton	38	10	14	14	41	51	44
West Ham	38	10	12	16	42	59	42
West Brom	38	6	8	24	29	65	26
Sunderland	38	4	7	27	21	65	19

FA CUP
Third round

WORTHINGTON CUP
Quarter-finals

Graham Taylor walked out of Villa Park with an attack on the board

THE GAMES

Sunday July 21
FC ZURICH (a)
InterToto Cup, 3rd rnd, 1st leg
Lost 0-2   HT 0-1   Att 4,560
Enckelman — Delaney, Dublin, Samuel, Wright — Stone, Boateng, Hitzlsperger (Hendrie 73), Barry (Kachloul 81) — Crouch, Boulding (Hadji 57) *Subs not used* Postma, Moore, Taylor, Ridgewell *Booked* Delaney, Samuel *Sent off* Samuel 82
Referee **F Meyer (Germany)**

After the shortest of summer breaks, Villa set off on the InterToto Cup trail at the third-round stage and not only lose to goals by Keita and Yasar, but also have Samuel sent off for a second bookable offence near the end.

Saturday July 27
FC ZURICH (h)
InterToto Cup, 3rd rnd, 2nd leg
Won 3-0 (win 3-2 on agg)   HT 1-0   Att 18,349
Enckelman — Delaney, Mellberg, Staunton, Barry — Hendrie, Taylor, Hitzlsperger — Boulding (Merson ht), Crouch, Allback (Moore 71) *Subs not used* Postma, Hadji, Balaban, Samuel, Ridgewell *Booked* Staunton
Scorers **Boulding 32, Allback 49, Staunton 77**
Referee **R Rosetti (Italy)**

Boulding, newly recruited from Grimsby Town, makes an immediate impact with the goal that sets in motion a tremendous second-leg fightback, Staunton venturing forward to complete the recovery 13 minutes from time. It proves to be a final appearance in a Villa shirt for Merson.

Wednesday July 31
LILLE (a)
InterToto Cup, semi-final, 1st leg
Drew 1-1   HT 0-0   Att 14,437
Postma — Delaney, Mellberg, Staunton, Samuel — Hadji (Vassell), Taylor, Hitzlsperger, Barry — Crouch, Allback (Stone) *Subs not used* Myhill, Wright, Boulding, Ridgewell, Moore *Booked* Samuel, Staunton
Scorer **Taylor 77**
Referee **M Sfiri (Croatia)**

Ahead through Taylor with only 13 minutes to go in France and looking to preserve a first-leg lead, Villa are stung when they concede an injury-time equaliser to D'Amico.

Wednesday August 7
LILLE (h)
InterToto Cup, semi-final, 2nd leg
Lost 0-2 (lose 3-1 on agg)   HT 0-1   Att 26,192
Enckelman — Mellberg, Dublin (Hendrie ht), Staunton — Delaney, Taylor (Hadji), Hitzlsperger, Barry — Vassell, Crouch (Moore 80), Allback *Subs not used* Postma, Boulding, Samuel, Ridgewell *Booked* Staunton, Taylor, Moore, Vassell
Referee **P Gomes Costa (Portugal)**

The week in which Merson (Portsmouth) and Boateng (Middlesbrough) depart for pastures new, Villa also depart the InterToto Cup when goals just before half-time and just after it, by Fahmi and Bonnal, earn Lille a deserved aggregate win.

FOR THE FIRST TIME SINCE the formation of the Premiership there were some special games for Villa fans to look out for when the fixtures were announced — the two derby games against Birmingham City and, as a bonus, a couple against West Bromwich Albion, too. West Midlands football was returning to its former glory, and Aston Villa would be standing proud as the top team come May. Or so they thought.

Derbies aside, there was not a great deal of excitement at Villa Park. By the time the season started the club had already been knocked out of the InterToto Cup by an average Lille side. George Boateng had followed the path that ambitious Villa players and coaches take to the Riverside Stadium (he would finish four points ahead of his previous employers) without being replaced.

The major summer signings, Marcus Allback and Ulises de la Cruz, were hardly the sort of players to sell season tickets. The feeling that Graham Taylor was building a team of workmanlike grinders was enhanced when Paul Merson left for Portsmouth — with him went all the team's creativity.

Still, Villa Park was full on the opening day, but then Liverpool were the visitors so it would be. For the first few games of the season Villa were overrun in midfield; Boateng, despite his limitations, was an excellent destructive midfielder and he was missed. Taylor attempted to rectify this by signing Mark Kinsella and Oyvind Leonhardsen, and it was at this point that Villa fans realised how far the club had fallen — a year earlier they were top of the table; now they were signing thirtysomething midfielders who were surplus to requirements at Charlton Athletic and Tottenham Hotspur.

Even after the average start to the season, Villa fans were not prepared for the shock that awaited them at St Andrew's on September 16. Despite the farcical nature of Birmingham City's second goal, when Peter Enckelman allowed a throw-in to roll past him into the net, the right team won. Birmingham played as a team, with passion and commitment, and Villa capitulated. This was perturbing, as Taylor's flair-free team could not match opponents who played with all the characteristics that he admires. Bizarre team selection, such as playing Ronny Johnsen in midfield that night, added to Villa's troubles. This was a problem all season — Taylor did not know his best side. Away to West Ham United in a crucial game in April, Villa started with three centre backs. This was not the usual formation, and the players were noticeably uncomfortable. Villa reverted to a back four when West Ham scored, which took all of 15 minutes.

This inconsistency in team selection was mirrored in results as Villa never managed to win more than two games in succession —

Gareth Barry, inspirational as ever in the victory over Blackburn Rovers

the pathetic record of one away win was matched only by Sunderland. What passed for a great run in January (winning 5-2 away to Middlesbrough and 3-0 at home to Blackburn Rovers) ignited false hope for the last third of the season. The arrival of Joey Gudjonsson, on loan from Real Betis, sparked this revival of sorts, but he quickly descended to the mediocre level of most of his team-mates, completing his fall with his sending off in the second Birmingham derby defeat. That was the one chance that Villa had to salvage some pride and they blew it spectacularly, with an indisciplined display that saw Dion Dublin precede Gudjonsson to the dressing-room for a headbutt on Robbie Savage and Enckelman hand Geoff Horsfield his second derby goal of the season. Taylor refused to speak to the press and he was right — nothing he could have said would have made up for being beaten twice by the Blues.

In what was a terrible season there were a few positives to give hope for the future. Gareth Barry played the best football of his career on the left side of midfield and there is a promising group of young players coming through — Villa won the FA Youth Cup in 2002 and Taylor gave debuts to five of those players this season, but it remains to be seen if they are going to save Villa. Having young prospects is like having games in hand — sometimes you would rather have the points. The regression of Lee Hendrie, booed off when he was substituted against Sunderland in the last home game of the season, is a sobering reminder of how few promising players become established first teamers.

It is doubtful if Villa will evolve while Doug Ellis remains entrenched in the boardroom, but the appointment of David O'Leary to succeed Taylor is a shrewd move. O'Leary's arrival offers some hope of improvement, but it remains to be seen whether he will have the resources to elevate Villa from their position as the second team in the second city.

Sunday August 18
LIVERPOOL (h)
Lost 0-1 HT 0-0 Att 41,183 Position 16th
Enckelman — Delaney, Mellberg, Alpay, Barry (Samuel 84) — Staunton — De La Cruz, Hendrie, Hitzlsperger (Hadji 76) — Crouch (Allback 64), Vassell *Subs not used* Postma, Boulding *Booked* Staunton, Alpay
Referee **A D'Urso**

Enckelman saves Owen's penalty after Riise's winner early in the second half, but Villa create little of note except for Staunton's shot against the crossbar. Banners criticising the club's supposed lack of ambition help to make for an unsettling start to Villa's Premiership campaign.

Saturday August 24
TOTTENHAM HOTSPUR (a)
Lost 0-1 HT 0-1 Att 33,494 Position 17th
Enckelman — Delaney, Mellberg, Staunton, Wright — De La Cruz (Allback ht) — Kinsella, Hendrie, Barry (Samuel 77) — Crouch (Angel ht), Vassell *Subs not used* Postma, Hadji
Report page 150

Wednesday August 28
MANCHESTER CITY (h)
Won 1-0 HT 0-0 Att 33,494 Position 13th
Enckelman — Delaney, Mellberg, Staunton, Wright (Samuel ht) — Hendrie, Kinsella, Barry — Angel (Allback 87), Crouch, Vassell *Subs not used* Hitzlsperger, Postma, De La Cruz *Booked* Barry
Scorer **Vassell 64**
Referee **D Pugh**

"We got off lightly. Five or six players went missing." Kevin Keegan goes on the attack after Manchester City's poor performance. Vassell makes amends for Crouch's string of misses by getting Villa's first league goal — and points — of the season.

Sunday September 1
BOLTON WANDERERS (a)
Lost 0-1 HT 0-0 Att 22,500 Position 16th
Enckelman — Delaney, Mellberg, Staunton, Wright (Samuel 63) — Hendrie, Kinsella, Angel (Allback 63), Crouch, Vassell (De La Cruz ht) *Subs not used* Hitzlsperger, Postma *Booked* Enckelman, Hendrie, Angel
Report page 234

Wednesday September 11
CHARLTON ATHLETIC (h)
Won 2-0 HT 0-0 Att 26,483 Position 9th
Enckelman — Mellberg, Alpay, Staunton — De La Cruz, Kinsella, Johnsen, Barry, Samuel — Allback (Moore 76), Angel (Crouch 88) *Subs not used* Postma, Hitzlsperger, Hendrie
Scorers **De La Cruz 70, Moore 83**
Referee **G Poll**

Back to 3-5-2 for Graham Taylor and Villa, who are denied by Kiely in the Charlton goal until De La Cruz pops up with his first goal for the club. Moore, a late substitute, then becomes an instant hit on his Premiership debut with the well-taken goal that seals victory.

Monday September 16
BIRMINGHAM CITY (a)
Lost 0-3   HT 0-1   Att **29,505**   Position **15th**
Enckelman — Mellberg, Alpay, Staunton — De La Cruz, Kinsella, Johnsen, Barry, Samuel — Allback (Dublin ht), Angel (Vassell ht) *Subs not used* Postma, Hendrie, Moore *Booked* Barry, Staunton, Alpay
Report page 187

Sunday September 22
EVERTON (h)
Won 3-2   HT 1-0   Att **30,023**   Position **10th**
Enckelman — Mellberg, Johnsen, Staunton — De La Cruz (Leonhardsen 75), Hendrie, Kinsella, Barry, Samuel — Crouch (Dublin 81), Vassell (Moore 81)
Subs not used Angel, Postma
Scorers **Hendrie 7, 48, Dublin 85**
Referee **J Winter**

Hendrie justifies his recall with two well-taken goals from midfield to put Villa in charge, but they need a scrambled late winner from Dublin, four minutes after coming on as a substitute, to take the points after Radzinski's fine shot and Campbell's header draw Everton level.

Saturday September 28
SUNDERLAND (a)
Lost 0-1   HT 0-0   Att **40,092**   Position **12th**
Enckelman — Mellberg, Johnsen, Staunton — Delaney (De La Cruz 77), Hendrie, Kinsella (Leonhardsen 86), Barry, Samuel — Dublin (Crouch 86), Vassell *Subs not used* Postma, Allback *Booked* Dublin, Hendrie, Staunton
Report page 271

Wednesday October 2
LUTON TOWN (h)
Worthington Cup, 2nd rnd
Won 3-0   HT 2-0   Att **20,833**
Enckelman — Mellberg, Johnsen, Staunton (Leonhardsen 68) — De La Cruz, Hendrie, Kinsella, Barry, Samuel — Dublin (Allback 82), Vassell (Moore ht) *Subs not used* Postma, Crouch
Scorers **De La Cruz 9, Dublin 25, 48**
Referee **C Webster**

Unlike many of their peers there is no dabbling with understrength, experimental sides in the Worthington Cup for Villa, who see off Nationwide League second division opposition with no alarms after De La Cruz sets them on their way. Dublin's second, a peach of a volley, is the pick of the goals.

MATCH OF THE SEASON

Middlesbrough 2   Aston Villa 5
Riverside Stadium, Tuesday January 28 2003
Martin Woods

ASTON VILLA SHED THEIR unenviable record of not having won away from home this season in a most appropriate manner when they defeated the only club in the Barclaycard Premiership with an unbeaten home record. Second-half goals from Gareth Barry, Darius Vassell and Dion Dublin secured an impressive victory after Villa had forfeited a two-goal lead in a first half replete with goalmouth incident and a goalkeeping blunder guaranteed a long shelf-life in the television archives.

Graham Taylor, the former England manager, and Steve McClaren, a putative national coach, are responsible for the two worst away records in the Premiership. That the culprits should provide a chilled Riverside Stadium crowd with a four-goal feast in the first half was, perversely, only to be expected. "Great credit to the players because after being two up we threw it away," Taylor said.

It was Middlesbrough, though, who were almost rewarded for their early enterprise when Jonathan Greening stabbed a shot just wide of Peter Enckelman's post after ten minutes. Szilard Nemeth then forced Enckelman to concede a corner in saving his stinging shot. Villa, however, were soon matching the home side with a series of composed attacks that culminated in Vassell's opening goal. "Playing the three forwards helped us," Taylor said.

Johannes Gudjonsson, signed from Real Betis this week, had blazed a shot inches over the crossbar a minute before Vassell cut past Stuart Parnaby, the full back, and calmly struck the ball into the right corner of Mark Schwarzer's net. Andrew Davies, an 18-year-old making his debut in the heart of the home defence in place of Gareth Southgate, who has flu, then made a brave tackle to deny Dublin. Gudjonsson then induced the comical error from Schwarzer when the Australia goalkeeper let his free kick from 35 yards through his hands and into the net.

The gift goal somehow galvanised McClaren's team and their response yielded two fine goals. First Massimo Maccarone dinked Joseph-Desire Job's headed flick over Enckelman into the net and, in their next attack, Jonathan Greening dribbled past a stunned defence before firing home. A game that had threatened to provide all the drama of a first-round InterToto Cup snooze now had the characteristics of a full-blooded cup tie.

The scoring frenzy recommenced 90 seconds into the second half when Barry, after an attack had broken down, found himself unmarked near the penalty spot. Thomas Hitzlsperger had intercepted the clearance and drove the ball into the area, where Barry not so much trapped the ball as failed to get out of its way

Vassell celebrates after scoring Villa's fourth goal, his second, at the Riverside

Sunday October 6
LEEDS UNITED (h)
Drew 0-0 **HT 0-0** Att **33,505** Position **14th**
Enckelman — Mellberg, Johnsen (Leonhardsen 13;
Angel ht), Staunton — De La Cruz, Hendrie, Kinsella,
Barry, Samuel — Dublin, Vassell *Subs not used* Postma,
Allback, Crouch *Booked* Vassell
Referee **M Halsey**

Villa enjoy the advantage in territory and possession,
but fail really to extend Robinson in the Leeds goal.
Bowyer, who learns later in the day that he has been
dropped by England for the European Championship
matches against Slovakia and Macedonia, wastes
Leeds's best chance.

Monday October 21
SOUTHAMPTON (h)
Lost 0-1 **HT 0-0** Att **25,817** Position **18th**
Enckelman — Mellberg, Alpay, Staunton — De La Cruz
(Hadji 58), Hendrie (Moore 83), Kinsella (Postma 47),
Barry, Samuel — Dublin, Vassell *Subs not used* Angel,
Leonhardsen *Booked* Hendrie, Staunton *Sent off*
Enckelman 46
Referee **S Bennett**

I don't like Mondays? After the nightmare of St
Andrew's, Enckelman suffers another televised calamity
when the Villa goalkeeper is harshly sent off for a foul
on Ormerod a few seconds into the second half, any
offence seemingly having been committed by Alpay.
The protests over, Beattie's penalty settles an otherwise
dull affair.

Saturday October 26
MANCHESTER UNITED (a)
Drew 1-1 **HT 1-0** Att **67,619** Position **11th**
Enckelman — Delaney, Mellberg, Staunton, Samuel —
Leonhardsen (Hitzlsperger 84), Taylor, Kinsella, Barry —
Dublin (Crouch 66), Moore (Angel 66) *Subs not used*
Postma, Allback
Scorer **Mellberg 35**
Report page 45

Sunday November 3
BLACKBURN ROVERS (a)
Drew 0-0 **HT 0-0** Att **23,004** Position **15th**
Enckelman — Delaney, Mellberg, Staunton, Samuel
— Leonhardsen, Taylor, Kinsella, Barry — Dublin
(Crouch 76), Angel (Moore 70) *Subs not used*
Hitzlsperger, Postma, Johnsen *Booked* Barry,
Moore
Report page 105

before sidefooting it home. "We got a little bit of good fortune with
our third goal because Thomas Hitzlsperger tried to score but it hit
Gareth [Barry]," Taylor said.

When Maccarone fell inside the area while tracked by Ronny
Johnsen just past the hour mark and sought a penalty, it was a first
sign of desperation by the home team, and the imperative to attack
regardless took its toll on the home defence.

Jlloyd Samuel curled a cross from the left flank into the area,
Vassell found the space to chest it down and shoot into the roof of
the net, then Dublin's headed goal from Barry's cross in the last
minute ended a move that seemed played out in slow motion.
Middlesbrough were spent but at least lost their record to a brace of
superior finishes from Vassell.

"It's very disappointing when you concede five goals," McClaren
said. "I've watched them again and there's a lot of mistakes. When
everything's going well it's OK, but when the chips are down you

Wednesday November 6
OXFORD UNITED (a)
Worthington Cup, 3rd rnd
Won 3-0 HT 0-0 Att 12,177
Postma — Delaney, Johnsen, Staunton, Samuel —
Leonhardsen (Angel ht), Taylor, Kinsella (Hitzlsperger
75), Barry — Dublin, Moore (Allback 87) *Subs not used*
Crouch, Henderson *Booked* Taylor
Scorers **Taylor 74, Barry 77, Dublin 86**
Referee **M Messias**

On the night that Arsenal, Spurs, Leeds and West Ham
are among those Premiership sides eliminated, Villa put
a dire first-half performance behind them to coast to
victory over Nationwide League third division opposition,
Taylor capitalising on a goalkeeping error to set them
on their way.

Saturday November 9
FULHAM (h)
Won 3-1 HT 1-0 Att 29,563 Position 13th
Enckelman — Delaney, Mellberg, Staunton (Johnsen
77), Samuel — Leonhardsen, Taylor, Kinsella
(Hitzlsperger 62), Barry — Dublin, Angel (Allback ht)
Subs not used Moore, Postma *Booked* Leonhardsen,
Taylor, Allback
Scorers **Angel 20, Allback 66, Leonhardsen 88**
Referee **A D'Urso**

Villa end their poor league run and inflict a fourth
successive Premiership defeat on Jean Tigana's side.
Angel's header gives Villa the lead and, after Boa
Morte's equaliser, Allback is introduced to restore the
advantage and set up Leonhardsen for a late third to
finish the contest.

Saturday November 16
WEST BROMWICH ALBION (a)
Drew 0-0 HT 0-0 Att 27,091 Position 13th
Enckelman — Delaney, Mellberg, Johnsen
(Staunton 39), Samuel (Hendrie 60) — Leonhardsen,
Taylor, Hitzlsperger, Barry — Dublin, Allback (Vassell 60)
Subs not used Postma, Angel *Booked* Barry, Taylor,
Johnsen
Report page 261

Saturday November 23
WEST HAM UNITED (h)
Won 4-1 HT 1-0 Att 33,279 Position 11th
Enckelman — Samuel, Mellberg, Staunton, Barry —
Leonhardsen, Taylor, Hendrie (Kinsella 85),
Hitzlsperger — Vassell (Allback 85), Dublin (Angel 85)
Subs not used Postma, Crouch *Booked* Dublin,
Staunton, Hitzlsperger
Scorers **Hendrie 29, Leonhardsen 59, Dublin 72,
Vassell 80**
Referee **C Foy**

Two months and several bad misses after hitting
Premiership goal No 99, Dublin reaches three figures
with the third goal in a comfortable win over struggling
West Ham, who are sent back to the bottom of the
table. Hendrie opens the floodgates with the first in an
expert display of finishing by Villa.

Dion Dublin turns to shoot as Middlesbrough become increasingly bedraggled

need your senior players. When we lose the likes of Ugo [Ehiogu]
and Gareth [Southgate] it hurts us. It's no excuse but we were very
young and inexperienced tonight. We always looked over our
shoulders even when we were in third place. We always knew where
reality was."

McClaren confirmed that the club is on the verge of signing
Malcolm Christie and Chris Riggott from Derby County but, given
their experience in trying to sign Seth Johnson from Leeds United,
he was reluctant to elaborate.

"We're not certain until that dotted line is signed," he said. "We
can't say anything until they're actually our players."

MIDDLESBROUGH (4-3-1-2): M Schwarzer — S Parnaby, A Davies, A Vidmar, F Queudrue — Geremi, G
Boateng, J Greening — J-D Job (D Murphy 69) — M Maccarone, S Nemeth. **Substitutes not used**: S
Downing, M Crossley, C Cooper, L Wilkshire. **Booked** Boateng.
ASTON VILLA (4-4-2): P Enckelman — M Delaney, O Mellberg, R Johnsen, J Samuel — S Moore (S
Staunton 78), T Hitzlsperger, J Gudjonsson (L Hendrie 89), G Barry — D Dublin, D Vassell. **Substitutes
not used**: S Postma, U De La Cruz, P Crouch. **Booked** Dublin.
Referee: D Gallagher.

THE MANAGER

Graham Taylor

Taylor's major achievement was in bringing to national consciousness the boardroom problems at Villa Park. Sadly (for him) he had to resign to do this after the board refused to back his radical plans to reform the team. He inherited a mess from John Gregory, but made some questionable signings and was by no means blameless. Taylor is a principled and dignified man who is fondly remembered by most Villa fans for what he did for the club a over decade ago, but he should have left it at that and not taken on the job again.

Richard Guy

APPEARANCES

	Prem	FAC	WC	Euro	Total
M Allback	9 (11)	-	0 (2)	3	12 (13)
Alpay Ozalan	5	-	-	-	5
J P Angel	8 (7)	1	0 (3)	-	9 (10)
G Barry	35	1	4	4	44
G Boateng	-	-	-	1	1
M Boulding	-	-	-	2	2
S Cooke	0 (3)	-	-	-	0 (3)
P Crouch	7 (7)	-	-	4	11 (7)
U De La Cruz	12 (8)	1	2 (1)	-	15 (9)
M Delaney	12	-	1	4	17
D Dublin	23 (5)	1	4	2	30 (5)
R Edwards	7 (1)	1	-	-	8 (1)
P Enckelman	33	-	3	3	39
J Gudjonsson	9 (2)	-	-	-	9 (2)
M Hadji	7 (4)	-	1	1 (2)	9 (6)
L Hendrie	22 (5)	1	3	1 (2)	27 (7)
T Hitzlsperger	24 (2)	-	2 (1)	4	30 (3)
R Johnsen	25 (1)	-	3	-	28 (1)
H Kachloul	-	-	-	0 (1)	0 (1)
M Kinsella	15 (4)	1	2 (2)	-	18 (6)
O Leonhardsen	13 (6)	-	3 (1)	-	16 (7)
O Mellberg	38	1	2	3	44
P Merson	-	-	-	0 (1)	0 (1)
S Moore	7 (6)	-	1 (1)	0 (2)	8 (9)
S Postma	5 (1)	1	1	1	8 (1)
L Ridgewell	-	0 (1)	-	-	0 (1)
J Samuel	33 (5)	1	4	2	40 (5)
S Staunton	22 (4)	-	3	3	28 (4)
S Stone	-	-	-	1 (1)	1 (1)
I Taylor	9 (4)	0 (1)	2	3	14 (5)
D Vassell	28 (5)	0 (1)	3	1 (1)	32 (7)
P Whittingham	1 (3)	-	-	-	1 (3)
A Wright	9 (1)	1	-	1	11 (1)

Saturday November 30
ARSENAL (a)
Lost 1-3 HT 0-1 Att 38,090 Position **14th**
Enckelman — Mellberg, Johnsen, Staunton, Samuel — Leonhardsen, Taylor, Hitzlsperger, Hendrie (De La Cruz ht) — Dublin, Vassell Subs not used Postma, Angel, Allback, Kinsella Booked Dublin, Hitzlsperger, Taylor
Scorer **Hitzlsperger 64**
Report page 58

Wednesday December 4
PRESTON NORTH END (h)
Worthington Cup, 4th rnd
Won 5-0 HT 1-0 Att 23,042
Enckelman — Samuel (De La Cruz 82), Staunton, Johnsen, Barry — Leonhardsen, Taylor (Kinsella 31), Hendrie, Hitzlsperger — Dublin, Vassell (Angel 82) Subs not used Postma, Allback
Scorers **Vassell 44, 55, Dublin 80, Angel 84, Hitzlsperger 87**
Referee **C Wilkes**

On the day that John Gregory feels compelled to issue a statement denying any wrongdoing over his transfer activity while Villa manager, one of his overseas signings, Angel, hits the goal of a game replete with cracking strikes, his spectacular bicycle kick topping a comprehensive victory.

Saturday December 7
NEWCASTLE UNITED (h)
Lost 0-1 HT 0-0 Att 33,446 Position **15th**
Enckelman — De La Cruz, Mellberg, Johnsen, Samuel — Leonhardsen, Hendrie, Hitzlsperger, Barry (Kinsella 42) — Dublin (Angel 67), Vassell Subs not used Postma, Allback, Ridgewell Booked Hendrie, Johnsen
Referee **S Bennett**

At the end of a week in which he has been talking about extending his playing career, Shearer proves his enduring worth by heading the only goal eight minutes from time. Three minutes earlier, Angel's header had hit the bar, Villa having previously been denied by Given's fine saves from Barry and Vassell.

Saturday December 14
WEST BROMWICH ALBION (h)
Won 2-1 HT 1-1 Att 40,391 Position **14th**
Enckelman — Samuel, Mellberg, Johnsen, Staunton — Leonhardsen, Hendrie, Hitzlsperger, Barry — Dublin, Vassell Subs not used Angel, Postma, Allback, De La Cruz, Kinsella Booked Samuel, Hendrie, Staunton Sent off Staunton 68
Scorers **Vassell 16, Hitzlsperger 90**
Referee **M Dean**

Hitzlsperger's third goal in four games, another long-range special but this time with the aid of a deflection, is cruel luck on an Albion side for whom Hoult earns more rave reviews with a brilliant performance in goal. Vassell's opener is cancelled out by Koumas, his first goal for Albion, from 20 yards.

Wednesday December 18
LIVERPOOL (h)
Worthington Cup, 5th rnd
Lost 3-4   HT 1-1   Att 38,530
Enckelman — De La Cruz (Angel 79), Samuel, Mellberg,
Barry — Leonhardsen, Hendrie (Kinsella 83),
Hitzlsperger, Hadji — Dublin, Vassell *Subs not used*
Postma, Allback, Edwards
Scorers **Vassell 23 (pen), Hitzlsperger 72,**
Henchoz 88 (og)
Referee **G Barber**

Supporter chaos outside the ground, goals queuing up
inside it: after an 80-minute delay to the kick-off while
thousands wait to collect their tickets, Villa's night of
embarrassment and misery is completed in the last
minute when, having fought back to 3-3, Murphy's
second goal of a protracted night puts Liverpool through
to the last four.

Saturday December 21
CHELSEA (a)
Lost 0-2   HT 0-1   Att 38,284   Position 15th
Enckelman — Samuel, Mellberg, Staunton, Barry —
Leonhardsen (Kinsella 61), Hendrie, Hitzlsperger,
Hadji — Dublin (Allback 61), Vassell (Angel 62) *Subs not
used* Postma, De La Cruz *Booked* Dublin, Hendrie,
Staunton
Report page 83

Thursday December 26
MANCHESTER CITY (a)
Lost 1-3   HT 1-1   Att 33,991   Position 16th
Enckelman — Mellberg, Staunton, Barry — De La Cruz,
Kinsella, Hitzlsperger (Leonhardsen 67; Hendrie 89),
Samuel — Hadji — Dublin, Vassell (Angel 63) *Subs not
used* Postma, Allback *Booked* De La Cruz
Scorer **Dublin 41**
Report page 143

Saturday December 28
MIDDLESBROUGH (h)
Won 1-0   HT 1-0   Att 33,637   Position 14th
Postma — Edwards, Mellberg, Johnsen (Wright ht),
Samuel — Hadji (De La Cruz 4; Allback 81), Kinsella,
Hitzlsperger, Barry — Dublin, Angel *Subs not used*
Moore, Henderson *Booked* Samuel, Barry, De La Cruz
Scorer **Dublin 11**
Referee **R Styles**

Dublin's looping, seemingly fluked goal at the near
post early on proves decisive in a dull affair. Barry
later hits the bar while, at the other end, Wright clears
off the line from Geremi's header. Middlesbrough's
humour is not improved by the unlucky sending-off of
Wilson.

PLAYER OF THE SEASON   Olof Mellberg

The Sweden centre half was the only
outfield Premiership player to feature in
every minute of every match and it is no
mean achievement for a defender to avoid
suspension in these card-happy days —
quite apart from the fact that he played a
lot of the season nursing an Achilles injury
that restricted his training. Possesses all
the qualities of the modern centre half and
has had to adapt to a number of different
partners. Given that Villa had no idea
where the opposition goal was, it was vital
that they conceded as few as possible.
The Mellberg-marshalled defence was the
eighth tightest in the Premiership.
Richard Guy

● Villa's televised 3-2 home win over Everton ended a run of six successive defeats in matches shown live.

● Villa had not met local rivals West Bromwich Albion in the league for 15 years before November 2002, but they then met twice in four weeks.

● Early in 2003 Villa won successive Premiership games by three-goal margins, 5-2 away to Middlesbrough and 3-0 at home to Blackburn Rovers. Before that they had only managed one three-goal victory in the previous two years.

● Villa did not play at home on a Saturday in the Premiership until November 9.

● Villa have lost just two of their past 23 games at home to West Ham United.

● Graham Taylor has not won on his ten league visits to Old Trafford as a manager, four with Villa and six with Watford.

● Villa finished beneath Tottenham Hotspur in the Premiership table for the first time in eight seasons.

● Villa against Everton is the most-played top-flight fixture and each side has won 67 times.

● Villa have won three of their past 35 league matches against Manchester United.

● And have won just two of their past 21 meetings with Arsenal.

● Nine of the past 12 meetings between Villa and West Ham United have been drawn.

Bill Edgar

GOALSCORERS

	Prem	FAC	WC	Euro	Total
M Allback	5	-	-	1	6
J P Angel	1	1	1	-	3
G Barry	3	-	1	-	4
M Boulding	-	-	-	1	1
U De La Cruz	1	-	1	-	2
D Dublin	10 (1p)	-	4	-	14 (1p)
J Gudjonsson	2	-	-	-	2
L Hendrie	4	-	-	-	4
T Hitzlsperger	2	-	2	-	4
O Leonhardsen	3	-	-	-	3
O Mellberg	1	-	-	-	1
S Moore	1	-	-	-	1
S Staunton	-	-	-	1	1
I Taylor	-	-	1	1	2
D Vassell	8 (1p)	-	3 (1p)	-	11 (2p)
Own goals	1	-	1	-	2

Wednesday January 1
BOLTON WANDERERS (h)
Won 2-0   HT 1-0   Att **31,838**   Position **14th**
Postma — Edwards, Mellberg, Samuel, Wright — De La Cruz (Cooke 88), Hendrie, Hitzlsperger (Kinsella 67), Barry — Dublin, Angel (Vassell 67) *Subs not used* Enckelman, Ridgewell *Booked* Hitzlsperger, Hendrie
Scorers **Dublin 8, Vassell 80**
Referee **M Messias**

Dublin's third goal in as many games and Vassell's clincher after Bergsson's dithering earn a deserved victory for Villa, but Bolton are furious that a clear penalty — for Edwards' pull on Ricketts's shirt at 1-0 down — is denied them "The referee bottled it," an angry Sam Allardyce claims.

Saturday January 4
BLACKBURN ROVERS (h)
FA Cup, 3rd rnd
Lost 1-4   HT 1-1   Att **23,884**
Postma — Edwards (Ridgewell 70), Mellberg, Samuel, Wright — De La Cruz, Kinsella (Taylor 64), Hendrie, Barry — Dublin, Angel (Vassell 64) *Subs not used* Hitzlsperger, Henderson
Scorer **Angel 41**
Referee **J Winter**

A thin crowd and a thinner performance from the home side, whose dismay at their FA Cup exit is heightened by the fact that Yorke, a Villa old boy, scores two of Blackburn's goals — at the Holte End to boot. Jansen also helps himself to a double, his first goals since almost losing his life in a summer motorbike accident.

Saturday January 11
LIVERPOOL (a)
Drew 1-1   HT 0-1   Att **43,210**   Position **13th**
Enckelman — Samuel, Mellberg, Johnsen, Barry — Hendrie (De La Cruz 52), Taylor, Hitzlsperger, Barry — Dublin, Vassell (Moore ht) *Subs not used* Edwards, Crouch, Postma *Booked* Wright, Taylor
Scorer **Dublin 49 (pen)**
Report page 96

Saturday January 18
TOTTENHAM HOTSPUR (h)
Lost 0-1   HT 0-0   Att **38,576**   Position **14th**
Enckelman — Delaney, Mellberg, Johnsen, Samuel — Hendrie (De La Cruz ht), Taylor, Hitzlsperger, Barry — Dublin (Crouch 78), Moore (Vassell ht) *Subs not used* Wright, Postma *Booked* Delaney
Referee **N Barry**

Villa's performance is summed up when the referee is named man of the match. However, Spurs are not complaining when, after Taylor's hapless near-post miss, Sheringham, adjudged just onside, seals victory at the other end 30 seconds later with a volley from Carr's cross.

Tuesday January 28
MIDDLESBROUGH (a)
Won 5-2 **HT 2-2** Att **27,546** Position **12th**
Enckelman — Delaney, Mellberg, Johnsen, Samuel —
Moore (Staunton 78), Hitzlsperger, Gudjonsson
(Hendrie 89), Barry — Dublin, Vassell *Subs not used*
Postma, De La Cruz, Crouch *Booked* Dublin,
Gudjonsson
Scorers **Vassell 24, 81, Gudjonsson 31, Barry 48,
Dublin 90**
Report page 169

Sunday February 2
BLACKBURN ROVERS (h)
Won 3-0 **HT 2-0** Att **29,171** Position **11th**
Enckelman — Delaney (Staunton 84), Mellberg,
Johnsen, Samuel — Moore (De La Cruz 78),
Gudjonsson (Hendrie 90), Hitzlsperger, Barry —
Dublin, Vassell *Subs not used* Postma, Crouch
Booked Barry
Scorers **Dublin 2, 40, Barry 80**
Referee **M Dean**

Suddenly there is no holding Villa, who follow their nap
hand against Middlesbrough in midweek with three
more against a Blackburn side who "weren't at the
races", according to Graeme Souness. Dublin, with a
clever header after 90 seconds, then takes his tally to
seven goals in seven league games before Barry
completes the demolition.

Saturday February 8
FULHAM (a)
Lost 1-2 **HT 1-2** Att **17,092** Position **12th**
Enckelman — Edwards (Hendrie ht), Mellberg, Johnsen,
Samuel — Moore (De La Cruz ht), Gudjonsson,
Hitzlsperger (Crouch 67), Barry — Dublin, Vassell
Subs not used Postma, Staunton *Booked* Edwards,
Barry, Gudjonsson
Scorer **Barry 3**
Report page 206

Saturday February 22
CHARLTON ATHLETIC (a)
Lost 0-3 **HT 0-0** Att **26,257** Position **12th**
Enckelman — Alpay, Mellberg, Johnsen, Wright
(Samuel 60) — De La Cruz (Hadji 60), Gudjonsson,
Kinsella, Barry — Crouch, Vassell (Allback 66)
Subs not used Postma, Hendrie *Booked* Crouch,
Kinsella
Report page 182

MARCUS ALLBACK
Forward
Born July 5, 1973, Stockholm
Ht 6ft 0in **Wt** 12st 0lb
Signed from Heerenveen, May
2002, £2m

ALPAY OZALAN
Defender
Born May 29, 1973, Izmir,
Turkey
Ht 6ft 2in **Wt** 13st 7lb
Signed from Fenerbahce, July
2000, £5.6m

JUAN PABLO ANGEL
Forward
Born October 21, 1975,
Medellin, Colombia
Ht 5ft 11in **Wt** 11st 3lb
Signed from River Plate, January
2001, £9.5m

GARETH BARRY
Midfield
Born February 23, 1981,
Hastings
Ht 6ft 0in **Wt** 12st 6lb
Signed from trainee, February
1998

GEORGE BOATENG
(see Middlesbrough)

MICHAEL BOULDING
Forward
Born February 8, 1975, Sheffield
Ht 5ft 10in **Wt** 11st 5lb
Signed from Grimsby Town, July
2002, free

STEPHEN COOKE
Midfield
Born February 15, 1983, Walsall
Ht 5ft 8in **Wt** 9st 8lb
Signed from trainee, February
2000

PETER CROUCH
Forward
Born January 30, 1981,
Macclesfield
Ht 6ft 7in **Wt** 11st 12lb
Signed from Portsmouth, March
2002, £5m

ULISES DE LA CRUZ
Defender
Born February 8, 1974,
Chota, Ecuador
Ht 5ft 11in **Wt** 11st 6lb
Signed from Hibernian, July 2002,
£1.5m

MARK DELANEY
Defender
Born May 13, 1976,
Haverfordwest
Ht 6ft 1in **Wt** 11st 7lb
Signed from Cardiff City, March
1999, £250,000

Juan Pablo Angel

DION DUBLIN
Forward
Born April 22, 1969, Leicester
Ht 6ft 2in **Wt** 12st 4lb
Signed from Coventry City,
November 1998, £5.75m

ROB EDWARDS
Defender
Born December 25, 1982, Telford
Ht 6ft 1in **Wt** 11st 10lb
Signed from trainee, December
2002

PETER ENCKELMAN
Goalkeeper
Born March 10, 1977,
Turku, Finland
Ht 6ft 2in **Wt** 12st 5lb
Signed from TPS Turku, February
1999, £200,000

JOEY GUDJONSSON
Midfield
Born May 25, 1980,
Akranes, Iceland
Ht 5ft 6in **Wt** 11st 5lb
Signed from Real Betis (loan),
January 2003

MOUSTAPHA HADJI
Midfield
Born November 16, 1971,
Ifrane, Morocco
Ht 6ft 0in **Wt** 12st 2lb
Signed from Coventry City, July
2001, £4.5m

LEE HENDRIE
Midfield
Born May 18, 1977, Birmingham
Ht 5ft 10in **Wt** 11st 0lb
Signed from trainee, May 1994

THOMAS HITZLSPERGER
Midfield
Born April 5, 1982, Munich
Ht 6ft 0in **Wt** 11st 12lb
Signed from Bayern Munich,
August 2000, free

RONNY JOHNSEN
Defender
Born June 10, 1969,
Sandefjord, Norway
Ht 6ft 3in **Wt** 13st 1lb
Signed from Manchester United,
August 2002, free

HASSAN KACHLOUL
Midfield
Born February 19, 1973,
Agadir, Morocco
Ht 6ft 1in **Wt** 12st 2lb
Signed from Southampton, July
2001, free

MARK KINSELLA
Midfield
Born August 12, 1972, Dublin
Ht 5ft 9in **Wt** 10st 10lb
Signed from Charlton Athletic,
August 2002, free

OYVIND LEONHARDSEN
Midfield
Born August 17, 1970,
Kristiansund, Norway
Ht 5ft 10in **Wt** 11st 2lb
Signed from Tottenham Hotspur,
August 2002, free

OLOF MELLBERG
Defender
Born September 3, 1977,
Gullspang, Sweden
Ht 6ft 1in **Wt** 12st 10lb
Signed from Racing Santander,
July 2001, £5m

PAUL MERSON
(transferred to Portsmouth,
August 2002)

Monday March 3
BIRMINGHAM CITY (h)
Lost 0-2 HT 0-0 Att 42,602 Position 14th
Enckelman — Samuel, Mellberg, Johnsen, Wright
(Crouch 90) — Moore (Hadji ht) Gudjonsson, Hendrie,
Barry — Dublin, Vassell *Subs not used* Hitzlsperger,
Postma, Edwards *Booked* Gudjonsson *Sent off* Dublin
51, Gudjonsson 81
Referee **M Halsey**

Dublin apologises the next day for the Savage headbutt
that leads to his dismissal on a sorry night all round for
Villa. Gudjonsson also sees red, collecting a second
booking for a two-footed tackle on Devlin, while crowd
disturbances during and after the match prompt an
inevitable FA investigation. Amid the mayhem,
Birmingham complete a tempestuous league double to
boot.

Saturday March 15
MANCHESTER UNITED (h)
Lost 0-1 HT 0-1 Att 42,602 Position 14th
Postma — Samuel, Mellberg, Johnsen, Wright — Hadji,
Hitzlsperger, Hendrie, Barry — Dublin (Cooke 79),
Vassell *Subs not used* Enckelman, Crouch, Kinsella,
Edwards *Booked* Wright, Hadji
Referee **M Dean**

Arsenal's lead at the head of the Premiership, eight
points at one stage, is cut to two as United capitalise on
the champions' defeat by Blackburn with a narrow
victory at Villa Park, courtesy of Beckham's early goal
from close range. Giggs, who provides the cross, later
hits the bar, but Villa create enough chances to take at
least a point.

Saturday March 22
SOUTHAMPTON (a)
Drew 2-2 HT 2-1 Att 31,888 Position 14th
Postma — Samuel, Mellberg, Johnsen, Wright — Hadji,
Hitzlsperger, Hendrie (Moore 88), Barry — Crouch
(Allback 70), Vassell *Subs not used* Enckelman,
De La Cruz, Edwards *Booked* Barry
Scorers **Hendrie 30, Vassell 36**
Report page 134

Saturday April 5
ARSENAL (h)
Drew 1-1 HT 0-0 Att 42,602 Position 15th
Enckelman — Mellberg, Johnsen, Barry — De La Cruz
(Edwards 66), Gudjonsson (Allback 66), Hendrie,
Hitzlsperger, Samuel — Vassell, Hadji (Leonhardsen 79)
Subs not used Postma, Moore *Booked* Allback
Scorer **Toure 71 (og)**
Referee **U Rennie**

Arsenal's Premiership advantage is now down to goal
difference after Graham Taylor is rewarded for
changing Villa's formation with a gritty, if dour, draw.
Ljungberg puts the champions ahead, but Toure slices
into his own net under pressure to earn Villa a
deserved point.

Saturday April 12
WEST HAM UNITED (a)
Drew 2-2 HT 1-1 Att 35,029 Position 14th
Enckelman — Edwards, Mellberg, Staunton, Samuel —
Hadji (Leonhardsen 52), Hendrie (Gudjonsson 26),
Hitzlsperger, Barry — Allback (Taylor 90), Vassell
Subs not used Postma, Moore *Booked* Barry
Scorers **Vassell 36 (pen), Leonhardsen 53**
Report page 255

Saturday April 19
CHELSEA (h)
Won 2-1   HT 1-0   Att **39,358**   Position **13th**
Enckelman — Edwards, Mellberg, Johnsen, Samuel —
Leonhardsen, Gudjonsson (Staunton 19), Hitzlsperger,
Barry — Allback, Vassell *Subs not used* Angel, Dublin,
Postma, Cooke *Booked* Leonhardsen
Scorer **Allback 11, 78**
Referee **R Styles**

On the day that Doug Ellis reveals he is battling
prostate cancer, Allback gives the Villa chairman a lift
with the two goals that reward their superiority over
Chelsea and deal a potentially damaging blow to the
Londoners' Champions League aspirations. Terry's
headed reply comes far too late for Claudio Ranieri's
team.

Monday April 21
NEWCASTLE UNITED (a)
Drew 1-1   HT 0-1   Att **52,015**   Position **14th**
Enckelman — Edwards (Taylor 33), Mellberg, Johnsen,
Samuel — Staunton — Leonhardsen, Hitzlsperger
(Dublin 65), Barry (Whittingham ht) — Allback, Vassell
Subs not used Angel, Postma *Booked* Barry
Scorer **Dublin 69**
Report page 76

Saturday April 26
EVERTON (a)
Lost 1-2   HT 0-0   Att **40,167**   Position **14th**
Enckelman — Edwards (Whittingham ht), Mellberg,
Johnsen (Taylor ht), Staunton — Leonhardsen (Vassell
67), Gudjonsson, Hitzlsperger, Samuel — Allback,
Dublin *Subs not used* Postma, Hendrie *Booked* Vassell
Scorer **Allback 49**
Report page 124

Saturday May 3
SUNDERLAND (h)
Won 1-0   HT 0-0   Att **36,963**   Position **14th**
Enckelman — Samuel, Mellberg, Johnsen, Staunton —
Leonhardsen (Gudjonsson 72), Taylor, Hendrie (Dublin
76), Hitzlsperger (Whittingham 57) — Vassell, Allback
Subs not used Postma, Moore
Scorer **Allback 80**
Referee **S Dunn**

Villa can celebrate safety after a late goal from Allback
that inflicts Sunderland's fourteenth successive league
defeat, but there is a mixed reaction from the stands
afterwards as Graham Taylor goes on to the pitch to
address the fans.

Sunday May 11
LEEDS UNITED (a)
Lost 1-3   HT 1-1   Att **40,205**   Position **16th**
Postma — Samuel (Taylor 84), Mellberg, Johnsen
(Dublin 89), Whittingham — Moore (Cooke 75),
Hitzlsperger, Gudjonsson, Barry — Vassell, Allback
Subs not used Enckelman, Ridgewell
Scorer **Gudjonsson 40**
Report page 220

STEFAN MOORE
Forward
Born September 28, 1983,
Birmingham
Ht 5ft 11in **Wt** 10st 12lb
Signed from trainee, July 2000

STEFAN POSTMA
Goalkeeper
Born June 10, 1976, Utrecht
Ht 6ft 7in **Wt** 14st 6lb
Signed from De Graafschap, May
2002, £1.5m

LIAM RIDGEWELL
Defender
Born July 21, 1984, London
Ht 5ft 10in **Wt** 10st 5lb
Signed from trainee, August 2001

JLLOYD SAMUEL
Defender
Born March 29, 1981,
San Fernando, Trinidad
Ht 5ft 11in **Wt** 11st 4lb
Signed from trainee, February
1999

STEVE STAUNTON
Defender
Born January 19, 1969, Drogheda
Ht 6ft 1in **Wt** 12st 12lb
Signed from Liverpool, December
2000, free

STEVE STONE
Midfield
Born August 20, 1971, Gateshead
Ht 5ft 9in **Wt** 11st 3lb
Signed from Nottingham Forest,
March 1999, £5.5m

IAN TAYLOR
Midfield
Born June 4, 1968, Birmingham
Ht 6ft 1in **Wt** 12st 0lb
Signed from Sheffield Wednesday,
December 1994, £1m

DARIUS VASSELL
Forward
Born June 30, 1980, Birmingham
Ht 5ft 7in **Wt** 12st 0lb
Signed from trainee, April 1998

PETER WHITTINGHAM
Defender
Born September 8, 1984,
Nuneaton
Ht 5ft 10in **Wt** 9st 13lb
Signed from trainee, April 2003

ALAN WRIGHT
Defender
Born September 28, 1971,
Ashton-under-Lyne
Ht 5ft 4in **Wt** 9st 9lb
Signed from Blackburn Rovers,
March 1995, £1m

Darius Vassell

BOLTON WANDERERS

PREMIERSHIP

	P	W	D	L	F	A	Pts
Man Utd	38	25	8	5	74	34	83
Arsenal	38	23	9	6	85	42	78
Newcastle	38	21	6	11	63	48	69
Chelsea	38	19	10	9	68	38	67
Liverpool	38	18	10	10	61	41	64
Blackburn	38	16	12	10	52	43	60
Everton	38	17	8	13	48	49	59
Southampton	38	13	13	12	43	46	52
Man City	38	15	6	17	47	54	51
Tottenham	38	14	8	16	51	62	50
Middlesbro	38	13	10	15	48	44	49
Charlton	38	14	7	17	45	56	49
Birmingham	38	13	9	16	41	49	48
Fulham	38	13	9	16	41	50	48
Leeds	38	14	5	19	58	57	47
Aston Villa	38	12	9	17	42	47	45
Bolton	**38**	**10**	**14**	**14**	**41**	**51**	**44**
West Ham	38	10	12	16	42	59	42
West Brom	38	6	8	24	29	65	26
Sunderland	38	4	7	27	21	65	19

FA CUP
Third round

WORTHINGTON CUP
Second round

Staying up: Sam Allardyce and Bernard
Mendy celebrate survival

THE GAMES

Saturday August 17
FULHAM (a)
Lost 1-4   HT 1-3   Att 16,338   Position 19th
Jaaskelainen — Mendy (Whitlow ht), N'Gotty,
Bergsson, Charlton — Okocha (Pedersen ht), Frandsen,
Nolan (Warhurst 69), Gardner — Ricketts, Djorkaeff
Subs not used Poole, Dean Holdsworth *Booked* Mendy,
N'Gotty
Scorer **Ricketts 4 (pen)**
Report page 199

Saturday August 24
CHARLTON ATHLETIC (h)
Lost 1-2   HT 1-1   Att 21,753   Position 20th
Jaaskelainen — Barness, N'Gotty, Whitlow, Charlton
— Gardner (Nolan 77), Frandsen (Walters 85),
Warhurst — Djorkaeff, Pedersen — Ricketts
(Dean Holdsworth 78) *Subs not used* Poole, Mendy
Booked N'Gotty
Scorer **Djorkaeff 2**
Referee **M Messias**

Ahead for the second successive match, Bolton are
still without a point. Djorkaeff's early strike is cancelled
out from the penalty spot after N'Gotty's push on
Rufus and the bravery of Stuart, who injures himself
winning the ball to set up Euell's winner, earns victory
for Charlton.

Sunday September 1
ASTON VILLA (h)
Won 1-0   HT 0-0   Att 22,500   Position 17th
Jaaskelainen — N'Gotty, Bergsson, Whitlow, Charlton
(Gardner 32) — Frandsen, Warhurst (Barness 38),
Nolan — Djorkaeff, Pedersen — Ricketts *Subs not used*
Poole, Mendy, Dean Holdsworth *Booked* Ricketts,
Pedersen
Scorer **Ricketts 56 (pen)**
Referee **S Dunn**

This time Bolton hang on to the lead given them when
Enckelman brings down Pedersen for Ricketts to
convert his second penalty of the season — and Bolton
are off the bottom of the table. It is a poor match,
though, in which Angel has an equaliser wrongly
disallowed for offside.

Wednesday September 11
MANCHESTER UNITED (a)
Won 1-0   HT 0-0   Att 67,623   Position 12th
Jaaskelainen — Barness, Bergsson, Whitlow, Charlton
— Frandsen (Dean Holdsworth 86) — Pedersen
(Campo 90), Nolan, Gardner — Ricketts, Djorkaeff
(Warhurst 72) *Subs not used* Walters, Poole *Booked*
Nolan, Holdsworth
Scorer **Nolan 76**
Report page 43

THE 2002-03 SEASON MARKED A crucial stage in the
development of Bolton Wanderers as a Premiership side to be
reckoned with. Nurtured and groomed by Sam Allardyce, the ugly
duckling finally became a swan. Not the finest swan in the realm,
but a nice-looking bird with the strength, speed and grace to look at
home with the high-flyers.

Over two seasons the Bolton manager turned what was derided
by one pundit as "a first division side with a couple of Premiership
players" into an attractive team that was difficult to beat and
perhaps a little unlucky still to be in relegation danger at the
beginning of May. In avoiding the drop, he secured for the club its
longest stay in the top division since the 1960s.

Now, it is no secret that, in achieving this, Allardyce sought
foreign help, and — let's not beat about the bush — brought in a few
more players on loan than many observers thought was decent or
proper. He has skilfully exploited the loan system, scouring Europe
for talented performers languishing in the reserves at some of the
Continent's top clubs and persuading them to leave the sunshine to
spend a few months freezing their socks off in the shadow of Winter
Hill. Central to his success has been his judgment in choosing men
who not only have the ability to shine in the Premiership, but who
also have the will to win. This cannot have been easy, but Allardyce
has the knack.

So far, so good. But it has been suggested that such dependence
on the loan market is unhealthy and even detrimental to English
football. It is doubtful that Allardyce has spent his summer holiday
bent double with guilt. Above all, football is entertainment. Is there a
single Bolton fan who did not hold his breath with nervous
excitement last season as Bernard Mendy, on loan from Paris Saint-
Germain, streaked down the right wing to spread panic among the
opposition defence? Did anyone fail to marvel at the rapier-like
tackling of Florent Laville, on loan from Lyons? Can any Bolton fan,
hand on heart, say that he was not brought to the brink of
incontinence every time that Ivan Campo, of Real Madrid, set about
playing the ball out of his own penalty area? Ah, but when the
manager moved him from central defence to midfield, the
Spaniard's control and distribution were an inspiring sight. A long,
cross-field pass by Campo is a thing of beauty.

For his trouble, Allardyce has had to contend with lurid stories of
his picking a team consisting entirely of foreigners and of having as
many as five loan players on the field at once. And it's all true. We
could be forgiven for thinking that he was trying to pull a fast one.
But here is another truth: the Wanderers beat Manchester United

Djorkaeff's goal against Arsenal helped to salvage a point and keep Bolton up

away with a team that contained nine players who had helped to win promotion from the first division two seasons previously. This was not a one-off. The same players were in the side that beat Newcastle United and five or six of them would feature in every game. Loan players come and go but some, like Youri Djorkaeff, the World Cup-winner, decide to stay. Allardyce's unconventional method of strengthening his squad seems to be working.

What next in this great adventure? Another struggle for Premiership survival, of course, but does it have to be so hard on the stomach lining? Bolton fans could do with a break after being distressed and debilitated by consecutive bouts of relegation sickness. It would be nice to be ensconced in mid-table and to have something else to talk about — perhaps a bit of a run in the FA Cup. The club has a great Cup tradition, but Allardyce has achieved a certain notoriety over the past two seasons for his apparent lack of respect for the competition (not to mention the League Cup, which he has been accused of helping to kill). He has been known to field cup teams containing seven or eight reserves, saving his best players for those all-important league matches.

But there is more to it than that. Allardyce knows that if he is not careful he could wake up one day and find himself in Europe, facing an undertaking that by his own reckoning requires an outlay of £20 million, without which his squad would be severely stretched and the club's Premiership status put in dire peril. Well, he should worry about that when the time comes. After all, he could always send out his reserves.

Saturday September 14
LIVERPOOL (h)
Lost 2-3 HT **0-1** Att **27,328** Position **13th**
Jaaskelainen — Barness (Livesey 31), Bergsson, Whitlow (Campo ht), Charlton — Nolan, Frandsen, Gardner, Djorkaeff (Walters 75) — Dean Holdsworth, Pedersen *Subs not used* Okocha, Poole *Booked* Bergsson, Gardner
Scorers **Gardner 54, Campo 87**
Referee **R Styles**

Baros makes a stunning full debut for Liverpool, twice putting them ahead, but Bolton fight back each time and look to have snatched a point through Campo three minutes from time. Heskey, though, has other ideas, replying immediately to prevent Liverpool's fourth successive 2-2 draw.

Saturday September 21
ARSENAL (a)
Lost 1-2 HT **0-1** Att **37,974** Position **17th**
Jaaskelainen — Barness, Bergsson, Whitlow, Charlton — Djorkaeff (Tofting 80), Campo, Frandsen, Pedersen (Ricketts ht), Farrelly — Dean Holdsworth (Okocha 66) *Subs not used* Livesey, Poole *Booked* Jaaskelainen, Bergsson, Holdsworth, Campo
Sent off Campo 80
Scorer **Farrelly 47**
Report page 55

Saturday September 28
SOUTHAMPTON (h)
Drew 1-1 HT **0-0** Att **22,692** Position **17th**
Jaaskelainen — Barness, Bergsson, Whitlow, Charlton — Farrelly (Pedersen 78), Campo, Frandsen — Djorkaeff — Dean Holdsworth (Okocha 78), Ricketts *Subs not used* Poole, Livesey, Tofting *Booked* Barness
Scorer **Djorkaeff 90**
Referee **U Rennie**

Defeat looms for Bolton when Bridge ventures forward from full back to score a rare goal for Southampton with only eight minutes remaining, but Djorkaeff, a class apart from his rivals and team-mates, poaches a last-gasp equaliser when a long throw is flicked on.

Wednesday October 2
BURY (h)
Worthington Cup, 2nd rnd
Lost 0-1 HT **0-0** Att **12,621**
Poole — Mendy, Campo, David Holdsworth, Smith — Tofting, Livesey, Bulent, Johnson (Nolan 59) — Walters (Dean Holdsworth 59), Armstrong (Pedersen 53) *Subs not used* Jaaskelainen, Richardson *Booked* Bulent
Sent off Bulent 64
Referee **H Webb**

Some big teams are taking the Worthington Cup seriously. Then there's Bolton. Sam Allardyce makes ten team changes and invites Bury, of the third division, to cause the upset of the night. With Mendy putting through his own goal early in the second half, that is precisely what they do. Bolton's nightmare is complete with the sending-off of Bulent, on his debut, for a second bookable offence.

Saturday October 5
MIDDLESBROUGH (a)
Lost 0-2 HT 0-1 Att **31,005** Position **18th**
Jaaskelainen — Barness, Bergsson, Whitlow, Charlton
(Farrelly ht) — Campo — Frandsen (Okocha 72), Nolan,
Djorkaeff — Dean Holdsworth (Ricketts ht), Pedersen
Subs not used Poole, Tofting *Booked* Nolan,
Djorkaeff, Campo
Report page 164

Sunday October 20
TOTTENHAM HOTSPUR (a)
Lost 1-3 HT 0-0 Att **35,909** Position **20th**
Jaaskelainen — Barness, Bergsson, Whitlow,
Charlton — Farrelly, Campo (Dean Holdsworth 77),
Nolan, Gardner — Ricketts, Djorkaeff (Okocha 74)
Subs not used Poole, Frandsen, Armstrong *Booked*
Nolan
Scorer **Djorkaeff 63**
Report page 152

Monday October 28
SUNDERLAND (h)
Drew 1-1 HT 0-1 Att **23,036** Position **20th**
Jaaskelainen — Mendy (Barness 70), N'Gotty, Campo,
Whitlow, Gardner — Nolan (Okocha 57), Frandsen,
Farrelly — Ricketts, Djorkaeff *Subs not used* Pedersen,
Dean Holdsworth, Poole *Booked* Campo
Scorer **Babb 80 (og)**
Referee **E Wolstenholme**

A genuine basement battle as twentieth takes on
nineteenth, and that's the way they stay after an
honourable draw. Gray gives Sunderland the lead on
the stroke of half-time, but they lose Myhre and Reyna
to injury and two points to an eightieth-minute own goal
headed past Macho, Myhre's replacement, by his own
defender, Babb.

Saturday November 2
BIRMINGHAM CITY (a)
Lost 1-3 HT 0-0 Att **27,224** Position **20th**
Jaaskelainen — N'Gotty, Campo, Whitlow (Nolan 77)
— Mendy, Okocha, Frandsen (Charlton 77), Farrelly,
Gardner — Djorkaeff, Ricketts (Dean Holdsworth 70)
Subs not used Poole, Tofting *Booked* Mendy, Gardner,
Djorkaeff, Whitlow *Sent off* Gardner 67
Scorer **Okocha 72**
Report page 189

MATCH OF THE SEASON

Bolton Wanderers 2   Middlesbrough 1
The Reebok Stadium, Sunday May 11 2003
Oliver Kay

THERE WAS A SOLE ST GEORGE'S flag on view as the many
nationalities of Bolton Wanderers took the opportunity to show
their colours during a jubilant lap of honour yesterday. The
Frenchmen and Spaniards embraced, the Nigerian and Jamaican
danced and the assorted Nordics, national flags on their shoulders,
smiled politely and enjoyed a more modest celebration. Survival was
toasted in a variety of tongues, perhaps least of all English, but all
knew the significance of what had just been achieved.

There is a school of thought which says that Bolton, with their
polyglot squad and propensity for short-term signings, are the worst
thing to have happened to English football in many years, but do
not expect anyone who was at the Reebok Stadium yesterday to
endorse that view. In years to come, Ivan Campo, Jay-Jay Okocha,
Youri Djorkaeff *et al* will be remembered almost as fondly as Nat
Lofthouse, Frank Worthington and John McGinlay. During the
post-match love-in between players and fans, the appreciation was
clearly mutual.

In the middle of it all was Gudni Bergsson, the Iceland defender
who first arrived on these shores as a Tottenham Hotspur player in
1988, when overseas imports formed a small minority. This was his
last appearance for Bolton before finally, having postponed his
retirement for three consecutive summers, returning to Reykjavik to
embark on a career as a lawyer. If his first of 316 matches for the
club, the League Cup final defeat by Liverpool in 1995, was
memorable, yesterday's farewell was an occasion that he will never
forget. It was an afternoon of high tension, with events at St
Andrew's relayed by those anxious supporters wielding transistor
radios, but, if it was billed as a day when Bolton's multinational
squad would be forced to display a traditional British fighting spirit,
it proved to be nothing of the sort. Always in control of their destiny
from the tenth minute, when Per Frandsen gave them the lead with
a spectacular goal, Okocha and company played as they always do,
with smiles on their faces and a carefree abandon that is still hard to
reconcile with their manager.

Sam Allardyce, a self-styled "big ugly bruiser" of a centre half
during his playing days, defies the convention that teams are
moulded in their manager's image. Unable to compete in the
inflated British market, he has used his knowledge of the European
scene to buy players such as Okocha and Djorkaeff, acquiring
others, such as Campo and Bernard Mendy, on loan. The result
could have been a faceless mish-mash, but Allardyce somehow has
blended these disparate talents into a team that have been beaten in
just one of their last nine matches of a memorable campaign.

Bolton ensured their safety with a last-day home victory over Middlesbrough

Relegation, he said, would have knocked Bolton back five years, with Okocha and Djorkaeff among those who had unashamedly indicated that they would jump ship, but, however tense it became briefly, midway through the second half, it was rarely an issue. Middlesbrough proved compliant opposition for the first 45 minutes, aware that their fair-play record may take them into the Uefa Cup at the expense of Manchester City, and only belatedly bared their teeth before Franck Queudrue was sent off for two senseless lunges on Campo in as many minutes.

With a better goal difference than West Ham United, Bolton were always in control of their destiny, but Allardyce admitted that it took two goals in 11 first-half minutes to begin to settle his nerves. Frandsen seized on a wayward pass from Jonathan Greening and sent an unstoppable shot past Mark Schwarzer, who was left clutching at thin air again on 21 minutes as Okocha's delightful free kick sailed past his right hand. With a two-goal margin against a team possessing a wretched record away from home, it seemed to be plain sailing regardless of what West Ham did.

Then came the threat of a twist in the tale. Michael Ricketts came

Saturday November 9
WEST BROMWICH ALBION (h)
Drew 1-1   HT 0-1   Att 23,630   Position 20th
Jaaskelainen — N'Gotty, Campo, Barness — Mendy, Okocha, Frandsen, Farrelly (Nolan 26), Gardner (Charlton 81) — Dean Holdsworth (Ricketts ht), Djorkaeff *Subs not used* Poole, Pedersen *Booked* Nolan, Campo *Sent off* N'Gotty 20
Scorer **Frandsen 89**
Referee **M Riley**

For the second weekend running Bolton are reduced to ten men, and for the second weekend running Sam Allardyce is unimpressed with the officials after N'Gotty pays seemingly too harsh a price for raising an arm in a challenge with Roberts. They snatch a draw, though, with Frandsen's late header cancelling out Dobie's opener for West Brom.

Sunday November 17
LEEDS UNITED (a)
Won 4-2   HT 1-1   Att 36,627   Position 18th
Jaaskelainen — N'Gotty (Tofting 59), Campo, Barness — Mendy, Frandsen, Nolan (Ricketts 77), Okocha, Charlton — Pedersen, Djorkaeff *Subs not used* Poole, Dean Holdsworth, Smith
Scorers **Pedersen 3, 90, Djorkaeff 80, Ricketts 90 (pen)**
Report page 214

Saturday November 23
CHELSEA (h)
Drew 1-1   HT 0-0   Att 25,476   Position 18th
Jaaskelainen — Barness, Campo, Charlton — Warhurst, Nolan (Ricketts 79), Frandsen (Tofting 79), Okocha, Gardner — Pedersen, Djorkaeff *Subs not used* Poole, Dean Holdsworth, Southall *Booked* Barness, Tofting
Scorer **Pedersen 63**
Referee **M Dean**

This time it is Bolton's opponents who are reduced to ten men, Babayaro seeing red for allegedly elbowing Djorkaeff off the ball, but Chelsea are not to be denied a point. Trailing to Pedersen's header, they produce one of their own in the last minute when Hasselbaink meets Zola's chipped pass. Sam Allardyce is "absolutely gutted".

Saturday November 30
MANCHESTER CITY (a)
Lost 0-2   HT 0-1   Att 34,860   Position 19th
Jaaskelainen — Barness, Campo, Charlton — Nolan (Livesey 75), Warhurst, Tofting (Ricketts 66), Gardner — Okocha — Pedersen (Johnson 68), Djorkaeff *Subs not used* Southall, Poole *Booked* Nolan, Gardner
Report page 142

Saturday December 7
BLACKBURN ROVERS (h)
Drew 1-1   HT 1-0   Att **24,556**   Position **18th**
Jaaskelainen — Barness, Campo, Bergsson, Charlton
— Frandsen, Warhurst (Nolan 50), Okocha (Tofting 75),
Gardner (Ricketts 54) — Pedersen, Djorkaeff
Subs not used Poole, Livesey *Booked* Frandsen,
Djorkaeff
Scorer **Okocha 8**
Referee **N Barry**

Another home match for Bolton, another 1-1 draw
— their fifth in succession. Okocha's sweet half-volley
gives them an early lead, but with the last of five
minutes of added time almost up, Short decides
that now would be a good time to score his first
Premiership goal for Blackburn, his header earning
a point.

Monday December 16
LEEDS UNITED (h)
Lost 0-3   HT 0-2   Att **23,378**   Position **19th**
Jaaskelainen — Bergsson, Campo, N'Gotty
(Whitlow 78) — Barness, Tofting (Farrelly 79),
Frandsen, Okocha (Walters 90), Charlton — Djorkaeff
— Pedersen *Subs not used* Smith, Poole *Booked*
Frandsen, Campo
Referee **G Poll**

The luck turns for Leeds and Terry Venables at last.
With many predicting that defeat will lead to his
dismissal, he sees Mills and Wilcox score with
long-range specials, Fowler net from an offside
position and Robinson brilliantly turn Djorkaeff's
penalty on to a post after Harte is harshly penalised
for handball.

Saturday December 21
WEST HAM UNITED (a)
Drew 1-1   HT 0-1   Att **34,892**   Position **19th**
Jaaskelainen — Barness, N'Gotty (Whitlow ht),
Bergsson, Charlton — Okocha, Frandsen, Nolan,
Gardner — Pedersen, Djorkaeff (Ricketts 55) *Subs
not used* Poole, Facey, Tofting *Booked* Whitlow
Scorer **Ricketts 65**
Report page 251

Frandsen settles Bolton's nerves with a stunning opening goal from distance

off the bench to convert Luke Wilkshire's cross, his first goal for
Middlesbrough since an acrimonious transfer from Bolton in
January, on 61 minutes. Allardyce, suddenly fearing the worst, left
the sanctuary of the directors' box and soon heard that West Ham
had taken the lead at St Andrew's. For 15 minutes, Bolton were a
mess, their composure lost in the heat of the battle, with Ricketts
apparently relishing the prospect of contributing to his former club's
downfall. The introduction of Kevin Nolan gave Bolton more
balance in midfield, though, while Middlesbrough's momentum was
lost as Queudrue was dismissed. News of Birmingham City's
fightback quickly filtered through from the stands and the final five
minutes were played out in a carnival atmosphere. In any language,
Bolton were safe.

BOLTON WANDERERS (4-1-4-1): J Jaaskelainen — B N'Gotty, G Bergsson, M Whitlow, R Gardner
— I Campo — B Mendy (sub: K Nolan, 72min), P Frandsen, A Okocha, Y Djorkaeff (sub: S Charlton, 90)
— H Pedersen (sub: P-Y Andre, 66). **Substitutes not used:** S Ballesta, K Poole. **Booked:** Mendy,
Frandsen, N'Gotty.

MIDDLESBROUGH (4-3-1-2): M Schwarzer — S Parnaby, C Riggott, G Southgate, F Queudrue
— L Wilkshire, G Boateng, J Greening (sub: S Downing, 46) — Juninho — M Maccarone (sub: M Ricketts,
46), M Christie (sub: Doriva, 46). **Substitutes not used:** A Davies, M Crossley. **Booked:** Greening,
Queudrue. **Sent off:** Queudrue.
Referee: R Styles.

THE MANAGER

Sam Allardyce

The best thing to happen to Bolton Wanderers since the days of Bill Ridding and Nat Lofthouse. His management style combines solid, old-fashioned values with an open-minded acceptance of new-fangled technologies and strange philosophies. He laments that football has become a "namby-pamby" game from which the art of tough tackling, at which he excelled as a player, has been lost, but welcomes the advantages afforded by computer wizardry and Chinese medicine. The fans adore him, but he may just have gone too far in deciding that this season his team should play in an all-white strip.

Alan Kay

APPEARANCES

	Prem	FAC	WC	Total
P-Y Andre	0 (9)	-	-	0 (9)
C Armstrong	-	-	1	1
S Ballesta	1 (5)	-	-	1 (5)
A Barness	21 (4)	1	-	22 (4)
G Bergsson	31	-	-	31
Akin Bulent	0 (1)	-	1	1 (1)
I Campo	28 (3)	2	1	31 (3)
S Charlton	27 (4)	-	-	27 (4)
Y Djorkaeff	36	1	-	37
D Facey	1 (8)	2	-	3 (8)
G Farrelly	6 (2)	2	-	8 (2)
P Frandsen	34	-	-	34
R Gardner	31 (1)	-	-	31 (1)
David Holdsworth	-	-	1	1
Dean Holdsworth	5 (4)	-	0 (1)	5 (5)
N Hunt	-	1 (1)	-	1 (1)
J Jaaskelainen	38	-	-	38
J Johnson	0 (2)	-	1	1 (2)
F Laville	10	-	-	10
D Livesey	0 (2)	1	1	2 (2)
B Mendy	20 (1)	1	1	22 (1)
B N'Gotty	23	1	-	24
K Nolan	15 (18)	1 (1)	0 (1)	16 (20)
A Okocha	26 (5)	0 (1)	-	26 (6)
H Pedersen	31 (2)	-	0 (1)	31 (3)
K Poole	-	2	1	3
M Ricketts	13 (9)	1	-	14 (9)
J Smith	-	2	1	3
S Tofting	2 (6)	2	1	5 (6)
J Walters	0 (4)	0 (1)	1	1 (5)
P Warhurst	5 (2)	0 (1)	-	5 (3)
M Whitlow	14 (3)	1 (1)	-	15 (4)

Thursday December 26
NEWCASTLE UNITED (h)
Won 4-3 HT **3-1** Att **27,314** Position **17th**
Jaaskelainen — Barness, Whitlow, Bergsson, Charlton — Djorkaeff (Nolan 65), Frandsen, Okocha, Gardner — Ricketts, Pedersen (Facey 76) *Subs not used* Poole, Campo, Tofting *Booked* Frandsen
Scorers **Okocha 5, Gardner 9, Ricketts 45, 63**
Referee **U Rennie**

Three goals in the opening nine minutes set the scene for a Boxing Day feast at the Reebok. Okocha and Gardner both find the top corner of Given's net early on and a double from Ricketts, to make it 4-1, proves just enough to withstand Newcastle's Shearer-led recovery.

Saturday December 28
EVERTON (a)
Drew 0-0 HT **0-0** Att **39,480** Position **17th**
Jaaskelainen — Barness, Campo, Bergsson, Charlton — Nolan, Frandsen, Okocha, Gardner — Ricketts (Tofting 60), Pedersen (Facey 84) *Subs not used* Poole, Walters, Livesey *Booked* Bergsson, Charlton, Frandsen, Ricketts
Report page 119

Wednesday January 1
ASTON VILLA (a)
Lost 0-2 HT **0-1** Att **31,838** Position **17th**
Jaaskelainen — Barness, Bergsson, Bergsson, Charlton — Nolan (Bulent 85), Frandsen (Tofting 76), Gardner — Okocha, Pedersen (Facey 61) — Ricketts *Subs not used* Poole, Livesey
Report page 229

Saturday, January 4
SUNDERLAND (h)
FA Cup, 3rd rnd
Drew 1-1 HT **1-0** Att **10,123**
Poole — Barness, Campo, Livesey (Whitlow 73) — Hunt, Bulent (Okocha 73), Tofting (Nolan 73), Farrelly, Smith — Ricketts, Facey *Subs not used* Jaaskelainen, Walters *Booked* Hunt
Scorer **Ricketts 18**
Referee **G Barber (rep D Pugh 70)**

In front of a crowd 13,000 down on the figure for the corresponding Premiership fixture in October, a Bolton side showing nine changes take the lead through Ricketts, but the same player misses two other chances and Sunderland earn a replay through Phillips's header after a dire encounter.

Saturday January 11
FULHAM (h)
Drew 0-0   HT 0-0   Att **25,156**   Position **17th**
Jaaskelainen — Barness, Bergsson, Campo, Charlton
— Okocha (Walters 83), Frandsen, Gardner — Djorkaeff
— Pedersen, Facey (Nolan 69) *Subs not used* Poole,
Whitlow, Tofting *Booked* Charlton
Referee **A Wiley**

A tense but scarcely tight match as two teams in
trouble take turns to miss chances. Pedersen puts
three over the bar for Bolton, Legwinski also clearing
off the line from Gardner, while Sava has a goal for
Fulham ruled out for a marginal offside and Malbranque
fluffs a close-range sitter.

Tuesday January 14
SUNDERLAND (a)
FA Cup, 3rd rnd replay
Lost 0-2 (aet)   HT 0-0   Att **14,550**
Poole — N'Gotty, Campo, Whitlow — Mendy (Hunt 81),
Tofting, Nolan, Farrelly (Walters 62), Smith — Facey
(Warhurst ht), Djorkaeff *Subs not used* Jaaskelainen,
Bulent
Report page 276

Saturday January 18
CHARLTON ATHLETIC (a)
Drew 1-1   HT 0-0   Att **26,057**   Position **17th**
Jaaskelainen — Barness (Facey 76), Bergsson, Whitlow,
Charlton — Nolan, Frandsen, Gardner — Djorkaeff —
Ricketts, Pedersen (Mendy 68) *Subs not used* Poole,
N'Gotty, Campo
Scorer **Djorkaeff 85**
Report page 180

Wednesday January 22
NEWCASTLE UNITED (a)
Lost 0-1   HT 0-1   Att **52,005**   Position **17th**
Jaaskelainen — Mendy, N'Gotty, Bergsson, Barness
— Nolan (Facey 81), Frandsen (Campo 10),
Gardner, Charlton — Pedersen (Ricketts 67),
Djorkaeff *Subs not used* Poole, Bulent *Booked*
Bergsson, Campo
Report page 73

Jay-Jay Okocha arrived with a reputation so big he must have pushed it through customs on a trolley. Unsurprisingly, he took a while to live up to it, but he went on to become a favourite with the Reebok crowd as well as with producers of television football programmes, who delighted in showing compilations of his sensational stunts. Although Okocha's
main asset is his match-winning creativity, his showmanship is rarely without purpose: if hemmed in by two or three defenders, he will trick his way out. Sadly, the Bolton fans know that, with these skills, it is only a matter of time before he gives them the slip as well.

Alan Kay

FACTS AND STATS

● Between September 28 and February 22, Bolton drew 1-1 in ten of their 25 games.

● Just 10,123 saw Bolton draw 1-1 at home to Sunderland in the FA Cup on January 4. The last time a home match in the league attracted so few people was in November 1994, in the first division.

● Bolton have recorded more wins over Manchester United (41) than vice versa (39).

● They did not score a first-half goal in 11 games between September 1 and November 9.

● Bolton's win over Birmingham City on February 1 was their first on a Saturday since the previous April.

● Nine of Bolton Wanderers' 19 Premiership games at home featured a decisive goal in the last five minutes.

Bill Edgar

Tuesday January 28
EVERTON (h)
Lost 1-2   HT 0-2   Att 25,119   Position 17th
Jaaskelainen — Mendy, N'Gotty (Facey 68), Bergsson, Charlton — Frandsen, Campo, Gardner — Djorkaeff — Ricketts, Pedersen (Nolan ht) *Subs not used* Poole, Whitlow, Barness *Booked* Mendy, Gardner
Scorer **Bergsson 90**
Referee **R Styles**

With a grand total of 18 league goals, Watson has hardly been prolific throughout a 12-year career, but his double for Everton — a spectacular shot hooked over his shoulder from 18 yards and a toe-poke from ten yards closer — is enough to keep Bolton in the Premiership relegation mire, despite Bergsson's last-minute reply.

Saturday February 1
BIRMINGHAM CITY (h)
Won 4-2   HT 1-1   Att 24,288   Position 17th
Jaaskelainen — N'Gotty, Campo, Bergsson, Charlton — Mendy, Frandsen, Okocha, Gardner — Pedersen (Facey 81), Djorkaeff *Subs not used* Poole, Nolan, Barness, Tofting *Booked* Frandsen, Gardner
Scorers **Cunningham 12 (og), Pedersen 46, Djorkaeff 84, Facey 87**
Referee **D Gallagher**

This is a "must-win" game for Sam Allardyce — and his Bolton team do just that. Pegged back twice by Birmingham, who contribute to their own downfall with Cunningham's own-goal opener and a nervous display in goal by Bennett, Bolton hit two in the last six minutes to drag the Midlands side back into the relegation fray.

Saturday February 8
WEST BROMWICH ALBION (a)
Drew 1-1   HT 1-0   Att 26,933   Position 17th
Jaaskelainen — Bergsson, Campo, N'Gotty — Mendy, Okocha (Andre 86), Frandsen, Gardner, Charlton — Pedersen (Ballesta 80), Djorkaeff (Nolan 74) *Subs not used* Poole, Barness *Booked* Jaaskelainen, Frandsen, Campo, Ballesta
Scorer **Pedersen 18**
Report page 265

GOALSCORERS

Name	Prem	FAC	WC	Total
G Bergsson	1	-	-	1
I Campo	2	-	-	2
Y Djorkaeff	7	-	-	7
D Facey	1	-	-	1
G Farrelly	1	-	-	1
P Frandsen	2	-	-	2
R Gardner	2	-	-	2
K Nolan	1	-	-	1
B N'Gotty	1	-	-	1
A Okocha	7 (1p)	-	-	7 (1p)
H Pedersen	7	-	-	7
M Ricketts	6 (3p)	1	-	7 (3p)
Own goals	3	-	-	3

Saturday February 22
MANCHESTER UNITED (h)
Drew 1-1 HT 0-0 Att 27,409 Position 16th
Jaaskelainen — N'Gotty, Laville, Bergsson, Charlton —
Campo — Mendy (Barness 82), Okocha, Gardner —
Pedersen (Ballesta 57), Djorkaeff (Nolan 85) *Subs
not used* Poole, Andre *Booked* Campo
Scorer **N'Gotty 61**
Referee **A D'Urso**

With "Sven-gate" still on everybody's minds after Sir
Alex Ferguson's revelations about the England head
coach in *The Times*, his team does what it is renowned
for — scoring a late (in this case last-minute) goal to
salvage a draw thanks to Solskjaer. Bolton, who led
through N'Gotty's scruffy header, once again drop vital
points at the death.

Saturday March 8
LIVERPOOL (a)
Lost 0-2 HT 0-1 Att 41,462 Position 17th
Jaaskelainen — N'Gotty, Laville, Bergsson, Charlton
— Campo — Mendy (Andre 61), Okocha, Gardner,
Djorkaeff — Ballesta (Nolan 71) *Subs not used*
Barness, Frandsen, Poole *Booked* Laville, Campo,
Ballesta
Report page 98

Saturday March 15
SUNDERLAND (a)
Won 2-0 HT 0-0 Att 42,124 Position 17th
Jaaskelainen — N'Gotty, Laville, Bergsson, Gardner —
Campo — Mendy, Frandsen, Okocha — Pedersen
(Ballesta 80), Djorkaeff (Nolan 88) *Subs not used*
Poole, Andre, Barness *Booked* Laville
Scorers **Okocha 50, Pedersen 55**
Report page 278

Monday March 24
TOTTENHAM HOTSPUR (h)
Won 1-0 HT 0-0 Att 23,084 Position 17th
Jaaskelainen — N'Gotty, Laville, Bergsson, Gardner
(Barness ht) — Campo — Mendy (Andre 73), Frandsen,
Okocha — Pedersen, Djorkaeff *Subs not used* Nolan,
Ballesta, Poole
Scorer **Okocha 90 (pen)**
Referee **G Poll**

Dumped back into the bottom three by West Ham's win
on Saturday, Bolton climb straight back out again
courtesy of a penalty, coolly dispatched by Okocha with
almost the last kick of the game, Doherty having
brought down Djorkaeff as Bolton's second-half
pressure finally reaps reward.

THE PLAYERS

PIERRE-YVES ANDRE
Midfield
Born May 14, 1974,
Lannion, France
Ht 6ft 1in **Wt** 12st 2lb
Signed from Nantes (loan),
February 2003

CHRIS ARMSTRONG
Forward
Born June 19, 1971, Newcastle
Ht 6ft 0in **Wt** 13st 3lb
Signed from Tottenham Hotspur,
August 2002, free

SALVA BALLESTA
Forward
Born May 25, 1975,
Paese, Spain
Ht 6ft 0in **Wt** 13st 3lb
Signed from Valencia (loan),
January 2003

ANTHONY BARNESS
Defender
Born February 25, 1973,
Lewisham
Ht 5ft 10in **Wt** 12st 1lb
Signed from Charlton Athletic,
July 2000, free

GUDNI BERGSSON
Defender
Born July 21, 1965, Reykjavik
Ht 6ft 1in **Wt** 12st 3lb
Signed from Tottenham Hotspur,
March 1995, £65,000

AKIN BULENT
Midfield
Born August 28, 1979, Belgium
Ht 6ft 1in **Wt** 12st 4lb
Signed from Galatasaray, August
2002, free

IVAN CAMPO
Defender
Born February 21, 1974,
San Sebastian, Spain

Ht 5ft 11in **Wt** 12st 11lb
Signed from Real Madrid (loan),
August 2002

SIMON CHARLTON
Defender
Born October 25, 1971,
Huddersfield
Ht 5ft 8in **Wt** 11st 4lb
Signed from Birmingham City,
July 2000, free

YOURI DJORKAEFF
Forward
Born March 9, 1968, Lyons
Ht 5ft 10in **Wt** 11st 7lb
Signed from 1FC Kaiserslautern,
February 2002, free

DELROY FACEY
Forward
Born April 22, 1980,
Huddersfield
Ht 6ft 0in **Wt** 13st 0lb
Signed from Huddersfield Town,
July 2002, free

Gudni Bergsson

GARETH FARRELLY
Midfield
Born August 28, 1975, Dublin
Ht 6ft 0in **Wt** 12st 7lb
Signed from Everton, November 1999, free

PER FRANDSEN
Midfield
Born February 6, 1970, Copenhagen
Ht 6ft 1in **Wt** 12st 6lb
Signed from Blackburn Rovers, July 2000, £1.6m

RICARDO GARDNER
Midfield
Born September 25, 1978, St Andrews, Jamaica
Ht 5ft 9in **Wt** 11st 0lb
Signed from Harbour View, Jamaica, August 1998, £1m

DAVID HOLDSWORTH
Defender
Born November 8, 1968, Walthamstow
Ht 6ft 1in **Wt** 12st 4lb
Signed from Birmingham City, August 2002, free

DEAN HOLDSWORTH
Forward
Born November 8, 1968, Walthamstow
Ht 5ft 11in **Wt** 13st 6lb
Signed from Wimbledon, October 1997, £3.5m

NICKY HUNT
Defender
Born September 3, 1983, Bolton
Ht 6ft 0in **Wt** 10st 6lb
Signed from trainee, August 2000

JUSSI JAASKELAINEN
Goalkeeper
Born April 17, 1975, Vaasa, Finland

Ht 6ft 4in **Wt** 12st 10lb
Signed from VPS Vaasa, November 1997, £100,000

JERMAINE JOHNSON
Midfield
Born June 25, 1980, Kingston, Jamaica
Ht 5ft 9in **Wt** 11st 5lb
Signed from Tivoli Gardens, Jamaica, September 2001, £750,000

FLORENT LAVILLE
Defender
Born August 7, 1973, Valence, France
Ht 6ft 1in **Wt** 13st 1lb
Signed from Lyons (loan), February 2003

DANIEL LIVESEY
Defender
Born December 31, 1984, Salford
Signed from trainee, August 2002

BERNARD MENDY
Defender
Born August 20, 1981, Evreux, France
Ht 5ft 11in **Wt** 12st 2lb
Signed from Paris Saint-Germain (loan), July 2002

BRUNO N'GOTTY
Defender
Born June 10, 1971, Lyons
Ht 6ft 1in **Wt** 13st 8lb
Signed from Marseilles, September 2001, £500,000

KEVIN NOLAN
Midfield
Born June 24, 1982, Liverpool
Ht 6ft 1in **Wt** 13st 5lb
Signed from trainee, January 2000

Saturday April 5
MANCHESTER CITY (h)
Won 2-0 HT 1-0 Att **26,949** Position **16th**
Jaaskelainen — N'Gotty, Laville, Bergsson, Gardner — Campo — Mendy, Frandsen, Okocha (Nolan 88) — Pedersen (Facey 76), Djorkaeff (Johnson 90) *Subs not used* Barness, Poole
Scorers **Pedersen 32, Campo 52**
Referee **M Dean**

Okocha puts a missed first-half penalty behind him to inspire Bolton to a third successive league win, setting up Pedersen for the opener before Campo kills off an outplayed City, for whom Anelka fluffs two great early chances, with a header. "Performances like that can get managers the sack," Kevin Keegan, the rueful Manchester City manager, says.

Saturday April 12
CHELSEA (a)
Lost 0-1 HT 0-0 Att **39,852** Position **17th**
Jaaskelainen — Barness (Andre 72), Laville, Bergsson, Gardner — Campo (Nolan 86) — Mendy, Frandsen (Charlton 68), Okocha — Pedersen, Djorkaeff *Subs not used* Poole, Facey *Booked* Bergsson, Laville
Report page 87

Saturday April 19
WEST HAM UNITED (h)
Won 1-0 HT 1-0 Att **27,160** Position **17th**
Jaaskelainen — N'Gotty, Laville, Bergsson, Charlton — Mendy, Frandsen, Campo, Okocha (Andre 89) — Pedersen, Djorkaeff (Nolan 83) *Subs not used* Poole, Facey, Barness *Booked* Mendy, Laville, Campo
Scorer **Okocha 38**
Referee **U Rennie**

The ultimate six-pointer ends with Bolton celebrating a huge win — secured by a wonderful goal, Okocha finding the top corner from distance after running from deep in his own half — and West Ham in complete disarray, with Pearce sent off for a wild foul on Andre and both Cole and Brevett facing an investigation into alleged incidents in the players' tunnel after the match.

Monday April 21
BLACKBURN ROVERS (a)
Drew 0-0 HT 0-0 Att **28,862** Position **16th**
Jaaskelainen — N'Gotty, Laville, Bergsson, Gardner — Mendy, Frandsen, Campo, Okocha — Pedersen (Nolan 84), Djorkaeff (Andre 60) *Subs not used* Whitlow, Barness, Poole *Booked* Mendy, Laville, Campo
Report page 112

Saturday April 26
ARSENAL (h)
Drew 2-2   HT 0-0   Att 27,253   Position 17th
Jaaskelainen — N'Gotty, Bergsson, Laville, Gardner — Campo (Nolan 71) — Mendy (Andre 71), Frandsen, Okocha — Pedersen (Ballesta 83), Djorkaeff *Subs not used* Charlton, Poole *Booked* Laville, Campo *Sent off* Laville 90
Scorers **Djorkaeff 74, Keown 84 (og)**
Referee **A D'Urso**

Neither side can afford the two points they drop here, but Bolton, with West Ham closing the gap at the bottom, will be less displeased, having fought back from 2-0 down with 16 minutes to go. Keown's glancing header into his own net hits Arsenal's title hopes the day after Campbell learns that he will miss the last four matches of the season, banned for his sending-off against Manchester United.

Saturday May 3
SOUTHAMPTON (a)
Drew 0-0   HT 0-0   Att 30,951   Position 17th
Jaaskelainen — N'Gotty, Laville, Bergsson, Gardner — Campo — Mendy (Andre 53), Frandsen, Okocha (Nolan 87) — Pedersen (Ballesta 79), Djorkaeff *Subs not used* Poole, Charlton *Booked* Campo, Djorkaeff
Report page 136

Sunday May 11
MIDDLESBROUGH (h)
Won 2-1   HT 2-0   Att 27,241   Position 17th
Jaaskelainen — N'Gotty, Bergsson, Whitlow, Gardner — Campo — Mendy (Nolan 72), Frandsen, Okocha, Djorkaeff (Charlton 90) — Pedersen (Andre 66) *Subs not used* Ballesta, Poole *Booked* Mendy, N'Gotty, Frandsen
Scorers **Frandsen 10, Okocha 21**
Referee **R Styles**

Finishing seventeenth has never tasted so sweet. Bolton know that victory will be enough for survival and they race into a 2-0 lead before a goal from Ricketts, their recently departed striker, prompts more than a few late nerves. Middlesbrough have Queudrue sent off for the third time this season.

AGUSTIN OKOCHA
Midfield
Born August 14, 1973, Enugu, Nigeria
Ht 5ft 10in **Wt** 11st 0lb
Signed from Paris Saint-Germain, July 2002, free

HENRIK PEDERSEN
Forward
Born June 10, 1975, Denmark
Ht 6ft 1in **Wt** 13st 5lb
Signed from Silkeborg, July 2001, £650,000

KEVIN POOLE
Goalkeeper
Born July 21, 1963, Bromsgrove
Ht 5ft 10in **Wt** 12st 11lb
Signed from Birmingham City, October 2001, free

MICHAEL RICKETTS
(see Middlesbrough)

JEFF SMITH
Midfield
Born June 28, 1980, Middlesbrough
Ht 5ft 10in **Wt** 11st 8lb
Signed from Bishop Auckland, March 2001, free

STIG TOFTING
Midfield
Born August 14, 1969, Aarhus, Denmark
Ht 5ft 9in **Wt** 12st 0lb
Signed from SV Hamburg, February 2002, £250,000

JONATHAN WALTERS
Forward
Born September 20, 1983, Birkenhead
Signed from Blackburn Rovers, August 2001, free

PAUL WARHURST
Midfield
Born September 26, 1969, Stockport
Ht 6ft 1in **Wt** 13st 6lb
Signed from Crystal Palace, November 1998, £800,000

MIKE WHITLOW
Defender
Born January 13, 1968, Northwich
Ht 6ft 0in **Wt** 12st 12lb
Signed from Leicester City, September 1997, £500,000

Mike Whitlow

WEST HAM UNITED

PREMIERSHIP

	P	W	D	L	F	A	Pts
Man Utd	38	25	8	5	74	34	83
Arsenal	38	23	9	6	85	42	78
Newcastle	38	21	6	11	63	48	69
Chelsea	38	19	10	9	68	38	67
Liverpool	38	18	10	10	61	41	64
Blackburn	38	16	12	10	52	43	60
Everton	38	17	8	13	48	49	59
Southampton	38	13	13	12	43	46	52
Man City	38	15	6	17	47	54	51
Tottenham	38	14	8	16	51	62	50
Middlesbro	38	13	10	15	48	44	49
Charlton	38	14	7	17	45	56	49
Birmingham	38	13	9	16	41	49	48
Fulham	38	13	9	16	41	50	48
Leeds	38	14	5	19	58	57	47
Aston Villa	38	12	9	17	42	47	45
Bolton	38	10	14	14	41	51	44
West Ham	**38**	**10**	**12**	**16**	**42**	**59**	**42**
West Brom	38	6	8	24	29	65	26
Sunderland	38	4	7	27	21	65	19

FA CUP
Fourth round

WORTHINGTON CUP
Third round

Paolo Di Canio waves goodbye after relegation is confirmed at St Andrew's

THE GAMES

Monday August 19
NEWCASTLE UNITED (a)
Lost 0-4 HT 0-0 Att **51,072** Position **20th**
James — Pearce, Repka, Dailly, Winterburn — Schemmel (Labant 71), Cisse (Moncur 71), Carrick, Sinclair — Cole — Defoe *Subs not used* Breen, Van der Gouw, Camara
Booked Winterburn, Cisse
Report page 66

Saturday August 24
ARSENAL (h)
Drew 2-2 HT 1-0 Att **35,048** Position **16th**
James — Schemmel, Repka, Dailly, Winterburn (Breen 69) — Cole (Moncur 83), Cisse, Carrick, Sinclair — Kanoute, Defoe *Subs not used* Van der Gouw, Pearce, Camara *Booked* Repka, Moncur
Scorers Cole 44, Kanoute 53
Referee N Barry

Arsenal's record-breaking run of 14 straight Premiership wins ends after an Upton Park thriller in which West Ham, having had their 2-0 lead halved by Henry's fantastic 25-yard shot, miss a penalty — Seaman saving Kanoute's weak effort — and concede an equaliser to Wiltord with two minutes left.

Saturday August 31
CHARLTON ATHLETIC (h)
Lost 0-2 HT 0-2 Att **32,424** Position **19th**
James — Schemmel, Repka, Dailly, Winterburn (Camara 78) — Cole (Lomas 64), Carrick, Sinclair — Kanoute, Defoe *Subs not used* Van der Gouw, Pearce, Breen *Booked* Repka, Carrick, Cole
Referee J Winter

The worrying aspect of this defeat for West Ham is the tame manner in which they surrender. There is no hint of a fightback after first-half goals for Jensen and Fortune put Charlton in command and they slip back to the bottom of the table when Bolton beat Aston Villa the next day.

Wednesday September 11
WEST BROMWICH ALBION (h)
Lost 0-1 HT 0-1 Att **34,957** Position **20th**
James — Schemmel, Repka, Breen, Winterburn (Dailly 85) — Cole, Cisse, Carrick (Lomas 75), Sinclair — Kanoute, Di Canio (Defoe 75) *Subs not used* Van der Gouw, Pearce *Booked* Cole
Referee A D'Urso

The return to fitness of Di Canio, who has missed the opening weeks of the campaign with a foot injury, fails to ignite West Ham, who are beaten when Roberts finishes expertly in the first half to give West Bromwich Albion their second successive win after opening the season with three defeats. James prevents a heavier reverse.

THOUGH THE WORD "TRAGIC" IS often misused in a sporting context, there may not be a better one to describe West Ham's loss of Premiership status. They were, after all, a group of talented players who brought relegation entirely upon themselves. Just like Brian Clough's Nottingham Forest ten years ago, they were clearly too good to go down ... but down they went.

The fact that they so very nearly managed to survive — their fate was decided on the last day of the season — made it even more painful. Rousing group huddles and heroic performances, most notably against Chelsea and Tottenham Hotspur, captivated their legion of loyal fans and the players salvaged a lot of pride, amassing 22 points in the last 11 games. But the fightback began too late; the damage had been done.

Finishing on 42 points was no disgrace, but not a single player could claim to have played well throughout the season. And the fact that after relegation no fewer than three players — David James, Joe Cole and Trevor Sinclair — were selected for the England squad to play South Africa underlined the absurdity of the club's position.

Watching them lead Arsenal 2-0 in their first home game with less than 30 minutes to go, who could have predicted that things would turn so sour? Not only did they let the Double-winners off the hook, they crumbled so alarmingly that by Christmas they had collected only 14 points. A climate of fear had set in and it was not until January 29 that they managed to win their first league game at what used to be known as Fortress Upton Park.

The defence, in particular, was a shambles, shipping countless bad goals, with James beginning to look shaky in goal. The temperamental Tomas Repka, who had cost £5 million, lost form, confidence and his head with referees, his colleagues and the fans. Gary Breen, having had a good World Cup with Ireland, proved to be a poor purchase and Sinclair was not the same player who had impressed so much for England in Japan in the summer. Frederic Kanoute, touted not so long ago as a £10 million striker, somehow managed to be out for four months with a groin injury. And for all his crowd-pleasing skills, Paolo Di Canio had become a nuisance, more interested in using the newspapers to attack Glenn Roeder and the directors.

Though he could offer no satisfactory explanation for the crisis, Roeder remained calm and dignified, winning admiration and sympathy from his fellow managers. It was not his fault that his ego-inflated players were not performing to their true potential, some said. To an extent this was true, but it was clear that his lack of experience at the top level had begun to tell. He was a hard-working

Victory over Sunderland in March raised hopes of survival that were dashed

coach, respected if not feared by his high-earning charges, but he seemed to lack the personality to instil mental strength in the side. They became a laughing stock, picking up just six points from a possible 42.

In the new year there was much hope that the arrival from Leeds United of Lee Bowyer would make a difference, but far more effective introductions were Glen Johnson and Rufus Brevett in defence and Les Ferdinand, that brave old trouper, up front. With Sinclair and Repka returning to form, they sparked a heartening revival. But the pressures took their toll on Roeder's health. Trevor Brooking valiantly stepped into the managerial breach for the last three matches and introduced a three-pronged attack, while Di Canio, restored to the bench, grabbed some dramatic farewell goals that would have saved the club had Bolton not staged a remarkable comeback of their own.

There were plenty of "if onlys" to ponder over for fans. "If only we hadn't capitulated at home to Birmingham and West Brom" would have to rank high among them. And, though it is an uncharitable thought, should the board have sacked Roeder before Christmas, when West Ham's woes began to pile up? It certainly might have been better for his health, as well as for the club's.

Fans can certainly blame the board for deciding not to give Roeder any money to buy new players at the start of the season. The board, which spent £30 million on the stadium, had shut down the tills partly to make up for extravagance in the transfer market on the part of Harry Redknapp, the man who so did much to raise standards at Upton Park before being sacked when his wheeler-dealing went wrong.

In May it was Redknapp who was celebrating promotion to the Premiership with Portsmouth, just as his old club's relegation was confirmed. That made the "tragedy" complete.

Sunday September 15
TOTTENHAM HOTSPUR (a)
Lost 2-3 **HT 0-0** Att **36,005** Position **20th**
James — Pearce, Repka (Winterburn 9), Breen, Dailly — Cole, Lomas, Cisse, Sinclair — Kanoute (Defoe 85), Di Canio (Carrick 79) *Subs not used* Van der Gouw, Camara *Booked* Sinclair, Kanoute *Sent off* Pearce 70
Scorers **Kanoute 66, Sinclair 77**
Report page 151

Saturday September 21
MANCHESTER CITY (h)
Drew 0-0 **HT 0-0** Att **35,550** Position **20th**
James — Schemmel, Repka, Breen, Minto — Cole (Pearce 88), Lomas, Cisse (Carrick 73), Sinclair — Kanoute, Di Canio (Defoe 73) *Subs not used* Van der Gouw, Winterburn *Booked* Cisse, Minto
Referee **G Barber**

Failing to win a desperately dull encounter confirms this as West Ham's worst start to a season in their history, the fans beginning to turn on Glenn Roeder as the manager withdraws Di Canio with 17 minutes to go. At least Kevin Keegan has something to smile about — his wife's horse, Funfair Wane, wins the Ayr Gold Cup at 16-1.

Saturday September 28
CHELSEA (a)
Won 3-2 **HT 1-1** Att **38,929** Position **20th**
James — Schemmel, Repka, Breen, Minto — Sinclair, Lomas, Carrick, Cole — Kanoute (Defoe 4), Di Canio (Cisse 87) *Subs not used* Van der Gouw, Pearce, Winterburn *Booked* Repka, Schemmel, Lomas, Minto
Scorers **Defoe 40, Di Canio 48, 84**
Report page 79

Tuesday October 1
CHESTERFIELD (a)
Worthington Cup, 2nd rnd
Drew 1-1 (aet; win 5-4 on pens) **HT 1-0** Att **7,102**
James — Schemmel, Repka, Breen, Minto — Cole, Lomas, Carrick, Sinclair — Defoe, Di Canio *Subs not used* Dailly, Cisse, Garcia, Camara, Van der Gouw *Booked* Repka, Schemmel, Di Canio
Scorer **Defoe 13**
Referee **A Hall**

Their first win of the season under their belts, West Ham forgo the custom of squad rotation for an awkward tie away to Chesterfield and need Carrick to keep his nerve in the shoot-out — in front of travelling supporters who have criticised him this season — after failing to build on Defoe's early goal.

Saturday October 5
BIRMINGHAM CITY (h)
Lost 1-2 HT 1-2   Att **35,010**   Position **20th**
James — Schemmel (Pearce 71), Repka, Breen, Minto
— Cole (Camara 71), Lomas, Carrick, Sinclair — Defoe,
Di Canio *Subs not used* Van der Gouw, Cisse,
Winterburn *Booked* Carrick, Minto
Scorer **Cole 17**
Referee **P Dowd**

The level of criticism aimed at Glenn Roeder by
supporters increases markedly after defensive blunders
by Breen and Repka lead directly to Birmingham's two
goals, although the second — his second of the game
— is nonetheless superbly taken by John. It proves to be
the winner after Cole had drawn West Ham level. "A
little bit of fear crept into our play for the first time,"
the manager admits.

Saturday October 19
SUNDERLAND (a)
Won 1-0 HT 1-0   Att **44,352**   Position **16th**
James — Dailly, Repka, Pearce (Breen 67), Minto —
Sinclair (Cisse 77), Lomas, Carrick, Cole — Defoe,
Di Canio *Subs not used* Van der Gouw, Winterburn,
Camara *Booked* Carrick
Scorer **Sinclair 23**
Report page 272

Wednesday October 23
FULHAM (a)
Won 1-0 HT 0-0   Att **15,858**   Position **14th**
James — Dailly, Repka, Pearce, Minto — Cisse, Carrick,
Sinclair — Cole — Defoe, Di Canio *Subs not used*
Van der Gouw, Breen, Winterburn, Garcia, Camara
Booked Repka, Dailly, Cisse
Scorer **Di Canio 90 (pen)**
Referee **R Styles**
Report page 201

Sunday October 27
EVERTON (h)
Lost 0-1 HT 0-0   Att **34,117**   Position **15th**
James — Repka, Dailly, Pearce, Minto (Camara 82)
— Sinclair, Lomas (Cisse 73), Carrick, Cole — Defoe,
Di Canio *Subs not used* Van der Gouw, Breen,
Winterburn
Referee **A Wiley**

Rooney may be the talk of the town, but his visit to the
capital with Everton reveals that the teenager is
capable of mistakes like everybody else. With only
James to beat in the West Ham goal, he misses the
target, but his team deservedly take all three points
nonetheless when Carsley heads their second-half
winner.

MATCH OF THE SEASON

West Ham United 1   Chelsea 0
Upton Park, Saturday May 3 2003
Matt Dickinson, Chief Football Correspondent

AS SAVIOURS GO, A COMBINATION OF Trevor Brooking and
Paolo Di Canio is about as good as it gets for West Ham United
supporters, their double act surpassable only if Bobby Moore were
to come down from the heavens to tap in the winning goal. On
Saturday, the fans trooped out of Upton Park believing that
anything was possible and the news that Glenn Roeder had listened
to a famous victory via a bedside radio seemed another small
miracle.

Then they arrived home to hear that Bolton Wanderers had
shoved them back into the bottom three of the Barclaycard
Premiership. One more miracle will be needed on Sunday and they
may have exceeded their allocation in this extraordinary win over
Chelsea. West Ham remain favourites for the drop and, if it
happens, a sick manager and an ailing club will be what remains
rather than stirring memories of Brooking and Di Canio.

At least they will take the fight into the last day of the season and
it is fair to ask what would have been the outcome had Roeder been
in charge. It is a terribly delicate topic, even though the latest
bulletin was upbeat at the weekend, the stricken manager at home
and expecting a visit from officials and players before going back to
hospital for neurosurgery that should restore him to full health.

Would Di Canio have been recalled to the squad by Roeder after
a ten-week exile for indiscipline as much as illness? Probably not.
Would Roeder have deployed the daring 4-3-3 formation that has
shown Brooking to be so much more than an understated pundit?
Again, the answer is almost certainly negative.

This is not to kick a man when he is down and, under Roeder,
West Ham had begun the revival that has reaped 21 points from the
past ten matches. It is to underline the impact of Brooking, who has
brought leadership, tactical nous and boldness to an almost
impossible task — qualities that, if we are honest, he has kept well
hidden through so many years of fence-sitting commentary that
Kevin Keegan recently called him "creosote".

Brooking has excelled as temporary manager from the moment
he called five senior players together and asked what they would
think if he selected Di Canio. "I asked the question and they all said
that if he was fit and available, then fine," he said. It was an
intelligent move. He could not have predicted that Di Canio would
score the only goal, in the 71st minute, cleverly lifting the ball over
Carlo Cudicini from close range, but he deserved the break for his
adventurous game-plan.

Di Canio was inconsolable in the dressing-room after what was
almost certainly his last appearance at Upton Park. He sat crying in

Ferdinand keeps Melchiot at bay in the victory against Chelsea at Upton Park

Kanoute holds off Gallas as West Ham battle for Premiership survival

Saturday November 2
LIVERPOOL (a)
Lost 0-2 HT 0-1 Att 44,048 Position 16th
James — Dailly, Repka, Pearce, Minto — Cisse, Lomas, Carrick, Cole — Defoe (Camara 67), Sinclair *Subs not used* Breen, Winterburn, Garcia, Van der Gouw
Report page 93

Wednesday November 6
OLDHAM ATHLETIC (h)
Worthington Cup, 3rd rnd
Lost 0-1 HT 0-1 Att 21,919
James — Pearce, Breen (Winterburn 55), Dailly — Lomas, Carrick, Cisse (Garcia 79), Cole, Minto (Schemmel 55) — Defoe, Camara *Subs not used* Van der Gouw, Sofiane *Booked* Pearce, Dailly, Schemmel, Defoe
Referee **U Rennie**

West Ham suffer their almost ritual annual cup humiliation by a lower-division side when Oldham Athletic, riding high in the second division under Iain Dowie, the former Upton Park forward, go through thanks to Corazzin's header just before half-time. Glenn Roeder's side is the only one in the country without a home win.

Sunday November 10
LEEDS UNITED (h)
Lost 3-4 HT 1-4 Att 33,297 Position 18th
James — Dailly, Repka (Schemmel ht), Pearce, Winterburn — Lomas (Cisse 50), Carrick, Cole, Sinclair — Defoe, Di Canio *Subs not used* Van der Gouw, Camara, Minto *Booked* Repka, Schemmel, Cisse, Cole, Di Canio
Scorers **Di Canio 21, 50 (pen), Sinclair 74**
Referee **S Dunn**

This is a meeting of two managers under increasing pressure and it is Terry Venables who earns some breathing space as his Leeds side, having romped into a 4-1 half-time lead, hang on in the face of a spirited West Ham recovery in the second half. "I won't walk away," Glenn Roeder insists later.

Sunday November 17
MANCHESTER UNITED (h)
Drew 1-1 HT 0-1 Att 35,049 Position 19th
James — Schemmel, Dailly, Pearce, Winterburn — Cole, Cisse, Carrick, Sinclair — Defoe, Di Canio *Subs not used* Van der Gouw, Repka, Breen, Camara, Garcia *Booked* Cisse, Di Canio
Scorer **Defoe 86**
Referee **M Halsey**

Sir Alex Ferguson hints that he may delay his planned retirement as his Manchester United side, ahead through Van Nistelrooy, are pegged back by Defoe's late equaliser for West Ham. One point, preserved by two fine late saves by James, is enough to take them off the bottom of the table once again.

Saturday November 23
ASTON VILLA (a)
Lost 1-4 HT 0-1 Att **33,279** Position **20th**
James — Schemmel, Pearce, Dailly, Winterburn — Cole,
Cisse, Carrick, Sinclair — Defoe, Di Canio *Subs not used*
Van der Gouw, Repka, Breen, Garcia, Camara *Booked*
Dailly, Pearce, Cisse
Scorer **Di Canio 70**
Report page 226

Monday December 2
SOUTHAMPTON (h)
Lost 0-1 HT 0-0 Att **28,844** Position **20th**
James — Schemmel, Dailly, Repka, Winterburn —
Sinclair, Carrick, Cole, Di Canio (Moncur 77) — Pearce,
Defoe *Subs not used* Van der Gouw, Minto, Breen,
Camara *Booked* Repka
Referee **M Riley**

The Southampton team bus arrives late — and so does
Beattie, the striker meeting Ormerod's cross in the
second minute of stoppage time for a barely
deserved winner. "Sack the board" and "Roeder out"
chants reflect the mood among West Ham fans after
seeing Defoe and Pearce miss the best of several
chances.

Saturday December 7
MIDDLESBROUGH (a)
Drew 2-2 HT 0-0 Att **28,283** Position **20th**
James — Schemmel, Dailly, Repka, Winterburn —
Sinclair, Cisse (Moncur 85), Carrick, Cole — Pearce
(Breen 90), Defoe *Subs not used* Van der Gouw, Minto,
Camara *Booked* Repka
Scorers **Cole 46, Pearce 76**
Report page 166

Saturday December 14
MANCHESTER UNITED (a)
Lost 0-3 HT 0-2 Att **67,555** Position **20th**
James — Schemmel, Repka, Dailly, Minto (Breen 89)
— Lomas (Moncur 85), Carrick, Cole, Sinclair — Pearce,
Defoe *Subs not used* A Ferdinand, Camara, Bywater
Booked Repka
Report page 47

Di Canio celebrates scoring against Chelsea, but can West Ham halt the slide?

the bath, ignoring the jokes of team-mates who had been happy to
see him cast into exile by Roeder. "It was brilliant to score, but what
gave me the greatest pleasure was being able to wear the West Ham
shirt again," Di Canio said. "I don't know if the goal will be
important or not, but the best thing for me was to say 'thank you' to
the supporters in person, to wear the shirt on my back and then to
go on and score the goal which keeps us alive."

The trouble for West Ham was that, because of goal difference, it
was not enough to keep their fate in their own hands — unlike Chelsea, who are lucky to remain fourth. Claudio Ranieri's team only
need to draw against Liverpool on Sunday to qualify for the Champions League, which is just as well because Jimmy Floyd Hasselbaink
has given up and they have hit wretchedly inconsistent form.

West Ham are on a roll and, according to Brooking, "if we get 44
points and go down, we will be desperately unlucky". But it is quite
possible, given that Bolton face a comparatively easy home match
against Middlesbrough while West Ham must travel to Birmingham
City. Before he departed, Brooking was asked if he had happy
memories of St Andrew's. "Not really, no."

WEST HAM UNITED (4-3-1-2): D James — G Johnson, C Dailly, T Repka, R Brevett — J Cole, S Lomas,
T Sinclair — J Defoe — F Kanoute, L Ferdinand (sub: P Di Canio, 56min). **Substitutes not used:**
R van der Gouw, D Hutchison, R Garcia, E Cisse. **Booked:** Sinclair, Defoe, Repka.

CHELSEA (4-4-2): C Cudicini — M Melchiot, W Gallas, M Desailly, C Babayaro — J Morris
(sub: B Zenden, 77), F Lampard, E Petit, G Le Saux — E Gudjohnsen (sub: J F Hasselbaink, 71), G Zola
(sub: C Cole, 71). **Substitutes not used:** E de Goey, M Stanic.
Referee: A D'Urso.

THE MANAGER

Glenn Roeder

Despite Glenn Roeder's protests that his side were simply having no luck and that injuries had taken their toll, his inability to motivate key players was always a worry. And given his background as a captain and centre back, it was surprising that he failed so dismally to marshal an effective defence. But he is a decent man who did not deserve to suffer as he did. Two wins and a draw were a great achievement for Trevor Brooking, his stand-in for the final three matches. He eased the pain of relegation for all the players and supporters.

Gavin Hadland

APPEARANCES

	Prem	FAC	WC	Total
L Bowyer	10	1	-	11
G Breen	9 (5)	2	2	13 (5)
R Brevett	12 (1)	-	-	12 (1)
T Camara	0 (4)	0 (1)	1	1 (5)
M Carrick	28 (2)	2	2	32 (2)
E Cisse	18 (7)	2	1	21 (7)
J Cole	36	2	2	40
C Dailly	23 (3)	1 (1)	1	25 (4)
J Defoe	29 (9)	2	2	33 (9)
P Di Canio	16 (2)	-	1	17 (2)
L Ferdinand	12 (2)	-	-	12 (2)
R Garcia	-	0 (1)	0 (1)	0 (2)
D Hutchison	0 (10)	-	-	0 (10)
D James	38	2	2	42
G Johnson	14 (1)	0 (1)	-	14 (2)
F Kanoute	12 (5)	-	-	12 (5)
V Labant	0 (1)	-	-	0 (1)
S Lomas	27 (2)	1	2	30 (2)
S Minto	9 (3)	1	2	12 (3)
J Moncur	0 (7)	-	-	0 (7)
I Pearce	26 (4)	2	1	29 (4)
T Repka	32	0 (1)	1	33 (1)
S Schemmel	15 (1)	1	1 (1)	17 (2)
T Sinclair	36 (2)	2	1	39 (2)
N Winterburn	16 (2)	1	0 (1)	17 (3)

Saturday December 21
BOLTON WANDERERS (h)
Drew 1-1 HT 1-0 Att **34,893** Position **20th**
James — Schemmel, Repka, Dailly, Winterburn — Sinclair, Lomas, Carrick, Cole — Pearce (Hutchison 80), Defoe *Subs not used* Bywater, Breen, Moncur, Johnson
Scorer **Pearce 17**
Referee **S Bennett**

West Ham know now that they must defy history as well as the sceptics if they are to survive. Ahead through Pearce, they concede a goal to Ricketts — the Bolton substitute scoring for the first time from open play for a year — and will be bottom at Christmas, a relegation predicament from which no Premiership side has ever escaped.

Thursday December 26
FULHAM (h)
Drew 1-1 HT 0-0 Att **35,025** Position **20th**
James — Schemmel, Repka, Dailly, Winterburn — Sinclair, Lomas (Hutchison 76), Carrick, Cole — Kanoute (Pearce 66), Defoe *Subs not used* Bywater, Breen, Moncur *Booked* Repka, Winterburn *Sent off* Repka 90
Scorer **Sinclair 65 (pen)**
Referee **D Gallagher**

As if their problems were not severe enough, West Ham face losing Repka to suspension after the defender talks himself into his tenth yellow card of the season and continues to harangue Dermot Gallagher, the referee, who then pulls out a red. "Inexcusable," is Glenn Roeder's verdict. Sinclair's penalty — and two great late saves by James — earn a point.

Saturday December 28
BLACKBURN ROVERS (a)
Drew 2-2 HT 1-1 Att **24,998** Position **20th**
James — Schemmel, Breen, Dailly, Winterburn (Minto 83) — Lomas (Defoe 73), Cisse (Moncur 77), Cole, Carrick, Sinclair — Pearce *Subs not used* Repka, Bywater *Booked* Dailly, Cole
Scorers **Taylor 24 (og), Defoe 86**
Report page 107

Saturday January 4
NOTTINGHAM FOREST (h)
FA Cup, 3rd rnd
Won 3-2 HT 1-1 Att **29,612**
James — Schemmel, Breen, Dailly, Winterburn (Repka 86) — Cisse, Carrick, Cole, Sinclair — Pearce (Camara 75), Defoe *Subs not used* Van der Gouw, Moncur, Sofiane
Scorers **Defoe 26, 83, Cole 61**
Referee **P Durkin**

At long last, West Ham win in front of their own supporters — and in dramatic FA Cup style. Twice behind to an attractive Forest side, they are indebted to Johnson's penalty miss at 2-2 before Defoe seals their passage to the fourth round with his second goal of the game.

Saturday January 11
NEWCASTLE UNITED (h)
Drew 2-2 **HT 2-1** Att **35,048** Position **19th**
James — Lomas, Breen, Dailly, Winterburn (Minto 56)
— Bowyer, Cisse (Hutchison 81), Carrick, Cole — Defoe,
Sinclair (Pearce 81). *Subs not used* Van der Gouw,
Moncur
Scorers **Cole 14, Defoe 45**
Referee **J Winter**

Anti-racism protests and scuffles outside the ground,
but an exciting match inside it as West Ham, with
Bowyer "back home" in the East End and on his best
behaviour on his debut, go behind, take the lead
before half-time and finally concede an exquisite
equaliser to Jenas, who volleys into the top corner.

Sunday January 19
ARSENAL (a)
Lost 1-3 **HT 1-1** Att **38,053** Position **20th**
James — Dailly, Breen, Pearce, Winterburn (Minto 80)
— Lomas, Bowyer, Cole, Cisse (Moncur 85), Sinclair —
Defoe *Subs not used* Hutchison, Van der Gouw,
Johnson *Booked* Breen *Sent off* Lomas 13
Scorer **Defoe 40**
Report page 60

Wednesday January 22
CHARLTON ATHLETIC (a)
Lost 2-4 **HT 1-2** Att **26,340** Position **20th**
James — Lomas, Breen, Dailly, Minto (Winterburn 71)
— Bowyer, Cisse (Johnson 62), Carrick, Sinclair —
L Ferdinand, Defoe *Subs not used* Van der Gouw,
Hutchison, Pearce *Booked* Bowyer, Ferdinand
Scorers **Rufus 19 (og), Fish 62 (og)**
Report page 180

Sunday January 26
MANCHESTER UNITED (a)
FA Cup, 4th rnd
Lost 0-6 **HT 0-2** Att **67,181**
James — Lomas, Breen (Dailly 80), Pearce, Minto
— Bowyer, Cisse (Garcia 80), Carrick, Sinclair (Johnson
80) — Cole — Defoe *Subs not used* Hutchison,
Van der Gouw *Booked* Defoe, Minto
Report page 49

Though his form was patchy early in
the season and his goal count
disappointing, the young England star
came of age when given the
captain's armband. Joe Cole worked
tirelessly all over the field and his
passion for the club shone through.
Abandoning his flicks, tricks and
fancy dannery, he transformed
himself into a combative ball of
energy who would no longer shy away
from tackles. No one showed more
urgency in the struggle for survival
than Cole and it was he who
introduced those group huddles.
Gavin Hadland

STATS AND FACTS

- In the 1977-78 season, West Ham had Trevor Brooking on the pitch and won six of their last nine games but were relegated from the old first division. Last season, with Brooking as the caretaker manager for the final couple of weeks, they won six of their last 11 matches and still went down.

- The 2-0 home win over Tottenham Hotspur on March 1 was their first clean sheet in 22 games.

- West Ham recorded minus goal differences every season during their ten-year stint in the Premiership, despite finishing in the top half five times.

- West Ham have won two of their past 16 home matches against Leeds United.

- In the space of 33 days around the new year, Jermain Defoe scored either the winner or an equaliser in the last ten minutes of a match for West Ham on three occasions — in a 2-2 draw away to Blackburn Rovers, the 3-2 home win over Nottingham Forest in the FA Cup and the 2-1 home win over Blackburn Rovers.

- West Ham United have won just two of their past 23 games away to Aston Villa.

- They finished below Everton in the Premiership for the first time in seven seasons.

- Paolo Di Canio and Frederic Kanoute, West Ham's main strike pairing, only started together five times last season.

- West Ham have not won any of their past 35 matches at Anfield.

- Nine of the past 12 meetings between West Ham United and Aston Villa have ended in draws.

Bill Edgar

GOALSCORERS

	Prem	FAC	WC	Total
M Carrick	1	-	-	1
J Cole	4	1	-	5
J Defoe	8	2	1	11
P Di Canio	9 (3p)	-	-	9 (3p)
L Ferdinand	2	-	-	2
F Kanoute	5	-	-	5
I Pearce	2	-	-	2
T Sinclair	8 (1p)	-	-	8 (1p)
Own goals	3	-	-	3

Wednesday January 29
BLACKBURN ROVERS (h)
Won 2-1   HT 0-1   Att 34,743   Position 18th
James — Johnson, Repka, Pearce, Winterburn — Bowyer (Defoe 84), Lomas, Carrick, Cole — L Ferdinand (Kanoute 59), Di Canio (Sinclair 88) *Subs not used* Van der Gouw, Schemmel *Booked* Cole
Scorers **Di Canio 58 (pen), Defoe 89**
Referee **A Wiley**

Unlucky 13? Not for West Ham, who finally win at Upton Park after 12 unsuccessful league attempts — and this despite going behind to Blackburn. The returning Di Canio wins and converts a penalty before Defoe, a late substitute, gets the goal that, with West Bromwich Albion losing at home to Charlton Athletic, takes them off the bottom.

Sunday February 2
LIVERPOOL (h)
Lost 0-3   HT 0-2   Att 35,033   Position 19th
James — Johnson, Repka, Pearce, Brevett (Brevett 59) — Sinclair (Defoe 68), Bowyer, Carrick, Cole — L Ferdinand (Kanoute 55), Di Canio *Subs not used* Van der Gouw, Schemmel *Booked* Cole
Referee **M Messias**

The bubbles of optimism are immediately blown away as West Ham suffer a more predictable Upton Park fate. Three corners, each delivered by Riise and met with abject defending, allow Liverpool to coast to victory, with Gerrard getting the second the day before incurring a three-match FA suspension for his tackle on Naysmith during the Merseyside derby.

Saturday February 8
LEEDS UNITED (a)
Lost 0-1   HT 0-1   Att 40,126   Position 19th
James — Johnson, Repka, Pearce, Brevett (Sinclair 83) — Bowyer, Carrick (Hutchison 90), Lomas, Cole — Kanoute, Di Canio (Defoe 73) *Subs not used* Van der Gouw, Dailly *Booked* Bowyer, Brevett
Sent off Kanoute 70
Report page 218

Sunday February 23
WEST BROMWICH ALBION (a)
Won 2-1   HT 1-0   Att 27,042   Position 18th
James — Johnson, Repka, Pearce, Brevett (Breen 85) — Bowyer (Breen 85), Carrick, Lomas, Sinclair — L Ferdinand (Hutchison 81), Di Canio (Defoe 49) *Subs not used* Van der Gouw, Moncur *Booked* Carrick
Scorer **Sinclair 45, 67**
Report page 266

Saturday March 1
TOTTENHAM HOTSPUR (h)
Won 2-0   HT 1-0   Att 35,049   Position 18th
James — Johnson, Repka, Pearce, Brevett — Bowyer, Carrick, Cole, Sinclair — L Ferdinand (Hutchison 82), Defoe *Subs not used* Van der Gouw, Breen, Cisse, Moncur *Booked* Cole, Johnson, Bowyer
Scorers **Ferdinand 31, Carrick 47**
Referee **N Barry**

With their own lack of firepower — and fighting spirit — acute, it is the striker that Spurs let go who inevitably causes their downfall, Les Ferdinand ignoring the pain from a suspected fractured eye socket to score the first goal and help to set up the second in a vital and thoroughly deserved victory.

Saturday March 15
EVERTON (a)
Drew 0-0   HT 0-0   Att 40,158   Position 18th
James — Johnson, Repka, Pearce, Brevett — Lomas, Carrick, Cole (Cisse 86), Sinclair — L Ferdinand (Dailly 83), Defoe. *Subs not used* Breen, Moncur, Van der Gouw
Report page 122

Saturday March 22
SUNDERLAND (h)
Won 2-0   HT 1-0   Att 35,033   Position 17th
James — Johnson, Repka, Pearce, Brevett — Lomas (Hutchison 87), Carrick, Cole (Cisse 84), Sinclair — L Ferdinand (Kanoute ht), Defoe. *Subs not used* Van der Gouw, Dailly *Booked* Johnson
Scorers **Defoe 24, Kanoute 65**
Referee **R Styles**

Sunderland's fate is surely sealed after an eighth straight league defeat, but for West Ham the road to salvation is now clear after goals from Defoe, set up by Ferdinand's leap, and Kanoute, who is released by Carrick, take them out of the bottom three for the first time since November 10.

Saturday April 5
SOUTHAMPTON (a)
Drew 1-1   HT 0-1   Att 31,941   Position 18th
James — Johnson, Repka, Pearce, Brevett — Bowyer, Lomas (Cisse ht), Cole, Sinclair — L Ferdinand (Kanoute 58), Defoe. *Subs not used* Van der Gouw, Hutchison, Dailly *Booked* Cole, Bowyer
Scorer **Defoe 83**
Report page 134

THE PLAYERS

LEE BOWYER
Midfield
Born January 3, 1977, Canning Town
Ht 5ft 9in **Wt** 10st 6lb
Signed from Leeds United, January 2003, £100,000

GARY BREEN
Defender
Born December 12, 1973, Hendon
Ht 6ft 1in **Wt** 12st 0lb
Signed from Coventry City, July 2002, free

RUFUS BREVETT
Defender
Born September 24, 1969, Derby
Ht 5ft 8in **Wt** 11st 6lb
Signed from Fulham, January 2003, undisclosed

TITI CAMARA
Forward
Born November 17, 1972, Conakry, Guinea
Ht 6ft 1in **Wt** 12st 8lb
Signed from Liverpool, December 2000, £1.5m

MICHAEL CARRICK
Midfield
Born July 28, 1981, Wallsend
Ht 6ft 0in **Wt** 11st 10lb
Signed from trainee, August 1998

EDOUARD CISSE
Midfield
Born March 30, 1978, Pau, France
Ht 6ft 1in **Wt** 12st 0lb
Signed from Rennes (loan), August 2002

JOE COLE
Midfield
Born November 8, 1981, Islington
Ht 5ft 9in **Wt** 11st 0lb
Signed from trainee, December 1998

CHRISTIAN DAILLY
Defender
Born October 23, 1973, Dundee
Ht 6ft 0in **Wt** 12st 10lb
Signed from Blackburn Rovers, January 2001, £1.75m

JERMAIN DEFOE
Forward
Born October 7, 1982, Beckton
Ht 5ft 7in **Wt** 10st 4lb
Signed from Charlton Athletic, July 1999, undisclosed

Rufus Brevett

PAOLO DI CANIO
Forward
Born July 9, 1968, Rome
Ht 5ft 9in **Wt** 11st 9lb
Signed from Sheffield Wednesday,
January 1999, £1.7m

LES FERDINAND
Forward
Born December 18, 1966,
Acton
Ht 5ft 11in **Wt** 13st 5lb
Signed from Tottenham Hotspur,
January 2003, nominal

RICHARD GARCIA
Forward
Born September 4, 1981,
Perth, Australia
Ht 5ft 11in **Wt** 12st 1lb
Signed from trainee, September
1998

DON HUTCHISON
Forward
Born May 9, 1971, Gateshead
Ht 6ft 2in **Wt** 11st 8lb
Signed from Sunderland, August
2001, £5m

DAVID JAMES
Goalkeeper
Born August 1, 1970,
Welwyn Garden City
Ht 6ft 5in **Wt** 14st 5lb
Signed from Aston Villa, June
1999, £3.5m

GLEN JOHNSON
Defender
Born August 23, 1984, London
Ht 5ft 10in **Wt** 11st 0lb
Signed from trainee, August 2001

FREDERIC KANOUTE
Forward
Born September 2, 1977,
Saint-Foy-les-Lyons, France
Ht 6ft 4in **Wt** 12st 10lb
Signed from Lyons, March 2000,
£4m

VLADIMIR LABANT
Defender
Born June 8, 1974, Zilina,
Slovakia
Ht 6ft 0in **Wt** 11st 7lb
Signed from Sparta Prague,
January 2002, £900,000

Frederic Kanoute

Saturday April 12
ASTON VILLA (h)
Drew 2-2 **HT 1-1** **Att 35,029** Position **18th**
James — Johnson, Repka, Pearce, Brevett — Bowyer
(L Ferdinand 62), Lomas, Cole, Sinclair — Kanoute
(Hutchison 85), Defoe. *Subs not used* Van der Gouw,
Dailly, Cisse *Booked* Repka, Cole, Lomas, Bowyer
Scorers **Sinclair 15, Kanoute 65**
Referee **M Dean**

The claret and blue confrontation ends with Villa edging
nearer safety and West Ham still deep in the mire. After
surrendering an early lead, Glenn Roeder's side at least
recover to take a point, and it would have been three
but for Enckelman's late heroics in the Villa goal and
bad misses from Defoe and Ferdinand.

Saturday April 19
BOLTON WANDERERS (a)
Lost 0-1 **HT 0-1** **Att 27,160** Position **18th**
James — Johnson, Repka, Pearce, Brevett — Lomas,
Cisse (L Ferdinand 65), Cole, Sinclair — Kanoute,
Defoe. *Subs not used* Van der Gouw, Hutchison, Dailly,
Breen *Booked* Defoe, Cole, Lomas, Johnson *Sent off*
Pearce 90
Report page 243

Monday April 21
MIDDLESBROUGH (h)
Won 1-0 **HT 0-0** **Att 35,019** Position **18th**
James — Johnson, Repka, Pearce, Brevett — Lomas,
Cisse, Cole, Sinclair — L Ferdinand, Defoe. *Subs not
used* Van der Gouw, Breen, Dailly, Garcia, Hutchison
Booked Brevett
Scorer **Sinclair 77**
Referee **A Wiley**

A must-win game for West Ham and they duly oblige
through Sinclair, but all celebrations are put on hold
with the news that Glenn Roeder has been rushed to
hospital after the manager complains of feeling unwell
after the match.

Sunday April 27
MANCHESTER CITY (a)
Won 1-0 **HT 0-0** **Att 34,815** Position **18th**
James — Johnson, Repka, Pearce (Dailly 85), Brevett
— Sinclair, Lomas, Cisse (Kanoute ht), Cole —
L Ferdinand (Hutchison 54), Defoe. *Subs not used*
Van der Gouw, Garcia *Booked* Defoe
Scorer **Kanoute 81**
Report page 148

Saturday May 3
CHELSEA (h)
Won 1-0 HT 0-0 Att **35,042** Position **18th**
James — Johnson, Repka, Dailly, Brevett — Cole,
Lomas, Sinclair — Defoe — Kanoute, L Ferdinand
(Di Canio 56). *Subs not used* Van der Gouw, Hutchison,
Garcia, Cisse *Booked* Repka, Defoe, Sinclair
Scorer **Di Canio 71**
Referee **A D'Urso**

It is now played two, won two for Trevor Brooking as
West Ham's acting manager recalls Di Canio and sees
the forward, exiled under Glenn Roeder, come off the
bench to score the scripted winner against Chelsea that
takes the relegation fight to the last day. Di Canio cries;
Chelsea's tears over their dented Champions League
ambitions are stemmed with the news that Liverpool
have been beaten as well.

Sunday May 11
BIRMINGHAM CITY (a)
Drew 2-2 HT 0-0 Att **29,505** Position **18th**
James — Johnson, Dailly, Repka, Brevett (Di Canio 82)
— Cole (Hutchison 88), Lomas, Sinclair — Defoe,
L Ferdinand, Kanoute. *Subs not used* Van der Gouw,
Cisse, Moncur *Booked* Brevett
Report page 196

STEVE LOMAS
Midfield
Born January 18, 1974, Hanover
Ht 6ft 0in **Wt** 12st 8lb
Signed from Manchester City,
March 1997, £1.6m

SCOTT MINTO
Defender
Born August 6, 1971, Heswall
Ht 5ft 9in **Wt** 12st 7lb
Signed from Chelsea, January
1999, £1m

JOHN MONCUR
Midfield
Born September 22, 1966,
Stepney
Ht 5ft 7in **Wt** 9st 10lb
Signed from Swindon Town, June
1994, £900,000

IAN PEARCE
Defender
Born May 7, 1974, Bury St
Edmunds
Ht 6ft 3in **Wt** 14st 4lb
Signed from Blackburn Rovers,
September 1997, £1.6m

TOMAS REPKA
Defender
Born January 2, 1974, Slavicin,
Czech Republic
Ht 6ft 0in **Wt** 12st 7lb
Signed from Fiorentina,
September 2001, £5.5m

SEBASTIEN SCHEMMEL
Defender
Born June 2, 1975, Nancy
Ht 5ft 10in **Wt** 11st 12lb
Signed from Metz, January 2001,
£465,000

TREVOR SINCLAIR
Midfield
Born March 2, 1973, Dulwich
Ht 5ft 10in **Wt** 12st 10lb
Signed from Queens Park
Rangers, January 1998, £2.3m

NIGEL WINTERBURN
Defender
Born December 11, 1963,
Nuneaton
Ht 5ft 9in **Wt** 11st 4lb
Signed from Arsenal, July 2000,
£250,000

Trevor Sinclair

WEST BROMWICH ALBION

PREMIERSHIP

	P	W	D	L	F	A	Pts
Man Utd	38	25	8	5	74	34	83
Arsenal	38	23	9	6	85	42	78
Newcastle	38	21	6	11	63	48	69
Chelsea	38	19	10	9	68	38	67
Liverpool	38	18	10	10	61	41	64
Blackburn	38	16	12	10	52	43	60
Everton	38	17	8	13	48	49	59
Southampton	38	13	13	12	43	46	52
Man City	38	15	6	17	47	54	51
Tottenham	38	14	8	16	51	62	50
Middlesbro	38	13	10	15	48	44	49
Charlton	38	14	7	17	45	56	49
Birmingham	38	13	9	16	41	49	48
Fulham	38	13	9	16	41	50	48
Leeds	38	14	5	19	58	57	47
Aston Villa	38	12	9	17	42	47	45
Bolton	38	10	14	14	41	51	44
West Ham	38	10	12	16	42	59	42
West Brom	**38**	**6**	**8**	**24**	**29**	**65**	**26**
Sunderland	38	4	7	27	21	65	19

FA CUP
Fourth round

WORTHINGTON CUP
Second round

**Jason Koumas looked every inch a
Premiership player**

THE GAMES

Saturday August 17
MANCHESTER UNITED (a)
Lost 0-1   HT 0-0   Att 67,645   Position **18th**
Hoult — Sigurdsson, Moore, Gilchrist — Balis, Gregan
(Taylor 82), McInnes, Johnson, Clement — Dichio
(Dobie 60), Roberts (Marshall 69) *Subs not used*
Jensen, Wallwork *Booked* McInnes *Sent off* McInnes
Report page 42

Saturday August 24
LEEDS UNITED (h)
Lost 1-3   HT 0-1   Att 26,618   Position **18th**
Hoult — Sigurdsson, Moore (Dichio 59), Gilchrist
— Balis, Gregan, McInnes (Wallwork 72), Johnson
(Marshall 72), Clement — Dobie, Roberts *Subs not
used* Taylor, Jensen *Booked* Sigurdsson
Scorer **Marshall 90**
Referee **S Dunn**

Having waited 16 years for top-flight football to return
to The Hawthorns — and then another 2½ hours for a
teatime kick-off — Albion's celebrations are instantly
deflated by an outstanding Leeds performance.
Bowyer's 25-yard shot is the pick of the visiting team's
three strikes.

Tuesday August 27
ARSENAL (a)
Lost 2-5   HT 3-0   Att 37,920   Position **20th**
Hoult — Sigurdsson, Moore, Gilchrist — Balis, Gregan,
McInnes (Marshall 62), Johnson, Clement — Dobie,
Roberts *Subs not used* Wallwork, Dichio, Taylor, Jensen
Booked McInnes, Clement
Scorers **Dobie 51, Roberts 87**
Report page 54

Saturday August 31
FULHAM (h)
Won 1-0   HT 0-0   Att 25,461   Position **17th**
Hoult — Gregan, Moore, Gilchrist — Balis, Marshall
(Koumas 53), Wallwork, Johnson, Clement — Hughes
(Taylor 78), Roberts (J Chambers 88) *Subs not used*
Jensen, Dichio *Booked* Moore, Johnson, Wallwork,
Hughes
Scorer **Moore 48**
Referee **R Styles**

After straight defeats against three of last season's
top five, Albion find Fulham more to their liking. The
signings of Hughes, a talisman at The Hawthorns, and
Koumas in midweek are followed by Moore's header
early in the second half as Jean Tigana's toothless side
suffer their first defeat of a season already comprising
ten league and cup matches.

PIGS WEARING LIPSTICK. THAT'S how West Bromwich Albion
were cruelly labelled as they took their first tentative steps into the
promised land after 16 years in the football wilderness. Experts were
convinced that the writing was on the wall before a ball had been
kicked. At 7-2 on, they were the shortest-priced favourites for relegation since the Premiership began. But Gary Megson, who had
"achieved the impossible" by hauling his team back into the big
time, valiantly shrugged off the merchants of doom. He urged his
players to react like top-class golfers. "The ones that are successful
are those who hole the putts," the manager reasoned.

And so Albion took their Premiership bow at Old Trafford's
Theatre of Dreams. The prospect was mouth-watering for the
long-suffering fans. Starved of glory for a decade and a half, they
now proudly stood shoulder to shoulder with Europe's finest. For a
while the fantasy continued. In September, three wins in a row put
Albion above Manchester United in the league and the supporters
were setting their sights on Europe. The pigs were preparing to fly.

Megson was flying too. His popularity in the Black Country
soared to such an extent that he was made Lord of the Manor of
West Bromwich. On his inauguration night he shuffled nervously
into the banqueting hall, flanked by two wandering minstrels.
Before him, a pair of cackling serving wenches were thrown
unceremoniously into the stocks by way of sacrifice. Unfortunately
for Lord Megson, the medieval tomfoolery marked the beginning of
the end of his wonderful Premiership adventure.

"The Premier League is bent — one penalty all season and the
referees against us every game. That's the price you pay for being an
unfashionable club," the Baggies diehards wailed as the team began
to fade away. Their frustrations were born out when Megson sent a
"video nasty" to Philip Don, the referees' supervisor, highlighting a
number of "questionable decisions" against his team. Don called the
game's 24 elite officials together for an emergency briefing. Nothing
seemed to change.

The transfer window was Albion's last hope. The "pigs" needed to
go to market — but they refused to spend a penny. It was a crushing
blow to supporters, who were now forced to buckle down for an
impossible relegation battle. In a way, the club had sealed its own
fate. "If we go bankrupt the fans won't have a team to support at all,"
the management argued. "You've blown our big opportunity — you
haven't even given us a chance," the downhearted faithful replied.

Even the previously untouchable Megson was coming in for
criticism. His stubborn reluctance to play Bob Taylor, the Black
Country folk hero, in his testimonial year was aggravating

A narrow victory over Southampton in September was Albion's third in a row

supporters. By the middle of March, the manager had resigned himself to relegation. "We're up the creek," he said after a 2-0 home defeat against Chelsea.

The final blow came away to Birmingham City. Geoff Horsfield's winning goal, four minutes into injury time, summed up Albion's luckless season. It was the end of the road — and everyone in the ground knew it. The players left St Andrew's dejected. Many of the fans were reduced to tears. Still, though, they kept their enthusiasm and sense of humour.

Albion suffered only one thrashing all season, a 6-0 drubbing by Liverpool at The Hawthorns — the worst home defeat in the club's history. But for all the near misses and debatable decisions, the team, with the exception of Russell Hoult and Jason Koumas, had nowhere near enough quality to compete at the highest level. Lee Hughes, on his return from Coventry City, was disappointing and Jason Roberts, billed by some as a possible successor to his uncle, Cyrille Regis, as the "new Messiah", scored just three goals.

On the last day of the season, with the team long since doomed, the paying customers again took centre stage. They were serenaded by their Newcastle United counterparts, who could not resist a few bars of the Dame Vera Lynn classic, *We'll Meet Again*.

At the final whistle, both sets of supporters gave each other a standing ovation. "I love you," screamed one heavily tattooed gentleman as he applauded the Baggies on their "lap of honour". Then he turned to his fellow fans. You could tell by his face that he had a point to make. "I'd watch this team in any division," he said. "I'd follow them out of the league and back again. It's in here, you see," he added, thumping his bare chest. "Anyone who is gutted that we're out of the Premiership was only ever here for the glamour in the first place."

Wednesday September 11
WEST HAM UNITED (a)
Won 1-0   HT 1-0   Att **34,957**   Position **13th**
Hoult — Gregan, Moore, Gilchrist — Balis, Koumas (Sigurdsson 63), Wallwork, Johnson, Clement — Hughes (Dobie 50), Roberts (J Chambers 86) *Subs not used* Jensen, Dichio
Scorer **Roberts 28**
Report page 246

Saturday September 14
SOUTHAMPTON (h)
Won 1-0   HT 0-0   Att **26,383**   Position **7th**
Hoult — Gregan, Moore, Gilchrist — Balis, Koumas (Dichio 63), Wallwork (Sigurdsson ht), Johnson, Clement — Hughes (Dobie ht), Roberts *Subs not used* Jensen, J Chambers *Booked* Moore, Hughes
Scorer **Gregan 79**
Referee **C Wilkes**

After opening with three straight defeats, Albion have now won three on the trot and are up to seventh position. Pahars misses two fine chances for Southampton, but with a poor game seemingly destined to finish goalless, Gregan's 35-yard shot catches Jones by surprise and, one fumble later, Albion are victorious.

Saturday September 21
LIVERPOOL (a)
Lost 0-2   HT 0-0   Att **43,830**   Position **9th**
Hoult — Sigurdsson, Moore, Gilchrist — Balis (Marshall 82), Koumas (Dichio ht), Gregan, Johnson, Clement — Dobie (Murphy 35), Roberts *Subs not used* Wallwork, J Chambers *Booked* Gregan, Dichio *Sent off* Hoult 35
Report page 91

Monday September 30
BLACKBURN ROVERS (h)
Lost 0-2   HT 0-0   Att **25,170**   Position **13th**
Hoult — Sigurdsson (Wallwork ht), Moore, Gilchrist — Balis, Koumas (Marshall ht), Gregan, Johnson, Clement — Taylor (Dobie 64), Roberts. *Subs not used* Murphy, J Chambers *Booked* Roberts
Referee **M Halsey**

Although the goal that sends them on the way to defeat — a penalty awarded for Wallwork's foul on Duff that clearly starts outside the box — is contentious, West Brom can have few complaints on the balance of play, Cole putting Duff through for the clinching strike in the 76th minute.

Wednesday October 2
WIGAN ATHLETIC (a)
Worthington Cup, 2nd rnd
Lost 1-3   HT 0-1   Att 6,558
Murphy — Sigurdsson, Lyttle, Wallwork — J Chambers
(Clement ht), Marshall, Koumas, Jordao, Dyer —
Hughes, Dichio (Dobie 60) *Subs not used* Jensen,
Turner, Collins
Scorer **Hughes 89**
Referee **L Cable**

A barely recognisable Albion team — Gary Megson
blames injury and fatigue rather than the need for
squad rotation — is humiliated by Wigan, flying high in
the second division, for whom Ellington, with a hat-trick
between the 31st and eightieth minutes, is
unstoppable. Hughes's first goal since his return
scarcely eases Albion's pain.

Saturday October 5
NEWCASTLE UNITED (a)
Lost 1-2   HT 1-1   Att 52,142   Position 15th
Murphy — Balis, Gregan, Moore, Gilchrist, Clement —
Marshall (Koumas 77), McInnes, Johnson — Dobie
(Hughes 67), Roberts *Subs not used* Wallwork,
Sigurdsson, Jensen *Booked* Gregan, Roberts
Scorer **Balis 27**
Report page 68

Saturday October 19
BIRMINGHAM CITY (h)
Drew 1-1   HT 0-0   Att 27,021   Position 15th
Hoult — Gregan, Moore, Gilchrist — Balis, Marshall,
Wallwork, Johnson, Clement — Hughes (Dobie 67),
Roberts *Subs not used* Murphy, Sigurdsson, Koumas,
J Chambers *Booked* Gilchrist, Clement, Marshall
Scorer **Roberts 87**
Referee **G Poll**

Down to ten men after Tebily's dismissal for two fouls
on Roberts, Birmingham are gifted an 86th-minute lead
via a cruel rebound off Moore, but Albion, on top in the
second half, get a deserved equaliser almost
immediately thanks to a classy finish from Roberts, who
finds space where only Tebily previously existed.

MATCH OF THE SEASON

West Ham United 0   West Bromwich Albion 1
Upton Park, Wednesday September 11 2002
By Alyson Rudd

Roberts, the goalscorer, has Repka worried in Albion's victory at Upton Park

Albion observe the silence for the first anniversary of September 11 attacks

EVERYONE wondered how long it would take West Bromwich Albion to adjust to the Barclaycard Premiership. It would have been more pertinent to consider how long it would take West Ham United to warm up this season. Glenn Roeder's team remain rooted to the bottom of the table, while Gary Megson's side, having held on to the lead taken through Jason Roberts in the first half, can consider themselves thoroughly awake to the demands of the league.

"Results often cloud people's judgment," Roeder said. But with just one point to their name, judgment will be coming thick and fast that West Ham are too fancy up front and too sloppy at the back.

Asked by helpful local police if they knew where they were going, a bunch of West Bromwich fans replied: "We're going to watch the Baggies win." On a visit to any other Premiership club, such a reply from a newly promoted team's supporters might have been considered cheeky. But West Bromwich have tasted victory in the Premiership this season and West Ham have not.

However, it seemed cheeky all the same when West Bromwich took the lead in the 27th minute. West Ham had been indulging in party tricks, drawing gasps of admiration with build-ups of real beauty prompted by Paolo Di Canio, back after a foot injury. But a couple of saves by Russell Hoult, to deny decent efforts from Joe Cole, and several wasted chances were punished when a ball through the middle from Ronnie Wallwork was pounced on by Roberts; his finish was Premiership class. "We've accepted that the

Saturday October 26
CHELSEA (a)
Lost 0-2 HT 0-1 Att **40,893** Position **18th**
Hoult — Gregan (Sigurdsson 67), Moore, Gilchrist — Balis, Marshall (Hughes 58), McInnes, Johnson, Clement — Dobie, Roberts *Subs not used* Murphy, Wallwork, Koumas *Booked* Johnson
Report page 80

Saturday November 2
MANCHESTER CITY (h)
Lost 1-2 HT 0-0 Att **27,044** Position **18th**
Hoult — Gregan, Moore, Gilchrist — Balis, A Chambers (Koumas 67), McInnes, Johnson, Clement — Dobie (Hughes 61), Roberts *Subs not used* Murphy, Wallwork, Sigurdsson *Booked* Gregan, McInnes
Scorer **Clement 62**
Referee **D Elleray**

With Anelka producing his best display since joining them, Manchester City dominate at The Hawthorns. The Frenchman gives Kevin Keegan's side the lead and sets up the winner for Goater after Clement's free kick had briefly raised Albion's hopes.

Saturday November 9
BOLTON WANDERERS (a)
Drew 1-1 HT 1-0 Att **23,630** Position **18th**
Hoult — Sigurdsson, Moore, Gregan — Balis, A Chambers, McInnes, Johnson, Clement — Dobie (Koumas 79), Roberts *Subs not used* Murphy, J Chambers, Wallwork, Hughes *Booked* McInnes, A Chambers
Scorer **Dobie 17**
Report page 237

Saturday November 16
ASTON VILLA (h)
Drew 0-0 HT 0-0 Att **27,091** Position **18th**
Hoult — Sigurdsson, Moore, Gilchrist (A Chambers 77) — Balis, McInnes, Gregan (Dichio 71), Johnson, Clement — Dobie (Hughes 67), Roberts *Subs not used* Murphy, Wallwork *Booked* Moore, Gregan, Dichio
Referee **D Gallagher**

A tale of two penalties — or make that one. Gilchrist's foul on Delaney is so clear-cut that even Albion fans must have felt like appealing, but Dermot Gallagher mysteriously waves play-on. The referee later awards one to Villa, for Moore's tackle on Barry, but Dublin's effort is saved by Hoult to earn Albion a deserved point.

Saturday November 23
EVERTON (a)
Lost 0-1 HT 0-0 Att 40,113 Position 19th
Hoult — Sigurdsson, Moore, Gregan — Balis (Koumas
72), Wallwork, McInnes, Johnson, Clement — Dobie
(Hughes 51), Roberts *Subs not used* Dichio,
J Chambers, Murphy *Booked* Clement, Koumas
Report page 118

Saturday November 30
MIDDLESBROUGH (h)
Won 1-0 HT 0-0 Att 27,029 Position 17th
Hoult — Sigurdsson, Moore (J Chambers 85), Gregan
— Balis, Koumas, McInnes, Johnson, Clement —
Roberts (Dobie 90), Hughes (Dichio 59) *Subs not used*
Murphy, Wallwork
Scorer **Dichio 72**
Referee **P Durkin**

Dichio is off the transfer list, off the bench and off on a
goal celebration after scrambling Albion's winner. Job
and Whelan both hit Hoult's crossbar with headers
late on, but the visiting team deserve nothing. "That
was our poorest performance of the season," Steve
McClaren, the Middlesbrough manager, says.

Sunday December 8
TOTTENHAM HOTSPUR (a)
Lost 1-3 HT 0-2 Att 35,958 Position 17th
Hoult — Sigurdsson, Wallwork, Gregan — Balis,
Koumas, McInnes, Johnson (A Chambers 84), Clement
— Roberts (Dichio 80), Hughes (Dobie 56) *Subs not
used* J Chambers, Murphy *Booked* Clement
Scorer **Doble 73**
Report page 154

Saturday December 14
ASTON VILLA (a)
Lost 1-2 HT 1-1 Att 40,391 Position 17th
Hoult — Sigurdsson, Moore, Gregan — Balis, Koumas,
McInnes, Johnson, Clement — Roberts (Dobie 83),
Hughes (Dichio 58) *Subs not used* Wallwork, A
Chambers, Murphy *Booked* Koumas
Scorer **Koumas 29**
Report page 227

Hughes displays the battling qualities that helped Albion to victory

stadiums are nice and there are more people here," Megson said of
his team's more confident recent displays in the top division.

The urge to move off the bottom of the table is always agonising
and in the second half the home fans began to lose patience. The
moment when Tomas Repka and Michael Carrick collided while
trying to clear the same ball was almost too much to bear. "Roeder,
sort it out," they chanted.

But West Ham were not the only side intent on streaming
forward. The visiting team, who might have been forgiven for
stacking men behind the ball, were just as threatening in the second
half as they had been in the first and Roberts was denied a second
goal only by the alertness of David James.

Roberts is "nowhere near the finished article", according to his
manager, but the former Bristol Rovers striker was sufficiently
accomplished to worry West Ham. As the teams trudged off, three
fans berated Repka for a weak display and he was hauled away by
Paul Aldridge, the club's managing director, as he squared up to the
disillusioned supporters.

WEST HAM UNITED (4-4-2): D James — S Schemmel, T Repka, G Breen, N Winterburn (sub: C Dailly,
85min) — J Cole, E Cisse, M Carrick (sub: S Lomas, 75), T Sinclair — F Kanoute, P Di Canio
(sub: J Defoe, 75). **Substitutes not used:** R van der Gouw, I Pearce. **Booked:** Cole.
WEST BROMWICH ALBION (3-5-2): R Hoult — S Gregan, D Moore, P Gilchrist — I Balis, J Koumas
(sub: L Sigurdsson, 63), R Wallwork, A Johnson, N Clement — L Hughes (sub: S Dobie, 50), J Roberts
(sub: J Chambers, 86). **Substitutes not used:** B Jensen, D Dichio.
Referee: A D'Urso.

THE MANAGER

Gary Megson

Gary Megson is on the cusp. His honeymoon in paradise has come to an end and the manager who became a Lord for leading his team into the Premiership has got to prove himself all over again. Megson likes to run West Bromwich Albion from top to bottom. He simply will not tolerate dissent if it threatens his iron grip on The Hawthorns. He has ambitions to manage at the highest level, but whether he is good enough will only become clear in the fullness of time. Is Megson one of Britain's finest young managers or a screaming bully who cannot quite cut it at the highest level? The jury is out.

Malcolm Boyden

APPEARANCES

	Prem	FAC	WC	Total
I Balis	27 (1)	0 (1)	-	27 (2)
A Chambers	10 (3)	1 (1)	-	11 (4)
J Chambers	2 (6)	-	1	3 (6)
N Clement	34 (2)	2	0 (1)	36 (3)
S Dobie	10 (21)	0 (2)	0 (1)	10 (24)
D Dichio	19 (9)	2	1	22 (9)
L Dyer	-	-	1	1
P Gilchrist	22	1 (1)	-	23 (1)
S Gregan	36	2	-	38
R Hoult	37	2	-	39
L Hughes	14 (9)	-	1	15 (9)
A Johnson	30 (2)	2	-	32 (2)
Jordao	0 (3)	-	1	1 (3)
J Koumas	27 (5)	2	1	30 (5)
D Lyttle	2 (2)	-	1	3 (2)
D McInnes	28 (1)	1	-	29 (1)
L Marshall	4 (5)	-	1	5 (5)
D Moore	29	2	-	31
J Murphy	1 (1)	-	2	3 (1)
J Roberts	31 (1)	2	-	33 (1)
L Sigurdsson	23 (6)	1 (1)	1	25 (7)
R Taylor	2 (2)	-	-	2 (2)
I Udeze	7 (4)	-	-	7 (4)
R Wallwork	23 (4)	2	1	26 (4)

Saturday December 21
SUNDERLAND (h)
Drew 2-2 HT 2-0 Att 26,703 Position 18th
Hoult — Sigurdsson, Moore, Gregan — Balis (A Chambers 64), Koumas, McInnes, Johnson, Clement — Roberts (Dobie 64), Dichio *Subs not used* Murphy, Wallwork, Hughes *Booked* Sigurdsson, Johnson
Scorers **Dichio 27, Koumas 33**
Referee **C Wilkes**

West Brom seem to have the measure of this relegation battle when they take a two-goal lead, but what Gary Megson describes as "abject defending" allows Phillips to cap a fine Sunderland recovery with both goals, first outmuscling Gregan and then finishing a jinking run.

Thursday December 26
ARSENAL (h)
Lost 1-2 HT 1-0 Att 27,025 Position 19th
Hoult — Sigurdsson, Moore, Gregan — A Chambers (Dobie 84), Koumas, Wallwork (J Chambers 83), Johnson, Clement — Roberts, Dichio *Subs not used* Murphy, Balis, Hughes *Booked* Dichio
Scorer **Dichio 3**
Referee **G Poll**

As all their championship rivals drop points, Arsenal come from behind — Dichio's bullet header having given West Brom a third-minute lead — to win through Jeffers, who punishes Sigurdsson's slip, and Henry, although Roberts had hit Seaman's post with the score at 1-1.

Saturday December 28
CHARLTON ATHLETIC (a)
Lost 0-1 HT 0-1 Att 26,196 Position 19th
Hoult — Sigurdsson, Moore, Gregan — A Chambers (Dobie 74), Koumas (Hughes 83), Wallwork, Johnson, Clement — Roberts, Dichio *Subs not used* Murphy, Gilchrist, J Chambers *Booked* Gregan, Dichio, Roberts
Report page 179

Saturday January 4
BRADFORD CITY (h)
FA Cup, 3rd rnd
Won 3-1 HT 3-0 Att 19,909
Hoult — Sigurdsson, Moore, Gregan (Gilchrist ht) — A Chambers, Koumas, Wallwork (Balis 85), Johnson, Clement — Roberts (Dobie ht), Dichio *Subs not used* Jensen, J Chambers *Booked* Roberts
Scorer **Dichio 4, 11, 19**
Referee **D Elleray**

No tie on FA Cup third-round day is effectively settled more quickly than this one, with the first hat-trick of Dichio's professional career seeing off Bradford City inside 20 minutes. The first two are headers, the third coming after a pass from Roberts. Danks's reply is little consolation to the losers.

Saturday January 11
MANCHESTER UNITED (h)
Lost 1-3 HT 1-2 Att **27,129** Position **20th**
Hoult — Sigurdsson (Dobie 75), Moore, Gilchrist —
A Chambers (Balis 86), Koumas, Wallwork, Johnson,
Clement — Roberts, Dichio *Subs not used* Murphy,
McInnes, J Chambers
Scorer **Koumas 6**
Referee **N Barry**

West Brom are allowed to dream of an unlikely victory
for all of 22 seconds. That is the time it takes for
Van Nistelrooy to cancel out the opener from Koumas,
Scholes and Solskjaer then rewarding United's
supremacy and sending Albion back to the bottom of
the table.

Saturday January 18
LEEDS UNITED (a)
Drew 0-0 HT 0-0 Att **39,708** Position **20th**
Hoult — Gregan, Moore, Gilchrist — Balis
(Wallwork 35), McInnes, Koumas (Sigurdsson 77),
Johnson, Clement — Dichio, Dobie (Hughes 63)
Subs not used Murphy, Udeze *Booked* Johnson
Sent off Johnson 74
Report page 217

Saturday January 25
WATFORD (a)
FA Cup, 4th rnd
Lost 0-1 HT 0-0 Att **16,975**
Hoult — Gregan, Moore (A Chambers 83), Gilchrist —
Wallwork, Koumas, McInnes (Sigurdsson 58), Johnson,
Clement — Dichio, Roberts (Dobie 67) *Subs not used*
Udeze, Murphy
Referee **J Winter**

Gary Megson is furious with Albion's dismal display,
questioning his side's motivation as much as their
ability after Helguson's long-overdue winner for the first
division side. Only Hoult, who had earlier saved Cox's
penalty, and the hard-working Koumas are exempt
from criticism.

PLAYER OF THE SEASON **Russell Hoult**

Russell Hoult had so little to do when Albion achieved promotion to the Barclaycard Premiership that his defenders used to ask the goalkeeper if he had remembered his deckchair. He relished every minute of life among the elite, even though the deckchair was well and truly discarded. Albion fans will say that he is unquestionably England's No 1. It is a great source of frustration that he is not considered to be in a fashionable enough league team to represent his country. Surely Sven-Goran Eriksson, the England head coach, would never consider a goalkeeper whose side had suffered relegation, would he? You had better ask David James.

Malcolm Boyden

STATS AND FACTS

● Lee Hughes failed to score in 23 Premiership appearances for Albion, yet he scored 79 league goals in the first division at more than one every two games.

● Albion won 1-0 on 15 occasions in gaining promotion to the Premiership and their first four victories back in the top flight were also by that scoreline.

● Albion followed Ipswich Town's example of a year earlier by losing 6-0 at home to Liverpool on the way to relegation.

● Adam and James Chambers, Albion's twins, made 13 and eight Premiership appearances respectively this season, but referees were spared any confusion. The pair were only on the pitch at the same time for two minutes, against Arsenal on Boxing Day.

Bill Edgar

Wednesday January 29
CHARLTON ATHLETIC (h)
Lost 0-1   HT 0-0   Att 26,113   Position 20th
Hoult — Gregan, Moore, McInnes 53), Gilchrist —
A Chambers, Koumas, Wallwork, Johnson, Udeze —
Dichio (Dobie 77), Roberts *Subs not used* Murphy,
Clement, Sigurdsson
Referee **A D'Urso**

A vastly improved performance from Albion, but no change in fortune. Kiely denies Wallwork with one of the saves of the season before Bartlett heads in for Charlton from Jensen's free kick. Then, at the death, Dobie heads against a post and Johnson misses a real sitter.

Saturday February 1
MANCHESTER CITY (a)
Won 2-1   HT 1-1   Att 34,765   Position 18th
Hoult — Gregan, Moore, Gilchrist — A Chambers,
Koumas (Sigurdsson 85), Wallwork, McInnes,
Clement — Hughes (Dichio 65), Roberts *Subs not used*
Murphy, Dobie, Jordao *Booked* Gregan, Wallwork
Sent off Roberts 81
Scorers **Clement 18, Moore 71**
Report page 145

Saturday February 8
BOLTON WANDERERS (h)
Drew 1-1   HT 0-1   Att 26,933   Position 18th
Hoult — Gregan, Moore, Gilchrist (Udeze 71) —
A Chambers, McInnes (Johnson 77), Wallwork,
Koumas, Clement — Dichio, Roberts (Hughes 77)
Subs not used Murphy, Sigurdsson *Booked* Gregan,
Chambers
Scorer **Johnson 90**
Referee **D Elleray**

Trailing from the eighteenth minute in a relegation match of huge significance, Albion lay siege to the Bolton goal, missing sitters (Roberts) and hitting the woodwork (Gregan) before Johnson forgets the pain of a broken toe to poach a last-gasp equaliser, his first goal for more than a year.

Wednesday February 19
FULHAM (a)
Lost 0-3   HT 0-0   Att 15,799   Position 18th
Hoult — Gregan, Moore, Gilchrist — A Chambers,
Koumas, Wallwork, McInnes, Clement (Udeze 90)
— Hughes (Dobie 72), Dichio (Jordao 81) *Subs not
used* Murphy, Sigurdsson *Booked* Gregan, Chambers
Report page 206

GOALSCORERS

	Prem	FAC	WC	Total
I Balis	2 (1p)	-	-	2 (1p)
N Clement	3	-	-	3
D Dichio	5	3	-	8
S Dobie	5	-	-	5
S Gregan	1	-	-	1
L Hughes	-	-	1	1
A Johnson	1	-	-	1
J Koumas	4	-	-	4
D McInnes	2	-	-	2
L Marshall	1	-	-	1
D Moore	2	-	-	2
J Roberts	3	-	-	3

Sunday February 23
WEST HAM UNITED (h)
Lost 1-2 HT 0-1 Att 27,042 Position **19th**
Hoult — Gregan, Moore, Gilchrist — A Chambers, Koumas, Wallwork (Sigurdsson 74), McInnes (Dobie 74), Udeze — Hughes, Dichio *Subs not used* Murphy, Lyttle, Clement *Booked* Gregan
Scorer **Dichio** 50
Referee **M Dean**

Despite almost coming to blows with Repka, his team-mate (Di Canio and Glenn Roeder also have a public falling-out), James is outstanding in the West Ham goal as Sinclair's double helps them to win the biggest "six-pointer" of the season to date. West Brom are again left to bemoan a succession of missed chances.

Saturday March 1
SOUTHAMPTON (a)
Lost 0-1 HT 0-1 Att 31,915 Position **19th**
Hoult — Sigurdsson, Moore, Gilchrist — Wallwork (Dobie ht), Koumas, Gregan, McInnes (Jordao 77), Udeze (Clement 25) — Hughes, Dichio *Subs not used* Murphy, A Chambers *Booked* Dichio, Gregan
Report page 133

Sunday March 16
CHELSEA (h)
Lost 0-2 HT 0-1 Att 27,024 Position **19th**
Hoult — Sigurdsson, Moore (J Chambers 15), Clement — Balis, Koumas, Gregan, McInnes (Wallwork 15), Udeze (Dichio ht) — Hughes, Roberts *Subs not used* Murphy, Dobie
Referee **A D'Urso**

With Moore, who may be out for up to nine months, and McInnes injured in the first 15 minutes, and Zola inspiring Chelsea to a convincing win, Gary Megson confesses that his Albion team are "up the creek", although he believes that they still have a paddle. Zola's goal, beautifully created and finished, is the highlight of the day.

Saturday March 22
BIRMINGHAM CITY (a)
Lost 0-1 HT 0-0 Att 29,449 Position **19th**
Hoult — Sigurdsson, Wallwork, Clement — Balis, Koumas (Hughes 86), Gregan, McInnes, Udeze — Dichio, Roberts *Subs not used* Dobie, Lyttle, J Chambers, Murphy
Report page 194

THE PLAYERS

IGOR BALIS
Midfield
Born January 5, 1970, Slovakia
Ht 5ft 11in **Wt** 11st 2lb
Signed from Slovan Bratislava, December 2000, £150,000

ADAM CHAMBERS
Midfield
Born November 20, 1980, Sandwell
Ht 5ft 9in **Wt** 10st 10lb
Signed from trainee, July 1998

JAMES CHAMBERS
Defender
Born November 20, 1980, Sandwell
Ht 5ft 9in **Wt** 10st 10lb
Signed from trainee, July 1998

NEIL CLEMENT
Defender
Born October 3, 1978, Reading
Ht 5ft 11in **Wt** 11st 3lb
Signed from Chelsea, March 2000, £100,000

SCOTT DOBIE
Forward
Born October 10, 1978, Workington
Ht 6ft 1in **Wt** 11st 2lb
Signed from Carlisle United, July 2001, £150,000

DANIELE DICHIO
Forward
Born October 19, 1974, Hammersmith
Ht 6ft 4in **Wt** 13st 10lb
Signed from Sunderland, November 2001, £1.25m

LLOYD DYER
Midfield
Born September 13, 1982, Birmingham
Ht 5ft 8in **Wt** 10st 2lb
Signed from trainee, July 2002

PHIL GILCHRIST
Defender
Born August 25, 1973, Stockton-on-Tees
Ht 5ft 11in **Wt** 12st 10lb
Signed from Leicester City, March 2001, £500,000

Neil Clement

SEAN GREGAN
Defender
Born March 29, 1974, Guisborough
Ht 6ft 2in **Wt** 14st 11lb
Signed from Preston North End, August 2002, £1.5m

RUSSELL HOULT
Goalkeeper
Born November 22, 1972, Ashby de la Zouch
Ht 6ft 3in **Wt** 12st 8lb
Signed from Portsmouth, January 2001, £500,000

LEE HUGHES
Forward
Born May 22, 1976, Smethwick
Ht 5ft 10in **Wt** 11st 7lb
Signed from Coventry City, August 2002, £2.5m

ANDY JOHNSON
Midfield
Born May 2, 1974, Bristol
Ht 6ft 0in **Wt** 12st 6lb
Signed from Nottingham Forest, September 2001, £200,000

JORDAO
Forward
Born August 30, 1971, Malange, Angola
Ht 6ft 3in **Wt** 12st 10lb
Signed from SC Braga, Portugal, August 2000, £350,000

JASON KOUMAS
Midfield
Born September 25, 1979, Wrexham
Ht 5ft 10in **Wt** 11st 6lb
Signed from Tranmere Rovers, August 2002, £2.25m

DES LYTTLE
Defender
Born September 24, 1971, Wolverhampton
Ht 5ft 9in **Wt** 12st 13lb
Signed from Watford, June 2000, free

DEREK McINNES
Midfield
Born July 5, 1971, Paisley
Ht 5ft 8in **Wt** 11st 5lb
Signed from Rangers, August 2000, £450,000

Andy Johnson

Saturday April 5
MIDDLESBROUGH (a)
Lost 0-3 **HT 0-1** Att **30,187** Position **19th**
Hoult — Sigurdsson, Wallwork, Gilchrist — Balis (Lyttle 85), Koumas, Gregan, McInnes (Johnson 60), Clement — Dichio, Roberts (Dobie 53) *Subs not used* Murphy, Hughes *Booked* Koumas
Report page 171

Saturday April 12
EVERTON (h)
Lost 1-2 **HT 1-2** Att **27,039** Position **19th**
Hoult — Sigurdsson, Wallwork, Gregan — Balis, McInnes (Dobie 78), Koumas, Johnson, Clement (Udeze 83) — Dichio, Hughes *Subs not used* Murphy, J Chambers, Lyttle *Booked* Sigurdsson, McInnes
Scorer **Balis 18 (pen)**
Referee **S Bennett**

The Hawthorns goes wild as Albion are finally awarded their first penalty of the season, for Stubbs's handball, and Balis converts it, but two errors by the normally reliable Hoult in goal allow Everton — whose manager, David Moyes, is sent to the stand — to come from behind for victory and only results elsewhere prevent the home side from joining Sunderland in relegation.

Saturday April 19
SUNDERLAND (a)
Won 2-1 **HT 2-0** Att **36,025** Position **19th**
Hoult — Sigurdsson, Wallwork, Gregan — Balis, Koumas, McInnes, Johnson, Clement — Dichio, Hughes (Roberts 36) *Subs not used* Murphy, Dobie, Lyttle, Udeze *Booked* Koumas
Scorer **McInnes 39, 42**
Report page 279

Monday April 21
TOTTENHAM HOTSPUR (h)
Lost 2-3 **HT 1-1** Att **26,899** Position **19th**
Hoult — Sigurdsson, Wallwork, Gregan — Balis, Koumas, McInnes, Johnson, Udeze (Clement 58) — Dichio (Dobie 67), Roberts *Subs not used* Murphy, J Chambers, Lyttle *Booked* Sigurdsson, Roberts
Scorers **Dichio 24, Clement 61**
Referee **P Dowd**

Their relegation confirmed two days earlier by Bolton's win over West Ham, West Brom twice take the lead against Spurs but end up with nothing as Keane's expert finishing proves the difference between the sides, his double helping to silence the Albion fans who give the former Wolves striker a hard time from the stands.

Saturday April 26
LIVERPOOL (h)
Lost 0-6 **HT 0-1** Att **27,128** Position **19th**
Hoult — Gregan (Jordao 87), Wallwork (J Chambers 54), Clement — Balis, Koumas, McInnes, Johnson, Udeze (Lyttle 73) — Dichio, Roberts *Subs not used* Murphy, Dobie *Booked* Dichio
Referee **D Gallagher**

Albion's magnificent fans keep up a barrage of noise, despite seeing their side subjected to the worst home defeat in the club's history. Their team simply has no answer to the predatory instincts of Baros and, especially, the four-goal Owen, whose one-man assault on the record books includes becoming the youngest player to reach a century of Premiership goals.

Saturday May 3
BLACKBURN ROVERS (a)
Drew 1-1 **HT 0-1** Att **27,470** Position **19th**
Hoult — Wallwork, J Chambers, Gregan — Lyttle, Koumas, McInnes, Johnson, Clement — Roberts, Dichio (Dobie 83) *Subs not used* Murphy, Balis, Hughes, Udeze *Booked* Johnson
Scorer **Koumas 54**
Report page 112

Sunday May 11
NEWCASTLE UNITED (h)
Drew 2-2 **HT 0-1** Att **27,036** Position **19th**
Hoult — Sigurdsson, J Chambers (Udeze 80), Wallwork — Lyttle, Koumas, McInnes, Johnson, Clement — Dichio, Taylor (Dobie 31) *Subs not used* Jensen, Balis, Roberts
Scorer **Dobie 57, 71**
Referee **G Barber**

Taylor limps into retirement as Albion limp out of the Premiership, although they show typical fighting qualities on the final day of the season to share the honours with Newcastle, Dobie's double coming between goals from Jenas and Viana.

LEE MARSHALL
Midfield
Born January 21, 1979, Islington
Ht 6ft 0in **Wt** 11st 11lb
Signed from Leicester City, August 2002, £700,000

DARREN MOORE
Defender
Born April 22, 1974, Birmingham
Ht 6ft 2in **Wt** 15st 6lb
Signed from Portsmouth, September 2001, £750,000

JOE MURPHY
Goalkeeper
Born August 21, 1981, Dublin
Ht 6ft 2in **Wt** 13st 1lb
Signed from Tranmere Rovers, July 2002, £320,000

JASON ROBERTS
Forward
Born January 25, 1978, Park Royal
Ht 6ft 0in **Wt** 12st 6lb
Signed from Bristol Rovers, July 2000, £2m

LARUS SIGURDSSON
Defender
Born June 4, 1973, Akureyri, Iceland
Ht 6ft 0in **Wt** 12st 4lb
Signed from Stoke City, September 1999, £325,000

BOB TAYLOR
Forward
Born February 1967, Horden
Ht 5ft 10in **Wt** 10st 12lb
Signed from Bolton Wanderers, March 2000, £90,000

IFEANI UDEZE
Midfield
Born July 21, 1980, Nigeria
Ht 5ft 10in **Wt** 11st 1lb
Signed from PAOK Salonika (loan), January 2003

RONNIE WALLWORK
Defender
Born September 9, 1977, Manchester
Ht 5ft 10in **Wt** 12st 10lb
Signed from Manchester United, July 2002, free

Ronnie Wallwork

SUNDERLAND

PREMIERSHIP

	P	W	D	L	F	A	Pts
Man Utd	38	25	8	5	74	34	83
Arsenal	38	23	9	6	85	42	78
Newcastle	38	21	6	11	63	48	69
Chelsea	38	19	10	9	68	38	67
Liverpool	38	18	10	10	61	41	64
Blackburn	38	16	12	10	52	43	60
Everton	38	17	8	13	48	49	59
Southampton	38	13	13	12	43	46	52
Man City	38	15	6	17	47	54	51
Tottenham	38	14	8	16	51	62	50
Middlesbro	38	13	10	15	48	44	49
Charlton	38	14	7	17	45	56	49
Birmingham	38	13	9	16	41	49	48
Fulham	38	13	9	16	41	50	48
Leeds	38	14	5	19	58	57	47
Aston Villa	38	12	9	17	42	47	45
Bolton	38	10	14	14	41	51	44
West Ham	38	10	12	16	42	59	42
West Brom	38	6	8	24	29	65	26
Sunderland	**38**	**4**	**7**	**27**	**21**	**65**	**19**

FA CUP
Fifth round

WORTHINGTON CUP
Fourth round

Kevin Phillips applauds fans who endured
a poor season at the Stadium of Light

THE GAMES

Saturday August 17
BLACKBURN ROVERS (a)
Drew 0-0   HT 0-0   Att **27,122**   Position **10th**
Sorensen — Wright, Bjorklund, Babb, Gray — Kilbane
(Quinn 90), McCann, McAteer, Reyna, Butler — Phillips
Subs not used Craddock, Kyle, Arca, Macho *Booked*
Wright, Kilbane
Report page 102

Saturday August 24
EVERTON (h)
Lost 0-1   HT 0-1   Att **37,698**   Position **14th**
Sorensen — Wright, Bjorklund, Babb, Gray — Reyna,
McCann, McAteer (Quinn 68), Butler — Phillips, Kyle
(Piper 63) *Subs not used* McCartney, Arca, Macho
Booked Wright
Referee **R Styles**

After a troubled summer, Sunderland get off to the
worst possible start with defeat in their first home
match. They hit the woodwork three times and even
squander a last-minute penalty when Wright, who had
fouled Quinn, then saves from Phillips. Campbell's
close-range goal for Everton in the 28th minute proves
decisive.

Wednesday August 28
LEEDS UNITED (a)
Won 1-0   HT 0-0   Att **39,929**   Position **10th**
Sorensen — Wright, Bjorklund, Babb, Gray — Piper
(Arca 71), Thirlwell, McAteer, Reyna, Butler — Phillips
(Kyle 78) *Subs not used* Macho, McCartney, Quinn
Scorer **McAteer 46**
Report page 210

Saturday August 31
MANCHESTER UNITED (h)
Drew 1-1   HT 0-1   Att **47,586**   Position **11th**
Sorensen — Wright, Bjorklund, Babb, Gray — Piper
(Thirlwell 89), Reyna, McAteer, Butler — Flo (Quinn 79),
Phillips *Subs not used* Kyle, McCartney, Myhre
Booked McAteer
Scorer **Flo 70**
Referee **U Rennie**

A match featuring a goal on his debut for Flo, who
equalises Giggs's early strike the day after signing, is
completely overshadowed by the antics of Keane.
The Manchester United captain is sent off for the tenth
time in his Old Trafford career when his running feud
with McAteer — a legacy of the Ireland fallout at the
World Cup finals — culminates in an elbow to his
compatriot's head, a red card and countless newspaper
headlines.

THAT SUNDERLAND ENDED THEIR season in relegation was of little surprise to their supporters, who had watched the team's decline with a sense of doom and morbid fascination. Demotion had only been narrowly avoided the previous year and a disappointing pre-season tour offered little hope that this latest campaign would provide another stay of execution. What could not have been foreseen was such a dramatic and complete collapse.

With a batch of moderately expensive signings, Peter Reid began with a mixed set of results that would compare favourably with the team's eventual capitulation. An away win against Leeds United (when that still had some kudos) and a draw against Manchester United suggested signs of life. But by October, a run of humiliating defeats that saw a slide down the table and, perhaps more significant, a drop in attendances, forced Bob Murray, the chairman, finally to revoke his rash claim that Reid was unsackable.

What happened next is still the stuff of myth and radio phone-in conspiracy theory. With a stellar cast of potential managers (David O'Leary, Gianluca Vialli, George Graham, Mick McCarthy) all playing coquette with the media, Murray announced that Reid's replacement would be the FA's technical director, Howard Wilkinson. The reaction in the North East was one of stunned disbelief. The club's PR machine went into meltdown trying to sell the new appointment, but the supporters had been hoping for and expecting much, much more. Wilkinson's mantle as the last English manager to win the title could not assuage the criticism of his dour personality, his six years out of club management and his reputation for the long-ball game.

An early run of five matches unbeaten briefly offered some hope, but thereafter the team sank deeper into a quagmire of mediocrity and, with nine games remaining, Sunderland were seven points adrift of safety. While the club persisted with talk of survival, the fans had accepted the inevitable and were hoping at least for a period of stability. A fortnight earlier, Murray had assured Wilkinson and his assistant, Steve Cotterill, that their positions were secure, yet in a startling turnabout, both were sacked and McCarthy brought in. While Murray had been criticised for persisting too long with Reid, this latest volte-face conveyed panic and rashness. Wilkinson had failed to turn around the team in five months, yet McCarthy was being given only eight weeks.

Predictably, he was unable to save them, although his failure to gain even a point must have raised doubts about his previously untested ability to manage in the Premiership. The Wearsiders ended their campaign in total disarray: an astonishing one point

Victory over Spurs in November, with Flo on target, offered a brief respite

from a possible 57 and a run of 15 consecutive defeats that was only halted by the season's merciful close. Their final tally of 19 points represents not just the worst performance in Premiership history, but almost the worst by a top-flight team since the Football League was formed in 1888.

With the likely enforced sale of the team's few quality players, Sunderland will face next season with a squad of youngsters and journeymen in a division that has shown little respect for those cast from the elite. While the club might point optimistically to Leicester City's immediate return to the Premiership, the continuing struggles of many relegated teams offer a more sobering and realistic prospect.

The challenge for the club is now not just on the pitch, but to survive as an institution. Sunderland have become a financial leviathan that is veering dangerously off course. Murray has estimated that relegation will add a further £20 million to the club's debts of £26 million and has refused to rule out the possibility of administration. The financial trials of the previous season's relegated teams, Leicester, Derby County and Ipswich Town, will have done little to ease his concerns.

The most galling aspect of Sunderland's plight is that it probably could have been so easily avoided. In January 2001, the club lay second in the table. Had Reid used this status to strengthen his workmanlike squad, or more tellingly had Murray forced him to do so, the team would undoubtedly have achieved at least the Uefa Cup place they so narrowly missed on the last day of the season. With Europe would have come the finance and prestige to attract real talent and engender real hope for the future. Instead, Reid did nothing, Murray stood back and the chance was lost. As Murray now contemplates Sunderland's bleak future, he might reflect that running a large Premiership club is not a *laissez-faire* affair.

Tuesday September 10
MIDDLESBROUGH (a)
Lost 0-3   HT 0-2   Att 32,155   Position 12th
Sorensen — Wright, Bjorklund, Babb, Gray — Piper, Reyna, McAteer, Butler (Bellion 74) — Flo, Stewart
Subs not used Macho, Williams, Kyle, Thirlwell
Booked Piper, McAteer, Stewart
Report page 163

Saturday September 14
FULHAM (h)
Lost 0-3   HT 0-1   Att 35,432   Position 18th
Sorensen — Wright, Bjorklund, Babb, Gray — Piper, Reyna, McAteer (McCann 56), Butler (Quinn 56) — Flo, Stewart *Subs not used* Bellion, Williams, Macho
Booked Wright, Gray
Referee **C Foy**

The pressure on Peter Reid increases with another dismal home display. Sunderland simply have no answer to the guile of Inamoto, the Japan playmaker rejected by Arsenal, who scores Fulham's first goal and helps to set up Marlet and Hayles in turn after the interval.

Saturday September 21
NEWCASTLE UNITED (a)
Lost 0-2   HT 0-2   Att 52,181   Position 19th
Sorensen — Wright, Bjorklund (Williams 71), Babb, Gray — Piper, McAteer (Quinn ht), McCann, Reyna, Kilbane — Flo (Stewart 86) *Subs not used* Myhre, Bellion *Booked* Wright, Bjorklund, McCann, Williams
Report page 67

Saturday September 28
ASTON VILLA (h)
Won 1-0   HT 0-0   Att 40,092   Position 16th
Sorensen — Wright (Williams 32), Craddock, Babb, Kilbane — Piper, Reyna, McCann, Arca — Flo (Quinn 69), Bellion (Stewart 78) *Subs not used* Thirlwell, Myhre
Booked McCann, Reyna, Stewart
Scorer **Bellion 70**
Referee **N Barry**

Aston Villa's dismal form on their travels extends to no points and no goals in four trips as they provide Sunderland with the much-needed tonic of a victory, secured when Bellion, the exciting French teenager, bursts clear to score the only goal on his first Premiership start.

Tuesday October 1
CAMBRIDGE UNITED (a)
Worthington Cup, 2nd rnd
Won 7-0   HT 2-0   Att 8,175
Myhre — Williams, Craddock, Babb, Kilbane (McCartney 78) — Bellion, McCann, Reyna (Thirlwell 66), Arca (Butler 61) — Flo, Stewart *Subs not used* Sorensen, Kyle *Booked* Williams
Scorers **Reyna 21, McCann 25, Arca 54, Stewart 63, 65, Flo 75, 83**
Referee **P Danson**

Some much-needed light relief for Sunderland as Bellion, who has a hand in five of their goals, leads the Worthington Cup rout of the third division side. Flo and Stewart, the recent arrivals, share four of them for a team that has previously managed only three in total in the league.

Sunday October 6
ARSENAL (a)
Lost 1-3   HT 0-3   Att 37,902   Position 17th
Sorensen (Myhre 16) — Williams, Craddock, Babb, Kilbane (Piper 59) — Bellion, McCann, Reyna, Arca — Flo (Quinn 74) *Subs not used* McCartney, Stewart
Scorer **Craddock 82**
Report page 56

Saturday October 19
WEST HAM UNITED (h)
Lost 0-1   HT 0-1   Att 44,352   Position 18th
Macho — Wright, Craddock, Babb, Gray — Piper (Bellion ht), McCann, Reyna (Thirlwell 79), Kilbane — Phillips, Stewart (Quinn 61) *Subs not used* Bjorklund, Ingham *Booked* Kilbane
Referee **G Barber**

The "under new management" signs are up at the Stadium of Light after the sacking of Peter Reid, but there is no change in fortune in the first match under Howard Wilkinson and Steve Cotterill as a superb finish by Sinclair from Di Canio's inspired pass allows West Ham to climb off the bottom with this narrow victory.

Monday October 28
BOLTON WANDERERS (a)
Drew 1-1   HT 1-0   Att 23,036   Position 19th
Myhre (Macho 27) — Wright, Craddock, Babb, McCartney — Kilbane, McCann, Reyna (Thirlwell 39), Gray — Phillips (Flo 76), Bellion *Subs not used* Bjorklund, Piper *Booked* Kilbane, McCann
Scorer **Gray 45**
Report page 236

Leeds United 0   Sunderland 1
Elland Road, Wednesday August 28 2002
Rick Broadbent

THERE WAS UNEXPECTED TROUBLE at the Terry Venables love-in last night. The man with the Midas touch was undone by a figure supposedly heading for a golden handshake. It was Sunderland's first league win at Elland Road for 41 years and a lifeline for Peter Reid, their beleaguered manager.

The result also provided Venables with a dose of cold reality. The fans who have been quick to take his attacking approach to heart booed their team off at the end. "Expectations are high everywhere," Venables said. "The crowd have to decide where they are, but you accept that if you lose at home."

As Reid is well aware, patience is a rare commodity in the Premiership. If Sunderland can summon up a similar level of resilience, then they may well save Reid his job. The whispers have grown to a clamour of late, but a few more results such as this and the gloves will come off only if the blinkers are on.

Leeds will reflect that they had enough pressure to salvage their unbeaten record, but even when Venables added a fourth striker, in the form of Robbie Keane, still yearning for a move to Tottenham Hotspur, they struggled to carve out clear openings.

The winner came 28 seconds after the restart. Thomas Butler, a lively figure throughout on the left flank, curled in a cross, Kevin Phillips, making his 200th start for Sunderland, nodded the ball down and Jason McAteer stabbed it in from six yards. It rallied Leeds into action and, with Olivier Dacourt replacing the ineffectual Eirik Bakke, they began to exert some belated pressure.

That should have resulted in a penalty when Michael Gray barged into the back of Mark Viduka as he steadied himself to meet Keane's deft cross — "a stone bonker" was Venables's florid description — but that was as close as they came. Too often they became confused by their own complex patterns and they posed a more genuine threat when they favoured the prosaic approach over the pretty.

An effort by Harry Kewell was blocked by Gray, Viduka had a header saved by Thomas Sorensen and Paul Thirlwell made a superbly timed clearance as Alan Smith bore down on a loose ball, but Sunderland stood firm. "We have some good players at the club, but there's a lot of anxiety about at the moment," Reid said. "That happens. People expect you to win every game, but I can't fault the players in the three matches we've had."

The alterations Venables has made to the team bequeathed him by David O'Leary have had mixed results. Paul Robinson has played well after being granted a deserved chance in goal and Nick Barmby has released Kewell from sentry duty on the wing, but Venables's

Reyna shields the ball from Bowyer during Sunderland's win at Elland Road . . .

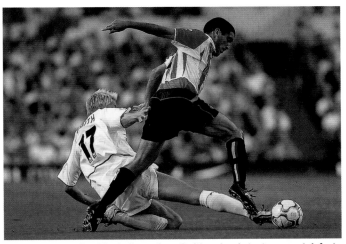
. . . but cannot resist this challenge from Smith as Leeds try to prevent defeat

preference for Bakke as the anchor in midfield is baffling. It was an elementary error by the Norwegian that handed Claudio Reyna the best chance of the first half and it took a smart save from Robinson to spare his blushes.

That proved to be a rare sight of goal in a turgid opening period. Leeds passed and probed, but, foiled by Reid's sensible tactic of flooding the midfield, had only a header by Kewell into the side-netting and a strike by Viduka that was deflected harmlessly wide to show for their bluster.

Frustration promptly turned to anxiety when McAteer scored and Leeds lost their heads. It took Keane's arrival to improve matters. Venables has said that the Ireland World Cup hero can leave, but he might wish to reconsider after seeing him leave Kewell,

Sunday November 3
CHARLTON ATHLETIC (a)
Drew 1-1   HT 1-0   Att 26,284   Position 18th
Macho — Wright, Bjorklund, Craddock, Babb — Thirlwell (Williams 65), McCann, Kilbane, Gray — Phillips (Piper 79), Flo *Subs not used* Ingham, McCartney, Stewart *Booked* Wright, Bjorklund, McCann, Williams
Scorer **Flo 15**
Report page 177

Wednesday November 6
ARSENAL (a)
Worthington Cup, 3rd rnd
Won 3-2   HT 0-2   Att 19,059
Macho — Rossiter, Varga, Thome, McCartney — Williams, Schwarz (Piper ht), Thirlwell — Stewart — Proctor, Kyle *Subs not used* Clark, Byrne, Dickman, Turns *Booked* Piper
Scorers **Kyle 56, Stewart 70, 72**
Report page 57

Sunday November 10
TOTTENHAM HOTSPUR (h)
Won 2-0   HT 0-0   Att 40,024   Position 16th
Macho — Wright, Craddock, Babb, McCartney — Proctor (Thirlwell 75), McCann, Kilbane, Gray — Phillips (Kyle 88), Flo *Subs not used* Ingham, Stewart, Bjorklund
Scorers **Phillips 60, Flo 62**
Referee **U Rennie**

A first goal of the season for Phillips, a header on the hour, and one by Flo almost immediately afterwards earn Sunderland their first league win under Howard Wilkinson after their Worthington Cup success in midweek, "We deserved nothing," Glenn Hoddle admits. Niall Quinn announces his retirement at half-time.

Sunday November 17
LIVERPOOL (a)
Drew 0-0   HT 0-0   Att 43,074   Position 17th
Macho — Bjorklund, Craddock, Babb, McCartney — Proctor (Stewart 85), McCann, Kilbane, Gray — Phillips (Thirlwell 66), Flo (Kyle 72) *Subs not used* Williams, Ingham *Booked* Bjorklund
Report page 94

Saturday November 23
BIRMINGHAM CITY (h)
Lost 0-1   HT 0-0   Att 38,803   Position 17th
Macho — Wright, Craddock, Babb, McCartney — Proctor (Bellion 56), McCann, Kilbane, Gray — Flo, Phillips *Subs not used* Poom, Stewart, Thirlwell, Bjorklund *Booked* Wright, Gray, McCann
Referee **R Styles**

Sunderland's brief revival ends when Craddock's slip is punished by Morrison with the winner in the 89th minute, the home side's nearest effort to a goal coming when Tebily hits his own crossbar. Only Savage's petulant reaction to being substituted spoils Birmingham's day.

Saturday November 30
CHELSEA (a)
Lost 0-3 **HT 0-0** Att **38,946** Position **18th**
Macho — Wright, Craddock, Babb, Gray — Bjorklund
(Bellion 62) — McCann, Thirlwell, Kilbane (McCartney 71)
— Flo, Phillips *Subs not used* Poom, Williams, Stewart
Booked Kilbane, McCann, Thirlwell
Report page 82

Tuesday December 3
SHEFFIELD UNITED (a)
Worthington Cup, 4th rnd
Lost 0-2 **HT 0-0** Att **27,068**
Macho — Rossiter, Thome, Varga, McCartney — Bellion,
McCann, Williams, Proctor — Kyle (Schwarz 65),
Stewart *Subs not used* Clark, Medina, Turns, Dickman
Booked McCartney
Referee **A Wiley**

Howard Wilkinson, suffering a first defeat of his
managerial career at Bramall Lane, has no regrets after
fielding a shadow side once again in the Worthington
Cup — there are nine changes from the defeat away to
Chelsea — and seeing them beaten by two goals early in
the second half.

Monday December 9
MANCHESTER CITY (h)
Lost 0-3 **HT 0-1** Att **36,511** Position **19th**
Macho — Wright, Bjorklund, Babb, McCartney — Proctor,
Thirlwell, Kilbane, Gray (Stewart 66) — Flo (Kyle 66),
Phillips (Bellion 66) *Subs not used* Poom, Williams
Booked Gray
Referee **S Dunn**

Things are going from bad to worse for Sunderland,
beaten with almost embarrassing ease by Kevin
Keegan's side after Phillips misses a great chance at
0-0. By the time that Goater scores City's third, the
Stadium of Light is almost deserted on a bitterly cold
night.

Sunday December 15
LIVERPOOL (h)
Won 2-1 **HT 1-0** Att **37,118** Position **17th**
Macho — Wright, Bjorklund, Babb, McCartney — Thirlwell,
McCann, Kilbane, Gray (Proctor 80) — Flo (Stewart 89),
Phillips *Subs not used* Ingham, Bellion, Thome
Scorers **McCann 36, Proctor 85**
Referee **M Halsey**

Sunderland may be in trouble, but this is also
Liverpool's fourth straight league defeat. McCann
has a penalty saved by Kirkland after having given
Sunderland the lead, but it is Macho's excellence that
catches the eye before and after Baros's equaliser.
Sunderland's winner comes from Proctor after an initial
air shot.

Even a first victory of the season cannot ease the pressure felt by Peter Reid

Viduka and Smith in the shade with an ebullient performance.
"There have been discussions, but there is nothing as yet," Venables
said.

How Sunderland would love to sign Keane to ease the burden on
Phillips's shoulders, but they can take solace from the promise
shown by Matt Piper on his full debut and Reyna's calming
influence in the engine room.

So the honeymoon is over for El Tel. He once claimed that
things are never as good as they seem when you are winning and
never as bad when losing. Both sets of fans might want to take note.

LEEDS UNITED (4-3-3): P Robinson — D Mills, L Radebe, D Matteo, I Harte — L Bowyer, E Bakke
(sub: O Dacourt, 55min), N Barmby (sub: R Keane, 55) — A Smith, M Viduka, H Kewell. **Substitutes
not used:** G Kelly, N Martyn, J Woodgate. **Booked:** Bowyer, Dacourt.

SUNDERLAND (4-5-1): T Sorensen — S Wright, J Bjorklund, P Babb, M Gray — M Piper (sub: J Arca,
71), P Thirlwell, J McAteer, C Reyna, T Butler — K Phillips (sub: K Kyle, 78). **Substitutes not used:**
J Macho, G McCartney, N Quinn.
Referee: M Halsey.

THE MANAGER

Howard Wilkinson

Wilkinson could claim that he inherited a poor squad, with little finance available for improvement, but while other managers swung exciting loan deals, he signed only a reserve keeper and an uninspiring centre back. His much-vaunted technical knowledge was possibly his undoing as his cerebral approach was never likely to motivate a team cast in the fire of Peter Reid's passion. Urging his players to adopt Tiger Woods's mental philosophy could not have sat easily with a side accustomed to "Get stook in and knock it to Quinny."

Richard Hakin

APPEARANCES

	Prem	FAC	WC	Total
J Arca	7 (6)	4	1	12 (6)
P Babb	26	3	1	30
D Bellion	5 (6)	0 (1)	2	7 (7)
J Bjorklund	19 (1)	1 (1)	-	20 (2)
C Black	2	-	-	2
T Butler	7	-	0 (1)	7 (1)
B Clark	0 (1)	1	-	1 (1)
J Craddock	25	4	1	30
J Dickman	0 (1)	-	-	0 (1)
T El Karkouri	8	0 (1)	-	8 (1)
T A Flo	23 (6)	1 (1)	1	25 (7)
M Gray	32	4	-	36
K Kilbane	30	3	1	34
K Kyle	9 (8)	2 (1)	2	13 (9)
J Macho	12 (1)	1	2	15 (1)
J McAteer	9	1	-	10
G McCann	29 (1)	3	2	34 (1)
G McCartney	16 (8)	1 (2)	2 (1)	19 (11)
N Medina	-	1	-	1
T Myhre	1 (1)	-	1	2 (1)
J Oster	1 (2)	1 (1)	-	2 (3)
K Phillips	32	4	-	36
M Piper	8 (5)	-	0 (1)	8 (6)
M Poom	4	-	-	4
M Proctor	11 (10)	3 (2)	2	16 (12)
N Quinn	0 (8)	-	-	0 (8)
C Reyna	11	-	1	12
M Rossiter	-	0 (1)	2	2 (1)
R Ryan	0 (2)	-	-	0 (2)
S Schwarz	-	-	1 (1)	1 (1)
T Sorensen	21	4	-	25
M Stewart	9 (10)	2	3	14 (10)
P Thirlwell	12 (7)	1	1 (1)	14 (8)
E Thome	1	2	2	5
S Thornton	11	3	-	14
S Varga	-	0 (1)	2	2 (1)
D Williams	12 (4)	2	3	17 (4)
S Wright	25 (1)	3	-	28 (1)

Saturday December 21
WEST BROMWICH ALBION (a)
Drew 2-2   HT 0-0   Att 26,703   Position 17th
Macho — Wright, Craddock, Babb, McCartney (Bellion ht) — Thirlwell, McCann, Kilbane, Gray — Flo, Phillips *Subs not used* Ingham, Bjorklund, Stewart, Proctor *Booked* Craddock
Scorer **Phillips 56, 64**
Report page 263

Thursday December 26
LEEDS UNITED (h)
Lost 1-2   HT 1-0   Att 44,029   Position 18th
Macho — Wright, Craddock, Babb, Gray — Proctor (Stewart 82), McCann, Thirlwell (McCartney 82), Kilbane — Flo (Kyle 82), Phillips *Subs not used* Ingham, Bjorklund *Booked* Proctor
Scorer **Proctor 34**
Referee **M Dean**

The ink has hardly dried on Rooney's record when Milner, at 16 years and 357 days, becomes the Premiership's youngest scorer, his goal cancelling out Proctor's opener for Sunderland. Proctor then concedes the penalty through which Fowler secures the points for Leeds with ten minutes to go.

Saturday December 28
SOUTHAMPTON (a)
Lost 1-2   HT 0-0   Att 31,423   Position 18th
Macho — Wright, Craddock, Babb, McCartney — Thirlwell, McCann, Kilbane, Gray (Kyle (Bjorklund 90), Phillips (Proctor ht) *Subs not used* Ingham, Stewart *Booked* Phillips, McCartney
Scorer **Flo 77**
Report page 130

Wednesday January 1
MANCHESTER UNITED (a)
Lost 1-2   HT 1-0   Att 67,609   Position 18th
Macho — Wright, Craddock, Babb, McCartney — Thirlwell — Flo (Proctor 72), McCann (Williams 14), Kilbane, Stewart (Oster 84) — Phillips *Subs not used* Sorensen, Bjorklund *Booked* Wright
Scorer **Veron 5 (og)**
Report page 48

Saturday January 4
BOLTON WANDERERS (a)
FA Cup, 3rd rnd
Drew 1-1   HT 0-1   Att 10,123
Macho — Wright (Rossiter 14; Bjorklund 27), Craddock, Babb, McCartney — Proctor, Williams, Thirlwell, Oster — Phillips, Kyle (Flo ht) *Subs not used* Sorensen, Stewart *Booked* Oster, McCartney
Scorer **Phillips 63**
Report page 239

Saturday January 11
BLACKBURN ROVERS (h)
Drew 0-0 HT **0-0** Att **36,529** Position **18th**
Sorensen — Williams, Craddock, Babb, McCartney —
Oster (Arca 60), McCann, Thirlwell, Proctor (Stewart 78)
— Phillips, Flo *Subs not used* Macho, Bjorklund, Kyle
Booked Williams
Referee **M Riley**

Both sides profess themselves happy with a point in a
featureless affair in which Cole and Yorke miss the
best openings for Blackburn, while Sunderland, who
finish the stronger, go close when Craddock hits the
post late on.

Tuesday January 14
BOLTON WANDERERS (h)
FA Cup, 3rd rnd replay
Won 2-0 (aet) HT **0-0** Att **14,550**
Sorensen — Williams, Bjorklund (Varga 60), Thome,
Gray (Proctor 67) — Thornton, McCann, Medina
(McCartney 90), Arca — Kyle, Stewart *Subs not used*
Macho, Oster
Scorers **Arca 99, Proctor 100**
Referee **N Barry**

All change at Sunderland, with eight alterations in each
line-up from Saturday's league fixtures. In front of the
second-lowest crowd at a windy Stadium of Light, a tie
that neither side seems particularly intent on winning is
finally settled in extra time with two goals in a minute.
"We weren't very good," Sam Allardyce, the Bolton
manager, admits.

Saturday January 18
EVERTON (a)
Lost 1-2 HT **1-0** Att **37,409** Position **18th**
Sorensen — Williams, Craddock, Babb, McCartney —
Thornton, McCann, Thirlwell (Arca 63), Kilbane — Flo
(Proctor 73), Phillips *Subs not used* Gray, Thome,
Macho *Booked* Babb, McCann, Craddock
Scorer **Kilbane 34**
Report page 121

Saturday January 25
BLACKBURN ROVERS (a)
FA Cup, 4th rnd
Drew 3-3 HT **1-1** Att **14,315**
Sorensen — Clark, Craddock, Babb, Gray — Kilbane,
McCann, Stewart, Arca — Phillips, Proctor *Subs
not used* Macho, Kyle, Medina, Oster, Thome
Booked Kilbane
Scorers **Stewart 2, Proctor 52, Phillips 70**
Report page 109

PLAYER OF THE SEASON Kevin Phillips

After such an appalling 2002-03, it seems inappropriate to nominate a player of the season. Certainly, the *Sunderland Echo* reduced the award to a farce when it chose Sean Thornton (first match: January; total Premiership appearances: 11). More deserving would have been the Stadium of Light crowd. An average home gate of almost 40,000, despite their team's disheartening displays, shames players, managers and directors alike. If one has to nominate someone on the field (and assuming Samson the Cat, the Sunderland mascot, is ineligible), it is difficult to look beyond Kevin Phillips. His goal tally (nine in total, with only six in the league) was modest, but his general play shone in an otherwise abject side.

Richard Hakin

STATS AND FACTS

● If Mick McCarthy had won eight of his nine games (while losing the other one against Bolton Wanderers. Sunderland would still have been relegated.

● Based on average attendances, Sunderland had 0.48 points per thousand fans (19 points; 39,698 fans), the worst Premiership ratio.

● The 2-2 draw with West Bromwich Albion on December 21 was only the second time in 15 months that a Premiership match involving Sunderland had featured both teams scoring more than once.

● Derby despair: Sunderland have won one of their past 11 games against Middlesbrough and two of their past 14 against Newcastle United.

Bill Edgar

GOALSCORERS

	Prem	FAC	WC	Total
J Arca	-	1	1	2
D Bellion	1	-	-	1
J Craddock	1	-	-	1
T A Flo	4	-	2	6
M Gray	1	-	-	1
K Kilbane	1	-	-	1
K Kyle	-	-	1	1
J McAteer	1	-	-	1
G McCann	1	1	1	3
K Phillips	6 (1p)	3	-	9 (1p)
M Proctor	2	2	-	4
C Reyna	-	-	1	1
M Stewart	1	1	4	6
S Thornton	1	-	-	1
Own goals	1	-	-	1

Tuesday January 28
SOUTHAMPTON (h)
Lost 0-1 **HT 0-0** Att **34,102** Position **18th**
Sorensen — Gray, Craddock, Babb (Thirlwell 64), McCartney — Stewart (Kyle 72), McCann (Clark 64), Kilbane, Arca — Phillips, Proctor *Subs not used* Macho, Oster *Booked* Proctor
Referee **N Barry**

The lowest crowd for a Premiership fixture at the Stadium of Light becomes increasingly discordant as Beattie, with his seventeenth goal of the season, secures Southampton's victory before Phillips misses a late chance for an equaliser from a similar position.

Saturday February 1
CHARLTON ATHLETIC (h)
Lost 1-3 **HT 0-3** Att **36,042** Position **20th**
Sorensen — Wright, Craddock, Babb, Gray — Proctor (Stewart 74), McCann, Kilbane (McCartney 89), Arca — Phillips, Flo *Subs not used* Macho, Oster, Thirlwell *Booked* Kilbane
Scorer **Phillips 81 (pen)**
Referee **A Wiley**

Never has a Premiership defeat been more cruelly self-inflicted. Not one, not two, but three own goals in a bizarre eight-minute spell, the unfortunate Proctor contributing two of them, gift Charlton victory and send a disbelieving Sunderland side to the bottom of the table for the first time. The fans vote with their feet, some leaving even before half-time.

Wednesday February 5
BLACKBURN ROVERS (h)
FA Cup, 4th rnd replay
Drew 2-2 (aet; win 3-0 on pens) **HT 1-0** Att **15,745**
Sorensen — Wright, Craddock, Thome, Gray (Oster 114) — Thornton, McCann, Kilbane, Arca (McCartney 87) — Phillips, Proctor (Kyle 116) *Subs not used* Macho, Thirlwell *Booked* Proctor
Scorers **Phillips 10, McCann 79**
Referee **A D'Urso**

Twice ahead but forced into overtime by Flitcroft's second goal of the game, in the ninetieth minute, Sunderland warm a depleted, frozen crowd by romping through the penalty shoot-out as Thompson, Cole and Grabbi all fail to beat Sorensen from the spot.

Saturday February 8
TOTTENHAM HOTSPUR (a)
Lost 1-4 **HT 1-2** Att **36,075** Position **20th**
Sorensen — Wright, Craddock, Thome (Piper 69), McCartney — El Karkouri — Thornton, McCann (Thirlwell 60), Arca — Phillips, Proctor (Flo 68) *Subs not used* Macho, Babb *Booked* McCann, Phillips
Scorer **Phillips 26**
Report page 157

Saturday February 15
WATFORD (h)
FA Cup, 5th rnd
Lost 0-1 HT 0-0 Att 26,916
Sorensen — Wright, Craddock, Babb (Proctor 73), Gray — Thornton, McAteer, Kilbane, Arca (El Karkouri 59) — Phillips, Flo (Bellion 59) *Subs not used* Macho, Thirlwell *Booked* Gray, Craddock
Referee **M Dean**

Sunderland's management and fans are not alone in feeling that their side have been unfairly treated after their Cup elimination at Watford's hands leaves them with only a relegation fight to contend with. Smith's twice-taken penalty, awarded for McAteer's innocuous foul on Helguson, proves decisive, Sorensen being adjudged to have moved off his line to save the first effort.

Saturday February 22
MIDDLESBROUGH (h)
Lost 1-3 HT 0-2 Att 42,134 Position 20th
Sorensen — Wright, Craddock, El Karkouri, Gray (Arca 72) — Bellion (Piper ht), McCann, McAteer, Kilbane (Proctor 84) — Phillips, Flo *Subs not used* Macho, Babb *Booked* Wright, Kilbane
Scorer **Phillips 56**
Referee **M Halsey**

Howard Wilkinson is forced to "clarify his position" after claiming before this derby that Sunderland are not in the relegation equation. Crowd disturbances add an unpleasant atmosphere to another thoroughly depressing day on Wearside as Riggott's double sets up an easy win for Middlesbrough.

Saturday March 1
FULHAM (a)
Lost 0-1 HT 0-0 Att 16,286 Position 20th
Sorensen — Wright, Craddock, El Karkouri, Gray (McCartney 83) — Piper (Proctor 79), McCann, McAteer, Kilbane — Phillips, Flo *Subs not used* Macho, Babb, Arca *Booked* McAteer, McCann
Report page 207

Saturday March 15
BOLTON WANDERERS (h)
Lost 0-2 HT 0-0 Att 42,124 Position 20th
Sorensen — Wright (Arca ht), Bjorklund, El Karkouri, McCartney — Proctor (Kyle 80), Williams, Thornton, Gray — Phillips, Flo (Stewart 66) *Subs not used* Poom, Babb *Booked* McCartney
Referee **J Winter**

An afternoon that begins full of optimism as Mick McCarthy is welcomed as Sunderland's new manager — Howard Wilkinson having been dismissed five days earlier — ends in despair as Okocha and Pedersen score the goals that take Bolton, one of the sides that Sunderland must overtake if they are to stay up, ten points clear of bottom place.

THE PLAYERS

JULIO ARCA
Midfield
Born January 31, 1981, Quilmes, Argentina
Ht 5ft 9in **Wt** 11st 6lb
Signed from Argentinos Juniors, August 2000, £3.5m

PHIL BABB
Defender
Born November 30, 1970, Lambeth
Ht 6ft 0in **Wt** 12st 3lb
Signed from Sporting Lisbon, July 2002, free

DAVID BELLION
Forward
Born November 27, 1982, Paris
Ht 6ft 0in **Wt** 11st 5lb
Signed from AS Cannes, August 2001, free

JOACHIM BJORKLUND
Defender
Born March 15, 1971, Vaxjo, Sweden
Ht 6ft 1in **Wt** 12st 8lb
Signed from Venezia, January 2002, £1.5m

CHRIS BLACK
Midfield
Born September 7, 1982, Ashington
Signed from trainee, May 2003

THOMAS BUTLER
Midfield
Born April 25, 1981, Dublin
Ht 5ft 8in **Wt** 10st 6lb
Signed from trainee, August 1998

BEN CLARK
Defender
Born January 24, 1983, Shotley Bridge
Ht 6ft 2in **Wt** 12st 6lb
Signed from trainee, August 1999

JODY CRADDOCK
Defender
Born July 25, 1975, Bromsgrove
Ht 6ft 1in **Wt** 12st 4lb
Signed from Cambridge United, August 1997, £300,000

JONJO DICKMAN
Midfield
Born September 22, 1981, Hexham
Ht 5ft 8in **Wt** 10st 5lb
Signed from trainee, August 1996

TALAL EL KARKOURI
Defender
Born July 8, 1976, Morocco
Ht 6ft 1in **Wt** 12st 10lb
Signed from Paris Saint-Germain (loan), January 2003

TORE ANDRE FLO
Forward
Born June 15, 1973, Stryn, Norway
Ht 6ft 4in **Wt** 13st 8lb
Signed from Rangers, August 2002, £6.75m

MICHAEL GRAY
Defender
Born August 3, 1974, Sunderland
Ht 5ft 7in **Wt** 10st 10lb
Signed from trainee, July 2002

Jody Craddock

KEVIN KILBANE
Midfield
Born February 1, 1977, Preston
Ht 6ft 0in **Wt** 12st 0lb
Signed from West Bromwich
Albion, December 1999, £2.5m

KEVIN KYLE
Forward
Born June 7, 1981, Stranraer
Ht 6ft 3in **Wt** 12st 0lb
Signed from trainee, August 2000

JURGEN MACHO
Goalkeeper
Born August 24, 1977, Vienna
Ht 6ft 4in **Wt** 13st 12lb
Signed from First Vienna, July
2000

JASON McATEER
Midfield
Born June 18, 1971, Birkenhead
Ht 5ft 10in **Wt** 11st 12lb
Signed from Blackburn Rovers,
October 2001, £1m

GAVIN McCANN
Midfield
Born January 10, 1978,
Blackpool
Ht 5ft 11in **Wt** 12st 8lb
Signed from Everton, November
1998, £500,000

GEORGE McCARTNEY
Defender
Born April 29, 1981, Belfast
Ht 5ft 11in **Wt** 12st 5lb
Signed from trainee,
August 1998

NICOLAS MEDINA
Midfield
Born February 17, 1982,
Buenos Aires
Ht 5ft 10in **Wt** 10st 4lb
Signed from Argentinos Juniors,
June 2001, £3.5m

THOMAS MYHRE
Goalkeeper
Born October 16, 1973,
Sarpsborg, Norway
Ht 6ft 2in **Wt** 13st 0lb
Signed from Besiktas, July 2002,
free

JOHN OSTER
Midfield
Born December 8, 1978, Boston
Ht 5ft 9in **Wt** 10st 8lb
Signed from Everton, August
1999, £1m

KEVIN PHILLIPS
Forward
Born July 25, 1973, Hitchin
Ht 5ft 7in **Wt** 11st 0lb
Signed from Watford, July 1997,
£325,000

MATTHEW PIPER
Midfield
Born September 29, 1981,
Leicester
Ht 6ft 1in **Wt** 13st 5lb
Signed from Leicester City, August
2002, £3.5m

MART POOM
Goalkeeper
Born February 3, 1972,
Tallinn, Estonia
Ht 6ft 5in **Wt** 13st 6lb
Signed from Derby County,
November 2002, £2.5m

MICHAEL PROCTOR
Forward
Born October 3, 1980, Sunderland
Ht 5ft 11in **Wt** 12st 7lb
Signed from trainee, October 1997

NIALL QUINN
Forward
Born October 6, 1966, Dublin
Ht 6ft 4in **Wt** 13st 10lb
Signed from Manchester City,
August 1996, £1.3m

Saturday March 22
WEST HAM UNITED (a)
Lost 0-2 HT **0-1** Att **35,033** Position **20th**
Sorensen — Williams, Bjorklund, El Karkouri, McCartney
(Proctor 64) — Butler (Stewart 80), Thornton, Kilbane,
Gray — Phillips, Flo (Kyle 58) *Subs not used* Poom,
Babb
Report page 254

Saturday April 5
CHELSEA (h)
Lost 1-2 HT **1-0** Att **40,011** Position **20th**
Sorensen — Williams, Bjorklund, El Karkouri, Gray —
Thornton, McCann, Kilbane (McCartney 86) — Phillips,
Kyle, Stewart *Subs not used* Poom, Babb, Proctor, Arca
Booked El Karkouri
Scorer **Thornton 12**
Referee **D Gallagher**

Sunderland give their best performance for months, but
it is still not enough to prevent a Premiership record
ninth successive defeat as Chelsea cancel out
Thornton's fine opener with Zola's deflected volley,
then win the match with a superb turn and shot by Cole,
their substitute.

Saturday April 12
BIRMINGHAM CITY (a)
Lost 0-2 HT **0-1** Att **29,132** Position **20th**
Poom — Williams, Bjorklund (McCartney 22), El Karkouri
(Wright 55), Gray — Thornton, McCann, Kilbane —
Phillips, Kyle, Stewart *Subs not used* Proctor, Arca,
Turns *Booked* McCartney *Sent off* Stewart 86
Report page 195

Saturday April 19
WEST BROMWICH ALBION (h)
Lost 1-2 HT **0-2** Att **36,025** Position **20th**
Poom — Williams, Craddock, El Karkouri
(McCartney 58), Gray — Thornton, McCann (Arca 19),
Kilbane — Phillips, Kyle (Proctor 82), Stewart *Subs not
used* Sorensen, Flo *Booked* Williams, El Karkouri, Kyle,
McCartney
Scorer **Stewart 70**
Referee **G Poll**

Their relegation confirmed seven days earlier, there is
no relief for Sunderland — and this time they take West
Brom with them. Despite ending a run of seven straight
losses with McInnes's first goals of the season, both
after mistakes by Poom, Albion's own Premiership
demotion is finally sealed by Bolton's victory against
West Ham on the same afternoon.

Monday April 21
MANCHESTER CITY (a)
Lost 0-3 HT 0-2 Att 34,357 Position **20th**
Poom — Williams, Craddock, McCartney, Gray —
Thornton, Kilbane, Arca (Dickman ht) — Phillips, Kyle
(Proctor 62), Stewart (Flo 62) *Subs not used* Sorensen,
Clark *Booked* McCartney
Report page 147

Saturday April 26
NEWCASTLE UNITED (h) Position **20th**
Lost 0-1 HT 0-1 Att 45,067 Position **20th**
Sorensen — Williams, Craddock, Bjorklund, Gray —
Bellion, Thornton, Kilbane, Arca (Flo 84) — Proctor (Ryan
76), Kyle *Subs not used* Poom, McCartney, Clark
Booked Williams, Kyle, Proctor, Bjorklund
Referee **S Bennett**

Sunderland's thirteenth successive league defeat is one
of the most painful in that sequence as Newcastle,
twice rescued earlier by Given, win the derby from the
penalty spot through Solano after Kilbane's trip on
Bellamy. Shearer, carrying three separate injuries, says
he will not play again this season.

Saturday May 3
ASTON VILLA (a)
Lost 0-1 HT 0-0 Att 36,963 Position **20th**
Poom — Williams, Bjorklund, Craddock, Gray — Black
(Proctor 84), Thornton, McCann, Kilbane — Phillips, Kyle
(Flo 84) *Subs not used* Sorensen, McCartney, Ryan
Booked Phillips
Report page 232

Sunday May 11
ARSENAL (h)
Lost 0-4 HT 0-2 Att 40,188 Position **20th**
Sorensen — Williams (McCartney ht), Bjorklund,
Craddock, Gray — Black (Oster ht), Thornton (Ryan ht),
McCann, Kilbane — Phillips, Kyle *Subs not used* Poom,
Proctor *Booked* McCann
Referee **P Durkin**

Mick McCarthy is "embarrassed" (and booed) after
Sunderland's farewell performance as they are taken
apart by an Arsenal side smarting at the loss of their
title and inspired by Henry, who scores the opener and
sets up two of Ljungberg's hat-trick.

CLAUDIO REYNA
Midfield
Born July 20, 1973, Livingston,
New Jersey
Ht 5ft 9in **Wt** 11st 3lb
Signed from Rangers, December
2001, £4.5m

MARK ROSSITER
Midfield
Born May 27, 1983, Sligo
Signed from trainee,
August 2002

RICHIE RYAN
Midfield
Born January 6, 1985, Kilkenny
Signed from trainee,
August 2001

STEFAN SCHWARZ
Midfield
Born April 18, 1969, Malmo
Ht 6ft 0in **Wt** 12st 6lb
Signed from Valencia, August
1999, £4m

THOMAS SORENSEN
Goalkeeper
Born June 12, 1976,
Odense, Denmark
Ht 6ft 4in **Wt** 13st 10lb
Signed from OB Odense, August
1998, £500,000

MARCUS STEWART
Forward
Born November 7, 1972, Bristol
Ht 5ft 10in **Wt** 11st 0lb
Signed from Ipswich Town, August
2002, £3.25m

PAUL THIRLWELL
Midfield
Born February 13, 1979,
Gateshead
Ht 5ft 11in **Wt** 11st 4lb
Signed from trainee, August 1997

EMERSON THOME
Defender
Born March 30, 1972,
Porto Alegre, Brazil
Ht 6ft 1in **Wt** 13st 4lb
Signed from Chelsea, September
2000, £4.5m

SEAN THORNTON
Midfield
Born May 18, 1983, Drogheda
Ht 5ft 10in **Wt** 11st 0lb
Signed from Tranmere Rovers,
July 2002, undisclosed

STANISLAV VARGA
Defender
Born October 8, 1972,
Lipany, Slovakia
Ht 6ft 2in **Wt** 14st 8lb
Signed from Slovan Bratislava,
August 2000, £650,000

DARREN WILLIAMS
Midfield
Born April 28, 1977,
Middlesbrough
Ht 5ft 10in **Wt** 11st 12lb
Signed from York City, October
1996, £50,000

STEPHEN WRIGHT
Defender
Born February 8, 1980, Liverpool
Ht 5ft 11in **Wt** 12st 0lb
Signed from Liverpool, August
2002, £3m

Stephen Wright

NATIONWIDE LEAGUE

FIRST DIVISION

CHAMPIONS
Portsmouth

RUNNERS-UP
Leicester City

PROMOTED VIA PLAY-OFFS
Wolverhampton Wanderers

Forever blowing bubbly: Harry Redknapp celebrates Portsmouth's championship

THE GAMES

Saturday August 10
Burnley 1 Brighton 3; Coventry 2 Sheff Utd 1; Derby 3 Reading 0; Leicester 2 Watford 0; Millwall 0 Rotherham 6; Norwich 4 Grimsby 0; Portsmouth 2 Nott'm Forest 0; Preston 1 C Palace 2; Sheff Weds 0 Stoke 0; Walsall 0 Ipswich 2; Wimbledon 0 Gillingham 1

Sunday August 11
Bradford 0 Wolves 0

Tuesday August 13
Brighton 0 Coventry 0; C Palace 1 Bradford 1; Gillingham 1 Derby 0; Grimsby 0 Wimbledon 0; Reading 2 Sheff Weds 1; Rotherham 1 Norwich 1; Sheff Utd 1 Portsmouth 1; Watford 0 Millwall 0

Wednesday August 14
Nott'm Forest 2 Preston 2; Stoke 0 Leicester 1; Wolves 3 Walsall 1

Saturday August 17
Brighton 0 Norwich 2; C Palace 2 Portsmouth 3; Gillingham 1 Millwall 0; Grimsby 1 Derby 2; Nott'm Forest 4 Sheff Weds 0; Reading 1 Coventry 2; Rotherham 0 Preston 0; Sheff Utd 1 Walsall 1; Stoke 2 Bradford 1; Watford 3 Wimbledon 2; Wolves 3 Burnley 0

Sunday August 18
Ipswich 6 Leicester 1

Saturday August 24
Bradford 0 Grimsby 0; Burnley 0 Sheff Utd 1; Coventry 1 C Palace 0; Derby 1 Wolves 4; Leicester 2 Reading 1; Millwall 1 Ipswich 1; Norwich 1 Gillingham 0; Portsmouth 3 Watford 0; Preston 4 Stoke 3; Sheff Weds 1 Rotherham 2; Walsall 2 Nott'm Forest 1; Wimbledon 1 Brighton 0

Monday August 26
Brighton 0 Walsall 2; Gillingham 1 Preston 1; Grimsby 0 Portsmouth 1; Ipswich 1 Bradford 2; Rotherham 2 Derby 1; Stoke 1 Norwich 1; Watford 5 Coventry 2

Tuesday August 27
C Palace 0 Leicester 0; Reading 3 Burnley 0; Sheff Utd 3 Millwall 1; Wolves 2 Sheff Weds 2

Wednesday August 28
Nott'm Forest 2 Wimbledon 0

Saturday August 31
Bradford 4 Rotherham 2; Burnley 0 C Palace 0; Coventry 0 Nott'm Forest 1; Derby 2 Stoke 0; Leicester 2 Gillingham 0; Millwall 2 Grimsby 0; Norwich 4 Watford 0; Portsmouth 4 Brighton 2; Walsall 0 Reading 2; Wimbledon 3 Wolves 2

Sunday September 1
Preston 0 Ipswich 0; Sheff Weds 2 Sheff Utd 0

Saturday September 7
Derby 1 Burnley 2; Gillingham 1 Portsmouth 3; Millwall 1 Brighton 0; Norwich 2 Sheff Utd 3; Rotherham 0 Reading 0; Watford 2 Walsall 0; Wimbledon 2 Leicester 3

TO PORTSMOUTH THE BOUQUETS; to Leicester City the bounty and the brickbats; to Wolverhampton Wanderers the champagne sweetened by deferred glory. But to Sheffield United? The most decorated wooden spoon the Nationwide League has awarded.

Portsmouth were barely out of the automatic promotion places all season and only lost one league game before Hallowe'en, so few would dispute that Harry Redknapp's champions were the best team in the division. Yet would United have pushed for a top-two place harder if they had not been chasing silverware on three fronts? To reach the semi-finals of the Worthington Cup and the FA Cup — and push Liverpool and Arsenal all the way once they got there — and then the first division play-off final but finish empty-handed seems cruel in the extreme. Perhaps Neil Warnock deserved the manager-of-the-year award as a consolation prize for his team winning 34 of their 61 matches.

Yet Warnock, one of the division's most entertaining managers, was unlikely to receive many pats on the back from his peers. His xenophobic outpourings at Anfield, after Liverpool had needed extra time to beat them 3-2 on aggregate, and his suggestion that Arsenal's winner in the FA Cup semi-final was down to the referee taking out a United player in the build-up, came across as the rantings of a bad loser. At Easter, with the top two all but home and dry, Warnock suggested that Leicester's promotion, after they had shed 90 per cent of their debt through four months in administration, was immoral.

In the play-off final defeat by Wolves, Warnock was dismissed from the dugout with United trailing 3-0 at half-time. At least that gave him time to calm down and the manager who had lifted his team ten places in 12 months finished the season by graciously praising Dave Jones's team. "They deserved it," he said. "Maybe our season went on a half too long, but I can't blame my players for mistakes after all they've given me this season." Michael Brown scored 22 times from midfield, Stuart McCall, at 38, led by example in front of the back four while the fledgeling talents of Phil Jagielka and the skilful Michael Tonge, both 20, shone through.

When it comes to wheeling and dealing, Redknapp has few equals. Having reluctantly inherited from Graham Rix in March 2002 a team that would only just avoid relegation, the former West Ham United manager ripped up the manual and started again. The signing of Paul Merson from Aston Villa was the most inspirational of his many and varied recruits, although Shaka Hislop and Arjan de Zeeuw, both free transfers, and Matthew Taylor, the wing back, a snip at £400,000 from Luton Town, were highly influential.

Redknapp also maintained Portsmouth's momentum with timely additions: Steve Stone, Tim Sherwood and Yakubu Aiyegbeni, the Nigeria forward from Maccabi Haifa. Only Nigel Quashie and Linvoy Primus played in both the final game in 2001-02, when Portsmouth finished seventeenth, and 2002-03, when Svetoslav Todorov's hat-trick helped to defeat Bradford City 5-0 and left him as the leading first division goalscorer with 26.

Redknapp, backed by the millions of Milan Mandaric, his chairman, played down the financial factor. "We've put a team together on a shoestring," he said. "It's a load of Bosmans and, all right, we may have spent more than Rotherham on wages, but it's still very little compared with four or five clubs in this division."

Leicester spent not a bean. While Portsmouth won promotion after 15 years out of the top flight, the East Midlanders had come down from the Premiership in 2002 and swiftly into the hands of the administrators. Yet while Gary Lineker, with Jon Holmes, his agent, acting as chairman, rode in on their white horses to help to secure the club's future, there was much resentment that a club that could tot up

FINAL TABLE

| | P | | HOME | | | | | AWAY | | | | | |
		W	D	L	F	A	W	D	L	F	A	P	G D
Portsmouth	46	17	3	3	52	22	12	8	3	45	23	98	52
Leicester	46	16	5	2	40	12	10	9	4	33	28	92	33
Sheffield Utd	46	13	7	3	38	23	10	4	9	34	29	80	20
Reading	46	13	3	7	33	21	12	1	10	28	25	79	15
Wolves	46	9	10	4	40	19	11	6	6	41	25	76	37
Nott'm Forest	46	14	7	2	57	23	6	7	10	25	27	74	32
Ipswich	46	10	5	8	49	39	9	8	6	31	25	70	16
Norwich	46	14	4	5	36	17	5	8	10	24	32	69	11
Millwall	46	11	6	6	34	32	8	3	12	25	37	66	-10
Wimbledon	46	12	5	6	39	28	6	6	11	37	45	65	3
Gillingham	46	10	6	7	33	31	6	8	9	23	34	62	-9
Preston	46	11	7	5	44	29	5	6	12	24	41	61	-2
Watford	46	11	5	7	33	26	6	4	13	21	44	60	-16
Crystal Palace	46	8	10	5	29	17	6	7	10	30	35	59	7
Rotherham	46	8	9	6	27	25	7	5	11	35	37	59	0
Burnley	46	10	4	9	35	44	5	6	12	30	45	55	-24
Walsall	46	10	3	10	34	34	5	6	12	23	35	54	-12
Derby County	46	9	5	9	33	32	6	2	15	22	42	52	-19
Bradford City	46	7	8	8	27	35	7	2	14	24	38	52	-22
Coventry	46	6	6	11	23	31	6	8	9	23	31	50	-16
Stoke	46	9	6	8	25	25	3	8	12	20	44	50	-24
Sheffield Weds	46	7	7	9	29	32	9	11	27	41	46	-17
Brighton	46	7	6	10	29	31	4	6	13	20	36	45	-18
Grimsby	46	5	6	12	26	39	4	6	13	22	46	39	-37

Saturday September 14
Brighton 2 Gillingham 4; Burnley 2 Stoke 1; Coventry 3 Grimsby 2; C Palace 4 Wolves 2; Leicester 3 Derby 1; Nott'm Forest 0 Watford 1; Portsmouth 1 Millwall 0; Preston 2 Sheff Weds 2; Reading 0 Wimbledon 1; Sheff Utd 1 Rotherham 0; Walsall 0 Bradford 1

Sunday September 15
Ipswich 1 Norwich 1

Tuesday September 17
Brighton 1 Stoke 2; Burnley 2 Millwall 2; C Palace 0 Derby 1; Leicester 4 Bradford 0; Portsmouth 4 Wimbledon 1; Preston 1 Watford 1; Sheff Utd 2 Grimsby 1; Walsall 3 Rotherham 4

Wednesday September 18
Coventry 1 Sheff Weds 1; Nott'm Forest 4 Gillingham 1; Reading 0 Norwich 2

Saturday September 21
Bradford 2 Burnley 2; Derby 0 Preston 2; Gillingham 1 Sheff Utd 1; Grimsby 0 Nott'm Forest 3; Millwall 0 Walsall 3; Norwich 1 Portsmouth 0; Rotherham 1 Brighton 0; Sheff Weds 0 Leicester 0; Watford 3 C Palace 3; Wimbledon 0 Coventry 1; Wolves 0 Reading 1

Sunday September 22
Stoke 2 Ipswich 1

Tuesday September 24
Bradford 1 Coventry 1; Wolves 4 Preston 0

Wednesday September 25
Sheff Weds 0 C Palace 0; Stoke 2 Nott'm Forest 2

Saturday September 28
Brighton 1 Grimsby 2; Burnley 1 Wimbledon 0; Coventry 2 Millwall 3; Ipswich 0 Derby 1; Leicester 1 Wolves 0; Nott'm Forest 3 Watford 3; Portsmouth 3 Bradford 0; Preston 1 Norwich 2; Reading 1 Stoke 1; Sheff Utd 1 Watford 2; Walsall 1 Sheff Weds 0

Sunday September 29
C Palace 2 Gillingham 2

Saturday October 5
Bradford 1 Preston 1; Derby 2 Walsall 2; Gillingham 0 Coventry 2; Grimsby 0 Reading 3; Millwall 1 Nott'm Forest 2; Norwich 0 Leicester 0; Rotherham 2 Portsmouth 3; Sheff Weds 1 Burnley 3; Stoke 1 C Palace 1; Watford 1 Brighton 0; Wolves 1 Sheff Utd 3

Sunday October 6
Wimbledon 0 Ipswich 1

Tuesday October 8
Grimsby 3 Ipswich 0

Saturday October 12
Bradford 0 Derby 0; Burnley 2 Walsall 1; Ipswich 2 Sheff Weds 1; Millwall 1 Wimbledon 1; Rotherham 1 Gillingham 1; Watford 2 Grimsby 0

Saturday October 19
Brighton 2 Sheff Utd 4; Gillingham 3 Watford 0; Grimsby 0 Rotherham 0; Leicester 0 Burnley 1; Norwich 3 Millwall 1; Portsmouth 1 Coventry 1; Reading 3 Ipswich 1; Sheff Weds 2 Bradford 1; Stoke 0 Wolves 2; Walsall 3 Preston 3; Wimbledon 2 C Palace 2

Sunday October 20
Derby 0 Nott'm Forest 0

Tuesday October 22
Ipswich 2 Burnley 2

Wednesday October 23
Coventry 1 Norwich 1; Sheff Utd 2 Stoke 1

Saturday October 26
Bradford 2 Norwich 1; Burnley 0 Portsmouth 3;
Coventry 0 Walsall 0; C Palace 5 Brighton 0; Ipswich
0 Gillingham 1; Millwall 3 Derby 0; Nott'm Forest 2
Leicester 2; Preston 1 Reading 0; Rotherham 4
Stoke 0; Sheff Utd 1 Wimbledon 1; Watford 1
Sheff Weds 0; Wolves 4 Grimsby 1

Tuesday October 29
Gillingham 0 Wolves 4; Grimsby 6 Burnley 5;
Leicester 2 Coventry 1; Norwich 0 Nott'm Forest 0;
Portsmouth 3 Preston 2; Reading 1 Bradford 0;
Walsall 3 C Palace 4; Wimbledon 2 Rotherham 1

Wednesday October 30
Derby 2 Sheff Utd 1; Sheff Weds 0 Millwall 1;
Stoke 1 Watford 2

Saturday November 2
Brighton 3 Bradford 2; Coventry 2 Rotherham 1;
Grimsby 1 Gillingham 1; Nott'm Forest 3 Sheff
Utd 0; Portsmouth 0 Leicester 2; Preston 3 Burnley
1; Reading 2 Millwall 0; Sheff Weds 1 Derby 3;
Wimbledon 4 Norwich 2; Walsall 4 Stoke 2;
Watford 1 Wolves 1

Sunday November 3
Ipswich 1 C Palace 2

Wednesday November 6
Wolves 1 Portsmouth 1

Saturday November 9
Bradford 3 Wimbledon 5; Burnley 3 Coventry 1;
C Palace 0 Nott'm Forest 0; Derby 1 Portsmouth 2;
Gillingham 0 Reading 1; Leicester 2 Walsall 0;
Millwall 2 Preston 1; Norwich 3 Sheff Weds 0;
Rotherham 2 Watford 1; Sheff Utd 0 Ipswich 0;
Stoke 1 Grimsby 2

Monday November 11
Wolves 1 Brighton 1

Saturday November 16
Brighton 1 Derby 0; Coventry 0 Wolves 2;
Gillingham 1 Sheff Weds 1; Grimsby 3 Preston 3;
Millwall 2 Leicester 2; Norwich 2 C Palace 0; Nott'm
Forest 3 Bradford 0; Portsmouth 3 Stoke 0;
Rotherham 0 Burnley 0; Wimbledon 3 Walsall 2

Sunday November 17
Watford 0 Ipswich 2

Saturday November 23
Bradford 0 Sheff Utd 5; Burnley 2 Norwich 0;
C Palace 2 Grimsby 0; Ipswich 2 Coventry 1;
Leicester 2 Rotherham 1; Preston 2 Brighton 2;
Reading 1 Watford 0; Sheff Weds 1 Portsmouth 3;
Stoke 0 Millwall 1; Walsall 1 Gillingham 0;
Wolves 2 Nott'm Forest 1

Monday November 25
Derby 3 Wimbledon 2

Tuesday November 26
C Palace 0 Reading 1; Preston 2 Leicester 0

Wednesday November 27
Nott'm Forest 3 Brighton 2

Alliance and Leicester: Adams and his back-room staff at the Walkers Stadium get the party started after securing promotion by beating Brighton on April 19

£50 million worth of debt while building a fine new stadium could call in the administrators and come out the other side, having retained enough playing quality to win promotion.

This, however, was not the fault of Muzzy Izzet, who stood out as Leicester's finest player, nor of Micky Adams, the manager, who won his third promotion with different clubs. Leicester's supporters remained loyal throughout, with the highest average attendance (29,230) outside the Premiership. Derby County pulled in 25,469 on average, despite the soap opera season that followed their relegation from the Premiership, while Sheffield Wednesday's supporters merit recognition. Despite the success of the team across the city, Wednesday outnumbered their rivals, averaging 20,326 as they prepared for life in the second division.

Finally, Wolves ended a 19-year exile from the top flight. Backed by an average league crowd of 25,744, they lost just three of the 28 games they played in 2003 in reaching the last eight of the FA Cup — memorably beating Newcastle United in the third round — and, via Cardiff, the Premiership. Paul Ince lifted the play-off trophy at the Millennium Stadium on May 26 after goals from Mark Kennedy, Nathan Blake and Kenny Miller eclipsed Sheffield United.

PLAYER OF THE SEASON
Paul Ince, Wolverhampton Wanderers

Paul Merson deserves his place as one of the five *Times Football Yearbook* players of the year, Muzzy Izzet was a tenacious and classy contributor to a Leicester City promotion campaign based on teamwork and Michael Brown scored many spectacular goals in Sheffield United's thrilling adventures. But Paul Ince's combination of drive and composure steered Wolves through waters that had hitherto proved too choppy. Once he regained full fitness, Ince, even at 35, reproduced quality from the highest level while never allowing his team-mates to rest on their laurels.

Peter Lansley

LEADING SCORERS

		League	FAC	WC	Total
David Johnson	Nott'm Forest	25+2	0	2	29
Svetoslav Todorov	Portsmouth	26	0	0	26
David Connolly	Wimbledon	24	0	0	24
Kenny Miller	Wolves	19+1	3	1	24
Neil Shipperley	Wimbledon	20	1	3	24
Michael Brown	Sheffield Utd	16+2	2	2	22
Marlon Harewood	Nott'm Forest	20	1	0	21
Paul Dickov	Leicester City	17	2	1	20
Steve Kabba	Sheffield Utd	14+1	3	0	18

Figures after the + sign indicate play-off goals
Kabba's total includes one league goal for Crystal Palace and six for Grimsby Town

PFA TEAM

Shaka Hislop
Portsmouth

Denis Irwin	**Michael Dawson**	**Joleon Lescott**	**Matthew Taylor**
Wolves	Nottingham Forest	Wolves	Portsmouth

Michael Brown	**Muzzy Izzet**	**Paul Merson**	**Michael Tonge**
Sheffield United	Leicester City	Portsmouth	Sheffield United

David Johnson	**Paul Dickov**
Nottingham Forest	Leicester City

Saturday November 30
Brighton 0 Reading 1; Coventry 1 Preston 2; Gillingham 1 Stoke 1; Grimsby 1 Leicester 2; Millwall 1 Bradford 0; Norwich 1 Derby 0; Nott'm Forest 2 Ipswich 1; Portsmouth 3 Walsall 2; Rotherham 0 Wolves 0; Sheff Utd 2 C Palace 1; Watford 2 Burnley 1; Wimbledon 3 Sheff Weds 0

Saturday December 7
Bradford 1 Gillingham 3; Burnley 1 Nott'm Forest 0; C Palace 1 Millwall 0; Derby 3 Watford 0; Ipswich 1 Rotherham 2; Leicester 0 Sheff Utd 0; Preston 3 Wimbledon 5; Reading 0 Portsmouth 0; Sheff Weds 1 Brighton 1; Stoke 1 Coventry 2; Walsall 3 Grimsby 1; Wolves 1 Norwich 0

Tuesday December 10
Brighton 1 Ipswich 1

Saturday December 14
Bradford 1 Nott'm Forest 0; Burnley 2 Rotherham 6; C Palace 2 Norwich 0; Derby 1 Brighton 0; Ipswich 4 Watford 2; Leicester 4 Millwall 1; Preston 3 Grimsby 0; Reading 0 Sheff Utd 2; Sheff Weds 0 Gillingham 2; Stoke 1 Portsmouth 1; Walsall 2 Wimbledon 0; Wolves 0 Coventry 2

Friday December 20
Brighton 0 Leicester 1

Saturday December 21
Coventry 3 Derby 0; Gillingham 4 Burnley 2; Grimsby 2 Sheff Weds 0; Millwall 1 Wolves 1; Norwich 2 Walsall 1; Nott'm Forest 2 Reading 0; Portsmouth 1 Ipswich 1; Sheff Utd 1 Preston 0; Watford 1 Bradford 0; Wimbledon 1 Stoke 1

Sunday December 22
Rotherham 1 C Palace 3

Thursday December 26
Bradford 4 Stoke 2; Burnley 2 Wolves 1; Coventry 2 Reading 0; Derby 1 Grimsby 3; Leicester 1 Ipswich 2; Millwall 2 Gillingham 2; Norwich 0 Brighton 1; Portsmouth 1 C Palace 1; Preston 2 Rotherham 2; Sheff Weds 2 Nott'm Forest 0; Walsall 0 Sheff Utd 1; Wimbledon 0 Watford 0

Saturday December 28
Brighton 2 Burnley 2; C Palace 2 Preston 0; Grimsby 1 Norwich 1; Ipswich 3 Walsall 2; Nott'm Forest 1 Portsmouth 2; Reading 2 Derby 1; Rotherham 1 Millwall 3; Sheff Utd 0 Coventry 0; Stoke 3 Sheff Weds 2; Watford 1 Leicester 2; Wolves 1 Bradford 2

Wednesday January 1
C Palace 1 Coventry 1; Ipswich 4 Millwall 1; Nott'm Forest 1 Walsall 1; Rotherham 0 Sheff Weds 2; Stoke 2 Preston 1; Watford 2 Portsmouth 2; Wolves 1 Derby 1

Saturday January 11
Burnley 1 Ipswich 1; Coventry 0 Brighton 0; Derby 1 Gillingham 1; Leicester 0 Stoke 0; Millwall 4 Watford 0; Norwich 1 Rotherham 1; Sheff Weds 3 Reading 2; Walsall 0 Wolves 1; Wimbledon 3 Grimsby 3

Monday January 13
Portsmouth 1 Sheff Utd 2

MATCH OF THE SEASON

Friday January 17
Sheff Utd 3 Sheff Weds 1

Saturday January 18
Brighton 1 Portsmouth 1; C Palace 1 Burnley 1;
Gillingham 3 Leicester 2; Grimsby 0 Millwall 2;
Ipswich 3 Preston 0; Nott'm Forest 1 Coventry 1;
Reading 0 Walsall 0; Rotherham 3 Bradford 2;
Stoke 1 Derby 3; Wolves 1 Wimbledon 1

Sunday January 19
Watford 2 Norwich 1

Saturday January 25
Grimsby 1 Bradford 2; Preston 1 Nott'm Forest 1

Tuesday January 28
Reading 1 Leicester 3

Saturday February 1
Bradford 2 Ipswich 0; Burnley 2 Reading 5; Derby 3
Rotherham 0; Coventry 0 Watford 1; Leicester 1
C Palace 0; Millwall 1 Sheff Utd 0; Norwich 2
Stoke 2; Portsmouth 3 Grimsby 0; Preston 3
Gillingham 0; Sheff Weds 0 Wolves 4; Walsall 1
Brighton 0; Wimbledon 2 Nott'm Forest 3

Tuesday February 4
Brighton 2 Wimbledon 3

Saturday February 8
Brighton 4 Wolves 1; Coventry 0 Burnley 1; Grimsby
2 Stoke 0; Ipswich 3 Sheff Utd 2; Nott'm Forest 2 C
Palace 1; Portsmouth 6 Derby 2; Preston 2 Millwall
1; Sheff Weds 2 Norwich 2; Walsall 1 Leicester 4;
Watford 1 Rotherham 2; Wimbledon 2 Bradford 2

Monday February 10
Reading 2 Gillingham 1

Saturday February 15
Bradford 0 Brighton 1; Derby 2 Sheff Weds 2;
Gillingham 3 Grimsby 0; Millwall 0 Reading 2;
Rotherham 1 Coventry 0

Monday February 17
Leicester 1 Portsmouth 1

Tuesday February 18
Sheff Utd 1 Reading 3

Wednesday February 19
Ipswich 2 Wolves 4

Saturday February 22
Brighton 1 Millwall 0; Burnley 2 Derby 0; Coventry 0
Bradford 2; C Palace 0 Sheff Weds 0; Ipswich 2
Grimsby 2; Leicester 4 Wimbledon 0; Nott'm Forest
6 Stoke 0; Portsmouth 1 Gillingham 0; Preston 0
Wolves 2; Reading 3 Rotherham 0; Sheff Utd 0
Norwich 1; Walsall 2 Watford 0

Tuesday February 25
Gillingham 1 Norwich 0; Wolves 0 Watford 0

Wednesday February 26
Stoke 1 Walsall 0

Friday February 28
Rotherham 1 Sheff Utd 2

Sheffield United 4   Nottingham Forest 3 *(Sheffield United win 5-4 on agg)*
Bramall Lane, Thursday May 15 2003
David McVay

IT WAS THIRD TIME LUCKY for Sheffield United at Bramall
Lane last night. The South Yorkshire club had suffered defeats in
the semi-finals of the Worthington Cup and the FA Cup this season,
but those disappointments receded as they overcame Nottingham
Forest in an undulating, compelling and immensely entertaining
second leg of this Nationwide League first division play-off
semi-final.

Either United or Wolverhampton Wanderers will be playing
Premiership football next season after the final at the Millennium
Stadium on May 26. Neil Warnock, the United manager, has yet to
lose in a play-off final, having prevailed with Notts County (twice),
Huddersfield Town and Plymouth Argyle. His unblemished record
may remain intact if the indomitable spirit that his players
demonstrated to retrieve a two-goal deficit against Forest is
anything to judge by. They will start favourites in Cardiff.

Extra time was required to separate the sides, who were as evenly
matched as they were in the 1-1 first-leg draw at the City Ground on
Saturday. United, though, proved the stronger, remarkably so since
this was their sixtieth competitive game of a long-haul campaign.

Paul Peschisolido nudged his side ahead for the first time over the
two legs in the 112th minute. The Canada forward had been on the
pitch as a substitute for only seven minutes. He is familiar with his
role as heroic saviour, but none of his previous late shows will
compare to the solo strike that finally broke Forest's resolve,
twisting and turning to score with a low, right-foot drive.

Five minutes later, Des Walker, the Forest captain, headed an
own goal to make it 4-2 — shades of 1991 and his FA Cup Final
howler that gifted Tottenham Hotspur the trophy, also in extra
time. Robert Page, the United captain, managed to emulate Walker
by turning the ball into his own net shortly afterwards, but any
thoughts Forest might have had of forcing a penalty shoot-out ran
out of time.

In the first leg, defensive naivety had cost Forest dear after David
Johnson's opening strike, but after the Jamaica forward's right-foot
finish, his 29th goal of the season, handed them the breakthrough
on the half-hour last night, it appeared that they had learnt their
lesson well. Andy Reid, nipping in at the far post, volleyed in
Matthieu Louis-Jean's cross to double their lead in the 58th minute
and Forest's travelling supporters were already making plans to
book their hotel rooms for Cardiff.

Once again, though, Forest conceded quickly. Walker fouled
Steve Kabba on the edge of the 18-yard area and, after a short delay,
Michael Brown's free kick found the net via a deflection.

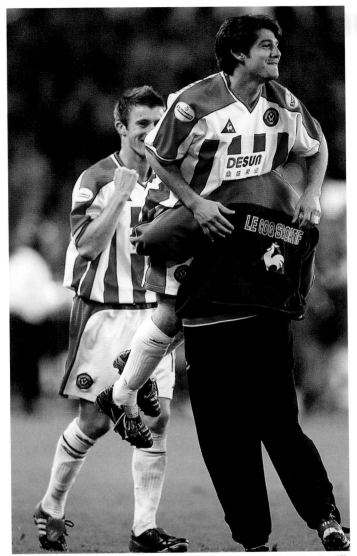

Lift-off: the diminutive Peschisolido hits the heights as United head for Cardiff

Suddenly, Forest's mask of composure was stripped away and it came as no surprise when Kabba, another substitute, levelled the score in the 68th minute. A long punt upfield was defended poorly, allowing the United player to control and volley beyond Darren Ward, the Forest goalkeeper.

SHEFFIELD UNITED (4-4-2): P Kenny — J Curtis, P Jagielka, R Page, R Kozluk — P Ndlovu (sub: P Peschisolido, 105min), M Rankine, M Brown, M Tonge — D Windass (sub: S Kabba, 46), C Asaba (sub: W Allison, 105). **Substitutes not used:** S McCall, N Montgomery. **Booked:** Tonge, Brown.
NOTTINGHAM FOREST (4-3-1-2): D Ward — M Louis-Jean, J Thompson, D Walker, J Brennan — G Williams (sub: J O Hjelde, 114), R Scimeca, A Reid — D Huckerby — M Harewood (sub: J Lester, 61), D Johnson. **Substitutes not used:** E Bopp, E Jess, B Roche. **Booked:** Walker, Huckerby.
Referee: P Walton.

Saturday March 1
Bradford 1 Walsall 2; Derby 1 Leicester 1; Gillingham 3 Brighton 0; Grimsby 0 Coventry 2; Millwall 0 Portsmouth 5; Sheff Weds 0 Preston 1; Stoke 0 Burnley 1; Watford 1 Nott'm Forest 1; Wimbledon 2 Reading 0; Wolves 4 C Palace 0

Sunday March 2
Norwich 0 Ipswich 2

Tuesday March 4
Bradford 0 Leicester 0; Gillingham 1 Nott'm Forest 4; Grimsby 1 Sheff Utd 4; Millwall 1 Burnley 1; Rotherham 0 Walsall 0; Watford 0 Preston 1; Wimbledon 2 Portsmouth 1

Wednesday March 5
Derby 0 C Palace 1; Norwich 0 Reading 1; Sheff Weds 5 Coventry 1; Stoke 1 Brighton 0; Wolves 1 Ipswich 1

Saturday March 8
Bradford 2 C Palace 1; Brighton 2 Rotherham 0; Coventry 2 Wimbledon 2; Ipswich 0 Stoke 0; Leicester 1 Sheff Weds 1; Preston 4 Derby 2; Walsall 1 Millwall 2

Monday March 10
Nott'm Forest 2 Grimsby 2

Tuesday March 11
C Palace 1 Ipswich 1; Gillingham 3 Wimbledon 3

Wednesday March 12
Portsmouth 3 Norwich 2; Reading 0 Wolves 1; Sheff Utd 4 Burnley 2

Saturday March 15
Brighton 1 Nott'm Forest 0; Derby 1 Bradford 2; Gillingham 1 Rotherham 1; Grimsby 1 Watford 0; Leicester 2 Preston 1; Norwich 2 Coventry 0; Portsmouth 1 Wolves 0; Reading 2 C Palace 1; Sheff Weds 0 Ipswich 1; Stoke 0 Sheff Utd 0; Walsall 3 Burnley 2; Wimbledon 2 Millwall 0

Tuesday March 18
Bradford 1 Sheff Weds 1; Burnley 1 Leicester 2; C Palace 0 Wimbledon 1; Ipswich 3 Reading 1; Millwall 0 Norwich 2; Preston 5 Walsall 0; Rotherham 0 Grimsby 1; Sheff Utd 2 Brighton 1; Watford 0 Gillingham 1; Wolves 0 Stoke 0

Wednesday March 19
Coventry 0 Portsmouth 4; Nott'm Forest 3 Derby 0

Saturday March 22
Bradford 0 Reading 1; Burnley 1 Grimsby 1; Coventry 1 Leicester 2; C Palace 2 Walsall 0; Ipswich 2 Brighton 2; Millwall 3 Sheff Weds 0; Nott'm Forest 4 Norwich 0; Preston 1 Portsmouth 1; Rotherham 2 Wimbledon 1; Sheff Utd 2 Derby 0; Watford 1 Stoke 2; Wolves 6 Gillingham 0

Tuesday March 25
Brighton 0 C Palace 0; Burnley 0 Bradford 2; Norwich 1 Wimbledon 0; Sheff Utd 2 Gillingham 2

Saturday March 29
Gillingham 1 Ipswich 3; Norwich 3 Bradford 2; Sheff Weds 2 Watford 2

Friday April 4
Reading 1 Brighton 2

Saturday April 5
Bradford 0 Millwall 1; Burnley 4 Watford 7; C Palace 2 Sheff Utd 2; Derby 2 Norwich 1; Ipswich 3 Nott'm Forest 4; Leicester 2 Grimsby 0; Preston 2 Coventry 2; Sheff Weds 4 Wimbledon 2; Stoke 0 Gillingham 0; Walsall 1 Portsmouth 2; Wolves 0 Rotherham 0

Monday April 7
Wimbledon 1 Sheff Utd 0

Tuesday April 8
Burnley 2 Preston 0; C Palace 0 Watford 1; Grimsby 0 Wolves 1; Leicester 1 Nott'm Forest 0

Wednesday April 9
Stoke 2 Rotherham 0

Friday April 11
Nott'm Forest 2 Wolves 2

Saturday April 12
Brighton 0 Preston 2; Coventry 2 Ipswich 4; Gillingham 0 Walsall 1; Grimsby 1 C Palace 4; Millwall 3 Stoke 1; Norwich 2 Burnley 0; Portsmouth 1 Sheff Weds 2; Rotherham 1 Leicester 1; Wimbledon 0 Derby 2

Tuesday April 15
Portsmouth 1 Burnley 0; Reading 5 Preston 1; Sheff Utd 1 Nott'm Forest 0; Walsall 0 Coventry 0

Wednesday April 16
Derby 1 Millwall 2

Friday April 18
Ipswich 3 Portsmouth 0; Reading 1 Nott'm Forest 0

Saturday April 19
Bradford 2 Watford 1; Burnley 2 Gillingham 0; C Palace 0 Rotherham 0; Derby 1 Coventry 0; Leicester 2 Brighton 0; Preston 2 Sheff Utd 0; Sheff Weds 0 Grimsby 0; Stoke 2 Wimbledon 1; Walsall 0 Norwich 0; Wolves 3 Millwall 0

Monday April 21
Brighton 1 Sheff Weds 1; Coventry 0 Stoke 1; Gillingham 1 Bradford 0; Grimsby 0 Walsall 1; Millwall 3 C Palace 2; Norwich 0 Wolves 3; Nott'm Forest 2 Burnley 0; Portsmouth 3 Reading 0; Rotherham 2 Ipswich 1; Sheff Utd 2 Leicester 1; Watford 2 Derby 0; Wimbledon 2 Preston 0

Saturday April 26
Brighton 4 Watford 0; Burnley 2 Sheff Weds 7; Coventry 0 Gillingham 0; C Palace 1 Stoke 0; Ipswich 1 Wimbledon 5; Nott'm Forest 3 Millwall 3; Preston 1 Bradford 0; Reading 2 Grimsby 1; Sheff Utd 3 Wolves 3; Walsall 3 Derby 2

Sunday April 27
Leicester 1 Norwich 1; Portsmouth 3 Rotherham 2

Tuesday April 29
Sheff Utd 3 Bradford 0

Wednesday April 30
Watford 0 Reading 3

Sunday May 4
Bradford 0 Portsmouth 5; Derby 1 Ipswich 4; Gillingham 2 C Palace 1; Grimsby 2 Brighton 2; Millwall 2 Coventry 0; Norwich 2 Preston 0; Rotherham 2 Nott'm Forest 2; Sheff Weds 2 Walsall 1; Stoke 1 Reading 0; Watford 2 Sheff Utd 0; Wimbledon 2 Burnley 1; Wolves 1 Leicester 1

PLAY-OFFS

SEMI-FINALS

First legs, May 10

NOTTINGHAM FOREST (0) **1**
Johnson 55
29,064

SHEFFIELD UNITED (0) **1**
Brown 58 (pen)

WOLVES (0) **2**
Murty 75 (og), Naylor 84
27,678

READING (1) **1**
Forster 25

Second leg, May 14

READING (0) **0**
24,060

WOLVES (0) **1**
Rae 81

(Wolves win 3-1 on aggregate)

Second leg, May 15

SHEFFIELD UNITED (0) **4**
Brown 60, Kabba 68
Peschisolido 112, Walker 117 (og)

NOTTINGHAM FOREST (1) **3**
Johnson 30, Reid 58, Page 119 (og)
30,212

(aet: 2-2 after 90min; Sheffield United win 5-4 on aggregate)

FINAL
May 26,   Millennium Stadium

SHEFFIELD UNITED (0) **0**
69,473

WOLVES (3) **3**
Kennedy 6, Blake 22, Miller 45

It had been a long, painful exile, incorporating four failures in the play-offs, a £50 million investment by Sir Jack Hayward, above right, their chairman, and countless broken dreams, but finally Wolverhampton Wanderers were back in the top flight. Their 19-year wait was ended as Sheffield United, already beaten in two cup semi-finals, came up short for the third time in a campaign that arguably made them the team of the season. It was also a final vindication for Dave Jones, the Wolves manager, left, who admitted that he had had to rebuild his life as well as his career after wholly unfounded allegations against him.

SHEFFIELD UNITED (4-4-2): P Kenny — J Curtis, P Jagielka, R Page, R Kozluk — P Ndlovu (sub: P Peschisolido, 64min), M Rankine (sub: S McCall, ht), M Brown, M Tonge — S Kabba, C Asaba (sub: W Allison, 74). **Substitutes not used:** G Kelly, N Montgomery. **Booked:** Tonge, Brown.

WOLVERHAMPTON WANDERERS (4-4-2): M Murray — D Irwin, P Butler, J Lescott, L Naylor — S Newton, P Ince, C Cameron, M Kennedy — N Blake (sub: A Proudlock, 88), K Miller (sub: D Sturridge, 76). **Substitutes not used:** M Oakes, A Rae, M Edworthy. **Booked:** Irwin.

Referee: S Bennett.

NATIONWIDE LEAGUE

SECOND DIVISION

CHAMPIONS
Wigan Athletic

RUNNERS-UP
Crewe Alexandra

PROMOTED VIA PLAY-OFFS
Cardiff City

Crowning glory: Paul Jewell guided Wigan Athletic on a record-strewn promotion run

THE GAMES

Saturday August 10
Bristol City 2 Blackpool 0; Cheltenham 0 Wigan 2; Colchester 1 Stockport 0; Huddersfield 0 Brentford 2; Luton 2 Peterborough 3; Mansfield 4 Plymouth 3; Northampton 1 Crewe 1; Notts Co 1 Wycombe 1; Oldham 1 Cardiff 2; Port Vale 1 Tranmere 4; QPR 3 Chesterfield 1; Swindon 3 Barnsley 1

Tuesday August 13
Barnsley 1 Cheltenham 1; Blackpool 5 Luton 2; Brentford 1 Bristol City 0; Cardiff 3 Port Vale 1; Chesterfield 2 Swindon 4; Crewe 0 Notts Co 3; Peterborough 0 Oldham 1; Plymouth 2 Huddersfield 1; Stockport 1 QPR 1; Tranmere 1 Colchester 1; Wigan 3 Mansfield 2; Wycombe 1 Northampton 1

Saturday August 17
Barnsley 1 QPR 0; Blackpool 0 Swindon 0; Brentford 0 Oldham 0; Cardiff 1 Northampton 2; Chesterfield 2 Port Vale 1; Crewe 2 Colchester 0; Peterborough 0 Huddersfield 1; Plymouth 2 Luton 1; Stockport 0 Notts Co 0; Tranmere 1 Cheltenham 0; Wigan 2 Bristol City 0; Wycombe 3 Mansfield 3

Friday August 23
Northampton 0 Blackpool 1

Saturday August 24
Bristol City 3 Wycombe 0; Cheltenham 1 Plymouth 2; Colchester 0 Brentford 1; Huddersfield 1 Crewe 1; Luton 2 Barnsley 3; Mansfield 0 Chesterfield 2; Notts Co 0 Wigan 2; Oldham 2 Tranmere 0; Port Vale 0 Stockport 1; QPR 2 Peterborough 0; Swindon 0 Cardiff 1

Monday August 26
Barnsley 0 Notts Co 0; Blackpool 0 Oldham 0; Brentford 3 Swindon 1; Cardiff 0 Luton 0; Peterborough 0 Colchester 0; Plymouth 2 Bristol City 0; Stockport 2 Mansfield 0; Tranmere 2 Huddersfield 1; Wigan 0 Port Vale 1; Wycombe 4 QPR 1

Tuesday August 27
Chesterfield 4 Northampton 0; Crewe 1 Cheltenham 0

Saturday August 31
Bristol City 2 Tranmere 0; Cheltenham 1 Cardiff 1; Colchester 1 Wigan 0; Huddersfield 0 Blackpool 0; Luton 3 Chesterfield 0; Mansfield 0 Crewe 5; Northampton 1 Barnsley 0; Notts Co 2 Brentford 2; Oldham 0 Wycombe 2; Port Vale 1 Peterborough 0; QPR 2 Plymouth 2; Swindon 0 Stockport 1

Friday September 6
Bristol City 3 Northampton 0

Saturday September 7
Blackpool 3 Tranmere 0; Brentford 0 Luton 0; Colchester 1 Cheltenham 1; Crewe 0 Chesterfield 0; Huddersfield 1 Barnsley 0; Mansfield 0 QPR 4; Notts Co 1 Oldham 3; Swindon 1 Port Vale 2; Wigan 3 Wycombe 0

Saturday September 14
Barnsley 1 Plymouth 1; Cardiff 2 Stockport 1; Cheltenham 2 Bristol City 3; Chesterfield 0 Wigan 0; Luton 2 Notts Co 2; Northampton 0 Huddersfield 0; Oldham 6 Mansfield 1; Peterborough 0 Crewe 0; Port Vale 1 Colchester 0; QPR 2 Swindon 0; Tranmere 3 Brentford 1; Wycombe 1 Blackpool 2

PATIENCE, AS BIRMINGHAM CITY and Ipswich Town can confirm, is a virtue when promotion is the ambition. Three times those two clubs were thwarted in the Nationwide League play-offs, only to realise their dream of reaching the Premiership at the fourth time of asking. If at first you don't succeed ...

Clearly, that philosophy was taken on board at the JJB Stadium, where Steve Bruce, now the Birmingham manager, had endured a short spell in charge in 2001, at the end of which Wigan Athletic discovered that it was not to be third time lucky in the play-offs. Bruce moved on to Crystal Palace, Paul Jewell was his replacement — and so began a beautiful relationship that, after a season of consolidation, swept the Lancashire club into the first division in May without recourse to the end-of-season lottery after a season in which 16 club records were broken and 100 points achieved.

Patience is all very well; having a few bob in the bank to spend on players helps, too, and David Whelan, the Wigan owner, has not shirked the duties that come with being a wealthy benefactor. Nathan Ellington (£1 million from Bristol Rovers) and Tony

FINAL TABLE

	P	W	D	L	F	A	W	D	L	F	A	P	GD
			HOME						AWAY				
Wigan	46	14	7	2	37	16	15	6	2	31	9	100	43
Crewe	46	11	5	7	29	19	14	6	3	47	21	86	36
Bristol City	46	15	5	3	43	15	9	6	8	36	33	83	31
QPR	46	14	4	5	38	19	10	7	6	31	26	83	24
Oldham	46	11	6	6	39	18	11	10	2	29	20	82	30
Cardiff	46	12	6	5	33	20	11	6	6	35	23	81	25
Tranmere	46	14	5	4	38	23	9	6	8	28	34	80	9
Plymouth	46	11	6	6	39	24	6	8	9	24	28	65	11
Luton	46	8	8	7	32	28	9	6	8	35	34	65	5
Swindon	46	10	5	8	34	27	6	7	10	25	36	60	-4
Peterborough	46	8	7	8	25	20	6	9	8	26	34	58	-3
Colchester	46	8	7	8	24	24	6	9	8	28	32	58	-4
Blackpool	46	10	8	5	35	25	5	5	13	21	39	58	-8
Stockport	46	8	8	7	39	38	7	2	14	26	32	55	-5
Notts County	46	10	7	6	37	32	3	9	11	25	38	55	-8
Brentford	46	8	8	7	28	21	6	4	13	19	35	54	-9
Port Vale	46	9	5	9	34	31	5	6	12	20	39	53	-16
Wycombe	46	8	7	8	39	38	5	6	12	20	28	52	-7
Barnsley	46	7	8	8	27	31	6	5	12	24	33	52	-13
Chesterfield	46	11	4	8	29	28	3	4	16	14	45	50	-30
Cheltenham	46	6	9	8	26	31	4	9	10	27	37	48	-15
Huddersfield	46	7	9	7	27	24	4	3	16	12	37	45	-22
Mansfield	46	9	2	12	38	45	3	6	14	28	52	44	-31
Northampton	46	7	4	12	23	31	3	5	15	17	48	39	-39

Dinning (£750,000 from Wolverhampton Wanderers) were among the high-profile acquisitions.

Few would dispute that it was in defence where Wigan stole a march over their rivals. Jason de Vos, the Canada centre half, and Matt Jackson, who collected a Cup-winner's medal with Everton, were at the central hub, while John Filan, the Australia goalkeeper, ensured that only nine league goals were conceded on their travels. Significantly, not one of the other top six teams scored against them on their own grounds.

Insiders point to a couple of 1-0 defeats, back-to-back matches against Colchester United and Port Vale in late August, that provided the catalyst for success. It was not until January 25 that Wigan would be beaten again, a juggernaut of a run in which they went 21 league games undefeated, conceding just 11 goals, including a sequence of eight matches without being breached. Those heady winter days and nights also delivered glory in the Worthington Cup with the Premiership scalps of West Bromwich Albion, Manchester City — the reviled foe from Maine Road — and Fulham. It seemed that it could not get much better, but it did. Crewe Alexandra, their nearest rivals, were unable to keep with the pace and Wigan's promotion was secured with plenty to spare.

At the other end of the table, newly promoted Cheltenham Town toiled in vain to catch Chesterfield — who finished just above the relegation zone — as did Northampton Town and Mansfield Town. Those two clubs sacked their managers, Northampton granting Terry Fenwick only seven matches as successor to Kevan Broadhurst. At least Keith Curle brought a touch of stability to Field Mill when he took over from Stuart Watkiss. However, the odds were against survival for a team whose ability to defend was diametrically opposed to that of Wigan. Certainly, the euphoria of promotion the previous season had waned by March, when a 1-0 away defeat to Cardiff City began a five-match losing sequence.

By that time the game was also just about up for Huddersfield Town, with losses on and off the pitch. Wigan arrived at the McAlpine Stadium on April 19 and a point in a 0-0 draw was sufficient to claim the title and send the Yorkshire club scurrying in the opposite direction. After Crewe's promotion as runners-up was confirmed, Queens Park Rangers sneaked into the top six, leaving Tranmere Rovers with nothing to show for reaching 80 points — a total that would have earned a play-off position in most seasons.

Tommy Doherty had been outstanding in central midfield for Bristol City, earning his first Northern Ireland caps against Italy and Spain in June. His team had tottered, though, after losing to

Tuesday September 17
Barnsley 2 Blackpool 1; Cardiff 2 Brentford 0; Cheltenham 2 Swindon 0; Chesterfield 1 Stockport 0; Luton 2 Mansfield 3; Northampton 4 Colchester 1; Oldham 1 Bristol City 0; Peterborough 2 Plymouth 0; Port Vale 3 Notts Co 2; QPR 3 Huddersfield 0; Tranmere 0 Wigan 2; Wycombe 1 Crewe 2

Saturday September 21
Blackpool 3 Port Vale 2; Brentford 1 Wycombe 0; Bristol City 1 QPR 3; Colchester 0 Oldham 1; Crewe 2 Tranmere 0; Huddersfield 2 Port Vale 2; Stockport 4 Barnsley 1; Swindon 2 Northampton 0; Wigan 2 Peterborough 2

Tuesday September 24
Plymouth 2 Cardiff 2

Saturday September 28
Barnsley 1 Wigan 3; Cardiff 2 Crewe 1; Cheltenham 1 Notts Co 4; Chesterfield 1 Blackpool 0; Luton 3 Swindon 0; Northampton 2 Mansfield 0; Oldham 4 Huddersfield 0; Peterborough 5 Brentford 1; Port Vale 2 Bristol City 3; QPR 2 Colchester 0; Tranmere 1 Stockport 0; Wycombe 2 Plymouth 1

Saturday October 5
Blackpool 3 Cheltenham 1; Brentford 1 Barnsley 2; Bristol City 4 Chesterfield 0; Colchester 0 Wycombe 1; Crewe 2 QPR 0; Huddersfield 2 Port Vale 2; Mansfield 6 Tranmere 1; Notts Co 2 Peterborough 2; Plymouth 0 Northampton 0; Stockport 2 Luton 3; Swindon 0 Oldham 1; Wigan 2 Cardiff 2

Tuesday October 8
Stockport 2 Peterborough 1

Saturday October 12
Barnsley 1 Bristol City 4; Cardiff 1 Wycombe 0; Chesterfield 1 Tranmere 0; Huddersfield 3 Notts Co 0; Luton 2 Cheltenham 1; Northampton 1 Brentford 2; Peterborough 0 Mansfield 0; Plymouth 1 Wigan 3; Port Vale 1 Oldham 1; Stockport 1 Crewe 4; Swindon 2 Colchester 2

Monday October 14
QPR 2 Blackpool 1

Friday October 18
Colchester 2 Chesterfield 0

Saturday October 19
Blackpool 1 Cardiff 0; Brentford 1 Port Vale 1; Bristol City 2 Swindon 0; Cheltenham 1 QPR 1; Crewe 0 Plymouth 1; Mansfield 0 Huddersfield 2; Notts Co 2 Northampton 1; Oldham 1 Luton 2; Tranmere 1 Barnsley 0; Wigan 2 Stockport 1; Wycombe 3 Peterborough 2

Saturday October 26
Barnsley 1 Wycombe 1; Cardiff 4 Tranmere 0; Chesterfield 0 Notts Co 0; Huddersfield 1 Colchester 1; Luton 1 Wigan 1; Northampton 1 Cheltenham 2; Peterborough 1 Bristol City 3; Plymouth 1 Blackpool 3; Port Vale 1 Crewe 2; QPR 1 Oldham 2; Stockport 2 Brentford 3; Swindon 2 Mansfield 1

Tuesday October 29
Blackpool 1 Stockport 3; Brentford 0 Plymouth 0;
Bristol City 1 Huddersfield 0; Cheltenham 0
Port Vale 1; Colchester 1 Barnsley 1; Crewe 0
Luton 1; Mansfield 0 Cardiff 1; Notts Co 1
Swindon 1; Oldham 4 Northampton 0;
Tranmere 1 Peterborough 1; Wycombe 2
Chesterfield 0; Wigan 1 QPR 1

Friday November 1
Mansfield 4 Colchester 2

Saturday November 2
Brentford 5 Blackpool 0; Cardiff 3 Peterborough 0;
Cheltenham 1 Huddersfield 0; Chesterfield 1
Barnsley 0; Northampton 3 Luton 0; Oldham 2
Stockport 0; Port Vale 0 QPR 0; Tranmere 2
Plymouth 1; Wigan 2 Crewe 0; Wycombe 2
Swindon 3

Saturday November 9
Barnsley 3 Cardiff 2; Blackpool 0 Wigan 2;
Colchester 2 Bristol City 2; Crewe 2 Brentford 1;
Huddersfield 0 Wycombe 0; Luton 0 Port Vale 0;
Notts Co 2 Mansfield 2; Peterborough 1
Chesterfield 0; Plymouth 2 Oldham 2; QPR 0
Northampton 1; Stockport 1 Cheltenham 1;
Swindon 1 Tranmere 1

Saturday November 23
Brentford 0 Wigan 1; Crewe 3 Blackpool 0;
Huddersfield 2 Swindon 3; Luton 0 QPR 0;
Mansfield 4 Bristol City 5; Northampton 3
Port Vale 0; Notts Co 2 Colchester 3; Oldham 0
Cheltenham 0; Peterborough 1 Barnsley 3;
Plymouth 4 Stockport 1; Wycombe 1 Tranmere 3

Sunday November 24
Cardiff 1 Chesterfield 0

Friday November 29
QPR 0 Cardiff 4

Saturday November 30
Barnsley 2 Oldham 2; Blackpool 1 Notts Co 1;
Bristol City 2 Crewe 2; Cheltenham 1 Brentford 0;
Chesterfield 1 Huddersfield 0; Colchester 0
Plymouth 0; Port Vale 4 Mansfield 2; Stockport 2
Wycombe 1; Swindon 1 Peterborough 1; Tranmere
1 Luton 3; Wigan 1 Northampton 0

Tuesday December 3
Bristol City 3 Notts Co 2

Saturday December 14
Brentford 2 Chesterfield 1; Cardiff 0 Bristol City 2;
Crewe 2 Barnsley 0; Huddersfield 2 Stockport 1;
Luton 1 Colchester 2; Mansfield 4 Blackpool 0;
Northampton 0 Tranmere 4; Notts Co 3 QPR 0;
Oldham 0 Wigan 2; Peterborough 4 Cheltenham 1;
Plymouth 1 Swindon 1; Wycombe 3 Port Vale 1

Friday December 20
Colchester 1 Cardiff 2; Stockport 4 Northampton 0

Crewe were unable to keep pace with Wigan, who stormed to the title, but they went up without having to endure the lottery of the play-offs

Leicester City in the FA Cup third round, despite playing their opponents off the pitch at the Walkers Stadium, but a resurgence at Ashton Gate brought third place and the label of favourites for the play-offs. Cardiff, though, ground out an aggregate win over City to secure a "home" match against QPR in the final.

Graham Kavanagh and Peter Thorne, Cardiff's £1 million men, were expected to lead the way in the Welsh capital, along with the prolific Robert Earnshaw. However, an unlikely hero emerged in the shape of Andy Campbell. He replaced Earnshaw from the bench and sent the city into a state of delirium when he lobbed the only goal in extra time.

If the second division waved a fond farewell to Cardiff, the Football League almost issued a curt goodbye to Notts County, the oldest league club in the world. They were given a deadline of the end of May to come out of administration or face expulsion. A consortium of former RAF pilots appeared to have flown to the rescue on the north banks of the Trent, but the forecast is for continued turbulence at Meadow Lane — and at several other venues at this impoverished level of the game.

PLAYER OF THE SEASON
Jason de Vos, Wigan Athletic

Any side that loses just four league games in a season and concedes 25 goals must have the sort of reliable backbone for which managers yearn. Matt Jackson has the experience, but it was his central defensive colleague, Jason de Vos, the Canada captain, who excelled in this pivotal position for the second division champions. His consistency saw him selected for the divisional team at the PFA awards. Paul Jewell, his manager, might also cite the eight goals, all of them crucial, that helped to maintain their advantage over the chasing pack and kept Wigan on course for the championship.

David McVay

LEADING SCORERS

		League	FAC	WC	Total
Robert Earnshaw	Cardiff City	31	1	3	35
Luke Beckett	Stockport County	27	1	1	29
Sam Parkin	Swindon Town	25	0	0	25
Mark Stallard	Notts County	24	0	1	25
Steven Howard	Luton Town	22	0	1	23
Rob Hulse	Crewe Alexandra	22	0	1	23
Simon Haworth	Tranmere Rovers	20	1	1	22
Scott Murray	Bristol City	19	3	0	22
Nathan Ellington	Wigan Athletic	15	2	5	22
Iyseden Christie	Mansfield Town	18	1	0	19
Andy Clarke	Peterborough Utd	17	1	0	18
John Murphy	Blackpool	16	2	0	18

PFA TEAM

John Filan
Wigan Athletic

Nicky Eaden
Wigan Athletic

Jason de Vos
Wigan Athletic

Fitz Hall
Oldham Athletic

Mickey Bell
Bristol City

Scott Murray
Bristol City

Jimmy Bullard
Wigan Athletic

Graham Kavanagh
Stoke City

Martin Bullock
Blackpool

Robert Earnshaw
Cardiff City

Rob Hulse
Crewe Alexandra

Saturday December 21
Barnsley 0 Mansfield 1; Blackpool 3 Peterborough 0; Bristol City 1 Luton 1; Cheltenham 0 Wycombe 0; Chesterfield 0 Oldham 1; Port Vale 1 Plymouth 2; QPR 1 Brentford 1; Swindon 1 Crewe 3; Tranmere 2 Notts Co 2; Wigan 1 Huddersfield 0

Thursday December 26
Bristol City 0 Plymouth 0; Cheltenham 0 Crewe 4; Colchester 1 Peterborough 1; Huddersfield 1 Tranmere 2; Luton 2 Cardiff 0; Mansfield 4 Stockport 2; Northampton 0 Chesterfield 1; Notts Co 3 Barnsley 2; Oldham 1 Blackpool 1; Port Vale 0 Wigan 1; QPR 2 Wycombe 1; Swindon 2 Brentford 1

Saturday December 28
Barnsley 2 Port Vale 1; Blackpool 3 Colchester 1; Brentford 1 Mansfield 0; Chesterfield 2 Cheltenham 2; Peterborough 0 Northampton 0; Plymouth 1 Notts Co 0; Stockport 1 Bristol City 4; Tranmere 3 QPR 0; Wigan 2 Swindon 0; Wycombe 1 Luton 2

Sunday December 29
Cardiff 4 Huddersfield 0; Crewe 1 Oldham 2

Wednesday January 1
Barnsley 1 Northampton 2; Blackpool 1 Huddersfield 1; Cardiff 1 Swindon 1; Chesterfield 2 Luton 1; Crewe 2 Mansfield 1; Peterborough 0 QPR 2; Plymouth 3 Cheltenham 1; Stockport 0 Port Vale 1; Tranmere 1 Oldham 2; Wigan 3 Notts Co 1; Wycombe 2 Bristol City 1

Saturday January 4
Colchester 2 Tranmere 2; Northampton 0 Wycombe 5; Oldham 0 Peterborough 0; QPR 1 Stockport 0; Swindon 3 Chesterfield 0

Friday January 10
Bristol City 0 Wigan 1

Saturday January 11
Colchester 1 Crewe 2; Huddersfield 0 Peterborough 1; Mansfield 0 Wycombe 0; QPR 1 Barnsley 0

Tuesday January 14
Oldham 2 Brentford 1

Saturday January 18
Barnsley 2 Luton 3; Blackpool 2 Northampton 1; Brentford 1 Notts Co 1; Cardiff 2 Cheltenham 1; Chesterfield 1 Mansfield 2; Crewe 1 Huddersfield 0; Peterborough 1 Port Vale 2; Plymouth 0 QPR 1; Stockport 2 Swindon 5; Tranmere 1 Bristol City 1; Wigan 2 Colchester 1; Wycombe 2 Oldham 2

Tuesday January 21
Notts Co 3 Stockport 2

Wednesday January 22
Swindon 1 Blackpool 1

Saturday January 25
Bristol City 1 Stockport 1; Cheltenham 0 Chesterfield 0; Colchester 0 Blackpool 2; Huddersfield 1 Cardiff 0; Luton 1 Wycombe 0; Northampton 0 Peterborough 1; Notts Co 0 Plymouth 2; Oldham 1 Crewe 3; Port Vale 0 Barnsley 0; QPR 1 Tranmere 2; Swindon 2 Wigan 1

Tuesday January 28
Mansfield 1 Wigan 2

Friday January 31
Cardiff 1 Oldham 1

Saturday February 1
Barnsley 1 Swindon 1; Blackpool 0 Bristol City 0;
Crewe 3 Northampton 3; Peterborough 1 Luton 1;
Plymouth 3 Mansfield 1; Stockport 1 Colchester 1;
Tranmere 1 Port Vale 0; Wigan 0 Cheltenham 0;
Wycombe 3 Notts Co 1

Sunday February 2
Chesterfield 2 QPR 4

Tuesday February 4
Cheltenham 3 Tranmere 1; Huddersfield 1
Plymouth 0; Mansfield 0 Brentford 0;
Northampton 0 Cardiff 1; Notts Co 2 Crewe 2

Saturday February 8
Brentford 1 Crewe 2; Bristol City 1 Colchester 2;
Cardiff 1 Barnsley 1; Cheltenham 0 Stockport 2;
Chesterfield 0 Peterborough 0; Mansfield 3 Notts
Co 2; Northampton 1 QPR 1; Oldham 0 Plymouth 1;
Port Vale 1 Luton 2; Tranmere 0 Swindon 1; Wigan
1 Blackpool 1; Wycombe 0 Huddersfield 0

Tuesday February 11
Bristol City 0 Brentford 0; Luton 1 Blackpool 3;
Port Vale 5 Chesterfield 2

Friday February 14
Colchester 1 Mansfield 0

Saturday February 15
Barnsley 2 Chesterfield 1; Blackpool 1 Brentford 0;
Huddersfield 3 Cheltenham 3; Luton 3
Northampton 2; Notts Co 2 Bristol City 0; Plymouth
0 Tranmere 1; QPR 4 Port Vale 0; Stockport 1
Oldham 2; Swindon 0 Wycombe 3

Tuesday February 18
Cheltenham 1 Barnsley 3

Friday February 21
Cardiff 1 Plymouth 1

Saturday February 22
Barnsley 0 Huddersfield 1; Cheltenham 1
Colchester 1; Chesterfield 0 Crewe 2; Luton 0
Brentford 1; Northampton 1 Bristol City 2;
Oldham 1 Notts Co 1; Peterborough 2 Stockport 0;
Port Vale 1 Swindon 1; QPR 2 Mansfield 2;
Tranmere 2 Blackpool 1; Wycombe 0 Wigan 2

Tuesday February 25
Brentford 1 Huddersfield 0; Crewe 0 Wigan 1;
Luton 1 Plymouth 0; Port Vale 0 Cardiff 2

Saturday March 1
Blackpool 1 Wycombe 0; Brentford 1 Tranmere 2;
Bristol City 3 Cheltenham 1; Colchester 4 Port Vale
1; Crewe 0 Peterborough 1; Huddersfield 2
Northampton 0; Mansfield 0 Oldham 1; Notts Co 2
Luton 1; Plymouth 1 Barnsley 1; Stockport 1
Cardiff 1; Swindon 3 QPR 1; Wigan 3 Chesterfield 1

MATCH OF THE SEASON

Queens Park Rangers 0   Cardiff City 4
Loftus Road, Friday November 29 2002
Tom Dart

THEY HAD HOPED FOR catharsis, but they ended up crushed. Queens Park Rangers were desperate to make amends for one of the worst results in their history, their midweek FA Cup defeat by Vauxhall Motors, but after an impressive first half that was an energetic release of pent-up frustration, Cardiff City's superior ability and self-belief saw them to an easy win.

The hooliganism that dogs Cardiff like an incurable disease threatened to divert attention from their rise to the top of the Nationwide League second division, however. A member of the stadium catering staff was treated for a minor abdomen cut after possibly being stabbed as he left the toilets in the Cardiff end.

The match had been moved to Friday night because of the fear that police would have been overstretched by the prospect of keeping order here as well as at Stamford Bridge, where Chelsea face Sunderland this afternoon. Six hundred officers were involved in maintaining order last night across West London. Five men were arrested inside Loftus Road and there were a number of incidents in the vicinity before and after the match.

QPR began in hyperactive fashion. Full of attacking intent and supported by an enthusiastic crowd, they stormed forward at every opportunity, but the standard of their finishing was not as impressive as their motivation.

They went a goal down early in the second half, however, after they failed to clear a corner and the ball pinged around the six-yard box before it was finally judged to have crossed the line. It was debatable as to whether it was really Robert Earnshaw's goal, but he claimed it.

There was no doubt about the second. Earnshaw collected a through-pass, sidestepped Danny Shittu and crashed a fine shot into the top corner. QPR disintegrated after that as the true fragility of their confidence was laid bare.

Lack of concentration led to two more goals shortly before the end. Terrell Forbes failed to put enough weight on a back-pass and Earnshaw took advantage, floating a chip over Simon Royce for his nineteenth goal of the season. In the final minute, Andy Campbell, a substitute, completed the rout when a horrible mistake by Tommy Williams put him clean through. His first attempt was saved, but he tucked away the rebound to crown Cardiff's third win in six days.

QPR have not won in ten matches. "We're reeling at the minute," Ian Holloway, the QPR manager, said. "Our team spirit is horrendous. At the moment the wheels have come off the wagon.""Goals change games," Lennie Lawrence, the Cardiff manager,

Earnshaw's hat-trick destroyed QPR and kept Cardiff in the promotion race

said. "In the first half, QPR were marginally the better team — the difference between the two teams is that our players always think we're going to win and they [QPR] are thinking, 'Here we go again.'" Cardiff's next challenge is Margate in the FA Cup next week. "We don't want to be a headline for the wrong reasons," Lawrence said. As the police continued to deal with trouble outside the ground, it would have been no surprise if he had been talking about something other than football.

QUEENS PARK RANGERS (4-4-2): S Royce — T Forbes, C Carlisle, D Shittu, T Williams — M Bircham, R Langley, S Palmer, C Willock (sub: D Oli, 68min) — B Angell (sub: P Furlong, 61), K Gallen. **Substitutes not used:** N Culkin, D Murphy, A Thomson. **Booked:** Bircham.

CARDIFF CITY (4-4-2): N Alexander — R Weston, S Prior, C Barker, G Croft — D Hamilton, W Boland, G Kavanagh, A Legg — R Earnshaw (sub: A Campbell, 86), P Thorne (sub: L Fortune-West, 88). **Substitutes not used:** M Margetson, J Bowen, L Maxwell. **Booked:** Boland, Weston, Hamilton. **Referee:** C Wilkes.

Tuesday March 4
Blackpool 1 Barnsley 2; Brentford 0 Cardiff 2; Bristol City 2 Oldham 0; Colchester 2 Northampton 0; Crewe 4 Wycombe 2; Huddersfield 0 QPR 3; Mansfield 3 Luton 2; Notts Co 1 Port Vale 0; Plymouth 6 Peterborough 1; Stockport 2 Chesterfield 1; Wigan 0 Tranmere 0

Saturday March 8
Barnsley 1 Stockport 0; Cardiff 0 Notts Co 2; Cheltenham 3 Mansfield 1; Chesterfield 3 Plymouth 2; Luton 3 Huddersfield 0; Northampton 1 Swindon 0; Oldham 2 Colchester 0; Peterborough 1 Wigan 1; Port Vale 1 Blackpool 0; QPR 1 Bristol City 0; Tranmere 2 Crewe 1; Wycombe 4 Brentford 0

Tuesday March 11
Brentford 1 Colchester 1

Wednesday March 12
Swindon 0 Cheltenham 3

Friday March 14
Tranmere 3 Cardiff 3

Saturday March 15
Blackpool 1 Plymouth 1; Brentford 1 Stockport 2; Bristol City 1 Peterborough 0; Cheltenham 1 Northampton 1; Colchester 2 Huddersfield 0; Crewe 1 Port Vale 1; Mansfield 2 Swindon 1; Notts Co 1 Chesterfield 1; Oldham 0 QPR 0; Wigan 1 Luton 1; Wycombe 2 Barnsley 2

Tuesday March 18
Barnsley 1 Tranmere 1; Cardiff 2 Blackpool 1; Chesterfield 0 Colchester 4; Huddersfield 1 Mansfield 1; Luton 0 Oldham 0; Northampton 2 Notts Co 0; Peterborough 1 Wycombe 2; Plymouth 1 Crewe 3; Port Vale 1 Brentford 0; QPR 4 Cheltenham 1; Stockport 1 Wigan 1

Wednesday March 19
Swindon 1 Bristol City 1

Friday March 21
Cardiff 1 Mansfield 0

Saturday March 22
Barnsley 1 Colchester 1; Chesterfield 4 Wycombe 0; Huddersfield 1 Bristol City 2; Luton 0 Crewe 4; Northampton 0 Oldham 2; Peterborough 0 Tranmere 0; Plymouth 3 Brentford 0; Port Vale 1 Cheltenham 2; QPR 0 Wigan 1; Stockport 2 Blackpool 2; Swindon 5 Notts Co 0

Saturday March 29
Blackpool 1 QPR 3; Brentford 3 Northampton 0; Bristol City 2 Barnsley 0; Colchester 1 Swindon 0; Crewe 1 Stockport 0; Mansfield 1 Peterborough 5; Notts Co 3 Huddersfield 2; Oldham 1 Port Vale 1; Tranmere 2 Chesterfield 1; Wigan 0 Plymouth 1

Friday April 4
Northampton 0 Wigan 2

Saturday April 5
Brentford 2 Cheltenham 2; Cardiff 1 QPR 2;
Huddersfield 4 Chesterfield 0; Luton 0 Tranmere 0;
Mansfield 0 Port Vale 1; Notts Co 3 Blackpool 1;
Oldham 2 Barnsley 1; Peterborough 1 Swindon 1;
Plymouth 0 Colchester 0; Wycombe 1 Stockport 4

Tuesday April 8
Cheltenham 2 Luton 2; Wycombe 0 Cardiff 4

Saturday April 12
Barnsley 1 Peterborough 2; Blackpool 0 Crewe 1;
Bristol City 5 Mansfield 2; Cheltenham 1 Oldham 1;
Colchester 1 Notts Co 1; Port Vale 3
Northampton 2; QPR 2 Luton 0; Stockport 2
Plymouth 1; Swindon 0 Huddersfield 1; Tranmere 1
Wycombe 0; Wigan 2 Brentford 0

Sunday April 13
Chesterfield 0 Cardiff 3

Tuesday April 15
Crewe 1 Bristol City 1

Wednesday April 16
Peterborough 2 Cardiff 0

Friday April 18
Northampton 0 Stockport 3

Saturday April 19
Brentford 1 QPR 2; Cardiff 0 Colchester 3;
Crewe 0 Swindon 1; Huddersfield 0 Wigan 0;
Luton 2 Bristol City 2; Mansfield 0 Barnsley 1;
Notts Co 0 Tranmere 1; Oldham 4 Chesterfield 0;
Peterborough 1 Blackpool 3; Plymouth 3
Port Vale 0; Wycombe 1 Cheltenham 1

Monday April 21
Barnsley 1 Crewe 2; Blackpool 3 Mansfield 3;
Cheltenham 1 Peterborough 1; Chesterfield 0
Brentford 2; Colchester 0 Luton 5; Port Vale 1
Wycombe 1; QPR 2 Notts Co 0; Stockport 2
Huddersfield 1; Tranmere 4 Northampton 0;
Wigan 3 Oldham 1

Tuesday April 22
Bristol City 2 Cardiff 0

Wednesday April 23
Swindon 2 Plymouth 0

Saturday April 26
Barnsley 1 Brentford 0; Cardiff 0 Wigan 0;
Cheltenham 3 Blackpool 0; Chesterfield 2
Bristol City 0; Luton 1 Stockport 1; Northampton 2
Plymouth 2; Oldham 4 Swindon 0; Peterborough 1
Notts Co 0; Port Vale 5 Huddersfield 1; QPR 0
Crewe 0; Wycombe 0 Colchester 0

Tuesday April 29
Tranmere 3 Mansfield 1

Saturday May 3
Blackpool 1 Chesterfield 1; Brentford 1
Peterborough 1; Bristol City 2 Port Vale 0;
Colchester 0 QPR 1; Crewe 1 Cardiff 1; Huddersfield
1 Oldham 1; Mansfield 2 Northampton 1; Notts Co 1
Cheltenham 0; Plymouth 1 Wycombe 0; Stockport 2
Tranmere 3; Swindon 2 Luton 1; Wigan 1 Barnsley 0

SEMI-FINALS

First legs, May 10

CARDIFF (0) **1**   **BRISTOL CITY** (0) **0**
Thorne 74   19,164

OLDHAM (1) **1**   **QUEENS PARK RANGERS** (0) **1**
Eyres 28   Langley 47
12,152

Second legs, May 13

BRISTOL CITY (0) **0**   **CARDIFF** (0) **0**
16,307
(Cardiff win 1-0 on aggregate)

Second leg, May 14

QUEENS PARK RANGERS (0) **1**   **OLDHAM** (0) **0**
Furlong 82   17,201
(Queens Park Rangers win 2-1 on aggregate)

FINAL
     May 25, Millennium Stadium

CARDIFF CITY (0) **1**   **QUEENS PARK RANGERS** (0) **0**
Campbell 114   66,096
(after extra time)

Cardiff City took another step towards fulfilling Sam Hammam's dream of establishing the club at the pinnacle of the game — which their chairman has backed with £10 million of his own cash — when a cleverly taken extra-time goal by Andy Campbell, a substitute, ended QPR's resistance. The strike also justified a brave gamble by Lennie Lawrence, the Cardiff manager, who had withdrawn the prolific Robert Earnshaw as QPR, defying predictions that they would wilt under pressure in the Welsh capital, defended stubbornly. Ian Holloway's side might even have won when, with extra time looming, Andy Thomson's header drifted wide.

CARDIFF CITY (4-4-2): N Alexander — R Weston (sub: G Croft, 70min), S Prior, D Gabbidon, C Barker — W Boland, G Kavanagh, G Whalley, A Legg (sub: M Bonner, 115) — P Thomas, R Earnshaw (sub: A Campbell, 79). **Substitutes not used:** J Bowen, M Margetson. **Booked:** Kavanagh.
QUEENS PARK RANGERS (4-4-2): C Day — S Kelly, C Carlisle, D Shittu, G Padula (sub: T Williams, 80) — K Gallen, M Bircham, S Palmer, K McLeod — R Pacquette (sub: A Thomson, 61), P Furlong. **Substitutes not used:** N Culkin, T Forbes, B Angell. **Booked:** Furlong, Palmer, Bircham.
Referee: H Webb.

NATIONWIDE LEAGUE

THIRD DIVISION

CHAMPIONS
Rushden & Diamonds

RUNNERS-UP
Hartlepool United

ALSO PROMOTED
Wrexham

PROMOTED VIA PLAY-OFFS
Bournemouth

Promotion set in stone: Brian Talbot celebrates Rushden & Diamonds' title

THE GAMES

Saturday August 10
Boston 2 Bournemouth 2; Cambridge 1 Darlington 2; Carlisle 1 Hartlepool 3; Hull 2 Southend 2; Kidderminster 1 Lincoln 1; Macclesfield 1 York 1; Oxford 2 Bury 1; Rochdale 1 L Orient 0; Scunthorpe 1 Wrexham 1; Shrewsbury 1 Exeter 0; Swansea 2 Rushden 2; Torquay 2 Bristol Rovers 1

Tuesday August 13
Bournemouth 0 Kidderminster 0; Bristol Rovers 1 Hull 1; Bury 0 Cambridge 1; Darlington 2 Swansea 2; Exeter 1 Scunthorpe 1; Hartlepool 2 Boston 0; L Orient 3 Macclesfield 2; Lincoln 2 Rochdale 0; Rushden 3 Torquay 0; Southend 0 Carlisle 1; Wrexham 1 Oxford 0; York 2 Shrewsbury 1

Saturday August 17
Bournemouth 1 Cambridge 1; Bristol Rovers 1 Rochdale 2; Bury 3 Swansea 2; Darlington 0 Oxford 1; Exeter 3 Hull 1; Hartlepool 0 Macclesfield 2; L Orient 2 Scunthorpe 0; Lincoln 0 Carlisle 1; Rushden 3 Kidderminster 1; Southend 2 Shrewsbury 3; Wrexham 1 Boston 1; York 4 Torquay 3

Saturday August 24
Boston 2 Lincoln 0; Cambridge 2 L Orient 1; Carlisle 0 Bristol Rovers 0; Hull 1 Bury 1; Kidderminster 4 Exeter 3; Macclesfield 0 Wrexham 1; Oxford 0 Southend 1; Rochdale 1 Darlington 1; Scunthorpe 2 York 1; Shrewsbury 1 Rushden 1; Swansea 2 Bournemouth 0; Torquay 1 Hartlepool 1

Monday August 26
Bury 4 Shrewsbury 3; Exeter 1 Torquay 2; Hartlepool 2 Hull 0; L Orient 0 Kidderminster 0; Lincoln 3 Macclesfield 0; Rushden 2 Scunthorpe 0; Southend 2 Cambridge 1; Wrexham 2 Rochdale 5; York 2 Boston 0

Tuesday August 27
Bournemouth 1 Oxford 1; Bristol Rovers 3 Swansea 1; Darlington 2 Carlisle 0

Saturday August 31
Boston 1 Bury 1; Cambridge 4 Rushden 1; Carlisle 0 Exeter 2; Hull 1 L Orient 1; Kidderminster 1 Darlington 1; Macclesfield 0 Bournemouth 1; Oxford 0 Hartlepool 1; Rochdale 1 Southend 2; Scunthorpe 2 Bristol Rovers 2; Shrewsbury 1 Swansea 1 York 2; Torquay 2 Wrexham 1

Friday September 6
Bury 2 York 1; Carlisle 0 Rochdale 2

Saturday September 7
Cambridge 1 Hull 2; Exeter 1 Bournemouth 3; Kidderminster 0 Boston 0; Lincoln 1 Scunthorpe 0; Oxford 2 Torquay 0; Rushden 3 Southend 0; Shrewsbury 2 L Orient 1; Swansea 2 Hartlepool 2

Sunday September 8
Macclesfield 2 Bristol Rovers 1

Saturday September 14
Boston 1 Oxford 3; Bournemouth 1 Bury 2; Bristol Rovers 1 Exeter 1; Hartlepool 4 Darlington 1; Hull 4 Carlisle 0; L Orient 1 Lincoln 1; Rochdale 1 Shrewsbury 1; Scunthorpe 1 Kidderminster 1; Southend 1 Macclesfield 0; Torquay 3 Cambridge 2; Wrexham 4 Swansea 0; York 0 Rushden 0

NO ONE GETS RICH WAGERING on the outcome of the third division. You would be better off investing your money in safer gambles, such as forecasting the weather in spring or guessing what David Beckham's next hairstyle will be. You know the small print in financial adverts that says "past performance is no guarantee of future results"? They should put it on the front of every team's programme on each season's opening day.

Supporters do not know what to expect: which means they can hope. Down here, the element of surprise lives on. Sure, money, talent, self-belief and squad depth help, — but not always. This egalitarian, semi-random division is like a weird fusion of a meritocracy and a fruit machine. The play itself? Caricatured as a gawky, kick-and-rush festival that bears only a limited relation to football. If the Premiership is Hollywood, the third division is reality TV. So there is plenty that is prosaic to endure. But some teams try to play football the right way. And sometimes they do.

Best story of the year? Keith Alexander, the new Lincoln City

FINAL TABLE

| | P | HOME | | | | | AWAY | | | | | P | GD |
		W	D	L	F	A	W	D	L	F	A		
Rushden & D	46	16	5	2	48	19	8	10	5	25	28	87	26
Hartlepool Utd	46	16	5	2	49	21	8	8	7	22	30	85	20
Wrexham	46	12	7	4	48	26	11	8	4	36	24	84	34
Bournemouth	46	14	7	2	38	18	6	7	10	22	30	74	12
Scunthorpe Utd	46	11	8	4	40	20	8	7	8	28	29	72	19
Lincoln City	46	10	9	4	29	18	8	7	8	17	19	70	9
Bury	46	8	8	7	25	26	10	8	5	32	30	70	1
Oxford Utd	46	9	7	7	26	20	10	5	8	31	27	69	10
Torquay Utd	46	9	11	3	41	31	7	7	9	30	40	66	0
York City	46	11	9	3	34	24	6	6	11	18	29	66	-1
Kidderminster H	46	8	8	7	30	33	8	7	8	32	30	63	-1
Cambridge Utd	46	10	7	6	38	25	6	6	11	29	45	61	-3
Hull City	46	9	10	4	34	19	5	7	11	24	34	59	5
Darlington	46	8	10	5	36	27	4	8	11	22	32	54	-1
*Boston Utd	46	11	6	6	34	22	4	7	12	21	34	54	-1
Macclesfield T	46	8	6	9	29	28	6	6	11	28	35	54	-6
Southend Utd	46	12	1	10	29	23	5	2	16	18	36	54	-12
Leyton Orient	46	9	6	8	28	24	5	5	13	23	37	53	-10
Rochdale	46	7	6	10	30	30	5	10	8	33	40	52	-7
Bristol Rovers	46	7	7	9	25	27	5	8	10	25	30	51	-7
Swansea City	46	9	6	8	28	25	3	7	13	20	40	49	-17
Carlisle Utd	46	5	5	13	26	40	8	5	10	26	38	49	-26
Exeter City	46	7	7	9	24	31	4	8	11	26	33	48	-14
Shrewsbury T	46	5	6	12	34	39	4	8	11	28	53	41	-30

*Boston Utd deducted four points for financial irregularities

Richie Humphreys, right, attacks to keep Hartlepool on course for promotion

manager, assembled a small squad largely accrued from non-league ranks and his team were accordingly installed as relegation favourites. That billing failed to take into account Alexander's pragmatism — or should that be cynicism? His team were organised, physical and no strangers to 1-0 wins. What seemed like an unambitious plan designed merely to achieve survival instead yielded a shock promotion campaign. Lincoln managed only 46 goals, but a defence that shipped just 37 was the bedrock of their success.

Simon Yeo, a former soldier and postman, turned into a goalscoring super-sub, netting spectacular late strikes that saw Lincoln into the post-season and past Scunthorpe United in the play-off semi-finals. Brian Laws, of Scunthorpe, had been one of several managers to gripe at Lincoln's tactics, but they went haywire at both ends at Sincil Bank in the first leg, Lincoln winning 5-3.

They were finally halted by Bournemouth, one of many clubs under the yoke of financial restraint, who beat them 5-2 in a wild match at the Millennium Stadium. Sean O'Driscoll, the Bournemouth manager, had been on the verge of the sack early in the season, but he guided his side to an immediate return to the second division.

Biggest flops? In August, Hull City, the bookmakers' choice for the title, seemed to have all the right ingredients. Jan Molby was a popular choice as manager, their squad was reckoned to be the division's most talented — certainly the most expensive — and they were due to move into a 25,000-seat stadium at the turn of the year. The new ground was the sole factor to live up to expectations.

Molby departed in October after Hull won two of their opening 12 league games. He was replaced by Peter Taylor, who had taken

Tuesday September 17
Bournemouth 3 Rushden 1; Bristol Rovers 2 Bury 1; Hartlepool 2 Lincoln 1; Hull 1 Macclesfield 3; L Orient 1 Oxford 2; Rochdale 4 Cambridge 3; Scunthorpe 3 Carlisle 1; Southend 0 Kidderminster 2; Torquay 2 Shrewsbury 1; Wrexham 4 Exeter 0; York 1 Darlington 0

Wednesday September 18
Boston 1 Swansea 0

Saturday September 21
Bury 1 Hartlepool 1; Cambridge 3 York 0; Carlisle 4 Boston 2; Darlington 2 Bournemouth 2; Exeter 1 L Orient 0; Kidderminster 0 Rochdale 0; Lincoln 2 Southend 1; Macclesfield 2 Scunthorpe 3; Oxford 0 Hull 0; Rushden 2 Wrexham 2; Shrewsbury 2 Bristol Rovers 5; Swansea 0 Torquay 1

Tuesday September 24
Darlington 0 Wrexham 1

Saturday September 28
Boston 1 Cambridge 3; Bournemouth 3 Carlisle 1; Bristol Rovers 1 Kidderminster 2; Hartlepool 1 Rushden 2; Hull 1 Swansea 0; L Orient 2 Darlington 1; Rochdale 3 Macclesfield 1; Scunthorpe 1 Shrewsbury 1; Southend 1 Exeter 0; Torquay 0 Lincoln 0; Wrexham 2 Bury 2; York 0 Oxford 1

Saturday October 5
Bury 1 Southend 3; Cambridge 2 Wrexham 2; Carlisle 1 Torquay 2; Darlington 1 Bristol Rovers 0; Exeter 0 York 1; Kidderminster 1 Hull 0; Lincoln 1 Bournemouth 2; Macclesfield 2 Oxford 0; Scunthorpe 1; Rushden 2 L Orient 0; Shrewsbury 0 Hartlepool 1; Swansea 1 Rochdale 1

Saturday October 12
Boston 2 Torquay 1; Bristol Rovers 2 Lincoln 0; Bury 2 Darlington 2; Carlisle 1 Shrewsbury 2; Exeter 1 Rushden 1; Hull 3 Rochdale 0; Kidderminster 0 Macclesfield 2; Oxford 1 Swansea 0; Scunthorpe 1 Cambridge 2; Southend 1 York 0; Wrexham 0 L Orient 0

Sunday October 13
Bournemouth 2 Hartlepool 1

Saturday October 19
Cambridge 1 Oxford 1; Darlington 2 Boston 3; Hartlepool 4 Wrexham 3; L Orient 0 Bournemouth 0; Lincoln 1 Exeter 0; Macclesfield 2 Carlisle 2; Rochdale 1 Scunthorpe 2; Rushden 1 Bury 1; Shrewsbury 2 Kidderminster 3; Swansea 1 Southend 0; Torquay 1 Hull 4; York 2 Bristol Rovers 2

Friday October 25
Southend 0 Hartlepool 1

Saturday October 26
Boston 3 Rochdale 1; Bournemouth 1 York 0; Bristol Rovers 1 L Orient 2; Bury 2 Macclesfield 1; Carlisle 2 Swansea 2; Exeter 0 Darlington 4; Hull 1 Rushden 1; Kidderminster 2 Cambridge 1; Oxford 2 Shrewsbury 2; Scunthorpe 5 Torquay 1; Wrexham 0 Lincoln 2

Tuesday October 29
Cambridge 2 Carlisle 1; Darlington 1 Scunthorpe 1; Hartlepool 2 Bristol Rovers 0; L Orient 2 Southend 1; Lincoln 1 Bury 1; Macclesfield 2 Oxford 1; Rochdale 3 Exeter 3; Rushden 1 Boston 0; Shrewsbury 1 Hull 1; Swansea 0 Kidderminster 4; Torquay 4 Bournemouth 0; York 1 Wrexham 1.

Friday November 1
Hartlepool 0 York 0

Saturday November 2
Boston 0 Exeter 3; Bournemouth 1 Bristol Rovers 0;
Cambridge 1 Swansea 0; Carlisle 1 Oxford 0;
Darlington 0 Lincoln 0; Hull 2 Scunthorpe 0;
L Orient 1 Bury 2; Macclesfield 1 Shrewsbury 2;
Rochdale 0 Rushden 1; Southend 0 Wrexham 1

Saturday November 9
Bristol Rovers 0 Southend 1; Bury 0 Torquay 1;
Exeter 1 Hartlepool 2; Kidderminster 1 Carlisle 2;
Lincoln 1 Hull 1; Oxford 2 Rochdale 0; Rushden 2
Darlington 0; Scunthorpe 2 Boston 0; Shrewsbury 3
Cambridge 1; Swansea 1 Macclesfield 0; Wrexham
3 Bournemouth 2; York 3 L Orient 2

Tuesday November 19
Torquay 2 Kidderminster 2

Saturday November 23
Bristol Rovers 0 Wrexham 3; Carlisle 1 Bury 2;
Exeter 1 Cambridge 2; Hull 1 Boston 0; L Orient 1
Hartlepool 2; Lincoln 1 Rushden 2; Macclesfield 3
Torquay 3; Rochdale 0 York 1; Scunthorpe 2
Swansea 0; Shrewsbury 2 Darlington 2; Southend 0
Bournemouth 1

Saturday November 30
Boston 0 L Orient 1; Bournemouth 2 Scunthorpe 1;
Bury 1 Exeter 0; Cambridge 3 Macclesfield 1;
Darlington 2 Southend 1; Hartlepool 2
Kidderminster 1; Oxford 1 Lincoln 0; Rushden 2
Bristol Rovers 1; Swansea 2 Shrewsbury 0; Torquay
2 Rochdale 2; Wrexham 0 Hull 0; York 2 Carlisle 1

Saturday December 14
Bristol Rovers 0 Oxford 2; Carlisle 1 Wrexham 2;
Exeter 1 Swansea 0; Hull 0 Darlington 1;
Kidderminster 1 York 2; L Orient 2 Torquay 0;
Lincoln 2 Cambridge 2; Macclesfield 0 Rushden 1;
Rochdale 4 Hartlepool 0; Scunthorpe 0 Bury 1;
Shrewsbury 0 Bournemouth 0; Southend 4 Boston 2

Friday December 20
York 1 Lincoln 1

Saturday December 21
Boston 6 Shrewsbury 0; Bournemouth 0 Hull 0;
Bury 1 Rochdale 1; Cambridge 3 Bristol Rovers 1;
Darlington 0 Macclesfield 0; Hartlepool 2
Scunthorpe 2; Oxford 2 Exeter 2; Rushden 1
Carlisle 1; Swansea 0 L Orient 1; Torquay 3
Southend 1; Wrexham 0 Kidderminster 2

Thursday December 26
Boston 3 York 0; Cambridge 1 Southend 1;
Carlisle 2 Darlington 2; Hull 2 Hartlepool 0;
Kidderminster 3 L Orient 2; Macclesfield 0
Lincoln 1; Oxford 3 Bournemouth 0; Rochdale 2
Wrexham 2; Scunthorpe 0 Rushden 0; Shrewsbury
4 Bury 1; Swansea 0 Bristol Rovers 1

Saturday December 28
Bournemouth 3 Rochdale 3; Bristol Rovers 1
Boston 1; Darlington 1 Torquay 1; Exeter 1
Macclesfield 1; Hartlepool 3 Cambridge 0; L Orient
2 Carlisle 1; Lincoln 1 Swansea 0; Rushden 0
Oxford 2; York 1 Hull 1

Sunday December 29
Bury 1 Kidderminster 1; Southend 1 Scunthorpe 2

Wednesday January 1
Bury 1 Hull 0; Hartlepool 2 Carlisle 1; Lincoln 1
Boston 1; Rushden 5 Shrewsbury 1; Wrexham 1
Macclesfield 3; York 1 Scunthorpe 3

charge of England just two years earlier. Big crowds flocked to the impressive stadium and results improved briefly, but Hull proved irredeemably mid-table.

The League's *nouveau riche* took the title. Rushden & Diamonds did not splash the cash as freely as in the past, but they could afford to sign Dean Holdsworth from Bolton Wanderers on transfer deadline day. Hartlepool United slowly faded under Mike Newell's stewardship but still finished second. Newell lost his job all the same. Wrexham's strong finish saw them grab third place, thanks in no small part to Andy Morrell, whose 34 league goals earned him a close-season move to Coventry City.

Boston United began their inaugural campaign with a four-point deduction for financial irregularities. The tone was set for a difficult season, but they ended up comfortably in mid-table. So did York City, who flirted with the top seven for a while — an admirable effort from a club that was hours from going out of business. Terry Dolan, the manager, was sacked in May as a cost-cutting measure.

Rochdale only missed out on automatic promotion by a point in 2001-02. The next season, though, was a different story. Paul Simpson took over as player-manager and led them in a memorable FA Cup run, but they spent much of the campaign near the foot of the table. Simpson left his post in May.

It was a year of financial and footballing ruin for Exeter City. The destitute club were relegated after 83 years in the Football League. Through Uri Geller's connections, Exeter hatched a lot of hype; but showbiz pretensions do not get you far in this earthy division. Lee Sharpe arrived but did not last long and the club even attempted to sign Paul Gascoigne, though didn't everyone?

Michael Knighton, the Carlisle United owner, was finally removed last summer, but that was as good as it got for the Cumbrians, save for an LDV Vans Trophy final appearance. The perennial strugglers finished only a point clear of Exeter, in the newly introduced second relegation place, having secured their survival in the penultimate game.

And what a game: a dramatic 3-2 win at Gay Meadow that relegated Shrewsbury Town. Shrewsbury were winless in their final 15 league matches, a run for which their porous defence was culpable. Still, their performances were hard to explain given the talent at their disposal.

The previous season they had finished one point off the play-offs. The next, four months after knocking Everton out of the FA Cup, the giantkillers flatlined and were bundled out of this capricious division through the trapdoor. And who could have predicted that?

PLAYER OF THE SEASON
Andy Morrell, Wrexham

A late bloomer, Andy Morrell enjoyed his best season for Wrexham at 28 and his 34 league goals earned a close-season move to Coventry City. The former gym instructor, who joined the club from Newcastle Blue Star after Rob McCaffrey, the Sky Sports presenter, fixed him up with a trial, scored seven times in one game against Merthyr Tydfil in 2000, but did not enjoy a sustained run as a first-choice striker until this season. In August and September he found the net in eight successive games, scoring 12 times in that spell.

Tom Dart

LEADING SCORERS

		League	FAC	WC	Total
Andy Morrell	Wrexham	34	0	1	35
Dave Kitson	Cambridge Utd	20	1	1	22
Martin Carruthers	Scunthorpe Utd	20	1	0	21
Bo Henriksen	Kidderminster H	20	0	0	20
Peter Duffield	Boston United	17	2	0	19
Barry Conlon	Darlington	15	2	0	17
Paul Hall	Rushden & D	16	0	0	16
Luke Rodgers	Shrewsbury Town	16	0	0	16
Lee McEvilly	Rochdale	15	1	0	16
Onandi Lowe	Rushden & D	15	1	0	16
Eifion Williams	Hartlepool Utd	15	0	1	16
Martin Gritton	Torquay Utd	13	3	0	16
Steve Torpey	Scunthorpe Utd	12	3	1	16
Nigel Jemson	Shrewsbury Town	11	5	0	16

Duffield's total includes 13 league and two FA Cup goals for York City

PFA TEAM

Alan Fettis
Hull City

Carlos Edwards
Wrexham

Graeme Lee
Hartlepool United

Chris Westwood
Hartlepool United

Paul Underwood
Rushden & Diamonds

Richie Humphreys
Hartlepool United

Mark Tinkler
Hartlepool United

Paul Hall
Rushden & Diamonds

Alex Russell
Torquay United

Andy Morrell
Wrexham

Dave Kitson
Cambridge United

Saturday January 4
Boston 0 Hartlepool 1; Carlisle 1 Southend 0; Hull 1 Bristol Rovers 0; Torquay 1 Rushden 1

Saturday January 11
Hull 2 Exeter 2; Kidderminster 0 Rushden 2; Scunthorpe 2 L Orient 1; Torquay 3 York 1

Tuesday January 14
Bristol Rovers 1 Torquay 1; Oxford 1 Darlington 1; Shrewsbury 0 Southend 1; Swansea 2 Bury 3

Saturday January 18
Bournemouth 2 Macclesfield 2; Bristol Rovers 2 Scunthorpe 1; Bury 0 Boston 0; Darlington 2 Kidderminster 1; Exeter 1 Carlisle 0; Hartlepool 3 Oxford 1; L Orient 2 Hull 0; Lincoln 1 Shrewsbury 1; Rushden 4 Cambridge 1; Southend 1 Rochdale 0; Wrexham 2 Torquay 1; York 3 Swansea 1

Tuesday January 21
Macclesfield 0 Hartlepool 1; Rochdale 0 Lincoln 1; Scunthorpe 1 Exeter 1; Southend 2 Oxford 1

Saturday January 25
Boston 0 Bristol Rovers 0; Cambridge 0 Hartlepool 0; Carlisle 3 L Orient 1; Hull 0 York 0; Kidderminster 3 Bury 2; Macclesfield 1 Exeter 3; Oxford 3 Rushden 0; Scunthorpe 4 Southend 1; Swansea 2 Lincoln 0; Torquay 3 Darlington 1

Tuesday January 28
Kidderminster 1 Oxford 3; L Orient 1 Cambridge 1

Saturday February 1
Bournemouth 2 Boston 1; Bristol Rovers 1 Carlisle 1; Exeter 1 Shrewsbury 2; Hartlepool 3 Torquay 2; Rushden 1 Swansea 1; Southend 3 Hull 0; Wrexham 2 Scunthorpe 1

Sunday February 2
York 2 Macclesfield 1

Tuesday February 4
Cambridge 1 Bury 2; Carlisle 1 Lincoln 4; Kidderminster 1 Bournemouth 0; Oxford 0 Wrexham 2; Swansea 1 Darlington 0

Saturday February 8
Boston 1 Scunthorpe 0; Bournemouth 2 Wrexham 0; Cambridge 5 Shrewsbury 0; Carlisle 2 Kidderminster 2; Darlington 2 Rushden 2; Hartlepool 2 Exeter 1; Hull 0 Lincoln 1; L Orient 0 York 1; Macclesfield 1 Swansea 3; Rochdale 2 Oxford 1; Southend 2 Bristol Rovers 2; Torquay 1 Bury 1

Tuesday February 11
Bournemouth 3 Swansea 0; Darlington 0 Rochdale 1; Shrewsbury 2 York 2; Torquay 1 Exeter 0

Saturday February 15
Bristol Rovers 0 Bournemouth 0; Bury 0 L Orient 1; Exeter 0 Boston 2; Kidderminster 2 Torquay 0; Lincoln 1 Darlington 1; Scunthorpe 3 Hull 1; Swansea 2 Cambridge 0; Wrexham 3 Southend 0; York 0 Hartlepool 0

Tuesday February 18
Exeter 2 Kidderminster 5

Saturday February 22
Boston 3 Kidderminster 0; Bournemouth 2 Exeter 0; Bristol Rovers 1 Macclesfield 1; Hartlepool 4 Swansea 0; Hull 1 Cambridge 1; L Orient 0 Shrewsbury 2; Rochdale 0 Carlisle 1; Scunthorpe 0 Lincoln 0; Southend 2 Rushden 1; Torquay 2 Oxford 3; York 1 Bury 1

Sunday February 23
Wrexham 0 Darlington 0

Tuesday February 25
L Orient 0 Rochdale 1

Saturday March 1
Bury 2 Bournemouth 1; Cambridge 0 Torquay 1;
Carlisle 1 Hull 5; Darlington 2 Hartlepool 2;
Exeter 0 Bristol Rovers 0; Kidderminster 1
Scunthorpe 3; Lincoln 1 L Orient 1; Macclesfield 2
Southend 1; Oxford 2 Boston 1; Rushden 2 York 1;
Shrewsbury 3 Rochdale 1; Swansea 0 Wrexham 0

Tuesday March 4
Bury 0 Bristol Rovers 1; Cambridge 2 Rochdale 2;
Darlington 2 York 1; Exeter 1 Wrexham 0;
Kidderminster 1 Southend 1; Lincoln 3 Hartlepool
0; Macclesfield 0 Hull 1; Oxford 0 L Orient 2;
Rushden 2 Bournemouth 1; Swansea 0 Boston 0

Friday March 7
Hartlepool 0 Bury 0

Saturday March 8
Boston 0 Carlisle 0; Bournemouth 2 Darlington 0;
Bristol Rovers 0 Shrewsbury 0; Hull 0 Oxford 0;
L Orient 1 Exeter 1; Scunthorpe 1 Macclesfield 1;
Southend 0 Lincoln 1; Torquay 0 Swansea 0;
Wrexham 3 Rushden 0; York 3 Cambridge 1

Tuesday March 11
Carlisle 1 Scunthorpe 2; Darlington 1 Cambridge 2;
Macclesfield 3 L Orient 1; Rochdale 1
Bournemouth 1; Wrexham 3 Shrewsbury 3

Saturday March 15
Cambridge 0 Kidderminster 2; Darlington 2
Exeter 2; Hartlepool 2 Southend 1; L Orient 1
Bristol Rovers 2; Lincoln 1 Wrexham 1;
Macclesfield 0 Bury 0; Rochdale 1 Boston 0;
Rushden 4 Hull 2; Shrewsbury 1 Oxford 2;
Swansea 1 Carlisle 2; Torquay 1 Scunthorpe 1;
York 1 Bournemouth 0

Tuesday March 18
Bournemouth 3 L Orient 1; Bristol Rovers 0 York 1;
Bury 0 Rushden 1; Carlisle 1 Macclesfield 0;
Exeter 2 Lincoln 0; Hull 1 Torquay 1;
Kidderminster 2 Shrewsbury 2; Oxford 1
Cambridge 1; Scunthorpe 3 Rochdale 1;
Southend 0 Swansea 2; Wrexham 2 Hartlepool 0

Wednesday March 19
Boston 1 Darlington 0

Saturday March 22
Boston 1 Rushden 1; Bournemouth 1 Torquay 1;
Bristol Rovers 1 Hartlepool 0; Bury 2 Lincoln 0;
Carlisle 0 Cambridge 1; Exeter 1 Rochdale 1; Hull 2
Shrewsbury 0; Kidderminster 2 Swansea 2;
Oxford 0 Macclesfield 1; Scunthorpe 0
Darlington 1; Southend 1 L Orient 0; Wrexham 1
York 1

Monday March 24
Rushden 3 Rochdale 3

Tuesday March 25
Bury 1 Oxford 1; Cambridge 2 Bournemouth 1;
Lincoln 1 Kidderminster 0; Shrewsbury 2
Torquay 3

Friday March 28
Swansea 3 Oxford 2

MATCH OF THE SEASON

Shrewsbury Town 2   Carlisle United 3
Gay Meadow, Tuesday April 29 2003
Peter Lansley

IT WAS A GHOULISH AFFAIR, but, as Carlisle United celebrated salvaging their status as a Football League club, Shrewsbury Town conceded theirs. Four months after knocking Everton out of the FA Cup, Kevin Ratcliffe's team had their relegation to the Nationwide Conference confirmed last night after this seventh successive defeat.

Brian Wake, formerly of Tow Law Town, should be the toast of Cumbria this morning after his hat-trick secured Carlisle's future as a league club. Roddy Collins's team can breathe easily on Saturday, when their final match of the Nationwide League third division campaign, against Bournemouth, will seem like a veritable carnival. Swansea City or Exeter City will go down with Shrewsbury.

Ratcliffe experienced the ultimate honour in league football as captain of the Everton side that won the first division championship in 1985. Last night he endured opposite emotions as Shrewsbury, after 53 years as a Football League club, departed. Three years ago, in his first season in charge at Gay Meadow, Ratcliffe kept the team up on the last day of the season by winning away to Exeter.

The former Wales captain asked to be allowed to go home and discuss matters with his family before making any announcement about his future, but his departure appears inevitable. "They're my players, I've brought the majority of them in, so at the end of the day you've got to take some responsibility," he said. Asked if players were shedding tears in the dressing-room, he said: "I'm sure there'll be one or two. I'm also sure there'll be one or two who weren't."

Shrewsbury, without a win since March 1, have conceded 90 league goals and earned just four points from the past 14 games. Nigel Jemson, the man whose two goals won that glorious third-round tie against Ratcliffe's former club in January, gave them the lead with a 31st-minute penalty last night. However, they went into their shell and allowed Wake to score twice within two minutes.

Ryan Lowe, a substitute, was dismissed within 90 seconds of his introduction, for butting Mark Summerbell, as Shrewsbury threatened to fall apart in the second period. They reclaimed some credibility and Luke Rodgers, their prize asset, scored with a spectacular volley six minutes from time. By then, however, Wake had taken advantage of more horrendous defending to complete his hat-trick.

Shrewsbury, paradoxically, will go into the non-league ranks in a relatively healthy financial state. Their Cup exploits, which culminated in a fourth-round visit from Chelsea, at least ensures that they start life in the Conference with some fiscal muscle. Roland Wycherley, the chairman, had announced on the eve of last night's game that the club is in the black for the first time after

Luke Rodgers leads Shrewsbury off in despair after relegation is confirmed

grossing £500,000 from the Cup adventure. Keith Sayfritz, a director, said: "What's happened here should not have happened, but we should not forget that Kevin is the man who saved us at Exeter three years ago and took us to within an inch of the play-offs last year. That is why we gave him the chance to keep the club up. It's the lowest point in our history and the worst day of my life."

The calls for Ratcliffe's dismissal rang out long and loud, but Sayfritz said: "Kevin Ratcliffe deserves to be treated with respect and he has our respect. We are committed to doing what is right for our supporters and for our football club."

On August 19, 1950, Shrewsbury played their first game in the Football League, a goalless draw against Scunthorpe United. With football's penchant for bitter irony, the same club will provide the opposition for Shrewsbury's wake at Gay Meadow on Saturday.

SHREWSBURY TOWN (4-4-2): M Cartwright — A Thompson (sub: D Moss, 52min), K Murray, P Wilding, A Holt — S Aiston, J Tolley, R Hulbert, I Woan (sub: S Watts, 56) — N Jemson (sub: R Lowe, 67), L Rodgers. **Substitutes not used:** D Artell, S Jagielka. **Booked:** Rodgers, Tolley, Hulbert, Murray. **Sent off:** Lowe.
CARLISLE UNITED (4-4-2): M Glennon — M Birch (sub: B Shelley, 68), P Raven (sub: L Andrews, 34), P Murphy, L Maddison — R Baldacchino, J McCarthy, M Summerbell, C Russell — B Wake, R Foran. **Substitutes not used:** P Keen, B McGill, C Farrell. **Booked:** Murphy, Birch, Wake, Summerbell, Foran.
Referee: B Curson.

Saturday March 29
Cambridge 1 Scunthorpe 1; Darlington 3 Bury 1; Hartlepool 0 Bournemouth 0; Lincoln 2 Bristol Rovers 1; Macclesfield 2 Kidderminster 0; Rushden 1 Exeter 0; Torquay 1 Boston 1; York 2 Southend 0

Tuesday April 1
Oxford 0 Carlisle 0

Wednesday April 2
Boston 3 Wrexham 3

Saturday April 5
Bristol Rovers 1 Rushden 2; Exeter 1 Bury 2; Hull 1 Wrexham 2; Kidderminster 2 Hartlepool 2; L Orient 3 Boston 2; Lincoln 0 Oxford 1; Macclesfield 1 Cambridge 1; Rochdale 0 Torquay 2; Scunthorpe 0 Bournemouth 2; Shrewsbury 0 Swansea 0; Southend 2 Darlington 0

Tuesday April 8
Rochdale 1 Bristol Rovers 1

Wednesday April 9
Shrewsbury 1 Wrexham 2

Saturday April 12
Boston 0 Hull 1; Bournemouth 1 Southend 0; Bury 1 Carlisle 1; Cambridge 2 Exeter 1; Darlington 5 Shrewsbury 1; Hartlepool 4 L Orient 1; Oxford 2 Kidderminster 1; Rushden 1 Lincoln 0; Swansea 1 Scunthorpe 1; Torquay 2 Macclesfield 2; Wrexham 3 Bristol Rovers 2; York 2 Rochdale 2

Tuesday April 15
Carlisle 1 York 1; Rochdale 0 Kidderminster 1; Shrewsbury 2 Macclesfield 3

Friday April 18
Rochdale 1 Bury 2

Saturday April 19
Bristol Rovers 3 Cambridge 1; Carlisle 1 Rushden 2; Exeter 2 Oxford 2; Hull 3 Bournemouth 1; Kidderminster 0 Wrexham 2; L Orient 3 Swansea 1; Lincoln 1 York 0; Macclesfield 1 Darlington 0; Scunthorpe 4 Hartlepool 0; Shrewsbury 1 Boston 2; Southend 3 Torquay 0

Monday April 21
Boston 1 Southend 0; Bournemouth 2 Shrewsbury 1; Bury 0 Scunthorpe 0; Darlington 2 Hull 0; Hartlepool 2 Rochdale 2; Oxford 0 Bristol Rovers 1; Rushden 3 Macclesfield 0; Swansea 0 Exeter 1; Torquay 2 L Orient 2; Wrexham 6 Carlisle 1; York 0 Kidderminster 0

Tuesday April 22
Cambridge 0 Lincoln 0

Saturday April 26
Boston 2 Macclesfield 1; Bournemouth 0 Lincoln 1; Bristol Rovers 2 Darlington 1; Hartlepool 3 Shrewbury 0; Hull 4 Kidderminster 1; L Orient 0 Rushden 0; Rochdale 1 Swansea 2; Scunthorpe 2 Oxford 0; Southend 1 Bury 2; Torquay 2 Carlisle 3; Wrexham 5 Cambridge 0; York 0 Exeter 2

Tuesday April 29
L Orient 0 Wrexham 1; Rochdale 2 Hull 1; Shrewsbury 2 Carlisle 3

Saturday May 3
Bury 0 Wrexham 3; Cambridge 1 Boston 2; Carlisle 0 Bournemouth 2; Darlington 2 L Orient 2; Exeter 1 Southend 0; Kidderminster 1 Bristol Rovers 1; Lincoln 1 Torquay 1; Macclesfield 3 Rochdale 2; Oxford 2 York 0; Rushden 1 Hartlepool 1; Shrewsbury 1 Scunthorpe 1; Swansea 4 Hull 2

A DEATH IN THE FAMILY . . .

TOM DART

CALL ME A TRAGEDY junkie, but if there's a possibility a game I'm watching as a neutral could go to penalties and it doesn't, I always feel a little disappointed. After all, what's drama without a thrilling climax? And one where the concept of the "team", of collective responsibility, is shredded because the result comes down to the actions of a couple of individuals?

As with all big games, as with life, history strips away the padding and leaves you with slivers. A match's free-form beats and rhythms are reduced to a few loud, percussive clangs. The orchestra defers to the soloists.

That's the thing about Great Escapes: last-day survival miracles that preserve a club's precious league status. Team efforts, no doubt; but they make heroes out of men who are, professionally, among the lowest of the low. Jimmy Glass for Carlisle United in 1999; Robbie Reinelt, who scored Brighton's equaliser against Hereford United in 1997; James Thomas, match-winner, Swansea City versus Hull City, Saturday, May 3, 2003.

Thomas is a talented young player who failed to make the grade at Blackburn Rovers. He was Swansea's hero, no question: local boy scores hat-trick to keep his favourite club in the league. His third was decisive. Clean through, 25 yards out, instead of dribbling headlong towards goal, he chipped the keeper. The perfectly placed shot arced into the net like it was painting a rainbow in the grey South Wales sky. It was ridiculous, irresponsible,

arrogant and sublime. Very un-third division. I bet storm clouds gathered over St James' Park the instant it left his foot. Until then Exeter had a chance. To escape the grasping tentacles of the Nationwide Conference they needed to better Swansea's result. Early on, things were going their way. Southend United, their opponents, missed a penalty. Up at the Vetch, Hull equalised, then took the lead, at which point they mentally decamped to some sun-kissed beach. It was still up for grabs until Thomas intervened. In that split second before foot met ball, he *knew* he was going to score. He had seen the future, and it was Swansea 4, Hull 2.

He faced his Conrad Moment, and he passed the test. And Swansea survived.

Two years before he penned *Heart of Darkness*, a novel about Sunderland under Howard Wilkinson, Joseph Conrad wrote *Lord Jim*. The crux of the book is how one man caves in under extreme pressure. As Conrad puts it, there is "nothing more awful than to watch a man who has been found out, not in a crime but in a more than criminal weakness ... And there are things — they look small enough sometimes too — by which some of us are totally and completely undone." Translated into football-speak, what Conrad is saying is that the lad had his own Final Day experience and bottled it big-time.

I'm not telling you anything you don't know when I say that supporting a football team is analogous to having a torrid love affair. All very Nick Hornby-esque, but in common with most third division teams, supporting Torquay United is like dating Grotbags, the fat green witch from Rod Hull's 1980s kids' TV show. There's excitement and occasional magic, but plans for domination always backfire and end in farce and ridicule.

I was in the away end when the Gulls travelled to Underhill in 2001 for the most recent last-day relegation face-off. Barnet had to win; Torquay had to draw. The weeks leading up to the game were not a happy time. I felt helpless, anxious, constantly on the cusp of utter doom. It was like being leader of the Conservative Party, basically. Think of the terror: your future is in the hands of 16 individuals who, over the course of the past nine months, have proved themselves to be brazen

Conference call: Exeter City fans despair after their relegation is confirmed on the last day of the season after 83 years in the League

incompetents. Playing down the Barnet slope, Torquay took a 2-0 lead. Then came the Conrad moment. Well, three of them, actually.

First, in his own box, Lord Jimmy Aggrey, an alleged defender, performed a manoeuvre not commonly seen outside the NBA. More than criminal: penalty to Barnet. Up steps the excellent Darren Currie. His effort is weak; he is totally and completely undone. Stuart Jones, who is only playing because his manager dreamt the previous night that he would save a penalty, stops it. Then Torquay go down the other end and make it 3-0. It ends 3-2; had Currie scored, I believe that Barnet would have gone on to win. Jones received the eternal gratitude of every Gulls fan and, nine months later, received a free transfer to Chester City. As for Barnet, who knows what happened to them.

At the end, my mind was an emotional blender. It swirled round a dozen incoherent thoughts and concocted them into a strange feeling that tasted overwhelmingly like relief mixed with a dash of joy and a hint of survivor guilt.

Two years ago I tried to imagine what Barnet fans were feeling. To them it must have felt like a death. In some ways it is. Going out of the league kills your pride. You lose that cherished place in the national consciousness,

the extra credibility of being a Member Of The Football League. It could even precipitate an identity crisis if your team is an important part of how you define yourself.

Following a struggling team that abruptly exits the third division, this happens. A present that you may not like, but one that is safe and familiar, suddenly becomes the past. Surrendered to history. How do you turn over a new leaf when you've reached the last page of the book? A humdrum supporting life and yet it seems a tragedy now that it's gone. Think of it like that and the joy you feel at clinging to league survival is a celebration of the beauty of the familiar. Sticking to what you know never felt so good.

Yes, football is about renewal — each season it does what life can't: perform a rebirth. Yes, existence, and your team, go on. But that isn't the point. The point is that if the Conrad Moment is flunked, things go on in a different way than before. It might be horrible; it might turn out better than expected. But it won't be the same.

And, in a funny way, that's positive news. Long live the last-day emotional mincing machine. I hope the tears and cheers flow freely at the final, final whistle next and every year. Because the way these games hold the power to hurt and heal is the ultimate affirmation that all this wonderful nonsense matters.

PLAY-OFFS

SEMI-FINALS

First legs, May 10

BURY (0) **0**
5,782

BOURNEMOUTH (0) **0**

LINCOLN CITY (2) **5**
Weaver 15, Mayo 18, Smith 55, Yeo 82, 90
8,902

SCUNTHORPE UTD (1) **3**
Calvo-Garcia 26, 69, Stanton 70

Second leg, May 13

BOURNEMOUTH (2) **3**
O'Connor 21, Hayter 38, 60
7,945

BURY (0) **1**
Preece 67

(Bournemouth win 3-1 on aggregate)

Second leg, May 14

SCUNTHORPE UTD (0) **0**
8,295

LINCOLN CITY (0) **1**
Yeo 88

(Lincoln win 6-3 on aggregate)

FINAL

May 24, Millennium Stadium

BOURNEMOUTH (2) **5**
S Fletcher 29, C Fletcher 45, 77
Purches 56, O'Connor 60

LINCOLN CITY (1) **2**
Futcher 35, Bailey 75
32,148

Rarely can the losers have had as much to cheer as the victors in a play-off final. As Bournemouth's players went on a lap of honour to celebrate their immediate return to the second division after a thumping triumph in Cardiff, the fans of Lincoln City, their beaten rivals, stayed to applaud the players of a club that had come out of administration only days before the season began, when its very existence was under threat, and mounted a wholly unexpected promotion campaign under the management of Keith Alexander. Carl Fletcher, the Bournemouth captain, scored twice as his side became the first to hit five goals in a final.

BOURNEMOUTH (4-4-2): N Moss — N Young, C Fletcher, A Gulliver, W Cummings — W Elliott (sub: D Thomas, 90min), M Browning, S Purches, G O'Connor (sub: B Stack, 80) — J Hayter, S Fletcher (sub: D Holmes, 85). **Substituites not used:** G Stewart, S McDonald.

LINCOLN CITY (3-4-3): A Marriott — S Weaver, P Morgan, B Futcher — M Bailey, P Gain, R Butcher, S Bimson (sub: C Connelly, 57) — P Smith (sub: S Yeo, 50), D Cropper (sub: S Willis, 73), P Mayo. **Substitutes not used:** B Sedgemore, M Bloomer. **Booked:** Weaver, Morgan. **Referee:** A Kaye.

AVERAGE ATTENDANCES

FIRST DIVISION

Leicester City	29,230
Wolverhampton Wanderers	25,744
Derby County	25,469
Ipswich Town	25,454
Nottingham Forest	24,436
Norwich City	20,352
Sheffield Wednesday	20,326
Portsmouth	18,933
Sheffield United	18,069
Crystal Palace	16,866
Reading	16,011
Coventry City	14,812
Stoke City	14,587
Burnley	13,976
Preston North End	13,853
Watford	13,404
Bradford	12,500
Millwall	8,512
Gillingham	8,078
Rotherham United	7,522
Walsall	6,978
Brighton and Hove Albion	6,650
Grimsby Town	5,883
Wimbledon	2,786

SECOND DIVISION

Queens Park Rangers	13,206
Cardiff City	13,050
Bristol City	11,889
Barnsley	9,757
Huddersfield Town	9,506
Plymouth Argyle	8,980
Tranmere Rovers	7,876
Wigan Athletic	7,287
Blackpool	6,990
Crewe Alexandra	6,761
Luton Town	6,746
Oldham Athletic	6,699
Notts County	6,153
Wycombe Wanderers	6,002
Brentford	5,759
Stockport County	5,488
Swindon Town	5,440
Northampton Town	5,210
Peterborough United	4,950
Mansfield Town	4,887
Cheltenham Town	4,655
Port Vale	4,436
Chesterfield	4,108
Colchester United	3,386

THIRD DIVISION

Hull City	12,843
Bristol Rovers	6,934
Oxford United	5,862
Bournemouth	5,828
Swansea City	5,159
Hartlepool United	4,943
Carlisle United	4,775
Rushden & Diamonds	4,329
Wrexham	4,265
Leyton Orient	4,257
York City	4,175
Cambridge United	4,172
Southend United	3,951
Lincoln City	3,923
Exeter City	3,762
Scunthorpe United	3,692
Shrewsbury Town	3,656
Darlington	3,312
Bury	3,226
Torquay United	3,131
Boston United	3,048
Kidderminster Harriers	2,895
Rochdale	2,739
Macclesfield Town	2,110

IN THE FIRING LINE

MANAGERIAL COMINGS AND GOINGS 2002-03

MAY 2002

13 John Hollins refuses new terms at Rochdale. Paul Simpson takes over as player-manager on May 29.

15 Five days after Stoke City's triumph in the second division play-off final, Gudjon Thordarsson departs.

27 Steve Cotterill resigns from Cheltenham Town to take over at Stoke.

31 Mick Wadsworth is dismissed by Oldham Athletic. Iain Dowie is installed the same day.

JUNE

6 Steve Coppell resigns from Brentford, to be replaced by Wally Downes.

14 Huddersfield Town sack Lou Macari while he is on holiday. Mick Wadsworth, recently departed from Oldham, takes over on July 1.

14 Watford, in dire financial straits, sack the big-spending Gianluca Vialli and replace him with Ray Lewington on July 11.

27 Leeds United announce that David O'Leary has left by "mutual consent", but it soon transpires that he was pushed. Terry Venables breezes into Elland Road on July 9.

JULY

4 Boston United, the third division newcomers, suspend Steve Evans pending an FA hearing into alleged financial irregularities. Neil Thompson is appointed caretaker manager.

9 Tranmere Rovers sack Dave Watson two days after a 7-0 defeat by Birmingham City ... in a friendly. Ray Mathias takes over on September 6.

SEPTEMBER

18 Neil Thompson, in temporary charge of Boston United, resigns, his position "untenable".

20 Steve Evans, Boston's suspended manager, resigns. Neil Thompson

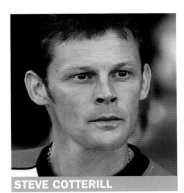

STEVE COTTERILL

TERRY YORATH

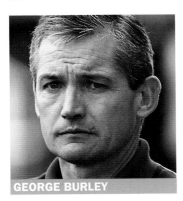

GEORGE BURLEY

withdraws his resignation the same day.

20 Nick Cusack quits as player-manager of Swansea City after the arrival of Brian Flynn as director of football.

OCTOBER

5 John Cornforth is dismissed by Exeter City, 21st in the third division. Neil McNab is appointed on October 17.

7 Peter Reid is sacked after 7½ years in charge at Sunderland, seventeenth in the Premiership. Howard Wilkinson replaces him three days later.

7 Martin Hinshelwood is sacked by Brighton after ten successive first-division defeats. Steve Coppell signs a one-year contract the same day.

9 Steve Cotterill quits Stoke City to go to Sunderland as Howard Wilkinson's No 2.

10 Jan Molby leaves Hull City. Peter Taylor takes over on October 16.

11 George Burley's near eight-year reign at Ipswich Town ends in the sack. Joe Royle moves in on October 28.

15 Barnsley, seventeenth in the second division, dismiss Steve Parkin and replace him with Glyn Hodges.

23 Darlington, seventeenth in the third division, sack Tommy Taylor and bring in Mick Tait.

31 Terry Yorath resigns from Sheffield Wednesday before he is pushed. Chris Turner appointed on November 7.

NOVEMBER

7 Chris Turner resigns from Hartlepool United in order to take over at Hillsborough. Mike Newell is appointed to succeed Turner a fortnight later.

DECEMBER

2 Mansfield Town dismiss Stuart Watkiss, Keith Curle succeeding him on December 4.

JANUARY 2003

6 A 5-0 home defeat costs Kevan Broadhurst his job at Northampton Town. Terry Fenwick takes over the next day.

13 Graham Allner's seven months in charge of Cheltenham Town end in the sack. Bobby Gould is appointed on January 22.

29 Steve Whitton leaves Colchester United by mutual consent. Phil Parkinson replaces him on February 25.

FEBRUARY

24 Terry Fenwick's reign at Northampton Town ends after seven games (won none, lost five). Martin Wilkinson is next in line.

25 Neil McNab, hired by Exeter City in October, is sacked, with the club bottom of the third division. Gary Peters replaces him the same day.

MARCH

10 Howard Wilkinson (20 league games, won two, lost 15) is sacked by Sunderland, seven points adrift of safety. Steve Cotterill goes, too, Mick McCarthy takes over two days later.

21 Leeds United announce the end of Terry Venables's reign to the Stock Exchange. The next day, Peter Reid is appointed for the final eight games of the season. He is given a one-year contract on May 9.

25 Southend United sack Rob Newman, appointing Steve Wignall on April 18.

26 Huddersfield Town, bottom of the second division, sack Mick Wadsworth and appoint Mel Machin.

APRIL

17 Jean Tigana, serving notice with Fulham, is dismissed. Chris Coleman, in caretaker charge for the last five games

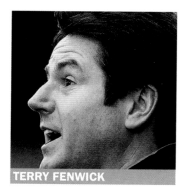

TERRY FENWICK

TREVOR FRANCIS

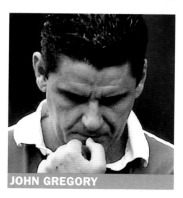

JOHN GREGORY

of the season, gets the job full time on May 15.

18 Trevor Francis leaves Crystal Palace by mutual consent. Steve Kember, the caretaker manager, gets the job on a permanent basis on May 23.

22 Dave Rushbury quits Chesterfield after being abused by fans. Roy McFarland replaces him on May 12.

24 With Glenn Roeder taken ill, Trevor Brooking takes charge for West Ham United's final three matches.

30 Kevin Ratcliffe resigns at Shrewsbury Town after their relegation to the Nationwide Conference.

MAY

7 Paul Simpson resigns from Rochdale. Alan Buckley is appointed on June 1.

9 John Gregory, suspended by Derby County since March 21, is dismissed over "serious allegations" levelled by his employer. George Burley, appointed "interim manager" on March 31, gets the job on a full-time basis on June 6.

14 Graham Taylor's second spell in charge of Aston Villa ends in his resignation. David O'Leary returns to management on May 20.

23 Joe Kinnear is sacked by Luton Town three days after a mystery consortium takes over.

30 Newly-promoted Hartlepool United fail to offer Mike Newell a new contract.

30 Terry Dolan is released by cash-strapped York City. Chris Brass, 27, becomes the youngest manager in the Football League.

JUNE

23 Mike Newell, winner of a fans' telephone poll, is appointed manager of Luton Town.

SCOTTISH FOOTBALL

CHAMPIONS
Rangers

TENNENT'S SCOTTISH CUP
Rangers

CIS INSURANCE CUP
Rangers

FIRST DIVISION
Falkirk

RUNNERS-UP
Clyde

SECOND DIVISION
Raith Rovers

RUNNERS-UP
Brechin City

THIRD DIVISION
Morton

RUNNERS-UP
East Fife

Make mine a treble: all-conquering
Rangers win the best title race . . . ever

"MONEY-MAKING AND MONEY-GRABBING." The accusation is not from 2003, but 1890. The Scottish League remains as divided by internecine feuding as it was 113 seasons ago — and just as dramatic.

The bitter words came from a critic of the league's creation over a century ago, who condemned the move towards elitism. Such talk was barely off the agenda last season as Celtic and Rangers pursued the idea of a move to England.

In the end they abandoned the project and even made up their differences with the other ten clubs in the Bank of Scotland Premierleague, who withdrew their notice to quit the SPL in protest at Old Firm demands for a greater share of television revenue — and served up the most exciting title race in the game's history. The destination of the championship was not decided until the 91st minute of the last game of the season.

The first championship was shared between Dumbarton and Rangers in 1890-91 after they had finished level on points and their play-off ended in a draw. Another play-off beckoned in 2002-03: the tickets had been printed for a showdown at Hampden Park on June 3 as Celtic and Rangers refused to be separated on the run-in.

Martin O'Neill's team showed the true hallmark of champions as the adrenalin surged through their veins after reaching the Uefa Cup final. Celtic came from eight points behind and made up an eight-goal difference in the final furlong. They went to Ibrox on April 27 knowing that defeat would see them surrender their title to Rangers and won the last derby of the season 2-1. Rangers then slipped up the following week away to Dundee, requiring a late penalty from Mikel Arteta to snatch a point. Celtic travelled to Motherwell — where both they and Rangers had lost earlier in the campaign — in midweek and won 4-0 to go top on goal difference.

The Glasgow pair swapped pole position on three more occasions as they stepped up a gear and demolished opposition in a blizzard of goals before the penultimate round of fixtures saw Rangers win 2-0 win away to Heart of Midlothian to go top by virtue of having scored one more goal — the third criteria used to determine the champions — as the title rivals entered the last weekend.

The contrast in the build-up could hardly have been greater. Rangers enjoyed a week of rest at home, free from any hype, as Celtic's first European final in 33 years hogged the limelight, before O'Neill's team returned drained by the searing heat in Seville and the trauma of losing 3-2 to FC Porto in extra time.

The importance of the occasion was underlined by the fact that the BBC, which stepped in with a rescue package to broadcast the SPL after Sky pulled out when its £45 million, four-season offer was rejected, used both terrestrial channels to screen the title deciders simultaneously. The unique experiment did not go unrewarded. Rangers floored Dunfermline Athletic 6-1 at home, but the last, vital goal — from Arteta's penalty — did not come until stoppage time. Just 25 miles away, down the A77 at Rugby Park — where the Old Firm had both previously dropped points — Celtic swept Kilmarnock aside 4-0.

For nine brief minutes, O'Neill's team controlled the destiny of the title when, at 3-0 up, they led Rangers on goal difference, but a missed penalty by Alan Thompson and Arteta's success from the spot allowed the pendulum to swing back to Ibrox once more.

It was a remarkable achievement for Alex McLeish, who had taken over as manager from Dick Advocaat 18 months earlier when Rangers were trailing 18 points in Celtic's wake. The trophy was just one of three for McLeish, who also won the Tennent's Scottish Cup and CIS Insurance Cup to become the sixth manager in Rangers' history to complete the treble.

For O'Neill and his players, to finish without any silverware was scant reward for a thrilling campaign in the Uefa Cup and SPL. However, the Celtic manager insisted: "In my first season at Celtic we won the treble and we were champions last season with a record points total — but this has been the most memorable of them all. I don't think our fans consider us to be failures."

Though Hearts finished 25 points adrift of the leading pair, it was something of a renaissance at Tynecastle. The Edinburgh club's thrilling 2-1 defeat of Celtic in April was something that neither Blackburn Rovers nor Liverpool could do to O'Neill's team in the Uefa Cup and secured European football for Craig Levein's team, despite the

Blue is the colour: Barry Ferguson, the Rangers captain, holds the trophy aloft after the conclusion to the most dramatic of title races

sale of their best asset, Antti Niemi, the goalkeeper, to Southampton for £2 million.

Motherwell finished bottom, despite their successes against the Old Firm, but Terry Butcher's side were spared relegation because Falkirk, the Bell's Scottish League first division champions, were not allowed into the top flight after failing to fulfil stadium criteria. Their ageing Brockville ground finally succumbed to the wrecking ball, but plans to share Airdrie United's all-seat Excelsior Stadium until a new ground was built were rejected by the SPL. Falkirk appealed, taking their case to the Scottish Parliament, and the accusation of a

"money-grabbing" cartel was part of the lexicon of Scottish football once more.

In truth, however, there was less money to grab. The total debt of the 12 SPL clubs soared to more than £160 million, with only Celtic making a profit. Rangers announced record losses to plunge £80 million into the red — a legacy of a decade of transfer frenzy — while clubs such as Hearts, Hibernian, Aberdeen and Dundee United radically pruned their wage-bills of expensive foreign players. That at least allowed some young Scottish talent to emerge, most notably James McFadden at Motherwell, who completed the entire season in

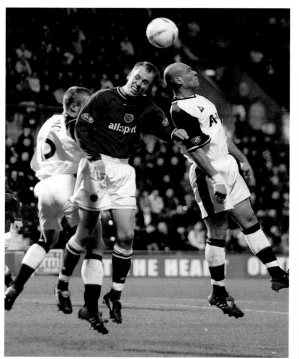

A renaissance at Tynecastle saw Hearts qualify for Europe in third

Though Barry Ferguson earned the SPL Player of the Year award for his driving force — and 18 goals — in helping Rangers to the title, Henrik Larsson continues to know no boundaries. The Celtic striker, Europe's top scorer in 2000-01, delivered another prolific campaign. His two goals in the Uefa Cup final hoisted the Swede's total to 44 goals, a figure that would have been much higher had he not broken his jaw in February. Larsson underlined his remarkable willpower by returning in only five weeks and netting a minute into his comeback, against Liverpool.

Celtic Park was truly his domain: only once did Larsson not score in a league game there — the day he suffered his injury against Livingston. Even if he never scored, though, Larsson would be a priceless asset because of his link play. It is no coincidence that his strike partner, John Hartson, hit 26 goals.

Phil Gordon

administration after John Boyle, their owner, walked away from debts of £11 million in April 2002.

Bankruptcy had stalked Raith Rovers for years. The Fife club paid a huge price for having to build a 10,000-seat stadium to be in the premier division before dropping out in 1997. However, after years of austerity, they took the second division title under the guidance of Antonio Calderon, their young Spanish manager.

The third division rivalled the top flight for title intensity. Four clubs — Morton, Peterhead, East Fife and Albion Rovers — had a chance of promotion going into the final day. Morton went up as champions, killing off Peterhead in front of nearly 9,000 fans at Cappielow — a third division record — while Albion were about to celebrate securing the runner-up position until a late goal from Kenny Deuchar, of East Fife, left spirits in Methil very much elated.

Stevie Crawford, right, who hit a total of 23 goals for Dunfermline Athletic last season, takes on Momo Sylla, the Celtic defender

LEADING SCORERS

PREMIERLEAGUE

		League	FAC	CIS	Euro	Total
Henrik Larsson	Celtic	28	2	2	12	44
John Hartson	Celtic	18	2	2	3	25
Stevie Crawford	Dunfermline	19	2	2	0	23
Ronald de Boer	Rangers	16	1	1	2	20
James McFadden	Motherwell	13	5	1	0	19
Chris Sutton	Celtic	15	0	0	4	19
Barry Ferguson	Rangers	16	2	0	0	18
*Alex Burns	Motherwell	16	0	1	0	17
Shota Arveladze	Rangers	15	1	0	0	16
Mark de Vries	Hearts	15	0	0	0	15

FIRST DIVISION

		League	FAC	CIS	Euro	Total
Dennis Wyness	Inverness CT	19	4	4	0	27
Owen Coyle	Falkirk	20	3	1	0	24
Paul Ritchie	Inverness CT	18	1	2	0	21
Lee Miller	Falkirk	16	0	1	0	17
Colin Samuel	Falkirk	11	4	1	0	16

SECOND DIVISION

		League	FAC	CIS	Euro	Total
Chris Templeman	Brechin	22	0	0	0	22
Ian Harty	Stranraer	12	4	3	0	19
Jerome Vareille	Airdrie Utd	18	1	0	0	19
Martin Bavidge	Forfar	15	3	0	0	18
Paul Tosh	Forfar	13	2	0	0	15

THIRD DIVISION

		League	FAC	CIS	Euro	Total
Alex Williams	Morton	23	3	0	0	26
Kenny Deucher	East Fife	21	0	2	0	23
Iain Stewart	Peterhead	21	0	0	0	21
Martin Johnston	Peterhead	16	0	0	0	16
Mark Dobie	Gretna	10	2	0	0	12

*Alex Burns scored all his goals for Partick Thistle

BANK OF SCOTLAND PREMIERLEAGUE

	P	W	D	L	F	A	Pts	GD
Rangers	38	31	4	3	101	28	97	+73
Celtic	38	31	4	3	98	26	97	+72
Hearts	38	18	9	11	57	51	63	+6
Kilmarnock	38	16	9	13	47	56	57	–9
Dunfermline	38	13	7	18	54	71	46	–17
Dundee	38	10	14	14	50	60	44	–10
Hibernian	38	15	6	17	56	64	51	–8
Aberdeen	38	13	10	15	41	54	49	–13
Livingston	38	9	8	21	48	62	35	–14
Partick	38	8	11	19	37	58	35	–21
Dundee Utd	38	7	11	20	35	68	32	–33
Motherwell	38	7	7	24	45	71	28	–26

BELL'S SCOTTISH LEAGUE FIRST DIVISION

	P	W	D	L	F	A	Pts	GD
Falkirk	36	25	6	5	80	32	81	+48
Clyde	36	21	9	6	66	37	72	+29
St Johnstone	36	20	7	9	49	29	67	+20
Inverness CT	36	20	5	11	74	45	65	+29
Queen of South	36	12	12	12	45	48	48	–3
Ayr	36	12	9	15	34	44	45	–10
St Mirren	36	9	10	17	42	71	37	–29
Ross County	36	9	8	19	42	46	35	–4
Alloa	36	9	8	19	39	72	35	–33
Arbroath	36	3	6	27	30	77	15	–47

SECOND DIVISION

	P	W	D	L	F	A	Pts	GD
Raith	36	16	11	9	53	36	59	+17
Brechin	36	16	7	13	63	59	55	+4
Airdrie Utd	36	14	12	10	51	44	54	+7
Forfar	36	14	9	13	55	53	51	+2
Berwick	36	13	10	13	43	48	49	–5
Dumbarton	36	13	9	14	48	47	48	+1
Stenhousemuir	36	12	11	13	49	51	47	–2
Hamilton	36	12	11	13	43	48	47	–5
Stranraer	36	12	8	16	49	57	44	–8
Cowdenbeath	36	8	12	16	46	57	36	–11

THIRD DIVISION

	P	W	D	L	F	A	Pts	GD
Morton	36	21	9	6	67	33	72	+34
East Fife	36	20	11	5	73	37	71	+36
Albion	36	20	10	6	62	36	70	+26
Peterhead	36	20	8	8	76	37	68	+39
Stirling	36	15	11	10	50	44	56	+6
Gretna	36	11	12	13	50	50	45	0
Montrose	36	7	12	17	35	61	33	–26
Queen's Park	36	7	11	18	39	51	32	–12
Elgin	36	5	13	18	33	63	28	–30
East Stirling	36	2	7	27	32	105	13	–73

Rangers 1   Celtic 2
Ibrox, Sunday April 27 2003
Phil Gordon

THE WIND OF CHANGE SWEPT through Martin O'Neill's thoughts yesterday — and blew the Bank of Scotland Premierleague title race wide open. The Celtic manager stopped being a creature of habit and abandoned his long-held principles to fashion a victory at Ibrox that breathes new life into the championship run-in.

Switching from 3-5-2 to 4-4-2 is not exactly radical, but it is for O'Neill, who has never deviated from his preferred back three since he walked into Celtic Park almost three years ago — even more so when the title was on the line.

Celtic not only crossed Glasgow and won the last Old Firm league game of the season, thanks to a penalty from Alan Thompson and a consummate finish by John Hartson in the first half, to narrow the gap on their rivals, but they did so when their nerve and their limbs were being questioned.

Just 58 hours after stepping off a plane from Portugal, O'Neill's players conjured a result and a performance many thought beyond them to trim Rangers' lead to five points, but with a match in hand. Ronald de Boer's header made it an intriguing last half-hour, but though Rangers are only four wins away from the finishing line, they appeared more drained than Celtic.

The Uefa Cup final was too much of a distraction for O'Neill's team, it had been claimed. The energy-sapping game with Boavista would have taken too great a toll. Celtic's recent dropped points against Heart of Midlothian and Dundee, along with the defeat in the Tennent's Scottish Cup by Inverness Caledonian Thistle, was the work of a side that had taken its eye off the domestic ball, argued others.

How wrong we all were. Celtic looked in no mood yesterday to abandon their pursuit of a third successive championship as they wrecked Rangers' unbeaten home record.

O'Neill has been under fierce scrutiny over his recent Old Firm record, with just one win in eight derbies against Alex McLeish before yesterday. The shrewdness of the Rangers manager in opting for a bold 4-3-3 unit has inflicted substantial damage over the past 14 months since he attained his inaugural win.

Heading for a showdown: Celtic keep the race alive

Yesterday, Celtic not only shut the back door with the introduction of Jackie McNamara — who went from the bench to captain in one move — and Ulrik Laursen in a back four alongside Bobo Balde and Joos Valgaeren, but they also exploited the space left by their counterparts at the other end.

Even without the rugged Johan Mjallby and Paul Lambert, the captain, who succumbed to injuries sustained against Boavista, Celtic possessed more muscle than Rangers, more ruthlessness in finishing, and even protected Javier Broto, the substitute goalkeeper, who was given an unexpected derby baptism after Robert Douglas damaged his groin after eight minutes.

"We wanted to try and win the game," O'Neill reflected later. "There was no point in doing anything else and, with the players we had left, I had to adjust.

"But it's nothing to do with tactics. It is about character and determination and I told my players later that they were terrific. Obviously, the championship is still within Rangers' grasp, but they have a lot of difficult games left and we have kept it alive."

Yet Celtic could easily have been behind after just two minutes when Claudio Caniggia slipped clear, thanks to De Boer's vision, and lobbed the ball over the advancing Douglas, but without the accuracy to find the empty net. Lorenzo Amoruso then thumped a header over the bar and the siege had not relented by the time that Broto took over.

Barry Ferguson was cut down by Valgaeren outside the box, allowing the Rangers captain a free kick which stole through the wall and fell into the path of De Boer, but the Holland player tugged his right-foot shot wide from eight yards.

Larsson, though, was finding equally threatening amounts of space between the Rangers defenders and it took Craig Moore's vigilant slide tackle in the box to rescue Rangers.

Rangers then survived a scare in the 26th minute, when McNamara's deep free kick was allowed to travel, without a touch from any player on either side, into the danger area. It even passed Stefan Klos, the goalkeeper, who knew little about it as the ball spun back

off the post and rebounded off his chest before Moore scrambled it clear.

However, there would be a reprieve for Klos two minutes later. Larsson robbed Ferguson and spread play out to Hartson, who ran at Amoruso, only for the defender naively to leave his body in the way and concede a penalty, which Thompson swept past Klos with his left boot, sending the goalkeeper the wrong way.

Three minutes before half-time, Celtic doubled their lead with a sweeping move. Didier Agathe and Hartson exchanged passes on the right, allowing the winger to skip past Arthur Numan's challenge and reach the byline, where his cutback was deftly touched on by Larsson for Hartson to score his first goal since that night at Anfield five weeks ago, by drilling a right-foot shot past Klos from ten yards for his 25th goal of the season.

Celtic had the spark, Rangers appeared one-paced and with Neil Lennon and Chris Sutton patrolling the midfield, there was little space for the leaders to find their passing fluency.

However, no team ever dominates an Old Firm game for 90 minutes. Rangers' pride carried them over the immense barrier that Celtic presented and De Boer halved the deficit in the 57th minute. Agathe failed to spot Numan's dash down the left and the Dutch defender found his compatriot with a fine cross that allowed De Boer to beat Broto with a downward header for his eighteenth goal of the season.

Yet it failed to reignite Rangers. There was another chance for De Boer, but his tame shot was saved by Broto and Celtic protected their stand-in goalkeeper as they ran the clock down. Indeed, it was Klos who prevented further scoring when he denied Larsson in the dying minutes. Celtic, though, are far from dead and Rangers are entering nervous territory.

RANGERS (4-3-3): S Klos — F Ricksen, C Moore, L Amoruso, A Numan — R de Boer, B Ferguson, B Konterman (sub: M Arteta, ht) — C Caniggia (sub: N McCann, 71), M Mols, P Lovenkrands (sub: S Thompson, 81). **Substitutes not used:** A McGregor, M Ross. **Booked:** Moore, De Boer, Lovenkrands.

CELTIC (4-4-2): R Douglas (sub: J Broto, 8) — J McNamara, B Balde, J Valgaeren, U Laursen — D Agathe, N Lennon, C Sutton, A Thompson — H Larsson, J Hartson (sub: S Petrov, 66). **Substitutes not used:** S Maloney, J Smith, S Crainey. **Booked:** Sutton, Hartson, Agathe.

Referee: H Dallas.

Redemption man: Amoruso turns to receive the acclaim of the Rangers fans at Ibrox after the defender, stripped of the captaincy by the previous manager, had headed the only goal of the Tennent's Scottish Cup final against Dundee

CIS INSURANCE CUP

SEMI-FINALS (Hampden Park)

Tuesday February 4
HEARTS (0) **0**   **RANGERS** (1) **1**
31,609   De Boer 27

Thursday February 6
CELTIC (0) **3**   **DUNDEE UTD** (0) **0**
Balde 52, 90   18,856
Larsson 80

FINAL (Hampden Park)

Sunday March 16
CELTIC (0) **1**   **RANGERS** (2) **2**
Larsson 57   Caniggia 23
52,000   Lovenkrands 35

Rangers take the first step towards the treble, but Celtic are left wondering what might have been after John Hartson has an equaliser wrongly disallowed and misses a last-minute penalty.

CELTIC (3-5-2): R Douglas — J Mjallby (sub: S Petrov, 88min), B Balde, J Valgaeren — J Smith (sub: M Sylla, 66), P Lambert, N Lennon, C Sutton (sub: S Maloney, 80), A Thompson — H Larsson, J Hartson. **Substitutes not used:** J McNamara, D Marshall. **Booked:** Lennon, Thompson. **Sent off:** Lennon.
RANGERS (4-3-3): S Klos — F Ricksen, C Moore, L Amoruso, J Bonnissei (sub: M Ross, 64) — R de Boer (sub: S Arveladze, 86), B Ferguson, M Arteta (sub: B Konterman, 78) — C Caniggia, M Mols, P Lovenkrands. **Substitutes not used:** N McCann, A McGregor. **Booked:** Amoruso.
Referee: K Clark.

TENNENT'S SCOTTISH CUP

SEMI-FINALS (Hampden Park)

Saturday April 19
RANGERS (1) **4**   **MOTHERWELL** (2) **3**
Konterman 2, Mols 56   Craig 15, McFadden 27
Amoruso 60, Partridge 73 (og) Adams 90
29,352

Sunday April 20
INVERNESS CT (0) **0**   **DUNDEE** (0) **1**
14,429   Nemsadze 78

FINAL (Hampden Park)

Saturday May 31
DUNDEE (0) **0**   **RANGERS** (0) **1**
47,136   Amoruso 66

Alex McLeish became the sixth Rangers manager to achieve the treble but admitted that the club would have to go on winning trophies if his reign was not to turn sour. That happened to Dick Advocaat, who also won the treble in 1998-99, and it was Lorenzo Amoruso, a symbol of Advocaat's subsequent decline, whose goal decided a taut final. The Italian defender was stripped of the captaincy by Advocaat amid a dressing-room atmosphere of bitching that eclipsed *Big Brother*, but he rose to thump home the decisive header from Neil McCann's free kick. However, had Barry Smith not hit the inside of the post with a third-minute volley that left Stefan Klos well beaten, Dundee may have gone on to lift the trophy for the first time in 93 years.

DUNDEE (4-3-1-2): J Speroni — D Mackay (sub: S Milne, 77min), L Mair, Z Khizanishvili, J Hernandez — G Rae (sub: G Brady, 84), G Nemsadze, B Smith — M Burchill (sub: N Novo, 70) — F Caballero, S Lovell. **Substitutes not used:** J Langfield, B Carranza. **Booked:** Novo.
RANGERS (4-4-2): S Klos — F Ricksen, L Amoruso, C Moore, A Numan (sub: K Muscat, 69) — S Arveladze (sub: S Thompson, 55), B Ferguson, R Malcolm, N McCann — R de Boer, M Mols (sub: M Ross, ht). **Substitutes not used:** A McGregor, S McLean. **Booked:** Arveladze, McCann.
Referee: K Clark.

NON-LEAGUE

NATIONWIDE CONFERENCE
Yeovil Town

PROMOTED VIA PLAY-OFFS
Doncaster Rovers

FA TROPHY
Burscough

FA VASE
Brigg Town

DR MARTENS LEAGUE
Tamworth

UNIBOND LEAGUE
Accrington Stanley

RYMAN LEAGUE
Aldershot Town

Up where we belong: Yeovil Town rejoice in a long-awaited step up to the League

FINAL TABLES

NATIONWIDE CONFERENCE

	P	W	D	L	F	A	Pts
Yeovil	42	28	11	3	100	37	95
Morecambe	42	23	9	10	86	42	78
Doncaster	42	22	12	8	73	47	78
Chester	42	21	12	9	59	31	75
Dag & Red	42	21	9	12	71	59	72
Hereford	42	19	7	16	64	51	64
Scarborough	42	18	10	14	63	54	64
Halifax	42	18	10	14	50	51	64
Forest Green	42	17	8	17	61	62	59
Margate	42	15	11	16	60	66	56
Barnet	42	13	14	15	65	68	53
Stevenage	42	14	10	18	61	55	52
Farnborough	42	13	12	17	57	56	51
Northwich	42	13	12	17	66	72	51
Telford	42	14	7	21	54	69	49
Burton Albion	42	13	10	19	52	77	49
Gravesend	42	12	12	18	62	73	48
Leigh RMI	42	14	6	22	44	71	48
Woking	42	11	14	17	52	81	47
Nuneaton	42	13	7	22	51	78	46
Southport	42	11	12	19	54	69	45
Kettering	42	8	7	27	37	73	31

YEOVIL TOWN'S PROMOTION to the Nationwide League should have been the abiding image of the season. The resounding quality of their football. The enthusiasm of their green-and-white clad supporters. Yet, week after week, the headlines were stolen by the activities of the Nationwide Conference administrators.

Having secured the prize of a second promotion place, there was first the matter of setting up the play-offs. They proved a notable success. Nothing about Yeovil's triumph could match the drama that saw Doncaster Rovers clinch their return to the League with a "promotion goal" in extra time at the Britannia Stadium. Then there was the politics. Under the courteous but hard-headed stewardship of John Moules, their chief executive, the Conference has reinvented itself as the fifth division. At the same time it is also seeking to change the landscape of non-league football.

By threatening to go it alone, the Conference pushed the FA into accepting a proposal for north and south feeder divisions. Two of their representatives and two each from the existing feeders — the Dr Martens League, the UniBond League and the Ryman League — formed a Football Alliance to establish the criteria for admission to the new divisions. To round off a momentous season, the Conference decided in June that teams falling into administration should be docked 12 points. Clubs will not be allowed to spend more than 65 per cent of their turnover on players' wages.

The Conference suffered one rebuff. The clubs voted in March to expand its ranks to 24 for next season. Only one club would have been relegated, which it had long been clear would have been Kettering Town, the lame duck of the campaign. The FA said no. Attention duly focused, the relegation struggle proved gripping. On the final Saturday, Southport and Nuneaton Borough, seemingly secure only weeks before, went down. Woking, by gaining a victory after a record run of nine draws, and Leigh RMI stayed up.

The narrow survival of Farnborough Town concluded the season's most extraordinary soap opera. The Hampshire club was thrust centre stage when drawn at home to Arsenal in the fourth round of the FA Cup. After two days of inflated debate, the tie was switched to Highbury. Farnborough lost 5-1 but acquitted themselves well. Three days later, Graham Westley, the club's owner and manager, decamped and resurfaced immediately as the manager of Stevenage Borough.

Westley maintained that he had not left Farnborough in the lurch, that despite his messy departure they were in better shape than when he took over in 1999. It was just that it did not seem so at the time. Seven players followed Westley to Broadhall Way. Ian

PLAYER OF THE SEASON
John Ryan

He was on the pitch for only four minutes. He did not touch the ball. Yet who could argue against John Ryan? The owner of Doncaster Rovers decided that £4 million put into the club entitled him to fulfil his lifelong ambition. So in the final league match of the season, away to Hereford United, Ryan, at 52 years and 360 days, trotted on to the grass and into football history — and in doing so proved that the Nationwide Conference had not entirely sold its non-league soul to professionalism

Walter Gammie

McDonald, the Farnborough caretaker manager, was unable to sign any replacements because of a transfer embargo that was a legacy from Westley. To keep them up was a considerable achievement. McDonald's reward was to be replaced by Tommy Taylor, a long-time friend of Victor Searle, the new owner. McDonald agreed to stay on as coach. Westley, meanwhile, made a good start. Taking over Stevenage with the club next to bottom, he lifted them to safety with a run of six victories.

Other candidates for the manager of the season abound. Terry Brown, previously successful with Hayes, in 1996, proved equal to the task that had unseated George Borg by sending Aldershot Town galloping to the Ryman League title. Darron Gee healed the wound of the previous season, when the title was snatched from their grasp on the final day, by taking Tamworth to the Dr Martens League title. John Coleman brought Accrington Stanley the UniBond League crown and took them to one step away from regaining the Football League place lost by its predecessor club in 1962.

Colin Addison dragged Forest Green Rovers out of the mire, while Jim Harvey and Mark Wright endured bitter disappointment as Morecambe and Chester City were beaten in penalty shoot-outs in the play-off semi-finals. Harvey can take pride in making the most of Morecambe's new full-time status. Wright ensured that Chester became a feared force. But the biggest blow was taken on the chin by Garry Hill. After yet another Cup run and a record string of 11 Conference victories that ignited a slow start, the play-off defeat for Dagenham & Redbridge was tough to take.

For every loser, of course, there is a winner and the palm has to go to Gary Johnson. Since their win over Sunderland in 1949, Yeovil had been the most famous name in non-league football. The nation had applauded as they took their Cup victims to a record 20, but expected more. Johnson made it happen. With a sure touch, he made the right moves at the right times. The joy in Somerset was unconfined. The pleasure was felt throughout the land.

DR MARTENS LEAGUE
PREMIER DIVISION

	P	W	D	L	F	A	Pts
Tamworth	42	26	10	6	73	32	88
Stafford R	42	21	12	9	76	40	75
Dover	42	19	14	9	42	35	71
Tiverton Tn	42	19	12	11	60	43	69
Chippenham Tn	42	17	17	8	59	37	68
Worcester C	42	18	13	11	60	39	67
Crawley Tn	42	17	13	12	64	51	64
Havant and W	42	15	15	12	67	64	60
Chelmsford	42	15	12	15	65	63	57
Newport Co	42	15	11	16	53	52	56
Hednesford	42	14	13	15	59	60	55
Moor Green	42	13	14	15	49	58	53
Hinckley U	42	12	16	14	61	64	52
Bath City	42	13	13	16	50	61	52
Welling	42	13	12	17	55	58	51
Grantham Town	42	14	9	19	59	65	51
Weymouth	42	12	15	15	44	62	51
Cambridge C	42	13	10	19	54	56	49
Halesowen	42	12	13	17	52	63	49
Hastings Utd	42	10	13	19	44	57	43
Ilkeston Tn	42	10	10	22	54	92	40
Folkestone I	42	7	7	28	57	105	28

EASTERN DIVISION

	P	W	D	L	F	A	Pts
Dorchester Town	42	28	9	5	114	40	93
Eastbourne Bor	42	29	6	7	92	33	93
Stamford	42	27	6	9	80	39	87
Salisbury City	42	27	8	7	81	42	86
Bashley	42	23	12	7	90	44	81
King's Lynn	42	24	7	11	98	62	79
Rothwell Town	42	22	10	10	77	52	76
Banbury United	42	21	11	10	75	50	74
Tonbridge Angels	42	20	11	11	71	54	71
Histon	42	20	7	15	99	62	67
Ashford Town	42	18	9	15	63	57	63
Sittingbourne	42	15	8	19	57	69	53
Burnham	42	15	7	20	62	79	52
Fisher Ath	42	15	5	22	57	80	50
Chatham Town	42	14	5	23	54	84	47
Newport (IOW)	42	12	6	24	53	87	42
Dartford	42	11	8	23	48	78	41
Erith & Belvedere	42	11	6	25	65	96	39
Corby Town	42	9	11	22	48	84	38
Fleet Town	42	8	8	26	34	80	32
Spalding United	42	4	6	32	40	108	18
St Leonards	42	4	4	34	38	116	16

WESTERN DIVISION

	P	W	D	L	F	A	Pts
Merthyr Tydfil	42	28	8	6	78	32	92
Weston-s-Mare	42	26	7	9	77	42	85
Bromsgrove Rov	42	23	7	12	73	41	76
Solihull Borough	42	21	13	8	77	48	76
Gloucester City	42	22	9	11	87	59	75
Mangotsfield Utd	42	21	10	11	106	53	73
Redditch United	42	22	6	14	76	42	72
Rugby United	42	20	9	13	58	43	69
Gresley Rovers	42	19	10	13	63	54	67
Taunton Town	42	20	7	15	76	78	67
Sutton Coldfield T	42	18	10	14	63	53	64
Evesham United	42	19	6	17	76	72	63
Clevedon Town	42	14	13	15	54	60	55
Cirencester Town	42	15	7	20	62	82	52
Cinderford Town	42	13	12	17	51	67	51
Shepshed Dynamo	42	12	6	24	48	76	42
Stourport Swifts	42	10	11	21	48	66	41
Bedworth United	42	11	7	24	46	74	40
Swindon S	42	11	5	26	52	85	38
Atherstone United	42	9	10	23	45	78	37
Rocester	42	9	10	23	34	74	37
Racing Club Warwck	42	3	9	30	33	104	18

UNIBOND LEAGUE

	P	W	D	L	F	A	Pts
Accrington S	44	30	10	4	97	44	100
Barrow	44	24	12	8	84	52	84
Vauxhall M	44	22	10	12	81	46	76
Stalybridge	44	21	13	10	77	51	76
Worksop	44	21	9	14	82	67	72
Harrogate Tn	44	21	8	15	75	63	71
Bradford P A	44	20	10	14	73	70	70
Hucknall Tn	44	17	15	12	72	62	66
Droylsden	44	18	10	16	62	52	64
Whitby	44	17	12	15	80	69	63
Marine	44	17	10	17	63	60	61
Wkfld & Emley	44	14	18	12	46	49	60
Runcorn	44	15	15	14	69	74	60
Altrincham	44	17	9	18	58	63	60
Gainsboro	44	16	11	17	67	66	59
Ashton Utd	44	15	13	16	71	79	58
Lancaster	44	16	9	19	71	75	57
Burscough	44	14	9	21	44	51	51
Blyth S	44	14	9	21	67	87	51
Frickley	44	13	8	23	45	78	47
Gateshead	44	10	11	23	60	81	41
Colwyn Bay	44	5	9	30	52	99	24
Hyde	44	5	8	31	40	98	23

FIRST DIVISION

	P	W	D	L	F	A	Pts
Alfreton Town	42	26	9	7	106	59	87
Spennymoor Utd	42	27	6	9	81	42	87
Radcliffe Borough	42	25	10	7	90	46	85
North Ferriby Utd	42	23	9	10	78	45	78
Chorley	42	21	10	11	80	51	73
Witton Albion	42	19	15	8	67	50	72
Belper Town	41	20	12	9	53	42	72
Matlock Town	42	20	10	12	67	48	70
Leek Town	42	20	9	13	63	46	69
Workington	42	19	10	13	73	60	67
Farsley Celtic	42	17	11	14	66	67	62
Kendal Town	42	18	7	17	68	58	61
Bamber Bridge	42	15	9	18	55	59	54
Guiseley	40	13	10	17	65	61	49
Bishop Auckland	42	13	10	19	58	83	49
Lincoln United	42	12	9	21	67	77	45
Stocksbridge PS	41	11	9	21	52	78	42
Rossendale United	42	12	5	25	58	88	41
Kidsgrove Athletic	42	9	11	22	49	71	38
Ossett Town	42	8	9	25	39	80	33
Eastwood Town	42	5	8	29	33	92	23
Trafford	42	5	6	31	34	99	21

MATCH OF THE SEASON

Doncaster Rovers 3   Dagenham & Redbridge 2 (aet)
Britannia Stadium, Saturday May 10 2003
Mark Venables

FIVE YEARS AFTER THEY WERE relegated from the Football League, Doncaster Rovers are back, courtesy of a "promotion goal", as the Nationwide Conference has copyrighted the golden goal, by Francis Tierney that ended a valiant fightback from Dagenham & Redbridge in the inaugural Nationwide Conference promotion final at the Britannia Stadium on Saturday. However, on such a momentous afternoon, once again the club's reputation was tainted by the behaviour of an element of their supporters.

The restart was delayed twice after some Doncaster supporters invaded the pitch. They did so again after Tierney's winning goal, this time in larger numbers, with several hundred running to confront Dagenham's fans. Only their restraint and a heavy police presence, unprecedented in non-league football, prevented the situation deteriorating further. As it was, the post-match ceremonies were held up as the pitch was cleared.

Such concerns were far from the mind of Dave Penney as he basked in the glow of success, just 14 months after taking over the managerial reins at Belle Vue.

"I think this one, getting into the Football League, is the second biggest promotion issue aside from division one to the Premiership," he said. "No disrespect to the Conference, but we will be playing at the likes of Huddersfield, Lincoln, Scunthorpe, York and Mansfield instead of Forest Green, Tamworth or Margate."

With an hour played, Doncaster were two goals to the good and cruising, outclassing their opponents on the pitch and outnumbering their supporters in the stand — in excess of 9,000 of the 13,092 supported the Yorkshire club.

Paul Green headed Doncaster in front after Tim Ryan's teasing cross had found him unmarked six yards out. Ten minutes into the second period it appeared to be all over when Dave Morley rose to head a corner from Tierney past the despairing efforts of John McGrath and Tony Roberts.

Dagenham are not the sort of side to accept defeat easily and when Mark Stein latched on to a flicked header from Steve West and slipped the ball under the advancing Andy Warrington, the game was back on.

With 12 minutes left it was all square, Tarkan Mustafa beating Tierney to Paul Terry's defence-splitting pass and guiding the ball past Warrington's dive and inside the far post.

As extra timed progressed, heavy legs were beginning to take their toll when Tierney, the former Crewe Alexandra midfield player, swept a cross from Paul Barnes past Roberts to bring the curtain down on a pulsating final. It was a gratifying end to a

Doncaster's scorers, from left Tierney, Morley and Green, glory in their victory

season blighted by injury for the Liverpool-born player, who had missed four months with a snapped Achilles. "I was running towards the goal with their lad and I knew that if I just got in front of him and the ball was anywhere along the six-yard box it was going in the net," Tierney said.

They say that lightning doesn't strike twice, but don't remind Garry Hill. It is the second consecutive season that Dagenham have missed out on promotion by the smallest of margins. Last year, Boston United beat them on goal difference in acrimonious circumstances — they were later fined and docked points for making illegal payments to players — and Tierney's strike consigned them to a double dose of distress.

"When you see the players at the end of the game it's clear that this is the hardest blow that we've had in my years as manager," Hill said. "It's very hard, but I've got to try and lead by example. It will probably affect me more tomorrow."

DONCASTER ROVERS (4-4-2): A Warrington — S Marples, D Morley, S Foster, T Ryan — J Paterson (sub: J Blunt, 83min), P Green, R Ravenhill, F Tierney — T Whitman (sub: G Blundell, 83), P Barnes. **Substitutes not used:** J Doolan, M Albrighton, S Nelson. **Booked:** Ryan, Ravenhill.

DAGENHAM & REDBRIDGE (4-4-2): A Roberts — L Goodwin (sub: M Smith, 70), L Matthews, T Cole, T Mustafa — J McGrath (sub: A Vickers, 70), D Shipp, P Terry (sub: S Heffer, 94), M Janney — S West, M Stein. **Substitutes not used:** P Gothard, D Hill. **Booked:** Matthews, McGrath, Smith.

Referee: A Marriner.

RYMAN LEAGUE
PREMIER DIVISION

	P	W	D	L	F	A	Pts
Aldershot	46	33	6	7	81	36	105
Canvey I	46	28	8	10	112	56	92
Hendon	46	22	13	11	70	56	79
St Albans	46	23	8	15	73	65	77
Basingstoke	46	23	7	16	80	60	76
Sutton Utd	46	22	9	15	77	62	75
Hayes	46	20	13	13	67	54	73
Purfleet	46	19	15	12	68	48	72
Bedford Tn	46	21	9	16	66	58	72
Maidenhead	46	16	17	13	75	63	65
Kingstonian	46	16	17	13	71	64	65
Billericay	46	17	11	18	46	44	62
B Stortford	46	16	11	19	74	72	59
Hitchin	46	15	13	18	69	67	58
Ford Utd	46	15	12	19	78	84	57
Braintree Tn	46	14	12	20	59	71	54
Aylesbury Utd	46	13	15	18	62	75	54
Harrow Boro	46	15	9	22	54	75	54
Grays Ath	46	14	11	21	53	59	53
Heybridge	46	13	14	19	52	80	53
Chesham	46	14	10	22	56	81	52
Boreham Wd	46	11	15	20	50	58	48
Enfield	46	9	11	26	47	101	38
Hampton & R	46	3	14	29	35	86	23

NORTH DIVISION

	P	W	D	L	F	A	Pts
Northwood	46	28	7	11	109	56	91
Hornchurch	46	25	15	6	85	48	90
Hemel Hempstead	46	26	7	13	70	55	85
Slough Town	46	22	14	10	86	59	80
Uxbridge	46	23	10	13	62	41	79
Aveley	46	21	14	11	66	48	77
Berkhamsted Tn	46	21	13	12	92	68	76
Thame United	46	20	12	14	84	51	72
Wealdstone	46	21	9	16	85	69	72
Harlow Town	46	20	12	14	66	53	72
Marlow	46	19	10	17	74	63	67
Barking & East Ham	46	19	9	18	73	76	66
Yeading	46	18	11	17	77	69	65
Great Wakering Rov	46	17	14	15	64	70	65
Oxford City	46	17	13	16	55	51	64
Arlesey Town	46	17	12	17	69	71	63
East Thurrock Utd	46	17	10	19	75	79	61
Wingate & Finchley	46	15	11	20	70	74	56
Barton Rovers	46	15	7	24	53	65	52
Tilbury	46	14	7	25	55	96	49
Wivenhoe Town	46	9	11	26	56	94	38
Leyton Pennant	46	9	7	30	38	81	34
Wembley	46	7	11	28	57	111	32
Hertford Town	46	6	6	34	46	119	24

SOUTH DIVISION

	P	W	D	L	F	A	Pts
Carshalton Ath	46	28	8	10	73	44	92
Bognor Regis Tn	46	26	10	10	92	34	88
Lewes	46	24	16	6	106	50	88
Dulwich Hamlet	46	23	12	11	73	49	81
Whyteleafe	46	21	13	12	74	51	76
Bromley	46	21	13	12	70	53	76
Walton & Hersham	46	20	13	13	87	63	73
Horsham	46	21	9	16	80	58	72
Epsom & Ewell	46	19	12	15	67	66	69
Egham Town	46	19	10	17	62	71	67
Tooting & Mitcham	46	18	9	19	83	78	63
Worthing	46	17	12	17	78	75	63
Windsor & Eton	46	18	9	19	66	65	63
Leatherhead	46	16	13	17	71	66	61
Staines Town	46	14	16	16	57	63	58
Banstead Athletic	46	14	15	17	58	59	57
Ashford Town (Mx)	46	14	11	21	47	70	53
Croydon	46	15	8	23	56	87	53
Croydon Athletic	46	13	13	20	52	66	52
Bracknell Town	46	12	16	18	57	74	52
Corinthian-Casuals	46	12	14	20	50	68	50
Molesey	46	13	9	24	52	79	48
Metropolitan Police	46	12	10	24	50	76	46
Chertsey Town	46	3	7	36	43	139	16

WIMBLEDON COMMONERS

NIGEL HENDERSON

"IT'S MY F****** TEAM, not yours Charlie Koppel." As an expression of eloquence it had all the subtlety of a Vinnie Jones tackle, but the cry of one supporter within moments of our opening Combined Counties League match provided a neat synopsis of what AFC Wimbledon was about.

Few of the 2,500 of us who had swelled Sandhurst's average attendance of 60 that warm August day could even put names to our players, but of greater importance was the fact that we had reclaimed our club from those who had treated it like a plaything or, misguidedly, thought that they could make money from it.

The concept of a renegade "Real Wimbledon" had first been mooted some years earlier when Sam Hammam, then the owner, had flirted with the idea of relocating to Dublin. But, when it happened, it was with a speed and sense of purpose that few could have anticipated. After

the FA commission decided to back the plans of Koppel, the chairman, to move to Milton Keynes, the clamour for change was strong — change that would broadcast a message of defiance in response to its laughable assertion that such action by the fans "was not in the interests of football"; franchising, however, obviously was. But also, by reverting to the bottom of the non-league pyramid, newer fans would be able to experience something of the essence of the club, while those of earlier vintage could revisit what they counted as their personal histories.

Sandhurst played at Bottom Meadow — as the name suggests, pretty enough, but essentially the type of roped-off parkland that most members of the CCL called home. It was no Plough Lane, which had been a decent Southern League stadium before we were forced to decamp to Selhurst Park, but what it did have in common with our spiritual home was a welcoming atmosphere, an atmosphere that was to be found amid most of the

You're in the army now: fans of AFC Wimbledon welcome their team out at Sandhurst's ground. Meanwhile (right), back at Selhurst . . .

byways of Surrey, Hampshire and Berkshire. In part because of this, the longer the season went on, the less we seemed to miss consorting with the game's aristocracy.

Who needed Old Trafford, its prawn sandwiches nibbled behind a glass partition, when you could scoop heaps of home-made lamb korma from a paper plate as you watched your side from an earthy mound as the sun set over Southall? Who needed Stamford Bridge when you could wander alongside the Thames before enjoying a closely fought cup-tie with Walton Casuals? It was certainly a pleasant change from what we were used to: a long, dreary train journey to a soulless stadium, culminating in a grim greeting from stewards who looked as if they would sooner smite you than show you to your seat. And that was just Selhurst Park.

There were other gratifying differences. We were no longer outnumbered by opposition supporters on our "own" turf, in this case the Kingsmeadow stadium we rented from Kingstonian; we were able to put something back into the grassroots teams, run on the goodwill of volunteers much fewer in number than our own; and we began to win regularly, sometimes by quite a few goals, all the time reassured to be standing alongside faces familiar to us from years at Plough Lane and Selhurst.

None of us had known what to expect of the CCL, but those who thought it would be a romp were swiftly disabused of the notion. Our squad, culled from 230 hopefuls who attended trials on Wimbledon Common, took its time to gel while our opponents, inspired by the sight of 3,000 people packed into Kingsmeadow, seemed to raise their games. As the standard of football proved to be better than we had dared hope, we became increasingly appreciative of the fact that a good goal was a good goal, whether sculpted at the Bernabeu or Bedfont.

Ten points from the first seven games was a return that probably cost us promotion to the Ryman League, but it was then that a club was emerging in reality as well as name. Volunteers, from the chairman down to fans selling merchandise from the back of a converted ambulance — the Wombulance — worked feverishly to make a success of things, while we began to develop a strange, symbiotic relationship with the players.

Receiving little financial reward, they were, in effect,

playing for love; love of the game, yes, but also the love of supporters desperate to start again after our rejection — and desperate not to be disappointed.

Not that all was rosy in the AFC Wimbledon garden: troublemakers unaffiliated to either side infiltrated a crucial match away to AFC Wallingford in November, the brief fighting that followed producing the unwelcome sight of a police helicopter hovering overhead for the second half. Then successive — and surprising — defeats in late January led to a wringing of hands on the club's internet chat sites, blame and counter-blame careering across cyberspace until Terry Eames, the manager (and a Wimbledon player in the late Seventies) entered the argument by offering to quit.

It was an action that brought us, ever grateful for the sacrifices he had made, to our senses, the defining moment in a season of a series of them, perhaps. It was the catalyst for a run of 14 wins in the last 15 games, not quite enough to deprive Withdean 2000, 31 games without defeat, of the title, nor Wallingford, whose 3-2 defeat at Kingsmeadow in March was the footballing highlight of the year, of second place. But it served to remind us of the special thing we had worked so hard to establish, and how easily we could throw it away.

FA VASE

SEMI-FINALS: First legs: Oadby Town 0 Brigg Town 2 (Drayton 61, Roach 73); Maldon Town 0 AFC Sudbury 1 (Wall 76 og). **Second legs:** Brigg Town 1 (Carter 15 pen) Oadby Town 1 (Horner 7). *Brigg win 3-1 on aggregate*. AFC Sudbury 2 (Claydon, 67, 80) Maldon Town 0. *AFC Sudbury win 3-0 on aggregate*

FINAL (Upton Park)

BRIGG TOWN (1) **2**   **AFC SUDBURY** (1) **1**
Housham 3, Carter 68   Rayner 30
6,634

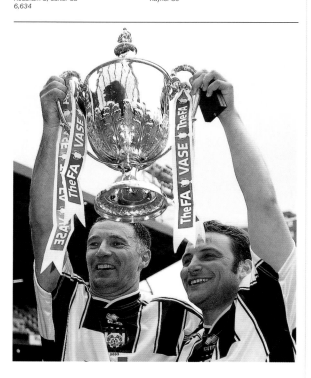

For the second time in seven years the FA Vase was won by Brigg Town. The team that beat Sudbury Town at Upton Park did not have the panache of the side that demolished Clitheroe 3-0 in 1996, but what it did have was the same astute guiding hand in Ralph Clayton. Lincolnshire's own larger-than-life legend won a duel of veteran managers with Keith Martin, the millionaire businessman who gave his time to football for nothing. He went into retirement empty-handed.

AFC SUDBURY (4-4-2): D Greygoose — D Head (sub: L Norfolk, 61min), C Tracey, J Bishop, A Spearing — T Rayner, A Gardiner (sub: S Banya, 78), W Anderson (sub: L Owen, 71), P Betson — A Claydon, G Bennett. **Substitutes not used:** R Taylor, S Hyde. **Booked:** Spearing.
BRIGG TOWN (5-3-2): D Steer — R Raspin, P Rowland, G Thompson, D Blanchard, S Carter — C Stones, S Housham, C Stead (sub: R Thompson, 41) — L Borman (sub: S Drayton, 86), S Roach. **Substitutes not used:** J Sherlock, R Nevis, R Gawthorpe. **Booked:** Raspin, Stones.
Referee: M Fletcher.

FA TROPHY

SEMI-FINALS: First legs: Aylesbury United 1 (Maskell 60) Burscough 1 (Martindale 69); Tamworth 1 (Rickards 43) Havant & Waterlooville 0. **Second legs:** Burscough 1 (Teale 90 pen) Aylesbury United 0. *Burscough win 2-1 on aggregate*. Havant & Waterlooville 1 (Taylor 42) Tamworth 1 (Rickards 111). *Tamworth win 2-1 on aggregate (aet)*

FINAL (Villa Park)

BURSCOUGH (1) **2**   **TAMWORTH** (0) **1**
Martindale 26, 55   Cooper 79
14,265

Hailing from a village in Lancashire and finishing eighteenth in the UniBond League, Burscough were shock winners, following a stunning 2-0 victory away to Yeovil Town in the quarter-finals by upsetting Tamworth in the final. Tamworth were hot favourites but were undone by two goals by Gary Martindale, back at the club from which he had launched his career in 1994. It was a dream return to Villa Park for Shaun Teale, 39, in his first season as Burscough player-manager.

BURSCOUGH (3-5-2): M Taylor — C Macauley (sub: M White, 77min), J Taylor, S Teale — M Byrne (sub: J Bluck, 84), J Norman, P Burns, J Lawless, R Bowen — G Martindale (sub: K McHale, 80), P Wright. **Substitutes not used:** G Maguire, M Molyneux. **Booked:** Lawless.
TAMWORTH (4-4-2): D Acton — R Warner, D Robinson, S Walsh, R Follett — N Colley, B McGorry, M Cooper, S Evans (sub: M Turner, 65) — S Rickards (sub: P Hatton, 88), M Sale (sub: M Hallam, 55). **Substitutes not used:** N Barnes, D Grocutt. **Booked:** Robinson, Walsh.
Referee: U Rennie.

FA CUP

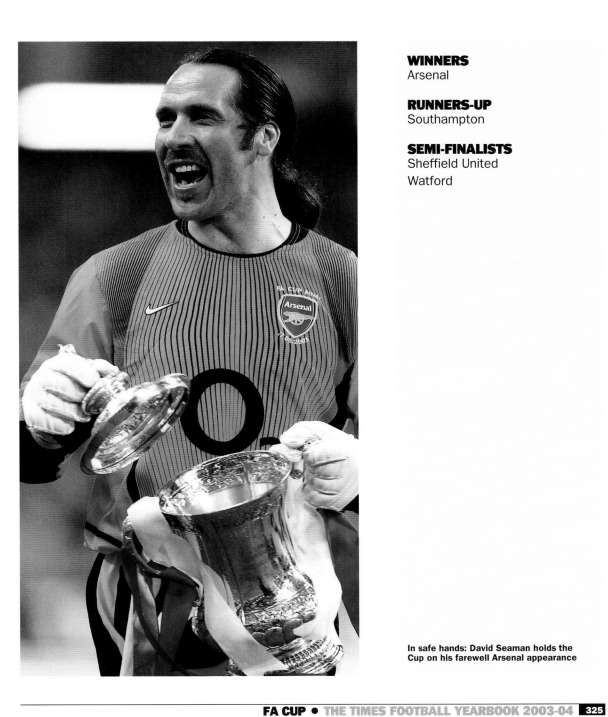

WINNERS
Arsenal

RUNNERS-UP
Southampton

SEMI-FINALISTS
Sheffield United
Watford

In safe hands: David Seaman holds the Cup on his farewell Arsenal appearance

EXTRA PRELIMINARY ROUND

Saturday August 24
Flixton 1 Goole 1; Holker Old Boys 0 Bridlington T 2; West Auckland T 2 Winsford Utd 1; Penrith 3 Brandon Utd 2; Marske Utd 1 Salford C 4; Maltby Main 0 Billingham Synthonia 6; Consett 4 Pontefract Collieries 1; Chester-le-Street T 3 Northallerton T 1; Morpeth 3 Curzon Ashton 2; Nelson 0 Norton & Stockton Ancients 0 (aet); Ramsbottom Utd 1 Thackley 0; Horden CW 2 Armthorpe Welfare 1; Bridgnorth T 4 Gedling T 2; Stratford T 4 Stourbridge 1; Mickleover Sports 3 Shirebrook T 1; Grosvenor Park 2 Stafford T 0; Newmarket T 2 Ely C 3 (tie awarded to Newmarket; Ely C disqualified for playing an ineligible player); Dereham T 1 AFC Wallingford 3; Saffron Walden T 0 Hullbridge Sports 1; Bedford Utd & Valerio 0 Brook House 1; Potters Bar T 1 Milton Keynes C 2; Sawbridgeworth T 2 Harwich & Parkeston 0; Raunds T 1 Ruislip Manor 0; Stotfold 0 Broxbourne Bor V&E 0; Tiptree Utd 1 Ipswich Wndrs 1; Ilford 3 Kempston Rov 0; Walton Casuals 0 Whitehawk 4; Greenwich Bor 1 Three Bridges 4; Deal T 2 Chichester C Utd 2; Lymington & New Milton 2 East Preston 2; Moneyfields 1 Burgess Hill T 0; Alton T 1 Didcot T 1; Horsham YMCA 1 Eastleigh 3; AFC Totton 3 Southwick 2; Ramsgate 1 Maidstone Utd 1; Chessington Utd 0 Ringmer 1; Reading T 3 Farnham T 1; Paulton Rov 5 Downton 1; Highworth T 2 Fairford T 2; Street 3 Keynsham T 1; Portland Utd 6 Welton Rov 2; Bishop Sutton 2 Melksham T 1; Christchurch 3 Willand Rov 0

Sunday August 25
Leek CSOB 0 Nantwich T 3; Littlehampton T 0 Godalming & Guildford 6

Replays

Tuesday August 27
Goole 0 Flixton 0 (aet; Goole win 5-4 on pens); Norton & Stockton Ancients 1 Nelson 2; Broxbourne Bor V&E 1 Stotfold 5; Ipswich Wndrs 3 Tiptree Utd 3 (aet; Ipswich Wndrs win 7-6 on pens); Chichester C Utd 2 Deal T 3; East Preston 1 Lymington & New Milton 2; Maidstone Utd 1 Ramsgate 0

Wednesday August 28
Didcot T 1 Alton T 0; Fairford T 1 Highworth T 4

PRELIMINARY ROUND

Friday August 30
Eastbourne T 1 Windsor & Eton 1

Saturday August 31
Shildon 2 Salford C 4; Morpeth T 1 Woodley Sports 0; Hatfield Main 0 Shotton Comrades 1; Selby T 0 Newcastle Blue Star 0; Fleetwood T 1 Workington 1; Skelmersdale Utd 1 Penrith 3; Brigg T 2 Kendal T 4; Whitley Bay 2 Harrogate Railway 0; Guisborough T 2 Blackpool Mechanics 0; Farsley Celtic 4 Seaham Red Star 4; Glasshoughton Welfare 1 Jarrow Roofing Boldon CA 3; Goole 0 Mossley 3; Nelson 2 Bishop Auckland 3; Ossett T 0 Worsbrough Bridge MW 2; Great Harwood T 0 Winterton Rgs 0; Horden CW 2 Trafford 0; Evenwood T 1 Durham C 4; Prescot Cables 3 Witton Alb 6; Parkgate 2 St Helens T 2; Squires Gate 1 Lincoln Utd 2; Tow Law T 2 Tadcaster Alb 1; Abbey Hey 0 Bamber Bridge 0; Louth Utd 4 Cheadle T 1; Ramsbottom Utd 3 Chadderton 0; Matlock 2 Pickering T 0; Maine Road 1 Guiseley 2; Spennymoor Utd 4 Consett 0; Chester-le-Street T 2 Hall Road Rgs 0; Atherton LR 0 Rossington Main 2; Ashington 7 Colne 0; Willington 0 Atherton Collieries 0; Chorley 5 Liversedge 0; Warrington T 2 Esh Winning 2; Bedlington Ter 3 Brodsworth MW 0; Alnwick T 1 Crook T 2; Garforth T 3 Yorkshire Amateur 1; Stocksbridge Park Steels 17 Oldham T 1; Rossendale Utd 0 Ossett Alb 1; Thornaby 1 Dunston FB 1; Clitheroe 1 Radcliffe Bor 3; Sheffield 0 West Auckland T 4; South Shields 1 Hallam 2; Easington Colliery 1 Hebburn T 3; Washington 0 North Ferriby Utd 2; Peterlee Newtown 2 Billingham Synthonia 1; Billingham T w/o Gretna; Darwen 1 Eccleshill Utd 3; Stourport Swifts 1 Alfreton T 4; Rocester 3 Congleton T 0; Kidsgrove Ath 4 Buxton 1; Rushall Olympic 1 Sutton Coldfield T 4; Staveley MW 0 Boston T 1; Halesowen H 1 Shepshed Dynamo 3; Newcastle T 0 Leek T 1; Belper T 0 Gresley Rov 1; Redditch Utd 2 Grosvenor Park 1; Bourne T 1 Eastwood T 1; Bedworth Utd 1 Causeway

---

THE OLDEST KNOCKOUT COMPETITION in world football has been in existence for so long that it has now become a medical curiosity. Each year, the wise and the good take turns with the stethoscope and debate whether the noise they can detect is the heartbeat of the FA Cup or its death rattle. The 2002-03 season offered succour to both points of view; alive, certainly, but still in good health?

There were contradictions everywhere. Those who predict annually the demise of the Cup chirped up when Craig Bellamy kissed his Barclaycard Premiership badge and mouthed "the only place to be" while Newcastle United were being beaten by Wolverhampton Wanderers. They did the same when Sam Allardyce, the Bolton Wanderers manager, spoke of "priorities" after just 14,550 supporters turned up at the Stadium of Light to see Sunderland stutter past his side. Yet while the Premiership accounted for just half of the clubs to reach the sixth round, note a few other statistics.

Nine of the past 11 finals have featured either Arsenal or Manchester United and the monoliths were to meet at Old Trafford on February 15; it may have taken place in the dressing-room, but the stray boot that smashed into David Beckham's forehead told of Sir Alex Ferguson's commitment to the competition.

And while their confrontation with Southampton in the Cup Final may not have been a match to linger in the memory, Arsenal, having already squandered the championship, ultimately dragged themselves to the Millennium Stadium, where they showed that they were desperate not to end empty-handed a campaign that had promised so much. Losers maybe, but Gordon Strachan's Southampton side contented themselves with the rich reward of European football.

There were the traditional and time-honoured nods to romance, too, when the draw comes up with something that scriptwriters for soap operas would reject as surreal. But it was not a dream when Kevin Ratcliffe managed Shrewsbury Town (eighteenth in the Nationwide League third division) to a 2-1 triumph over Everton (fifth in the Premiership), the club he had captained to FA Cup glory 19 years earlier.

Was it fantasy when Vauxhall Motors, of the UniBond League premier division, did for Queens Park Rangers (finalists in 1982), or when Harrogate Railway, representing the Northern Counties East League, earned themselves a home tie against Bristol City? Rochdale's victory over Coventry City replicated their finest hour, 32 years earlier. They reached the fifth round for only the second

Arsenal won a scrappy final to ensure that they did not finish empty-handed

time and Paul Simpson, the manager, was awarded a contract as a result.

Farnborough Town topped it all. Saved from bankruptcy three seasons earlier, the Hampshire club eased past Harrogate Town, Southport and Darlington. Danny Carroll, a teacher who had scored the winning goal at Feethams, took a day off work to hear the draw — home, to Arsenal, the champions of England. They were trounced 5-1 (has there ever been a better-named consolation goalscorer than Rocky Baptiste?), but loved the experience.

But precious few of those remarkable stories were told without rancour. Shrewsbury subsequently endured a run of eight consecutive defeats and, after a stay of 53 years, bade farewell to the Football League. Members of the Harrogate Railway squad went on strike for a larger share of the £100,000 the club had made from television receipts. Simpson's permanent employment proved short-lived. However, most consternation was reserved for Farnborough and, particularly, Graham Westley, their ambitious manager and millionaire owner. Instead of facing Arsenal at Cherrywood Road, Westley, citing safety reasons, took his team to Highbury for their fourth-round match. It was anti-romance. About £450,000 was banked from the Cup run, enough to clear debts, but Westley left

Utd 1; Histon 2 Quorn 3; Oadby T 2 Rugby Utd 2; Atherstone Utd 3 Studley 0; Stratford T 3 Ludlow T 1; Nantwich T 4 Holbeach Utd 0; ChaseT 0 Spalding Utd 1; Corby T 0 Stamford 6; Arnold T 1 RC Warwick 0; King's Lynn 1 Deeping Rgs 0; Willenhall T 1 Glapwell 0; Pelsall Villa 1 Borrowash Vic 1; Shifnal T 1 Blackstones 4; Glossop North End 1 Boldmere St Michaels 0; Solihull Bor 2 Oldbury Utd 0; Barwell 1 Bromsgrove Rov 1; Long Buckby 0 Marlow 2; Newmarket T 1 Ilford 3; Barking & East Ham Utd 4 Soham T Rgs 3; Hullbridge Sports 2 Edgware T 5; Great Yarmouth T 2 Holmer Green 1; Desborough T 1 Romford 2; Southall T 1 Wroxham 6; Northampton Spencer 1 Yaxley 1; Banbury Utd 1 Berkhamsted T 1; Hoddesdon T 0 AFC Sudbury 2 (at Hertford Town FC); Cheshunt 3 Wembley 0; Maldon T 1 Flackwell Hth 1; Leighton T 2 Royston T 2; Chalfont St Peter 0 Hemel Hempstead T 3; Clacton T 3 Sawbridgeworth T 1; Wealdstone 1 Leyton 3; Cogenhoe Utd 0 Diss T 2; Bowers Utd 1 Arlesey T 4; Wivenoe T 0 Yeading 3; Stotfold 1 Hornchurch 1; St Neots T 6 Stansted 0; Bury T 2 Barton Rov 3; Lowestoft T 0 Uxbridge 2; Raunds T 5 Burnham R 1; Wootton Blue Cross 3 Brackley T 1; Stewarts & Lloyds 1 Ford Sports Daventry 0; Harlow T 0 Aveley 1; Stowmarket T 1 Southall 6; Wisbech T 3 Woodbridge T 1; Brook House 2 Burnham 3; Hanwell T 0 Great Wakering Rov 3; Mildenhall T 0 London Colney 0; Tilbury 4 Gorleston 3 (at Aveley FC); Concord Rgs 2 Hertford T 3; Ware 5 Milton Keynes C 1; Haringey Bor 0 Northwood 1; Ipswich Wndrs 2 Leyton Pennant 3; Letchworth 1 Staines T 1; Clapton 0 Beaconsfield SYCOB 3; Witham T 0 Wingate & Finchley 5; St Margaretsbury 2 Dunstable T 0 (at Dunstable Town FC); East Thurrock Utd 1 Harefield Utd 2; Buckingham T 3 Tring T 0; Rothwell T 3 Kingsbury T 1; Brentwood 2 AFC Wallingford 2; Fakenham T 1 Southend Manor 3; Wick 1 Abingdon Utd 4; Merstham 3 St Leonards 4; Three Bridges 3 Didcot T 1; Erith T 0 Ringmer 3; North Leigh 0 Cowes Sports 5; Bromley 3 Abingdon T 2; Lymington & New Milton 1 Dulwich Hamlet 1; Redhill 1 Peacehaven & Telscombe 3; Gosport Bor 2 Wantage T 1; Oxford C 0 Cray Wndrs 1; Deal T 4 Hythe T 2; Eastleigh 5 Erith & Belvedere 0; Fisher Ath 7 Wokingham T 0; Whyteleafe 1 Reading T 0; Whitstable T 1 Chipstead 2; Croydon Ath 0 Eastbourne Bor 0; AFC Totton 2 Thamesmead T 0; Molesey 3 Hassocks 0; Bedfont 3 Whitehawk 1; Saltdean Utd 0 VCD Ath 3; Beckenham T 1 Croydon 2; Brockenhurst 3 Fleet T 2; Newport (IoW) 1 Blackfield & Langley 1; Moneyfields 0 BAT Sports 2; Chertsey T 4 Arundel 1; Tunbridge Wells 2 Ashford T (Middx) 1; Fareham T 1 Tooting & Mitcham Utd 1; Godalming & Guildford 3 Whitchurch Utd 0; Thame Utd 1 Slough T 2; Sandhurst T 2 Herne Bay 6; Sittingbourne 2 Slade Green 2; Metropolitan Police 4 Lancing 0; Camberley T 0 Cove 1; Horsham 2 Lordswood 2; Lewes 1 Thatcham T 0; Chatham T 0 Egham T 0; Bognor Regis T 1 Worthing 0; Banstead Ath 1 Leatherhead 4; Westfield 1 Dorking 2; Tonbridge Angels 2 Maidstone Utd 3; Hillingdon Bor 2 Chessington & Hook Utd 2; Corinthian Casuals 1 Epsom & Ewell 1; Walton & Hersham 2 Andover 1; Ashford T 1 Carshalton Ath 3; AFC Newbury 2 Hailsham T 1; Selsey 3 Ash Utd 0; Eastbourne Utd 0 Cobham 3; Chard T 2 Swindon Supermarine 0; Frome T 0 Shortwood Utd 1; Bishop Sutton 1 Cinderford 7; Torrington 2 Westbury Utd 1; Odd Down 0 Paulton Rov 2; Clevedon T 2 Bitton 2; Highworth T 2 Cirencester T 2; Hungerford T 2 Shepton Mallet 0; Bridport 2 Taunton T 3; Elmore 1 Backwell Utd 2; Bashley 2 Mangotsfield Utd 2; Salisbury C 1 Bideford 2; Barnstaple T 0 Team Bath 3; Corsham T 3 Portland Utd 1; Devizes T 5 Ilfracombe T 2; Bournemouth 3 Bridgwater T 0; Falmouth T 2 Bristol Manor Farm 0; Merthyr Tydfil 3 Christchurch 0; Porthleven 0 Dorchester T 5; Tuffley Rov 0 St Blazey 1; Minehead T 0 Gloucester C 2; Weston-super-Mare 4 Calne T 0; Yate T 4 Hallen 2; Dawlish T 0 Wimborne T 3; Brislington 2 Evesham Utd 2; Street 1 Bemerton Hth Harlequins 3

Sunday September 1
Bacup Bor 1 Bridlington T 2 (at Rossendale Utd FC); Mickleover Sports 2 Cradley T 1; Biddulph Vic 2 Bridgnorth T 0; Pagham 3 Bracknell T 2; Dartford 2 Carterton T 2

Replays

Monday September 2
Harrogate Railway 5 Whitley Bay 4; Atherton Collieries 5 Willington 1; Bitton 1 Clevedon T 2

Tuesday September 3
Newcastle Blue Star 2 Selby T 4; Workington T 1 Fleetwood 0 (aet); Seaham Red Star 1 Farsley Celtic 6; St Helens T 3 Parkgate 1; Bamber Bridge 2 Abbey Hey 2 (aet: Abbey Hey win 4-2 on pens); Pickering T 0 Matlock T 1; Dunston FB 2 Thornaby 1; Eastwood T 3 Bourne T 1; Rugby Utd 2 Oadby T 3; Borrowash Vic 1 Pelsall Villa 4; Bromsgrove Rov 4 Barwell 3; Yaxley 5 Northampton Spencer 1 (aet); Berkhamsted T 1 Banbury Utd 4; Flackwell Hth 1 Maldon T 0; Hornchurch 4 Stotfold 4 (aet: Stotfold win 5-4 on pens); AFC Wallingford 4 Brentwood 1; Dulwich Hamlet 1 Lymington & New Milton 3; Eastbourne Bor 4 Croydon Ath 1; Blackfield & Langley 0 Newport (IoW) 3; Tooting & Mitcham 1 Fareham T 0; Slade Green 3 Sittingbourne 1; Lordswood 1 Horsham 2; Egham T 0 Chatham T 1; Chessington & Hook Utd 1 Hillingdon Bor 3; Epsom & Ewell 1 Corinthian Casuals 2; Carterton T 1 Dartford 0; Mangotsfield Utd 0 Bashley 1; Evesham Utd 3 Brislington 2

Wednesday September 4
St Margaretsbury 2 Dunstable T 0 (at Dunstable Town FC); Winterton Rgs 0 Great Harwood T 0 (aet: Great Harwood win 4-3 on pens); Esh Winning 3 Warrington T 1 (aet); Causeway Utd 1 Bedworth Utd 2; Royston T 3 Leighton T 0; London Colney 1 Mildenhall T 0; Staines T 1 Letchworth 0 (at Egham Town FC); Windsor & Eton 3 Eastbourne T 2

FIRST QUALIFYING ROUND

Saturday September 14
Eccleshill Utd 3 St Helens T 2; Bedlington Ter 1 Ossett Alb 0; Radcliffe Bor 4 Abbey Hey 1; Esh Winning 1 Harrogate Railway 2; Horden CW 4 Shotton Comrades 1; Dunston FB 2 Selby T 0; Kendal T 2 North Ferriby Utd 1; Workington 2 Mossley 3; Bishop Auckland 3 Rossington Main 3; Jarrow Roofing Boldon CA 2 Billingham T 4; Morpeth T 0 Guisborough T 1; West Auckland T 6 Chorley 3; Chester-le-Street T 2 Penrith 0; Great Harwood T 1 Crook T 1; Bridlington T 1 Garforth T 0; Tow Law T 5 Matlock T 4; Witton Alb 1 Ramsbottom Utd 1; Farsley Celtic 3 Lincoln Utd 1; Durham C 5 Worsbrough Bridge MW 1; Guiseley 3 Hebburn T 0; Peterlee Newtown 4 Louth Utd 0; Spennymoor Utd 1 Ashington 1; Atherton Collieries 1 Salford C 0; Alfreton T 0 Kidsgrove Ath 1; Nantwich T 2 Rocester 0; Eastwood T 1 Redditch Utd 2; Stamford 3 Oadby T 1; Boston T 1 Sutton Coldfield T 1; King's Lynn 4 Quorn 1; Blackstone 2 Pelsall Villa 2; Bromsgrove Rov 5 Gresley Rov 0; Solihull Bor 9 Glossop North End 0; Willenhall T 0 Atherstone Utd 2; Mickleover Sports 0 Shepshed Dynamo 1; Arnold T 1 Biddulph Vic 1; Leek T 2 Spalding Utd 1; Stratford T 1 Bedworth Utd 2; Stewarts & Lloyds 0 Burnham 1; Rothwell T 3 Southend Manor 2; Cheshunt 4 Edgware T 0; Hertford T 1 AFC Wallingford 4; Royston T 3 London Colney 2; Hemel Hempstead T 7 St Neots 1; Ilford 2 Clacton T 3; Wootton Blue Cross 2 Wroxham 1; Raunds T 1 AFC Sudbury 3; Barking & East Ham Utd 1 Banbury Utd 0; Leyton Pennant 3 Great Yarmouth T 3; Staines T 1 Uxbridge 2 (at Egham Town FC); Harefield Utd 2 Barton Rov 1; Tilbury 0 Yeading 2 (at East Thurrock Utd FC); Beaconsfield SYCOB 5 Great Wakering Rov 0; Northwood 1 Wisbech T 2; Aveley 2 Stotfold 1; Diss T 3 Romford 0; St Margaretsbury 1 Arlesey T 2; Southall 2 Yaxley 3; Flackwell Hth 2 Buckingham T 1; Leyton 0 Marlow 1; Wingate & Finchley 2 Ware 0; Bromley 2 BAT Sports 1; Herne Bay 3 Cowes Sports 2; Peacehaven & Telscombe 1 Carterton T 2; Walton & Hersham 3 Cove 0; Horsham 3 Slade Green 0; Lewes 2 Brockenhurst 1; Eastleigh 2 Croydon 0; Abingdon Utd 2 Leatherhead 3; Chatham T 2 Godalming & Guildford 3; Molesey 3 Fisher Ath 0; Bognor Regis T 4 Windsor & Eton 1; VCD Ath 2 Bedfont 1; Tunbridge Wells 2 Selsey 2; Newport (IoW) 0 Maidstone Utd 4; Metropolitan Police 1 Corinthian Casuals 0; Hillingdon Bor 2 Lymington & New Milton 3; Gosport Bor 2 Deal T 1; Eastbourne Bor 6 AFC Newbury 2; St Leonards 1 Slough T 2; Tooting & Mitcham 0 Cobham 0; AFC Totton 3 Pagham 1; Carshalton Ath 4 Dorking 0; Ringmer 1 Chertsey T 2; Chipstead 1 Three

Newcastle's visit to Molineux in January produced a thrilling third-round tie

immediately for Stevenage Borough, taking several players with him. More heartening was Watford's surge to the semi-finals, where they lost 2-1 to Southampton. Since their single season in the Premiership and the unproductive reign of Gianluca Vialli, financial meltdown had appeared their destination. On St Valentine's Day, they announced that the contracts of five professionals were being cancelled. What did Watford's heroics mean to Ray Lewington? "Survival," the manager said.

The undoubted Cup kings were Sheffield United, who were pipped by Liverpool in the last four of the Worthington Cup, were runners-up to Wolves in the first division play-offs (which almost counts) and were beaten by Arsenal at Old Trafford in the FA Cup semi-finals. Neil Warnock, the United manager, typically monopolising controversy, accused Graham Poll, the referee, of being Arsenal's "best midfield player".

So a mixed year was followed by a scrappy final, which was just about right. Match of the season? Wolves 3, Newcastle 2, a televised third-round tie crammed with goals, errors and intrigue. A meeting convened by a furious Sir Bobby Robson the next day may have persuaded Bellamy that his gesture was mistaken. The Newcastle manager was guest of honour in Cardiff and when he passed the trophy to David Seaman, his look said a lot: I wish that was me.

PLAYER OF THE SEASON

Michael Brown

Of the 22 goals that Michael Brown scored for Sheffield United, a colossal return for a midfield player, only two came in the Cup — albeit in a 4-3, fourth-round thriller against Ipswich Town — but no player was more consistently excellent for Neil Warnock's team during a magnificent season. The former England Under-21 international was Warnock's first cash purchase in 2000, when he left Manchester City for £400,000. and at 26 is a thoroughbred who seems sure to play in the Premiership sooner or later.

George Caulkin

LEADING FA CUP GOALSCORERS 2002-03

10: Paul Jackson (Stocksbridge Park Steels)

9: Kevin Smith (Harrogate Railway)
Jody Banim (Radcliffe Borough)

8: Steve Davey (Harrogate Railway)

7: Rocky Baptiste (Farnborough Town)

6: Andrew Claydon (AFC Sudbury)
Marvin Samuel (Arlesey Town)
Michael Midwood (Farsley Celtic)
Eric Tomlinson (Metropolitan Police)

TOP ATTENDANCES ROUND BY ROUND

Extra preliminary round	747	Ramsgate v Maidstone United
Preliminary round	1,027	Tonbridge Angels v Maidstone United
First qualifying round	732	Bromsgrove Rovers v Gresley Rovers
Second qualifying round	1,681	Aldershot Town v Aylesbury United
Third qualifying round	1,870	Aldershot Town v Lewes
Fourth qualifying round	3,470	Bath City v Yeovil Town
First round	7,803	Hull City v Macclesfield Town
Second round	11,645	Oxford United v Swindon Town
Third round	67,222	Manchester United v Portsmouth
Fourth round	67,181	Manchester United v West Ham United
Fifth round	67,209	Manchester United v Arsenal
Sixth round	41,456	Chelsea v Arsenal
Semi-finals	59,170	Arsenal v Sheffield United, at Old Trafford

MOST FA CUP WINS

10	Manchester United
9	Arsenal
8	Tottenham Hotspur
7	Aston Villa
6	Blackburn Rovers, Liverpool, Newcastle United
5	Everton, The Wanderers, West Bromwich Albion
4	Bolton Wanderers, Manchester City, Sheffield United, Wolverhampton Wanderers
3	Chelsea, Sheffield Wednesday, West Ham United

MOST FINAL APPEARANCES

16	Arsenal
15	Manchester United
13	Newcastle United
12	Everton, Liverpool
10	Aston Villa, West Bromwich Albion
9	Tottenham Hotspur
8	Blackburn Rovers, Manchester City, Wolverhampton Wanderers
7	Bolton Wanderers, Chelsea, Preston North End
6	Old Etonians, Sheffield United, Sheffield Wednesday
5	Huddersfield Town, The Wanderers
4	Derby County, Leeds United, Leicester City, Oxford University, Royal Engineers, Southampton, Sunderland, West Ham United
3	Blackpool, Burnley, Nottingham Forest, Portsmouth

Bridges 3; St Blazey 1 Bournemouth 0; Team Bath 3 Backwell Utd 1; Torrington 0 Hungerford T 1; Yate T 0 Bideford 4; Bemerton Hth H 2 Shortwood Utd 1; Merthyr Tydfil 2 Chard T 0; Weston-super-Mare 3 Wimborne T 1; Clevedon T 2 Dorchester T 0; Gloucester City 3 Bashley 0; Devizes T 0 Taunton T 1; Falmouth T 1 Evesham Utd 2; Highworth T 2 Cinderford T 3; Paulton Rov 2 Corsham T 1

Sunday September 15
Hallam 2 Stocksbridge Park Steels 3; Cray Wndrs 1 Whyteleafe 0

Replays

Tuesday September 17
Rossington Main 1 Bishop Auckland 1 (aet; Rossington win 4-1 on pens); Ramsbottom Utd 2 Witton Alb 3; Ashington 1 Spennymoor Utd 2; Sutton Coldfield T 2 Boston T 0; Pelsall Villa 3 Blackstone 2; Biddulph Vic 1 Arnold T 2; Great Yarmouth T 5 Leyton Pennant 1; Stotfold 0 Aveley 2; Cobham 1 Tooting & Mitcham Utd 3

Wednesday September 18
Crook T 1 Great Harwood T 1 (aet; Great Harwood T win 8-7 on pens); Selsey 2 Tunbridge Wells 1

SECOND QUALIFYING ROUND

Saturday September 28
Chester-le-Street 5 Harrogate Railway 5; Colwyn Bay 4 West Auckland T 0; Hyde Utd 7 Tow Law T 3; Guisborough T 3 Guiseley 3; Stocksbridge Park Steels 0 Ashton Utd 2; Stalybridge Celtic 2 Workington 2; Bedlington Ter 1 Vauxhall M 2; Durham City 3 Peterlee Newton 0; Gainsborough Trinity 3 Frickley Ath 2; Whitby T 0 Bradford Park Avenue 4; Harrogate T 2 Great Harwood T 0; Marine 2 Eccleshill Utd 2; Runcorn 2 Wakefield & Emley 0; Bridlington T 3 Witton Alb 1; Droylsden 4 Farsley Celtic 3; Altrincham 1 Kendal T 0; Accrington Stanley 2 Billingham T 1; Spennymoor Utd 5 Atherton Collieries 0; Horden CW 0 Worksop T 4; Rossington Main 0 Radcliffe Bor 7; Lancaster City 2 Blyth Spartans 4; Dunston FB 2 Burscough 0; Gateshead 3 Barrow 4; Shepshed Dynamo 0 Stafford Rgs 2; Bedford T 6 Pelsall Villa 1; King's Lynn 1 Cambridge City 0; Bromsgrove Rov 2 Tamworth 2; Bedworth Utd 1 Moor Green 4; Ilkeston T 7 Atherstone Utd 0; Sutton Coldfield T 0 Halesowen T 2; Hednesford T 0 Hucknall T 0; Redditch Utd 1 Leek T 1; Nantwich T 0 Arnold T 3; Solihull Bor 0 Grantham T 2; Worcester City 3 Stamford 0; Hinckley Utd 3 Kidsgrove Ath 0; Walton & Hersham 1 Chesham Utd 0; Harefield Utd 4 AFC Sudbury 4; Grays Ath 1 Marlow 0; Molesey 3 Hitchin T 1; Hendon 3 Tooting & Mitcham 0; Leatherhead 1 Bromley 1; Godalming & Guildford 0 Hampton & Richmond 1; AFC Wallingford 0 Eastbourne Bor 1; Clacton T 2 Kingstonian 3; Billericay T 3 Yeading 1; Hayes 6 Bognor Regis T 0; AFC Totton 2 Slough T 2; Rothwell T 1 Barking & East Ham Utd 0; Maidenhead Utd 1 Welling Utd 2; Lewes 0 Eastleigh 0; Horsham 2 Yaxley 0; Havant & Waterlooville 2 Harrow Bor 1; Diss T 2 Chertsey T 3; Canvey Is 2 Folkestone Invicta 1; Carshalton Ath 1 Chelmsford C 1; Heybridge Swifts 1 Sutton Utd 1; Uxbridge 1 Braintree T 2; Hastings Utd 4 Selsey 1; Flackwell Hth 2 Royston T 2; Hemel Hempstead T 3 Cray Wndrs 1; Enfield 1 Bishop's Stortford 5; Beaconsfield SYCOB 1 Gosport Bor 2; Burnham 0 Herne Bay 1; Aldershot T 3 Aylesbury Utd 1; Dover Ath 2 Basingstoke T 0; Lymington & New Milton 3 Cheshunt 1; Carterton T 0 Arlesey T 6; Crawley T 3 Great Yarmouth 0; Wisbech T 6 VCD Ath 1; Wootton Blue Cross 0 Purfleet 4; Three Bridges 1 Aveley 3; Ford Utd 4 Metropolitan Police 2; St Albans C 2 Wingate & Finchley 0; Tiverton T 1 Taunton T 1; Bath C 5 Merthyr Tydfil 1; Weston-super-Mare 2 Clevedon T 0; Gloucester C 1 Newport County 1; Team Bath 6 Bemerton Hth Harlequins 1; Bideford 3 St Blazey 1; Hungerford T 2 Paulton Rov 1; Evesham Utd 1 Cinderford T 1; Chippenham T 1 Weymouth 4

Sunday September 29
Maidstone Utd 2 Boreham Wood 5

Replays

Monday September 30
Harrogate Railway 7 Chester-le-Street 2 (aet); Guiseley 1 Guisborough T 0; Newport County 4 Gloucester C 0

Tuesday October 1
Workington T 3 Stalybridge Celtic 1; Eccleshill Utd 2 Marine 3 (aet); Hucknall T 3 Hednesford T 3 (aet; Hucknall win 6-5 on pens); Leek T 1 Redditch Utd 2; Stamford 1 Worcester C 2; AFC Sudbury 5 Harefield Utd 0; Bromley 2 Leatherhead 4; Slough T 2 AFC Totton 0; Sutton Utd 1 Heybridge Swifts 2; Newport County 4 Gloucester C 0; Cinderford T 0 Evesham Utd 5

Wednesday October 2
Eastleigh 2 Lewes 4 (aet); Chelmsford C 1 Carshalton Ath 1 (aet; Royston T 0 Flackwell Hth 0 (aet; Flackwell Hth win 5-3 on pens); Taunton T 0 Tiverton T 2

THIRD QUALIFYING ROUND

Saturday October 12
Harrogate Railway 4 Workington 0; Droylsden 0 Spennymoor Utd 0; Accrington Stanley 0 Harrogate T 0; Bradford Park Avenue 3 Bridlington T 5; Vauxhall M 6 Gainsborough Trinity 1; Durham C 1 Blyth Spartans 1; Barrow 3 Hyde Utd 1; Ashton Utd 0 Runcorn 3; Dunston FB 0 Marine 1; Colwyn Bay 1 Radcliffe Bor 2; Guiseley 2 Altrincham 1; Ilkeston T 6 King's Lynn 1; Redditch Utd 0 Arnold T 1; Hinckley Utd 1 Tamworth 3; Moor Green 3 Halesowen T 1; Wisbech T 1 Bedford T 0; Hucknall T 1 Worcester C 0; Grantham T 1 Worksop T 0; Stafford Rgs 3 Rothwell T 0; Canvey Is 2 Aveley 0; Billericay T 4 Braintree T 0; Heybridge Swifts 1 Herne Bay 0; Hemel Hempstead 1 Arlesey T 2; Dover Ath 2 Welling Utd 2; Molesey 3 Chertsey T 1; Bishop's Stortford 1 Eastbourne Bor 0; Flackwell Hth 1 Purfleet 0; Grays Ath 2 Hayes 1; AFC Sudbury 2 Walton & Hersham 0; Hastings Utd 2 Hendon 1; Slough T 4 Hampton & Richmond 2; St Albans C 1 Chelmsford C 0; Boreham Wood 2 Kingstonian 0; Leatherhead 1 Ford Utd 2; Horsham 1 Hungerford T 0; Havant & Waterlooville 4 Evesham Utd 0; Weston-super-Mare 0 Bath C 5; Bideford 3 Gosport Bor 1; Aldershot T 2 Lewes 0; Newport County 0 Team Bath 3; Lymington & New Milton 0 Crawley T 2; Tiverton T 4 Weymouth 2

Replays

Tuesday October 15
Spennymoor Utd 3 Droylsden 2; Harrogate T 3 Accrington Stanley 2; Welling Utd 1 Dover Ath 3

Thursday October 17
Blyth Spartans 3 Durham C 1

FOURTH QUALIFYING ROUND

Saturday October 26
Wisbech T 0 Harrogate T 2; Blyth Spartans 1 Runcorn 3; Morecambe 3 Grantham T 1; Ilkeston T 0 Stafford Rgs 1; Burton Alb 2 Halifax T 1; Moor Green 2 Leigh RMI 1; Harrogate Railway 4 Marine 2; Arnold T 0 Scarborough 2; Northwich Vic 3 Spennymoor Utd 1; Hucknall T 1 Vauxhall M 1; Guiseley 3 Tamworth 3; Southport 4 Bridlington T 1; Radcliffe Bor 2 Chester C 4; Nuneaton Bor 1 Barrow 1; AFC Sudbury 1 St Albans C 2; Bishop's Stortford 1 Boreham Wood 1; Heybridge Swifts 2 Bideford T 0; Slough T 3 Canvey Is 2; Aldershot T 0 Dagenham & Redbridge 4; Hastings Utd 0 Kettering T 0; Havant & Waterlooville 3 Billericay T 1; Hereford Utd 1 Arlesey T 0; Horsham 0 Team Bath 0; Gravesend & Northfleet 1 Margate 2; Forest Green Rov 2 Ford Utd 1; Flackwell Hth 1 Crawley T 4; Dover Ath 1 Woking 1; Barnet 0 Tiverton T 2; Grays Ath 1 Stevenage Bor 2; Molesey 0 Farnborough T 6

Sunday October 27
Telford Utd 0 Doncaster Rov 2; Bath C 1 Yeovil T 1

Replays

Monday October 28
Boreham Wood 4 Bishop's Stortford 1; Team Bath 1 Horsham 1 (aet: Team Bath win 4-2 on pens)

Tuesday October 29
Vauxhall M 5 Hucknall T 1; Barrow 4 Nuneaton Bor 3; Yeovil T 3 Bath C 1; Kettering T 0 Hastings Utd 5; Woking 1 Dover Ath 2; Tamworth 2 Guiseley 3

MATCH OF THE SEASON

Shrewsbury Town 2   Everton 1
Gay Meadow, Saturday January 4 2003
Nick Szczepanik

THERE IS SOMETHING SURREAL about the crowd at a football match chanting "Are you watching, BBC?" as a TV crew records the match for broadcast on *Match of the Day*. The Shrewsbury Town supporters' point, however, was that this tie, which encapsulated the spirit of the FA Cup third round, should have been televised live instead of one of the two all-Premiership matches, Southampton v Tottenham Hotspur and Manchester City v Liverpool, that the BBC chose instead.

Perhaps the Beeb is still peeved about losing the rights to cover Premiership matches to ITV, so went for the next-best thing. Or maybe it thought that a match between the team eighteenth in the Nationwide League third division and the side in fifth place in the Premiership might be too one-sided — unlike Southampton v Tottenham, for instance.

Shrewsbury's margin of victory could have been wider, but otherwise the people were proved right and the BBC wrong. As an occasion, it had promise: Wayne Rooney's first FA Cup tie; two managers trying to beat clubs they once captained; and a leafy riverside setting as different from Goodison Park as it is possible to imagine. And, as a match, it had everything: good football and plenty of chances, including a late winner; Rooney outshone by a veteran; and, of course, a giant-killing of some magnitude.

The scale of Shrewsbury's achievement was illustrated by the match programme, which listed their 25 previous appearances in the third round alongside Everton's 35 semi-finals and finals. Everton, though, struggled on the bumpy pitch and seldom opened up a defence that went into the match as the worst in the third division.

Tomasz Radzinski did his best, having first-half shots blocked by Ian Dunbavin and Pete Wilding and watching as Li Tie miskicked when he put a late chance on a plate, but it all added up to David Moyes's biggest setback as Everton manager. "When you win you take the applause, and when you lose you have to take the boos," Moyes said. "We deserved the boos today."

Moyes, though, was gracious enough to admit that Shrewsbury had merited victory. As Kevin Ratcliffe, the Shrewsbury manager, said: "It all clicked together." His team were the more composed, kept possession better and had the outstanding finisher. Nigel Jemson, 33, scored both goals, was denied a third by the reflexes of Richard Wright, the Everton goalkeeper, and left with a shirt belonging to Rooney that will be auctioned for charity — one of the few positive impressions made by the 17-year-old boy wonder of the Barclaycard Premiership.

Jemson, whose winning goal for Nottingham Forest in the 1990

Jemson, Shrewsbury's FA Cup hero against Everton, is mobbed by team-mates

Littlewoods Cup final at Wembley was arguably the highlight of a career that has taken him to 13 different clubs, put Shrewsbury ahead from a free kick seven minutes before the interval. Everton equalised through Niclas Alexandersson on the hour and looked likely to prevail as Shrewsbury tired, but the underdogs rallied and Jemson headed the winner in the 89th minute from another free kick, taken by Ian Woan, his former Forest team-mate.

It was no surprise that free kicks were Everton's downfall. Time and again they were forced to use illegal means to stop the Shrewsbury forwards, especially Luke Rodgers, a 21-year-old youth team product. Quick and aggressive, he had a shot touched on to a post by Wright, earned the free kick for Jemson to hit the first goal and was denied a clear penalty when Peter Clarke brought him down three minutes after half-time.

However, for a club that has to confront the realities of existence in the third division, with plans to abandon their picturesque but antiquated ground for more modern facilities, the performance of Rodgers and others means that there could be a chance to cash in beyond the possibilities offered by today's draw for the fourth round. Shrewsbury had done their bit for the romance of the Cup, in other words, and now it was time to look on the practical side.

Roland Wycherley, the chairman, had only one regret — that Jemson's late winner had denied the club an estimated £500,000 from its share of the gate for a second match at Goodison. "I've just had a chat with the manager and I've sacked him," Wycherley joked.

SHREWSBURY TOWN (4-4-2): I Dunbavin — D Moss, D Artell, P Wilding, A Smith — R Lowe (sub: S Aiston, 84min), J Tolley, I Atkins, I Woan — L Rodgers (sub: S Jagielka, 80), N Jemson (sub: L Drysdale, 90). **Substitutes not used:** L Kendall, M Redmile. **Booked:** Lowe.
EVERTON (4-4-2): R Wright — P Clarke, D Weir, A Stubbs, D Unsworth (sub: K McLeod, 90) — L Carsley, S Gemmill (sub: Li Tie, 75), T Gravesen (sub: N Alexandersson, ht), G Naysmith — W Rooney, T Radzinski. **Substitutes not used:** M Pembridge, E Baardsen. **Booked:** Gravesen, Stubbs, Rooney.

FIRST ROUND

Saturday November 16

Farnborough T 5 Harrogate T 1; Tiverton T 1 Crawley T 1; Dover Ath 0 Oxford Utd 1; Northwich Vic 0 Scunthorpe Utd 3; Bury 0 Plymouth Argyle 3; Wycombe Wndrs 2 Brentford 4; Yeovil T 0 Cheltenham T 2; Hull C 0 Macclesfield T 3; York C 2 Swansea C 1; Chesterfield 1 Morecambe 2; Kidderminster H 2 Rushden & Diamonds 2; AFC Bournemouth 2 Doncaster Rov 1; Dagenham & Redbridge 3 Havant & Waterlooville 2; Team Bath 2 Mansfield T 4; Swindon T 1 Huddersfield T 0; Bristol Rov 0 Runcorn 0; Barnsley 1 Blackpool 4; Leyton Orient 1 Margate 1; Oldham Ath 2 Burton Alb 2; Barrow 2 Moor Green 0; Shrewsbury T 4 Stafford Rgs 0; Southend Utd 1 Hartlepool Utd 1; Hereford Utd 0 Wigan Ath 1; Port Vale 0 Crewe Alexandra 1; Scarborough 0 Cambridge Utd 0; Stevenage Bor 1 Hastings Utd 0; Colchester Utd 0 Chester C 1; Torquay Utd 5 Boreham Wood 0; Vauxhall M 0 QPR 0; Slough T 1 Harrogate Railway 2; Carlisle Utd 2 Lincoln C 1; Heybridge Swifts 0 Bristol C 7; Rochdale 3 Peterborough Utd 2; Wrexham 0 Darlington 2; Luton T 4 Guiseley 0; Southport 4 Notts County 2; Tranmere Rov 2 Cardiff C 2; Northampton T 3 Boston Utd 2; Stockport County 4 St Albans C 1

Sunday November 17
Forest Green Rov 0 Exeter C 0

Replays

Tuesday November 26
Crawley T 3 Tiverton T 2; Rushden & Diamonds 2 Kidderminster H 1; Runcorn 1 Bristol Rov 3; Margate 1 Leyton Orient 0; Hartlepool Utd 1 Southend Utd 2; Exeter C 2 Forest Green Rov 1; Cambridge Utd 2 Scarborough 1; QPR 1 Vauxhall M 1 (aet; Vauxhall M win 4-3 on pens); Cardiff C 2 Tranmere Rov 1

Wednesday November 27

Burton Alb 2 Oldham Ath 2 (aet; Oldham Ath win 5-4 on pens)

SECOND ROUND

Saturday December 7
Morecambe 3 Chester C 2; Shrewsbury T 3 Barrow 1; Darlington 4 Stevenage Bor 1; Oldham Ath 1 Cheltenham T 2; Macclesfield T 2 Vauxhall M 0; Cambridge Utd 2 Northampton T 2; Exeter C 3 Rushden & Diamonds 1; Southport 0 Farnborough T 3; Crawley T 1 Dagenham & Redbridge 2; Bristol Rov 1 Rochdale 1; Wigan Ath 3 Luton T 0; Stockport County 0 Plymouth Argyle 3; Southend Utd 1 Bournemouth 1; York C 1 Brentford 2; Margate 0 Cardiff C 3; Scunthorpe Utd 0 Carlisle Utd 0; Blackpool 3 Torquay Utd 1; Crewe Alexandra 3 Mansfield T 0

Sunday December 8
Harrogate Railway 1 Bristol C 3; Oxford Utd 1 Swindon T 0

Replays

Tuesday December 17
Rochdale 3 Bristol Rov 2; Northampton T 0 Cambridge Utd 1; Bournemouth 3 Southend Utd 2

Monday December 23

Carlisle Utd 0 Scunthorpe Utd 1

THIRD ROUND

Saturday January 4
Leicester C 2 Bristol C 0; Scunthorpe Utd 0 Leeds Utd 2; Gillingham 4 Sheffield Wednesday 1; Chelsea 1 Middlesbrough 0; Ipswich T 4 Morecambe 0; Preston North End 1 Rochdale 2; Shrewsbury T 2 Everton 1; Bournemouth 0 Crewe Alexandra 0; Plymouth Argyle 2 Dagenham & Redbridge 2; Cambridge Utd 1 Millwall 1; Bolton Wndrs 1 Sunderland 1; Darlington 2 Farnborough T 3; Walsall 0 Reading 0; Stoke C 3 Wigan Ath 0; West Ham Utd 3 Nottingham Forest 2; Charlton Ath 3 Exeter C 1; Sheffield Utd 4 Cheltenham T 0; Aston Villa 1 Blackburn Rov 4; Cardiff C 2 Coventry C 2; Southampton 4 Tottenham Hotspur 0; Arsenal 2 Oxford Utd 0; Grimsby T 2 Burnley 2; West Bromwich Alb 3 Bradford C 1; Rotherham Utd 0 Wimbledon 3; Brentford

1 Derby County 0; Blackpool 1 Crystal Palace 2;
Manchester Utd 4 Portsmouth 1; Macclesfield T 0
Watford 2

Sunday January 5
Wolverhampton Wndrs 3 Newcastle Utd 2; Manchester
C 0 Liverpool 1; Fulham 3 Birmingham C 1

Tuesday January 14
Norwich C 3 Brighton & Hove Alb 1

Replays

Tuesday January 14
Crewe Alexandra 2 Bournemouth 2 (aet; Bournemouth
win 3-1 on pens); Dagenham & Redbridge 2 Plymouth
Argyle 0; Millwall 3 Cambridge Utd 2; Sunderland 2
Bolton Wndrs 0; Reading 1 Walsall 1 (aet; Walsall win
4-1 on pens); Burnley 4 Grimsby T 0

Wednesday January 15
Coventry C 3 Cardiff C 0

FOURTH ROUND

Saturday January 25
Norwich City 1 Dagenham & Redbridge 0
Southampton 1 Millwall 1
Walsall 1 Wimbledon 0
Blackburn Rovers 3 Sunderland 3
Rochdale 2 Coventry City 0
Sheffield United 4 Ipswich Town 3
Brentford 0 Burnley 3
Farnborough Town 1 Arsenal 5
(at Highbury)
Wolverhampton Wanderers 4 Leicester City 1
Watford 1 West Bromwich Albion 0
Gillingham 1 Leeds United 1

Sunday January 26
Stoke City 3 Bournemouth 0
Manchester United 6 West Ham United 0
Shrewsbury Town 0 Chelsea 4
Fulham 3 Charlton Athletic 0
Crystal Palace 0 Liverpool 0

Replays

Tuesday February 4
Leeds United 2 Gillingham 1

Wednesday February 5
Millwall 1 Southampton 2
Sunderland 2 Blackburn Rovers 2
(aet; Sunderland win 3-0 on pens)
Liverpool 0 Crystal Palace 2

FIFTH ROUND

Saturday February 15
Sunderland 0 Watford 1
Sheffield United 2 Walsall 0
Manchester United 0 Arsenal 2
Southampton 2 Norwich City 0

Sunday February 16
Crystal Palace 1 Leeds United 2
Wolverhampton Wanderers 3 Rochdale 1
Fulham 1 Burnley 1
Stoke City 0 Chelsea 2

Replay

Wednesday February 26
Burnley 3 Fulham 0

SIXTH ROUND

Saturday March 8
Arsenal 2 Chelsea 2

Sunday March 9
Watford 2 Burnley 0
Southampton 2 Wolverhampton Wanderers 0
Sheffield United 1 Leeds United 0

Replay

Tuesday March 25
Chelsea 1 Arsenal 3

SEMI-FINALS

Sunday, April 13   Villa Park

WATFORD (0) **1**　　　　　**SOUTHAMPTON** (1) **2**
Gayle 88　　　　　　　　　　Ormerod 43, Robinson 80 (og)
42,602

WATFORD (4-4-2): A Chamberlain — G Mahon, N Cox, M Gayle, P Robinson — N Ardley, P Vernazza
(sub: A Nielsen, 55min), M Hyde, S Glass (sub: L Cook, 76) — M Chopra (sub: T Smith, 70), H Helguson.
Substitutes not used: S Dyche, R Lee. **Booked:** Cox, Gayle, Robinson, Helguson.
SOUTHAMPTON (4-4-2): P Jones — P Telfer, C Lundekvam, M Svensson, W Bridge — F Fernandes,
A Svensson (sub: R Delap, 77), M Oakley, C Marsden — B Ormerod (sub: J Tessem, 90), J Beattie.
Substitutes not used: K Davies, D Higginbotham, A Blayney. **Booked:** Fernandes.
Referee: M Riley.

Sunday, April 13   Old Trafford

ARSENAL (1) **1**　　　　　**SHEFFIELD UNITED** (0) **1**
Ljungberg 34　　　　　　　　　59,170

ARSENAL (4-4-2): D Seaman — Lauren, M Keown, S Campbell, A Cole — R Parlour, P Vieira
(sub: Gilberto, 57), Edu, F Ljungberg — F Jeffers (sub: T Henry, 66), S Wiltord (sub: D Bergkamp, 82).
Substitutes not used: O Luzhny, S Taylor. **Booked:** Cole.
SHEFFIELD UNITED (4-3-3): P Kenny — J Curtis, P Jagielka, R Page, R Kozluk — M Tonge, S McCall
(sub: A Montgomery, 60), M Brown — S Kabba (sub: P Peschisolido, 77), W Allison (sub: C Asaba, 60),
P Ndlovu. **Substitutes not used:** S Murphy, G Kelly. **Booked:** McCall, Brown, Asaba.

FINAL　　　　　　　　　　May 25, Millennium Stadium

ARSENAL (0) **1**　　　　　**SOUTHAMPTON** (0) **0**
Pires 38　　　　　　　　　　　73,726

The appearance in the Southampton line-up of Chris Baird, the
young full back making only his second senior start, was as near
as the Cup Final got to producing a shock. Arsenal, only the
seventh team to reach three successive finals, could have had a
penalty inside 20 seconds, took the lead through a close-range
finish from Robert Pires and never looked like surrendering it to a
Southampton team who failed to reach the high standards they
had set themselves during the season. David Seaman was hardly
tested on what turned out to be his farewell game for Arsenal.

ARSENAL (4-4-2): D Seaman — Lauren, M Keown, O Luzhny, A Cole — F Ljungberg, P Parlour, Gilberto,
R Pires — T Henry, D Bergkamp (sub: S Wiltord, 77min). **Substitutes not used:** Taylor, Van Bronckhorst,
Kanu, Toure. **Booked:** Keown, Henry.
SOUTHAMPTON (4-4-2): A Niemi (sub: P Jones, 65) — C Baird (sub: F Fernandes, 86), C Lundekvam,
M Svensson, W Bridge — P Telfer, M Oakley, A Svensson (sub: J Tessem, 75), C Marsden — J Beattie,
B Ormerod. **Substitutes not used:** P Williams, D Higginbotham. **Booked:** Telfer, M Svensson, Beattie,
Marsden.
Referee: G Barber.

WORTHINGTON CUP

**Spray it again: Michael Owen
toasts Liverpool's record victory**

WINNERS
Liverpool

RUNNERS-UP
Manchester United

SEMI-FINALISTS
Blackburn Rovers
Sheffield United

THE GAMES

PRELIMINARY ROUND

August 20

Bristol Rovers 0 Boston United 2

FIRST ROUND

September 10

Bournemouth 3 Brentford 3
(aet; Brentford win 4-2 on pens)
Bristol City 0 Oxford United 1
Burnley 3 Blackpool 0
Bury 1 Stoke City 0
Crystal Palace 2 Plymouth Argyle 1 *(aet)*
Cambridge United 3 Reading 1
Grimsby Town 0 Chesterfield 1 *(aet)*
Hartlepool United 1 Tranmere Rovers 2
Huddersfield Town 2 Darlington 0
Hull City 2 Leicester City 4 *(aet)*
Leyton Orient 3 Queens Park Rangers 2
Lincoln City 1 Stockport County 3
Mansfield Town 1 Derby County 3
Northampton Town 0 Wigan Athletic 1
Norwich City 0 Cheltenham Town 3
Oldham Athletic 3 Notts Co 2
Port Vale 0 Crewe Alexandra 2
Portsmouth 2 Peterborough United 0
Rotherham United 3 Carlisle United 1
Rushden & Diamonds 0 Millwall 0
(aet; Rushden win 5-3 on pens)
Sheffield United 1 York City 0
Southend United 1 Wimbledon 4
Torquay United 0 Gillingham 1
Walsall 1 Shrewsbury Town 0
Watford 1 Luton Town 2
Wrexham 2 Bradford City 1

September 11

Boston United 1 Cardiff City 5
Brighton and Hove Albion 2 Exeter City 1 *(aet)*
Coventry City 3 Colchester United 0
Macclesfield Town 4 Barnsley 1 *(aet)*
Nottingham Forest 4 Kidderminster Harriers 0
Preston North End 2 Scunthorpe United 1 *(aet)*
Sheffield Wednesday 1 Rochdale 0
Swansea City 2 Wolverhampton Wndrs 3
Swindon Town 1 Wycombe Wndrs 2 *(aet)*

SECOND ROUND

September 24

Ipswich Town 3 Brighton and Hove Albion 1

October 1

Brentford 1 Middlesbrough 4
Cambridge United 0 Sunderland 7
Charlton Athletic 0 Oxford United 0
(aet; Oxford win 6-5 on pens)
Chesterfield 1 West Ham United 1
(aet; West Ham win 5-4 on pens)
Huddersfield Town 0 Burnley 1 *(aet)*
Macclesfield Town 1 Preston North End 2
Manchester City 3 Crewe Alexandra 2
Portsmouth 1 Wimbledon 3
Rotherham United 4 Wolverhampton Wndrs 4
(aet; Rotherham win 4-2 on pens)

THE NOISE ALMOST RAISED the closed roof of the Millennium Stadium. A competition that had revived in recent months was now enjoying the perfect climax, a final that paired Liverpool and Manchester United, England's most famous and successful clubs. The passion of their fans in Cardiff indicated that the Worthington Cup had become worthy again.

The League Cup, in its various guises, has attracted nearly as much ridicule as the InterToto Cup since the big clubs began to lose interest in the mid-1990s, yet attendances last season were the highest since 1979-80, long before managers dreamt of fielding weakened teams to save senior players for the pursuit of potentially more lucrative league points.

The figures were boosted by the fact that Old Trafford staged three games, which drew a total of nearly 170,000 people to watch Manchester United face Leicester City, Chelsea and Blackburn Rovers. Large numbers were encouraged by the decision of Sir Alex Ferguson, the United manager, to field a full-strength side from the quarter-finals onwards. Similarly, Gerard Houllier also selected his best players once his Liverpool team reached the last eight.

The renaissance, of course, may prove to be a temporary reprieve for a tournament that many feel should be scrapped. Furthermore, there were several negative signs last season. Liverpool and United, after all, fielded under-strength sides in their first two ties, as most leading Premiership sides did in the early stages, while the final had to share the limelight with another televised match that day (Arsenal v Charlton Athletic in the Premiership).

Peter Reid might also question the Worthington Cup's value, having been dismissed as Sunderland manager less than a week after guiding them to a 7-0 win away to Cambridge United. The club clearly considered the result to be insufficient compensation for his team's poor league form.

Sunderland eventually fell to Sheffield United, of the first division, who were arguably the team of the tournament in what was a remarkable season for them. Neil Warnock's men were lucky to draw five home ties, but they produced a sensational late comeback against Leeds United, when two goals in stoppage time earned a 2-1 win. A double from Michael Tonge produced a similar turnaround against Houllier's side in the first leg of the semi-final and they only succumbed at Anfield after extra time.

Other Nationwide League representatives to excel were Wigan Athletic. Nathan Ellington scored a hat-trick in the win over West Bromwich Albion before the second division side completed a hat-trick of their own — three Premiership victims — by knocking

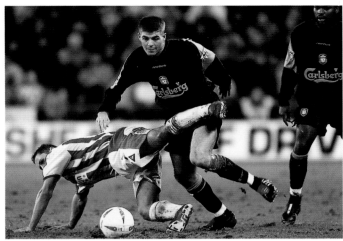
Sheffield United proved an awkward obstacle for Liverpool in the semi-finals

out Manchester City and Fulham. West Ham United and Charlton, both at full strength, were also taken to penalties by Chesterfield and Oxford United respectively, West Ham going through but promptly losing at home to Oldham Athletic in the third round.

Macclesfield Town avoided spot-kicks when Danny Whitaker achieved the rare distinction of recording a hat-trick in extra time to see off Barnsley, but there was an even more unusual tale at Selhurst Park. Wimbledon were immune to the Worthington Cup's rising attendances, their match against Rotherham United attracting just 664 supporters.

The continental engagements of Liverpool and Manchester United meant that they entered the competition in the third round and their journeys to the final were unconvincing. Liverpool only beat Southampton at home after a fine display from Chris Kirkland, their goalkeeper, and they needed a penalty shoot-out to see off Ipswich Town, also at Anfield. They edged out Aston Villa at Villa Park in the competition's most exciting game before scraping through their semi-final against Sheffield United.

Manchester United had little difficulty in defeating Leicester at Old Trafford, but were lucky to beat Burnley away and Chelsea at home. Their semi-final win over Blackburn Rovers was ultimately comfortable, even though they had to come from behind after Andrew Cole had scored against his former club in the second leg.

United dominated the final for long periods but were foiled by the excellence of Jerzy Dudek, the Liverpool goalkeeper, who, until Kirkland's injury, had seemed likely to be left out for the rest of the season after a howler against United in the Premiership in December. Goals from Steven Gerrard and Michael Owen ensured that, after five difficult years, the Worthington Cup finished on a high. The Carling Cup, its successor, has something to live up to.

Sheffield United 4 Wycombe Wndrs 1
Stockport County 1 Gillingham 2 (aet)
Tottenham Hotspur 1 Cardiff City 0
Wrexham 0 Everton 3

October 2

Aston Villa 3 Luton Town 0
Bolton Wndrs 0 Bury 1
Crystal Palace 7 Cheltenham Town 0
Coventry City 8 Rushden & Diamonds 0
Derby County 1 Oldham Athletic 2 (aet)
Leyton Orient 2 Birmingham City 3
Nottingham Forest 1 Walsall 2
Sheffield Wednesday 1 Leicester City 2 (aet)
Southampton 6 Tranmere Rovers 1
Wigan Athletic 3 West Bromwich Albion 1

THIRD ROUND

November 5

Birmingham City 0 Preston North End 2
Manchester United 2 Leicester City 0
Wigan Athletic 1 Manchester City 0
Wimbledon 1 Rotherham United 3

November 6

Arsenal 2 Sunderland 3
Blackburn Rovers 2 Walsall 2
(aet; Blackburn win 5-4 on pens)
Burnley 2 Tottenham Hotspur 1
Crystal Palace 3 Coventry City 0
Chelsea 2 Gillingham 1
Fulham 3 Bury 1
Ipswich Town 3 Middlesbrough 1
Liverpool 3 Southampton 1
Newcastle United 3 Everton 3
(aet; Everton win 3-2 on pens)
Oxford United 0 Aston Villa 3
Sheffield United 2 Leeds United 1
West Ham United 0 Oldham Athletic 1

FOURTH ROUND

December 3

Burnley 0 Manchester United 2
Crystal Palace 2 Oldham Athletic 0
Sheffield United 2 Sunderland 0

December 4

Aston Villa 5 Preston North End 0
Blackburn Rovers 4 Rotherham United 0
Chelsea 4 Everton 1
Liverpool 1 Ipswich Town 1
(aet; Liverpool win 5-4 on pens)
Wigan Athletic 2 Fulham 1

QUARTER-FINALS

December 17

Manchester United 1 Chelsea 0
Sheffield United 3 Crystal Palace 1
Wigan Athletic 0 Blackburn Rovers 2

December 18

Aston Villa 3 Liverpool 4

Semi-finals and final details, page 338

MATCH OF THE SEASON

Aston Villa 3   Liverpool 4
Villa Park, Wednesday December 18 2002
David McVay

BETTER LATE THAN NEVER, perhaps, although Aston Villa might disagree with that sentiment after failing at the last in this pulsating Worthington Cup quarter-final at Villa Park last night.

By the final whistle, those inside the stadium had almost forgotten the ticket fiasco that delayed this match by 80 minutes as Liverpool and Villa produced a compelling contest, the pace and tempo of which seldom slackened as the clock ticked towards the midnight hour.

In the final seconds, Danny Murphy seized on a loose ball in Villa's penalty area and drove it through a ruck of players for his second goal of the evening to decide a memorable cup-tie.

The match had seemed destined for an even more protracted finale when Dion Dublin, appearing to be in an offside position, volleyed home an equaliser via a huge deflection off Stephane Henchoz in the 88th minute. The scoreline, however, reflects the relative weaknesses of these teams this season. Between them they have lifted this trophy ll times in its various guises, but it is Liverpool who will seek to establish further success this season and

add to their record of six final victories.

Whether it is the end of what Gerard Houllier, their manager, has described as his worst period in charge at Anfield — five league defeats have been suffered in the past five weeks — or merely a false dawn remains to be seen.

"We needed a win," Houllier said. "There are times when we have been unlucky in some league games and, indeed, we might have avoided defeat in three of them. Some things were not going our way and maybe we have put an end to it. I am so proud of their performance and I am pleased we scored, because the last thing we wanted was extra time [ahead of the Merseyside derby at home to Everton on Sunday]."

Even so, defensive frailty remains at the heart of Liverpool's back four and had Villa capitalised when they were in the ascendancy in the first half, it would surely have been the West Midlands club that progressed into the semi-final draw. Moreover, they would have been handed the easier of the two ties, opposing Sheffield United.

"Anything that could go wrong has gone wrong for us," Graham Taylor, the Villa manager, said. "[Steve] Staunton was injured this morning, then [Ronny] Johnsen before kick-off and then the referee knocks on my door to say the kick-off was delayed. If it was a conspiracy, it was complete when Jlloyd [Samuel] slipped for their winning goal."

Delays, apologetic public-address announcements promising the imminent resumption of normal service, then more delays. Fans lucky enough to be inside the stadium long before kick-off must have felt a certain empathy with frustrated train commuters when the leaves are falling on the nation's railway lines.

Thus, the collective sense of relief when a football match finally arrived at the station was overwhelming, not to mention therapeutic in that it gave both sets of supporters something to think about other than the bitter cold. There was plenty to sustain them, too, because the tie did not disappoint after its pre-match billing.

Villa drew first blood and deservedly so, not only because their early enterprise was encouraging, but also because they had suffered an eleventh-hour disruption to

Murphy's double for Liverpool proved decisive in a protracted tie

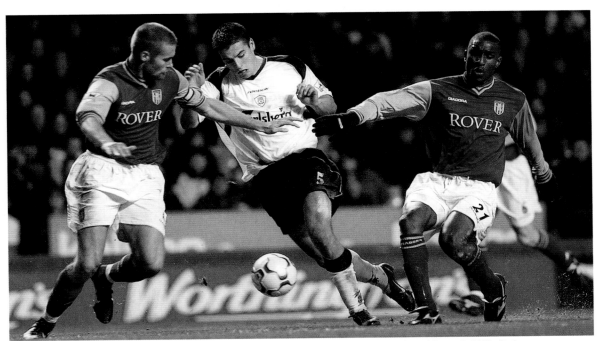

Leading man: Baros, who put Liverpool ahead early in the second half, takes on Mellberg, left, and Samuel at Villa Park

their preparations. Johnsen, the former Manchester United defender, pulled up during a warm-up routine and was replaced by Moustapha Hadji, the Morocco playmaker, whose role has been mainly to make up the numbers on the substitutes' bench this season.

Darius Vassell's pace embarrassed Henchoz and Sami Hyypia. The England forward showed both international defenders a clean pair of heels repeatedly and it was fitting that he should secure the lead in the 23rd minute from the penalty spot, after Lee Hendrie had been fouled by the sluggish Djimi Traore. Chris Kirkland, the Liverpool goalkeeper, dived early and Vassell's shot, true and down the middle, was the first successful spot kick by a Villa player this season.

Liverpool were not behind for long, though, Murphy curling in a free kick from 20 yards, via a slight deflection off the wall, to restore parity in the 27th minute.

Villa's response was impressive. Oyvind Leonhardsen unwittingly blocked a cross bound for Dublin and Kirkland proved his mettle with two splendid saves to deny Dublin and Hadji.

The feeling was that Liverpool had been let off lightly in the first half and, suitably chastened, they emerged the stronger after the interval, a superiority that was translated into a goal nine minutes into the second period. John Arne Riise's pass found Milan Baros lurking on the fringes of the Villa penalty area and, allowed time and space, the Czech Republic forward delivered a low drive beyond Peter Enckelman to give Liverpool the lead.

It seemed impossible that the tempo could increase, but it did. Olof Mellberg halted Baros's progress in the 67th minute, but, when the ball ran free, there was Steven Gerrard to pounce with conviction and make it 3-1 with an angled right-foot shot. "It was probably his best all-round performance of the season," Houllier said. "His energy and stamina are back."

Villa reduced the arrears courtesy of Thomas Hitzlsperger's left foot — "The Hammer", as it is known, finding its target with a low, 25-yard drive that fizzed unerringly into the corner of the net. The revival seemed complete after Dublin's fortunate volley. Perhaps an unexpected curtailment at the end of such a long night could be considered an act of mercy for the fans.

ASTON VILLA (4-4-2): P Enckelman — U De La Cruz (sub: J P Angel, 79min), O Mellberg, J Samuel, G Barry — O Leonhardsen, T Hitzlsperger, L Hendrie (sub: M Kinsella, 83), M Hadji — D Dublin, D Vassell. **Substitutes not used:** S Postma, M Allback, R Edwards.
LIVERPOOL (4-4-2): C Kirkland — M Babbel (sub: J Carragher, 39), S Henchoz, S Hyypia, D Traore — D Murphy, S Gerrard, S Diao, J A Riise — M Owen (sub: E Heskey, 76), M Baros. **Substitutes not used:** J Dudek, V Smicer, E-H Diouf. **Booked:** Murphy, Hyypia, Henchoz.
Referee: G Barber.

SEMI-FINALS, FIRST LEGS

MANCHESTER UTD (0) 1   BLACKBURN ROVERS (0) 1
Scholes 58
62,740
    Thompson 61

MANCHESTER UNITED (4-4-2): F Barthez — G Neville, R Ferdinand, W Brown, M Silvestre — D Beckham, P Neville (sub: D Forlan, 83min), J S Veron, R Giggs (sub: O G Solskjaer, 74) — R van Nistelrooy, P Scholes. **Substitutes not used:** L Blanc, J O'Shea, Ricardo. **Booked:** P Neville.
BLACKBURN ROVERS (4-4-2): B Friedel — L Neill, M Taylor, A Todd, J McEveley — D Thompson (sub: M Jansen, 66), Tugay, G Flitcroft, D Dunn (sub: K Gillespie, 19) — A Cole, D Yorke. **Substitutes not used:** N-E Johansson, E Ostenstad, A Kelly. **Booked:** Neill, McEveley.
Referee: U Rennie.

Wednesday January 8

SHEFFIELD UTD (0) 2   LIVERPOOL (1) 1
Tonge 76, 82
30,095
    Mellor 35

SHEFFIELD UNITED (4-4-2): P Kenny — P Jagielka, S Murphy, R Page, W Quinn — P Ndlovu, S McCall, M Brown, M Tonge — W Allison, C Asaba (sub: N Montgomery, 51min). **Substitutes not used:** R Kozluk, P Peschisolido, J-P McGovern, W de Vogt. **Booked:** Tonge, Asaba, Brown.
LIVERPOOL (4-5-1): C Kirkland — J Carragher, S Henchoz, S Hyypia, D Traore — E-H Diouf, D Murphy, S Gerrard, S Diao, V Smicer (sub: E Heskey, 57) — N Mellor (sub: M Owen, 71). **Substitutes not used:** J A Riise, B Cheyrou, J Dudek. **Booked:** Henchoz, Traore, Diouf, Diao.
Referee: M Dean.

PLAYER OF THE SEASON
Nathan Ellington

Long considered a future Premiership player, Nathan Ellington gave two top-flight clubs an exhibition of his talents in the Worthington Cup. Having produced an FA Cup hat-trick for Bristol Rovers away to Derby County the previous season, the 21-year-old striker scored all of Wigan Athletic's goals in the 3-1 second-round win over West Bromwich Albion. His two goals also brought a 2-1 victory for the second division side against Fulham. **Bill Edgar**

TOP SCORERS 2002-03

5   **Nathan Ellington** (Wigan Athletic)

4   **Dion Dublin** (Aston Villa), **Andrew Cole** (Blackburn Rovers), **Gary McSheffrey** (Coventry City)

3   **El-Hadji Diouf** (Liverpool), **Robert Earnshaw** (Cardiff City), **Rodney Jack** (Crewe Alexandra), **Stern John** (Birmingham City), **Andy Johnson** (Crystal Palace), **Lee Mills** (Coventry City), **Andy Monkhouse** (Rotherham United), **Brett Ormerod** (Southampton), **Dimitrios Papadopoulos** (Burnley), **Paul Scholes** (Manchester United), **Neil Shipperley** (Wimbledon), **Marcus Stewart** (Sunderland), **Darius Vassell** (Aston Villa), **Danny Whitaker** (Macclesfield Town)

LEAGUE CUP WINNERS

7   Liverpool
5   Aston Villa
4   Nottingham Forest
3   Leicester City, Tottenham Hotspur
2   Arsenal, Chelsea, Manchester City, Norwich City, Wolverhampton Wanderers
1   Blackburn Rovers, Birmingham City, Leeds United, Luton Town, Manchester United, Oxford United, Queens Park Rangers, Sheffield Wednesday, Stoke City, Swindon Town, West Bromwich Albion

SECOND LEGS

Tuesday January 21

LIVERPOOL (1) 2   SHEFFIELD UTD (0) 0
Diouf 9, Owen 107
43,837

(aet; 1-0 after 90min; Liverpool win 3-2 on agg)

LIVERPOOL (4-4-2): C Kirkland — J Carragher, S Henchoz, S Hyypia, J A Riise — E-H Diouf, S Gerrard, D Murphy, V Smicer (sub: B Cheyrou, 96min) — E Heskey, M Owen. **Substitutes not used:** S Diao, M Baros, N Mellor, J Dudek. **Booked:** Smicer, Kirkland.
SHEFFIELD UNITED (4-1-4-1): P Kenny — P Jagielka, S Murphy, R Page, W Quinn (sub: L Ten Heuvel, 115) — S McCall — P Ndlovu, N Montgomery (sub: T Mooney, 45), M Brown, M Tonge — W Allison (sub: P Peschisolido, 105). **Substitutes not used:** R Kozluk, W de Vogt. **Booked:** Quinn, Page.
Referee: A Wiley.

Wednesday January 22

BLACKBURN ROVERS (1) 1   MANCHESTER UTD (2) 3
Cole 12
29,048
    Scholes 30, 42, Van Nistelrooy 77 (pen)

(Manchester United win 4-2 on agg)

BLACKBURN ROVERS (4-4-2): B Friedel — L Neill, A Todd, M Taylor, J McEveley — D Thompson, Tugay, G Flitcroft, D Duff (sub: K Gillespie, 35min) — A Cole, D Yorke. **Substitutes not used:** M Jansen, C Short, E Ostenstad, R Robinson. **Booked:** Friedel, Thompson.
MANCHESTER UNITED (4-4-2): F Barthez — G Neville, R Ferdinand, W Brown, M Silvestre — D Beckham, R Keane, P Scholes (sub: N Butt, 80), J S Veron — R van Nistelrooy (sub: D Forlan, 84), R Giggs. **Substitutes not used:** P Neville, J O'Shea, Ricardo.
Referee: J Winter.

FINAL

          March 2, Millennium Stadium

LIVERPOOL (1) 2   MANCHESTER UTD (0) 0
Gerrard 39, Owen 86   74,500

With Arsenal extending their Premiership lead to eight points on the same day, Sir Alex Ferguson may have felt that his Manchester United side had lost two trophies in one afternoon as Liverpool captured the League Cup for the seventh time with their sixth victory over the old enemy in the past seven attempts. But if it was a day of regrets for United, it was an afternoon of redemption for two Liverpool players. Jerzy Dudek, whose error against United in the league match at Anfield in December eventually cost him his place in goal, was rightly named man of the final, having regained his place from the injured Chris Kirkland, while Steven Gerrard, publicly criticised by Gerard Houllier earlier in the season, capped an all-action display with the opening goal, scored with the aid of a sizeable deflection off David Beckham. Michael Owen ended any hopes that United may still have harboured when he sprinted clear on to Dietmar Hamann's pass to score the second four minutes from time.

LIVERPOOL (4-4-2): J Dudek — J Carragher, S Henchoz, S Hyypia, J A Riise — E-H Diouf (sub: I Biscan, 90min), D Hamann, S Gerrard, D Murphy (sub: V Smicer, 89), M Owen. **Substitutes not used:** P Arphexad, D Traore. **Booked:** Henchoz.
MANCHESTER UNITED (4-4-1-1): F Barthez — G Neville, R Ferdinand, W Brown (sub: O G Solskjaer, 74), M Silvestre — D Beckham, R Keane, J S Veron, R Giggs — P Scholes — R van Nistelrooy. **Substitutes not used:** J O'Shea, P Neville, N Butt, R Carroll.
Referee: P Durkin.

WOMEN'S FOOTBALL

Treble chance: Mary Phillip, the Fulham captain, holds the FA Women's Cup aloft

PREMIER LEAGUE
Fulham

RUNNERS-UP
Doncaster Belles

NORTHERN DIVISION
Aston Villa

RUNNERS-UP
Sunderland

SOUTHERN DIVISION
Bristol Rovers

RUNNERS-UP
Ipswich Town

FA CUP
Fulham

RUNNERS-UP
Charlton Athletic

LEAGUE CUP
Fulham

RUNNERS-UP
Arsenal

FINAL TABLES

FA WOMEN'S PREMIER LEAGUE
NATIONAL DIVISION

	P	W	D	L	F	A	GD	Pts
Fulham	18	16	2	0	63	13	+50	49*
Doncaster Belles	18	13	2	3	34	19	+15	41
Arsenal	18	13	1	4	53	21	+32	40
Charlton Athletic	18	10	4	4	44	20	+24	34
Birmingham City	18	6	3	9	26	31	-5	21
Tranmere Rovers	18	6	3	9	25	48	-23	21
Leeds United	18	5	4	9	33	42	-9	19
Everton	18	5	1	12	18	38	-20	16
Southampton S	18	2	5	11	10	30	-20	11
Brighton & HA	18	1	1	16	18	62	-44	4

*one point deducted

NORTHERN DIVISION

	P	W	D	L	F	A	GD	Pts
Aston Villa	22	16	4	2	59	18	+41	52
Sunderland	22	15	4	3	48	25	+23	49
Oldham Curzon	22	14	2	6	48	29	+19	44
Bangor City	22	11	4	7	46	37	+9	37
Wolverhampton	22	9	5	8	28	26	+2	32
Liverpool	22	7	8	7	37	32	+5	29
Lincoln City	22	6	7	9	38	46	-8	25
Manchester City	22	5	6	11	31	37	-6	21
Middlesbrough	22	6	2	14	25	44	-19	20
Sheffield Wed	22	5	5	12	15	36	-21	20
Ilkeston Town	22	5	4	13	24	44	-20	19
Garswood Saints	22	4	7	11	26	51	-25	19

SOUTHERN DIVISION

	P	W	D	L	F	A	GD	Pts
Bristol Rovers	20	17	1	2	76	19	+57	52
Ipswich Town	20	11	2	7	49	36	+13	35
Bristol City	20	10	5	5	47	34	+13	35
Millwall Lionesses	20	10	4	6	41	33	+8	34
Barnet	20	10	4	6	29	24	+5	34
Chelsea	20	10	2	8	33	31	+2	32
Merthyr Tydfil	20	9	3	8	30	34	-4	30
Langford	20	8	5	7	38	35	+3	29
Wimbledon	20	5	1	14	27	48	-21	16
Enfield	20	3	2	15	32	59	-27	11
Barking	20	2	1	17	22	71	-49	7

FA NATIONWIDE PREMIER LEAGUE CUP
FIRST ROUND
Barking 1 Garswood 4; Brighton 2 Barnet 0; Bristol R 3 Southampton 0; Charlton 7 Enfield 1; Doncaster 3 Everton 0; Fulham 6 Langford 2; Lincoln 2 Leeds Utd 4; Manchester C 5 Ilkeston 2; Middlesbrough 0 Ipswich 1; Sunderland 4 Chelsea 0; Tranmere 4 Millwall 0; Wolves 1 Liverpool 4; Arsenal 11 Sheff Weds 0; Bangor 2 Aston Villa 3; Wimbledon 0 Birmingham C 4
SECOND ROUND
Arsenal 3 Leeds Utd 0; Brighton 1 Birmingham 4; Bristol R 2 Oldham 0; Charlton 10 Garswood 1; Doncaster 2 Manchester C 1; Fulham 12 Liverpool 0; Sunderland 2 Aston Villa 3; Tranmere 6 Ipswich 0
THIRD ROUND
Arsenal 1 Tranmere 0; Aston Villa 1 Charlton 0; Fulham 5 Birmingham 0; Doncaster 7 Bristol R 0
SEMI-FINALS
Aston Villa 1 Fulham 2; Doncaster Belles 1 Arsenal 2
FINAL
Fulham 1 Arsenal 1 (aet; Fulham win 3-2 on penalties)

FULHAM'S FIRST SEASON IN THE top flight was also their last — for the time being, at least — as a professional entity. They carried off the domestic treble to boot, as if to prove the benefit of operating as a full-time team, but whether Mohamed Al Fayed's decision to reduce his financial commitment to Fulham Ladies marks the end of a dream or the start of a more competitive era in the women's game in England remains to be seen. This was supposed to be the season that a professional league was introduced in England, but Fulham's downscaling erased the red pencil mark that Adam Crozier, the former chief executive of the FA, had circled around the year 2003.

Another five-figure crowd watched Gaute Haugenes's team complete the treble by defeating Charlton Athletic 3-0 at Selhurst Park in the FA Women's Cup Final on May 5, but while there can be no doubting the women's game continues to rise in popularity, it is primarily as a participation sport than as a spectacle. In the long term, as this breeds more — and better — players, such numerical support will surely spill on to the terraces.

Football overtook netball as the most popular women's sport in 2002. According to an official FA audit, the number of affiliated girls' teams doubled to 4,200 in the past year, while the overall number of female players participating in affiliated league and cup competitions increased by 38 per cent, to 85,000. Ten years ago, before the FA started running the game, there were 11,000 players in around 80 teams. Now, 1.4 million girls under 15 play regularly.

The success of *Bend It Like Beckham*, the box-office hit film that featured women's football, has helped to glamorise the sport and was mirrored in the numbers watching the BBC's live coverage of the Women's Cup Final. An audience of 1.9 million tuned in to watch Fulham beat Charlton.

On March 30 they had retained the FA Nationwide Women's Premier League Cup when they beat Arsenal in a penalty shoot-out at Swindon Town's County Ground after the 90 minutes had ended with the score at 1-1, Rachel Yankey scoring for Fulham two minutes from time before Ciara Grant equalised in the final 60 seconds. Kim Jerray-Silver, the defender, scored the deciding penalty.

Haugenes's team remained unbeaten throughout the season, their third campaign as professionals, and only Charlton took points off them. Ten years after their formation, Fulham had eclipsed Arsenal and Doncaster Belles as the dominant team in the country.

Arsenal failed to win a trophy for the first time since 1996. Vic Akers's team were beaten in the semi-final of the FA Women's Cup by Charlton, for whom Justine Lorton scored a late penalty in a 1-0

Rachel Yankey, of Fulham, is sent flying during the FA Women's Cup Final

win at The Valley in front of a 3,031 crowd, on March 23. On the same day, Fulham won 7-2 away to Bristol Rovers at the Memorial Stadium, which had a gate of 2,442.

Arsenal also lost at the penultimate stage of the Uefa Women's Cup, having been knocked out in the quarter-finals in the inaugural event the previous season. On April 27, Fortuna Hjorring, from Denmark, won 5-1 at Barnet's Underhill ground in the second leg to complete an 8-2 aggregate victory.

After Marieanne Spacey's defection to Fulham 12 months earlier, Arsenal have now lost Angela Banks, the leading domestic goalscorer two years ago, who has retired. Jayne Ludlow, the Wales attacking midfield player, was named as the Nationwide players' player of the year in the end-of-season awards.

As FA Women's Premier League national division champions, Fulham will be England's representatives in the 2003-04 European campaign. Doncaster finished runners-up, eight points adrift. The Belles, with their lucrative backing from Green Flag, will henceforth be known as Doncaster Rovers Belles after they relinquished their status as the last independent top-flight club in order to merge with the men's club. Julie Chipchase, their manager, left to take over at Leeds United after Mark Hodgson's departure.

Birmingham City, promoted with Fulham 12 months previously, enjoyed a highly creditable season by finishing fifth, a feat that earned Marcus Bignot the Nationwide manager-of-the-year award. Brighton & Hove Albion, after two years in the top division, were relegated back to the FA Women's Premier League southern division, along with Southampton.

FA WOMEN'S CUP

FIRST ROUND

Chester-le-Street 4 Darwen 2; Parkgate 5 Liverpool 4; Darlington 1 Huddersfield 3; Stockport 4 Blackpool 0; Preston 2 Barnsley 3; Blackburn 6 Chesterfield 0; Southport 0 Chester 2; Newsham 2 East Durham 4; Durham 0 Newcastle 6; Gretna 3 Manchester Utd 6; Scunthorpe 5 Leeds Vixens 1; Thorpe 5 Hopwood 1; Loughborough 1 Coventry 0; Shrewsbury 10 Great Wyrley 1; Highfield 5 Lichfield 6; Rushden 4 Loughborough 1; Ilkeston 6 Kesteven 2; Peterborough 2 Northampton 1; Cambridge U w/o Telford; Leicester 4 Stafford 1; Hitchin 0 Reading 3; Chesham 0 Brook House 2; Aylesbury 1 Watford 6; Luton 1 Denham 2; West Ham 0 Norwich 1; QPR 3 Crowborough 0; Dagenham 7 Tring 1; Woking 2 Reading Royals 2 (aet; Reading Royals win 3-2 on pens); Gillingham 2 Crystal Palace 1; Colchester 4 Westbourne 0; Portsmouth 3 Bedford 0; Brentford 1 Stowmarket 2; Haywood 4 Clapton Orient 0; Newquay 7 Keynsham 2; Newton Abbot 4 Exeter 3 (aet); Cardiff 10 Okeford 2; Plymouth 0 Torbay 4; Rover Oxford 2 Swindon 1; Yeovil 0 Clevedon 1

SECOND ROUND

Parkgate 4 Thorpe 1; Newcastle 7 Chester-le-Street 1; Chester 2 Huddersfield 0; East Durham 2 Stockport 1; Blackburn 4 Barnsley 0; Manchester Utd 8 Scunthorpe 0; Peterborough 1 Ilkeston 6; Cambridge U 3 Lichfield 4; Leicester 5 Loughborough 1; Rushden 5 Shrewsbury 2; Norwich 2 Stowmarket 1; Reading Royals 8 Colchester 1; Redbridge 1 Reading 0; Dagenham 3 Brook House 0; Denham 0 Portsmouth 1; QPR 0 Watford 1; Haywood 1 Gillingham 3; Newquay 4 Newton Abbot 2; Torbay 2 Rover Oxford 0; Cardiff 2 Clevedon 1 (aet)

THIRD ROUND

Newcastle 3 Rushden 0; Manchester Utd 3 Ilkeston 0; Liverpool 5 Chester 0; Wolves 5 Sheff Weds 0; East Durham 7 Garswood 0; Blackburn 4 Bangor 0; Oldham 2 Sunderland 0; Leicester 1 Manchester C 0 (aet); Lincoln 4 Ilkeston 1; Parkgate 2 Aston Villa 7; Middlesbrough 5 Lichfield 1; Portsmouth 3 Ipswich 4; Dagenham 0 Bristol R 4; Gillingham 1 Torbay 3; Bristol C 2 Millwall 0; Reading Royals 2 Wimbledon 1; Merthyr T 2 Norwich 1; Chelsea 3 Langford 1; Enfield 0 Cardiff 1; Newquay 1 Watford 4; Barking 1 Redbridge 2

FOURTH ROUND

Bristol R 4 Chelsea 3; Arsenal 2 Tranmere 0; Blackburn 3 Middlesbrough 2; Reading 2 Aston Villa 3; Bristol C 1 Oldham 1 (aet; Oldham win 4-3 on pens); Lincoln 2 Leicester 1; Watford 1 Liverpool 1 (aet; Watford win 6-5 on pens); Newcastle 0 Birmingham 5; Barnet 1 East Durham 6; Torbay 0 Manchester Utd 2; Redbridge 0 Ipswich 4; Charlton 4 Brighton 0; Leeds Utd 4 Merthyr T 0; Cardiff 2 Wolves 2 (aet; Wolves win 2-1 on pens); Southampton 2 Everton 1; Fulham 2 Doncaster 0

FIFTH ROUND

Lincoln 0 Watford 0; East Durham 1 Fulham 3; Birmingham 7 Blackburn 2; Wolves 0 Arsenal 4; Manchester Utd 0 Charlton 8; Leeds Utd 0 Aston Villa 3; Ipswich 2 Oldham 3; Bristol R 1 Southampton 1 (aet; Bristol R win 3-1 on pens)

SIXTH ROUND

Arsenal 6 Aston Villa 0; Fulham 1 Oldham 0; Bristol R 3 Lincoln 2; Birmingham 1 Charlton 3

SEMI-FINALS

Bristol R 2 Fulham 7; Charlton 1 Arsenal 0

FINAL

Charlton 0 Fulham 3

ENGLAND

THE 2003 WOMEN'S WORLD Cup finals, to be staged in September and October, were switched to the United States because the Sars outbreak ruled China, the original hosts, out of contention, but England's interest in the tournament ended on a Saturday afternoon in St Etienne the previous November.

The transitional team being forged by Hope Powell performed well to earn the runners-up spot behind Germany in their qualifying group, Kelly Smith and Fara Williams starring in crucial wins over Holland and Portugal, and they overcame Iceland in the play-off semi-finals. Karen Walker, the captain, scored twice in the drawn first leg in Reykjavik before Amanda Barr claimed the only goal in the return at St Andrew's in Birmingham.

France, however, deservedly won both legs of the final, when England badly missed Smith, their injured Philadelphia Charge striker, and Katie Chapman, the Fulham midfield player, who was pregnant. Walker announced her retirement from international football after a 17-year run in which she scored a record 40 goals in 83 appearances, leaving England to set their sights on hosting the 2005 European Championship.

Karen Walker goes close against Iceland at St Andrew's

CHAMPIONS LEAGUE

Just champion: Shevchenko's penalty has won the European Cup for AC Milan

WINNERS
AC Milan

RUNNERS-UP
Juventus

SEMI-FINALISTS
Real Madrid
Inter Milan

THE GAMES

FIRST QUALIFYING ROUND

First leg, July 17
Tampere United 0 Pyunik 4; Skonto Riga 5 Barry Town 0; Portadown 0 Belshina 0; F91 Dudelange 1 Vardar 1; FBK Kaunas 2 Dinamo Tirana 3; FC Flora Tallinn 0 Apoel Nicosia 0; Zeljeznicar 3 Akranes 0; Hibernians 2 Shelbourne 2; Torpedo Kutaisi 5 B36 Torshavn 2; Sheriff Tiraspol 2 Zhenis 1

Second leg, July 24
Pyunik 2 Tampere United 0 (Pyunik win 6-0 on agg); Barry Town 0 Skonto Riga 1 (Skonto Riga win 6-0 on agg); Belshina 3 Portadown 2 (Belshina win 3-2 on agg); Vardar 3 Dudelange 0 (Vardar win 4-1 on agg); Dinamo Tirana 0 Kaunas 0 (Dinamo win 3-2 on agg); Apoel Nicosia 1 FC Flora 0 (Apoel win 1-0 on agg); Akranes 0 Zeljeznicar 1 (Zeljeznicar win 4-0 on agg); Shelbourne 0 Hibernians 1 (Hibernians win 3-2 on agg); B36 Torshavn 0 Torpedo Kutaisi 1 (Torpedo win 6-2 on agg); Zhenis 3 Sheriff Tiraspol 2 (5-5 on agg; Sheriff Tiraspol win on away goals)

SECOND QUALIFYING ROUND

First leg, July 31
Zalaegerszeg 1 Zagreb 0; FC Bruges 3 Dinamo Bucharest 1; Zilina 1 FC Basle 1; Skonto Riga 0 Levski 0; Dinamo Kiev 4 Pyunik 0; Brondby 1 Dinamo Tirana 0; Maribor 2 Apoel Nicosia 1; Vardar 1 Legia Warsaw 3; Boavista 4 Hibernians 0; Maccabi Haifa 4 Belshina 0; Lillestrom 0 Zeljeznicar 1; Hammarby 1 FK Partizan 1; Sparta Prague 3 Torpedo Kutaisi 0; Sheriff Tiraspol 1 GAK 4

Second leg, August 7
Zagreb 2 Zalaegerszeg 1 (2-2 on agg; Zalaegerszeg win on away goals); Dinamo Bucharest 0 FC Bruges 1 (FC Bruges win 4-1 on agg); FC Basle 3 Zilina 0 (FC Basle win 4-1 on agg); Levski 2 Skonto Riga 0 (Levski win 2-0 on agg); Pyunik 2 Dinamo Kiev 2 (Dinamo win 6-2 on agg); Dinamo Tirana 0 Brondby 4 (Brondby win 5-0 on agg); Apoel Nicosia 4 Maribor 2 (Apoel win 5-4 on agg); Legia Warsaw 1 Vardar 1 (Legia win 4-2 on agg); Hibernians 3 Boavista 3 (Boavista win 7-3 on agg); Belshina 0 Maccabi Haifa 1 (M Haifa win 5-0 on agg); Zeljeznicar 1 Lillestrom 0 (Zeljeznicar win 2-0 on agg); FK Partizan 4 Hammarby 0 (FK Partizan win 5-1 on agg); Torpedo Kutaisi 1 Sparta Prague 2 (Sparta win 5-1 on agg); GAK 2 Sheriff Tiraspol 0 (GAK win 6-1 on agg)

THIRD QUALIFYING ROUND

First leg, August 13
Maccabi Haifa 2 Sturm Graz 0; Apoel Nicosia 2 AEK Athens 3; Genk 2 Sparta Prague 0; Boavista 0 Auxerre 1; Feyenoord 1 Fenerbahce 0

August 14
Sporting Lisbon 0 Inter Milan 0; FK Partizan 0 Bayern Munich 3; Zalaegerszeg 1 Manchester United 0; Celtic 3 FC Basle 1; GAK 0 Lokomotiv Moscow 2; AC Milan 1 Sloven Liberec 0; Rosenborg 1 Brondby 0; Shakhtar Donetsk 1 FC Bruges 1; Barcelona 3 Legia Warsaw 0; Levski 0 Dinamo Kiev 1; Zeljeznicar 0 Newcastle Utd 1

Second leg, August 27
Fenerbahce 0 Feyenoord 2 (Feyenoord win 3-0 on agg); Manchester United 5 Zalaegerszeg 0 (Manchester United win 5-1 on agg); Bayern Munich 3 FK Partizan 1 (Bayern win 6-1 on agg); Sparta Prague 4 Genk 2 (4-4 on agg; Genk win on away goals); Inter Milan 2 Sporting Lisbon 0 (Inter Milan win 2-0 on agg).

August 28
Sturm Graz 3 Maccabi Haifa 3 (M Haifa win 5-3 on agg); Auxerre 0 Boavista 0 (Auxerre win 1-0 on agg); AEK Athens 1 Apoel Nicosia 0 (AEK win 4-2 on agg); FC Basle 2 Celtic 0 (3-3 on agg; Basle win on away goals); Lokomotiv Moscow 3 GAK 3 (Lokomotiv win 5-3 on agg); Sloven Liberec 2 AC Milan 1 (2-2 on agg; Milan win on away goals); Brondby 2 Rosenborg 3 (Rosenborg win 4-2 on agg); FC Bruges 1 Shakhtar Donetsk 1 (2-2 on agg; Bruges win 4-1 on pens); Legia Warsaw 0 Barcelona 1 (Barcelona win 4-0 on agg); Dinamo Kiev 1 Levski Sofia 0 (Dinamo win 2-0 on agg); Newcastle United 4 Zeljeznicar 0 (Newcastle win 5-0 on agg)

MORE THAN THE ODD MANAGER across Europe may have breathed a sigh of relief when Real Madrid, having briefly threatened to go back to basics, announced the capture of David Beckham from Manchester United. Real's policy of adding a *galactico* to their star-studded squad every year was once regarded with fear by their competitors, but, as their focus has drifted towards entertainment and the emerging football markets in the Far East, it has become a godsend. For as long as Real continue to neglect the art of defence, the rest of Europe still has a chance.

AC Milan ultimately proved themselves worthy winners of the European Cup in May, beating Juventus in a penalty shoot-out after a disappointing spectacle at Old Trafford, yet few would dare to venture that they were the outstanding team in the competition. Real, with their unrivalled collection of superstars, should have breezed towards their fourth trophy in six seasons, but their devotion to attacking football cost them dear as the Italian teams, built on far sturdier foundations, gave them and the rest of Europe a sobering lesson in the importance of traditional defensive values.

The laudable ambition of Florentino Perez, the Real president, mirrors that of Bill Shankly at Liverpool: to create a team so strong that "they'd have to send a team from Mars to beat us". The acquisition of Luis Figo, Zinedine Zidane, Ronaldo et al was intended to elevate Real on to another planet, to coin a popular football phrase, but it may take more than the replacement of Vicente Del Bosque by Carlos Queiroz, the former United assistant manager, to address their numerous flaws.

Real conceded 22 goals in their 16 matches, more than any of the other teams who reached the last eight. In the supposed fortress of the Bernabeu they were held to 2-2 draws by AEK Athens and Lokomotiv Moscow in the group stages. In the knockout phase, their defence went missing. They rode their luck during a breathless 4-3 defeat by United in the second leg of the quarter-final at Old Trafford before finally getting their comeuppance in the semi-finals, overrun in Turin by Juventus's high-octane performance.

There were other notable victims of such a cavalier approach, not least United, whose defence was unconvincing throughout. Newcastle United's naivety was rather more understandable. After losing their first three matches, they provided great drama in reaching the second group stage, but Liverpool, quarter-finalists the previous season, were a disappointment, shipping goals at an alarming rate as they were edged out by FC Basle in the first phase.

As for Arsenal, whose commitment to attack would cost them dear in their unsuccessful defence of the Premiership title, the reverse applied in the Champions League. After winning their first

Close encounter: it took a penalty shoot-out to settle the European Cup final

three matches in some style, the goals dried up. They won only once more in nine matches before they were eliminated in the second group stage, even if the nature of that victory, with Thierry Henry scoring all three goals away to AS Roma, was impressive.

Achieving the balance between defence and attack will always be the key to success in the Champions League and it was only the Italians, who had failed to provide even a quarter-finalist in the two previous years, who appeared able to manage it. Juventus, though fortunate to scrape through the second group stage, improved in the knockout stages, beating Barcelona 3-2 on aggregate before peaking in the second leg of the semi-final against Real. Their performance that night was inspired by Pavel Nedved, whom they would miss at Old Trafford after he picked up a needless suspension.

It was Milan who emerged triumphant. After an enterprising start to the final, they settled for the lottery of the penalty shoot-out, but even that failed to produce an abundance of goals as Dida and Gianluigi Buffon repelled five of the ten kicks between them. It was Dida, though, who saved more, with Milan's success confirmed when Andriy Shevchenko rolled home his kick.

It left many suggesting that the "real" final had taken place when United met Real in the quarter-finals. Until those teams start to invest their considerable resources in top-class defenders, however, the trophy will continue to be shared around.

FIRST GROUP STAGE

Group A
September 17
Auxerre 0 PSV Eindhoven 0
Arsenal 2 Borussia Dortmund 0
September 25
Borussia Dortmund 2 Auxerre 1
PSV Eindhoven 0 Arsenal 4
October 2
PSV Eindhoven 1 Borussia Dortmund 3
Auxerre 0 Arsenal 1
October 22
Borussia Dortmund 1 PSV Eindhoven 1
Arsenal 1 Auxerre 2
October 30
PSV Eindhoven 3 Auxerre 0
Borussia Dortmund 2 Arsenal 1
November 12
Auxerre 1 Borussia Dortmund 0
Arsenal 0 PSV Eindhoven 0

	P	W	D	L	F	A	Pts
Arsenal	6	3	1	2	9	4	10
Bor Dortmund	6	3	1	2	8	7	10
Auxerre	6	2	1	3	4	7	7
PSV Eindhoven	6	1	3	2	5	8	6

Group B
September 17
Valencia 2 Liverpool 0
FC Basle 2 Spartak Moscow 0
September 25
Spartak Moscow 0 Valencia 3
Liverpool 1 FC Basle 1
October 2
Liverpool 5 Spartak Moscow 0
Valencia 6 FC Basle 2
October 22
Spartak Moscow 1 Liverpool 3
FC Basle 2 Valencia 2
October 30
Liverpool 0 Valencia 1
Spartak Moscow 0 FC Basle 2
November 12
Valencia 3 Spartak Moscow 0
FC Basle 3 Liverpool 3

	P	W	D	L	F	A	Pts
Valencia	6	5	1	0	17	4	16
FC Basle	6	2	3	1	12	12	9
Liverpool	6	2	2	2	12	8	8
Spartak Moscow	6	0	0	6	1	18	0

Group C
September 17
Genk 0 AEK Athens 0; AS Roma 0 Real Madrid 3
September 25
Real Madrid 6 Genk 0; AEK Athens 0 AS Roma 0
October 2
AEK Athens 3 Real Madrid 3; Genk 0 AS Roma 1
October 22
Real Madrid 2 AEK Athens 2; AS Roma 0 Genk 0
October 30
AEK Athens 1 Genk 1; Real Madrid 0 AS Roma 1
November 12
Genk 1 Real Madrid 1; AS Roma 1 AEK Athens 1

	P	W	D	L	F	A	Pts
Real Madrid	6	2	3	1	15	7	9
AS Roma	6	2	3	1	3	4	9
AEK Athens	6	0	6	0	7	7	6
Genk	6	0	4	2	2	9	4

Group D
September 17
Rosenborg 2 Inter Milan 2; Ajax 2 Lyons 1
September 25
Lyons 5 Rosenborg 0; Inter Milan 1 Ajax 0
October 2
Inter Milan 1 Lyons 2; Rosenborg 0 Ajax 0
October 22
Lyons 3 Inter Milan 3; Ajax 1 Rosenborg 1

October 30
Inter Milan 3 Rosenborg 0; Lyons 0 Ajax 2
November 12
Rosenborg 1 Lyons 1; Ajax 1 Inter Milan 2

	P	W	D	L	F	A	Pts
Inter Milan	6	3	2	1	12	8	11
Ajax	6	2	2	2	6	5	8
Lyons	6	2	2	2	12	9	8
Rosenborg	6	0	4	2	4	12	4

Group E

September 18
Feyenoord 1 Juventus 1
Dinamo Kiev 2 Newcastle United 0
September 24
Newcastle United 0 Feyenoord 1
Juventus 5 Dinamo Kiev 0
October 1
Juventus 2 Newcastle United 0
Feyenoord 0 Dinamo Kiev 0
October 23
Newcastle United 1 Juventus 0
Dinamo Kiev 2 Feyenoord 0
October 29
Juventus 2 Feyenoord 0
Newcastle United 2 Dinamo Kiev 1
November 13
Feyenoord 2 Newcastle United 3
Dinamo Kiev 1 Juventus 2

	P	W	D	L	F	A	Pts
Juventus	6	4	1	1	12	3	13
Newcastle United	6	3	0	3	6	8	9
Dinamo Kiev	6	2	1	3	6	9	7
Feyenoord	6	1	2	3	4	8	5

Group F

September 18
Manchester United 5 Maccabi Haifa 2
Olympiakos 6 Bayer Leverkusen 2
September 24
Bayer Leverkusen 1 Manchester United 2
Maccabi Haifa 3 Olympiakos 0
October 1
Maccabi Haifa 0 Bayer Leverkusen 2
Manchester United 4 Olympiakos 0
October 23
Bayer Leverkusen 2 Maccabi Haifa 1
Olympiakos 2 Manchester United 3
October 29
Maccabi Haifa 3 Manchester United 0
Bayer Leverkusen 2 Olympiakos 0
November 13
Manchester United 2 Bayer Leverkusen 0
Olympiakos 3 Maccabi Haifa 3

	P	W	D	L	F	A	Pts
Manchester Utd	6	5	0	1	16	8	15
Bayer Leverkusen	6	3	0	3	9	11	9
Maccabi Haifa	6	2	1	3	12	12	7
Olympiakos	6	1	1	4	11	17	4

Group G

September 18
Bayern Munich 2 Deportivo 3; AC Milan 2 Lens 1
September 24
Lens 1 Bayern Munich 1; Deportivo 0 AC Milan 4
October 1
Deportivo 3 Lens 1; Bayern Munich 1 AC Milan 2
October 23
Lens 3 Deportivo 1; AC Milan 2 Bayern Munich 1
October 29
Deportivo 2 Bayern Munich 1; Lens 2 AC Milan 1
November 13
Bayern Munich 3 Lens 3; AC Milan 1 Deportivo 2

MATCH OF THE SEASON

Real Madrid 3   Manchester United 1
Bernabeu Stadium, Wednesday April 8 2003
Matt Dickinson, Chief Football Correspondent, in Madrid

SIR ALEX FERGUSON SECURED the away goal that he craved on a privileged evening in the Bernabeu last night. Shame about the three — and it could have been six — that flew into Manchester United's net in the European Cup quarter-final first leg.

On a night that should have been billed as *An Audience with Zinedine Zidane*, the last representatives of the Barclaycard Premiership were sliced apart by a Real Madrid team that will surely retain the trophy. The world's best side can acclimatise for the final at Old Trafford on May 28 when they come to Manchester in a fortnight and finish off the demolition of Ferguson's ambitions. Real hardly need any help, but their task will be aided by the suspension of Paul Scholes and Gary Neville, both booked last night.

Only this Real team could make Ronaldo look as clumsy as Emile Heskey and only this side of peerless talents could reduce United to periods of helplessness, as they did for most of a breathtaking first hour. Ferguson will claim that the tie is not over after Ruud van Nistelrooy reduced the deficit and his team will always create chances against a side as intent on attack as Real, but the United manager was left to rue his claim that the 0-0 here three years ago was the worst possible result. It was much better than last night's 3-1.

Luis Figo scored the first goal before two from Raul, but every touch from Zidane proved why, in a squad of prodigious talent, he still manages to tower above his gifted team-mates. In a universal game played by billions, the Frenchman has a feathery touch and balance that makes him unique. "He is my favourite," Steve McManaman has said, although Zidane was enemy No1 among a United midfield that was always a step behind his feints and flicks.

Roy Keane's decline as a colossus of the European game was sadly made evident by Zidane's mastery, but the United captain was not alone in his frustration. David Beckham, who missed a good chance in the second half, was overshadowed by Figo on a night when he will have been desperate to win over the *Madridistas*. Van Nistelrooy was his team's most potent force, but he could have had a hat-trick if he had shown the ruthlessness of Raul.

In Europe's finest theatre of football, the Continent's best team set out as if determined to teach United a lesson. Ferguson's bullying might work in his own domestic playground, but he picked a fight that he could never hope to win. Two goals by half-time might have been three if Anders Frisk, the referee, had not missed the clearest penalty of the season, when Ronaldo was upended by Wes Brown. "Was that the power of Real at work?" Ferguson was asked pointedly by one Spanish journalist after the Scot's suggestion that the home team operated above the laws. Real do not need to bend

Opening shots: Figo's curling effort leaves Barthez helpless

the rules when they ally potency to their class. "They mesmerise you at times with their control and passing," Ferguson said, "but I am disappointed with the first two soft goals." Figo will vehemently disagree about his opener after 12 minutes that will prompt as much debate as Ronaldinho's free kick for Brazil against England in last summer's World Cup. Was he crossing or shooting from the left corner of the penalty box? Figo deserves the benefit of the doubt.

United certainly responded as if they were struck down by genius rather than misfortune, struggling to get to grips with a team that produced its best 45 minutes of the season in that opening half. Real were rampant and, after Scholes surrendered possession just outside his own area, Zidane slipped the ball to Raul. It has not been a good season for Rio Ferdinand and he failed to nick the ball away. Raul's deft turn left the defender kicking at thin air and the forward struck a low, left-foot shot inside Fabien Barthez's near post.

Regret at a first-half chance squandered by Van Nistelrooy seemed the least of United's problems when they fell 3-0 behind four minutes into the second half. Taking the ball from Figo 22 yards out, Raul was given far too much space to pick his spot.

The crowd was revelling in the rout, but it was not the job of Real's players to join in the celebrations, a mistake that they paid for when United claimed the goal that reduced an impossible task at Old Trafford to the need for a highly improbable 2-0 victory. After Iker Casillas had tipped away Ryan Giggs's shot, Van Nistelrooy nodded in the rebound. The Holland striker might have added a second soon afterwards but for a brave block by Casillas. It was something for United to cling to when they return to Old Trafford.

REAL MADRID (4-2-2-2): I Casillas — M Salgado, I Helguera, F Hierro, Roberto Carlos — C Makelele, F Conceicao — L Figo, Z Zidane — Raul, Ronaldo (sub: Guti, 83min). **Substitutes not used:** D Cesar, S McManaman, F Morientes, J Portillo, S Solari, F Pavon.
MANCHESTER UNITED (4-4-1-1): F Barthez — G Neville (sub: O G Solskjaer, 86), R Ferdinand, W Brown, M Silvestre (sub: J O'Shea, 59) — D Beckham, R Keane, N Butt, R Giggs — P Scholes — R van Nistelrooy. **Substitutes not used:** Ricardo, L Blanc, D Forlan, Q Fortune, D Fletcher. **Booked:** Neville, Scholes, Van Nistelrooy.
Referee: A Frisk (Sweden).

	P	W	D	L	F	A	Pts
AC Milan	6	4	0	2	12	7	12
Deportivo La Coruna	6	4	0	2	11	12	12
Lens	6	2	2	2	11	11	8
Bayern Munich	6	0	2	4	9	13	2

Group H
September 18
Lokomotiv Moscow 0 Galatasaray 2
Barcelona 3 FC Bruges 2
September 24
FC Bruges 0 Lokomotiv Moscow 0
Galatasaray 0 Barcelona 2
October 1
Galatasaray 0 FC Bruges 0
Lokomotiv Moscow 1 Barcelona 3
October 23
FC Bruges 3 Galatasaray 1
Barcelona 1 Lokomotiv Moscow 0
October 29
Galatasaray 1 Lokomotiv Moscow 2
FC Bruges 0 Barcelona 1
November 13
Lokomotiv Moscow 2 FC Bruges 0
Barcelona 3 Galatasaray 1

	P	W	D	L	F	A	Pts
Barcelona	6	6	0	0	13	4	18
Lokomotiv Moscow	6	2	1	3	5	7	7
FC Bruges	6	1	2	3	5	7	5
Galatasaray	6	1	1	4	5	10	4

SECOND GROUP STAGE

Group A
November 27
Bayer Leverkusen 1 Barcelona 2
Newcastle United 1 Inter Milan 4
December 10
Inter Milan 3 Bayer Leverkusen 2
December 11
Barcelona 3 Newcastle United 1
February 18
Barcelona 3 Inter Milan 0
Bayer Leverkusen 1 Newcastle United 3
February 26
Inter Milan 0 Barcelona 0
Newcastle United 3 Bayer Leverkusen 1
March 11
Barcelona 2 Bayer Leverkusen 0
Inter Milan 2 Newcastle United 2
March 18
Bayer Leverkusen 0 Inter Milan 2
Newcastle United 0 Barcelona 2

	P	W	D	L	F	A	Pts
Barcelona	6	5	1	0	12	2	16
Inter Milan	6	3	2	1	11	8	11
Newcastle United	6	2	1	3	10	13	7
Bayer Leverkusen	6	0	0	6	5	15	0

Group B
November 27
AS Roma 1 Arsenal 3
Valencia 1 Ajax 1
December 10
Arsenal 0 Valencia 0
Ajax 2 AS Roma 1
February 18
Arsenal 1 Ajax 1
AS Roma 0 Valencia 1
February 26
Ajax 0 Arsenal 0
Valencia 0 AS Roma 3
March 11
Arsenal 1 AS Roma 1
Ajax 1 Valencia 1
March 18
AS Roma 1 Ajax 1
Valencia 2 Arsenal 1

	P	W	D	L	F	A	Pts
Valencia	6	2	3	1	5	6	9
Ajax	6	1	5	0	6	5	8
Arsenal	6	1	4	1	6	5	7
AS Roma	6	1	2	3	7	8	5

MILAN'S IDOL CURIOSITY

SIMON KUPER

This article was first published in The Times on May 26

ON WEDNESDAY, HE could win his third European Cup with his third club. He is still only 27. He is a complete footballer. Yet in his native Netherlands he is despised. "That Clarence Seedorf might win three Champions Leagues means nothing to me," Henk Spaan, compiler of the authoritative top 100 of his country's best footballers and a guardian of Dutch football culture, said.

Even Simon Zwartkruis, the author of a hagiography that is published this month (*Clarence Seedorf: De Biografie*), said that the player has "pissing-post status" at

Seedorf "plays like a chief when he could be a great Indian"

home. Seedorf was always going to win lots of European Cups. On October 28, 1992, aged 16 years and 211 days, he became Ajax's youngest player, ahead of Johan Cruyff, Marco van Basten, Dennis Bergkamp, etc. "For me, Clarence Seedorf is the footballer of the year 2000," Louis van Gaal, the Ajax manager, said.

Playing at centre back, left half, winger, wherever Ajax needed him, Seedorf seemed to have nothing left to learn. Already he had a much bigger build than most footballers, not to say the most prominent backside in the game. In interviews — there was never any question of Rooneyesque protection — Seedorf sounded like a retired Cabinet Minister, pontificating about discipline, responsibility and respect. It emerged, inevitably, that he had been *de facto* manager of his kindergarten, been asked to skip a year at primary school and voted on to the pupils' council at high school, as well as captaining all the national youth teams.

He belonged to a brilliant generation. Since childhood he had played in Ajax's youth teams with Patrick Kluivert, enjoying the best football education possible. In the first team they joined the De Boer twins, Edgar Davids, Frank Rijkaard, Edwin van der Sar, Kanu, Jari Litmanen and the others who, in 1995, would win the European Cup, Seedorf's first.

However, a warning of future troubles, documented by Zwartkruis, came when Seedorf was substituted during the final against AC Milan. While the match raged on, he rose from the bench to go and debate his substitution with Van Gaal. An alert reserve goalkeeper caught him and held him down until Seedorf, always an obliging character, decided to drop the matter. He was leaving Ajax anyway. After all, he was already 19. Sven-Goran Eriksson took him to Sampdoria, where Seedorf took four seconds to adjust. "I was able to develop my personality further, largely thanks to Eriksson," Seedorf told Zwartkruis. "He is not a man who imposes things on you, not a man for whom there is no vision besides his own."

Innocuous as all this sounds, a problem was emerging. Football is a hierarchy topped by the manager, but Seedorf understood it as a sort of discussion group in which people could grow their personalities. Even more than football, he loves communication. His favourite mode is abstract speech about "positive energy" and how certain events are predestined and assist personality growth. This was calculated to irritate Dutch fans (who dislike psychobabble), other footballers (ditto) and managers (who hate players saying anything at all). Yet when Seedorf joined Real Madrid after a year at Sampdoria, five years after they had first tried to sign him, he took his psychobabble with him. A polite and painfully well-meaning man, he did not imagine that it would upset anyone. When he tried to explain tactics during one half-time to Fabio Capello, the Real manager, Capello tore off his jacket and chucked it at him, shouting: "If you know it all so well, you be the coach!"

Although Seedorf won the European Cup with Real in 1998, beating Juventus in the final, he was not really accepted. At training sessions, one Real player said, after the manager had spoken, Seedorf would step forward and say: "You don't want to do it like that, you want to do it like this. And then you want to pass to me." He was sold to Inter Milan in January 2000.

Meanwhile, despite being a regular international since the age of 18, he had alienated virtually his entire home country. One problem was his "Zidane complex". A wonderful athlete, a sort of extremely fast concrete wall who could play one-touch, Seedorf wanted to be an old-fashioned playmaker. Some footballers have a personality that matches their style of play. Davids and Roy Keane are extremely aggressive men and extremely aggressive players. Cruyff was a bossy man and a bossy footballer. But Seedorf's personality — an extreme version of the responsible eldest son — impels him to play like a chief when he could be a great Indian.

Holland managers would usually put him at right half, but Seedorf, in the spirit of personality growth, would constantly pop up at No 10 instead. Because he can outrun opponents without any apparent effort and never seems to tire, he often seems not to be trying. His penchant for humourlessly declaiming boring abstractions in a monotone also annoyed the Dutch, as did his habit of taking and missing other people's penalties and his activities as spokesman for black players.

Seedorf was seen as the leader of a Surinamese separatist movement within the team. This was unfair.

He was speaking for Kluivert only because he thought Kluivert was too dumb to speak for himself and for Davids because Davids was too tactless. The widely held opinion that he and Davids are best friends — "twins" — is a misconception derived from the fallacy that all black people are the same.

"Edgar and I are two different personalities," Seedorf said politely. Holland's white players are mostly fond of Seedorf. When I asked Van der Sar about splits within the team, he said: "Those players you're talking about — we've been through a lot with each other." When Van der Sar and Davids were at Juventus, it was Van der Sar whom Seedorf used to phone. Yet Seedorf is often jeered during international matches (by Holland's mostly white crowds) and in a poll during Euro 2000, 81 per cent of the public voted him out of the national team. No Dutch footballer of recent decades has been more despised.

Seedorf went through hard years. His mother would cry in the stands during international matches while his father begged him to stop playing for Holland. Even Seedorf was affected. One Christmas he considered writing a poem to the Dutch people. (Speech not being enough for him, Seedorf is always doing extra communication through poems and songs.) At Inter he was getting up people's noses, too. He was often left on the bench. He has won nothing since the World Club Cup of 1998.

Yet since he joined Milan last summer, everything seems to have come together for him. He was put in left midfield, with orders to attack and defend, but allowed to drift to the centre when his personality impelled him. Milan loved his body — the club's computer programme found that he had the maximum desirable amount of muscle and he was banned from doing weight training. The club can also live with his growing personality.

When Seedorf joined the club, Bruno de Michelis, Milan's sports psychologist, told Zwartkruis: "He talked 10 per cent like a player, 70 per cent like a coach and 20 per cent like a general manager. But I also saw that he was doing it with a positive intention. In the years I've been working with Milan, I've never seen such a strong personality." Football is not yet ready for him, but after a few more European Cups, recognition awaits as a psychotherapist or Prime Minister.

Group C

November 26
L Moscow 1 B Dortmund 2; AC Milan 1 Real Madrid 0
December 11
B Dortmund 0 AC Milan 1; Real Madrid 2 L Moscow 2
February 19
Real Madrid 2 B Dortmund 1; AC Milan 1 L Moscow 0
February 25
L Moscow 0 AC Milan 1; B Dortmund 1 Real Madrid 1
March 12
Real Madrid 3 AC Milan 1; B Dortmund 3 L Moscow 0
March 19
AC Milan 0 B Dortmund 1; L Moscow 0 Real Madrid 1

	P	W	D	L	F	A	Pts
AC Milan	6	4	0	2	5	4	12
Real Madrid	6	3	2	1	9	6	11
B Dortmund	6	3	1	2	8	5	10
Lokomotiv Moscow	6	0	1	5	3	10	1

Group D

November 26
FC Basle 1 Manchester United 3
Deportivo La Coruna 2 Juventus 2
December 11
Juventus 4 FC Basle 0
Manchester United 2 Deportivo La Coruna 0
February 19
Manchester United 2 Juventus 1
FC Basle 1 Deportivo La Coruna 0
February 25
Juventus 0 Manchester United 3
Deportivo La Coruna 1 FC Basle 0
March 12
Manchester United 1 FC Basle 1
Juventus 3 Deportivo La Coruna 2
March 19
FC Basle 2 Juventus 1
Deportivo La Coruna 2 Manchester United 0

	P	W	D	L	F	A	Pts
Manchester Utd	6	4	1	1	11	5	13
Juventus	6	2	1	3	11	11	7
FC Basle	6	2	1	3	5	10	7
Deportivo	6	2	1	3	7	8	7

QUARTER-FINALS, FIRST LEGS
April 13
Ajax 0 AC Milan 0
Real Madrid 3 Manchester United 1
April 14
Inter Milan 1 Valencia 0
Juventus 1 Barcelona 1

Second legs
April 22
Barcelona 1 Juventus 2 (aet; 1-1 after 90min;
Juventus win 3-2 on agg)
Valencia 2 Inter Milan 1 (2-2 on agg; Inter Milan
win on away goals)
April 23
Manchester United 4 Real Madrid 3
(Real Madrid win 6-5 on agg)
AC Milan 3 Ajax 2 (AC Milan win 3-2 on agg)

SEMI-FINALS, FIRST LEGS
May 6
Real Madrid 2 Juventus 1
May 7
AC Milan 0 Inter Milan 0
Second legs
Inter Milan 1 AC Milan 1 (1-1 on agg; AC Milan win
on away goals)
Juventus 3 Real Madrid 1 (Juventus win 4-3 on agg)
FINAL
Details right

PLAYER OF THE SEASON
Paolo Maldini, AC Milan

If 2003 was the year that proved there is no substitute for experience, there was no oldie more golden than Paolo Maldini. Four weeks short of his 35th birthday, he was only the third-oldest player on the pitch in the European Cup final behind Alessandro Costacurta and Ciro Ferrara, but the match will be remembered as a masterclass in defending from the AC Milan veteran. Aside from the sentimental aspect of his fourth winner's medal, 14 years after his first, Maldini was named man of the match for a majestic performance in keeping in with the standards he had shown throughout the competition and, indeed, his career.

Oliver Kay

EUROPEAN CUP

FINAL
May 28, Old Trafford

JUVENTUS (0) **0**   **AC MILAN** (0) **0**
63,215

(aet; AC Milan win 3-2 on penalties)

JUVENTUS (4-4-2): G Buffon — L Thuram, I Tudor (sub: A Birindelli, 42min), C Ferrara, P Montero — M Camoranesi (sub: A Conte, 46), A Tacchinardi, E Davids (sub: M Zalayeta, 70), G Zambrotta — A Del Piero, D Trezeguet. **Substitutes not used:** A Chimenti, G Pessotto, M Iuliano, M Di Vaio. **Booked:** Tacchinardi, Conte.
AC MILAN (4-4-2): Dida — A Costacurta (sub: Roque Junior, 70), A Nesta, P Maldini, K Kaladze — Rui Costa (sub: M Ambrosini, 87), G Gattuso, A Pirlo (sub: Serginho, 76), C Seedorf — F Inzaghi, A Shevchenko. **Substitutes not used:** C Abbiati, Rivaldo, M Laursen, C Brocchi. **Booked:** Costacurta. **Referee:** M Merk (Germany).

LEADING SCORERS

		Total
Ruud van Nistelrooy	Manchester United	12
Filippo Inzaghi	AC Milan	10
Hernan Crespo	Inter Milan	9
Roy Makaay	Deportivo La Coruna	9
Raul	Real Madrid	9
Jan Koller	Borussia Dortmund	8
Thierry Henry	Arsenal	7
Javier Saviola	Barcelona	7
Alan Shearer	Newcastle United	6

UEFA CUP

WINNERS
FC Porto

RUNNERS-UP
Celtic

SEMI-FINALISTS
Boavista
Lazio

THE GAMES

QUALIFYING ROUND
First legs, August 15

Vaduz 1 Livingston 1; Sliema 1 Polonia 3; Anorthosis 3 Grevenmacher 0; Levski Tallinn 0 Maccabi Tel-Aviv 2; Leixoes 2 Belasica 1; Stabaek 4 Linfield 0; Sigma 2 FK Sarajevo 1; Zimbru 3 Gothenburg 1; Ki Klavsvik 2 Ujpest 2; MyPa 1 Odense 0; Dinamo Minsk 1 CSKA Sofia 4; Dinamo Tbilisi 4 TVMK Tallinn 1; Araka 0 Servette 2; Shamrock Rovers 1 Djurgardens 3; Varteks 5 Dundalk 0; Gomel 1 HJK Helsinki 0; Aberdeen 1 Nistru 0; AIK Solna 2 IBV Vestmannaeyjar 0; Rapid 2 Gorica 0; Domagnano 0 Viktoria Zizkov 2; Kairat 0 Crvena Zvezda 2; Zaporizhzhya 3 Birkirkara 0; Bangor 1 Sartid 0; Senec 1 Siroki Brijeg 2; Tirana 0 National 1; Avenir 0 Ipswich Town 1; Fylkir 1 Mouscron 1; Litex 5 Atlantas 0; Encamp 0 Zenit 5; Atyrau 0 Puchov 2; Glentoran 0 Wisla Krakow 2; Pobeda 2 Midtjylland 0; Primorje 6 Zvartnots 1; Ventspils 3 Lugano 0; Hapoel Tel-Aviv 1 Partizani 0; Ferencvaros 4 AEL Limassol 0; Hajduk Split 3 GI Gotu 0; Brann 2 Amica 5 TNS Llansantffraid 0; FC Copenhagen 3 Lokomotivi 1; Metalurgs 0 Karnten 2

Second legs, August 29

Livingston 0 Vaduz 0 (1-1 on agg; Livingston win on away goals); Polonia 2 Sliema 0 (Polonia win 5-1 on agg); Grevenmacher 2 Anorthosis 0 (Anorthosis win 3-2 on agg); Maccabi Tel-Aviv 2 Levski Tallinn 0 (Maccabi Tel-Aviv win 4-0 on agg); Belasica 1 Leixoes 2(Leixoes win 4-3 on agg); Linfield 1 Stabaek 1 (Stabaek win 5-1 on agg); FK Sarajevo 2 Sigma 1 (aet; 3-3 on agg; FK Sarajevo win 5-3 on pens); Gothenburg 2 Zimbru 2 (Zimbru win 5-3 on agg); 1 KI Klaksvik 0 (Ujpest win 3-2 on agg); Odense 2 MyPa 0 (Odense win 2-1 on agg); CSKA Sofia 1 Dinamo Minsk 0 (CSKA win 5-1 on agg); TVMK Tallinn 0 Dinamo Tbilisi 1 (Dinamo Tbilisi win 5-1 on agg); Servette 3 Araka 0 (Servette win 5-0 on agg); Djurgardens 2 Shamrock Rovers 0 (Djurgardens win 5-1 on agg); Dundalk 0 Varteks 4 (Varteks win 9-0 on agg); HJK Helsinki 0 Gomel 4 (Gomel win 5-0 on agg); Nistru 0 Aberdeen 0 (Aberdeen win 1-0 on agg); IBV Vestmannaeyjar 1 AIK Solna 3 (AIK win 5-1 on agg); Gorica 1 Rapid Bucharest 3 (Rapid Bucharest win 5-1 on agg); Viktoria Zizkov 3 Domagnano 0 (Viktoria Zizkov win 5-0 on agg); Crvena Zvezda 3 Kairat 0 (Crvena Zvezda win 5-0 on agg); Birkirkara 0 Zaporizhzhya 0 (Zaporizhzhya win 3-0 on agg); Sartid 2 Bangor 0 (Sartid win 2-1 on agg); Siroki Brijeg 3 Senec 0 (Siroki Brijeg win 5-1 on agg); National 3 Tirana 2 (National win 3-2 on agg); Ipswich Town 8 Avenir 1 (Ipswich win 9-1 on agg); Mouscron 3 Fylkir 1 (Mouscron win 4-2 on agg); Atlantas 1 Litex 3 (Litex win 8-1 on agg); Zenit 8 Encamp 0 (Zenit win 13-0 on agg); Puchov 0 Atyrau 0 (Puchov win 2-0 on agg); Wisla Krakow 4 Glentoran 0 (Wisla win 6-0 on agg); Midtjylland 3 Pobeda 0 (aet; Midtjylland win 3-2 on agg); Zvartnots 2 Primorje 0 (Primorje win 6-3 on agg); Lugano 1 Ventspils 0 (Ventspils win 3-1 on agg); Partizani 1 Hapoel Tel-Aviv 4 (Hapoel Tel-Aviv win 5-1 on agg); AEL Limassol 2 Ferencvaros 1 (Ferencvaros win 5-2 on agg); GI Gotu 0 Hajduk Split 8 (Hajduk win 11-0 on agg); Suduva 3 Brann 2 (Suduva win 6-4 on agg); TNS Llansantffraid 2 Amica 7 (Amica win 12-2 on agg); Lokomotiv Tbilisi 1 FC Copenhagen 4 (Copenhagen win 7-2 on agg); Karnten 4 Metalurgs 2 (Kartnten win 6-2 on agg)

ROD STEWART CHARTERED A private jet from his home in Los Angeles to join in the fun. He had turned down an invitation to a Buckingham Palace garden party to be there. Tony Blair sent a good-luck message to Martin O'Neill and his players. The Estadio Olimpico in Seville rocked, probably as never before. But there was no tumultuous climax for the green-and-white hordes. Instead, with five minutes of the Uefa Cup final remaining, Derlei, the FC Porto striker, rifled in his twelfth goal of the competition. It was football's first "silver goal" winner. For O'Neill it felt like a silver bullet.

Celtic had come so far, the ghosts of the Lisbon Lions, the European champions of 1967, haunting their every step. Billy McNeill, Jimmy Johnstone, Tommy Gemmell, Jock Stein — legends all. But this was the chance to exorcise those ghosts, to erase the burden of constant comparison.

O'Neill had recognised it. "I'm aware of the glorious history of this club and it's time to do something about it ourselves," he said. "We should not be frightened by history. We should enhance it and aspire to it." Enhancement was achieved — the 3-2 defeat after extra time made for compelling viewing and wonderful memories — but aspirations were dashed. It was heart-rending stuff, the Celtic players lying distraught on the Spanish turf. Yet still their fans saluted them, a serenade of undying admiration. It was magnificent theatre.

It had been some journey, too, in a competition initially made up of European nobodies but which also took in fair-play qualifiers, including Ipswich Town, three InterToto Cup victors (Fulham among them) and a bevy of Champions League discards along the way.

Ipswich started off in the qualifying round with the likes of TNS Llansantffraid, IBV Vestmannaeyjar and Domagnano. Avenir Beggen, of Luxembourg, were humbled 9-1 on aggregate and although Sartid, of Yugoslavia, were disposed of next, the financially stricken Suffolk club went out to Slovan Liberec on penalties in the second round. Fulham did better, reaching the third round before succumbing to Hertha Berlin, while Leeds United overcame Zaporizhzhya and Hapoel Tel-Aviv — as well as the corrosive infighting within the club — before going out to Malaga. Rangers slipped up at the first hurdle and Chelsea did their usual trick of underestimating their opponents, this time Viking Stavanger.

Celtic's foray into Europe did not open encouragingly, an away-goals defeat against FC Basle ejecting them from the Champions League in the third qualifying round. Still, Suduva, of Lithuania, were hammered 10-1 on aggregate in the first round of

O'Neill could take pride in his team's performance in Seville

their consolation prize, the Uefa Cup, and Blackburn Rovers were brushed aside with surprising ease. A "Battle of Britain" it was not.

Porto had seen off Polonia Warsaw and Austria Vienna, then Lens and Denizlispor, to reach the quarter-finals. Celtic gathered momentum, sneaking past Celta Vigo on away goals and VfB Stuttgart 5-4 over two legs. A meeting with Liverpool awaited in the last eight. Gerard Houllier's side had been eliminated from the Champions League, finishing behind Valencia and Basle in group B, and had seen off Vitesse Arnhem and Auxerre. A 1-1 draw in Glasgow handed them the initiative, but a re-energised Celtic won 2-0 at Anfield to earn a semi-final against Boavista.

Porto progressed courtesy of a 2-0 triumph against Panathinaikos in Greece — as impressive as Celtic's victory on Merseyside — and then met Lazio. A 4-1 first-leg success as good as guaranteed their place in Seville. O'Neill's men faltered against Boavista, drawing 1-1 at home, but Henrik Larsson's eightieth-minute goal in the second leg ended any hopes of an all-Portuguese final.

The final ebbed and flowed: frantic, fascinating. Derlei scored, Larsson equalised, his 200th Celtic goal. Dmitri Alenichev scored, Larsson equalised again — another header, his eleventh goal in the competition. Bobo Balde, the Celtic defender, was sent off in extra time, his team-mates tired and Derlei pounced with the winner.

O'Neill bit his tongue, angered at Porto's time-wasting tactics and theatrics. Yet he kept it together. No tears, no shame. Celtic had given everything. The Lions of Lisbon would have been proud of them. And were.

FIRST ROUND
First legs, September 19
Aberdeen 0 Hertha Berlin 0; Austria Vienna 5 Shakhtar 1; Leixoes 2 PAOK 1; Viktoria Zizkov 2 Rangers 0; Vitesse Arnhem 1 Rapid Bucharest 1; Bordeaux 6 Puchov 0; Servette 2 Amica 3; Sturm Graz 5 Livingston 2; Ferencvaros 4 Kocaelispor 0; Zeljeznicar 0 Malaga 0; Liberec 3 Dinamo Tbilisi 2; Leeds United 1 Zaporizhzhya 0; Litex 0 Panathinaikos 1; Crvena Zvezda 0 Chievo Verona 0; Hajduk Split 0 Fulham 1; Primorje 0 Wisla Krakow 2; APOEL Nicosia 2 Grazer AK 0; Celta Vigo 2 Odense 0; Metalurg Donetsk 2 Werder Bremen 2; Celtic 8 Suduva 1; Porto 6 Polonia 0; Gomel 1 Schalke 4; Grasshopper 3 Zenit 1; Ankaragucu 1 Alaves 2; Iraklis 4 Anorthosis 2; Midtjylland 1 Varteks 0; Blackburn Rovers 1 CSKA Sofia 1; Mouscron 2 Slavia 2; Denizlispor 2 Lorient 0; Chelsea 2 Viking 1; Karnten 0 Hapoel Tel-Aviv 4; Stuttgart 4 Ventspils 1; Dinamo Zagreb 6 Zalaegerszeg 0; FC Copenhagen 0 Djurgardens 0; Ipswich Town 1 Sartid 1; Maccabi Tel-Aviv 1 Boavista 0; AIK Solna 3 Fenerbahce 3; Sparta Prague 3 Siroki Brijeg 0; Paris Saint-Germain 3 Ujpest 0; Sporting Lisbon 1 Partizan 1; Legia Warsaw 4 Utrecht 1; Zimbru 0 Real Betis 2; Besiktas 2 FK Sarajevo 2; CSKA Moscow 1 Parma 1; Levski Sofia 4 Brondby 1; Anderlecht 0 Stabaek 1; National 3 Heerenveen 0; Lazio 4 Xanthi 0

Second legs, October 3
Hertha Berlin 1 Aberdeen 0 (Hertha win 1-0 on agg); Shakhtar 1 Austria Vienna 0 (Vienna win 5-2 on agg); PAOK 4 Leixoes 1 (PAOK win 5-3 on agg); Rangers 3 Viktoria Zizkov 1 (aet; 3-3 on agg; Zizkov win on away goals); Rapid Bucharest 1 Vitesse Arnhem 0 (Vitesse win 2-1 on agg); Puchov 1 Bordeaux 4 (Bordeaux win 10-1 on agg); Amica 1 Servette 2 (aet; 4-4 on agg; Amica win on away goals); Livingston 4 Sturm Graz 3 (Graz win 8-6 on agg); Kocaelispor 0 Ferencvaros 1 (Ferencvaros win 5-0 on agg); Malaga 0 Zeljeznicar 1 (Zeljeznicar win 1-0 on agg); Dinamo Tbilisi 0 Liberec 1 (Liberec win 4-2 on agg); Zaporizhzhya 1 Leeds United 1 (Leeds win 2-1 on agg); Panathinaikos 2 Litex 1 (aet; Panathinaikos win 3-1 on agg); Chievo Verona 0 Crvena Zvezda 2 (Crvena Zvezda win 2-0 on agg); Fulham 2 Hajduk Split 2 (Fulham win 3-2 on agg); Wisla Krakow 6 Primorje 1 (Wisla win 8-2 on agg); Grazer AK 1 APOEL Nicosia 1 (APOEL win 3-1 on agg); Odense 1 Celta Vigo 0 (Vigo win 2-1 on agg); Werder Bremen 8 Metalurg Donetsk 0 (Bremen win 10-2 on agg); Suduva 0 Celtic 2 (Celtic win 10-1 on agg); Polonia 2 Porto 0 (Porto win 6-2 on agg); Schalke 4 Gomel 0 (Schalke win 8-1 on agg); Zenit 2 Grasshopper 1 (Grasshopper win 4-3 on agg); Alaves 3 Ankaragucu 1 (Alaves win 5-1 on agg); Varteks 1 Midtjylland 1 (Midtjylland win 2-1 on agg); CSKA Sofia 3 Blackburn Rovers 3 (aet; 4-4 on agg; Blackburn win on away goals); Slavia Prague 5 Mouscron 1 (Slavia win 7-3 on agg); Lorient 3 Denizlispor 1 (aet; 3-3 on agg; Denizlispor win on away goals); Viking 4 Chelsea 2 (Viking win 5-4 on agg); Hapoel Tel-Aviv 0 Karnten 1 (Hapoel win 4-1 on agg); Stuttgart 4 Ventspils 1 (Stuttgart win 8-2 on agg); Zalaegerszeg 1 Dinamo Zagreb 3 (Dinamo win 9-1 on agg); Djurgardens 3 FC Copenhagen 1 (Djurgardens win 3-1 on agg); Sartid 0 Ipswich Town 1 (Ipswich win 2-1 on agg); Boavista 4 Maccabi Tel-Aviv 1 (Boavista win 4-2 on agg); Fenerbahce 3 AIK Solna 1 (Fenerbahce win 6-4 on agg); Siroki Brijeg 0 Sparta Prague 1 (Sparta win 4-0 on agg); Ujpest 0 Paris Saint-Germain 1 (PSG win 4-0 on agg); Partizan 3 Sporting Lisbon 3 (aet; Partizan win 6-4 on agg); Utrecht 1 Legia Warsaw 3 (Warsaw win 7-2 on agg); Real Betis 2 Zimbru 1 (Betis win 4-1 on agg); FK Sarajevo 0 Besiktas 5 (Besiktas win 7-2 on agg); Parma 3 CSKA Moscow 2 (Parma win 4-3 on agg); Brondby 1 Levski Sofia 1 (Sofia win 5-2 on agg); Stabaek 1 Anderlecht 2 (aet; 2-2 on agg; Anderlecht win on away goals); Heerenveen 2 National 0 (National win 3-2 on agg); Xanthi 0 Lazio 0 (Lazio win 4-0 on agg)

MATCH OF THE SEASON

SECOND ROUND

First legs, October 31

Djurgardens 0 Bordeaux 1; Viktoria Zizkov 0 Real Betis 1; Legia Warsaw 2 Schalke 3; APOEL Nicosia 0 Hertha Berlin 1; Malaga 2 Amica 1; Ferencvaros 0 Stuttgart 0; Boavista 2 Anorthosis 1; Dinamo Zagreb 0 Fulham 3; Parma 2 Wisla Krakow 1; Anderlecht 3 Midtjylland 1; Partizan 3 Slavia Prague 1; Lazio 1 Crvena Zvezda 0; Ipswich Town 1 Liberec 0; Alaves 1 Besiktas 1; Leeds United 1 Hapoel Tel-Aviv 0; Austria Vienna 0 Porto 1; Sparta Prague 1 Denizlispor 0; National 0 Paris Saint-Germain 2; Celtic 1 Blackburn Rovers 0; Vitesse 2 Werder Bremen 1; Celta Vigo 3 Viking 0; Sturm Graz 1 Levski Sofia 0; PAOK 3 Grasshopper 1; Fenerbahce 2 Panathinaikos 1

Second legs, November 14

Bordeaux 2 Djurgardens 1 (Bordeaux win 3-1 on agg); Real Betis 3 Viktoria Zizkov 0 (Real Betis win 4-0 on agg); Schalke 0 Legia Warsaw 0 (Schalke win 3-2 on agg); Hertha Berlin 4 APOEL Nicosia 0 (Hertha Berlin win 5-0 on agg); Amica 1 Malaga 2 (Malaga win 4-2 on agg); Stuttgart 2 Ferencvaros 0 (Stuttgart win 2-0 on agg); Anorthosis 0 Boavista 1 (Boavista win 3-1 on agg); Fulham 2 Dinamo Zagreb 1 (Fulham win 5-1 on agg); Wisla Krakow 4 Parma 1 (aet; Wisla Krakow win 5-3 on agg); Midtjylland 0 Anderlecht 3 (Anderlecht win 6-1 on agg); Slavia Prague 5 Partizan 1 (aet; Slavia Prague win 6-4 on agg); Crvena Zvezda 1 Lazio 1 (Lazio win 2-1 on agg); Liberec 1 Ipswich Town 0 (aet; 1-1 on agg; Liberec win 4-2 on penalties); Besiktas 1 Alaves 0 (Besiktas win 2-1 on agg); Hapoel Tel-Aviv 1 Leeds United 4 (Leeds United win 5-1 on agg); Porto 2 Austria Vienna 0 (Porto win 3-0 on agg); Denizlispor 2 Sparta Prague 0 (Denizlispor win 2-1 on agg); Paris Saint-Germain 1 National 0 (Paris Saint-Germain win 3-0 on agg); Blackburn Rovers 0 Celtic 2 (Celtic win 3-0 on agg); Werder Bremen 3 Vitesse Arnhem 3 (Vitesse Arnhem win 5-4 on agg); Viking 1 Celta Vigo 1 (Celta Vigo win 4-1 on agg); Levski Sofia 1 Sturm Graz 1 (aet; 1-1 on agg; Sturm Graz win 8-7 on penalties); Grasshopper 1 PAOK 1 (PAOK win 5-0 on agg); Panathinaikos 4 Fenerbahce 1 (Panathinaikos win 5-2 on agg)

THIRD ROUND

First legs, November 28

Paris Saint-Germain 2 Boavista 1; Hertha Berlin 2 Fulham 1; Wisla Krakow 1 Schalke 1; Sturm Graz 1 Lazio 3; Real Betis 1 Auxerre 0; Besiktas 3 Dinamo Kiev 1; AEK Athens 4 Maccabi Haifa 0; Porto 3 Lens 0; Celtic 1 Celta Vigo 0; FC Bruges 1 Stuttgart 2; Vitesse Arnhem 0 Liverpool 1; Liberec 2 Panathinaikos 2; Denizlispor 0 Lyons 0; Bordeaux 0 Anderlecht 2; Malaga 0 Leeds United 0; PAOK 1 Slavia Prague 0

Second legs, December 12

Boavista 1 Paris Saint-Germain 0 (aet; 2-2 on agg; Boavista win on away goals); Fulham 0 Hertha Berlin 0 (Hertha Berlin win 2-1 on agg); Schalke 1 Wisla Krakow 4 (Wisla Krakow win 5-2 on agg); Lazio 0 Sturm Graz 1 (Lazio win 3-2 on agg); Auxerre 2 Real Betis 0 (Auxerre win 2-1 on agg); Dinamo Kiev 0 Besiktas 0 (Besiktas win 3-1 on agg); Maccabi Haifa 1 AEK Athens 4 (Maccabi Haifa win 8-1 on agg); Lens 1 Porto 0 (Porto win 3-1 on agg); Celta Vigo 2 Celtic 1 (aet; 2-2 on agg; Celtic win on away goals); Stuttgart 1 FC Bruges 0 (Stuttgart win 3-1 on agg); Liverpool 1 Vitesse Arnhem 0 (Liverpool win 2-0 on agg); Panathinaikos 1 Liberec 0 (Panathinaikos win 3-2 on agg); Lyons 0 Denizlispor 1 (Denizlispor win 1-0 on agg); Anderlecht 2 Bordeaux 2 (Anderlecht win 4-2 on agg); Leeds United 1 Malaga 2 (Malaga win 2-1 on agg); Slavia Prague 4 PAOK 0 (Slavia Prague win 4-1 on agg)

Liverpool 0   Celtic 2 *(Celtic win 3-1 on agg)*
Anfield, Thursday March 20 2003
Oliver Kay

DURING A WEEK IN WHICH Arsenal and Newcastle United have been sent packing from the Champions League by the aristocrats from Italy and Spain, the last thing English football needed last night was to have its face rubbed in the dirt by its oldest rival. Celtic may have given the Scottish game a much-needed shot in the arm by reaching their first European semi-final since 1974, but the disintegration of Liverpool's Uefa Cup campaign leaves Manchester United as the Barclaycard Premiership's sole representatives in European competition.

Liverpool will not give a damn about the wider repercussions of this defeat, but the manner of it was symptomatic of their failings in the Premiership and in Europe this season. Slipshod defending, uninspired midfield play and erratic finishing contributed to their elimination from the Champions League in November and it was those traits, exposed by a Celtic team excelling in all departments, that resurfaced last night. They were not only outfought, but outplayed and even outwitted by the Scottish champions.

The damage was done by Alan Thompson and John Hartson, whose goals allowed Celtic to build on the platform that Martin O'Neill's game-plan had afforded them, but Liverpool's failure to exploit home advantage and build on their 1-1 draw in Glasgow seven days earlier was no less of a factor. Their one-dimensional approach was exposed by a visiting team who showed, particularly with Hartson's spectacular goal nine minutes from time, that there is inspiration in their game to go alongside the perspiration for which they are renowned.

"I'm like the players; I'm hurt," Gerard Houllier, the Liverpool manager, said. "But that's football. We battled and we competed, but the first goal, coming just before half-time, changed a lot. It was a great time for them to score and a bad time for us. But I refute the assertion that we were overconfident. We were very focused and very committed. We played with pride, but it was difficult in the second half, when we were trying to push forward and they had all their players behind the ball."

Anfield was made for evenings such as this, the atmosphere heightened before kick-off by a stirring communal rendition of *You'll Never Walk Alone*, but the wall of noise was by no means entirely hostile to Celtic, whose supporters had arrived in far greater numbers than their official allocation of 2,700 tickets suggested.

Whereas Liverpool had briefly been overwhelmed at Celtic Park, falling behind within two minutes, it quickly became apparent that their visitors were in no mood to be overawed. Henrik Larsson tested Jerzy Dudek with a free kick, while Hartson, desperate to

Thompson, right, holds off Heskey as Celtic rule the roost at Anfield

atone for a late penalty miss in Sunday's CIS Cup final defeat by Rangers, twice headed narrowly wide. Liverpool's pace and power have been enough to account for several European opponents at Anfield in recent seasons, but against Celtic, a team built on similar principles, it was proving harder. With Paul Lambert giving the visiting team more aggression in midfield, Liverpool's best efforts came from long range, Dietmar Hamann shooting just wide and Steven Gerrard forcing Robert Douglas into an excellent save.

It was proving a more compelling spectacle than the teams' previous competitive meeting on this ground, in September 1997, when Liverpool gained the 0-0 draw they needed to progress to the Uefa Cup second round on away goals, but any thoughts of doing likewise last night evaporated in the final minute of the first half, when Thompson gave Celtic the lead they deserved. After Djimi Traore tugged Larsson's shirt, Thompson stepped forward to send a low free kick through the wall and past the unsighted Dudek.

A 1-1 draw would have forced extra time, but only once, when Gerrard galloped forward and shot too close to Douglas, was Celtic's three-man defence stretched. A nervous last ten minutes looked in prospect, but it was Celtic who finished with a flourish, Hartson cutting in from the left wing and finding the top corner from 25 yards. "I had a real low on Sunday when I missed that penalty against Rangers," Hartson said, "but this is a real high and a night I'll never forget."

LIVERPOOL (4-4-2): J Dudek — J Carragher, D Traore, S Hyypia, J A Riise — D Murphy, S Gerrard, D Hamann, V Smicer (sub: M Baros, 56min) — E Heskey, M Owen. **Substitutes not used:** I Biscan, S Diao, P Berger, B Cheyrou, N Mellor, P Arphexad.
CELTIC (3-4-1-2): R Douglas — J Mjallby, B Balde, J Valgaeren — M Sylla (sub: J Smith, 86), N Lennon, P Lambert (sub: J McNamara, 73), A Thompson — S Petrov — J Hartson, H Larsson. **Substitutes not used:** U Laursen, S Maloney, S Guppy, S Crainey, D Marshall. **Booked:** Mjallby, Sylla, Thompson, Douglas.
Referee: M Merk (Germany).

FOURTH ROUND
First legs, February 20
Slavia Prague 1 Besiktas 0; Hertha Berlin 3 Boavista 2; Malaga 0 AEK Athens 0; Panathinaikos 3 Anderlecht 0; Celtic 3 Stuttgart 1; Porto 6 Denizlispor 1; Auxerre 0 Liverpool 1; Lazio 3 Wisla Krakow 3

Second legs, February 27
Besiktas 4 Slavia Prague 2 (Besiktas win 4-3 on agg); Boavista 1 Hertha Berlin 0 (aet; 3-3 on agg; Boavista win on away goals); AEK Athens 0 Malaga 1 (Malaga win 1-0 on agg); Anderlecht 2 Panathinaikos 0 (Panathinaikos win 3-2 on agg); Stuttgart 3 Celtic 2 (Celtic win 5-4 on agg); Denizlispor 2 Porto 2 (Porto win 8-3 on agg); Liverpool 2 Auxerre 0 (Liverpool win 3-0 on agg); Wisla Krakow 1 Lazio 2 (Lazio win 5-4 on agg)

QUARTER-FINALS
First legs, March 13
Malaga 1 Boavista 0
Celtic 1 Liverpool 1
Porto 0 Panathinaikos 1
Lazio 1 Besiktas 0

Second legs, March 20
Boavista 1 Malaga 0
(aet; 1-1 on agg; Boavista win 4-1 on penalties)
Liverpool 0 Celtic 2
(Celtic win 3-1 on agg)
Panathinaikos 0 Porto 2
(aet; Porto win 2-1 on agg)
Besiktas 1 Lazio 2
(Lazio win 3-1 on agg)

SEMI-FINALS
First legs, April 10
Celtic 1 Boavista 1
Porto 4 Lazio 1

Second legs, April 24
Boavista 0 Celtic 1
(Celtic win 2-1 on agg)
Lazio 0 Porto 0
(Porto win 4-1 on agg)

Final details overleaf

PLAYER OF THE SEASON
Derlei, FC Porto

Signed from Uniao Leiria during the summer, Derlei scored only six goals as FC Porto won the Portuguese championship. "I have other duties, defensive ones, and I play a little farther from the goal," he explained. In the Uefa Cup, though, when thrust into a more forward role by Jose Mourinho, the Porto coach, he came alive, doubling his tally and breaking Celtic hearts in Seville. "We paid peanuts for him, not millions, and I'm very proud of him," Mourinho said. Derlei, 27, a Brazilian, missed the Portuguese Cup final against Leiria after breaking his jaw in a collision on the training ground with Edgaras Jankauskas, the Lithuania striker.

Russell Kempson

FINAL

May 21, Seville

CELTIC (0) **2**
Larsson 47, 57
52,972

FC PORTO (1) **3**
Derlei 45, 115
Alenichev 54

(aet; 2-2 after 90min)

Henrik Larsson's double for Celtic in the final against FC Porto was in vain

CELTIC (3-5-2): R Douglas — J Mjallby, D Balde, J Valgaeren (sub: U Laursen, 64min) — D Agathe, P Lambert (sub: J McNamara, 76), N Lennon, S Petrov (sub: S Maloney, 104), A Thompson — H Larsson, C Sutton. **Substitutes not used:** M Hedman, M Sylla, D Fernandez, J Smith. **Booked:** Balde, Lennon, Petrov, Valgaeren. **Sent off:** Balde.
FC PORTO (4-4-2): V Baia — P Ferreira, J Costa (sub: P Emanuel, 71), R Carvalho, N Valente — Deco, Costinha (sub: R Costa, 9), D Alenichev, Maniche — Derlei, Capucho (sub: M Ferreira, 98). **Substitutes not used:** Nuno, C Peixoto, Clayton, Tiago. **Booked:** Valente, Derlei, Maniche, Ferreira. **Sent off:** Valente.
Referee: L Michel (Slovakia).

LEADING SCORERS

		Total
Derlei	FC Porto	12
Henrik Larsson	Celtic	11
Maciej Zurawski	Wisla Krakow	9
Nenad Jestrovic	Anderlecht	7
Mustafa Ozkan	Denizlispor	6

EUROPEAN FOOTBALL

All white on the night: Raul, left, and Ronaldo celebrate Real Madrid's title triumph on the final day in Spain

SPAIN
Real Madrid

ITALY
Juventus

GERMANY
Bayern Munich

FRANCE
Lyons

THE NETHERLANDS
PSV Eindhoven

PORTUGAL
FC Porto

BELGIUM
FC Bruges

FINAL TABLES

SPAIN

	P	W	D	L	F	A	Pts
Real Madrid	38	22	12	4	86	42	78
Real Sociedad	38	22	10	6	71	45	76
Deportivo	38	22	6	10	67	47	72
Celta Vigo	38	17	10	11	45	36	61
Valencia	38	17	9	12	56	35	60
Barcelona	38	15	11	12	63	47	56
Athletic Bilbao	38	15	10	13	63	61	55
Real Betis	38	14	12	12	56	53	54
Real Mallorca	38	14	10	14	49	56	52
Sevilla	38	13	11	14	38	39	50
Osasuna	38	12	11	15	40	48	47
Atletico Madrid	38	12	11	15	51	56	47
Malaga	38	11	13	14	44	49	46
Valladolid	38	12	10	16	37	40	46
Villarreal	38	11	12	15	44	53	45
Racing Santander	38	13	5	20	54	64	44
Espanyol	38	10	13	15	48	54	43
Recreativo Huelva	38	8	12	18	35	61	36
Alaves	38	8	11	19	38	68	35
Rayo Vallecano	38	7	11	20	31	62	32

ITALY

	P	W	D	L	F	A	Pts
Juventus	34	21	9	4	64	29	72
Inter Milan	34	19	8	7	64	38	65
AC Milan	34	18	7	9	55	30	61
Lazio	34	15	15	4	57	32	60
Parma	34	15	11	8	55	36	56
Udinese	34	16	8	10	38	35	56
Chievo	34	16	7	11	51	39	55
Roma	34	13	10	11	55	46	49
Brescia	34	9	15	10	36	38	42
Perugia	34	10	12	12	40	48	42
Bologna	34	10	11	13	39	47	41
Empoli	34	9	11	14	36	46	38
Atalanta	34	8	14	12	35	47	38
Reggina	34	10	8	16	38	53	38
Modena	34	9	11	14	30	48	38
Piacenza	34	8	6	20	44	62	30
Como	34	4	12	18	29	57	24
Torino	34	4	9	21	23	58	21

EUROPE'S FOUR LEADING LEAGUES are almost certain to produce the continental champions each year in these times of financial polarisation and last season the quartet also witnessed predictability at home. While Manchester United triumphed in the Barclaycard Premiership, Real Madrid, Juventus and Bayern Munich each extended their records for title wins in their own countries.

Real recorded their 29th Spanish championship, Juventus managed a 27th title in Italy and Bayern's success was their eighteenth in Germany, but their paths to the top were markedly different. Bayern destroyed the Bundesliga field and Juventus prevailed with some comfort, but Real needed a final-day victory over Athletic Bilbao to secure their trophy.

By signing Ronaldo shortly after he had inspired Brazil to their World Cup win in Japan, Real became arguably the strongest club team ever assembled, having acquired Zinedine Zidane and Luis Figo during the previous two summers. With Raul and Roberto Carlos already at the Bernabeu, the potential was mind-boggling. Yet the club's ambition is such that Vicente Del Bosque was eased aside as coach just hours after the league had been won, to be replaced by Carlos Queiroz, who was lured from Old Trafford. Del Bosque was asked to leave despite having turned the club into champions of either Spain or Europe in each of his four years in charge.

Del Bosque paid for the European Cup semi-final defeat by Juventus, but, although he might have coaxed even better results from the remarkable talent at his disposal, he deserves sympathy for having had his requests to sign more defenders ignored by the club. The resulting top-heavy team produced some wonderful attacking but was often hopeless at the back. The release of the ageing and ailing Fernando Hierro at the end of the season was no great surprise.

After a poor start, during which the overweight Ronaldo was criticised by many of the club's fans, Real eventually came good to regain the title that they had lost to Valencia a year before. Thus David Beckham, signed during the summer from Manchester United, is moving from one set of champions to another and he will hope to appear more often than Steve McManaman, another England midfield player, who made just six league starts.

That Real only scraped home owed much to an extraordinary effort by Real Sociedad, who had finished in the bottom half of La Liga in the previous three seasons. With two Liverpool cast-offs in Sander Westerveld, the goalkeeper, and Bjorn Kvarme, the central

No 1 hit: Ciro Ferrara enjoys the Juventus championship party in Italy

GERMANY

	P	W	D	L	F	A	Pts
Bayern Munich	34	23	6	5	70	25	75
VfB Stuttgart	34	17	8	9	53	39	59
B Dortmund	34	15	13	6	51	27	58
SV Hamburg	34	15	11	8	46	36	56
Hertha Berlin	34	16	6	12	52	43	54
Werder Bremen	34	16	4	14	51	50	52
Schalke 04	34	12	13	9	46	40	49
VfL Wolfsburg	34	13	7	14	39	42	46
VfL Bochum	34	12	9	13	55	56	45
TSV 1860 Munich	34	12	9	13	44	52	45
Hannover 96	34	12	7	15	47	57	43
B Moncheng'bach	34	11	9	14	43	45	42
Hansa Rostock	34	11	8	15	35	41	41
Kaiserslautern	34	10	10	14	40	42	40
Bayer Leverkusen	34	11	7	16	47	56	40
Arminia Bielefeld	34	8	12	14	35	46	36
Nuremberg	34	8	6	20	33	60	30
Energie Cottbus	34	7	9	18	34	64	30

FRANCE

	P	W	D	L	F	A	Pts
Lyons	38	19	11	8	63	41	68
AS Monaco	38	19	10	9	66	33	67
Marseilles	38	19	8	11	41	36	65
Bordeaux	38	18	10	10	57	36	64
FC Sochaux	38	17	13	8	46	31	64
AJ Auxerre	38	18	10	10	38	29	64
Guingamp	38	19	5	14	59	46	62
RC Lens	38	14	15	9	43	31	57
FC Nantes	38	16	8	14	37	39	56
Nice	38	13	16	9	39	31	55
PSG	38	14	12	12	47	36	54
Bastia	38	12	11	15	40	48	47
Strasbourg	38	11	12	15	40	54	45
Lille	38	10	12	16	29	44	42
Rennes	38	10	10	18	35	45	40
Montpellier	38	10	10	18	37	54	40
Ajaccio	38	9	12	17	29	49	39
Le Havre	38	10	8	20	27	47	38
Sedan	38	9	9	20	41	59	36
Troyes	38	7	10	21	23	48	31

THE NETHERLANDS

	P	W	D	L	F	A	Pts
PSV Eindhoven	34	26	6	2	87	20	84
Ajax	34	26	5	3	96	32	83
Feyenoord	34	25	5	4	89	39	80
NAC Breda	34	13	13	8	42	31	52
NEC	34	14	9	11	41	40	51
Roda JC	34	14	8	12	58	54	50
SC Heerenveen	34	13	8	13	61	55	47
Utrecht	34	12	11	11	49	49	47
RKC Waalwijk	34	14	4	16	44	51	46
AZ Alkmaar	34	12	8	14	50	69	44
Willem II	34	11	9	14	48	51	42
FC Twente	34	10	11	13	36	45	41
RBC Roosendaal	34	10	6	18	33	54	36
Vitesse Arnhem	34	8	9	17	37	51	33
FC Groningen	34	7	11	16	28	44	32
FC Zwolle	34	8	8	18	31	62	32
Excelsior	34	5	8	21	38	72	23
De Graafschap	34	6	5	23	35	84	23

PORTUGAL

	P	W	D	L	F	A	Pts
FC Porto	34	27	5	2	73	26	86
Benfica	34	23	6	5	74	27	75
Sporting Lisbon	34	17	8	9	52	38	59
Vitoria Guimaraes	34	14	8	12	47	46	50
Uniao Leiria	34	13	10	11	49	47	49
Pacos de Ferreira	34	12	9	13	40	47	45
CS Maritimo	34	13	5	16	36	48	44
Gil Vicente	34	13	5	16	42	53	44
Belenenses	34	11	10	13	47	48	43
Boavista	34	10	13	11	32	31	43
CD Nacional	34	9	13	12	40	46	40
Moreirense	34	9	12	13	42	46	39
SC Beira Mar	34	10	9	15	43	50	39
SC Braga	34	8	14	12	34	47	38
Academica	34	8	13	13	38	48	37
Varzim	34	10	6	18	38	51	36
Santa Clara	34	8	11	15	39	54	35
Vitoria Setubal	34	6	13	15	40	53	31

BELGIUM

	P	W	D	L	F	A	Pts
FC Bruges	32	25	4	3	96	33	79
Anderlecht	32	23	2	7	72	31	71
Lokeren	32	18	6	8	69	51	60
Sint-Truiden	32	16	8	8	63	44	56
Lierse	32	16	8	8	51	41	56
Genk	32	16	7	9	73	52	55
Standard Liege	32	14	8	10	53	39	50
AA Gent	32	15	2	15	49	55	47
Mons	32	13	4	15	45	45	43
Westerlo	32	12	4	16	39	46	40
Beveren	32	12	2	18	50	69	38
Royal Antwerp	32	9	7	16	44	55	34
Mouscron	32	9	5	18	42	72	32
Germinl Beerscht	32	8	7	17	49	57	31
La Louviere	32	7	9	16	34	44	30
Charleroi	32	6	9	17	39	66	27
KV Mechelen	32	4	6	22	18	86	18
Lommel	0	0	0	0	0	0	0

☐ *Lommel expelled from league; results expunged*

defender — and with Darko Kovacevic, who failed to settle at Sheffield Wednesday, up front — a side coached by Raynald Denoueix came within two points of a most unlikely title.

Almost as dramatic was the decline of Barcelona, who were in danger of relegation with a quarter of the season left, despite making imperious progress to the European Cup quarter-finals. The decision to hire Louis van Gaal for a second spell in charge at the Nou Camp proved a mistake and the Dutchman left in January, after which the team recovered under Raddy Antic, although he was replaced in turn at the end of the season by Frank Rijkaard.

Barcelona were eliminated from Europe by Juventus, one of a trio of Italian clubs that reached the semi-finals as well as challenging for the Serie A title. The Turin side did not match the transfer activity of AC Milan and Inter Milan in the run-up to the season, but the contributions of Gianluigi Buffon, Lilian Thuram and especially the outstanding Pavel Nedved, all in their second campaigns at the Stadio Delle Alpi, were decisive.

Milan had signed Rivaldo but made little use of the Brazil forward, an unused substitute in the European Cup final win over Juventus. Still, the team managed to provide considerable entertainment, in contrast to Inter, whose coach, Hector Cuper, reinforced his reputation as a producer of dour sides. In finishing fourth, Lazio overcame the enforced sales of Alessandro Nesta and Hernan Crespo before the season started to book a Champions League place that will ease their financial strife.

The advantage bestowed by wealth was illustrated by Bayern, who had signed Michael Ballack and Ze Roberto from Bayer Leverkusen after finishing third, one place below their rivals, in 2001-02, when Borussia Dortmund won the title by a point. Partly as a result, the Munich club won the league and Leverkusen collapsed, ending 14 places and 35 points behind them.

Bayern had long clinched the league when Leverkusen stood two points from safety with two games left, both of which they won. It was a comedown for a side that concluded the previous season in the European Cup final.

A shaky autumn for Bayern, in which they suffered an early Champions League exit, prompted much speculation that Ottmar Hitzfeld would be dismissed as coach. Similarly, a premature departure from Europe's senior competition almost persuaded Paul Le Guen to resign as the coach of Lyons, yet he stayed and saw his side become the first to retain the French title since Marseilles in 1992. As Del Bosque would acknowledge, management is a precarious business.

PLAYER OF THE SEASON — Pavel Nedved

Denied a place on the biggest stage by the Czech Republic's surprising failure to reach the World Cup finals, Pavel Nedved made amends by inspiring an outstanding campaign for Juventus. The hard-working attacking midfield player, signed from Lazio for £25 million in 2001, was the main creative spark in an unspectacular team. He was rewarded with a championship medal, but suspension ruled him out of the European Cup final and his absence was significant in his team's defeat by AC Milan.

Bill Edgar

SWITZERLAND

	P	W	D	L	F	A	Pts
Grasshopper	14	9	5	0	37	15	57
FC Basle	14	10	2	2	38	17	56
Neuchatel Xamax	14	5	4	5	18	17	35
Young Boys	14	6	1	7	21	29	34
FC Zurich	14	4	3	7	20	23	31
Servette	14	4	4	6	16	26	31
FC Thun	14	3	3	8	18	30	28
FC Wil	14	2	4	8	19	30	26

WALES

	P	W	D	L	F	A	Pts
Barry Town	34	26	5	3	84	26	83
TNS Llansantffraid	34	24	8	2	68	21	80
Bangor City	34	22	5	7	75	34	71
Aberystwyth Town	34	17	9	8	54	38	60
Connah's Quay	34	18	5	11	55	46	59
Rhyl	34	17	7	10	52	33	58
Afan Lido	34	14	10	10	44	34	52
Caersws	34	15	6	13	57	52	51
Cwmbran Town	34	14	8	12	51	40	50
Newtown	34	12	6	16	48	54	42
Port Talbot Town	34	11	6	17	36	51	39
Flexys CD	34	11	5	18	37	51	38
Haverfordwest	34	10	5	19	40	68	35
Caernarfon Town	34	8	10	16	43	53	34
Carmarthen Town	34	9	5	20	33	66	32
Oswestry Town	34	6	10	18	36	67	28
Welshpool Town	34	7	7	20	30	62	28
Llanelli	34	4	5	25	42	89	17

NORTHERN IRELAND

	P	W	D	L	F	A	Pts
Glentoran	38	28	6	4	78	22	90
Portadown	38	24	8	6	89	36	80
Coleraine	38	21	10	7	66	38	73
Linfield	38	17	12	9	70	41	63
Omagh Town	38	15	6	17	47	57	51
Institute	38	12	6	20	44	75	42
Ards	38	12	10	16	27	39	46
Lisburn Distillery	38	12	6	20	39	49	42
Cliftonville	38	9	14	15	37	43	41
Glenavon	38	8	12	18	41	67	36
Crusaders	38	9	9	20	26	61	36
Newry Town	38	8	7	23	33	69	31

LEADING SCORERS

FRANCE

26 Shabani Nonda (AS Monaco)
23 Pauleta (Bordeaux)
17 Didier Drogba (Guingamp)
14 Henri Camara (Sedan), Djibril Cisse (AJ Auxerre)
13 Juninho (Lyons)

GERMANY

21 Thomas Christiansen (VfL Bochum), Giovane Elber (Bayern Munich)
16 Ailton (Werder Bremen)
15 Kevin Kuranyi (VfB Stuttgart), Claudio Pizarro (Bayern Munich)

ITALY

24 Christian Vieri (Inter Milan)
18 Adrian Mutu (Parma)

17 Filippo Inzaghi (AC Milan)
16 Alessandro Del Piero (Juventus)
15 Adriano (Parma), Claudio Lopez (Lazio)

PORTUGAL

18 Simao Sabrosa (Benfica)
17 Fary Faye (Beira Mar)
16 Adriano (Nacional)
15 Eric Gaucho (CS Maritimo)

SPAIN

29 Roy Makaay (Deportivo La Coruna)
23 Nihat Kahveci (Real Sociedad), Ronaldo (Real Madrid)
20 Darko Kovacevic (Real Sociedad)
16 Raul (Real Madrid)

CHAMPIONS LEAGUE

Albania SK Tirana
Armenia Pyunik
Austria Austria Vienna, Grazer AK
Belarus BATE Borisov
Belgium FC Bruges, Anderlecht
Bosnia-Herzegovina Leotar
Bulgaria CSKA Sofia
Croatia Dinamo Zagreb
Cyprus Omonia Nicosia
Czech Republic Sparta Prague, Slavia Prague
Denmark FC Copenhagen
England Manchester United, Arsenal, Newcastle United, Chelsea
Estonia Flora Tallinn
Faeroe Isles HB Torshavn
Finland HJK Helsinki
France Lyons, AS Monaco, Marseilles
Georgia Dinamo Tbilisi
Germany Bayern Munich, VfB Stuttgart, Borussia Dortmund
Greece Olympiakos, Panathinaikos, AEK Athens
Hungary MTK Hungaria
Iceland KR Reykjavik
Ireland Bohemians
Israel Maccabi Tel-Aviv
Italy AC Milan, Juventus, Inter Milan, Lazio
Kazakhstan Irtysh Pavlodar
Latvia Skonto Riga
Lithuania FBK Kaunas
Luxembourg CS Grevenmacher
Macedonia Vardar
Malta Sliema Wanderers
Moldova Sheriff Tiraspol
The Netherlands PSV Eindhoven, Ajax
Northern Ireland Glentoran
Norway Rosenborg
Poland Wisla Krakow
Portugal FC Porto, Benfica
Romania Rapid Bucharest
Russia Lokomotiv Moscow, CSKA Moscow
Scotland Rangers, Celtic
Serbia and Montenegro Partizan Belgrade
Slovakia MSK Zilina
Slovenia Maribor

Roy Makaay was top goalscorer in Spain

Spain Real Madrid, Real Sociedad, Deportivo La Coruna, Celta Vigo
Sweden Djurgardens
Switzerland Grasshopper
Turkey Besiktas, Galatasaray
Ukraine Dinamo Kiev, Shakhtar Donetsk
Wales Barry Town

UEFA CUP

Albania KS Vllaznia, Dinamo Tirana
Andorra Santa Coloma
Armenia Banants, Shirak
Austria Karnten, SV Salzburg
Belarus Dinamo Minsk, Neman Grodno
Belgium Lokeren, RAA Louvieroise
Bosnia-Herzegovina Zeljeznicar, FK Sarajevo
Bulgaria Litex Lovech, Levski Sofia
Croatia Varteks, Kamen Ingrad, Hajduk Split
Cyprus Anorthosis Famagusta, APOEL Nicosia
Czech Republic Viktoria Zizkov, SK Teplice
England Liverpool, Blackburn Rovers, Southampton, Manchester City
Estonia Levadia Maardu, TVMK Tallinn
Faeroe Isles Kl Klaksvik, NSI Runavik
Finland MyPa, Haka

France Bordeaux, Sochaux, AJ Auxerre, RC Lens
Georgia Cioni Bolnisi, Torpedo Kutaisi
Germany SV Hamburg, Hertha Berlin, 1FC Kaiserslautern
Greece PAOK, Panionios, Aris Saloniki
Hungary Debreceni VSC, Ferencvaros
Iceland Fylkir, Grindavik
Ireland Derry City, Shelbourne
Israel Hapoel Tel-Aviv, Maccabi Haifa, Hapoel Ramat Gan
Italy Parma, AS Roma, Udinese
Kazakhstan FC Zhenis Astana, Atyrau
Latvia FK Ventspils
Liechtenstein Vaduz
Lithuania Atlantas, FK Ekranas
Luxembourg Etzella Ettelbruck, F91 Dudelange
Malta Valletta, Birkirkara
Macedonia Belasica GC, Cementarnica 55
Moldova Zimbru Chisinau, Nistru Otoci
The Netherlands Feyenoord, Utrecht, NAC Breda, NEC Nijmegen
Northern Ireland Portadown, Coleraine
Norway Molde FK, SFK Lyn, Valerenga
Poland Wisla Plock, Groclin Drodzisk, GKS Katowice
Portugal Uniao Leiria, Sporting Lisbon
Romania Steaua Bucharest
Russia Torpedo Moscow, Spartak Moscow
Scotland Dundee, Heart of Midlothian
Serbia and Montenegro FK Sartid, Crvena Zvezda
Slovakia SKM Puchov, Artmedia Petrzalka
Slovenia Publikum, Olimpija Ljubljana
San Marino Domajnano
Spain Valencia, Barcelona, Real Mallorca
Sweden AIK Solna, Malmo FF
Switzerland Neuchatel Xamax, Young Boys, FC Basle
Turkey Trabzonspor, Genclerbirligi, Gaziantepspor, Malatyaspor
Ukraine Dnipro Dnipropetrovsk, Metalurg Donetsk
Wales TNS, Cwmbran Town

INTERNATIONAL FOOTBALL

Down under: Michael Owen and England
are brought to their knees by Australia

THE GAMES

Saturday September 7
Friendly
PORTUGAL (h)
Villa Park
Drew 1-1   HT 1-0   Att 40,058
ENGLAND D James (West Ham United) — **D Mills**
(Leeds United; sub: **O Hargreaves**, Bayern Munich, ht),
R Ferdinand (Manchester United; sub: **J Woodgate**,
Leeds United, ht), **G Southgate** (Middlesbrough), **A Cole**
(Arsenal; sub: **W Bridge**, Southampton, ht) — **L Bowyer**
(Leeds United; sub: **T Sinclair**, West Ham United, 72), **S**
Gerrard (Liverpool; sub: **D Dunn**, Blackburn Rovers, ht),
N Butt (Manchester United; sub: **D Murphy**, Liverpool,
62), **E Heskey** (Liverpool) — **A Smith** (Leeds United), **M**
Owen (Liverpool; sub: **J Cole**, West Ham United, 62)
Sub not used **P Robinson** (Leeds United)
Scorer **Smith 40**
PORTUGAL V Baia (FC Porto; sub: **R Pereira**, Boavista,
ht) — **Beto** (Sporting Lisbon; sub: **Nuno Gomes**,
Benfica, ht), **F Meira** (VfB Stuttgart; sub: **J Silva**,
Boavista, 78), **F Couto** (Lazio; sub: **P Ferreira**, FC Porto,
ht) — **S Conceicao** (Inter Milan; sub: **N Valente**, FC
Porto, ht), **A Petit** (Benfica; sub: **L Vidigal**, Napoli, 65),
R Jorge (Sporting Lisbon; sub: **N Capucho**, FC Porto,
ht), **R Costa** (AC Milan; sub: **L Boa Morte**, Fulham, ht) —
L Figo (Real Madrid; sub: **H Viana**, Newcastle United,
ht), **P Pauleta** (Bordeaux; sub: **J Pinto**, Benfica, ht),
Simao (Benfica; sub: **Costinha**, FC Porto, ht)
Scorer **Costinha 79**
Referee **T H Ovrebo (Norway)**

Saturday October 13
European Championship qualifier
SLOVAKIA (a)
Bratislava
Won 2-1   HT 0-1   Att 30,000
SLOVAKIA M Konig (FC Zurich) — **P Dzurik** (Slovan
Bratislava), **V Leitner** (FK Teplice), **M Petras** (Sparta
Prague) — **P Hlinka** (SW Bregenz), **V Janocko** (Austria
Vienna; sub: **M Mintal**, MSK Zilnia, 89min), **M Zeman**
(Vitesse Arnhem), **A Pinte** (Panionios; sub: **J Kozlej**,
Olympiakos Nicosia, 89), **M Karhan** (VfL Wolfsburg) — **R**
Vittek (Slovan Bratislava; sub: **L Reiter**, Olomouc
Sigma, 81), **S Nemeth** (Middlesbrough) *Subs not used*
J Bucek (Xanthi), **M Cisovsky** (Inter Bratislava), **R**
Michalik (Sparta Prague), **M Klimpi** (Viktoria Zizkov)
Scorer **Nemeth 24**
Booked **Zeman, Leitner, Vittek**
ENGLAND D Seaman (Arsenal) — **G Neville**
(Manchester United), **J Woodgate** (Leeds United), **G**
Southgate (Middlesbrough), **A Cole** (Arsenal) — **S**
Gerrard (Liverpool; sub: **K Dyer**, Newcastle United, 77),
D Beckham (Manchester United), **N Butt** (Manchester
United), **P Scholes** (Manchester United) — **E Heskey**
(Liverpool; sub: **A Smith**, Leeds United, 90), **M Owen**
(Liverpool; sub: **O Hargreaves**, Bayern Munich, 87) *Subs
not used* **D Mills** (Leeds United), **D James** (West Ham
United), **U Ehiogu** (Middlesbrough), **D Vassell** (Aston
Villa)
Scorers **Beckham 65, Owen 82**
Booked **Gerrard, Beckham, Scholes**
Referee **D Messina (Italy)**

FOUR WINS AND A DRAW IN competitive fixtures sounds a straightforward kind of season, but it is a long time since results were the be-all and end-all around the England camp. A shooting outside the squad's hotel, an upsurge in hooliganism and questions about the England coach's love life — that all happened in 24 hours in Slovakia, even before the European Championship qualifying campaign had begun.

In a typical year in the job once knowingly described as the second most important in the country, Sven-Goran Eriksson lost his best coach, his closest ally at the FA and a few rounds of sparring with Sir Alex Ferguson. At times, he must have felt that some people wanted him to lose his job, but he continued to disarm his critics with an ability to win the big matches, and most of the small ones, as the season finished with the Swede more secure than at any time in the previous 12 months.

Comfortable with his simple tactics, enamoured with his calming demeanour and respectful of the way he treats them as adults, the players continue to strive to impress Eriksson and their eagerness has been reflected in results. The 2-2 draw at home to Macedonia was the one significant black mark in a season that they finished two points behind Turkey in the race to qualify for Euro 2004, but with a game in hand.

The good results kept putting out fires for Eriksson, some of his own making but others that were mischievously set ablaze. On more than one occasion, a ruddy-faced Scotsman was seen hurrying away from the scene.

Ferguson set the tone for a year of confrontation as early as last September, when he brought the club versus country issue bubbling to the surface. It was to stay there for much of the next nine months. His scandalous decision to pick Paul Scholes for a club fixture only 48 hours after declaring that he was unfit to play for his country against Portugal was deliberately provocative.

A few months later, Ferguson waded in with another two-footed tackle when he all but confirmed in an interview in *The Times* that, in early 2002, Eriksson had considered walking out on England to manage Manchester United. "I think they'd done the deal all right," Ferguson said. His incendiary comment was accompanied by an unflattering appraisal of the England head coach.

"I think Sven Eriksson would have been a nice easy choice for them [the United directors] in terms of nothing really happens, does it?" Ferguson said. "He doesn't change anything. He sails along, nobody falls out with him. He comes out and says, 'the first half we were good, second half we were not so good. I am very pleased with

Off night: Rooney is replaced after a disappointing display in Middlesbrough

the result'. I think he'd have been all right for United, you know what I mean? The acceptable face."

It says much for Eriksson's talents that he sailed through all the turbulence, including the storm that threatened to engulf him even before England's first competitive game, when the serialisation of Ulrika Jonsson's memoirs was timed to coincide with the trip to Slovakia. A year on, unsold copies of the former weather girl's autobiography can be found gathering dust in bargain buckets, but, at the time, the FA's hierarchy was bracing itself for damning revelations. While they scurried around, Eriksson remained unruffled. "My private life has never been so exposed like it is at the moment," he said. "I always told you that as long as I cope with it, it is OK, until I wake up one morning and say 'enough is enough'. I am coping — and winning helps."

And winning is what he did do in all but one of the games that mattered as England finished the season with an established starting XI, even if, to Eriksson's frustration, it never played together. Ten of them did against Turkey and, if fit, Ashley Cole would have replaced Wayne Bridge alongside David James, Gary Neville, Rio Ferdinand, Sol Campbell, David Beckham, Nicky Butt, Scholes, Steven Gerrard, Wayne Rooney and Michael Owen. When the tournament kicks off, the average age of the outfield players will still be under 26, so it is a team that can prosper in Portugal and beyond.

The fine-tuning of his side made it all the more senseless for Eriksson to be so promiscuous in his team selection, with 25 players used on top of the XI who lost to Brazil in the World Cup quarter-finals. Restoring Gary Neville and Gerrard, who was

Wednesday October 16
European Championship qualifier
MACEDONIA (h)
St Mary's Stadium
Drew 2-2   HT 2-2   Att 32,095
ENGLAND **D Seaman** (Arsenal) — **G Neville** (Manchester United), **J Woodgate** (Leeds United), **S Campbell** (Arsenal), **A Cole** (Arsenal) — **D Beckham** (Manchester United), **S Gerrard** (Liverpool; sub: **N Butt**, Manchester United, 56min), **P Scholes** (Manchester United), **W Bridge** (Southampton; sub: **D Vassell**, Aston Villa, 58) — **A Smith** (Leeds United), **M Owen** (Liverpool) *Subs not used* **D James** (West Ham United), **D Mills** (Leeds United), **G Southgate** (Middlesbrough), **O Hargreaves** (Bayern Munich), **F Lampard** (Chelsea) Scorers **Beckham 14, Gerrard 36** Booked **Beckham, Smith** Sent off **Smith 90**

MACEDONIA **P Milosevski** (Malatyaspor) — **R Popov** (FC Belasica GC), **G Sedloski** (Dynamo Zagreb), **A Vasoski** (Vardar), **R Petrov** (PFC Lokomotiv Plovdiv) — **V Grozdanovski** (FK Cementarnica), **V Sumulikoski** (Synot), **A Mitreski** (Grasshopper), **A Sakiri** (CSKA Sofia) — **V Trajanov** (PFC Lokomotiv Plovdiv; sub: **M Stojanovski**, FK Partizan, 90) — **G Toleski** (FK Napredok; sub: **G Pandev**, Inter Milan, 62) *Subs not used* **J Nikoloski** (PFC Slavia Sofia), **B Grncarov** (OFK Beograd), **M Vajs** (NK Rijeka), **S Ignatov** (Samsunspor), **D Nacevski** (FK Vardar) Scorers **Sakiri 11, Trajanov 25** Booked **Vasoski** Referee **A Ibanez (Spain)**

Wednesday February 12
Friendly
AUSTRALIA (h)
Upton Park
Lost 1-3   HT 0-2   Att 34,590
ENGLAND **D James** (West Ham United; sub: **P Robinson**, Leeds United, ht) — **G Neville** (Manchester United; sub: **D Mills**, Leeds United, ht), **R Ferdinand** (Manchester United; sub: **L King**, Tottenham Hotspur, ht), **S Campbell** (Arsenal; sub: **W Brown**, Manchester United, ht), **A Cole** (Arsenal; sub: **P Konchesky**, Charlton Athletic, ht) — **D Beckham** (Manchester United; sub: **D Murphy**, Liverpool, ht), **F Lampard** (Chelsea; sub: **O Hargreaves**, Bayern Munich, ht), **P Scholes** (Manchester United; sub: **J Jenas**, Newcastle United, ht), **K Dyer** (Newcastle United; sub: **W Rooney**, Everton, ht) — **M Owen** (Liverpool; sub: **F Jeffers**, Arsenal, ht), **J Beattie** (Southampton; sub: **D Vassell**, Aston Villa, ht) Scorer **Jeffers 70**

AUSTRALIA **M Schwarzer** (Middlesbrough) — **L Neill** (Blackburn Rovers), **T Popovic** (Crystal Palace), **C Moore** (Rangers), **S Lazaridis** (Birmingham City) — **B Emerton** (Feyenoord), **P Okon** (Leeds United), **K Skoko** (Genk; sub: **M Bresciano**, Parma, ht), **S Chipperfield** (FC Basle; sub: **V Grella**, Empoli, 76) — **H Kewell** (Leeds United; sub: **J Aloisi**, Osasuna, 56), **M Viduka** (Leeds United; sub: **M Sterjovski**, Lille, 84) *Subs not used* **K Muscat** (Rangers), **A Vidmar** (Middlesbrough), **Z Kalac** (Perugia) Scorer **Popovic 17, Kewell 42, Emerton 84** Booked **Lazaridis** Referee **M E Mejuto Gonzalez (Spain)**

Saturday March 29
European Championship qualifier
LIECHTENSTEIN (a)
Vaduz
Won 2-0 HT 1-0 Att 3,548
LIECHTENSTEIN P Jehle (Grasshopper) — **M Telser** (FC Vaduz), **D Hasler** (FC Wil 1900), **Michael Stocklasa** (FC Vaduz), **F D'Elia** (Chur 97) — **A Gerster** (FC Vaduz), **Martin Stocklasa** (FC Vaduz), **H Zech** (USV Eschen/Mauren; sub: **F Burgmeier**, FC Vaduz, 62min) — **M Frick** (Ternana), **R Buchel** (FC Vaduz; sub: **M Beck**, USV Eschen/Mauren, 86), **T Beck** (FC Vaduz) *Subs not used* **M Heeb** (USV Eschen/Mauren), **J Ospelt** (Chur 97), **F Gigon** (FC Baulmes), **C Ritter** (FC Vaduz), **T Nigg** (USV Escen/Mauren)
Booked **Zech**

ENGLAND D James (West Ham United) — **G Neville** (Manchester United), **R Ferdinand** (Manchester United), **G Southgate** (Middlesbrough), **W Bridge** (Southampton) — **D Beckham** (Manchester United; sub: **D Murphy**, Liverpool, 70), **S Gerrard** (Liverpool; sub: **N Butt**, Manchester United, 66), **P Scholes** (Manchester United), **K Dyer** (Newcastle United) — **E Heskey** (Liverpool; sub: **W Rooney**, Everton, 80), **M Owen** (Liverpool) *Subs not used* **P Robinson** (Leeds United), **D Mills** (Leeds United), **J Woodgate** (Newcastle United), **D Vassell** (Aston Villa)
Scorers **Owen 28, Beckham 53**
Referee **G Kasnaferis (Greece)**

Wednesday April 2
European Championship qualifier
TURKEY (h)
Stadium of Light
Won 2-0 HT 0-0 Att 47,667
ENGLAND D James (West Ham United) — **G Neville** (Manchester United), **R Ferdinand** (Manchester United), **S Campbell** (Arsenal), **W Bridge** (Southampton) — **D Beckham** (Manchester United), **N Butt** (Manchester United), **P Scholes** (Manchester United), **S Gerrard** (Liverpool) — **W Rooney** (Everton; sub: **K Dyer**, Newcastle United, 89min), **M Owen** (Liverpool; sub: **D Vassell**, Aston Villa, 58) *Subs not used* **D Mills** (Leeds United), **P Robinson** (Leeds United), **J Woodgate** (Newcastle United), **F Lampard** (Chelsea), **E Heskey** (Liverpool)
Scorers **Vassell 76, Beckham 90 (pen)**
Booked **Beckham**

TURKEY R Recber (Fenerbahce) — **Fatih** (Fenerbahce; sub: **H Sukur**, Blackburn Rovers, 79), **Alpay** (Aston Villa), **K Bulent** (Galatasaray), **P Ergun** (Galatasaray) — **Okan** (Inter Milan; sub: **D Umit**, Galatasaray, 59), **Tugay** (Blackburn Rovers), **Y Basturk** (Bayer Leverkusen; sub: **H Sas**, Galatasaray, 71), **Emre** (Inter Milan) — **K Nihat** (Real Sociedad), **M Ilhan** (Besiktas) *Subs not used* **C Omer** (Gaziantepspor), **B Deniz** (Genclerbirligi), **Y Ahmet** (Besiktas), **K Tayfun** (Real Sociedad)
Booked **Okan, Fatih**
Referee **U Meier (Switzerland)**

England's outstanding player of the second half of the season, were necessary changes, but the net did not need to be cast so wide that it gave first full caps to Lee Bowyer, Paul Konchesky and James Beattie.

Eriksson gave 25 new caps in his first 29 games in charge and it might have been even more if Scott Parker, Sean Davis and David Thompson had been used when called up. His attitude to friendlies was encapsulated in the match against Serbia and Montenegro, when, in a second half of changes, the captain's armband was tossed between Owen, Emile Heskey, Phil Neville and Jamie Carragher.

The 3-1 defeat to Australia in February, when Eriksson changed all 11 players at half-time, was farcical, but he remains committed to his policy of compromise with the clubs. He toughened up for the tug-of-war over Rooney at the end of the season and it is difficult to be critical when set aside his record in competitive fixtures. "I will always defend using players for 45 minutes in friendlies," he said. "Someone has to put the players first."

Friendlies could be forgotten as long as he kept winning the qualifiers and, after some harsh reviews of England's decent showing in the World Cup finals, the last thing that Eriksson needed was a bad start. The trip to Slovakia was already fraught because of Jonsson's memoirs and fighting in Bratislava. By half-time, England were 1-0 down on a bog of a pitch. "If you stood still for long enough, you sunk," Owen said.

It was just one of the occasions when Eriksson would justify his £3.5 million salary as he swapped to the midfield diamond that brought out the best in Scholes and negated the need for an orthodox left winger. "From the first minute of the second half it was another music," he said, and a free kick from Beckham and a header by Owen got the campaign off to a solid start.

No sooner had England found their way out of trouble than they were back in it five days later, when Eriksson had his worst day in the job against Macedonia, then ranked ninetieth in the world. The decision to abandon the diamond and introduce Bridge on the left flank was a mistake, although by no means the only one on a night when David Seaman and Campbell made calamitous errors. Goals from Beckham and Gerrard salvaged a draw, but Alan Smith's late dismissal was an ugly finale. Neither Smith nor Seaman played again last season, the Arsenal goalkeeper almost certainly ushered into belated international retirement as Eriksson turned to James.

Four months without a game was a long time to dwell on that performance, particularly when Eriksson lost Adam Crozier as his chief ally within the FA and Steve McClaren as his right-hand man.

James is beaten by Popovic's header as Australia take the lead at Upton Park

Ferguson's interview in *The Times* and the defeat to Australia exacerbated a long, frustrating winter and so Eriksson went into the games against Liechtenstein and Turkey in need of victories to respond to the criticism. A header from Owen and a free kick from Beckham secured an efficient victory in the tiny principality, but Eriksson had a surprise up his sleeve as England went on to the most decisive match of the campaign.

Playing Rooney from the start against Turkey was the boldest choice by an England manager for many years because, for all the Everton prodigy's gifts, the teenager had still made fewer than a dozen professional starts in his short but meteoric career. Eriksson's daring was rewarded with a team performance that began decently and reached a thrilling climax in a second half that ranked as the best 45 minutes of his reign. Darius Vassell, an effective substitute for England all season, tucked in the first before a penalty by Beckham eased their nerves. however, a stirring win was soured by the pitch invasions and racist chanting that brought a fine of around £70,000 from Uefa and, far more significantly, a "final warning" as to future conduct.

The team is progressing, a fact confirmed by the 2-1 victory over Slovakia at the Riverside Stadium in June, when Eriksson's substitutions and Owen's goals allowed a depleted team to recover from a half-time deficit, but the hooligan fringe continues to hold England's fate in Portugal in its hands every bit as much as Eriksson. "We have got a team which can win a major championship," Owen said. "It would be a real shame if that was thrown away by the minority of fans."

Thursday May 22
Friendly
SOUTH AFRICA (a)
Durban
Won 2-1 HT 1-1 Att 52,000
SOUTH AFRICA **B Baloyi** (Kaizer Chiefs) — **M Mabizela** (Orlando Pirates), **L Radebe** (Leeds United), **A Mokoena** (Germinal Beerschot), **T Molefe** (Jomo Cosmos) — **S Fredericks** (Kaizer Chiefs; sub: **C Mazibuko**, Umtata Bush Bucks, 77min), **M Sibaya** (Rubin FC), **T Mokoena** (Jomo Cosmos; sub: **J Mendu**, Moroka Swallows, 69), **D Buckley** (VfL Bochum) — **S Bartlett** (Charlton Athletic), **B McCarthy** (Celta Vigo; sub: **L Manyathela**, Orlando Pirates, 68) *Subs not used* **L Lekgwathi** (Orlando Pirates), **T Coyle** (Wits University), **M Khanyeza** (Lamontville Golden Arrows), **M Josephs** (Ajax Cape Town), **B Evans** (Ajax Cape Town)
Scorer **McCarthy 18 (pen)**
Booked **Mabizela, Molefe**

ENGLAND **D James** (West Ham United; sub: **P Robinson**, Leeds United, ht) — **D Mills** (Leeds United), **R Ferdinand** (Manchester United; sub: **M Upson**, Birmingham City, ht), **G Southgate** (Middlesbrough), **P Neville** (Manchester United) — **D Beckham** (Manchester United; sub: **J Jenas**, Newcastle United, 51), **S Gerrard** (Liverpool; sub: **G Barry**, Aston Villa, 82), **P Scholes** (Manchester United; sub: **J Cole**, West Ham United, 75), **T Sinclair** (West Ham United; sub: **F Lampard**, Chelsea, 58) — **E Heskey** (Liverpool; sub: **D Vassell**, Aston Villa, 65), **M Owen** (Liverpool) *Sub not used* **I Walker** (Leicester City)
Scorers **Southgate 1, Heskey 64**
Booked **Mills**
Referee **L K Chong (Mauritius)**

Tuesday June 3
Friendly
SERBIA AND MONTENEGRO (h)
Walkers Stadium
Won 2-1 HT 1-1 Att 30,900
ENGLAND **D James** (West Ham United) — **D Mills** (Leeds United; sub: **J Carragher**, Liverpool, 61min), **G Southgate** (Middlesbrough; sub: **J Terry**, Chelsea, ht), **M Upson** (Birmingham City; sub: **G Barry**, Aston Villa, 84), **A Cole** (Arsenal; sub: **W Bridge**, Southampton, ht) — **S Gerrard** (Liverpool; sub: **O Hargreaves**, Bayern Munich, ht), **P Neville** (Manchester United; sub: **J Beattie**, Southampton, 87), **F Lampard** (Chelsea; sub: **J Cole**, West Ham United, 61) — **P Scholes** (Manchester United; sub: **J Jenas**, Newcastle United, ht) — **M Owen** (Liverpool; sub: **W Rooney**, Everton, ht), **E Heskey** (Liverpool; sub: **D Vassell**, Aston Villa, 61) *Subs not used* **P Robinson** (Leeds United), **I Walker** (Leicester City)
Scorers **Gerrard 35, J Cole 82**
SERBIA AND MONTENEGRO **D Jevric** (Vitesse Arnhem; sub: **D Zilic**, FK Sartid, 67) — **Z Mirkovic** (Fenerbahce; sub: **N Brnovic**, FK Zeta, ht), **N Vidic** (Crvena Zvezda; sub: **D Kovacevic**, Real Sociedad, 82), **D Stefanovic** (Vitesse Arnhem; sub: **M Krstajic**, Werder Bremen, 50) — **S Markovic** (FC Zeleznik; sub: **Z Njegus**, Seville, 67), **I Duljaj** (Partizan Belgrade; sub: **B Boskovic**, Crvena Zvezda, ht), **N Kovacevic** (Crvena Zvezda; sub: **N Malbasa**, Partizan Belgrade, ht), **B Dmitrovic** (Sturm Graz; sub: **G Trobok**, Partizan Belgrade, ht) — **Z Vukic** (Partizan Belgrade; sub: **N Djordevic**, FK Obilic, ht), **S Ilic** (Partizan Belgrade; sub: **P Mijatovic**, Levante, 67) — **N Jestrovic** (Anderlecht; sub: **S Milosevic**, Espanyol, 75)
Scorer **Jestrovic 45**
Booked **Vidic**
Referee **P Allaerts (Belgium)**

Wednesday June 11
European Championship qualifier
SLOVAKIA (h)
Riverside Stadium
Won 2-1   HT 0-1   Att 35,000
ENGLAND D James (West Ham United) — **D Mills** (Leeds United; sub: **O Hargreaves**, Bayern Munich, 43min), **G Southgate** (Middlesbrough), **M Upson** (Birmingham City), **A Cole** (Arsenal) — **P Neville** (Manchester United) — **S Gerrard** (Liverpool), **P Scholes** (Manchester United), **F Lampard** (Chelsea) — **W Rooney** (Everton; sub: **D Vassell**, Aston Villa, 58), **M Owen** (Liverpool) *Subs not used* **P Robinson** (Leeds United), **W Bridge** (Southampton), **J Terry** (Chelsea), **J Cole** (West Ham United), **E Heskey** (Liverpool)
Scorer **Owen 62 (pen), 73**
SLOVAKIA M Konig (FC Zurich) — **M Hanek** (Moscow Dinamo), **M Zeman** (Vitesse Arnhem), **M Petras** (Sparta Prague), **V Labant** (Sparta Prague; sub: **O Debnar**, Artmedia Petrzalka, 38) — **V Janocko** (Austria Vienna), **I Demo** (Borussia Monchengladbach; sub: **M Mintal**, MSK Zilina, 55), **R Zabavnik** (MSK Zilina), **R Michalik** (Sparta Prague) — **R Vittek** (Slovan Bratislava), **S Nemeth** (Middlesbrough; sub: **L Reiter**, Sigma Olomouc, 75) *Subs not used* **B Rzeszoto** (Zlin), **M Karhan** (VfL Wolfsburg), **K Kisel** (Bohemians Prague), **J Kozlej** (Olympiakos Nicosia)
Scorer **Janocko 31**
Booked **Hanek, Vittek, Debnar**
Referee **W Stark (Germany)**

PLAYER OF THE SEASON   Michael Owen

Any striker is valuable for his goals, but Michael Owen can be regarded as priceless for scoring the ones that matter, a knack that the England forward maintained to demonstrate that Wayne Rooney has some way to go to usurp the first-choice forward in Sven-Goran Eriksson's team. The saviour in Slovakia, when he nodded in the winner, the Liverpool striker came to his country's rescue against the same opponents nine months later on home soil. Four goals in five competitive matches took his tally to 22 by the time that he won his fiftieth England cap. At the age of 23, Owen is ahead of schedule to beat Bobby Charlton's record of 49 international goals.
Matt Dickinson

MATCH OF THE SEASON

England 2   Turkey 0
Stadium of Light, Wednesday April 2 2003
Matt Dickinson, Chief Football Correspondent

THE MOST DARING SELECTION of Sven-Goran Eriksson's career was rewarded with one of its most important victories last night as England put an end to their post World Cup slump with a performance as bold as the head coach's choice of Wayne Rooney.

The notion of a grey, conservative manager and passionless players could not have looked more misguided as England's campaign for the 2004 European Championship was revitalised on a wild, raucous night.

Eriksson's selection of Rooney, the 17-year-old prodigy, had an element of recklessness that was echoed in England's performance but, on an unforgettable night for the teenager who departed to a standing ovation on his full England debut, this was an evening when every gamble paid off. England's diamond sparkled in a thrilling second half. The choice of Nicky Butt, the rock of the midfield and the man of the match, was as inspired as Eriksson's decision to dump Emile Heskey and give Rooney only his eleventh professional start.

The Swede rolled the dice and everything came up sixes, including the decision to bring on Darius Vassell for the injured Michael Owen as the Aston Villa forward rolled in the opening goal in the 76th minute. David Beckham added England's second from the penalty spot in injury time after Ergun tumbled into Kieron Dyer.

When he sat down with a pen and paper 12 days ago, Eriksson had no intention of picking Rooney in his squad, still less his starting XI for one of the defining matches of his reign. It was a selection as bold as any by an England coach for more than a decade. Glenn Hoddle's gamble on Matt Le Tissier against Italy and Kevin Keegan's punt on Gareth Southgate in midfield against Germany were stunning for their ineptitude but Rooney's place in the starting line-up was worrying no one. It could not have done more to raise the mood after depressing reports of fighting on the streets outside.

Rooney would never have been here at all had he not played against Arsenal on the day Eriksson selected his

David Beckham marshals England's defensive wall of Gerrard, Butt, Ferdinand and Scholes as Turkey threaten from a set-piece

In the first half of an explosive match, Beckham lost his temper several times and picked up a booking that led to a suspension

party, and even that was fortuitous. Tomasz Radzinski's hamstring strain left an opening and, as is his wont, Rooney charged through it and kept on running. He was still going last night when, after a slow start for the teenager and the rest of the team, he suddenly took over for a five-minute burst before half-time.

Moments after impudently juggling the ball in midfield — when did you ever see Heskey do that? — he broke forward with a swaying run that seemed certain to end in a shot on goal. The fact that he did not shoot was evidence enough that Eriksson had been right to go with him ahead of the Liverpool forward. A clever ball threaded through to Owen showed intelligence and maturity and would have yielded a goal had Rustu not been so alert.

That little spell going into the interval was England's best period of a feisty half in which Eriksson's men, and their captain in particular, were doing too much of the kicking against tricky, elusive opponents who lured them into fouls.

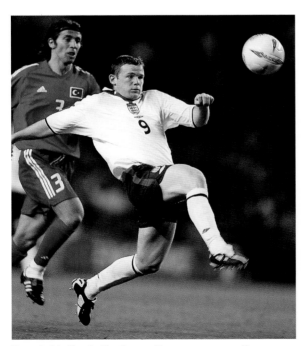

Promoted to the starting line-up, Rooney was a sensation

Beckham was booked for his third wild challenge after just nine minutes, a caution that will rule him out of the qualifying match against Slovakia in June. Flattened straight from kick-off by Emre, the England captain must still have been overheating when he snatched at a wonderful opportunity to put England ahead in the twelfth minute. After a neat chip forward by Paul Scholes, Steven Gerrard's looping cross was fumbled by Rustu and fell at the feet of Rooney. A fairytale come true? Only Ergun's block ruined the script but the ball came to Beckham who had a corner of the goal to aim at but sent an ugly, bobbling shot wide from eight yards.

Eriksson needed to remind his team of their shape at half-time because, with Gerrard prone to wander from his position in the diamond, there were spells of raggedness. It was a gung-ho performance, but one which had the Stadium of Light screaming England on as they pushed Turkey deep back inside their own half in a spell of sustained pressure after the interval.

Even when Owen was forced to withdraw after a cynical tackle by Alpay, England maintained the intensity. Beckham twice went close with free kicks, Gerrard headed narrowly wide from a corner, Scholes saw a powerful drive blocked and Vassell had a shot tipped over the crossbar by the busy and erratic Rustu.

There was nothing wrong with England's passion or ambition. What was needed was a touch of composure to add a goal to all their hard work and it came when Rio Ferdinand's half-volley was blocked and Vassell rolled in the rebound. Just when he needed it, the senior players, such as Beckham, Gerrard and Scholes, rose to the occasion for their coach. Eriksson deserved it for picking Rooney and taking a chance.

ENGLAND (4-4-2): **D James** (West Ham United) — **G Neville** (Manchester United), **R Ferdinand** (Manchester United), **S Campbell** (Arsenal), **W Bridge** (Southampton) — **D Beckham** (Manchester United), **N Butt** (Manchester United), **P Scholes** (Manchester United), **S Gerrard** (Liverpool) — **W Rooney** (Everton; sub: **K Dyer**, Newcastle United, 89min), **M Owen** (Liverpool; sub: **D Vassell**, Aston Villa, 58) **Substitutes not used: D Mills** (Leeds United), **P Robinson** (Leeds United), **J Woodgate** (Newcastle United), **F Lampard** (Chelsea), **E Heskey** (Liverpool). **Booked:** Beckham.
TURKEY (4-4-2): **R Recber** (Fenerbahce) — **Fatih** (Fenerbahce; sub: **H Sukur**, Blackburn Rovers, 79), **Alpay** (Aston Villa), **K Bulent** (Galatasaray), **P Ergun** (Galatasaray) — **Okan** (Inter Milan; sub: **D Umit**, Galatasaray, 59), **Tugay** (Blackburn Rovers), **Y Basturk** (Bayer Leverkusen; sub: **H Sas**, Galatasaray, 71), **Emre** (Inter Milan) — **K Nihat** (Real Sociedad), **M Ilhan** (Besiktas). **Substitutes not used: C Omer** (Gaziantepspor), **B Deniz** (Genclerbirligi), **Y Ahmet** (Besiktas), **K Tayfun** (Real Sociedad). **Booked:** Okan, Fatih.
Referee: U Meier (Switzerland).

THE GAMES

Wednesday August 21
Friendly
CYPRUS (h)
Windsor Park
Drew 0-0 HT 0-0 Att 6,922
NORTHERN IRELAND M Taylor (Fulham) — **D Griffin**
(Dundee United; sub: **M Duff**, Cheltenham Town, ht), **M
Williams** (Wimbledon), **C Murdock** (Preston North End),
G McCartney (Sunderland) — **K Gillespie** (Blackburn
Rovers), **D Johnson** (Birmingham City), **K Horlock**
(Manchester City), **P Kennedy** (Wigan Athletic) — **D
Healy** (Preston North End), **J Quinn** (Willem II) *Subs not
used* **M Ingham** (Sunderland), **W Feeney**
(Bournemouth), **G McCann** (West Ham United), **S
Robinson** (Luton Town)
CYPRUS N Panayiotou (Anorthosis) — **S Okkarides**
(APOEL Nicosia), **P Konnafis** (Omonia), **D Daskalakis**
(APOEL Nicosia; sub: **M Nikaladu**, Omonia, ht) — **G
Theodotou** (Omonia), **M Satsias** (APOEL Nicosia), **L
Eleftheriou** (AEK Athens), **N Nikolaou** (Anorthosis; sub:
C Michail, Aris, 43), **P Spyrou** (Olympiakos) — **I Okkas**
(PAOK), **Y Yiasoumi** (PAOK; sub: **M Agathokleous**,
APOEL Nicosia, 60) *Subs not used* **M Shimitras** (Alki
Larnaca), **C Kaiafas** (Omnia)
Booked **Eleftheriou**.
Referee **S Jones (Wales)**

Saturday October 12
European Championship qualifier
SPAIN (a)
Albacete
Lost 0-3 HT 0-1 Att 14,000
SPAIN I Casillas (Real Madrid) — **M Salgado** (Real
Madrid), **C Puyol** (Barcelona), **I Helguera** (Real Madrid),
R Bravo (Real Madrid) — **Joaquin** (Real Betis; sub: **G
Mendieta**, Barcelona, 76min), **Xavi** (Barcelona), **R
Baraja** (Valencia), **Vicente** (Valencia) — **Guti** (Real
Madrid; sub: **Capi**, Real Betis, 83) — **Raul** (Real Madrid;
sub: **F Morientes**, Real Madrid, 63) *Subs not used* **J
Capdevila** (Deportivo La Coruna), **P Contreras**
(Malaga), **D Albelda** (Valencia), **G Calvo** (Atletico
Madrid)
Scorers **Baraja 19, 89, Guti 59**
Booked **Helguera**
NORTHERN IRELAND M Taylor (Fulham) — **A Hughes**
(Newcastle United), **G Taggart** (Leicester City; sub: **G
McCann**, West Ham United, 70), **C Murdock** (Preston
North End), **G McCartney** (Sunderland) — **D Johnson**
(Birmingham City), **P Mulryne** (Norwich City), **S Lomas**
(West Ham United), **K Horlock** (Manchester City; sub: **M
Hughes**, Wimbledon, 65), **P McVeigh** (Norwich City;
sub: **D Healy**, Preston North End, 65) — **K Gillespie**
(Blackburn Rovers) *Subs not used* **R Carroll**
(Manchester United), **A Kirk** (Heart of Midlothian), **S
Holmes** (Wrexham), **C Toner** (Leyton Orient)
Booked **Gillespie**
Referee **L Michel (Slovakia)**

MALCOLM BRODIE, THE VENERABLE sports journalist whose
attendance at World Cup tournaments has been unblemished for
more than 50 years, was holding court. It was during the trip to
Campobasso in June, when Northern Ireland played Italy in a
match to raise funds for the bereaved of San Giuliano after a
devastating earthquake in the mountain village the previous
October.

Brodie was recalling the "Battle of Belfast", when the countries
first opposed one another, in the winter of 1957. It was supposed to
be a World Cup qualifying game, but since the referee, one Istvan
Zolt, the manager of the Budapest Opera House, was fogbound at
London — later Heathrow — airport, the Italians refused to
acknowledge it as anything but a friendly contest. A bruising 2-2
draw ensued at Windsor Park, the prelude to a riot by home
supporters and questions being asked in the Italian parliament.

A month later, on January 15, 1958, the Italians turned up once
more; and so did an acceptable match official. Suitably motivated,
the Irish, with Danny Blanchflower, of Tottenham Hotspur, Peter
McParland, the Aston Villa forward, Jimmy McIlroy, the Burnley
midfield playmaker, Wilbur Cush, of Leeds United, and Billy
Bingham, the Sunderland winger, all inspired, prevailed in a
relatively tame encounter, an historic 2-1 victory that carried them
to the finals in Sweden that year.

The history lesson was an appropriate one in that Northern
Ireland's unlikely quest to qualify for the 2004 European
Championship finals in Portugal began with a sentimental journey.
Unfortunately, Sammy McIlroy, the manager, soon discovered that
nostalgia is not what it used to be.

That voyage of stark discovery began in Valencia in October
2002, when the squad camped out at the same hotel that was the
headquarters for the Northern Ireland team throughout their feted
appearance in the World Cup finals of 1982. Gerry Armstrong
scored the only goal of the game against Spain that swept his
colleagues through to the second phase of the competition.

To mark the 20th anniversary, McIlroy, who was playing on that
momentous night, ensured that his present young charges sported
white shirts like the ones that had served their predecessors so well.
However, even with the imposing presence of Gerry Taggart, the
Leicester City centre half, returning to the fold, any chances of a
repeat scoreline were dashed by Spain's effortless superiority
throughout the game, which was played in Albacete, a small
industrial town two hours by car inland from Valencia. Two late
goals did justice to Spain's superior possession in a 3-0 victory. It

PLAYER OF THE SEASON   **Aaron Hughes**

The surging runs of Keith Gillespie were a feature of Northern Ireland's season, but for consistency, Aaron Hughes stood head and shoulders above his colleagues. The emergence of the Newcastle United defender has been one of the most encouraging aspects for Sammy McIlroy. Hughes's ability to play right back or centre half has allowed his manager to shuffle his limited pack. McIlroy believes that Hughes — who has been elevated to captain — and George McCartney, of Sunderland, will provide the backbone of the side for another ten years.

David McVay

Wednesday October 16
European Championship qualifier
UKRAINE (h)
Windsor Park
Drew 0-0   HT 0-0   Att 9,288
NORTHERN IRELAND M Taylor (Fulham) — **S Lomas** (West Ham United), **A Hughes** (Newcastle United), **G McCartney** (Sunderland), **K Horlock** (Manchester City) — **K Gillespie** (Blackburn Rovers), **P Mulryne** (Norwich City; sub: **G McCann**, West Ham United, 90min), **M Hughes** (Wimbledon), **D Johnson** (Birmingham City; sub: **C Murdock**, Preston North End, 84) — **P McVeigh** (Norwich City; sub: **A Kirk**, Heart of Midlothian, 65), **D Healy** (Preston North End) *Subs not used* **R Carroll** (Manchester United), **S Holmes** (Wrexham), **C Toner** (Leyton Orient), **C Baird** (Southampton)
Booked **Hughes**

UKRAINE V Reva (Dinamo Kiev) — **M Starostyak** (Shakhtar Donetsk), **O Luzhny** (Arsenal), **A Tymoschuk** (Shakhtar Donetsk) — **S Kormyltsev** (Torpedo Moscow; sub: **V Lysytski**, Dinamo Kiev, 89), **A Gusin** (Dinamo Kiev) — **H Zubov** (Shakhtar Donetsk), **M Kalynychenko** (Spartak Moscow; sub: **S Rebrov**, Tottenham Hotspur, 54), **A Voronin** (Mainz 05), **O Radchenko** (Dinamo Kiev) — **A Vorobey** (Shakhtar Donetsk; sub: **O Melashchenko**, Dinamo Kiev, 76) *Subs not used* **D Shutkov** (Shakhtar Donetsk), **S Matiukhih** (Dnipro Dnepropetrovsk), **O Venhlynsky** (Dnipro Dnepropetrovsk), **S Konovalov** (Dinamo Kiev)
Booked **Gusin**
Referee **C Bolognino (Italy)**

Wednesday February 12
Friendly
FINLAND (h)
Windsor Park
Lost 0-1   HT 0-0   Att 6,137
NORTHERN IRELAND M Taylor (Fulham; sub: **R Carroll**, Manchester United, ht) — **A Hughes** (Newcastle United), **M Williams** (Wimbledon), **G McCartney** (Sunderland; sub: **S Craigan**, Partick Thistle, 66), **P Kennedy** (Wigan Athletic) — **K Gillespie** (Blackburn Rovers), **S Lomas** (West Ham United), **D Johnson** (Birmingham City), **P McVeigh** (Norwich City; sub: **S Elliott**, Hull City, 76) — **J Quinn** (Willem II; sub: **A Kirk**, Heart of Midlothian, 60), **D Healy** (Preston North End) *Subs not used* **M Duff** (Cheltenham Town), **G McCann** (Cheltenham Town), **S Jones** (Crewe Alexandra)

FINLAND J Jaaskelainen (Bolton Wanderers) — **T Kuivasto** (Viking Stavanger), **S Hyypia** (Liverpool; sub: **M Heikkinen**, Portsmouth, 69), **H Tihinen** (Anderlecht), **J Hietanen** (Denzilspor) — **M Nurmela** (SC Heerenveen), **A Riihilahti** (Crystal Palace), **M Vayrynan** (SC Heerenveen; sub: **J Johansson**, Charlton Athletic, 62), **S Valakari** (Derby County), **J Kolkka** (Panathinaikos; sub: **P Kopteff**, Viking Stavanger, 76) — **M Forssell** (Chelsea; sub: **S Kuqi**, Sheffield Wednesday, ht) *Subs not used* **A Niemi** (Southampton), **P Basanen** (Ajax), **J Saarinen** (Rosenborg BK)
Scorer **Hyypia 49**
Booked **Hietanen**
Referee **D McDonald (Scotland)**

Saturday March 29
European Championship qualifier
ARMENIA (a)
Yerevan
Lost 0-1   HT 0-0   Att 10,321
ARMENIA R **Berezovsky** (Dinamo Moscow) — H **Vardanyan** (Young Boys), S **Hovsepyan** (Zenit St Petersburg), J A **Bilibio** (Pyunik) — A **Sarkisian** (Torpedo Moscow; sub: **Artur Mkrtchyan**, Pyunik, 90min), A **Voskanyan** (Digenis Morfu), K **Dokhoyan** (Krilya Sovetov), E **Melikyan** (Metalurg Donetsk), **Artravad Karamyan** (Panahaiki; sub: **Agvan Mkrtchyen**, Pyunik, 89) — A **Petrosyan** (Young Boys; sub: **H V Mkhitaryan**, Tadamon Sur, 90) — **Arman Karamyan** (Panahaiki)
Subs not used A **Ambertsumyan** (Marek), V **Minasyan** (Pyunik), E **Partiskyan** (Pyunik), A **Akopyan** (Banants)
Scorer **Petrosian 86**
Booked **Melikyan, Hovsepyan**

NORTHERN IRELAND M **Taylor** (Fulham) — A **Hughes** (Newcastle United), S **Craigan** (Partick Thistle), M **Williams** (Stoke City), G **McCann** (Cheltenham Town) — K **Gillespie** (Blackburn Rovers), S **Lomas** (West Ham United), D **Johnson** (Birmingham City), P **McVeigh** (Norwich City) — D **Healy** (Norwich City), J **Quinn** (Willem II; sub: S **Elliott**, Hull City, 71) *Subs not used* A **Fettis** (Hull City), C **Baird** (Southampton), C **Toner** (Leyton Orient), A **Kirk** (Heart of Midlothian), M **Duff** (Cheltenham Town), M **Hughes** (unattached)
Booked **Craigan**
Referee **R Bezke (Liechtenstein)**

Wednesday April 2
European Championship qualifier
GREECE (h)
Windsor Park
Lost 0-2   HT 0-1   Att 7,196
NORTHERN IRELAND M **Taylor** (Fulham) — A **Hughes** (Newcastle United), S **Craigan** (Partick Thistle), M **Williams** (Stoke City), G **McCartney** (Sunderland) — K **Gillespie** (Blackburn Rovers), S **Lomas** (West Ham United), D **Johnson** (Birmingham City), G **McCann** (Cheltenham Town; sub: P **McVeigh**, Norwich City, 68min) — J **Quinn** (Willem II), D **Healy** (Norwich City; sub: A **Kirk**, Heart of Midlothian, 68) *Subs not used* A **Fettis** (Hull City), S **Elliott** (Hull City), M **Duff** (Cheltenham Town), C **Toner** (Leyton Orient), C **Baird** (Southampton)
Booked **Gillespie, Williams, Lomas**
Sent off **Quinn 38, Gillespie 69**

GREECE A **Nikopolidis** (Panathinaikos) — N **Dabizas** (Newcastle United), S **Kyrgiakos** (Panathinaikos), K **Konstantinidis** (Hannover 96) — S **Giannakopoulos** (Olympiakos), T **Zagorakis** (AEK Athens), V **Tsartas** (AEK Athens; sub: P **Kafes**, PAOK Salonica, 75), G **Karagounis** (Panathinaikos), S **Venetidis** (Olympiakos, sub: P **Fissas**, Panathinaikos, 71) — A **Charisteas** (Werder Bremen), T **Nikolaidis** (AEK Athens; sub: Z **Vrizas**, Perugia, 41) *Subs not used* K **Chalkias** (Iraklis Salonica), G **Georgiadis** (PAOK Salonica), I **Amanatidis** (VfB Stuttgart), V **Lakis** (AEK Athens)
Scorer **Charisteas 3, 56**
Booked **Venetidis, Karagounis, Kyrgiakos**
Referee **G Gilewski (Poland)**

had been an unsatisfactory trip all round, punctuated by a flight delay at Heathrow, the players' boots going missing in transit and then the final ignominy: the senior squad's training kit ended up in Madrid.

The gremlins that manifested themselves during the preparations were apposite. Even before the qualifying games began, the cause was riddled with difficulties. Typically of Northern Ireland, too, they were not small teething problems. A religious zealot in Belfast had issued a death threat against Neil Lennon, the Northern Ireland captain, before the friendly against Cyprus at Windsor Park in August. Lennon boarded a plane back to Glasgow and never returned.

The Celtic midfield player's premature international retirement was compounded by similar decisions taken by Jim Magilton, the experienced Ipswich Town midfield anchor, and Kevin Horlock, of Manchester City. To that list of absentees of Premiership quality can be added Taggart. Valiantly though he defended in Albacete, it is probably in his body's best interests that it remains his international swansong.

A draw at home to Ukraine, then the desperately disappointing defeat to Armenia in Yerevan, saw the team plunge to the bottom of the table without a goal scored. To underline that unwelcome consistency, they capitulated 2-0 at home to Greece — when they also had two players sent off — after returning from the bitterly cold Armenian capital. It is 16 months, and 972 minutes of official play, since the side last scored a goal. They have not won in 11 matches and have been described as the worst Northern Ireland team in history by newspapers in Belfast.

Yet, on June 11, after the 0-0 European Championship draw with Spain at Windsor Park, McIlroy and his squad of novices received a rapturous ovation, having held the team placed second in Fifa's world rankings by virtue of a tenacious and inspired performance.

"The Irish people love to see a committed and passionate team and there was an abundance of it out there," McIlroy, positively beaming after the game, said. "There is a team coming through here and I want to be around to see it mature."

That could need a ten-year plan, but his wishes are reciprocated by the Irish FA. Given the tragedy and heartache that the people of this troubled province have had to endure over the years, optimism would appear to have become endemic.

Nearly four years into the job, perhaps the gremlins are at last beginning to give McIlroy and his eager rookies a break. They deserve it.

MATCH OF THE SEASON

Northern Ireland 0   Spain 0
Windsor Park, Wednesday June 11 2003
David McVay

Kennedy, left, and Doherty thwart Sergio in Northern Ireland's stirring 0-0 draw against Spain

AT LONG LAST, A RARITY arrived at Windsor Park last night. Not a Northern Ireland goal, but a gathering of Spaniards apparently not interested in the future of David Beckham. Despite the lack of a home goal — it is now 484 days since they scored — this was by some distance the most encouraging performance, coursing with tenacity and guile, that Northern Ireland have delivered for years. "We have a team coming through here and I was proud to be the manager tonight," Sammy McIlroy said.

Maik Taylor's reflex save from Raul in the closing minutes epitomised the spirit of the home team. Throughout, the Fulham goalkeeper denied the best that Spain could muster while, at the other end, Iker Casillas saved two headers from George McCartney.

However, the Real Madrid goalkeeper's best stop thwarted David Healy in the 64th minute when the Preston North End forward was presented with a clear chance to end his personal search for a goal at this level that has now lasted for two years. "We rode our luck at times but I thought we could have won it with the best chance of the night," McIlroy said.

A standing ovation awaited Northern Ireland at the final whistle. Seldom has a goalless draw been more glorious or rapturously embraced.

NORTHERN IRELAND (4-5-1): **M Taylor** (Fulham) — **C Baird** (Southampton), **A Hughes** (Newcastle United), **G McCartney** (Sunderland), **P Kennedy** (Wigan Athletic) — **D Healy** (Preston North End), **D Johnson** (Birmingham City), **D Griffin** (Dundee United), **T Doherty** (Bristol City; sub: **C Toner**, Leyton Orient, 80min), **S Jones** (Crewe Alexandra; sub: **P McVeigh**, Norwich City, 73) — **A Smith** (Glentoran; sub: **M Williams**, Stoke City, 90). **Substitutes not used:** R Carroll (Manchester United), G McCann (Cheltenham Town), G Hamilton (Portadown), S Elliott (Hull City). **Booked:** Johnson.
SPAIN (4-4-1-1): **I Casillas** (Real Madrid) — **C Puyol** (Barcelona), **C Marchena** (Valencia), **I Helguera** (Real Madrid), **Juanfran** (Celta Vigo) — **J Etxeberria** (Athletic Bilbao; sub: **J De Pedro**, Real Sociedad, 78), **R Baraja** (Valencia), **Sergio** (Deportivo La Coruna; sub: **Joaquin**, Real Betis, 66), **Vicente** (Valencia; sub: **F Morientes**, Real Madrid, 66) — **J C Valeron** (Deportivo La Coruna) — **Raul** (Real Madrid). **Substitutes not used:** M Salgado (Real Madrid), S Canizares (Valencia), R Bravo (Real Madrid), Gabriel (Barcelona). **Booked:** De Pedro.
Referee: C Larsen (Denmark).

Wednesday June 3
Friendly
ITALY (a)
Campobasso
Lost 0-2   HT 0-1   Att 22,000
ITALY F Toldo (Inter Milan) — **M Oddo** (Lazio), **N Legrottaglie** (Chievo Verona; sub: **D Bonera**, Parma, 57min), **F Cannavaro** (Inter Milan; sub: **M Ferrari**, Parma, ht), **F Grosso** (Perugia; sub: **A Birindelli**, Juventus, 69) — **S Fiore** (Lazio), **S Perrotta** (Chievo Verona; sub: **D Tommasi**, AS Roma, 57), **M Ambrosini** (AC Milan), **M Di Vaio** (Juventus; sub: **C Nervo**, Bologna, 69) — **B Corradi** (Lazio; sub: **M Delvecchio**, AS Roma, ht), **F Miccoli** (Perugia; sub: **A Di Natale**, Empoli, 57) *Sub not used* **C Abbiati** (AC Milan)
Scorers **Corradi 31, Delvecchio 67**

NORTHERN IRELAND M Taylor (Fulham; sub: **R Carroll**, Manchester United, 55) — **C Baird** (Southampton), **A Hughes** (Newcastle United), **G McCartney** (Sunderland), **P Kennedy** (Wigan Athletic; sub: **M Williams**, Wimbledon, 55) — **D Johnson** (Birmingham City; sub: **C Toner**, Leyton Orient, 69), **D Griffin** (Dundee United), **T Doherty** (Bristol City; sub: **S Elliott**, Hull City, 87), **P McVeigh** (Norwich City; sub: **S Jones**, Crewe Alexandra, 55) — **D Healy** (Preston North End; sub: **G Hamilton**, Portadown, 76), **A Smith** (Glentoran) *Subs not used* **S Craigan** (Partick Thistle), **G McCann** (Cheltenham Town)
Booked **Johnson**
Referee **L Baptista (Portugal)**

Wednesday June 11
European Championship qualifer
SPAIN (h)
Windsor Park
Drew 0-0   HT 0-0   Att 11,365
NORTHERN IRELAND M Taylor (Fulham) — **C Baird** (Southampton), **A Hughes** (Newcastle United), **G McCartney** (Sunderland), **P Kennedy** (Wigan Athletic) — **D Healy** (Preston North End), **D Johnson** (Birmingham City), **D Griffin** (Dundee United), **T Doherty** (Bristol City; sub: **C Toner**, Leyton Orient, 80min), **S Jones** (Crewe Alexandra; sub: **P McVeigh**, Norwich City, 73) — **A Smith** (Glentoran; sub: **M Williams**, Stoke City, 90) *Subs not used* **R Carroll** (Manchester United), **G McCann** (Cheltenham Town), **G Hamilton** (Portadown), **S Elliott** (Hull City)
Booked **Johnson**

SPAIN I Casillas (Real Madrid) — **C Puyol** (Barcelona), **C Marchena** (Valencia), **I Helguera** (Real Madrid), **Juanfran** (Celta Vigo) — **J Etxeberria** (Athletic Bilbao; sub: **J De Pedro**, Real Sociedad, 78), **R Baraja** (Valencia), **Sergio** (Deportivo La Coruna; sub: **Joaquin**, Real Betis, 66), **Vicente** (Valencia; sub: **F Morientes**, Real Madrid, 66) — **J C Valeron** (Deportivo La Coruna) — **Raul** (Real Madrid) *Subs not used* **M Salgado** (Real Madrid), **S Canizares** (Valencia), **R Bravo** (Real Madrid), **Gabriel** (Barcelona)
Booked **De Pedro**
Referee **C Larsen (Denmark)**

Wednesday August 21
Friendly
DENMARK (h)
Hampden Park
Lost 0-1 HT 0-1 Att 28,766
SCOTLAND R Douglas (Celtic) — **D Weir** (Everton; sub: **S Severin**, Heart of Midlothian, 77min), **C Dailly** (West Ham United), **M Ross** (Rangers) — R Stockdale (Middlesbrough; sub: **G Alexander**, Preston North End, 71), **K McNaughton** (Aberdeen; sub: **S Crainey**, Celtic, ht), **P Lambert** (Celtic; sub: **D McInnes**, West Bromwich Albion, 81), **B Ferguson** (Rangers), **G Naysmith** (Everton; sub: **A Johnston**, Middlesbrough, 71) — **K Kyle** (Sunderland), **S Thompson** (Dundee United; sub: **S Dobie**, West Bromwich Albion, 55) *Subs not used* N Sullivan (Tottenham Hotspur), L Wilkie (Dundee), G Williams (Nottingham Forest), P Gallacher (Dundee United)
DENMARK T Sorensen — K Bogelund (sub: **J Michaelson**, ht), **M Laursen** (sub: **M Wieghorst**, 66), R Henriksen (sub: **S Lustu**, 83), N Jensen — D Rommedahl (sub: **J Gronkjaer**, ht), **T Gravesen** (sub: **C Jensen**, ht), C Poulsen, P Lovenkrands (sub: **M Silberbauer**) — J D Tomasson, E Sand *Sub not used* P Skov-Jensen
Scorer **Sand 8**
Referee **L Irvine (Northern Ireland)**

Saturday September 7
European Championship qualifier
FAEROE ISLES (a)
Toftir
Drew 2-2 HT 0-2 Att 4,000
FAEROE ISLES J Knudsen (NSI) — P Thorsteinsson (NSI), O Johannesen (TB), J Jacobsen (HB), J Hansen (B36) — J A Borg (B36), J Johnsson (B36), F Benjaminsen (B68), H Elittor (KI; sub: **H Lakjuni**, KI, 89min) — C Jacobsen (Vejle; sub: **R Jacobsen**, HB, 75), J Petersen (B36; sub: **A Flotum**, HB, 78) *Subs not used* H F Hansen (B68), J Joensen (HB), J Mikkelsen (Molde), S Jacobsen (NSI)
Scorer **Petersen 6, 12**
Booked **Borg, Knudsen**

SCOTLAND R Douglas (Celtic) — **M Ross** (Rangers; sub: **G Alexander**, Preston North End, 75), **D Weir** (Everton), **C Dailly** (West Ham United), **S Crainey** (Celtic) — P Dickov (Leicester City; sub: **S Crawford**, Dunfermline Athletic, ht), **B Ferguson** (Rangers), **P Lambert** (Celtic), **A Johnston** (Middlesbrough) — K Kyle (Sunderland), **S Dobie** (West Bromwich Albion; sub: **S Thompson**, Dundee United, 83) *Subs not used* P Gallacher (Dundee United), K McNaughton (Aberdeen), L Wilkie (Dundee), G Williams (Nottingham Forest)
Scorers **Lambert 61, Ferguson 83**
Booked **Ross, Weir**
Referee **J Granat (Poland)**

Saturday October 12
European Championship qualifier
ICELAND (a)
Reykjavik
Won 2-0 HT 1-0 Att 7,000
ICELAND A Arason (Rosenborg BK) — B Thorsteinsson (Molde), L Sigurdsson (West Bromwich Albion), H Hreidarsson (Ipswich Town), A Vidarsson (Lokeren; sub: **M Baldvinsson**, Stabaek, 66min) — H Gudnason (Keflavik; sub: **B Gudjonsson**, Stoke City, 76), I Ingimarsson (Wolverhampton Wanderers), R Kristinsson (Lokeren), B Gunnarsson (Stoke City) — E Gudjohnsen (Chelsea) — H Sigurdsson (SFK Lynn; sub: **H Helguson**, Watford, ht) *Subs not used:* B Kristinsson (IBV), G Einarsson (Lillestrom), O Stigsson (Molde), J Gudjonsson (Real Betis)
Booked **Kristinsson**

THE NORTH ATLANTIC ALMOST claimed Berti Vogts, just as it did the German fleet. That Toftir did not become his Scapa Flow is evidence that Scotland's national coach is a survivor.

Scotland plunged deeper under Vogts, to No 64 in the Fifa rankings, in his first year in charge than under any previous manager. Rock bottom came on an ignominious day in the Faeroe Isles last autumn, yet those powers of recovery were witnessed by his own nation ten months later as he guided Scotland to a draw against Germany that kept alive hopes of reaching Euro 2004.

Seven years ago, Vogts was lifting the trophy itself. His compatriots, though, gave a lukewarm response and Germany's achievement in becoming European champions was laid solely at the feet of the players, prompting Vogts to say: "If I walked on water, my critics would say it is because I cannot swim." Wembley and Euro 96 could not have offered a more contrasting occasion for Vogts than the Svangaskard Stadium did on September 7, 2002. With the icy waves that pound this outcrop in the North Atlantic visible behind each goal, Vogts and his new team were sinking fast.

Just 13 minutes into the opening match of their European Championship qualifying campaign, the scoreline read: Faeroe Isles 2, Scotland 0. Both goals had come from John Petersen, a teacher. Vogts never had as much cause to ponder the merits of his swimming ability as that day. The squad had taken a two-hour ferry trip from the capital, Torshavn, to reach Toftir and ignominious defeat might have prompted an invitation to walk the plank on the return journey. Fortunately for Vogts, it was a mutiny on dry land that saved his skin. The shouts from the Scotland dressing-room were clearly heard by spectators. Paul Lambert and Barry Ferguson, the respective captains of Celtic and Rangers, railed against the insipid show from their colleagues. When they returned to the pitch, Lambert and Ferguson were as good as their word. Lambert reduced the deficit just after the hour and, seven minutes from time, Ferguson scored from the edge of the area.

A month earlier, Scotland had lost 1-0 to Denmark at Hampden Park in a friendly. It was the fifth successive defeat of Vogts's reign and questions were being asked of a man who had climbed the highest peaks as a player. Vogts, too, was asking questions. David Weir did not like their tone. The Everton defender quit the national side after being partly blamed by Vogts for the two Faeroe goals. His co-accused, Christian Dailly, stuck with it and was rewarded in October with the opening goal in Scotland's 2-0 win over Iceland in Reykjavik in the next qualifying tie. Vogts's players had endured a month of scathing criticism and responded with spirit. After Dailly's

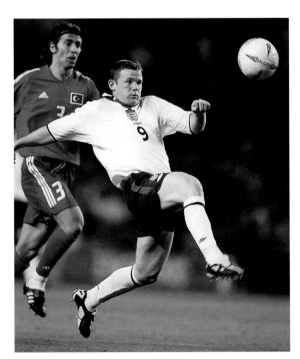

PLAYER OF THE SEASON
Paul Lambert

The search for players who distinguished themselves in Scotland's colours last season was hardly intense. Some, such as Steve Crawford, Gary Naysmith and Steven Pressley, deserve credit for their progress, but only one man could truly say that he made the others rise to his level: Paul Lambert. The Scotland captain is 33, yet he belied his age with a series of tireless displays that vindicated his decision to come out of international retirement. His goal dragged Scotland out of the mire in the Faeroe Isles and his peerless passing ensured that he overshadowed Michael Ballack when Germany came to Hampden.

Phil Gordon

early header, they controlled the game and Gary Naysmith sealed the success with a spectacular goal.

That result relieved the pressure on Vogts, and though victory over Canada was followed by defeats against Portugal and Ireland in friendlies, Scotland lifted themselves again for the serious business. Iceland were polished off to put Scotland briefly on top of their Euro 2004 qualifying group. Four days later, they went to Lithuania and kept the hosts, who had drawn in Germany the previous weekend, in check until a dubious late penalty.

After another friendly defeat, Austria winning at Hampden Park in front of fewer than 13,000 spectators, Vogts was under severe pressure again from a hostile media and the mood did not improve after a draw against New Zealand at Tynecastle. However, Vogts had demanded that he should be judged by the real thing. The visit of Germany on June 7 saw Scotland play with passion, energy and skill and left the group five leaders grateful for a point in a 1-1 draw.

Though Fredi Bobic put Germany ahead with a header midway through the first half, Scotland's second-half pressure told when Colin Cameron's swiftly taken free kick allowed Kenny Miller to thread his shot past Oliver Kahn. The Germany players blamed the ferocity of the Hampden crowd for forcing them into mistakes. "Hampden found its voice again," Vogts said. Progress has been painfully slow under him. However, Scotland had given themselves a platform to qualify for the Euro 2004 play-offs — more than could have been expected on that dark day in Toftir.

SCOTLAND R Douglas (Celtic) — **C Dailly** (West Ham United), **S Pressley** (Heart of Midlothian), **L Wilkie** (Dundee) — **M Ross** (Rangers), **B Ferguson** (Rangers), **P Lambert** (Celtic), **J McNamara** (Celtic; sub: **C Davidson**, Leicester City, 36), **G Naysmith** (Everton; sub: **R Anderson**, Aberdeen, 90) — **S Crawford** (Dunfermline Athletic), **S Thompson** (Dundee United; sub: **S Severin**, Heart of Midlothian, 90) *Subs not used* **P Gallacher** (Dundee United), **J McFadden** (Motherwell), **S Gemmill** (Everton), **P Devlin** (Birmingham City)
Scorers Dailly 7, Naysmith 62
Booked Ross, Thompson, Davidson
Referee **A Sars** (France)

Tuesday October 15
Friendly
CANADA (h)
Easter Road
Won 3-1   HT 1-1   Att 16,207
SCOTLAND P Gallacher (Dundee United) — **R Anderson** (Aberdeen), **S Pressley** (Heart of Midlothian), **L Wilkie** (Dundee; sub: **I Murray**, Hibernian, 75min) — **G Alexander** (Preston North End), **P Devlin** (Birmingham City), **C Dailly** (West Ham United), **S Gemmill** (Everton; sub: **S Severin**, Heart of Midlothian, 65), **M Ross** (Rangers; sub: **C Davidson**, Leicester City, ht) — **S Thompson** (Dundee United; sub: **J McFadden**, Motherwell, 81), **S Crawford** (Dunfermline Athletic; sub: **K Kyle**, Sunderland, 87) *Subs not used* **N Alexander** (Cardiff City), **G Caldwell** (Newcastle United), **G Williams** (Nottingham Forest)
Scorers **Crawford 11, Thompson 49, Crawford 73**

CANADA L Hirschfeld — **P Fenwick, K McKenna, R Hastings** — **C Pozniak, T Nsaliwa, D Imhof** (sub: **D Xausa**, 82), **P Stalteri, J de Guzman** — **T Radzinski, D de Rosario** *Subs not used* **M Nash, A Hutchinson, P Onstad**
Scorer **De Rosario 9 (pen)**
Booked **Fenwick**
Referee **L Huyghe** (Belgium)

Wednesday November 20
Friendly
PORTUGAL (a)
Braga
Lost 0-2   HT 0-2   Att 8,000
PORTUGAL Quim (sub: **Nelson**, 88min) — **F Couto, F Meira, R Rocha** — **S Conceicao, L Figo** (sub: **M Ferreira**, ht), **R Costa** (sub: **P Mendes**, 58), **R Jorge** (sub: **J Ribeiro**, 58) — **Tiago** (sub: **N Assis**, 84) — **Pauleta** (sub: **Nuno Gomes**, ht), **S Sabrosa** (sub: **Neca**, 77) *Subs not used* **R Silva, M Sergio**
Scorer **Pauleta 7, 18**
Booked **Couto**

SCOTLAND R Douglas (Celtic) — **R Anderson** (Aberdeen; sub: **D McInnes**, West Bromwich Albion, 23), **S Pressley** (Heart of Midlothian), **L Wilkie** (Dundee; sub: **S Severin**, Heart of Midlothian, 84) — **G Alexander** (Preston North End), **C Dailly** (West Ham United), **P Lambert** (Celtic; sub: **G Williams**, Nottingham Forest, 68), **G Naysmith** (Everton), **M Ross** (Rangers; sub: **P Devlin**, Birmingham City, ht) — **S Crawford** (Dunfermline Athletic), **S Dobie** (West Bromwich Albion; sub: **K Kyle**, Sunderland, 68) *Subs not used* **P Gallacher** (Dundee United), **S Caldwell** (Newcastle United), **N Alexander** (Cardiff City)
Referee **V Anghelieni** (Romania)

Wednesday February 12
Friendly
IRELAND (h)
Hampden Park
Lost 0-2   HT 0-1   Att 33,337

SCOTLAND N Sullivan (Tottenham Hotspur; sub: **P Gallacher**, Dundee United, ht) — **R Anderson** (Aberdeen), **S Caldwell** (Newcastle United), **C Dailly** (West Ham United) — **G Alexander** (Preston North End), **B Ferguson** (Rangers; sub: **C Cameron**, Wolverhampton Wanderers, 64), **P Lambert** (Celtic; sub: **S Gemmill**, Everton, ht), **G Naysmith** (Everton) — **N McCann** (Rangers; sub: **J Smith**, Celtic, 64) — **D Hutchison** (West Ham United; sub: **P Devlin**, Birmingham City, ht), **S Crawford** (Dunfermline Athletic; sub: **S Thompson**, Rangers, 64) *Subs not used* **K Miller** (Wolverhampton Wanderers), **S Dobie** (West Bromwich Albion), **K Kyle** (Sunderland), **J McNamara** (Celtic), **N Alexander** (Cardiff City), **R Malcolm** (Rangers)

Referee **E Braamhaar (the Netherlands)**
Ireland team, page 385

Saturday March 29
European Championship qualifier
ICELAND (h)
Hampden Park
Won 2-1   HT 1-0   Att 37,938
SCOTLAND R Douglas (Celtic) — **C Dailly** (West Ham United), **S Pressley** (Heart of Midlothian), **L Wilkie** (Dundee) — **G Alexander** (Preston North End), **P Lambert** (Celtic), **B Ferguson** (Rangers), **G Naysmith** (Everton), **D Hutchison** (West Ham United; sub: **P Devlin**, Birmingham City, 65min) — **K Miller** (Wolverhampton Wanderers; sub: **J McNamara**, Celtic, 81), **S Crawford** (Dunfermline Athletic) *Subs not used* **P Gallacher** (Dundee United), **R Malcolm** (Rangers), **A Gray** (Bradford City), **C Cameron** (Wolverhampton Wanderers), **S Gemmill** (Everton)
Scorers **Miller** 10, **Wilkie** 70
Booked **Pressley, Crawford, Lambert**

ICELAND A Arason (Rosenborg) — **L Sigurdsson** (West Bromwich Albion), **G Bergsson** (Bolton Wanderers), **I Ingimarsson** (Brighton) — **B Gunnarsson** (Stoke City; sub: **T Gudjohnson**, Stabaek IF, 73), **B Thorsteinsson** (Molde), **A Gretarsson** (Lokeren), **J Gudjonsson** (Aston Villa), **A Vidarsson** (Lokeren; sub: **I Sigurdsson**, Lillestrom, 82) — **R Kristinsson** (Lokeren), **E Gudjohnsen** (Chelsea; sub: **T Gudmundsson**, Stabaek IF, 88) *Subs not used* **B Kristinsson** (IBV Vestmannaeyjar), **P Marteinsson** (Stoke City), **G Einarsson** (Lillestrom), **M Baldvinsson** (Lokeren)
Scorer **Gudjohnsen** 48
Booked **I Sigurdsson**
Referee **R Temmink (the Netherlands)**

Wednesday April 2
European Championship qualifier
LITHUANIA (a)
Kaunas
Lost 0-1   HT 0-0   Att 6,400
LITHUANIA G Stauce (Forstiras Athens) — **D Gleveckas** (Shakhtar Donetsk), **T Zvirgzdasukas** (Halmstad), **I Dedura** (FKB Kaunas), **A Barasa** (unattached) — **I Morinas** (Mainz 05), **V Petrenko** (FKB Kaunas; sub: **D Maciulevicius**, Vilnius Sviesa, 72min), **D Semberas** (CSKA Moscow), **S Mikalajunas** (unattached; sub: **R Dziaukstas**, Saturn, 89) — **E Jankauskas** (FC Porto; sub: **A Fomenko**, Rostov, 65), **T Razanauskas** (Akritiros Athens) *Subs not used* **Z Karcemarskas** (Dinamo Moscow), **O Buitkas** (Skonto Riga), **T Papeckys** (FKB Kaunas), **E Poderis** (FKB Kaunas)
Scorer **Razanauskas** 73 (pen)

SCOTLAND P Gallacher (Dundee United) — **C Dailly** (West Ham United), **S Pressley** (Heart of Midlothian), **L Wilkie** (Dundee) — **G Alexander** (Preston North End), **J McNamara** (Celtic; sub: **S Gemmill**, Everton, 81), **P Lambert** (Celtic), **D Hutchison** (West Ham United),

---

MATCH OF THE SEASON

Scotland 1   Germany 1
Hampden Park, Saturday June 7 2003
Phil Gordon

THE T-SHIRTS BEING WORN by Scotland supporters on their way to Hampden Park on Saturday seemed more concerned with cheap point-scoring than any belief in obtaining one. A picture of the prostrate Oliver Kahn, after the goalkeeper's fumble last summer had presented the World Cup to Brazil, was accompanied by the message: "Yes we Kahn!" No doubt some entrepreneurial mind will replace that image with the moment Kenny Miller left him in despair before Scotland and Germany reconvene in Dortmund on September 10.

The T-shirt pledge proved authentic as Scotland cast aside the air of pantomime that has characterised the reign of Berti Vogts to deliver a performance that not only gave the World Cup runners-up a jolt, but restored some hope that there may yet be a door left open to gain entry into Euro 2004.

Germany are likely to regain control of group five when they play the Faeroe Isles in Torshavn on Wednesday, but even they will be unnerved by the way they failed to cope with a torrid day of Scots passion on and off the pitch.

Television cameras were trained on Vogts during the national anthems: the man who won the World Cup as a player with Germany and then led them to success in Euro 96 as a coach did not flinch when *Deutschland Uber Alles* was played, but *Flower of Scotland* proved irresistible.

He was not the only German. Many were blown away by the revamped anthem, just as the amp was by the electric guitarists leading the three Scots tenors. It was naff, it was kitsch, but it probably did the trick. Scotland took their cue from a pumped-up crowd and never dropped the tempo all day.

"The Scottish players were lifted by the crowd," Carsten Ramelow, the Germany defender, grumbled. "We had problems. The incredible noise made some of our players make bad mistakes." The decibel level went off the scale when Miller struck a composed equaliser in the 68th minute to cancel out Fredi Bobic's first-half header. Colin Cameron seized the loose ball to thread a swift free kick into the path of his Wolverhampton Wanderers colleague and Miller resisted the pack of Germans snapping at his heels to steer a finish beyond Kahn.

Scotland's rousing display even carried a hint of victory in the later stages. Miller suggested that is possible in Dortmund, a scenario that would offer automatic qualification instead of the play-off route for second place that the entire nation would settle for. Vogts might have tempered such boldness had he heard the striker, yet it was exactly the kind of self-belief he craved before this

Dailly calmly steers a path through midfield in Scotland's draw against Germany at Hampden

encounter. Led by the peerless Paul Lambert, any inferiority complex was cast aside as Germany were confronted by a team whose hunger was evident in every tackle.

Vogts deserved his moment of vindication after the welter of criticism from his adopted land as well as his native one, and would have needed plastic surgery to remove his grin afterwards. However, the inescapable fact is that Scotland's honourable draw rested upon two players who would probably not have featured had Vogts's hand not been forced. Miller and Cameron have required the kind of tenacity they showed against Germany simply to make a point to Vogts. Miller would not have played had Don Hutchison been fit. Cameron's case is more damning. One of the few genuine legacies left by Craig Brown, the midfield player was instantly discarded by Vogts after the 5-0 mauling by France. Vogts was also keen to praise Robert Douglas. The Celtic goalkeeper exorcised the torment of the Uefa Cup final defeat with a stunning save from Bernd Schneider's late free kick to preserve the scoreline.

"I told the players before they went out 'please leave your pressure in the dressing-room — it's all on Germany'," Vogts explained. "I asked them to go out and play with their heart, to play simple passes, but to play real Scottish football. The pressure is all on Germany now. When we arrived at the stadium, I knew it would be special. The atmosphere was incredible and the fans did not put pressure on us after Germany scored and I have to thank them for that — it was a great day for Scottish football."

SCOTLAND (4-4-2): R Douglas (Celtic) — M Ross (Rangers; sub: J McNamara, Celtic, 74min), S Pressley (Heart of Midlothian), A Webster (Heart of Midlothian), G Naysmith (Everton) — P Devlin (Birmingham City; sub: G Rae, Dundee, 59), C Cameron (Wolverhampton Wanderers), C Dailly (West Ham United), P Lambert (Celtic) — K Miller (Wolverhampton Wanderers; sub: S Thompson, Rangers, 89), S Crawford (Dunfermline Athletic). **Substitutes not used:** N Alexander (Cardiff City), G Alexander (Preston North End), L Wilkie (Dundee), A Gray (Bradford City). **Booked:** Devlin, Dailly, Pressley, Thompson.
GERMANY (3-5-2): O Kahn (Bayern Munich) — A Friedrich (Hertha Berlin), C Ramelow (Bayer Leverkusen), C Worns (Borussia Dortmund) — T Frings (Borussia Dortmund), B Schneider (Bayer Leverkusen; sub: S Kehl, Borussia Dortmund, 84), J Jeremies (Bayern Munich), M Ballack (Bayern Munich), T Rau (VfL Wolfsburg; sub: P Freier, VfL Bochum, 56) — F Bobic (Hannover 96), M Klose (1FC Kaiserslautern; sub: O Neuville, Bayer Leverkusen, 74). **Substitutes not used:** F Rost (Schalke 04), M Rehmer (Hertha Berlin), A Hinkel (VfB Stuttgart), K Kuranyi (VfB Stuttgart). **Booked:** Frings, Freier, Ballack.
Referee: D Messina (Italy).

G Naysmith (Everton) — S Crawford (Dunfermline Athletic; sub: P Devlin, Birmingham City, 57), K Miller (Wolverhampton Wanderers) *Subs not used* K Arthur (Partick Thistle), R Malcolm (Rangers), C Cameron (Wolverhampton Wanderers), A Gray (Bradford City), M Ross (Rangers)
Referee F Stuchlik (Austria)

Wednesday April 30
Friendly
AUSTRIA (h)
Hampden Park
Lost 0-2 HT 0-2 Att **12,189**
SCOTLAND P Gallacher (Dundee United) — L Wilkie (Dundee), A Webster (Heart of Midlothian), S Pressley (Heart of Midlothian) — P Devlin (Birmingham City; sub: J Smith, Celtic, 84min), C Burley (Derby County; sub: C Cameron, Wolverhampton Wanderers, 63), G Naysmith (Everton), C Dailly (West Ham United; sub: S Gemmill, Everton, ht) — D Hutchison (West Ham United; sub: K Miller, Wolverhampton Wanderers, 61) — S Thompson (Rangers; sub: S Crawford, Dunfermline Athletic, ht), J McFadden (Motherwell) *Subs not used* N Alexander (Cardiff City), G Alexander (Preston North End), R Malcolm (Rangers), M Ross (Rangers), K Arthur (Partick Thistle)
Booked **Wilkie**

AUSTRIA T Mandl — P Scharner, A Ehmann, M Stranzl, E Dospel — R Aufhauser, M Schopp, T Flogel (sub: M Hieblinger, 90), M Wagner, R Kirchler (sub: A Herzog, 84) — M Haas (sub: R Brunmayr, 63) *Subs not used* H Payer, E Pogatetz, T Holler, R Wallner
Scorers Kirchler 27, Haas 32
Booked **Scharner, Schopp**
Referee N Vollquartz (Denmark)

Tuesday May 27
Friendly
NEW ZEALAND (h)
Tynecastle
Drew 1-1 HT 0-0 Att **10,016**
SCOTLAND R Douglas (Celtic) — M Ross (Rangers; sub: G Alexander, Preston North End, ht), S Pressley (Heart of Midlothian), A Webster (Heart of Midlothian), G Naysmith (Everton) — P Devlin (Birmingham City), C Dailly (West Ham United), J McNamara (Celtic, sub: B Kerr, Newcastle United, 82), J McFadden (Motherwell) — K Kyle (Sunderland; sub: A Gray, Bradford City, 59), S Crawford (Dunfermline Athletic) *Subs not used* N Alexander (Cardiff City), S Caldwell (Newcastle United), G Caldwell (Newcastle United), I Murray (Hibernian), K Arthur (Partick Thistle)
Scorer Crawford 10
Booked Dailly, Webster, G Alexander, Devlin

NEW ZEALAND M Utting (sub: J Batty, ht) — D Mulligan (sub: D Oughton, ht), C Zoricich (sub: S Smith, 69), R Nelson, G Davis — C Jackson (sub: R De Gregorio, 54), S Elliott, M Burton, V Coveny — A Lines (sub: C Bouckenrooghe, 80), N Hickey *Sub not used* M Paston
Scorer Nelsen 47
Booked Mulligan
Referee M Ingvarsson (Sweden)

Saturday June 7
European Championship qualifier
GERMANY (h)
Hampden Park
Drew 1-1 HT 0-1 Att **48,047**
Scotland scorer **Miller 68**
Germany scorer **Bobic 22**
See left for full line-ups

THE GAMES

Wednesday August 21
Friendly
CROATIA (a)
Zagreb
Drew 1-1   HT 1-0   Att 6,500
CROATIA S Pletikosa (Hajduk Split; sub: **T Butina**, Dinamo Zagreb, 60min) — **B Zivkovic** (Bayer Leverkusen), **F Tapalovic** (VfL Bochum; sub: **M Babic**, Bayer Leverkusen, 60), **J Simunic** (Hertha Berlin) — **R Kovac** (Bayern Munich; sub: **J Vranjes**, Bayer Leverkusen, 60), **N Kovac** (Bayern Munich; sub: **J Leko**, Dinamo Zagreb, ht), **D Saric** (Panathinaikos), **D Vugrinec** (Lecce; sub: **S Maric**, Dinamo Zagreb, ht), **M Rapaic** (Fenerbahce; sub: **M Bazina**, GAK Graz, 60) — **G Vlaovic** (Panathinaikos; sub: **M Petric**, Grasshopper, ht), **T Maric** (VfL Wolfsburg; sub: **S Tomas**, Vicenza, 60) *Sub not used:* **D Hrman** (Varteks)
Scorer **Petric** 79

WALES P Jones (Southampton) — **M Delaney** (Aston Villa), **D Gabbidon** (Cardiff City), **A Melville** (Fulham), **D Barnard** (Grimsby Town; sub: **R Weston**, Cardiff City, 59) — **M Pembridge** (Everton), **C Robinson** (Portsmouth; sub: **P Evans**, Bradford City, 70), **A Johnson** (West Bromwich Albion) — **J Hartson** (Celtic; sub: **G Taylor**, Burnley, 58), **R Earnshaw** (Cardiff City; sub: **P Trollope**, Northampton Town, 79) *Subs not used* **M Crossley** (Middlesbrough), **C Llewellyn** (Norwich City), **D Ward** (Nottingham Forest), **D Vaughan** (Crewe Alexandra)
Scorer **Davies** 11
Booked **Delaney, Hartson**
Referee **M Frolich** (Germany)

Saturday September 7 2002
European Championship qualifier
FINLAND (a)
Helsinki
Won 2-0   HT 1-0   Att 35,833
FINLAND A Niemi (Southampton) — **V Nylund** (HJK Helsinki; sub: **J Johansson**, Charlton Athletic, 69min), **H Tihinen** (Anderlecht), **S Hyypia** (Liverpool), **J Saarinen** (Rosenborg; sub: **P Kopteff**, Viking Stavanger, 78) — **A Riihilahti** (Crystal Palace), **T Tainio** (Auxerre) — **M Nurmela** (Heerenveen; sub: **M Kottila**, HJK Helsinki, 86), **J Litmanen** (Ajax), **J Kolkka** (Panathinaikos) — **S Kuqi** (Sheffield Wednesday) *Subs not used* **J Hietanen** (Denizlispor), **T Kuivasto** (Viking Stavanger), **J Ilola** (HJK Helsinki), **J Jaaskelainen** (Bolton Wanderers)
Booked **Tihinen, Hyypia, Tainio**

WALES P Jones (Southampton) — **M Delaney** (Aston Villa), **A Melville** (Fulham), **D Gabbidon** (Cardiff City), **G Speed** (Newcastle United) — **A Johnson** (West Bromwich Albion; sub: **C Bellamy**, Newcastle United, 76), **M Pembridge** (Everton), **R Savage** (Birmingham City) — **S Davies** (Tottenham Hotspur), **R Giggs** (Manchester United) — **J Hartson** (Celtic) *Subs not used:* **R Weston** (Cardiff City), **C Robinson** (Wolverhampton Wanderers), **J Koumas** (West Bromwich Albion), **N Blake** (Wolverhampton Wanderers), **R Earnshaw** (Cardiff City), **M Crossley** (Middlesbrough)
Scorers **Hartson** 31, **Davies** 73
Booked **Pembridge, Johnson**
Referee **K Plautz** (Austria)

WERE IT NOT FOR THE FACT that there are so many positives on which to draw, it would be tempting to paint Wales's European Championship qualifying campaign as a valiant fight against adversity and the fates that the international community has thrown at them. Some of the obstacles have been of their own making, but it should be noted — to put their heroics into an even clearer context — that Wales's astonishing surge to the top of group nine came against a backdrop of several unwanted distractions.

There have been the constant club versus country battles, a recognised hazard but compounded in this case by mixed signals from the sport's governing body. There was the postponement of the match in Serbia and Montenegro because of political insecurity in Belgrade and its switch to the opening week of the Premiership season. There was the near expulsion of Azerbaijan, a decision that would have had severe consequences for Wales. And then there was the team's time-honoured tendency to shoot itself in the foot.

Mark Hughes and his players, though, rose above it all, winning their first four qualifying matches and preserving their record as the only team other than France to boast an unblemished record at the halfway stage. It is an astonishing feat for a country of Wales's means and dubious pedigree. They have not reached the finals of a leading tournament since the World Cup in 1958, but will guarantee at least a play-off place by picking up three points from their last four matches, or by drawing either home or away against Serbia.

So deeply ingrained is the feel-good factor in Welsh football, though, that Hughes and his players will view anything less than automatic qualification ahead of Italy as a disappointment. From the moment that John Hartson shot them into an early lead against Finland in Helsinki in September, there has been a belief that Wales are on the verge of something big. The 2-1 victory over Italy on an unforgettable evening in Cardiff a month later raised the bar considerably, but Hughes's team have soared above every challenge.

That game may come to be seen as the defining point of Hughes's reign as manager, the night that they announced their long-overdue return to the international scene. For 12 months, his team had been content to remain the best-kept secret in international football, slowly moving up the Fifa rankings, in which they had at one stage stood below Mali and Burkina Faso. But, on October 16, the Welsh dragon roared like never before, a vibrant performance crowned by goals from Simon Davies and Craig Bellamy.

The goalscorers, two of the Premiership's outstanding younger players, are at the sharp end of the revolution in Welsh football, even eclipsing Ryan Giggs as the team's most potent attacking

PLAYER OF THE SEASON   Simon Davies

Players tend to sink or swim when thrown in at the deep end of international football and Simon Davies, since a daunting baptism in Kiev in 2001, has looked at home in those hazardous waters. The midfield player has started Wales's past 14 games, a run that has more than merely coincided with the team's transformation under Mark Hughes. Blessed with all the raw materials — pace and poise, silk and steel — he has flourished on the international scene while demonstrating a genuine sense of pride in his country.
Oliver Kay

forces. Their style and verve, though, are allied to the experience of Paul Jones, Andy Melville, Robert Page, Mark Pembridge, Gary Speed and Hartson, all of whom have finally come to recognise that there is far more to international football than ritual beatings.

Presiding over the whole affair is Hughes, who faced calls for his head after a difficult start to his time in charge but who is now arguably their greatest asset. By his own admission, the former Manchester United forward did not look like a manager in the making during his playing days, but he appears to have all the requirements: a softly spoken authority, the ability to mould his players into a formidable unit, a keen eye for detail and, not least, the strength to make light of the inevitable problems.

Hughes has been far more impressive than Sven-Goran Eriksson, the England head coach, in standing up to the bullying of the Premiership managers, but it has been more difficult to gain the respect of Fifa. If its decision to stop Wales invoking the five-day rule before the match in Azerbaijan in November was possibly the right one, as the date was not designated for competitive matches, the lack of co-operation over the game in Belgrade on August 20, rearranged at Fifa's behest, was harder to accept.

No matter how high the odds are stacked against them, however, Wales, after so many near-misses, believe that 2004 will be their year. The reinstatement of Azerbaijan in May, after they had briefly been suspended from international football for "repeated violations of the code of conduct", hinted that Wales's luck may finally have turned, as did two defeats suffered by Serbia and Montenegro in June. Perhaps Lady Luck, tired of seeing her malevolent efforts rebuffed, has finally decided to smile on the Principality.

Wednesday October 16
European Championship qualifier
ITALY (h)
Millennium Stadium
Won 2-1   HT 1-1   Att 70,000
WALES P Jones (Southampton) — **M Delaney** (Aston Villa), **A Melville** (Fulham), **D Gabbidon** (Cardiff City), **G Speed** (Newcastle United) — **S Davies** (Tottenham Hotspur), **M Pembridge** (Everton), **R Savage** (Birmingham City) — **C Bellamy** (Newcastle United; sub: **N Blake**, Wolverhampton Wanderers, 90min), **R Giggs** (Manchester United) — **J Hartson** (Celtic) *Subs not used* **R Page** (Sheffield United), **R Weston** (Cardiff City), **C Robinson** (Portsmouth), **A Johnson** (West Bromwich Albion), **R Earnshaw** (Cardiff City), **M Crossley** (Middlesbrough)
Scorers **Davies 12, Bellamy 71**
Booked **Savage**

ITALY G Buffon (Juventus) — **C Panucci** (AS Roma), **A Nesta** (AC Milan), **F Cannavaro** (Inter Milan), **L Zauri** (Atalanta) — **D Tommasi** (AS Roma), **L Di Biagio** (Inter Milan; sub: **G Gattuso**, AC Milan, 65; sub: **M Marazzina**, Chievo Verona, 85), **A Pirlo** (AC Milan), **M Ambrosini** (AC Milan) — **A Del Piero** (Juventus), **V Montella** (AS Roma; sub: **M Maccarone**, Middlesbrough, 70) *Subs not used* **C Abbiati** (AC Milan), **D Adani** (Inter Milan), **M Iuliano** (Juventus), **M Oddo** (Lazio)
Scorer **Del Piero 32**
Booked **Di Biagio**
Referee **G Veissiere** (France)

Wednesday November 20
European Championship qualifier
AZERBAIJAN (a)
Baku
Won 2-0   HT 1-0   Att 8,000
AZERBAIJAN J Hassanzade (OMIK) — **A Kerimov** (Karabakh-Azersun; sub: **F Mamedov**, Shamkir, ht), **T Akhmedov** (Karabakh-Azersun; sub: **A Asadov**, Karabakh-Azersun, 74), **I Yadullayev** (Karabakh-Azersun), **A Niftaliyev** (Karabakh-Azersun) — **E Imamaliyev** (Shafa), **R Sadygov** (FK Neftchi) — **V Vasilyev** (FK Neftchi), **M Gurbanov** (Shankir; sub: **F Ismaylov**, Karabakh-Azersun, 61), **S Aliyev** (Volin Litsk) — **G Gurbanov** (Fakel-Voronezh) *Subs not used* **H Mahommedov** (Shamkir), **R Musayev** (Terek), **E Gambarov** (Novbakhor), **A Mamedov** (Shamkir)
Booked **Sadygov, Ismaylov**

WALES P Jones (Southampton) — **M Delaney** (Aston Villa; sub: **R Weston**, Cardiff City, 71), **A Melville** (Fulham), **R Page** (Sheffield United), **D Barnard** (Grimsby Town) — **S Davies** (Tottenham Hotspur), **G Speed** (Newcastle United), **C Robinson** (Portsmouth; sub: **P Trollope**, Northampton Town, 90) — **R Earnshaw** (Cardiff City; sub: **N Roberts**, Wigan Athletic, 89), **R Giggs** (Manchester United) — **J Hartson** (Celtic) *Subs not used* **A Williams** (Reading), **P Evans** (Bradford City), **J Thomas** (Swansea City), **M Crossley** (Middlesbrough)
Scorers **Speed 9, Hartson 68**
Booked **Page, Barnard**
Referee **L Huyghe** (Belgium)

Wednesday February 12
Friendly
BOSNIA-HERZEGOVINA (h)
Millennium Stadium
Drew 2-2 HT 1-1 Att **22,000**
WALES D Ward (Nottingham Forest; sub: **M Crossley,** Middlesbrough, ht) — R Weston (Cardiff City; sub: **M Jones,** Leicester City, 61), A Melville (Fulham), R Page (Sheffield United), **G Speed** (Newcastle United) — **S Davies** (Tottenham Hotspur), R Savage (Birmingham City; sub: **J Oster,** Sunderland, 88), **M Pembridge** (Everton) — R Earnshaw (Cardiff City; sub: **J Koumas,** West Bromwich Albion, 76), **C Bellamy** (Newcastle United) — J Hartson (Celtic; sub: G Taylor, Burnley, 82) *Subs not used* K Symons (Crystal Palace), D Barnard (Barnsley)
Scorers **Earnshaw** 8, **Hartson** 74

BOSNIA-HERZEGOVINA K Hasagic (Zeljeznicar Sarajevo) — D Berberovic (FK Sarajevo), **M Konjic** (Coventry City), M Hibic (Atletico Madrid), V Music (Como) — **M Beslija** (Genk), **B Biscevic** (Zeljeznicar Sarajevo; sub: A Velagic, Velez Mostar, 90), V Grujic (Borac Banja Luka; sub: **S Mulina,** Leotar Treblnje, 77), **S Barbarez** (SV Hamburg; sub: **N Miskovic,** Partizan Belgrade, 78), E Baljic (Galatasaray; sub: **M Hrgovic,** Siroki Brijeg, 78) — **E Bolic** (Rayo Vallecano; sub: N Halilovic, Varteks, 90) *Subs not used* A Tolja (Casino Bregtenz), B Krunic (Leotar Treblnje)
Scorers **Baljic** 5, **Barbarez** 64
Referee D Malcolm (Northern Ireland)

Saturday March 29
European Championship qualifier
AZERBAIJAN (h)
Won 4-0 HT 3-0 Att **72,500**
WALES P Jones (Southampton) — S Davies (Tottenham Hotspur), A Melville (Fulham), R Page (Sheffield United), **G Speed** (Newcastle United; sub: P Trollope, Northampton Town, ht) — J Oster (Sunderland), **M Pembridge** (Everton), R Savage (Birmingham City; sub: **C Robinson,** Portsmouth, 19) — **C Bellamy** (Newcastle United; sub: R Edwards, Aston Villa, 71), R Giggs (Manchester United) — J Hartson (Celtic) *Subs not used:* N Blake (Wolverhampton Wanderers), **R Earnshaw** (Cardiff City), G Taylor (Burnley), D Ward (Nottingham Forest)
Scorers **Akhmedov** 1 (og), **Speed** 40, **Hartson** 44, **Giggs** 52

AZERBAIJAN J Hassanzade (Volin Litsk) — K Guliyev (Volin Litsk), E Guliyev (Alania Vladikavkaz; sub: I Yadullayev, Neftabadan, ht), T Akhmedov (Karabakh-Azersun), E Imamaliyev (Shafa) — R Musayev (Shafa), R Mammadov (Pevkan), A Hajiyev (Shafa; sub: **F Mahammadov,** Mashinsazi, ht), M Gurbanov (Poladahvaz) — S Aliyev (Volin Litsk; sub: Z Tagizada, Shafa, 74) — G Gurbnaov (Volgar-Gazprom Astrakhan) *Subs not used* Z Zeynalov (Gomrukcu Baku), K Mammadov (Mashinsazi), S Musayev (Volin Litsk), H Mahammadov (Mashinsazi)
Booked R Mammadov, F Mahammadov, M Gurbanov
Referee P Leuba (Switzerland)

MATCH OF THE SEASON

Wales 2   Italy 1
Millennium Stadium, Wednesday October 16 2002
Oliver Kay

SUDDENLY, MARK HUGHES'S vision of football replacing rugby union in the hearts of the Welsh people does not seem quite so outlandish. After this astonishing result, on an unforgettable evening of patriotic fervour at the Millennium Stadium, anything, not least qualification for the 2004 European Championship, is possible. As Hughes's renascent team humiliated Italy, with Simon Davies and Craig Bellamy scoring goals that will secure their place in Welsh folklore, it was tempting to reflect that things will never be the same again in a country where football has always been synonymous with failure.

"Friends, Welshmen, countrymen, lend me your ears," the stadium announcer roared at the final whistle. "We came, we saw, we conquered." The Roman parody may not have been appreciated by Giovanni Trapattoni, whose position as Italy coach now seems untenable, but, had the stadium roof not been closed, the ensuing roar would have resounded through the valleys and across the River Severn. "Are you watching, England?" delirious fans shrieked. Maybe not before now, but this is a result that will make the rest of Europe, let alone Sven-Goran Eriksson's rabble, take notice.

Wales's glorious night was briefly threatened by Alessandro Del Piero, whose deflected free kick restored parity in the 32nd minute, but Bellamy's goal in the 71st minute embellished an unbeaten sequence of seven matches, which now includes victories over Italy and Germany.

There have been false dawns before, but Hughes believes this one is real. Wales are two points clear in group nine and will travel to Baku to play Azerbaijan next month believing that qualification for their first leading tournament since 1958 is within their grasp.

Hughes has not gained the recognition he deserves since taking charge of Wales three years ago, but no more. He said that the evening ranked alongside any of his achievements as a player with Manchester United and, while adding a note of caution, he concluded that the result would change people's perceptions of Welsh football. "It's been a wonderful evening," he said. "But I'm hoping there are more highs to come. Our campaign is off to a perfect start, but the secret is to keep our heads and make sure we complete the job."

The manager declined to single out individuals, paying tribute to a remarkable team effort, but John Hartson merits a special mention. Alessandro Nesta, reputedly one of the world's finest defenders, had no answer to the Celtic forward's strength and aggression. It was Hartson who released Bellamy for the winning goal, although there was no shortage of heroes in red. Robbie

Savage's aggression in midfield played a vital part in an epic win for Wales over Italy

Monday May 26 2003
Friendly
UNITED STATES (a)
San Jose
Lost 0-2   HT 0-1   Att 12,282

UNITED STATES N Rimando (DC United) — **R Suarez** (Dallas Burn; sub: **M Petke**, DC United, 78min), **C J Brown** (Chicago Fire), **J Agoos** (San Jose Earthquakes), **G Vanney** (Bastia) — **E Stewart** (DC United; sub: **M Lagos**, San Jose Earthquakes, 83), **B Convey** (DC United; sub: **B Ching**, San Jose Earthquakes, 75), **R Mulrooney** (San Jose Earthquakes), **E Lewis** (Preston North End) — **L Donovan** (San Jose Earthquakes), **J Kirovski** (Birmingham City; sub: **A Eskandarian**, DC United, 89) *Subs not used* **J Cannon** (Lens), **B Olsen** (DC United), **C Reyna** (Sunderland) Scorers **Donovan 41 (pen), Lewis 59** Booked **Suarez**

WALES P Jones (Southampton; sub: **D Ward**, Nottingham Forest, ht) — **M Jones** (Leicester City), **A Melville** (Fulham), **A Williams** (Reading), **D Vaughan** (Crewe Alexandra) — **S Davies** (Tottenham Hotspur), **J Oster** (Sunderland; sub: **D Pipe**, Coventry City, 70), **M Pembridge** (Everton; sub: **C Robinson**, Portsmouth, 79), **A Johnson** (West Bromwich Albion), **J Koumas** (West Bromwich Albion) — **G Taylor** (Burnley) *Subs not used* **P Trollope** (Northampton Town), **C Roberts** (Bristol City), **R Day** (Mansfield Town), **M Rees** (Millwall) Booked **M Jones, Oster, Pembridge** Sent off **M Jones 49** Referee **B Tellez (Mexico)**

Savage and Mark Pembridge dominated a midfield comprising the best that Serie A has to offer, while Danny Gabbidon, the young Cardiff City defender, shaded his individual duel with Del Piero. Aside from a breakdown of communication that, to the dismay of Hughes and his players, saw the roof left open during Monday's downpour, the Football Association of Wales did everything to set the scene for an evening that will live long in the memory. The combined efforts of the country's finest musicians and of John Charles, the finest Welsh footballer of them all, whipped an expectant crowd into a frenzy.

Eager anticipation gave way to euphoria in the twelfth minute as Davies put Wales ahead. Everyone in the stadium expected him to lay the ball off, but Davies had other ideas, sending an unstoppable right-foot shot past Gianluigi Buffon. Cue bedlam.

That goal could have deflated Italy, but the dead-ball delivery of Del Piero ensured that they remained a threat. In the 32nd minute his free kick took a deflection off the wall and looped over Paul Jones. Perhaps luck was shining on Trapattoni.

That seemed to be the case shortly before the interval, as a free kick from Ryan Giggs hit the woodwork, but Wales remained confident that it would be their night. The second half was a fractious affair, but, as the night wore on, gaps began to appear in the Italy defence. Hartson spotted one of them, passing the ball to Bellamy, who left Nesta and company trailing in his wake, skipped around the advancing Buffon and stroked the ball into the empty net. A remarkable end to a remarkable evening.

WALES (4-3-2-1): P Jones (Southampton) — **M Delaney** (Aston Villa), **A Melville** (Fulham), **D Gabbidon** (Cardiff City), **G Speed** (Newcastle United) — **S Davies** (Tottenham Hotspur), **M Pembridge** (Everton), **R Savage** (Birmingham City) — **C Bellamy** (Newcastle United; sub: **N Blake**, Wolverhampton Wanderers, 90min), **R Giggs** (Manchester United) — **J Hartson** (Celtic). Substitutes not used: **R Page** (Sheffield United), **R Weston** (Cardiff City), **C Robinson** (Portsmouth), **A Johnson** (West Bromwich Albion), **R Earnshaw** (Cardiff City), **M Crossley** (Middlesbrough). Booked: Savage.
ITALY (4-4-2): G Buffon (Juventus) — **C Panucci** (AS Roma), **A Nesta** (AC Milan), **F Cannavaro** (Inter Milan), **L Zauri** (Atalanta) — **D Tommasi** (AS Roma), **L Di Biagio** (Inter Milan; sub: **G I Gattuso**, AC Milan, 65; sub: **M Marazzina**, Chievo, 85), **A Pirlo** (AC Milan), **M Ambrosini** (AC Milan) — **A Del Piero** (Juventus), **V Montella** (AS Roma; sub: **M Maccarone**, Middlesbrough, 70). Substitutes not used: **C Abbiati** (AC Milan), **D Adani** (Inter Milan), **M Iuliano** (Juventus), **M Oddo** (Lazio). Booked: Di Biagio. Referee: G Veissiere (France).

THE GAMES

Wednesday August 21
Friendly
FINLAND (a)
Helsinki
Won 3-0 HT 1-0 Att 12,225
FINLAND J Jaaskelainen — P Pasanen, H Tihinen, S
Hyypia (sub: T Kuivasto, ht), J Saarinen — M Nurmela
(sub: P Kopteff, 69), J Ilola (sub: A Riihilahti, 59), T
Tainio (sub: J Hietanen, 80), J Kolkka (sub: M Kottila,
78) — J Litmanen — J Johansson (sub: S Kuqi, 59)
Subs not used A Niemi, M Heikkinen
IRELAND D Kiely (Charlton Athletic; sub: S Given,
Newcastle United, 75) — G Kelly (Leeds United), G
Breen (West Ham United), K Cunningham (Birmingham
City; sub: G Doherty, Tottenham Hotspur, ht), I Harte
(Leeds United; sub: G Barrett, Arsenal, 75) — T Butler
(Sunderland; sub: K Kilbane, Sunderland, ht), L Carsley
(Everton; sub: M Holland, Ipswich Town, 87), M
Kinsella (Charlton Athletic; sub: S McPhail, Leeds
United, ht), J McAteer (Sunderland; sub: C Healy,
Celtic, ht) — D Duff (Blackburn Rovers; sub: R Delap,
Southampton, ht), R Keane (Leeds United; sub: J
Goodwin, Stockport County, 83)
Scorers **Keane** 12, **Healy** 74, **Barrett** 83
Referee R Pedersen (Norway)

Saturday September 7
European Championship qualifier
RUSSIA (a)
Moscow
Lost 2-4 HT 0-2 Att 22,000
RUSSIA S Ovchinnikov (Lomomotiv Moscow) — S
Ignashevich (Lokomotiv Moscow), V Onopko (Rayo
Vallecano), G Nizhegorodov (Lokomotiv Moscow) — D
Loskov (Lokomotiv Moscow), Y Aldonin (Rotor
Volgograd), I Yanovsky (CSKA Moscow) — A Kariaka
(Krylya Sovietov Samara), R Gusev (CSKA Moscow; sub:
A Solomatin, CSKA Moscow, 28min) — V
Beschastnykh (Spartak Moscow; sub: A Kerzhakov,
Zenit St Petersburg, ht), S Semak (CSKA Moscow; sub:
D Khokhlov, Real Sociedad, 75) *Subs not used* R
Nigmatullin (CSKA Moscow), Y Kovtun (Spartak
Moscow), I Semshov (Torpedo Moscow), A Arshavin
(Zenit St Petersburg)
Scorers **Kariaka** 20, **Beschastnykh** 24, **Kerzhakov** 69,
Babb 86 (og)
Booked Ovchinnikov
IRELAND S Given (Newcastle United) — S Finnan
(Fulham), G Breen (West Ham United), K Cunningham
(Birmingham City), I Harte (Leeds United) — J McAteer
(Sunderland; sub: G Doherty, Tottenham Hotspur, 65),
M Kinsella (Aston Villa), M Holland (Ipswich Town), K
Kilbane (Sunderland; sub: P Babb, Sunderland, 85) — D
Duff (Blackburn Rovers; sub: C Morrison, Birmingham
City, 18), R Keane (Tottenham Hotspur) *Subs not used*
D Kiely (Charlton Athletic), G Kelly (Leeds United), C
Healy (Celtic), L Carsley (Everton)
Referee C Colombo (France)

Wednesday October 16
European Championship qualifier
SWITZERLAND (h)
Lansdowne Road
Lost 1-2 HT 0-1 Att 40,000
IRELAND S Given (Newcastle United) — G Kelly (Leeds
United), G Breen (West Ham United), K Cunningham
(Birmingham City), I Harte (Leeds United; sub: G
Doherty, Tottenham Hotspur, 86) — C Healy (Celtic), M
Holland (Ipswich Town), M Kinsella (Aston Villa), K
Kilbane (Sunderland; sub: C Morrison, Birmingham City,
61) — D Duff (Blackburn Rovers; sub: T Butler,
Sunderland, 82), R Keane (Tottenham Hotspur)

SMALL IN STATURE, PERHAPS, yet Brian Kerr is now the little
big man of Irish football, a rookie international manager no more.
And as he danced a jig of joy at Lansdowne Road on June II, Ireland
having eased past Georgia 2-0 in a European Championship
qualifying match, hope had been restored.

Eight months earlier, Ireland's chances of reaching the finals in
Portugal in 2004 had lain in tatters. A 2-1 home defeat against
Switzerland, hot on the heels of the 4-2 humiliation in Moscow, had
left Ireland not so much staring into the abyss but slithering into it.
Mick McCarthy, then the manager, had ridden the rage in Saipan,
when his row with Roy Keane had led to his captain taking an early
flight home. It proved to be the story of a World Cup finals that had
not even started. Yet although Keane walked, his former
team-mates still reached the second round and deservedly accepted
the plaudits.

The 3-0 friendly victory against Finland in Helsinki in August
confirmed McCarthy's judgment. His Ireland remained a
formidable force, but the sores from the Keane saga continued to
fester and, after the losses against Russia and Switzerland, they had
formed a gaping wound. A cussed character, ever ready to confront
his critics, McCarthy hung on. Only when the rabble-rousing from
sections of the Irish press affected his players, he said, would he go.
And when it did, he went, in November. Ireland had imploded.

Into the wreckage strode Kerr, 49, a softly-spoken, wispy-haired
figure born in Dublin. One of their own. It was time to rebuild from
within, to promote the man whose success at age-level football was
unparalleled in Ireland's history. His first job was to address the
Keane issue, to deal with the baggage. He did so privately,
persuasively and almost fruitfully. But with Keane ready to bury the
hatchet that he had kept honed for McCarthy, the medical advice
from Old Trafford decreed otherwise. No, Keane would stick with
Manchester United. The single-minded son of Cork who had
divided a country bade farewell to his beloved Ireland.

That "His Corkness" — the nickname often used to deride Keane
in his native land — chose to announce his decision on the eve of
Kerr's first game, a friendly against Scotland at Hampden Park,
showed a typical lack of respect. Me No l, the rest nowhere. Kerr
dealt with it deftly and moved on, perhaps glad to be rid of the
lingering malevolence that had brought down McCarthy. A poor
Scotland side were dispatched 2-0 and, by the end of the season,
Kerr had eked out a six-match unbeaten record, which included five
wins, that had restored not only Ireland's health but also their pride.
They lay two points off the top of qualifying group ten.

PLAYER OF THE SEASON — Damien Duff

The wizard of the dribble has replaced Roy Keane at the heart of Ireland's affections. Damien Duff effervescently filled the void left by the absent Keane at the World Cup finals and continued in the same vein throughout the European Championship qualifying campaign. His trickery is often bewitching, whether used up front alongside Robbie Keane, wide on the left or just behind the central strikers. His directness and versatility is invaluable to Brian Kerr, the Ireland manager. Fitness is a problem, but Duff is Dublin's diamond.
Russell Kempson

First up competitively was a daunting double-header, trips to Georgia and Albania. Amid the knife-throwing and bottle-chucking in Tbilisi — and without Robbie Keane, who was back home mourning the death of his father, — Ireland emerged with a 2-1 victory. Stirring stuff.

On to Tirana, another venture into the unknown. Albania, no longer the whipping boys of Europe, had recently beaten Russia, but a goalless draw represented a fair reward for Ireland's resilience under fire. To escape from the seething Qemal Stafa Stadium unbowed needed courage. And they had it.

A 1-0 friendly win against Norway in April franked that progress, with Kerr proving a flexible operator in his first home match in charge. His use of an alien 4-3-1-2 formation, giving Damien Duff a free role behind Robbie Keane and David Connolly, provided more encouraging signs of progress.

Not so against Albania at Lansdowne Road on June 7, when a below-par Ireland needed an injury-time own goal to sneak the three points. Good fortune played a significant part and that Duff, their fleet-footed talisman, limped off injured — and would not play against Georgia four days later — dampened spirits further.

Kerr had to reshuffle his pack. Duff-less maybe, but Ireland were still dogged and determined. Georgia were ground down impressively and Kerr, in a rare show of emotion, danced his jig. "I was just so elated," he said. "I'm just so happy that we're back in the picture to qualify. That's all I wanted to do when I took over and that's what we've done." Ireland's rehabilitation was on target. Confidence was returning, the belief restored — and the results duly forthcoming.

Saturday March 29
European Championship qualifier
GEORGIA (a)
Tbilisi
Won 2-1 HT 1-0 Att 15,000
GEORGIA G Lomaia (Lokomotiv Tbilisi) — **O Khizaneishvili** (Dinamo Tbilisi), **G Shashiashvili** (Dinamo Tbilisi), **A Amisulashvili** (Dinamo Tbilisi) — **L Tskitishvili** (SC Freiburg), **G Nemsadze** (Dundee), **G Jamarauli** (Metalurg Donetsk), **L Kobiashvili** (SC Freiburg) — **G Kinkladze** (Derby County; sub: **G Didava**, Kocaelispor, 71min) — **A Iashvili** (SC Freiburg), **T Ketsbaia** (Anorthosis Famagusta; sub: **G Demetradze**, Real Sociedad, ht) Subs not used **D Gvaramadze** (Dinamo Tbilisi), **D Kvirkvelia** (Dinamo Tbilisi), **R Kemoklidze** (Kocaelispor), **A Rekhviashvili** (Torpedo Moscow), **M Ashvetia** (FC Copenhagen)
Scorer **Kobiashvili 61**
Booked **Khizaneishvili**

IRELAND S Given (Newcastle United) — **S Carr** (Tottenham Hotspur), **G Breen** (West Ham United), **K Cunningham** (Birmingham City), **J O'Shea** (Manchester United) — **L Carsley** (Everton), **M Holland** (Ipswich Town), **M Kinsella** (Aston Villa), **K Kilbane** (Sunderland) — **G Doherty** (Tottenham Hotspur), **D Duff** (Blackburn Rovers) Subs not used **D Kiely** (Charlton Athletic), **J Kenna** (Birmingham City), **A O'Brien** (Newcastle United), **C Healy** (Celtic), **S McPhail** (Leeds United), **D Connolly** (Wimbledon), **A Lee** (Rotherham United)
Scorers **Duff 18, Doherty 84**
Booked **Doherty**
Referee **K Vassaras** (Greece)

Wednesday April 2
European Championship qualifier
ALBANIA (a)
Tirana
Drew 0-0 HT 0-0 Att 20,000
ALBANIA F Strakosha (Kalfea) — **E Beqiri** (KS Vllaznia), **G Cipi** (Ghent), **A Aliaj** (SK Tirana) — **K Duro** (Steaua Bucharest), **A Lala** (Hannover 96), **B Hasi** (Anderlecht), **E Murati** (Iraklis; sub: **A Bellaj**, Panionos, 67min) — **E Skela** (Eintracht Frankfurt; sub: **A Bushi**, Trabzonspor, 86) — **A Raklli** (Unterhaching; sub: **F Myrtaj**, Cesena, 69), **I Tare** (Brescia) Subs not used **A Beqaj** (OFI Crete), **A Duro** (Majatispor), **N Dede** (SK Tirana), **M Dragusha** (Eintracht Trier)
Booked **Bushi**

IRELAND S Given (Newcastle United) — **S Carr** (Tottenham Hotspur), **G Breen** (West Ham United), **K Cunningham** (Birmingham City), **J O'Shea** (Manchester United) — **L Carsley** (Everton), **M Holland** (Ipswich Town), **M Kinsella** (Aston Villa), **K Kilbane** (Sunderland) — **R Keane** (Tottenham Hotspur; sub: **G Doherty**, Tottenham Hotspur, 67), **D Duff** (Blackburn Rovers) Subs not used **D Kiely** (Charlton Athletic), **J Kenna** (Birmingham City), **A O'Brien** (Newcastle United), **C Healy** (Celtic), **A Quinn** (Sheffield Wednesday), **D Connolly** (Wimbledon)
Referee **S Farina** (Italy)

Wednesday April 30
Friendly
NORWAY (h)
Lansdowne Road
Won 1-0 HT 1-0 Att 32,643
IRELAND S Given (Newcastle United; sub: **N Colgan**, Hibernian, 60) — **S Carr** (Tottenham Hotspur), **G Breen** (West Ham United), **R Dunne** (Manchester City), **I Harte** (Leeds United; sub: **S Finnan**, Fulham, 60) — **M Holland** (Ipswich Town), **M Kinsella** (Aston Villa; sub: **L Carsley**, Everton, 65), **K Kilbane** (Sunderland; sub: **A Quinn**,

MATCH OF THE SEASON

Georgia 1 Ireland 2
Lokomotiv Stadium, Saturday March 29 2003
Russell Kempson in Tbilisi

AMID A HAIL OF BOTTLES, coins, ball-bearings and, most sinister of all, an open-bladed penknife, Ireland resurrected their hopes of qualifying for the European Championship finals in the naked hostility of the Lokomotiv Stadium here. They may have plumbed the depths since the intoxicating high of the World Cup finals last summer, subsequent events forcing the inevitable resignation of Mick McCarthy, their manager, but they are back on track. The navel-gazing is over.

Bottle was called for, not of the variety that rained from the seats of the animated Georgia fans after Levan Kobiashvili's equaliser in the 61st minute, but of the kind that is dredged straight from the soul. Brian Kerr, McCarthy's genial successor, resisted the urge to replace any of his players and, panic measures sensibly declined, they responded with a winner from Gary Doherty six minutes from time. Group ten, after Albania's 3-1 defeat of Russia on the same night, is a veritable conundrum.

Ireland travel to Albania today for the second part of their double-header from hell, in Tirana on Wednesday. More poverty, squalid surroundings and dodgy dealers lurking in hotel lobbies can be expected. Yet they are reinvigorated, refocused.

They have points on the board, after demoralising defeats by Russia and Switzerland, and have rejoined the hunt for honours in Portugal next year. Albania will not be easy. The Ireland squad is still depleted, although Robbie Keane, their talisman, will join them this afternoon, and the display here was not easy on the eye. However, the McCarthy era has been consigned to history, the nagging self-doubt that comes with successive defeats has gone and Kerr, after the 2-0 win against Scotland last month, has a blemish-free two-match record.

"I felt that we'd prepared as well as we could and you just hope that it all comes together," Kerr said. "The lads have been a class act over the past few days and I'm just so pleased for them. There is a sense of joy but also a sense of relief after they had worked so hard."

What Ireland lacked in flair and imagination, they made up for in grit. When the firmly struck free kick from Kobiashvili had squirmed through the hands of Shay Given at his near post, they could have capitulated and for ten minutes the Georgia players became as frenzied as their supporters. Portugal appeared but a pipe-dream. Gradually, though, the fervour of the home fans subsided. When Damien Duff rose alone to head Stephen Carr's cross goalwards, they held their breath. Giorgi Lomaia saved easily. When Doherty nodded in Gary Breen's knock-down from Duff's cross,

Carsley was an industrious figure as Ireland rediscovered their self-belief against Georgia in Tbilisi

they fell silent. Many streamed to the exits. On Monday, Doherty, the makeshift striker, had conceded the injury-time penalty that gave Bolton Wanderers a 1-0 victory against Tottenham Hotspur in the Barclaycard Premiership. From villain to hero. "I was devastated, but football has two sides and today I can celebrate," he said.

Georgia almost equalised again, when Givi Didava burst through, but Breen quickly changed from goal-maker to goal-saver. It was a perfectly-timed challenge. "I saw Gary coming into view," Kerr said, "and said to myself, 'Make it, just make the tackle'. And he did. He saved the day."

The banner proclaiming "God Bless Mick McCarthy" had offered a blast from the past, but Kerr's team of the present sauntered into an eighteenth-minute lead. Kevin Kilbane crossed from the left, Lee Carsley's shot was touched on to a post by Lomaia and Duff snaffled the rebound.

It got ugly when John O'Shea fouled Giorgi Demetradze. A bout of childish jostling followed, the home fans hurling an array of objects on to the pitch. Kilbane was struck on his left arm by the handle of a penknife and Kyros Vassaras, the Greek referee, had to ask Giorgi Nemsadze, the Georgia captain, to signal to the crowd to calm down.

They did not. Georgia scored from the free kick and, at regular intervals, more objects hurtled through the cold night air. A glass bottle narrowly missed Doherty as he celebrated his goal and Carsley was struck on the head by a plastic bottle as he tried to waste time near a corner flag. No matter. Ireland had regained that lust for championship points.

GEORGIA (3-4-1-2): **G Lomaia** (Lokomotiv Tbilisi) — **O Khizaneishvili** (Dinamo Tbilisi), **G Shashiashvili** (Dinamo Tbilisi), **A Amisulashvili** (Dinamo Tbilisi) — **L Tskitishvili** (SC Freiburg), **G Nemsadze** (Dundee), **G Jamarauli** (Metalurg Donetsk), **L Kobiashvili** (SC Freiburg) — **G Kinkladze** (Derby County; sub: **G Didava**, Kocaelispor, 71min) — **A Iashvili** (Freiburg), **T Ketsbaia** (Anorthosis Famagusta; sub: **G Demetradze**, Real Sociedad, ht). Substitutes not used: **D Gvaramadze** (Dinamo Tbilisi), **D Kvirkvelia** (Dinamo Tbilisi), **R Kemoklidze** (Kocaelispor), **A Rekhviashvili** (Torpedo Moscow), **M Ashvetia** (FC Copenhagen). Booked: **Khizaneishvili**.

IRELAND (4-4-2): **S Given** (Newcastle United) — **S Carr** (Tottenham Hotspur), **G Breen** (West Ham United), **K Cunningham** (Birmingham City), **J O'Shea** (Manchester United) — **L Carsley** (Everton), **M Holland** (Ipswich Town), **M Kinsella** (Aston Villa), **K Kilbane** (Sunderland) — **G Doherty** (Tottenham Hotspur), **D Duff** (Blackburn Rovers). Substitutes not used: **D Kiely** (Charlton Athletic), **J Kenna** (Birmingham City), **A O'Brien** (Newcastle United), **C Healy** (Celtic), **S McPhail** (Leeds United), **D Connolly** (Wimbledon), **A Lee** (Rotherham United). Booked: Doherty.

Referee: K Vassaras (Greece).

Sheffield Wednesday, 85) — **D Duff** (Blackburn Rovers; sub: **A Lee**, Rotherham United, 74) — **R Keane** (Tottenham Hotspur; sub: **G Crowe**, Bohemians, 90), **D Connolly** (Wimbledon; sub: **C Healy**, Celtic, 74) Subs not used **S McPhail** (Leeds United), **J Murphy** (West Bromwich Albion)
Scorer **Duff 16**

NORWAY F Olsen (sub: **E Holtan**, ht) — **C Basma** (sub: **A Aas**, 56), **B Hangeland, R Johnsen** (sub: **T Hansen**, ht), **A Bergdolmo** — **T Andersen** (sub: **F Johnsen**, 90) — **J Carew, T Svindal Larsen, O Leonhardsen, S Iversen** (sub: **P Rudi**, 65) — **S Rushfeld** (sub: **T A Flo**, ht) Sub not used **F Winsnes**
Referee **M McCurry (Scotland)**

Saturday June 7
European Championship qualifier
ALBANIA (h)
Lansdowne Road
Won 2-1 HT 1-1 Att 33,000
IRELAND S Given (Newcastle United) — **S Carr** (Tottenham Hotspur), **G Breen** (West Ham United), **K Cunningham** (Birmingham City), **J O'Shea** (Manchester United) — **M Holland** (Ipswich Town), **M Kinsella** (Aston Villa; sub: **L Carsley**, Everton, 55min), **K Kilbane** (Sunderland; sub: **S Reid**, Millwall, 75) — **D Duff** (Blackburn Rovers) — **D Connolly** (Wimbledon; sub: **G Doherty**, Tottenham Hotspur, 65), **R Keane** (Tottenham Hotspur) Subs not used **I Harte** (Leeds United), **R Dunne** (Manchester City), **N Colgan** (Hibernian), **C Healy** (Celtic)
Scorers **Keane 6, Aliaj 90 (og)**
Booked **Carr, Kinsella**

ALBANIA F Strakosha (Kalfea; sub: **A Beqaj**, OFI Crete, 75) — **E Beqiri** (KS Vllaznia), **G Cipi** (Ghent), **A Aliaj** (SK Tirana) — **B Hasi** (Anderlecht) — **K Duro** (Steaua Bucharest), **A Lala** (Hannover 96), **E Skela** (Eintracht Frankfurt), **E Murati** (Iraklis; sub: **A Bellaj**, Panionos, 57) — **I Tare** (Brescia), **A Raklli** (Unterhaching; sub: **F Myrtaj**, Cesena, 85) Subs not used **R Dabulla** (SK Tirana), **E Fakaj** (MSV Duisberg), **L Cana** (Paris Saint-Germain), **E Bogdani** (Reggina)
Scorer **Skela 8**
Booked **Lala, Beqiri, Cipi**
Referee **T Mikulski (Poland)**

Wednesday June 11
European Championship qualifier
GEORGIA (h)
Won 2-0 HT 1-0 Att 36,000
IRELAND S Given (Newcastle United) — **S Carr** (Tottenham Hotspur), **G Breen** (West Ham United), **K Cunningham** (Birmingham City), **J O'Shea** (Manchester United) — **L Carsley** (Everton), **M Holland** (Ipswich Town), **C Healy** (Celtic; sub: **M Kinsella**, Aston Villa, 86min), **K Kilbane** (Sunderland) — **R Keane** (Tottenham Hotspur), **G Doherty** (Tottenham Hotspur; sub: **A Lee**, Rotherham United, 88) Subs not used **I Harte** (Leeds United), **S Reid** (Millwall), **S McPhail** (Leeds United), **N Colgan** (Hibernian), **D Connolly** (Wimbledon)
Scorers **Doherty 43, Keane 58**

GEORGIA G Lomaia (Lokomotiv Tbilisi) — **Z Khizanishvili** (Dundee), **O Khizelashvili** (Dinamo Tbilisi), **K Kaladze** (AC Milan) — **A Rekhviashvili** (Torpedo Moscow) — **V Burduli** (Dinamo Tbilisi), **G Didava** (Kocaelispor; sub: **R Aleksidze**, Dinamo Tbilisi, 76), **M Asatiani** (Lokomotiv Moscow), **A Amisulashvili** (Dinamo Tbilisi) — **G Demetradze** (Metalurg Donetsk; sub: **V Daraselia**, Dinamo Tbilisi, 62), **S Arveladze** (Rangers) Subs not used **D Gvaramadze** (Dinamo Tbilisi), **D Siradze** (Lokomotiv Tbilisi), **G Shashiashvili** (Dinamo Tbilisi), **L Akhalaia** (Dinamo Tbilisi)
Booked **Khizaneishvili**
Referee **E Iturralde Gonzalez (Spain)**

INTERNATIONAL DATES

AUGUST 2003

Tuesday 19
Friendly
Ireland v Australia
Under-21 Championship qualifier
Serbia and Montenegro v Wales
Under-21 friendlies
England v Croatia
Poland v Ireland
Wednesday 20
Euro 2004 qualifier
Serbia and Montenegro v Wales
Friendlies
England v Croatia
Norway v Scotland

SEPTEMBER

Friday 5
Under-21 Championship qualifiers
Italy v Wales
Macedonia v England
Ireland v Russia
Ukraine v Northern Ireland
Saturday 6
Euro 2004 qualifiers
Italy v Wales
Macedonia v England
Ireland v Russia
Scotland v Faeroe Isles
Ukraine v Northern Ireland
Tuesday 9
Under-21 Championship qualifiers
England v Portugal
Germany v Scotland
Northern Ireland v Armenia
Wales v Finland
Women's friendly
Scotland v Italy
Wednesday 10
Euro 2004 qualifiers
England v Liechtenstein
Germany v Scotland
Northern Ireland v Armenia
Wales v Finland
Thursday 11
Women's friendly
Germany v England

OCTOBER

Friday 10
Under-21 Championship qualifiers
Greece v Northern Ireland
Turkey v England
Scotland v Lithuania
Switzerland v Ireland
Wales v Serbia and Montenegro
Saturday 11
Euro 2004 qualifiers
Greece v Northern Ireland
Scotland v Lithuania
Switzerland v Ireland
Turkey v England
Wales v Serbia and Montenegro
Sunday 19
*Women's European
Championship qualifier*
Czech Republic v Scotland

**Frank Leboeuf holds the trophy aloft
after France's victory at Euro 2000**

NOVEMBER

Saturday 15 and Wednesday 19
*Euro 2004 and Under-21
Championship play-offs*
Sunday 30
Euro 2004 finals draw

FEBRUARY 2004

Tuesday 17 and Wednesday 18
Friendlies, including
Portugal v England (tbc)

MARCH

Tuesday 30 and Wednesday 31
Friendlies

APRIL

Saturday 10
*Women's European
Championship qualifier*
Ukraine v Scotland
Tuesday 27 and Wednesday 28
Friendlies

MAY

Sunday 2
*Women's European
Championship qualifier*
Scotland v Germany
Sunday 23
*Women's European
Championship qualifier*
Scotland v Portugal
Thursday 27 to Tuesday June 8
Under-21 Championship finals

JUNE

Saturday 12
*Euro 2004 finals opening match
(Oporto)*
Saturday 12 to Wednesday 23
Group stages
Thursday 24 to Sunday 27
Quarter-finals
Wednesday 30 to Thursday July 1
Semi-finals

JULY

Sunday 4
Euro 2004 final (Lisbon)

OBITUARIES

Compiled by Daniel Crewe

IAN HUTCHINSON
1948-2002

Ian Hutchinson winds up for another one of the long throw-ins with which he will always be associated. A talented striker and the perfect foil for Peter Osgood, he was one of the stars of the glamorous Chelsea team of the early Seventies. He died in September 2002, aged 54

LIVES IN BRIEF

JULINHO

Born August 5, 1929
Died January 11, 2003

Ranking alongside Jairzinho and Garrincha, Julinho was one of Brazil's great wingers, scoring 13 goals in 31 games for his country. This total included a cracker in the "Battle of Berne", the infamous World Cup quarter-final against Hungary in 1954 which Brazil lost 4-2. Born in Sao Paulo, he later moved to Italy, where he helped Fiorentina to a league championship.

FRITZ WALTER

Born October 31, 1920
Died June 17, 2002

Feted as a hero after he captained West Germany to their surprise 1954 World Cup final victory over Hungary, Walter went on to lead the side in the 1958 World Cup finals at the age of 37 — having won his first cap in 1940 — and ended up with 33 international goals in 61 games. He spent his league career at Kaiserslautern and ended the war as a prisoner of the Russians. His wartime experiences made him refuse to fly to matches in his later years.

Trevor Ford cost Sunderland a British record fee of £30,000 in the autumn of 1950. Pictured here on his debut, he scored regularly, but the club still failed to win the trophies that the high-spending directors and fanatical supporters craved

BOBBIE BEATTIE

Born January 24, 1916 **Died** September 21, 2002
Career Kilmarnock, Preston North End/Scotland

After the 5ft 6in Beattie scored 18 goals in 34 games for Kilmarnock in 1936-37, he was snapped up by Preston and at the end of his first season at Deepdale he played in the FA Cup Final victory over Huddersfield Town at Wembley. Preston won the wartime north championship in 1940, with a young Tom Finney now in the team, and Beattie scored both goals in a replayed wartime cup final against Arsenal. During his time at Preston he also played alongside Bill Shankly and Tommy Docherty.

LEN DUQUEMIN

Born July 17, 1924 **Died** April 20, 2003
Career Vauxbelets, Tottenham Hotspur

A hard-working forward, Duquemin's running off the ball was crucial to the "push-and-run" style that took Arthur Rowe's Tottenham to the second division title in 1949-50 and the first division championship the following season. He was born in Guernsey — during the German occupation he worked as a gardener in a monastery — and moved to Spurs on the recommendation of a local hotelier. He scored 184 goals in 374 games for Spurs and, after playing non-league football, worked as a newsagent and pub landlord.

MARC-VIVIEN FOE
Born May 1, 1975 **Died** June 26, 2003
Career Lens, West Ham United, Lyons, Manchester City/Cameroon

The depth of the tributes paid to Foe after he collapsed and died during the Confederations Cup semi-final between Cameroon and Colombia in June were testament to his immense popularity. A hard-tackling and combative midfield player, he spent the 2002-03 season on loan at Manchester City, who were in the process of trying to make the move permanent. "He did not have an enemy in the game," Harry Redknapp, his former manager at West Ham, said.

TREVOR FORD
Born October 1, 1923 **Died** May 29, 2003
Career Swansea City, Aston Villa, Sunderland, Cardiff City, PSV Eindhoven, Newport County/Wales

An aggressive centre forward who was a potent cocktail of flair, pace and shooting ability, Ford became the idol of the Holte End at Villa Park before moving to Sunderland for a British record £30,000 in 1950. At Roker Park he scored regularly but was involved in a clash of personalities with Len Shackleton and joined Cardiff City for the same fee in 1953, so becoming the costliest player in the world. Allegations that he made in a Sunday newspaper about under-the-counter payments led to him being banned from English football for three years. He scored a record 23 goals in 38 games for Wales.

PETER HARRIS
Born December 19, 1925 **Died** January 2, 2003
Career Portsmouth/England

Harris was a modest legend of the great postwar Portsmouth side that won the league in 1948-49, when he scored 17 goals, and then

SIR BERT MILLICHIP
Born August 5, 1914
Died December 18, 2002

During his period as chairman of the Football Association — between 1981 and 1996 — Bert Millichip presided over the aftermath of the tragedies at Hillsborough and Heysel and the wrangling that led to the establishment of the FA Premier League. A decent amateur player, he joined his local club, West Bromwich Albion, and after the war succeeded his uncle as the club's solicitor, becoming chairman in 1976. After the Heysel disaster his smooth diplomacy played a significant role in the election of Lennart Johansson as president of Uefa, which led to the return of English clubs to Europe in 1990.

Peter Harris, a local boy who made good for Portsmouth in their golden era

ALAN ASHMAN
Manager who took West Bromwich Albion to the FA Cup in 1968 and Carlisle United to the top of the first division in 1974, died on November 30, 2002, aged 74.

SAID BELQOLA
Moroccan referee who took charge of the World Cup final in 1998, died on June 15, 2002, aged 45.

REG DRURY
Football Correspondent of the *News of the World* and one of the most widely respected journalists in the game, died on June 12, 2003, aged 74.

KEN GALLACHER
Chief football writer of *The Herald* and one of Scotland's best known writers, died on January 16, 2003, aged 63.

RON GRAY
Manager of Millwall and scout at Ipswich Town, died on October 11, 2002, aged 82.

MAURO RAMOS DE OLIVEIRA
Captain of Brazil's World Cup-winning team of 1962, died on September 18, 2002, aged 72.

JULIO PEREZ
Uruguayan who set up the goal that won the World Cup in 1950, died on September 21, 2002, aged 76.

DENIS SAUNDERS
Twice led Pegasus to the Amateur Cup, died on February 16, 2003, aged 78.

JUAN SCHIAFFINO
Scored Uruguay's equaliser in the deciding match of the 1950 World Cup, died on November 13, 2002, aged 77.

HARRY SHARRATT
Goalkeeper who helped Bishop Auckland to the Amateur Cup in three successive seasons, died on August 19, 2002, aged 72.

FRANK TAYLOR
Journalist who survived the Munich air crash and wrote *The Day A Team Died*, died on July 19, 2002, aged 81.

in 1949-50, when he scored 16. Although a winger, he scored 208 goals in 516 games for Portsmouth. His dedication to the club was not surprising, having been born close to Fratton Park, and he trained as a carpenter before signing for them in 1944. He won two England caps.

IAN HUTCHINSON
Born August 4, 1948 **Died** September 19, 2002
Career Chelsea

It was with two of his specialities that Hutchinson helped Chelsea to win the FA Cup against Leeds United in 1970. At Wembley, it was one of his headers that grabbed a late equaliser, and in the replay at Old Trafford his trademark "windmill" long throw-in led to the winner. A professor who experimented on Hutchinson found that he was double-jointed in both shoulders, enabling him to throw the ball long distances. He scored 58 goals in 144 games for the club, but constant injuries forced him to retire at the age of 27.

BILLY McPHAIL
Born February 2, 1928 **Died** April 4, 2003
Career Queen's Park, Clyde, Celtic

McPhail ensured legendary status at Celtic Park by scoring a hat-trick inside half an hour in the 7-1 victory over Rangers in the 1957 Scottish League Cup final. The three cup final goals were all headers and this was his speciality. He later sought compensation, unsuccessfully, for pre-senile dementia, which he said was caused by contact with heavy leather balls.

Albert Stubbins was prolific during Liverpool's 1946-47 title campaign

BILLY MORRIS

Born July 30, 1918 **Died** December 31, 2002
Career Burnley/Wales

Having survived being shot in the neck during the war, Morris became one of the great Burnley team of the late 1940s, the only member of the side to win international recognition. In 1946-47 the Clarets were promoted to the first division and also reached the FA Cup Final, where they were beaten by Charlton Athletic after extra time. He went on to help to develop the club's youth players and managed Wrexham.

ARTHUR ROWLEY

Born April 21, 1926 **Died** December 18, 2002
Career Wolverhampton Wanderers, West Bromwich Albion, Fulham, Leicester City, Shrewsbury Town

Although Rowley scored more Football League goals than any player in history, and in 13 successive seasons scored 20 or more, most were outside the top division and he never won a full England cap. He scored 251 in 303 games for Leicester — including 16 hat-tricks — and 152 in 236 games for Shrewsbury Town, where he transformed the side as player-manager. At a reunion of former Shrewsbury players he was given a light, modern ball to examine and said: "I hate to think what shape I would have kicked that into."

PAT SAWARD

Born August 17, 1928 **Died** September 20, 2002
Career Millwall, Aston Villa, Huddersfield Town/Ireland

Took advantage of an injury to Vic Crowe to cement his place at left half in the Aston Villa team that won the FA Cup in 1957. He went on to captain Villa in their 1959-60 second division championship season and managed Brighton when they won promotion from the third division in 1971-72. He played 18 times for his country.

ALBERT STUBBINS

Born July 17, 1919 **Died** December 28, 2002
Career Newcastle United, Liverpool

Starring alongside Karl Marx, Albert Einstein and Marilyn Monroe, Stubbins appeared on the cover of The Beatles' *Sgt Pepper's Lonely Hearts Club Band* album, the only footballer to do so. He joined Liverpool from Newcastle United for a club-record fee and in the first season after the war scored 24 goals, including the decisive one against Wolverhampton Wanderers that secured the title. In one game that season he struck a

Ray Wood won two championship medals during his time as Manchester United's first-choice goalkeeper

penalty so hard that it broke the goalkeeper's arm. He retired in 1952 and later worked as a newspaper journalist and for local radio.

RAY WOOD

Born June 11, 1931 **Died** July 7, 2002
Career Darlington, Manchester United, Huddersfield Town, Bradford City, Barnsley

One of the survivors of the Munich air crash, Wood had won championship medals with United in 1956 and 1957 but had lost his place as first-choice goalkeeper to Harry Gregg by the time of the disaster, in February 1958. Wood played only once more for United after the crash but then moved to Huddersfield Town, for whom he made more than 200 appearances. In the FA Cup Final of 1957 he was carried off after his jaw was broken by a charge from Peter McParland, the Aston Villa winger. Wood once said of the Busby Babes: "We weren't afraid of anybody."

KEY DATES

AUGUST 2003

Saturday 9
Nationwide League and Nationwide Conference start

Sunday 10
FA Community Shield: Arsenal v Manchester United

Tuesday 12
InterToto Cup finals (first legs)

Tuesday 12 and Wednesday 13
Champions League third qualifying round (first legs)
Carling Cup first round

Thursday 14
Uefa Cup qualifying round (first legs)

Saturday 16
Barclaycard Premiership starts

Sunday 17
FA Women's Premier League starts

Saturday 23
FA Cup extra preliminary round

Tuesday 26
InterToto Cup finals (second legs)

Tuesday 26 and Wednesday 27
Champions League third qualifying round (second legs)

Thursday 28
Uefa Cup qualifying round (second legs)

Friday 29
Super Cup: AC Milan v FC Porto

Saturday 30
FA Cup preliminary round
FA Youth Cup preliminary round

Sunday 31
FA Women's Premier League Cup preliminary round

SEPTEMBER

Saturday 6
FA Vase first qualifying round
FA Youth Cup first qualifying round

Sunday 7
FA Women's Cup first qualifying round

Saturday 13
FA Cup first qualifying round

Sunday 14
FA Women's Premier League Cup first round

Tuesday 16 and Wednesday 17
Champions League group matches

Saturday 20
FA Vase second qualifying round
FA Youth Cup second qualifying round

Tuesday 23 and Wednesday 24
Carling Cup second round

Wednesday 24
Uefa Cup first round (first legs)

Saturday 27
FA Cup second qualifying round

Sunday 28
FA Women's Cup second qualifying round

Tuesday 30
Champions League group matches

OCTOBER

Wednesday 1
Champions League group matches

Saturday 4
FA Trophy preliminary round
FA Youth Cup third qualifying round
FA County Youth Cup first round

Sunday 5
FA Sunday Cup first round

Saturday 11
FA Cup third qualifying round

Sunday 12
FA Women's Premier League Cup second round

Wednesday 15
Uefa Cup first round (second legs)
LDV Vans Trophy first round

Saturday 18
FA Vase first round

Tuesday 21 and Wednesday 22
Champions League group matches

Saturday 25
FA Cup fourth qualifying round
FA Youth Cup first round

Sunday 26
FA Women's Cup first round

Tuesday 28 and Wednesday 29
Carling Cup third round

NOVEMBER

Saturday 1
FA Trophy first round

Sunday 2
FA Sunday Cup second round
FA Women's Premier League Cup third round

Tuesday 4 and Wednesday 5
Champions League group matches

Wednesday 5
LDV Vans Trophy second round

Thursday 6
Uefa Cup second round (first legs)

Saturday 8
FA Cup first round
FA Youth Cup second round
FA County Youth Cup second round

Sunday 9
FA Women's Cup second round

Saturday 22
FA Vase second round

Tuesday 25 and Wednesday 26
Champions League group matches

Thursday 27
Uefa Cup second round (second legs)

Saturday 29
FA Trophy second round

Sunday 30
FA Sunday Cup third round

DECEMBER

Tuesday 2
Intercontinental Cup

Tuesday 2 and Wednesday 3
Carling Cup fourth round

Saturday 6
FA Cup second round
FA Youth Cup third round

Sunday 7
FA Women's Cup third round

Tuesday 9 and Wednesday 10
Champions League group matches

Wednesday 10
LDV Vans Trophy quarter-finals

Saturday 13
FA Vase third round
FA County Youth Cup third round

Sunday 14
FA Women's Premier League Cup semi-finals

Tuesday 16 and Wednesday 17
Carling Cup fifth round

Who will succeed Portsmouth as Nationwide League first division champions in May?

JANUARY 2004

Saturday 3
FA Cup third round
Sunday 4
FA Women's Cup fourth round
Saturday 10
FA Trophy third round
Sunday 11
FA Sunday Cup fourth round
Saturday 17
FA Vase fourth round
Tuesday 20 and Wednesday 21
Carling Cup semi-finals (first legs)
Wednesday 21
LDV Vans Trophy semi-finals
Saturday 24
FA Cup fourth round
Sunday 25
FA Women's Cup fifth round
Wednesday 28
Carling Cup semi-finals (second legs)
Saturday 31
FA Trophy fourth round
FA Youth Cup fourth round
FA County Youth Cup fourth round

FEBRUARY

Sunday 1
FA Sunday Cup fifth round
Saturday 7
FA Vase fifth round
Sunday 8
FA Women's Cup sixth round
Wednesday 11
LDV Vans Trophy final (first leg)
Saturday 14
FA Cup fifth round
FA Trophy fifth round
Saturday 21
FA Vase sixth round

FA Youth Cup fifth round
Tuesday 24 and Wednesday 25
Champions League second round
(first legs)
Wednesday 25
LDV Vans Trophy final (second leg)
Thursday 26
Uefa Cup third round (first legs)
Saturday 28
FA Trophy sixth round
Sunday 29
Carling Cup final

MARCH

Wednesday 3
Uefa Cup third round (second legs)
Saturday 6
FA Cup sixth round
FA County Youth Cup semi-finals
Tuesday 9 and Wednesday 10
Champions League second round
(second legs)
Thursday 11
Uefa Cup fourth round (first legs)
Saturday 13
FA Vase semi-finals (first legs)
FA Youth Cup sixth round
Sunday 14
FA Women's Cup semi-finals
Saturday 20
FA Vase semi-finals (second legs)
Sunday 21
FA Sunday Cup semi-finals
Tuesday 23 and Wednesday 24
Champions League quarter-finals
(first legs)
Thursday 25
Uefa Cup fourth round (second legs)
Saturday 27
FA Trophy semi-finals (first legs)

Sunday 28
LDV Vans Trophy final
FA Women's Premier
League Cup final

APRIL

Saturday 3
FA Trophy semi-finals (second legs)
FA Youth Cup semi-finals (first legs)
Sunday 4
FA Cup semi-finals
Tuesday 6 and Wednesday 7
Champions League quarter-finals
(second legs)
Thursday 8
Uefa Cup quarter-finals (first legs)
Wednesday 14
Uefa Cup quarter-finals
(second legs)
Saturday 17
FA Youth Cup semi-finals
(second legs)
Tuesday 20 and Wednesday 21
Champions League semi-finals
(first legs)
Thursday 22
Uefa Cup semi-finals (first legs)
Saturday 24
FA County Youth Cup final
Nationwide Conference ends
Sunday 25
FA Sunday Cup final
FA Women's Premier League ends

MAY

Monday 3
FA Women's Cup final
Tuesday 4 and Wednesday 5
Champions League semi-finals
(second leg)
Thursday 6
Uefa Cup semi-finals (second legs)
Saturday 8
Nationwide League ends
Saturday 15
FA Vase final
Barclaycard Premiership ends
Wednesday 19
Uefa Cup final
Saturday 22
FA Cup Final
Sunday 23
FA Trophy final
Wednesday 26
Champions League final
Saturday 29 to Monday 31
Nationwide League play-off finals

TIMES £150,000
FANTASY FOOTBALL
2003|04

I **Pick your team**

I **Give it a comedy name**

I **Win more prizes than ever**

I **It's not hard**

Look out for details in the paper, or visit:
www.timesonline.co.uk/fantasyfootball

WHAT'S IMPORTANT
THE TIMES